The Celtic Inscriptions of Britain

Phonology and Chronology, *c.* 400–1200

Publications of the Philological Society, 37

The Celtic Inscriptions of Britain

Phonology and Chronology, *c.* 400–1200

Patrick Sims-Williams

Publications of the Philological Society, 37

Oxford UK & Boston USA

ISBN 1-4051-0903-3

First published 2003

Blackwell Publishers
108 Cowley Road, Oxford, OX4 1JF, UK

and
350 Main Street,
Malden, MA 02148, USA.

British Library Cataloguing in Publication Data
A catalogue record for this publication is available from the British Library

Library of Congress Cataloging-in-Publication Data
Applied for

Typeset by Joshua Associates Ltd., Oxford
Printed in Great Britain by
the Alden Group, Oxford

To Professor William Gillies

CONTENTS

LIST OF TABLES AND FIGURES

PREFACE

The fifth- to twelfth-century inscriptions studied in this book include almost all the roman-letter and ogam inscriptions of Britain that were listed in Macalister's *Corpus Inscriptionum Insularum Celticarum*, plus eighty-two additions (i.e. the inscriptions with numbers higher than 1069 listed in Appendix 1 below). Account has been taken of earlier and later readings, including those in Nash-Williams's *Early Christian Monuments of Wales*, Okasha's *Corpus of Early Christian Inscribed Stones of South-West Britain*, the multi-authored *The Inscriptions of Early Medieval Brittany/Les inscriptions de la Bretagne du Haut Moyen Âge* by Wendy Davies and others, and a draft of the new *Corpus of Early Medieval Inscribed Stones and Stone Sculpture in Wales*, edited by Nancy Edwards, Mark Redknap, and John Lewis.

The purpose of this book is to provide the linguistic analysis of the Brittonic and Irish inscriptions of Britain that is lacking in the volumes by Macalister, Nash-Williams, and Okasha. It is directed primarily at those concerned with the early history of the Celtic languages and at philologists interested in methods and problems of historical phonology and onomastics. I hope that it will also be useful to archaeologists, historians, and art historians seeking guidance about the linguistic dating of the monuments and the nature of the personal names preserved on them.

This work was necessitated by a commission from the Art and Archaeology Committee of the University of Wales Board of Celtic Studies to write the linguistic commentary in the *Corpus of Early Medieval Inscribed Stones and Stone Sculpture in Wales*. I am most grateful to the three editors for sharing their drafts with me, to the Board for funding the work for a year, to Damian McManus for supporting the application, and to the Royal Commission on Ancient and Historical Monuments in Wales for sight of some of the fine new photographs being taken for the *Corpus*.

I am grateful to my wife, Marged, and children, Gwen and Gwilym, for their patience and interest on many field trips. Canon J. M. Riley was helpful at Tywyn church, and Nia Llwyd came to my rescue at Llangefni. Rosemary Cramp and the Corpus of Anglo-Saxon Stone Sculpture funded my visit to the Wareham inscriptions.

William Gillies made available the late Kenneth Jackson's copy of Macalister's *Corpus*, as described in Chapter 1 below, and gave me a copy of Pedersen's grammar many years earlier. Wendy Davies provided pre-publication drafts of *The Inscriptions of Early Medieval Brittany* and of material on her Celtic Inscribed Stones Project website. Oliver Padel commented as reader for the Philological Society, Keith Brown handled the manuscript, and Jon Coe corrected various errors. In the University of Wales, Aberystwyth, Elgan Davies and the Old College Library staff were as helpful and efficient as ever. My students Meredith Cane and Jon Coe provided material from their dissertations. Finally, the following kindly answered queries of various kinds: Lindsay Allason-Jones, Francesco Benozzo, Patrizia de Bernardo Stempel, Gareth Bevan, Barry Cunliffe, Joaquín Gorrochategui, Graham Isaac, Carlo Tedeschi, Charles Thomas, R. S. O. Tomlin, and Jürgen Uhlich.

I am most grateful to all those named above.

May 2002

1

INTRODUCTION

1.1 THE CORPUS

The corpus of 371 inscriptions examined in this book comprises nearly all the inscriptions listed by R. A. S. Macalister in his *Corpus Inscriptionum Insularum Celticarum* (1945–49), other than those in Ireland and Iona (CIIC 1–317, 521–967, 1070–95),[1] with the addition of 25 inscriptions from Brittany,[2] plus a large number of inscriptions from western Britain and Man which were unknown to Macalister. The non-Breton additions are referred to by numbers in the 1200s and 1400s, following Charles Thomas's extension of the CIIC numbering system,[3] and where Thomas's runs out I have provided numbers in the 2000s or, for the Breton stones, the 3000s (see Appendix 1). Thus every stone has a unique 'CIIC'-style number. When a stone bears more than one inscription and there is reason to believe that they are of significantly different dates, I have subdivided them into 348/a and 348/b, 368/a and 368/b, and so on.[4] As a result, total numbers of stones and of inscriptions vary.

After the unique 'CIIC' number I usually refer after a slash to other current systems of numbering for particular regions, e.g. 968/5; 993/124/18; 489/b/Ok13. These can be explained region by region as follows:

Brittany

In references like 3006/C1, 'C1' is the designation in Wendy Davies et al., *Inscriptions of Early Medieval Brittany* (IEMB). In the case of 3017/M8, I ignore the ancient Gaulish part of the inscription.[5]

---

[1] I also exclude a few Welsh inscriptions in CIIC (such as CIIC 969) which were not admitted by Nash-Williams into ECMW (Dr Nancy Edwards also regards 969 as Romanesque). All references to Macalister's CIIC are by number, with the exception of 'p. 397' which refers to an unnumbered Welsh inscription on p. 397 of Volume i of CIIC. Note that this first volume was reprinted in Ireland in 1996 by Four Courts Press, with a judicious Preface by Damian McManus on Macalister's strengths and much-derided weaknesses (cf. the reviews of CIIC by Williams and Jackson listed in my Bibliography).

[2] These are edited by Wendy Davies et al. in IEMB (2000). Prof. Davies kindly let me have a draft version of the 'Catalogue' section of IEMB in 1999.

[3] In his *Mute Stones* of 1994, with the addition of a no. 1212 from his later *Christian Celts*, pp. 62–63.

[4] This also applies to 407, 427, 473, 489, 1068 and 2002. I have not included the earlier, Roman portion of 2017. Not everyone agrees on dividing 473 into two; see below, p. 361.

[5] i.e. M8a in IEMB. Cf. *Recueil des inscriptions gauloises* (RIG), ii/1, no. L15. Note that I do not include the two problematic inscriptions from the Channel Islands discussed in IEMB.

Cornwall, Devon, and Somerset

In references like 489/a/Ok13, 'Ok13' refers to the number in Elisabeth Okasha's *Corpus of Early Christian Inscribed Stones of South-West Britain* (1993). Okasha collates numerous earlier readings of the stones, and although these are cited as 'Okasha' this does not imply that she endorses them. Frequent reference is also made to alternative readings by Charles Thomas in his *And Shall These Mute Stones Speak?* (1994). There is only one inscription from Somerset (499/Ok77).[6]

Dorset

In references like 1061/Dor.iii, 'Dor.iii' refers to the 1970 numbering of the stones at Wareham by the Royal Commission on Historical Monuments (England).[7]

Hampshire

The solitary ogam inscription from Silchester is referred to by its CIIC number alone (496), but I take account of the latest reading.[8]

Isle of Man

These inscriptions (500–505, 1066–68, and 2038) also have no further reference number. Note that 1068 bears a collection of Brittonic and Irish names which are here only differentiated into 1068/a (ogam script) and 1068/b (roman script).

Scotland and Northumberland

In references like 2025/Scot.12 and 498/Nb7, the '12' and '7' refer to Charles Thomas's numbering in his 'Early Christian Inscriptions of Southern Scotland'.[9] Like Macalister and Thomas, I do not attempt to include Pictish (or so-called Pictish) inscriptions,[10] on which other scholars are working, but I have retained those which Macalister did include, giving references such as '509/Ok.Pict3' when they are enumerated in Okasha's 'Non-Ogam

---

[6] I omit the Somerset inscription published by Foster, *Med. Arch.*, 32 (1988), 208–11, as being doubtfully Celtic.

[7] See under Radford & Jackson in the Bibliography, and for further literature see ‡25 of Ch. 2 below.

[8] Fulford et al., *Med. Arch.*, 44 (2000), 10–11; I do not accept their interpretation, however (see below, Ch. 2, ‡17).

[9] *GAJ*, 17 (1991–92), 1–10.

[10] Even though some of them are arguably Celtic: see e.g. Forsyth, *PSAS*, 125 (1995), 677–96, and in *Dunadd*, pp. 264–72.

Inscriptions of Pictland' (1985).[11] Thomas excludes various other non-Brittonic inscriptions from mainland Scotland (Macalister's 506–508 and 512), but I have retained these, since after all my corpus already contains many certain or arguably non-Brittonic inscriptions in the other 'Brittonic' areas. The Cumberland stone (2026) is doubtfully relevant.

Wales, Herefordshire, and Shropshire

In references like 968/5, the '5' refers to the numbering in Nash-Williams's *Early Christian Monuments of Wales* (1950) – there is a concordance in Appendix 2 below. In the case of inscriptions from Cardiganshire and Glamorgan (ECMW nos. 108–133 and 191–270) a third number, as in 990/108/1 or 409/198/849, refers to the numbering by W. Gwyn Thomas in his contributions to the *Cardiganshire County History*, i (1994), and to the Royal Commission on Ancient and Historical Monuments in Wales's inventory *Glamorgan*, i, part 3, *The Early Christian Period* (1976).[12] I do not refer to the numbering in the forthcoming Welsh *Corpus* (see Preface) as this is still in flux; however, I do refer to it from time to time simply as '*Corpus*'.

1.2 THE READINGS OF THE INSCRIPTIONS

Unlike the forthcoming Welsh *Corpus*, the present work is not intended, and does not claim, to establish new readings of the inscriptions (a good many of which I have not examined personally) or to adjudicate between old readings, except in a few cases. This is why many variant readings are cited, especially from CIIC, even when they seem linguistically unlikely. The simplified readings which I reviewed when writing the Phonology chapters below are given in Appendix 1. This is based on CIIC and (mostly) later publications, and makes no claim to consistency in the conventions for uncertain letters and so on (where various conventions are current); the relevant publications, in particular their illustrations, should be consulted for the fine detail. Note that ogam script is indicated by the use of **BOLD CAPITALS**. Appendix 1 is included, with some misgivings, first for the convenience of readers without easy access to the *corpora*, and secondly to

---

[11] *CMCS*, 9 (1985), 43–69.

[12] Four Glamorgan inscriptions in the Royal Commission volume (2029/p.39i, 2030/p.39ii, 2031/p.68, and 2034/871) were not in ECMW, and only the last has a number as opposed to a page reference. I have not accepted the new Glamorgan inscription proposed by Holder and Wardle, *Med. Arch.*, 43 (1999), 216–22. I have not included the lost inscription from Meliden, Flintshire because I could not decipher the copy by William Jones printed by Edwards, *Church Archaeology*, 3 (1999), 12.

make clear what was and was not systematically reviewed in the phonology chapters. I drafted those sections, for reasons which will emerge below, on the basis of Appendix 1 itself rather than the illustrated corpora, so as to avoid the epigraphically 'early' or 'late' appearance of the inscriptions influencing the linguistic analysis.

1.3 PREVIOUS LINGUISTIC WORK ON THE INSCRIPTIONS

Apart from the linguistic commentary in *Inscriptions of Early Medieval Brittany*,[13] Brittonic inscriptions have not received much attention from recent philologists – unlike those in the Irish ogam script, which have been intensively studied by McManus, Harvey, Ziegler, Uhlich, and others.[14] Nevertheless, I am fortunate in being able to build on the pioneering work of three gifted Brittonic Celticists: Sir John Rhys (1840–1915), Sir Ifor Williams (1881–1965), and Kenneth Jackson (1909–91). Rhys interpreted Celtic inscriptions throughout Britain and Ireland, not only in his *Lectures on Welsh Philology* (LWP), but also in articles published from 1873 onwards and throughout his career: 'epigraphy was the one subject which he never dropped; he would go anywhere to see a newly found inscribed stone.'[15] Ifor Williams focused more narrowly, but also more intensely, than Rhys on the inscriptions within Wales, treating them as documents in the Welsh linguistic corpus, and some of his epigraphic studies were quite appropriately included in Rachel Bromwich's collection of his papers, *The Beginnings of Welsh Poetry* (BWP).[16] Kenneth Jackson, systematically building on the work of Rhys and Williams, exploited the whole corpus of British inscriptions in his reconstruction of Brittonic historical phonology up to the twelfth century in his massive *Language and History in Early Britain* (LHEB) of 1953. His own heavily annotated copy of CIIC, frequently quoted below through the good offices of his successor in the Edinburgh Chair of Celtic, Professor William Gillies, shows that epigraphy was a subject which Jackson too never dropped. The substance of many of these annotations found their way

---

[13] The IEMB commentary is principally by Dr John T. Koch.

[14] See Bibliography. On the og(h)am script itself, see my 1992 and 1993 articles cited there. Prof. Jost Gippert has established an ogam website: http://titus.uni-frankfurt.de/ogam. For bibliography on Insular inscriptions see Bonser, *Anglo-Saxon and Celtic Bibliography*, i, 456–79; Nash-Williams, *BBCS*, 8 (1935–37), 62–84 and 161–88; Hughes & Williams, *Llyfryddiaeth yr Iaith Gymraeg*, pp. 150–53; the Index volumes of *AC*; and the website of the Celtic Inscribed Stones Project (University College London): http://www.ucl.ac.uk/archaeology/cisp (available from July 2000). A consolidated index to *BBCS* is being prepared by Dr Simon Rodway.

[15] Morris-Jones, *PBA*, 11 (1924–25), 196, with bibliography of Rhys's writings on pp. 198–208.

[16] A bibliography of his writings is given by Davies, *SC*, 4 (1969), 1–55, including an index of his references to inscriptions (p. 55) subsequent to those indexed by Parry, *Mynegai i Weithiau Ifor Williams*, p. 63 (a rather incomplete index).

into print in LHEB and elsewhere,[17] but I have gleaned a number of unpublished linguistic gems and cite them here – always as 'KHJ' rather than 'Jackson', to emphasize that Professor Jackson did not intend them for publication and would not necessarily have held to the views expresssed.

1.4 THE CHRONOLOGY OF THE INSCRIPTIONS: THE PROBLEM

A burning issue for some years has been the chronology of the Brittonic inscriptions. They have rarely been dated on linguistic grounds (as opposed to linguistic developments being dated on the basis of the stones). Fairly typical is Nash-Williams's relative and absolute chronology for the 444 inscribed and uninscribed Welsh monuments in ECMW: he classified them relatively in four groups, and dated them absolutely in periods between the fifth and the thirteenth centuries.[18] This scheme reflects the consensus at the time (1950): Ralegh Radford (from 1937 onwards) and Kenneth Jackson were operating with broadly similar systems, which they also applied to the Brittonic monuments of north and south-west Britain. Nash-Williams's scheme, in his own words, rested 'mainly on internal or typological considerations. The crucial features here are monumental form, decoration, and epigraphy, all of which undergo changes as time goes on' (p. 2). For brevity's sake I refer to these various non-linguistic dating criteria as 'epigraphic' throughout this book. It is notable (and advantageous from our point of view) that philology was not apparently a dating factor for Nash-Williams, despite the fact that he was in touch with linguists like Ifor Williams and Kenneth Jackson.

More recently, the epigraphers' consensus has been under attack. In 1990 I myself criticized the validity of the absolute dates for the handful of early monuments on which Nash-Williams's and Jackson's absolute dating of the British corpus ultimately rests – in my view there were no externally datable monuments before the ninth century – and this critique has been regarded by Harvey (2001) as if anything too mild.[19] The typological schemes for the

---

[17] See bibliography of Jackson's publications by J. E. C. Williams, *SC*, 14/15 (1979–80), 5–11, and 26/27 (1991–92), 211–12. By agreement with Professor Gillies, I have religiously cited 'KHJ' for all plausible points gleaned from his notes, while passing over in silence any that seemed to have been superseded. Eventually his copy of CIIC will be deposited in the National Library of Scotland.

[18] ECMW, p. 2, Table I. See discussion by Edwards, *Med. Arch.*, 45 (2001), 15–39. Cf. the remarks on the replacement of capital by cursive letters by Hughes, *AC*, 7th ser. 4 (1924), 42–45, Alcock, *Arthur's Britain*, pp. 243–45, Charles-Edwards, in *The Celtic World*, p. 715, n. 65, and in *Literacy in Medieval Celtic Societies*, p. 63, and Handley, in IEMB, pp. 50–51 and 53, and *EME*, 10 (2001), 196.

[19] For Nash-Williams's absolute dates, see ECMW, p. 1, n. 3. Cf. Sims-Williams, in *Britain 400–600*, pp. 226 and 236–37, and below, Table 3.5; Harvey, in *Roman, Runes and Ogham*, pp. 42–44. I followed Jackson in regarding *c.* 625 (death of King Cadfan) as only a *terminus post quem* for 970/13 CATAMANUS, not a fixed date.

development of letter forms (and other visual variables) have also been criticized, notably by Ken Dark (1992), Elisabeth Okasha (1993), Catherine Swift (1997), and Mark Handley (2001), who are all sceptical or agnostic about relative dating by typology. On the other hand, Carlo Tedeschi (1995, 2001) has defended and refined the typological system.[20] What is badly needed is an *independent* check on its validity. Can philology provide an independent relative or even absolute chronology? This is the principal problem addressed in this book.

It might seem that the absolute linguistic chronology has already been established by Jackson in LHEB: after all, he mentions 144 of our 371 inscriptions[21] and offers precise dates such as 'early sixth century' and 'seventh century' for many of them. It must therefore be stressed, as Okasha does,[22] that Jackson honestly and explicitly arrived at these dates not on *linguistic* but on *epigraphic* grounds, following the same sort of procedure as Nash-Williams (with whom he discussed letter forms in correspondence). He then used these epigraphic dates to help put absolute dates on his relative chronology of sound changes. For example, in discussing the change of /a:/ > /ɔ:/ > /au/ in Welsh (a relative chronology which was already well-established)[23] and the absolute date when /ɔ:/ > /au/ would have been shown in writing, Jackson pays particular attention to inscription 427/b/301 CATUOCONI which 'still has' /ɔ:/ and to inscription 986/62 RUALLAUN, which was the oldest case of /au/ known to him (see Fig. 1.1).

These inscriptions were important to Jackson because he had dated both stones to the eighth century on *epigraphic* grounds, and indeed justified the dating with reference to his correspondence with Nash-Williams.[24] Thus the epigraphy is dating the O to AU changeover to the eighth century; the linguistic changeover is not dating the stones. The same applies throughout LHEB, and partly[25] explains why Jackson only cited half of the available British inscriptions there: he only needed to identify the epigraphically

---

[20] Charles Thomas is a special case; in his *Mute Stones* (1994) he gives dates 'based on context, form, epigraphic *and linguistic* nature', etc. (p. 262 [my italics]; cf. pp. 289, 299, and 327).

[21] 142 of our inscriptions are cited in the index to LHEB, pp. 751–52, to which add the citations of 2038 BRANHUI and 2007/10 MAILISI on pp. 721 and 739.

[22] *Corpus*, p. 52 (cf. Thomas, *Mute Stones*, p. 71). This is amply confirmed by KHJ's notes and corrections to CIIC, which show the minute care he took in epigraphical fieldwork. It is in fact notable that the epigraphical work of Rhys, Williams, and Jackson surpassed that of most of their non-philological contemporaries. While no one would venture into Latin or Greek epigraphy without knowing the languages, knowledge of Celtic has never been regarded a *sine qua non* in Celtic epigraphy.

[23] e.g. VKG i, 47. Unlike Jackson, I use the colon rather than the macron to indicate long vowels, and /ɔ/ and /ɛ/ rather than his hooked *o* and *e* to indicate a open /o/ and /e/. I write /o̧/ and /ȩ/ for the corresponding close vowels.

[24] LHEB, pp. 291, n. 2, 293–94, and 294, n. 1.

[25] Other reasons are that many of the inscriptions contain irrelevant Latin, Irish, or non-diagnostic Brittonic names.

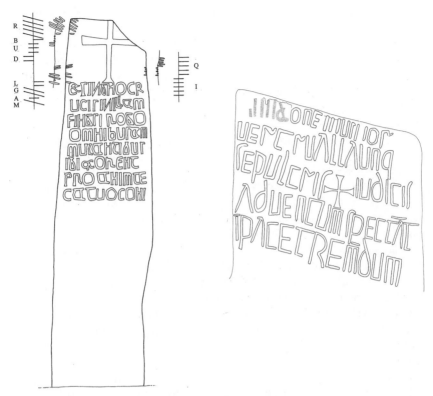

Figure 1.1 Caldey Island (427/b/301) and Llanlleonfel (986/62) inscriptions
(Crown copyright: RCAHMW; and courtesy of National Museum of Wales)

earliest and latest forms that attested to any given sound.[26] This was a
completely rational procedure, but its validity depends on the accuracy of
the non-linguistic typology for the monuments, which is now in question.

What I propose to do is to reverse the process. Instead of using the
epigraphy to date the sound changes, I intend to use the relative chronology
of the sound changes to date the epigraphy, or at least to see whether the
Nash-Williams/Jackson/Tedeschi relative chronology holds up. This has not
been done so far, presumably for fear of what Okasha calls a 'circular
argument'.[27] Actually, that danger can be avoided, so long as one does not
simply take dates from Jackson's Chronological Table,[28] such as 'eighth
century' for /ɔː/ > /au/, and use them to 'confirm' the eighth century as the
terminus ante quem for 427/b/301 CATUOCONI and terminus post quem
for 986/62 RUALLAUN.

[26] In practice, however, he was more generous with examples; see the lists in Ch. 2 below.
[27] *Corpus*, p. 52. Similarly Handley, *EME*, 10 (2001), 196.
[28] LHEB, §210, and Appendix 3 below.

In the first place, philologists are well capable of establishing free-standing *relative* chronologies of sound changes on internal linguistic grounds, and the Brittonic languages are no exception. In fact, their trajectory is very well known, thanks to the remains of Old Welsh, Cornish, and Breton from *c.* 800 onwards plus triangulation from ancient Continental Celtic and Old Irish evidence and from the other Indo-European languages. The *relative* chronology is already implicit in Holder Pedersen's grammar of 1909–1913 (VKG), and has since been refined, with very little dependence on the inscriptions, by Morris-Jones, Jackson, Hamp, Schrijver, and others. The *absolute* chronology of the sound changes (which is of lesser interest to most of these philologists) is more tricky, but I must stress that the approximate absolute dates given in Jackson's *Language and History* and his *Historical Phonology of Breton* (HPB) do not wholly depend on the inscriptions; indeed, the Breton inscriptions do not seem to be used at all in the 904 pages of HPB.[29] Jackson's absolute dates depended principally on: the phonetics of words and names borrowed from Latin into Brittonic, and from the latter into Irish and Anglo-Saxon; names quoted in Latin texts; and, from *c.* 800 onwards, the Old Welsh, Cornish, and Breton glosses. There is some room for manoeuvre with these absolute dates, taking into account developments in the relevant auxiliary sciences,[30] not to mention the truism that sound changes do not occur overnight or uniformly (either geographically or demographically). Nevertheless, the fact remains that much of Jackson's relative and absolute chronology does not depend on the inscriptions and *can* therefore be applied to them without circularity.

It is important to start with relative chronology before proceding to absolute chronology. In his chronological table in LHEB §210, Jackson arranged 98 (unnumbered!) Brittonic sound changes in approximate chronological order between the first century BC and the twelfth AD. (In this book I number them from ‡1 to ‡98; see Appendix 3.) Philologists thrive on controversy, so it is reassuring to report that on the whole his scheme has lasted well.[31] In ‡‡1–98 of my 'Brittonic Phonology' chapter I have looked

---

[29] Breton inscriptions were already available in Loth's *Chrestomathie bretonne* [Chrest.], pp. 82–86, but none of them figure in the index to HPB. In LHEB, p. 67, Jackson describes the Breton inscriptions as 'of no special importance to this book'.

[30] See Sims-Williams, in *Britain 400–600*, pp. 217–61. I argued that the sound changes had taken place orally earlier than Jackson supposed, but this may affect the inscriptions less than might be supposed, since they are native written records and can be expected to be orthographically conservative. See Ch. 3 below. On conservatism in general see Harvey, in *Roman, Runes and Ogham*. He raises the theoretical problem that a late but linguistically knowledgeable inscriber might have been able to create a linguistically 'early-looking inscription' (p. 42). The independent epigraphic evidence discussed below undermines this hypothesis, unless we suppose that such a skilled inscriber could also simulate early letter forms. A perfect forgery is by definition undetectable.

[31] Various possible or certain modifications will be reported passim. Note that some of Jackson's sound changes are not ordered but simply grouped in batches, and that some are ordered only on the basis of epigraphy; this will be borne in mind below as appropriate.

through the corpus of inscriptions in Appendix 1 for evidence for all ninety-eight sound changes, and have listed *all* the probable and possible examples, not just those on the epigraphically 'earliest' or 'latest' stones. This will make it possible, in the 'Brittonic Chronology' chapter, to say whether or not there is any correlation between the linguistic and non-linguistic relative chronologies. For instance, does Nash-Williams place the Welsh inscriptions reflecting /aː/, /ɔː/, and /au/ respectively in three successive epigraphical periods – in which case philology would indeed confirm his typology – or is there no correlation, confirming the fears of the sceptics? If there is a significant correlation, it will then be worthwhile to examine the distribution of *a*, *o*, and *au* spellings in datable *non-epigraphic* sources, and to use the latter to check on Nash-Williams's *absolute* chronology – always bearing in mind that the orthography of non-epigraphic and epigraphic texts *may* have developed at differing speeds.[32] There is no element of circularity in this procedure.

Since many inscriptions provide evidence of more than one sound change, we can attempt placing them in a relative order which, if it is coherent, should be sufficiently complex as to be almost self-confirming. I take as an example the six sound changes listed, in Jackson's chronological order, in Table 1.1. One or more of the six is relevant to 191 of our 371 inscriptions. In Table 1.1, the six are numbered 2–7 down the left, and, in column A, I give one example of an inscription where the sound change is *not* shown in the spelling, while in column B I give one example where it *is* shown. The working assumption is that stage B is always later than stage A, although we may find exceptions, a couple of examples being given in row 2:

(i) The first problem noted there is that some names are ambiguously Irish or British. For example, is 399/176 TOVISACI 'leader' (genitive) the ancestor of W. *tywysog*, with A still written, or is it the ancestor of Ir. *taoiseach*? If it is Irish, we would not expect the change /aː/ > /ɔː/ ever to happen, and we ought to leave it out of consideration. This is a serious problem in view of the extent of Irish settlement in western Britain.[33] In order to identify such cases I have systematically searched the various Irish onomastic corpora,[34] and I have also used various studies of Continental Celtic names to try and predict which names may have formed part of a common Insular Celtic stock.[35] In the Index of Forms

---

[32] Cf. p. 275 below.

[33] See e.g. Richards, *JRSAI*, 90 (1960), 133–62, and Thomas, *Mute Stones*; cf. Sims-Williams, *CMCS*, 44 (2002).

[34] Principally Meyer's *Contributions* and DIL (for A–E only); CGH and CGSH; LEIA (A–D and M–U); Ziegler; and the publications by O'Brien and Uhlich listed in my Bibliography.

[35] In particular KPN, GPN, Grauf., Oswald, RIG, Holder's *Alt-celtischer Sprachschatz* (cited as 'Holder'), Birkhan's *Germanen und Kelten*, Alföldy's *Noricum*, and Weisgerber's *Rhenania Germano-Celtica*. On comparison between Continental and Insular Celtic names see esp. Evans, *BBCS*, 24 (1970–72), 415–34. A source which I have not exploited fully, for reasons of

Discussed I have attempted to single-underline possible Irish names, and double-underline probable ones.

(ii) The second problem is raised by Latin names: although many Roman names became naturalized in British – *Marciānus* becoming W. *Meirchion*, *Vītālis* and *Vītālīnus* becoming W. *Gwidol* and *Gwidolin*, people may have been slower to write a change like A /a:/ to O /ɔ:/ in Roman names than in native names (such as *Maglākos becoming Archaic OW *Mailoc*), because of the weight of the classical tradition. In trying to identify the less common Roman names, I have paid particular attention to selected sources from Roman Britain.[36]

In short, then, we have to expect some problems both with ambiguously Irish/British names and with Latin names, and these need to be deferred until the straightforwardly native Brittonic names have been dealt with.

Whether or not Jackson's absolute dates for our six sample sound changes are precise,[37] nobody doubts that he has them in the right relative order: his scheme has an internal linguistic logic – for example, he argues that VENDESETLI must have become VENNISETLI (our sound change 3) before syncope (sound change 6) or the result would have been W. **Gwyntoedl rather than the attested Welsh name *Gwynnhoedl*.[38] We can therefore try using our six sound changes to put the 191 relevant inscriptions in sequence.

In an ideal world, where every inscription witnessed to every sound change, we would end up with an arrangement as in Table 1.2a. Col. 1 shows the number of the imaginary inscription, and cols. 2–7 are our six sound changes in chronological order. If we put A where the change has not happened and B where it has, the inscriptions should fall neatly into seven periods as shown. In Period 1, no changes have happened, as the row of As show. In Period 2, the first change (/a:/ > /ɔ:/) has happened, hence the B in column 2. In Period 3, the first two changes have happened (/a:/ > /ɔ:/ and

---

time, is Whatmough's *Dialects of Ancient Gaul* (DAG). Our Aberystwyth digital index to Holder was not advanced enough to be used.

[36] RIB i–ii; Tab.Vindol. ii; Tab.Luguval.; Tab.Sulis (see Abbreviations); and inscriptions published in *JRS* between 1955 and 1969 and in *Britannia* up to 2001. Needless to say, the persons mentioned in these sources were not all Britons in any sense (cf. PRB), but they give an idea of the names that may have survived the Roman empire in Britain. For the Continent I relied on Kajanto and Mócsy, and also used some of the databases listed by Bodel, *Epigraphic Evidence*, especially the Epigraphische Datenbank Heidelberg. Mócsy's data is now incorporated with additions in the *Onomasticon Provinciarum Europae Latinarum* (OPEL), but I only refer to this sporadically as publication was not completed until 2002.

[37] LHEB, §210, and Appendix 3 below. Here, and for most of this book, I avoid citing Jackson's absolute dates, in order to avoid the suggestion of a circular argument. Occasionally, however, I cite them when Jackson expresses relative chronology in terms of absolute dates as a sort of shorthand.

[38] LHEB, p. 512; cf. Sims-Williams, in *Britain 400–600*, p. 239, n. 81 (but see below, Ch. 3, p. 283, n. 88). When we come to deal with all 98 changes, however, the possibility will arise of making minor adjustments to Jackson's order. See pp. 258 and 352 below.

Table 1.1 Examples of sound changes ('A' > 'B')

1		A >	B
2	a: > ɔ: ‡18	363/143 CARANT<u>A</u>CVS Problems: e.g. 399/176 TOVIS<u>A</u>CI (Irish?) 473/a/Ok46 VIT<u>A</u>LI (Latin)	427/b/301 CATUOC<u>O</u>NI
3	nd > nn ‡22	390/96 VE<u>ND</u>ESETLI	376/174 VE<u>NN</u>ISETLI
4	-Σ- > -h- ‡36	376/174 VENNI<u>S</u>ETLI	365/149 MAVO<u>H</u>ENI
5	apocope ‡37	322/27 CAMVLOR<u>IS</u> (excluding possibly Latinate -VS, -I, -A, -E)	350/116/3 IDNERT (i.e. with ending lost)
6	syncope ‡38	342/70 CVN<u>O</u>CENNI	1000/182 C<u>O</u>NCENN
7	internal *i*-affection ‡‡57 and 64	329/42 C<u>A</u>NNTIANI (i.e. /a/ > /ei/ not shown)	1014/231/908 <u>E</u>NNIAUN (i.e. /a/ > /ei/ shown)

/nd/ > /nn/), hence the two Bs. In Period 4 /-Σ-/ > /-h-/ has happened as well – and so on until Period 7 includes the inscriptions where all six changes have occurred.

In the real world we can expect a more patchy pattern, as in Table 1.2b. Some inscriptions will bear no information one way or other about some changes, but we can still periodize them broadly. In Table 1.2b the *capital* As and Bs show the expected patchy data. Giving the inscriptions the benefit of the doubt, I have put a small *a* in any spaces to the *right* of every capital A, on the grounds that if the inscription fails to show an earlier change it is unlikely that it would show a later one, supposing that a diagnostic form turned up in it. For example, since in inscription 103 /a:/ > /ɔ:/ has not happened in col. 2, nor apocope in col. 5, I am assuming that if another fragment of it turned up that was relevant to the other variables it would in each case show the earlier form: ND rather than NN in col. 3, S rather than H in col. 4, and so on. This is the justification for the small letters *a*. Rather similarly I have put a small *b* in any spaces to the *left* of every capital B, on the grounds that if the inscription shows a later change it would also show an earlier one if it could, so to speak. For example, I am assuming that since imaginary inscription 51 shows -S- > -H- in col. 4, it would have shown ND > NN in col. 3 if that sequence of letters had occurred in it. – The mnemonic, then, is 'a *after* A and b *before* B'.

Once we have added in the lower-case letters, we are still left with various 'black holes' where we do not know whether to put *a* or *b*. These black holes mean that some inscriptions must be listed as spanning more than one

Table 1.2a Ideal attestation of sound changes

		sound changes					
		2	**3**	**4**	**5**	**6**	**7**
Period	*ins.*						
1	103	A	A	A	A	A	A
1	124	A	A	A	A	A	A
2	109	B	A	A	A	A	A
2	10	B	A	A	A	A	A
3	114	B	B	A	A	A	A
3	213	B	B	A	A	A	A
4	51	B	B	B	A	A	A
4	59	B	B	B	A	A	A
5	28	B	B	B	B	A	A
5	30	B	B	B	B	A	A
6	9	B	B	B	B	B	A
6	97	B	B	B	B	B	A
7	18	B	B	B	B	B	B
7	385	B	B	B	B	B	B

Table 1.2b Expected attestation of sound changes

		sound changes					
		2	**3**	**4**	**5**	**6**	**7**
Period	*ins.*						
1	103	A	a	a	A	a	a
1	124	A	a	A	a	A	a
2	109	B	A	A	a	a	a
2-4	10	B			A	a	A
3-4	114	B	B		A	a	a
3-5	213	b	B			A	A
4-7	51	B	b	B			
4-5	59	B	B	B		A	a
5	28	B	b	B	B	A	a
5-6	30	b	b	b	B		A
6	9	b	b	b	b	B	A
6-7	97	b	B	b	B	B	
7	18	B	b	b	B	b	B
7	385	b	b	B	b	b	B

period. For example, inscription 30 would be Period 5 if we put *a* in the black hole, but Period 6 if we put *b*. As we cannot decide which to put, we have to call it Period 5–6.

But should we give the inscriptions the benefit of the doubt when inserting the lower-case letters? Why should we assume that the *a*s and *b*s would not occur in a random fashion, with *a* coming before *b* (the unacceptable permutation) as often as *b* before *a* (the acceptable one)? Here some statistics are consoling. In our corpus of 191 inscriptions relevant to our six sound changes, there are only five problem cases (discussed below) where A comes before B. By contrast

> There are 105 inscriptions with only one (capital) A (55) or one B (50). There are forty-eight inscriptions with either two A (13) or two B (35). There are eighteen inscriptions with either three A (3) or three B (15).[39]

These 171 'same-letter' inscriptions present no problem without being especially revealing methodologically. It is more interesting that

> There are twenty inscriptions which combine one or more capital A with one or more capital B.

If we are right to give the inscriptions the benefit of the doubt, as I am doing, we should find that *all* the Bs precede *all* the As. In fact

> All Bs precede all As in fifteen of the twenty inscriptions.

This is not perfect, but is better than what one might expect by chance. The twenty break down as follows (starring the unacceptable permutations):

*AB	2 examples
*ABA	3 examples
BA	9 examples
BAA	2 examples
BBA	3 examples
BBBA	1 example
Total	20

We shall have look at the five problems, but just to sum up the statistics, we have eighty-six inscriptions (48 + 18 + 20) with at least two capitals, that is, data on at least two sound changes; and among these eighty-six, there are only five irregular inscriptions where an A occurs *before* a B, that is, where an early sound change is not shown but a later one is. Obviously the pattern is not a random one.

The five problem cases (starred in Table 1.3) are as follows:

(i) 448/370 RINACI NOMENA shows retention of /a:/ in the well-known Celtic *-ākos* suffix (> OW -*oc*, -*auc*), but /nd/ already having become /nn/, assuming that it is a Welsh cognate of Ir. *Rindach*, as Rhys suggested. The obvious solution is that Rhys's etymology was wrong, and that the name, if Welsh, has some other first element, perhaps the *Rin-* that appears in Old Breton names such as *Rinuiu* (: W. *rhin*?).[40] In this case the sound

---

[39] No inscriptions have 4 or more of the same capital letter. I do not give details of the inscriptions on which the above statistics are based since all the data are incorporated in the full tables in Ch. 3 below. Compare 'seriation' in Tyers, *Pottery*, p. 39.

[40] See ‡22.

change /nd/ > /nn/ is irrelevant, and the B that denotes it can be changed to *a*.

(ii) 2029/p.39i ERECOR / MAGLORI / CVNIIAC / FICIT again shows retention of /aː/ in CVNIIAC, assuming it is Welsh, but also the later apocope in this name and ERECOR. This stone is only known from an 1827 drawing, however, and rather than use the latter to overturn the tenets of Celtic philology, it is safer to use the philology to cast doubt on the drawing: possibly the terminations of ERECOR and CVNIIAC were either broken off the stone or were not recognized by the 1827 copyist (who would have been unfamiliar with the convention of writing final I horizontally, for instance). In this case the B denoting apocope can be changed to *a*.

To make such a change is not to manipulate the evidence, but simply to make explicit and formalize the sort of procedure that historical linguists are bound to adopt in such circumstances. The remaining three problem cases can be taken together:

(iii) 355/128/8 SILBANDVS IACIT is counted as pre- /aː/ > /ɔː/ but post- /nd/ > /nn/ on the basis of Jackson's tentative suggestion than the name is *Silbānus* (a Vulgar Latin form of *Silvānus*), with ND as a hypercorrect Welsh spelling of /n/, after /nd/ had become /nn/.[41] Since hypercorrection is a kind of conservatism, the *a*-spelling could also be conservative.

(iv) 365/149, when complete, read MAVOHENI FILI LVNARI HIC OCCISUS according to Lhuyd. Here we have -S- > -H- having happened in the first name (cf. W. *hen* 'old' < Celtic *seno*-), but LVNARI not yet showing A > O. The obvious explanation is the conservative Latin spelling tradition regarding /aː/; Latin *Lunāris* is still being spelt as it was in Romano-British inscriptions.[42]

(v) 419/284 FILIAE SALVIA[N]I HIC IACET VE[ ]MAIE UXSOR TIGIRNICI ET FILIE EIUS ONERATI [UXSOR IA]CIT RIGOHENI [ ]OCETI [ ]ACI. Exactly the same applies here. RIGOHENI has -H- < -S-, but the well-known Latin name *Salviānus* is spelt in the traditional way with A rather than O.

The root of the trouble with these last three exceptions seems to be that /aː/ > /ɔː/ was not always shown in Latin names, as we anticipated, and therefore cannot be relied upon. I therefore change A to *b* in col. 2 in each case, on the grounds that it should not have been assumed that /ɔː/ < /aː/ would not sometimes still have been spelled A in Latin names.

The patterns that occur in the twenty inscriptions that mix A and B are shown in Table 1.3. With the adjustments suggested above, the pattern in Table 1.3 is acceptable: B always occurs before A.

---

[41] However, see ‡‡ 18 and 22, and p. 321 for the suggestion that SILBANDVS may be Hiberno-Latin.

[42] See e.g. RIB i 786 and 1521.

Table 1.3 Inscriptions with both innovations and conservations

'CIIC' nos.	Sound changes						Period	ECMW etc. nos.	Data from Appendix 1
	2	3	4	5	6	7			
*448	A	B	a	a	a	a	1	370	1. **RINACI** {or PINACI} NOMENA
*2029	A	a	a	B	a	A	1	p. 39i	2. **ERECOR** MAGLORI CVNIAC FICIT
385	B				A	a	2–5	89	3. FILI LOVERNII ANATEMORI
477	B				A	a	2–5	Ok11	4. CONETOCI FILI TEGERNOMALI
487	B				A	a	2–5	Ok10	5. ....HIC IACIT CVNOMORI FILIVS
2028	B				A	A	2–5	Corn.	6. PATER COLIAVIFICIT ARTOGNOV[
3006	B				A	a	2–5	C1	7. DISIDERI FILI BODOGNOVS
376	b	B	A	a	A	a	3	174	8. VENNISETLI FILIVS ERCAGNI
400	b	B			A	a	3–5	177	9. VINNEMAGLI FILI SENEMAGLI
970	b	B			A	a	3–5	13	10. CATAMANUS REX SAPIENTISIMUS OPINATISIMUS OMNIUM REGUM
3005	b	B			A	a	3–5	F5	11. ?]NOMAILI FILIUS VENOMAILI
*355	A	B					3–7	128/8	12. **SILBANDVS** IACIT
*365	A	b	B		A	a	4–5	149	13. **MAVOHENI** FILI LVNARI HIC OCCISUS {Lhuyd}
*419	A	b	B		A	a	4–5	284	14. FILIAE **SALVIA[N]I** HIC IACIT VE[ ]MAIE UXSOR TIGIRNICI ET FILIE EIUS ONERATI [UXSOR {?} IA]CIT **RIGOHENE** [ ]OCETI [ ]ACI
486	b	b	b	B	B	A	6	Ok56	15. CVMREGNI { or: CVMRECINI } FILI MAVCI
490	B	b	B	b	B	A	6	Ok29	16. DATUIDOCI CONHINOCI FILIVS
493	b	b	b	b	B	A	6	Ok58	17. NEPRANI FILI CONBEVI
1044	b	b	b	B	B	A	6	Ok7	18. + LEUIUT IUSIT HEC ALTARE PRO ANIMA SUA
1054	b	b	b	B	B	A	6	Ok43	19. DONIERT ROGAVIT PRO ANIMA
3013	b	b	b	b	B	A	6	M4	20. CROX BRIT[ ] ET MULIER*IS* [ ] DRILEGO [ ] *FILI* CONB*RITI* HOC OPUS EORUM QUICUMQUE LIGAVIRIT

Table 1.4 Examples of the periodization of the 191 Brittonic inscriptions which show *at least one* of the sound changes 2–7

Period	*Sound changes*						Quantity of inscriptions
	2	3	4	5	6	7	
1	A	a	a	a	a	A	28
1–2		A	A	a	A	a	5
3	b	B	A	a	A	a	1
1–3			A	a	A	a	2
1–4				A	a	a	4
4–5	*b*	b	B		A	a	2
3–5	b	B			A	a	3
2–5	B				A	a	5
1–5					A	a	24
6	B	b	B	b	B	A	6
1–6						A	10
7	B	b	b	B	b	B	12
6–7	b	b	B	B	B		49
5–7	b	B	b	B			32
3–7	B	B					4
2–7	B						4
							191 total

With these five adjustments made, one can now complete the periodization of all 191 of the relevant Brittonic inscriptions. The patterns that occur are shown in Table 1.4, with the quantity of inscriptions showing each pattern listed on the right.[43] There are twenty-eight from Period 1; five from Period 1–2; one from Period 3; and so on. Obviously it is not very useful to date ten inscriptions so vaguely as 'Period 1–6', but some of these ought to fall into place when the rest of the ninety-eight sound changes are taken into account in Chapter 3.

Since Nash-Williams included and offered dates for 115 of these 191 inscriptions,[44] it should not be difficult to see whether or not there is any significant correlation between his epigraphic relative chronology and our quite independent linguistic relative chronology. In Table 1.5, the rows show our linguistic periods and the columns show Nash-Williams's dates. The periodization of the inscriptions shown in italics at the top and bottom is too vague to be useful, but the remainder show a clear correlation between language and epigraphy, as indicated by the three boxes.

---

[43] Note that the 28 examples of **A**aaaa**A** etc. will have various permutations of upper and lower case, and the 6 examples of **B**bBb**BA** etc. will sometimes have B instead of b, and so on. What is important for the periodization is that the **A**s and **B**s shown in **bold** occur as capitals in the relevant position in every instance.

[44] Nash-Williams also included, but did not date, the lost stone 333/50, counted in my Period 5–7 in Table 1.4.

Table 1.5 The 115 linguistically periodized Welsh inscriptions that are also dated typologically by Nash-Williams in ECMW

Per.	5c	5-6c	6c	6-7c	7c	7-9c	9c	9-10c	10c	10-11c	11c	11-12c	12c
1-5		318 319 342 362 370 401 413 435 446 449 455	325 349 358 361 387 436 447										
1-6		341 346 352A 394 442	409										
1	[1-4]	329 330 344 379 381 391 392 399 418 426 432 445 448	363 389 397 408 424 451	334	**404**								
1-2		328 368/b 429 454	390	1028									
1-3		377 417											
1-4	322	354											
2-5		385		[2-5]									
3		376											
3-5		400			970								
4-5			365 419										
7						995 1033 984 986 992 993 998 1004 1025	427/b 979 994 1000 1005	1014 348/b 1041 1065	1013 997	2008 1012 1015 1016 1027	1009 1022 1018 1019 1023 1024 1035	1008 2022	1032
6-7	**p397**		**324** **350**										
5-7			**440**			971	1011	1001	978	985 1036	1039	337 980 988 996	[5-7]
3-7		355	398										
2-7		366 412											
	5c	5-6c	6c	6-7c	7c	7-9c	9c	9-10c	10c	10-11c	11c	11-12c	12c

In fact the two schemes only conflict in five cases as opposed to 110 cases where they are compatible:[45]

(a) 404/270/843 is in our Period 1 because of the apparent /a:/ in TEGERNACUS, but is relatively late ('seventh-century') according to Nash-Williams. This is the most problematic case. There are three possible explanations. First, Nash-Williams's date may be too late; Tedeschi prefers the second half of the sixth century.[46] Secondly, TEGERNACUS may be the ancestor not of W. *Teyrnog* but of the well-known Irish cognate *Tighearnach*, which would still have been spelt with an A in the seventh century and indeed down to this day.[47] Thirdly, it may be that the ending -*acus* was sometimes conserved, owing to its frequent occurrence in Latinized Celtic names.[48]

The remaining four problem cases are all early according to Nash-Williams, but appear relatively late linguistically. It may be significant that our texts of them all depend on antiquarian transcripts of doubtful reliability (see Fig. 1.2).

(b) p. 397/285 BARRECTI, from Tomen y Mur, appears to be sub-Roman in Westwood's engraving, but is post-syncope if it derives from *Barro-rect-*. My linguistic analysis may be incorrect, however,[49] or the engraving may be unreliable.

(c) 324/34 is as late as Period 6–7 on account of the apparent syncope in CO[N]BURRI < *Kuno-burrī*. This lost Llantrisant inscription is known only from an appallingly bad eighteenth-century transcript, and either the reading of the syncope may be wrong or Nash-Williams's admittedly tentative epigraphic dating may be mistaken.[50]

(d) 440/335 is as late as Period 5–7 on the grounds that the second name shows apocope (-CAN rather than -CANI). Here again we are relying on a copy of this lost stone at Llanychaer, made by or for Edward Lhuyd. The inscription may have been miscopied (the reading may have been -CAVI with ligatured VI, or -CAN– with horizontal I) or the edge of the stone may even have been broken.[51]

(e) 350/116/3, the IDNERT stone at Llanddewibrefi, is in my Period 6–7 on account of the apocope and syncope but is early ('sixth century')

---

[45] I do not give details of the 110 'compatible' inscriptions, since all this information is subsumed into Ch. 3 below and there greatly refined. Inevitably, some inscriptions which are in the present 'compatible' category will emerge as problems when a larger number of sound changes is taken into account there; but the present sampling of 6 sound changes retains its overall value.

[46] *Scrittura e civiltà*, 19 (1995), 119.

[47] In this case the vocalism of TEG- would probably be due to Welsh influence; see Ch. 3 below, p. 272.

[48] See below, p. 272.

[49] See below, p. 273.

[50] See below, p. 294.

[51] See Ch. 2 below, ‡17n.

Figure 1.2 Tomen y Mur, Llantrisant, Llanychaer, and Llanddewibrefi stones
(Sources: LW, plate 78; Hübner (see p. 128, n. 727 below); British Library, Stowe MS 1023,
fo. 139r; Crown copyright: RCAHMW)

according to Nash-Williams in ECMW. At that time only a fragment of the stone was known; when Lhuyd's complete transcript turned up in 1961 (see Fig. 1.2), it was obviously epigraphically more advanced, by Nash-Williams's own criteria, than he had been able to see.[52]

It is striking that Nash-Williams's relative dating, in 110 out of 115 cases, is broadly in line with the linguistic evidence for relative dating which he preferred to ignore – and that the five disparities are not difficult to explain away. This encourages one to compare the epigraphic and linguistic chronologies in closer detail, to see whether they can be used to refine each other, and to see whether linguistic evidence from non-epigraphic sources can be used to transform these relative chronologies into absolute chronologies. These tasks must be postponed, however, until the evidence for the rest of the ninety-eight sound changes has been collected in the following chapter.

[52] See below, p. 274.

2

BRITTONIC PHONOLOGY

In his Chronological Table in *Language and History in Early Britain*, §210 (pp. 695–99),[1] Jackson lists ninety-eight Brittonic sound changes between the first century BC and the twelfth century AD. These will here be numbered from ‡1 to ‡98 and will be adopted as sub-headings, along with the LHEB page or paragraph numbers to which he refers in §210 for supporting argumentation (e.g. '‡1 *st* perhaps already > *ss*; LHEB §122'). The absolute dates to which Jackson assigns ‡‡ 1–98 (see Appendix 3 below) are not quoted, since here we are more concerned with ‡‡ 1–98 as offering an approximate *relative* chronology for the sound changes (*absolute* chronology being discussed in the next chapter). While there is room for dispute about details and for further refinement,[2] Jackson's relative chronology is undoubtedly broadly correct and there is no generally agreed alternative. Points in dispute will be noted passim below.

For most sound changes from the fifth century onwards some inscriptional evidence is cited by Jackson. Generally he cites only a few examples, usually (A) the (epigraphically) latest inscriptions in which a sound change has *not* occurred and (B) the (epigraphically) earliest inscriptions in which a sound change *has* occurred. In what follows I have attempted to enlarge Jackson's list to include all probable examples of (A) and (B) stages, partly because I am not taking for granted the accuracy of his epigraphical dates, and partly with a view to providing complete lists of forms for analysis in Chapter 3 below. (The order in which I list inscriptions is not significant, but tends to follow the order in ECMW and then that in CIIC for inscriptions absent from ECMW.)

As well as providing lists of probable examples under (A) and (B) below, I also discuss borderline and ambiguous forms which have to be excluded from the lists for one reason or another. A particular problem is raised by Latin forms, as already noted in Chapter 1. Although many Latin names were fully naturalized and show the same orthographical changes as native Brittonic names, the classical tradition probably acted as a brake on showing sound changes in spelling so soon as in the case of native names (and, of course, in both cases, we have to expect a degree of conservatism). We might expect, then, a Latin name such as *MARCIANI to appear as *MARCIONI later than a native name such as *CATACI would appear as *CATOCI. I can see no clear way of predicting this, however, and there is

---

[1] Cf. HPB, pp. 846–48.
[2] See esp. Sims-Williams, in *Britain 400–600*; Schrijver, SBCHP; McCone, TRC.

therefore an element of arbitariness in the treatment of Latin names below; I will return to this matter in Chapter 3. A further problem is raised by names which are ambiguously Irish or Brittonic, and here again it is difficult to be wholly consistent, especially as the spelling of names in one language may often have been influenced by the phonology of the other language. Instances will be discussed as they arise, but on the whole I have given dubious cases the benefit of the doubt in this chapter and treated them as Brittonic or at least as potentially relevant to Brittonic phonology and orthography. The opposite policy will be followed in Chapter 4 on Irish phonology. In the Index of Forms Discussed, probable Irish forms are double-underlined and possible Irish forms are single-underlined.

Jackson's assumed starting point is a Common Celtic phonological system with the following phonemes:[3]

Vowels: a e i o u   a: e: (< *ei) i: u:
Semi-vowels: i̯ u̯
Short diphthongs:[4] ai oi au eu ou (on the last three cf. ‡8 below).
Consonants: m n r l s (with allophone z) k^w (> p in Brittonic) t k (usually written c in LHEB, and with allophone x, usually written χ in LHEB) b d g. To these Jackson later added g^w (< IE g^{w}h).[5]

For ‡‡ 1–13 there is no inscriptional evidence in our corpus, clearly because these sound changes had been completed and were already shown orthographically before the start of the 'Early Christian' monumental tradition.

‡1 *st perhaps already > ss; LHEB §122*

‡2 *s > Σ; LHEB §115*
On the nature of Σ see ‡‡ 36 and 44 below.

‡3 *Internal -Σ- > nil; LHEB §117*

‡4 *ai already > ɛ [I use this symbol for open ē instead of Jackson's hooked ē]; LHEB §27.3*

‡5 *Vowels of proclitics already reduced; LHEB pp. 663–4*

‡6 *Vowels of final syllables already reduced; LHEB §151*
The evidence for this reduction is questionable.[6]

---

[3] Cf. Sims-Williams, in *Gaulois et celtique continental*, and for a general introduction, see Sims-Williams, in *The Indo-European Languages*, pp. 345–79.
[4] The long diphthongs are of marginal importance here; cf. LHEB, p. 336.
[5] HPB, pp. 480–81. Cf. Sims-Williams, in Evans FS, pp. 196–218, and ‡‡ 66 and 73 below.
[6] For some objections see Sims-Williams, in *Gaulois et celtique continental*.

‡7 χs *already* > X^s; *LHEB p. 538*

Jackson argues that the velar element was weakened rather than strengthened in auslaut, but see ‡14 below.

‡8 *au, eu, ou* > ǭ; *LHEB §22.1*

It is now widely believed, however, that /eu/ and /ou/ had already fallen together as /ou/ in Common Celtic, and Lambert has established that /au/ remained distinct and eventually fell together with /a:/ as /ɔ:/ (cf. ‡18 below).[7]

‡9 *Internal and final CC.* ū > ǖ; *LHEB §23.1*

‡10 *oi* > ū; *LHEB §22.2*

‡11 ị > j; *LHEB §38 A.3*

‡12 ǭ *(and Latin internal* ō) > ū; *LHEB §22.2*

375/166 TOTAVALI (cf. W. *tud*) is probably Irish (: OI *túath*). See ‡38 (BC) below.

‡13 *j* > δ *[I use* δ *instead of Jackson's barred d]; LHEB §38 A.3*

Jackson notes (p. 355) that this is first seen in 413/272 MONEDORIGI (cf. W. *mynydd*), but as there is no example within the corpus of inscriptions where /δ/ has *not* yet developed, it is not a useful criterion for dividing them up chronologically.[8] Further possible examples are 320/26 CVLIDOR(I), if < *Kö-lliδ-o-rīX^s < *Kon-sliị-o-rīgs, and more certainly 394/103 [V]ENEDOTIS (> MW *Gwyndot: Gwynedd* < * *Wēnija*).[9]

‡14 *-x [i.e.* -χ^s, *cf.* ‡7 *above] already* > *-s; LHEB, p. 625 [recte pp. 619, n. 1, and 627–28]*

The phonology seems to me to be incorrect here.

[14] The alleged change concerns British /χs/ (< *-*ks*, *-*gs*, *-*ps* cf. ‡7 above) rather than Latin -*x*. According to the argument in LHEB §§ 125–26, the latter (originally [ks]), came to Britain with the Gaulish [χs]

---

[7] Sims-Williams, in *Gaulois et celtique continental*; Lambert, in *Britain 400–600*, pp. 203–15; SBCHP, p. 195.

[8] It could be argued that /j/ > /δ/ occurred after a phoneme or allophone /δ/ had arisen by lenition of /d/ (‡17 below); cf. Sims-Williams, in *Gaulois et celtique continental*. The same probably applies to /z/ > /δ/; see Watkins, in Meid FS, p. 541. MONEDORIGI has been compared with place names of the 'Montreal' type, but is best taken as a patronymic; cf. LW, pp. 162–63; Holder ii, 623; Watson, *Celtic Place-Names of Scotland*, pp. 396–97.

[9] See ‡‡ 16, 40, and 58 below.

pronunciation,[10] and then developed to [ɪs] (‡52 below), perhaps in about the late sixth century (after the Anglo-Saxons had borrowed the Worcestershire place name Pensax = W. *pen Saeson). Jackson shows that this Latin x must have been distinct from the strongly velar native British sound which he denotes /X^s /, /-χ^s/ even though this had also to be written x in Romano-British sources (e.g. Romano-British TANCORIX).[11]

[14] The fate of this native /X^s/ in auslaut is inevitably obscured by the loss of final syllables, but between vowels it clearly developed to WCB *ch* [x] (also to *h* and nil), 'at some period between the fourth and the sixth to seventh centuries' according to Jackson.[12] Contrast, for example, the fate of Latin x in *Saxo, Saxones* > W. *Sais, Saeson* with the fate of British /X^s/ in W. *dehau* 'south': OI *dess*, Gaulish *Dexsiva*, Greek δεξιός.[13] Unless there is good evidence to the contrary, one should assume that the two sounds developed in the same ways in auslaut, and this is indicated by Latin *crux* > W. *crwys* (with /ɪs/), versus Celtic **su̯eks* > W. *chwech* 'six' (with /x/). Jackson, however, explains away *chwech* as an antevocalic sandhi form (and similarly MW *ech* < **eks*),[14] and maintains that 'in IE. final position *-x* > *-χs* seems to have given *-s* in Brit. by the fifth century, later lost'. The only evidence cited for this doctrine, which goes back to John Rhys and Ifor Williams, is the inscriptions themselves.[15] Their testimony, however, is ambiguous, as we shall see.

[14] Jackson's two examples of his *-s* stage (p. 619) are 322/27 CAMVLORIS < **Camulorīx* on an Anglesey lead coffin (already cited by Rhys and Williams), and 354/126/6 ORDOVS < **Ordovix* in Ceredigion. These names contain the two most common of the relevant Celtic name

---

[10] Jackson notes the possibility (no more) that some cases of *xs* instead of *x* in Gaul 'may be intended to represent χs' (LHEB, p. 536, n. 3; cf. ibid., p. 192; GPN, pp. 398–99; Hamp, *Britannia*, 6 (1975), 158–59; VLRB, pp. 919–20). Examples of *xs* in Roman Britain include *Alexsander* [modern import?] (cf. OPEL i, 75–76), *Maxsima* [ditto], *Maxsimus*, [*Max*]*sumus* (RIB i), *Mocux*[*s*]*oma* and]*xsmus* (RIB ii), *Exsactoris* and *Exsibuus* (Tab.Sulis). In connection with the names discussed below, note the Gaulish coin legends in -RIXS and -VIXS listed in RIG iv, 527. VXSOR for *uxor* (cf. RIB i 169) occurs in the Welsh inscriptions 419/284 and 451/401 (and cf. 321/25]SORIS cited in n. 49 below).

[11] RIB i 908, cited with other examples in LHEB, p. 536, n. 2; cf. MW *Tyngyr* (Lloyd-Jones, BBCS, 14 (1950–52), 36; DLG, p. 244; CBT iii, 126), and possibly *Tyncryn/Tyngryn* in *Merioneth Lay Subsidy*, ed. Williams-Jones, p. 135. Note also *Rianorix* (RIB i), *Maporix*, *Senorix*, *Sintorix* (RIB ii), *Deomiorix*, *Vindiorix* (Tab.Sulis).

[12] LHEB, p. 539. Schrijver, BBCS, 39 (1992), 2, suggests **xs* > **xh* > *ch*. Cf. SBCHP, p. 415; Schrijver, in Beekes FS, pp. 298–300.

[13] LEIA D-62; cf. De Bernardo Stempel, in Meid FS, p. 64.

[14] i.e., to use modern spelling, on the analogy of *chwech afal* 'six apples', *chwech* arose for 'six' *in pausa*, rather than regular ***chwes, later *chwe*. Instead of Jackson's implied **-eχ^s* > **-es* > **-e* → *-ech*, I would prefer **-eχ^s* > **-eχ* > *-e* ~ *-ech*. For the variation between *chwech* and *chwe* see Thomas, BBCS, 37 (1990), 28–29 (basically accepting Jackson).

[15] LHEB, pp. 535, 619, n. 1, 625, n. 2, 627, and 637 (and review by Watkins, AC, 104 (1956), 177); LWP, p. 365; BWP, pp. 7 and 15.

elements: *rīks 'king' and *wiks 'fighter'.[16] Jackson envisages *Ordovix passing through a stage *Ordoŭəs (cf. ‡6 above), but it is simpler to invoke Schrijver's doctrine that /ŭik/ became /ŭug/ (as in MW amwc 'fights for') and to suppose that ORDOVS is a spelling of *ORDOVVS, similar to Vulgar Latin spellings such as serus for servus and Bellaus for *Bellavus in the Romano-British tablets from Bath; -u- for -uu- is still frequent in Insular Latin.[17] We can now contrast CAMVLORIS and ORDOVS with 2006 CVNORIX, which was discovered at Wroxeter after the publication of LHEB, but could on the face of it be regarded as showing a stage earlier than CAMVLORIS and ORDOVS, before the alleged British -x > -s. Unfortunately, however, there are two reasons why we cannot take these two inscriptions at face value as evidence for -x > -s.

[14] First, Jackson himself points out that -S in CAMVLORIS and ORDOVS could be 'a VL. spelling, since Latin -x in polysyllables had become -s by the second to third century, resulting in constant confusions like felis for felix and felix for felis' (p. 619, n. 1). An instance of this is the Breton inscription 3001/F1 HEC CRUX BUDNOUENUS ABAX IUBSIT FACERE ISTAM, where both crux and abbas are spelt with -x. The implication is that spellings such as *CAMVLORIX and CVNORIX could have alternated in Vulgar Latin orthography with CAMVLORIS and *CVNORIS so that the variation in spelling between -X and -S tells us nothing about British sound change. (One might have supposed the analogy of Latin rex would have been a powerful reason for spelling with -X, but in fact this does not seem to have been felt strongly, to judge by the absence of Romano-British forms in *-rex.[18] Possibly -ris would be felt to be acceptably comparable to the -aris termination of names such as Apol(l)inaris, Familiaris, Ianuaris, Lunaris, Peculiaris, Salutaris, Saecularis, Singularis, Vidaris?)[19] A variant of this Vulgar Latin explanation would be to attribute CAMVLORIS to Gaulish spelling habits, since in

---

[16] GPN, pp. 243–49 and 281–85; RIG iv, 541 and 544; McManus, Guide, p. 178, nn. 21 and 23; Ziegler, pp. 115 and 118. *Ordovix is probably an ethnonym, 'an Ordovician, member of the Ordovices.' On the Ordovices see Gruffydd, THSC, 2 (1996), 18–19; Sims-Williams, in Ptolemy, p. 8 and n. 26.

[17] SBCHP, pp. 156–57 (cf. Schumacher, Historical Morphology, p. 199); Tab.Sulis, pp. 121 and 147. On Vulgar Latin V for VV see VLRB, p. 916. This is already invoked by Rhys, LWP, p. 206, in his discussion of ORDOVS. Cf. Holder i, 297 and ii, 892 on -aus and -ous. Le Blant, Nouveau recueil, p. 316, gives examples like SERVS, PERPETVS, and FLAVS (cf. OPEL ii, 147 and 219). Insular Latin examples from Wales such as fraudatius for fraudatiuus are cited by Lambert, Revue de Philologie, 57 (1983), 42 and n. 11.

[18] RIB indexes MORIREX for i 861, but the stone has genitive MORI REGIS. For -REX in Gaulish see GPN, p. 243.

[19] For these see indexes to RIB i–ii and Tab.Vindol. ii. Note also the Cunaris from Housesteads below.

Gaul -RIS occurs beside -RIX, presumably owing to a tendency to reduce /χs/ to /ss/.[20]

[14] Another, more likely, possibility, I suggest, is Irish influence. In Primitive Irish /ss/ < /xs/ < /ks/ 'was weakened to s when intervocalic and to /h/ in final position, falling together with original -s and the fricatives /ð/, /θ/, and /x/ which were also weakened to /h/ in this position'.[21] The only way of writing this sound in ogam (whether at the /-ss/ or /-s/ or /-h/ stage) was with the S symbol (*Sail*). In roman script, there was perhaps the possibility of writing -H, however,[22] or of reversion to -X as in 2006 CVNORIX at Wroxeter, assuming this *is* an Irish name (> *Conr(a)i*), as seems probable from the Irish patronymic MACVS MAQVI COLINE which follows – the thoroughly Romano-British context of Wroxeter may have favoured the -RIX spelling and British composition vowel -O-, however 'Cunorix' or *Cunaris* himself may have pronounced his own name.[23] On the other hand, it would be equally reasonable to carry over the ogam S[*ail*] spelling into roman script and write -S. A possible example of this, which has not received any attention, is an inscription CVNARIS on a 'buff sandstone building-stone reddened by fire, 0.24 by 0.12 by 0.17 m, found in 1976 unstratified' during excavations at Barrack XIII at Housesteads fort on Hadrian's Wall.[24] One wonders, judging from the composition vowel -A- as well as from the

---

[20] Examples in GPN, pp. 243–49; for the reason for specifying /ss/ (rather than /s/ as in Primitive Irish) see below, n. 54. According to Smith, VLRB, p. 919, Italian-type assimilation of [ks] to [ss] was not typical of Roman Britain, *Alesan(der)* at Caerleon (RIB i 375) being one exception.

[21] McManus, *Guide*, p. 85. Cf. TRC, p. 105 (*-xs* > *-ss* (> *-s* ?) > *-h*); GOI, p. 136.

[22] But -H was more certainly used for /x/ < /k/ as in CIIC 1 MENUEH < *-wikas*; see McManus, *Guide*, pp. 88 and 178, nn. 23 and 25; Sims-Williams, *CMCS*, 23 (1992), 46, and *TPS*, 91 (1993), 162–64; and ‡42 below.

[23] A non-Irish engraver is suggested by (Wright &) Jackson, *AntJ*, 48 (1968), 300, to explain COLINE instead of COLINI. British influence could also explain why the O is not raised to U (cf. W. *celyn* 'holly' < *kolino*-), although Jackson suggests that the inscription could predate Irish raising. See further McManus, *Guide*, p. 77; Uhlich, *Morphologie*, p. 219, and the discussion below in Ch. 5, p. 333, in the light of which it seems probable that CVNORIX represents Irish *Kunari* with the final consonant already lost. It could, however, be a British name, despite the patronymic, and the ancestor of W. *Cynyr/Cynri* (Lloyd-Jones, *BBCS*, 14 (1950–52), 36). Note that Wright & Jackson imply COLIVE, COIIVE, and COIINE as less likely but posssible readings. A possible parallel to COLINE in Wales is the old name of Diserth Castle, Flints., *Dincolyn*, also known as *Caer Faelan* (a name which also suggests an Irish connection cf. ‡48); see DP iv, 558–60; Lloyd-Jones, *Geirfa*, p. 358; WATU, p. 58. This is an obvious area for foreign settlement; cf. Viking evidence in Davies, *Patterns of Power*, p. 54.

[24] Hassall & Tomlin, *Britannia*, 8 (1977), 432; archaeological summary by Frere, ibid., pp. 372–73. Miss Lindsay Allason-Jones, Director of the Archaeological Museums, Newcastle upon Tyne, and literary executor of the excavator, Charles M. Daniels, kindly informed me (11.7.00) that the stone was in store awaiting its transfer to Housesteads Museum, and that the excavations were soon to be published: 'Although the stone is from an unstratified context it is likely to have been carved in either the initial building phase under Hadrian or the later phases under Antoninus Pius or Septimius Severus. There are indications of 5th century occupations at Housesteads, but this is not a period which tends

-S, whether this CVNARIS was an Irish immigrant comparable to CVNORIX at Wroxeter. If the stone is indeed as early as the time of Severus (d. 211), it provides the earliest evidence so far for both sound changes in Irish.

[14] There is in any case evidence that 322/27 CAMVLORIS (on the lead coffin from Anglesey) is from an Irish context, for the full inscription is CAMVLORIS HOI. The latter is *not* attested as a Latin abbreviation for *hic ossa iacent* or the like, but is a reasonable roman-letter spelling of Primitive Irish XOI 'here', a common formula word in the ogam inscriptions, where it always occurs in second position.[25] Camuloris himself was perhaps not Irish himself, unless he had adopted a British name, for the element *Camul-* is typically Gaulish and British,[26] but at least the patron or inscriber of his coffin was probably Irish.

[14] The subject of Jackson's other inscription with -S, 354/126/6 CORBALENGI IACIT ORDOVS, purports to be an Ordovican from north Wales. The inscription is incised vertically on a megalith at Dyffryn Bern[27] with a commanding view over the cove at Penbryn in Ceredigion, perhaps a trading or raiding station which he controlled.[28] In view of the

---

to produce inscriptions on Hadrian's Wall, except for the very occasional tombstone.' (Compare the case of 498/Nb7 BRIGOMAGLOS, a tombstone at Vindolanda, discussed by Swift, *Ogam Stones*, pp. 113–17 and 125.) R. S. O. Tomlin kindly confirms that it is not a tombstone, but pecked onto the face of a small building-stone with a mason's pick; 'I could not date it by the lettering, but a 2nd/3rd century date is likely. At Housesteads one would expect a Roman, Celtic or even German name, not an Irish.' He thinks the reading has to be CVNARIS not LVNARIS. See his drawing apud Sims-Williams, *CMCS*, 44 (2002).

[25] Sims-Williams, *CMCS*, 23 (1992), 48–49 (on the significance of the possible *theta* symbol (ibid., n. 69) see further Watson, *JRS*, 42 (1952), 56–62, and Tomlin & Hassall, *Britannia*, 29 (1998), 436, n. 17). For a survey of stones with XOI (>< OI) see Swift, *Ogam Stones*, pp. 97–111. It is preceded by names in the genitive in the ogam inscriptions, but this simply reflects the prevalence of that case in the corpus and does not mean that XOI requires or 'governs' the genitive case. It certainly seems preferable to take CAMVLORIS as a nominative form (even if functioning syntactically as genitive) rather than as a genitive form replacing *Camulorigis* or similar (cf. Sims-Williams, *CMCS*, 23 (1992), 48–49).

[26] Holder i, 725–28 and iii, 1067–69; LEIA C-287; GPN, pp. 160–61; Birkhan, *Germanen und Kelten*, pp. 336–43. In RIB note *Camulius* and *Camulogenus* (also [C]amulus if not [F]amulus), and especially *Camulorigi* (gen.) on a *defixio* from Nottinghamshire, which Hassall & Tomlin, *Britannia*, 24 (1993), 312, n. 8, regard as *Camulorīx* treated as a second-declension noun in -*us*. Compare 455/403 CAMVL(L)ORIGI FILI FANNVCI in Pembrokeshire, which has a probably Irish-influenced patronymic; see below, ‡18. Nash-Williams follows Macalister in reading 455/403 CAMVLORIGI, but LL or CL was conjectured in 1861 (cf. LW, p. 110) and the horizontal stroke of the first L (definitely not a C) is visible on the stone, more deeply incised than is shown by Macalister. The etymologically incorrect doubling suggests influence from the ogam spelling tradition.

[27] Cf. Ir. *bern* 'gap, mountain pass' (without certain British cognates) or, more likely, CB *bern* 'heap (of stones)', referring to the reused Bronze Age cairn where the inscription was found. See LEIA B-41 and 87; Hamp, *ÉC*, 26 (1989), 64.

[28] On finds from Penbryn see *Cardiganshire County History*, i, ed. Davies & Kirby, p. 435, s.n., and Edwards, *Med. Arch.*, 45 (2001), 21.

existence of Irish settlements in Wales, it is quite possible that this 'Ordovican' was of Irish birth – one of the Irish expelled by the sons of Cunedda perhaps[29] – for his name certainly appears Irish, as we shall see. The native Ordovican claim implied by ORDOVS can be compared with the Demetian claim implied by the name DEMETI, the patronymic of an Irishman on a bilingual ogam in Pembrokeshire (450/390, cf. ‡27n.). Personal names in **CORB**- (possibly 'part of a chariot', 'saddle', < Latin *corbis?*) are frequent in Irish (e.g. *Cor(b)mac*, *Cú Chorb*), including the ogam corpus,[30] but apparently unknown elsewhere (*corf* being only attested as a common noun in Welsh). The composition vowel -A- is typically Irish and is most naturally taken as such.[31] Lastly, the second element -*leng*- ('leap' or, according to some, 'long') is typical of Irish names such as *Conlang* and *Dúnlang*,[32] and does not seem to occur in British and Gaulish names. In Wales it appears in the name EVOLENGI, Ir. *Éolang*,[33] on the bilingual ogam stone 431/308 and on the roman-letter 436/316 EUOLENGGI, both in Pembrokeshire, and in the *Corpus* Dr Nancy Edwards follows Rhys's suggestion that this name may also appear in 424/299 at Brawdy in the same county. The only other instance of -L(A)(E)(I)NG- in Britain is 461/Ok66 ERCILINGI in Cornwall, which may well be Irish too (the OI gen. sg. *Erclaingi* is attested).[34] CORBALENGI is probably the Irish name *Corbleng*,[35] perhaps referring to a hero who 'leaps' into or out of the 'chariot' or the 'saddle'. In view of the Irish milieu, then, it possible that the spelling ORDOVS (for British **Ordou̯əX(ˢ)* or **Ordou̯u̯χ(ˢ)* ?) is influenced by Irish pronunciation and/or spelling. Names in nominative **-RIS* and **-VIS* must have been common in Irish, although only genitive forms are preserved in the ogam formulae.

---

[29] By contrast, Gruffydd, *THSC*, 2 (1996), 19, sees him as belonging to 'the first wave of Brittonic incursion south of the Dyfi and Ystwyth, an incursion associated . . . with Ceredig ap Cunedda.' Similarly Rhys, LWP, p. 159, in his attack on attempts to identify too many Welsh inscriptions as Irish, argued that an Ordovican could not be Irish, 'whether he came there as an invader or as an ally'. In 'On some of our inscribed stones', *AC*, 4th ser. 8 (1877), 137, he calls him 'our *Corbalengi*'.

[30] Ziegler, pp. 109–10 and 155. 357/136 CORBAGNI FILIVS AL[is presumably Irish; on -AGNI names see below, ‡48. Rhys, LWP, p. 379, identified CORB- with OI *corb* '[part of a] chariot' (< Latin *corbis*, 'basket', LEIA C-207), as in Cormac's explanation of his own name (LEIA C- 209); cf. W. *cor(o)f* 'saddle-bow' < *corbis* (French *courbet* 'bow of pack-saddle'), GPC. LEIA C-209 rejects the explanation of CORB- as 'raven' (EIHM, p. 283, n. 5) or 'defiles' (e.g. Ó Corráin & Maguire, *Gaelic Personal Names*, p. 59). Cf. Holder i, 1117.

[31] Although it *could* be a development of British -*o*- as Jackson assumes, LHEB, p. 645.

[32] Uhlich, *Morphologie*, pp. 112 and 131. Rhys, LWP, p. 379, favoured 'long'.

[33] Uhlich, *Morphologie*, p. 240; Ziegler, p. 189; see also McManus, *Ériu*, 37 (1986), 24, n. 33. The spelling with NGG may indicate the pronunciation [ŋg].

[34] CGSH, p. 160, §711.70. See below, ‡27. Thomas, *Mute Stones*, p. 283, reads ERCILINCI, as does Rhys, LWP, p. 404 (but segmenting *Ercil-inci*: W. -*ing*, see ‡48 n. 935).

[35] *Corbleng* is cited by Uhlich, *Morphologie*, p. 112. Dr Uhlich kindly informs me by letter that his source is *Corblinge* (gen. sg., retaining original *ā*-inflection) in the genealogical tract edited by Dobbs, *ZCP*, 21 (1938–39), 311.

[14] We thus have two possible explanations – Vulgar Latin or, more likely, Irish influence – for the -S of CAMVLORIS and ORDOVS,[36] and these weaken these forms' validity as evidence for a sound change -x > -s in British. The simplest view is that British -X^s became -ch (the regular internal treatment) and that this eventually disappeared with the apocope in polysyllables and also in monosyllables (e.g. Welsh *rhi* 'king'), with the exception of the forms *chwech* (beside *chwe*) and *ech* where sandhi and analogy may have helped to preserve the -ch. There is one (lost) inscription which seems to confirm this. 1205/Ok44, at Redruth, was transcribed by Borlase as MAVOUIH/VITO[.[37] This can be taken as a reflex of *$Maguvix$ (or *$Magurix$ if Borlase's U was an R as Thomas suggests) with the development *-X^s > -ch (> -h ?) hypothesized above – the -H standing for either /x/ (*ch*) or /h/ (cf. CIIC 1 MENUEH, n. 22 above). This is compatible with Jackson's chronology, whereby ‡17 /g/ > /ɣ/ and ‡25 /ɣ/ > /u̯/ occur before ‡37 'completion of the loss of final syllables'.

[14] To sum up, then, presumably the following can be grouped together as in various ways reflecting a stage before the reflex of final -X^s had been lost:

1. 2006 CVNORIX [but for -X as a possible pseudo-archaism here see n. 23 above]
2. 322/27 CAMVLORIS
3. 354/126/6 ORDOVS
4. 1205/Ok44 MAVOUIH (or MAVORIH)

[14] There is one further name in Cornwall which possibly belongs here. If Jackson is right to read the Castle Dore stone 487/Ok10 as DRVSTAVS (with ligatured AV), to reject the usual identification with Brittonic *Drystan* < *$Drustagnos$ because '-*agn*- could hardly have become -*an*- so early as the early sixth century', and to state that 'the interpretation of the

---

[36] In the case of CAMVLORIS it might be argued that the *$Camulorix$ had already been apocopated to *$Camulor$ (but *$Camulir$ with vowel-affection would have been expected, cf. ‡19) and that the -*is* is a Latin genitive (comparable to the patronymic (?) in Tab.Sulis no. 9 *Catinius Exsactoris*). This would not explain ORDOVS, however.

[37] See Okasha's plate. Oliver Padel (pers. comm.) points out that Borlase's U is distinct from his V. Thomas, *Mute Stones*, pp. 284–85, suggests MAVORI FI[LI] VITO[RI]. In *CA*, 24 (1985), 174, he had suggested that the 'U' was a damaged 'thin' R plus an I, but now (letter 1.3.01) he suggests that it is an inverted R, comparing 1212 MACARI (a very uncertain reading, however, judging by the photograph he kindly showed me). Whether the 'U' is V or R does not affect the phonological matter under consideration. Here the question of the H is crucial, and it has to be admitted that Borlase *could* have miscopied an FI ligature like that on 470/Ok78; but the H does make sense as it stands. For the possibility that 454/402 DEN[O]VI is a similar formation see ‡18 below. Theoretically VRIVI, both on 369/153 (not necessarily acephalous) and on 463/Ok15, could be another (since there seem to be no Latin names in -*uriuus*): a Celtic name *$Virivix$ (cf. *Viruico*, GPN, pp. 285 and 287) could yield a British nominative VRIVI, with *$Wiri$ > *Uri- as in the name of *U(i)riconium* (‡28 below) – although this is implausible if 463/Ok15 is as late as the date given by Thomas, *Mute Stones*, p. 328.

stone as DRVSTANVS is doubtful and begs the question',[38] it might be preferable to see DRVSTAVS as a reflex of *Drustavix comparable with ORDOVS < *Ordovix above. The preserved /st/ would be either Pictish or British, while the /s(s)/ treatment of /ks/ would be either Irish or Pictish;[39] putting them together, DRVSTAVS would be Pictish (as has often been assumed for other reasons), and the non-British composition vowel -A- would not be incompatible with this in view of our lack of information about pre-syncope Pictish.[40] All this depends on the questionable correctness of Jackson's reading, interpretation, and dating of the inscription.

[14] As candidates with -S for consideration here we can rule out the following:

325/33 BIVOTIS [recte BIVATIS?] FAMVLVS DEI, if comparable with moritex, moritix 'sailor', since Macalister's BIVOTIS + punctuation mark has been generally rejected in favour of -TISI or -TIGI;[41]
971/35 CUURI[S], where the -S besides being uncertain is probably not in the old final syllable;[42]
415/278, where Macalister's restored TARRONERIS[43] is not accepted by Nash-Williams, who reads IARRI[, which is acceptable as a name. One might compare OW iar, Mod.W. iâr 'hen' (as a nickname?), with which Holder and Pedersen compare Gaulish Iarilla; and note also Gaulish IIAROS or EAROS, unless this is acephalous.[44] There is also 156 MAQQI-IARI (OI Mac-Iair), which has been compared inter alia with OI íaru 'stoat, squirrel', probably from the stem *isar- 'swift' (as in the Gaulish

---

[38] Jackson, review of TYP, WHR, 1, special no. (1963), 85; see further below, ‡48. Note, however, that Jackson does not actually reject the DRVSTANVS interpretation here. In fact, compare KHJ's note: 'In conversation with Radford, 7.4.52, I put it to him that if the person is Trystan it would have had to be DRVSTANVS, and he agreed that the ligature AV might quite well stand for ANV – he had not thought of this problem and solution, but agreed.' Note that Lhuyd's drawing in BL Stowe MS 1023, fo. 20r (not cited by Okasha) reads CIRVSIVS or dRVSIVS, and that this could be interpreted as *DRVSTVS.

[39] See Jackson, in Problem of the Picts, p. 165, on both *st and *ks. EIHM, pp. 366–67, would connect Ir. trost, W. trwst 'noise' (cf. LEIA T-152). According to Holder i, 297 and 316, and iii, 759 and 777–78, there was an -aus suffix < -a(:)vos. Cf. KGP, p. 143. See also ‡60 below on 482/Ok71 NEMIAVS.

[40] Cf. Jackson, in Problem of the Picts, p. 166, on Bede's Meilochon. His derivation of Pictish Drostan (beside Drosten) from *Drustagnos (pp. 163–64) implies the composition vowel /a/, as in Irish (cf. ‡38 below).

[41] See ‡27 below. Cf. DLG, p. 194; Tomlin, in prep.

[42] BWP, pp. 11 and 17; LHEB, p. 671.

[43] Under misprinted no. '416'. In the printed version of Lhuyd, Parochialia, ii, 96, the reading is 'I . . APP', from NLW MS Llanstephan 185, fo. 89, but see the better copy in RCAHMW, Merioneth, p. 62. A photograph of the stone, lent by Dr Edwards, could be read IARBI but is unclear.

[44] Holder ii, 13; VKG i, 65; DLG, p. 157. [D]IAROS is queried in RIG iv, 249–50 and 536. W. iâr is feminine but forming the plural ieir like an o-stem, VKG i, 283, and ii, 86; Lewis & Pedersen, pp. 78 and 168. The Irish cognate is éirín(e) (DIL).

river name *Isara*).[45] A Welsh parallel may be the name *Iarddur* (also > *Arddur*) 'swift steel?', although this is usually regarded as a form of *Iarnddur* < **isarno-* 'iron'.[46] If Macalister's TARRONERIS were right (< **Tarr-ŏn-o-rīks* ??), a possible parallel would be the Aberhydfer ogam 2002/b **TARICORO**.[47]

321/25]SORIS (lost) could be a name in *-s-o-rix* such as *Vassorix*,[48] but [UX]SORIS or the genitive of a name in *-sor* are equally possible. Note that Henry Rowlands read 'the name OSORII'.[49]

2007/10 MAILIS (as opposed to MAILISI with horizontal -I) is an unlikely reading,[50] and in any case ****Mailix** can be ruled out as unattested and inexplicable.

[14] This seems the appropriate place to mention that, following Ifor Williams (who was following Rhys), Jackson notes[51] that a weakening of the nominative *-rīx* ending – via /-riːs/ according to Williams and Jackson, but /-riːx/ (/x/ = *ch*) is preferable as we have seen – may possibly be seen in 394/103 CANTIORI HIC IACIT (cf. Gaulish CANTORIX)[52] and 380/84 **ICORIGAS/ICORI FILIVS POTENTINI**,[53] and in Gildas's *Vortipori*.

---

[45] Ziegler, pp. 186–87 (short /i/ according to O'Rahilly, *Ériu*, 13 (1940–42), 119, n. 4, and DLG, p. 161). For this stem in Celtic river names see also LHEB, p. 523, and PNRB, p. 380.

[46] See ‡36 below on 1065/410 HAERDUR.

[47] **TARICORO** is compared by Thomas, *Mute Stones*, pp 119 and 128, n. 12, with OI *Tairmesc*, etc. in CGH, pp. 740–41 (where the *Tair-* is prepositional, LEIA T-1, 12 and 14); but note also names such as *Tar(r)a* in RIB ii and Grauf., p. 269, and *Tar(r)onius* in Holder ii, 1736–37.

[48] SBCHP, pp. 121 and 128.

[49] Owen, *AC*, 5th ser. 13 (1896), 140; LW, p. 198; RCAHMW, *Anglesey*, pp. cvi and cxvii ('SORIS (*or* SORII)'); Edwards, *ArchJ*, 154 (1997), 114–15. Holder ii, 1617 notes SORIS in CIL xiii 645 (= DAG, p. 418), but it is doubtful whether the words on this inscription from Bordeaux (*Duetil, Tiblik* [*Tilblik*, DAG, p. 419], and *Eppimus*) are genuine names. If SORIS is genuine, compare *Sorex* in Narbonensis (OPEL iv, 88), perhaps with *So-* 'good' (GPN, pp. 257–58), if not Latin *sorex* (cf. RIB i 1821).

[50] BWP, p. 23, LHEB, p. 329, n. 1, and below, ‡37. Nash-Williams, Jackson, and earlier writers were not aware that the stone still existed, as first reported by Williams, *TAAS*, 1945, p. 24, and confirmed to me (with a photograph showing horizontal -I) by Dr Nancy Edwards. MAILISI may have a suffix -IS as in MW *Glywys* (below, ‡58) and *Pelis* (Williams, *Canu Llywarch Hen*, p. 180). On the other hand, the other name from Llanfaelog is Irish (319/9 CVNOGVS(I)) and it resembles Irish names like *Máel Ísu* or *Máel-Inse* (could MAILISI be a brutal Latinization of *Máel Ísu*?). For *Máel-* names see O'Brien, *Celtica*, 10 (1973), 229; DIL s.v. *Máel*; CGH, pp. 684–95; MLH v/1, pp. 240–41. Is there any connection between MAILISI and the name *Llanfaelog*?

[51] LHEB, pp. 625 and 627; LWP, p. 365; BWP, pp. 7–8. In BWP, p. 9, Williams cites 413/272 CAELEXTI (for *Caelestis*, ?or < *Caelestius*, Kajanto, p. 338) for Latin *x* = /s/ and for loss of final *-s*. Note, however, that Lewis Morris's drawing 'adds to the proper name a character which may be an *s*, making *Cælextis*' (Owen, *AC*, 5th ser. 13 (1896), 137). Cf. 402/84 NOBILI for *Nobilis* (or *Nobilius*, n. 86 below).

[52] LWP, p. 369; LHEB, p. 624; RIG iv, 549 and references; Lambert, *ÉC*, 31 (1995), 118–19.

[53] This unique name presumably derives from the sparsely attested Celtic element **Ico-* (Rhys, *AC*, 6th ser. 7 (1907), 101; GPN, pp. 351–53; DLG, p. 158; *Icotagus*, ‡25 below). It may be attested in Gaul as Ικορ[(Lejeune, *ÉC*, 19 (1982), 15). Should the Rhineland place name *Icorigium* be derived from **Icorīx* (as by Rhys, *AC*, 6th ser. 7 (1907), 101) rather than

These spellings cannot be attributed to Gallo-Latin habits, since, as Ellis Evans notes,[54] the common loss of -*s* in Gaul never affects this -*s* (which was evidently [-ss]) < /-x/. Jackson argues, however, that these examples of -*ori* may well be genitives – or vocative in the Gildas instance – of Latinizing -*orius* replacing Celtic -*orīx* (with short [o] in both). An example to be grouped with the above, assuming it is not Irish, is 388/94 DERVORI HIC IACET, which, while it could be nominative from *Dervorīx*,[55] could also be the genitive of a Latinized *Dervorius*. Note also 361/140 TALORI . . . FILIVS (the terminations were recorded by Lhuyd).[56] As Jackson says, such a genitive in -*ori(i)* clearly occurs in the roman-letter part of 446/353 **MAGLICUNAS MAQI CLUTA[RIGAS]**/MAGLOCVNI(?) FILI CLVTORI,[57] and possibly in 320/26 CVLIDORI IACIT (if that is the reading rather than CVLIDOR) and 396/104 FILI AVITORI (if this is not genitive of a masculine *jo*-stem equivalent of 362/142 AVITORIA, assuming the latter *is* a *ja*-stem).[58] Further possible examples, reasonably

---

segmented *Ico-rigium*, as by Holder ii, 23 and Weisgerber, *Rhenania*, p. 350? It seems unlikely that OI *Echrí* continues *Ikorīks* rather than *Ek^worīks* (cf. Uhlich, *Morphologie*, p. 237, Ziegler, p. 187). Williams, *AC*, 106 (1957), 121, comments on the ending: 'Was there a feeling that the archaic old-fashioned Irish genitive had to be rendered into Latin as -*i*, like so many nouns of the second Declension?'

[54] GPN, p. 99 s.n. *Luguri* – his one exception, now in fact read as LVGVRIX in RIG ii/1, p. 87.

[55] Cf. Sims-Williams, *TAAS*, 1999, p. 147, comparing 344/73 DERVACI from *derwo*- 'oak' (LWP, p. 381) or 'true' (LEIA D-55). DERVACI and DERVORI could also be Irish, with -O- as composition vowel in the latter after the labial V. Cf. Holder i, 1270–71; LEIA D-12 and D-55 (*Derwo*- names, cf. NWÄI, p. 237, n. 114). See Williams, *Pedeir Keinc*, p. 286, for *Maeldderw* = *Derf(a)el*.

[56] Camden, *Britannia* (1695), col. 623. See also GPN, p. 260.

[57] In LHEB, p. 626 he notes that *Clutorīx* is implied by gen. CLVTORIGI FILI PAVLINI in 435/315. See also GPN, p. 181, Uhlich, *Morphologie*, p. 204, and MLH v/1, pp. 185–86, for OW *Clotri*, OI *clothrí*, etc. Cf. Frankish *Hlodericus*, Holder i, 1051.

[58] LHEB, pp. 624–25. On AVITORIA/**AVITTORIGES** see also pp. 185–86 and 625; and ‡17 below. The ogam -**ES** may be an error for -**EAS** (Uhlich, *Morphologie*, pp. 24 and 173, and McManus, *Guide*, p. 117) or equivalent to ><S = -**EAS** < -**IAS** (on >< = **EA** see Sims-Williams, *CMCS*, 23 (1992), 54). May it not be simpler, however, to regard -**RIGES** as weakened form of *-RIGIS, the genitive that appears in Britain in place of original *-*rīgos*, as in 358/138 VOTEPORIGIS/**VOTECORIGAS**? Jackson takes AVITORIA as a *ja*-stem, while Ziegler, p. 133, suggests -RIA is from *-RIGA (a VL rather than Celtic change? cf. ‡65), but *A(V)ITORIX is possible as a feminine name (despite the existence of the separate word for 'queen' discussed by McCone, *Ériu*, 49 (1998), 1–12), comparable with TANCORIX MVLIER at Old Carlisle in RIB i 908 and Gaulish *Aduorix* (GPN, p. 130). For -RIX in female names, and -RIGA in two feminine theonyms, see Lejeune, *ÉC*, 19 (1982), 112 and 119, also Zimmer, in Evans FS, pp. 325, 327 and 332, n. 42, e.g. on 1032/281 WLEDER (= *Gwledyr*, LW, p. 165) < *Wlatorīx*. Similar formations may be 395/102]ORIA IC IACIT, 1062/Dor.v GONGORIE (a completely obscure genitive(?)), and 349/121/4 VELVOR[IA] FILIA (if correctly restored – compare VELVE in RIB i 688 and *Velvalis* and *Velvinna* in Tab.Sulis, nos 53 and 4; cf. W. *gwelw*?). Note also 511/Scot.10 CONINIE and]RTIRIE (probably with Latinate -*i(a)e*, see LHEB, p. 188, and below, ‡‡ 48n and 57); 1024/255 BRANCIE; 419/284 VE[ ]MAIE; 508 FRYMIA COESIA; 1068/b HIPIA or NIPIA. 3020/I1 BELADORE may be a similar name to AVITORIA according to IEMB, p. 263. On -IA see further, ‡‡ 15 and 19n. below.

omitted by Jackson, are 458/Ok9 RANOCORI or NANOCORI which is obscure,[59] and 443/349 CAMVLORI (or less likely CAMVMORI), which only has to be genitive if the preceding word is read as FILI rather than HIC IACIT. To these uncertain cases we can now add 2001 (Carmarthenshire, Laugharne 2), which may have read C(?) . . . . . . CRET/ORBIORI + in Lhuyd's day,[60] and 2029/p.39i MAGLORI (cf. *Maglorius* below). 1205/Ok44, read by Borlase as MAVOUIH/VITO . . ., is emended by Charles Thomas to MAVORI FI[LI] VITO[RI].[61] If Thomas were right to take the H as FI(*li*) – and we have seen that Borlase's MAVOUIH can be taken at face value as from *Maguvix* – *MAVORI would have to be a genitive of the name seen in Scotland in the inscription which Thomas compares, 516/Scot.1 VIVENTIVS ET MAVORIVS, a British cognate of Gaulish *Magurix*, which is possibly also attested in the Latinized form *Magurius*, feminine *Maguria*.[62]

[14] In favour of such Latinizing -*orius* forms of -*orix* names, Jackson cited 409/198/849 PVMPEIVS CARANTORIVS (cf. *Carantorīx* > OW *Cerenhir*, W. *Cerennhyr*) and the Breton saint's name *Maglorius* (cf. *Maglorīx* > MW *Meilyr*).[63] To these we can add 516/Scot.1 MAVORIVS above (cf. Gaulish *Magurix*); and it seems plausible that 362/142 AVITORIA above is a comparable feminine formation. These Latin -*orius*/-*oria* forms are not demonstrably earlier than the -ORI inscriptions they are intended to explain, so particular importance can be attached to Romano-British parallels. The feminine VELORIGAM at Bath (Tab.Sulis, no. 53), which no doubt implies a masculine *Velorīx*, has been compared with the nomen *Velorius* attested in Germany.[64] More significantly, a

---

[59] Compare perhaps Gaulish CELECORIX, treated as a *rīx*-name in GPN, p. 246, and RIG iv, 541 and 550. Thomas, *Mute Stones*, pp. 128, n. 12, and 274, n. 24 says the R- is peculiar and compares the Aberhydfer ogam 2002/b **TARICORO** (on TARI- see above, n. 47). Here perhaps compare **kor-* 'cast' or **kor-* 'army', LEIA C-275. Jackson, *Speculum*, 21 (1946), 523, rejected RANOCORI in favour of NANOCORI. For Ligurian(?) *Nano-* see Holder ii, 683.

[60] Dr Edwards notes an alternative ORBIORIT, on which see below, ‡‡ 37 and 57. For the element *Orbio-* see GPN, p. 238.

[61] See n. 37 above.

[62] For *Magu-* see LHEB, pp. 440, 444 and 521. For *Magurix* see GPN, pp. 100 and 222; RIG i, 157–58, and iv, 326 and 539. For *Magur(i)us/a* see Holder ii, 386, Alföldy, *Noricum*, p. 235, Mócsy, p. 174, and OPEL iii, 47 (see n. 65 below). 464/Ok65 MAVISIR (medieval according to Thomas, *Mute Stones*, p. 328) is presumably something else, perhaps **Magesturīx*, W. *Meisyr* (see ‡25). MAVILODUO in RIB ii [fasc. 8] 2503.337 may rather read MAI BODC. Handley, *EME*, 10 (2001), 194, quotes other examples of *Viventius* but notes that *Mavorius* is not attested elsewhere. Thomas, *Mute Stones*, p. 284, notes 'there is a Roman name *Mavortius*' (see Kajanto, p. 212).

[63] LHEB, p. 625. Cf. Loth, *Noms des saints bretons*, p. 86, s.n. *Magloire*. *Maglōrius* with a long /o:/ would give the form *Maelur* cited without reference by Lloyd-Jones, *Y Geninen*, 44 (1926), 8. Tanguy, in *Cartulaire de Redon*, p. 64, notes that CARANTORIVS corresponds to the Breton parochial name *Carantoir*.

[64] Tab.Sulis, p. 181, and Holder iii, 154; cf. GPN, p. 276 correcting DAG, p. 831, and comparing 349/121/4 VELVOR[IA].

Romano-British lead tablet from Bravonium (Leintwardine, Hereford-shire) includes the name MAGLORIV[S] (alongside SENORIX), which shows that such a Latinization of *Maglorīx* occurred in Britain c. 200, well before the period of the 'Early Christian' inscriptions.[65] This suggests that a name like CANTIORIVS may not be merely a Latinization of British *Cantiori* (< *Cantiorīx*) created either by the addition of Latin *-us*, as Ifor Williams argued,[66] or by mistaking *Cantiori* (< *Cantiorīx*) as a Latin genitive, as argued by Jackson,[67] but rather a long-established by-form of *Cantiorīx*, of which CANTIORI would be the genitive.[68] If this is correct, forms such as *Meilyr* may descend directly from *Maglorius* as well as or instead of *Maglorīx* – just as W. *Pyr* undoubtedly descends from Latin(?) *Porius* (cf. 420/289 PORIVS) rather than from a non-existent **Porīx*.[69] The one proviso is that the *o* was short (as in *memoria* > *myfyr*, etc.) rather than long (as in *testimonium* > *testun* and *Artorius* > *Arthur*). This was not the case in Classical Latin for many of the possible models for the termination (e.g. *Censorius, Messorius, Caesoria, Victoria*).[70]

[14] The upshot of the above is that while a form such as CANTIORI *may* reflect an intermediate stage in the loss of final syllables, when the final consonant of [-i:X^s] had disappeared but the vowel [i(:)] remained, it can *equally well* be a Latin genitive of CANTIORIVS, a Latinate by-form of *Cantiorīx*. This ambiguity means that the chronology of CANTIORI, ICORI, and the like in relation to the loss of final syllables (‡‡ 21 and 37) is quite uncertain.

‡15 *ā-affection; LHEB §154*

This change, which lies behind masculine/feminine alternations in Welsh such as *gwyn, gwen* and *crwn, cron*, involved /i/ > /e/ and /u/ > /o/ in the accented penult before /a(:)/ in the final syllable. Jackson denies that British /a/ (as opposed to /a:/ and Latin /a(:)/) caused affection, arguing that the

---

[65] RIB ii [fasc. 8] 2504.20 (reading MASLORIV[S], but the preferable alternative is cited in the Index; PRB, p. 96; it is listed as a curse tablet in Tab.Sulis, p. 61). Another possibility is that MAGLORIVS is not a Latinization of *Maglorīx* but a related form; cf. ancient Continental forms such as *Magurius* beside *Magurix* if the former is more than a Latinization of the latter (GPN, p. 222; Rhys, *PBA*, 1911–12, pp. 262–63; see n. 62 above).

[66] BWP, p. 8.

[67] LHEB, p. 626. *Cantiorix* is 'King of Hosts' rather than 'King of the Borderland' according to Jackson, *JRS*, 37 (1947), 55. See further Lambert, *ÉC*, 31 (1995), 118–19.

[68] But if its MW descendant is *Cennur* (Gruffydd, *SC*, 24/25 (1989–90), 9), the *o* would have been long (as in *Artorius* > *Arthur*).

[69] BWP, p. 8; LHEB, p. 598. Williams takes *Porius* in Suetonius, *Caligula*, 35 (Holder ii, 1037), to be a Classical Latin name, but see Rhys & Brynmor-Jones, *Welsh People*, p. 503, n. 1: 'an *essedarius* who was probably a Gaul'. A distinct form is MW *Pyr* < *Pyrrhus*, CBT v, 168.

[70] All from RIB, where other names in *-orius* are *Florius, Litorius, Platorius*, and *Statorius*.

British /a/ had already been reduced (cf. ‡6), but this has been disputed;[71] I shall therefore refer to *a*-affection rather than *ā*-affection.

[15] According to Jackson 'there no evidence either for or against *ā*-affection in the Dark Age inscriptions'.[72] This may be too sweeping, although certain evidence is hard to find. One is basically concerned with female names with /a:/ in the old final syllable. The latter appears either as -A, which could be British or Latin, or frequently as -E, which is the regular spelling for Latin genitive -*ae*, as still in the Old Welsh female names in the Lichfield Gospels.[73] Nash-Williams usually notes that -E = -(*a*)*e*, even in the case of an Irish name like 378/169 BODIBEVE,[74] although he fails to do so with some of the less obvious examples.[75] Female names in -IA, whether classified as British or Latin, can be disregarded here, the former since it is agreed that native /-i̯a:/ did not cause *a*-affection.[76] Schrijver has argued that it could itself undergo affection to '*-ea* (with non-syllabic *e*)'.[77] No examples of such an -EA occur in the inscriptions, but it is difficult to classify any of the examples of -IA spellings as meaningfully pre-*a*-affection, because, as Schrijver shows, -*ia* was maintained to some extent in *Latin* words, sometimes even giving rise to *i*-affection (e.g. W. *myfyr* with *i*-affection beside OB *memor*, both from *memoria*).[78] A further possibility with /-i̯a:/ was a development via /-i̯i̯a:/ > /-eja:/ > /-eða:/ > W. -*edd*.[79] This might be expected to turn up as -IDA or -ED(A) in the inscriptions, but the only possible instance with *a*-affection is 394/103 [V]ENEDOTIS (‡13); but compare 413/272 MONEDORIGI, which cannot belong here as the vowel in the syllable following the *apparently* lowered /e/ < /i/ is the non-affecting composition vowel /o/ (cf. W. *mynydd*). Jackson explains the E as a

---

[71] LHEB, pp. 574–75; cf. SBCHP, pp. 255–57 and 467; Sims-Williams, in *Gaulois et celtique continental*.

[72] LHEB, p. 577. I shall of course be ignoring presumably Irish names in ogam script. For example, 405/228/845 |LICA is unlikely to be a Roman name like *Publica* or *Peruica* (RIB) rather than something like the Irish **GRAVICA** read by Macalister (cf. 150 **GRAVICAS** and Ziegler, pp. 185–86). Nash-Williams reads **L** instead of the **G**-, and after the lacuna, **LICA** instead of **VICA**. This goes back to Rhys, *AC*, 5th ser. 12 (1895), 182–83, who equated **LICA** with OI *lecc*, W. *llech* 'flagstone'; LEC is attested in the later Irish inscriptions CIIC 796 and 857–59. Cf. a non-Roman masculine cognomen *Licca* in Holder ii, 206–7.

[73] BWP, pp. 22–23; LHEB, p. 188; Sims-Williams, *BBCS*, 38 (1991), 59.

[74] Possibly genitive of a masculine *a*-stem (or a feminine theonym according to Orel, *BBCS*, 34 (1987), 7), although suggested to be an *o*-stem by McManus, *Guide*, pp. 103 and 177, n. 9; cf. LHEB, p. 181; Ziegler, p. 139; Uhlich, *Morphologie*, p. 187.

[75] Such as his 346/75 ADIVNE (= W. *Eiddun*, Holder i, 42, and Williams, *BBCS*, 10 (1939–41), 42; KHJ: 'Désirée'); however, this is now read ADIVNETI by Knight; cf. *Eidduned*, OB *Ediunet* in Loth, *RC*, 11 (1890), 136 and 141, and *Noms des saints bretons*, p. 36, comparing ADIVNE. For the masculine cf. 3003/F3 ADIVNI. Rhys, LWP, p. 385, notes *Eidyn* as a male name in the Triads (citing *Eiddyn* in Iolo Morganwg's Third Series), but this may rather be *He(i)dyn*; see TYP, p. 405.

[76] LHEB, p. 575; SBCHP, pp. 259–64 and 468. Cf. ‡19 n. 327.

[77] SBCHP, pp. 263–64.

[78] SBCHP, p. 263.

[79] LHEB, pp. 349–51.

Vulgar Latinism.[80] Alternatively, it could be a spelling of /ï/ < /i/ if the inscription is not too early.[81] [V]ENEDOTIS *may* be a similar case.

[15] The affection, or lack of affection, will only appear in names with original short /i/ or /u/ in the old penult. We can therefore ignore names with long vowels, diphthongs, the vowel A, and original /e/ and /o/. This eliminates, for example, 346/75 ADIVNE with /u:/ > /ü:/ (cf. W. *Eiddun(ed)*) – in any case now read ADIVNETI.[82] 419/284 RIGOHENE has original /e/ (< *Rīgosenā*) and is thus irrelevant. Similarly, while 2019 RIGELLA (if not a fake) could be from *Rīg-illā* it could also be from *Rīg-ellā*,[83] and it could equally well contain the same element *gell-* as 433/313 and 441/345 ANDAGELLI may do.[84] In any case, it may be an *Irish* name *Rigell*.[85] 402/184 MVLIER BONA is presumably Latin *bona* or *Bona*;[86] anyway, there is no reason to derive it from **Buna*. 512 QATTIDONA is quite obscure, and anyway not classifiable among the Brittonic inscriptions of Scotland according to Thomas.[87] 356/132/9 POTENINA MVLIIER, a female version of *Potentinus*, a name well established in Britain as 'a "Roman" cognomen (e.g. *RIB* [i] 334) derived from *potens*',[88] presumably had a long vowel like *Aventinus*, *Augustinus*, *Florentinus*, *Frontinus*, *Quartinus*, *Iustinus*, *Latinus*, and so on,[89] as probably did 325/33]INA SANCTISSIMA MATER, if that, rather than]IVA, is the correct reading. On the other hand, if]IVA is the correct reading, we may have a Celtic name in -[B]IVA (W. *-fyw* 'living'), with a short /i/ that should undergo *a*-affection.[90]

---

[80] LHEB, p. 355.

[81] See below, ‡34.

[82] See n. 75 above.

[83] For *-illā* > *-ell* see J. E. C. Williams, *Celtica*, 15 (1983), 156. For both *-ell-* and *-ill-* see Holder i, 1415, and ii, 34; he gives *Reg-illus*, *Reg-illa* and *Rig-illus*, but only cites sources (ii, 1107) for *Regili(us)* and *Regilia*. *Regillus/-a* was a well-known Roman cognomen: Kajanto, p. 316. Bowen & Gresham, *History of Merioneth*, i, 289, translate RIGELLA as 'Queenie'.

[84] If RIGELLA is a genuine name, a possible etymology would be *Rīgo-gellā*; see further ‡74 below. For *gell-* see LWP, p. 388 (wrongly comparing *Annell* cf. EANC, p. 95); Williams, *Canu Aneirin*, pp. 225–26; Ziegler, p. 128; Uhlich, *Morphologie*, pp. 162–63. Cf. ogam GELAGNI, n. 945 below, which, if = OI *Gelán*, could be the source of the OW *Gellan* noted in LWP, p. 388 (although it could = OI *Gíallán*). Schmidt, KGP, p. 216, compares only Gaulish *Adgelei* (gen., OPEL i, 21), as KHJ mentions, himself preferring OI *andach* (VKG ii, 9), with which compare British *Andaga* (n. 111 below). In this case segment *An-dag-elli* 'little bad one'.

[85] See ‡74.

[86] Such a personal name is noted by Nash-Williams, Lebel, p. 104, and Kajanto, p. 274. Cf. *Bonus* in *Historia Brittonum*, §49 (EWGT, p. 8). Nash-Williams translates HIC IACIT MVLIER BONA NOBILI 'Here lies Bona, the wife of Nobilis', but note that it may be 'the good woman Nobilis'; for *Nobilis* as a male and female name see Kajanto, p. 279, and OPEL iii, 103, where *Nobilius* is also attested.

[87] *GAJ*, 17 (1991–92), 4.

[88] See Tab.Sulis, p. 147, and RIB indexes.

[89] Names in indexes to RIB, and assuming Classical quantities.

[90] LEIA B-37. For this element see Evans, *BBCS*, 24 (1970–72), 427–29; Uhlich, *Morphologie*, p. 187; Ziegler, p. 100. But I am not aware of it in Welsh female names; no examples are

But this is quite uncertain; a Latin name like *Primitiva*, with /iː/, would also fit.[91] There was also original /iː/ in 461/Ok66 NONNITA to judge by the Middle Welsh form *Ystrad Ninhid* rhyming with *rydid* 'freedom' in Gwynfardd Brycheiniog.[92] On the other hand, 3025/I6 MELITA, which is obviously a Breton feminine counterpart of 382/86 MELITVu, must be from the Celtic or Greek stem *meli-* 'honey' with /i/,[93] here not affected to *e*. We must allow, however, for possible conservatism[94] and Classical influence

---

indexed in Cane, *Personal Names of Women*. Following Low, she regards the second element of OC *Haluiu* as cognate with W. *gwiw* rather than *byw* (pp. 121, 126, 127, and 134). As well as *Haluiu*, compare *Moruiw, Guenguiu*, and *Wenwiu* in Bodmin, pp. 83, 90, 96, and 98; the sex of these is mostly unclear. Orel, *BBCS*, 34 (1987), 7, sees a feminine form of **Katubiwos* in Κατουβηα in Maroneia and compares 378/169 BODIBEVE (see n. 74 above).

91 *Primitiva* and *Primitivus* are both in RIB. Cf. *Festivus, Lascivus, Finitivus*, ibid.. Thomas, *Christian Celts*, p. 85, and Howlett, *Cambro-Latin Compositions*, p. 27, favour [AVD]IVA ('*Auda* with feminine adjectival suffix *-iua*', Howlett), while Ifor Williams, in RCAHMW, *Anglesey*, p. cxi, noted *Dotiva* and *Lasciva*, as well as suggesting a Latinization of *Elliw*, or a feminine form of *-bivos*.

92 CBT ii, 443, line 107. The point still holds if *Nynnid* is a masculine name, as argued by Richards, *AC*, 118 (1969), 144–45, and ETG, pp. 151–52 and 212–13. For a Cornish *Sanctus Nunet* or *Nunit* see Padel, *Popular Dictionary of Cornish Place-Names*, p. 132, Orme, *Dedications*, p. 109, and *Saints of Cornwall*, p. 207. The name NI(*n*)ID may also occur in 979/46 (so Macalister, *AC*, 77 (1922), 201), though this is slightly doubted by Ifor Williams, *AC*, 90 (1935), 92. In CIIC ii Macalister, influenced by Williams's criticism, adopted the reading 'Pro ANiMa ID est [*est* = Insular '÷' abbreviation] ANIma GURHI'. (For use of *id est* cf. 516/Scot.1.) This was published too late to be considered in ECMW. *Nonnita*, as well as being the name of St David's mother (connected with Latin *nonna* 'nun' or with the name *Nonnus* cf. Ó Riain, in *Cardiganshire County History*, i, 385 and 394), already occurs in the Early Christian inscriptions of Gaul, as noted by Rhys, LWP, p. 404, and Okasha, *Corpus*, p. 300, both citing Le Blant, *Inscriptions chrétiennes de la Gaule antérieures au viiie siècle*, i, nos. 273, 278, and 326. Cf. Holder ii, 758–59; OPEL iii, 104 and 178. NONNITA in 461/Ok66 is generally assumed to be a female name (e.g. LHEB, p. 188), but in LBS iv, 22, n. 1, it is deduced from the context ('TRIS FILI') that it is a male Goidelic name in the genitive (i.e. with -A(S), cf. e.g. CIIC 29 **BRAN[I]TTAS**, McManus, *Guide*, p. 108, and Ziegler, pp. 108 and 140). It might be easier to regard **NONNITA(S)* as a *nominative* Hibernicization of a Latin *Nonnitus*; see further Chs. 4 and 5 below, pp. 303 and 333. KHJ notes (but evidently did not accept in LHEB) Rhys's unsatisfactory suggestion in *Englyn*, pp. 20–21, that NONNITA is a preform of the Irish *male* name *Nannid (Naindid* in *Patrician Texts*, ed. Bieler, p. 262); one problem is that this is an *i*-stem (O'Brien, *Celtica*, 10 (1973), 224), on the declension of which class in gen. -OS see McManus, *Guide*, p. 116.

93 For what it is worth, the MW form *Melyd, esgob Llundain* (Bede's Mellitus) in EWGT p. 70 (cited in IEMB, p. 287) supports /i/; cf. *Gallt Melyd* in LBS iii, 474.

94 Cf. the *Melito* cited in GPN, p. 115, n. 7, from DAG, p. 1287, § 244; cf. Holder ii, 538. Note 386/92 MELI and 453/399 MELI (also KHJ's reading); and cf. 351/115/2 DVMELVS and W. *Dyfel* (Ziegler, p. 175). Cf. *Me[li]tine* (for Greek *Me[li]tene)* in RIB ii [fasc. 8] 2503.342. Rhys, *AC*, 4th ser. 5 (1874), 173, compared MELI with the place name *Mellteyrn*; but for other possibilities see Lloyd-Jones, *Enwau Lleoedd Sir Gaernarfon*, pp. 55–56, and Williams, *BBCS*, 10 (1939–41), 41. (Subsequently, in *AC*, 5th ser. 12 (1895), 24–25, Rhys noted that the older form was *Mayltern, Maelteern.*) As noted by Swift, *Ogam Stones*, p. 93, Tírechán mentions a bishop *Melus: Patrician Texts*, ed. Bieler, pp. 128 and 136. He was probably Mel of Ard Achad, allegedly Patrick's nephew (ibid., p. 220; cf. CGSH, p. 255, s.n. *Mel*; LBS iii, 461–63; cf. *Merioneth Lay Subsidy*, ed. Williams-Jones, p. 5: *Wasmel*, probably = *gwas Mael* however cf. LBS iii, 400, and n. 976 below). MELI could be genitive of the well-attested *Melius* or *Maelius* (Holder ii, 538–39; OPEL iii, 44 and 74).

on the orthography. These are also extremely likely factors in the case of the Classicizing 414/271 AETERN[E], although it is possible that in speech Latin /ern/ was raised to /irn/ here before undergoing *a*-affection to /ern/ again (see ‡27 (ii)).

[15] A more significant example of non-affection is 320/26 ORVVITE MVLIERI. Since Rhys this has always been compared with W. *Erwyd* (as in *Ponterwyd*, Ceredigion, Rhys's native village).[95] The latter's *y* must derive from short, rather than long, /i/. If Rhys's comparison is correct, *Erwyd* is presumably masculine, from **Orwitos*, since **Orwitā* would have given Mod.W.**Orwed*; ORVVITE will be the precursor of this feminine **Orwed*, not yet showing *a*-affection. A Cornish cognate is perhaps visible in the name *capella beati Erviti* at Marazion in 1397, although this patron saint came to be equated with the Roman martyr *Hermes* (gen. *Hermetis*).[96] It is a problem, however, that the etymology of **Orwitos* is obscure (hardly Latin *orbĭtus* or Celtic *Orbio-*).[97] The best possibility I can find is the Latin name *Orfitus*, which is well attested, though in Roman Britain found only as the name of the consul of AD 149 on an imported amphora. The feminine form *Orfita* is attested on a third-century inscription from Trier: *Orfitae coniugi*.[98] If this is the same as our ORVVITE, the latter may have British /rw/ sound-substituted for /rf/, assuming that the name was borrowed earlier than the advent of a native /rf/ < /rp/ (‡43 below). If ORVVITE is Irish, on the other hand, we can compare the Irish female names in *Ór-* 'gold' (< Latin *aurum*): *Órna(i)t* and *Órlaith*.[99] *Órna(i)t* has the feminine diminutive element *-na(i)t*, as in *Damnat* 'little doe' etc.[100] Could the five minims of

95 LWP, p. 363; BWP, pp. 17 and 22; LHEB, p. 610; Richards, *Atlas of Anglesey*, p. 29 ('the *Erwyd* found in place names like Pont Erwyd' – was Richards also thinking of Erwd (Erwood) in Brycheiniog, WATU, p. 67?). Lloyd-Jones has a possible *erwyt* 'spear' (*Geirfa*, s.v.). It is perhaps not impossible that **Orwitā* derives from Vulgar Latin **Orivinda* < *Orienda* (cf. n. 108); for examples of loss of /n/ in /nd/, such as RIB i 621 VERECVD for *Verecund(a)*, see VLRB, p. 921. (Incidentally, the deceptively similar Italian place name *Orvieto* < *Orbivieto* probably derives from *urbs vetus*: Prati, *Archivio glottologico italiano*, 24 (1930), 56–59. I owe this reference to Dr F. Benozzo.)

96 See Olson & Padel, *CMCS*, 12 (1986), 49; cf. Orme, *Dedications*, pp. 80–81.

97 For the latter see GPN, pp. 238–39. Holder i, 229, and ii, 881, refers to Ptolemy's promontory 'Ορουιον (2.6.2) in Galicia, and tentatively identifies it with *Aryium prominens* in Avienus, *Ora Maritima*, lines 160–62 (see pp. 54 and 79 of Murphy's edition) – an identification not accepted in *Tabula Imperii Romani*, K-29, pp. 64 and 81, nor by Talbert, *Barrington Atlas*, map 24C2 and *Map-by-Map Directory*, i, 377, s.n. *Orouion Pr.*, and 385. García Alonso, *La geografía de Claudio Ptolomeo*, p. 181, is also doubtful and suggests derivation from **Orb-io-*.

98 OPEL iii, 116; RIB ii [fasc. 6] 2493.69, as corrected by Tomlin, *Britannia*, 28 (1997), 472; Nesselhauf, *27. Bericht des römisch-germanischen Kommission*, 1937 (Berlin, 1939), 56, §14 = DAG, p. 739. Holder ii, 881–82 seems to suggest that a masculine(?) ORVITA lies behind the potter's stamp OBVIT.F from Trion, Lyon (Oswald: *Obvivs* (?)), as given by Allmer & Dissard, *Musée de Lyon, inscriptions antiques*, iv, 384, no. 497–907 (indexed under *Obvitus*). Note an *Antonius Orfitus*, ibid., iii, 169, no. 258.

99 Ó Corráin & Maguire, *Gaelic Personal Names*, p. 150; Ó Cuív, *Celtica*, 18 (1986), 161–62.

100 DIL s.n.; O'Brien, *Celtica*, 10 (1973), 230; Meid, *Romanze*, p. 211; NWÄI, pp. 83, n. 55, and 341–43.

ORVVIT- be read as ORNΛT- for *Órnat* (+ Latin -*(a)e*) or, as is palaeographically easier, as ORINIT- for *Órn(a)it* with epenthetic vowel or reduced or archaizing composition vowel as in 106 **CORIBIRI** = *Coirbri?*[101]

[15] We can perhaps contrast ORVVITE with 332/40 [P]ETA FIL[IA]. I can find no name in RIB in -*petus*, -*peta* (or in -*metus*, -*meta*, Macalister's unlikely alternative reading being [M]ETA), and the only such name with *i* is *Cupitus* (for example, CVPITI (gen.) in a fourth-century list of tilemakers(?) from Binchester, Durham).[102] Compare also 514/Scot.8 CVPITIANI. This suggests [CVP]ETA FIL[IA] as a possible reading. If so, the E could be due to *a*-affection; note, however, 418/283 CVPETIAN[I], where the E cannot be so explained and – if correctly read – must be Vulgar Latin, like HEC for *hic* in the same inscription.[103] If Macalister is right about [M]ETA, another possibility is [DEM]ETA, a female version of 450/390 DEMETI (gen.). A more plausible example of *a*-affection, noted by Rhys, is 421/294 R[V]STECE FILIA PATERNINI;[104] the masculine *Rusticus* is attested in RIB, and Jackson notes a *Rustica* near Vienne in the sixth century.[105]

[15] 454/402 CVNIOVENDE MATER appears to contain *-windā* 'white', and is listed without special comment by Jackson along with names with *Windo-* such as 390/96 VENDESETLI and 376/174 VENNISETLI (> *Gwynnhoedl*) and 400/177 VINNEMAGLI (cf. 3005/F5 VENOMAILI, OB *Uuinmael/Uuenmael*, MB *Guenmael*, *Guenvael*).[106] Presumably he did

---

101 Cf. MacNeill, *PRIA*, 39 C (1931), 34–37; McManus, *Guide*, p. 178, n. 28; Ziegler, pp. 155–56; Uhlich, *Morphologie*, p. 49. It might be suggested that scholars have wrongly divided ETORVVITE MVLIERI, and that ETORVVITE is an Irish name like 318/6 ETTO-RIGI and 179 **ETO-RIGAS** (below, ‡38); but I can see no way of explaining an element -RVVIT- (hardly: OI *rús*, LEIA R-54). Hughes, *AC*, 7th ser. 4 (1924), 46–48, notes on ET ORVVITE that 'there is a considerable space between the R and the following letter and there certainly are some markings in this position'.

102 See n. 108 below. Kajanto, p. 296, notes that *Cupitus/Cupita* was particularly popular in Celtic areas. Looking outside Britain there are more possibilities: cf. *Hospita*, *Popita*, *Lucapetus*, *Agapetus*, *Scelepetus*, *Alpetus*, *Carpetus*; *Maeta*, *Pameta*, *Nemeta*, *Amita*, *Mitus*, *Suramitus*, *Domitus*, *Edomitus*, *Eumitus*, *Admetus*, *Imetus*, *Atimetus*, *Adrumetus*, *Epithymetus* (Mócsy, pp. 330 and 393–94).

103 For the variant *Cupitianus* see Kajanto, pp. 145 and 296. Note that 418/283 CVPITIAN(I) with -I- has also been read and is probably preferable: LWP, p. 377, and Edwards, *Med. Arch.*, 45 (2001), 26, n. 57.

104 LWP, p. 374. The [V] is uncertain but there is no reason to prefer a more vulgar [O] with Nash-Williams (though for a reverse confusion cf. 519/Scot.6 APVSTOLI for *apostoli*) and certainly not Macalister's [A]. But cf. Rhys, *Englyn*, p. 90, referring to Lewis Morris's drawing, in Hübner's *Inscriptiones Britanniae Christianae*, no. 125: 'had the vowel been other than *o* one would expect to find traces of a straight line.' The second E in -STE{E}CE seen by Macalister is illusory, I think.

105 LHEB, p. 191, n. 1. Weisgerber, *Rhenania*, p. 222, has one in the Moselle region.

106 LHEB, p. 512; cf. p. 325. Rhys, LWP, p. 372, says VINNEMAGLI > W. *Gwenfael*, citing *Iolo Manuscripts*, ed. Williams, p. 144 (Gwenfael daughter of Brychan, cf. *Enfael*, LBS ii, 455), but I have not found it in a respectable Welsh source; but for the Breton cognate see IEMB, p. 135, and Loth, *Noms des saints bretons*, pp. 54 and 133. For forms of *Gwynhoedl*, *Gwennoedyl*, etc. see Rhys, *AC*, 4th ser. 8 (1877), 143–44, and LBS iii, 231, n. 2.

not count CVNIOVENDE as a form with *a*-affection on account of the E also appearing, without etymological justification, in the *Windo-* forms. This is properly cautious, although in theory the latter forms could be using E to spell /ï/ < /i/ (see ‡34 below), whereas in CVNIOVENDE the E could really mean /e/ (it cannot mean /ï/, as this did not develop in the feminine form). Curiously, the ogam spelling of the cognate Irish name element **VEND-** is also problematic, since according to the handbooks OI *find* m.f. 'white' shows that lowering of /i/ did not take place across /nd/ in Irish. The handbooks may, however, be wrong about this, as Ziegler suggests (see ‡20 below). Whatever the explanation of the Irish names in **VEND-**, it is possible that they influenced the spelling of the British names – unless, that is, the ogam spelling convention was influenced by British practice, which is not impossible. Another possibility is that British VEND- is not always the same element as *windo-* or that it was an alternative spelling of it. In Roman Britain, as well as forms such as VINDOMORVCI, '*Vindutius*' (Caerleon), *Cunovindus*, and *Vindiorix*,[107] we have ORIVENDVS (??) on an altar from Gloucester, CVNOVENDI (gen.) in the fourth-century list of tile-makers(?) from Binchester, mentioned above, *Britivenda* on two Bath tablets, a possible [C]VNOVE[NDI] from Monmouth, and CVNOVEN stamped on lead ingots from the wreck at Ploumanac'h, cargo from the Brigantes and Iceni.[108] Note also *vendicas* for Classical *vindicas* on a London *defixio* which 'may be the first instance of a change found in some, but not all, Romance languages; cf. Italian *vengiare*, French *venger*, Spanish *vengar*, but Sardinian *vindicare*, Portuguese *vingar*'.[109] Continental Celtic names in *Vend-* are also widespread,[110] and can perhaps be best explained, along with the ogam and British examples, as spelling confusions due to a pan-Celtic tendency to raise /e/ to /ɪ/ before /nd/ (see ‡27). Whatever the precise explanation of the Roman-period forms like CVNOVENDI, they obviously cast doubt on CVNIOVENDE as an instance of *a*-affection.

[15] 2021 GVINNDA CAR[A?] CONIUN[X?] may be from *Windodag-* or *Windotam-*,[111] and so not contain *gwen*, and the same may be true of the

---

[107] RIB i 2053 and 353 (lost), and (for the last two) Wright & Hassall, *Britannia*, 2 (1971), 292 (Northumberland tombstone) and Tab.Sulis, no. 18.

[108] RIB i 119 (but this appears to be ORIVINDVS in the drawing) and ii [fasc. 5] 2491.78 (Binchester); Tab.Sulis, nos 2–3; Hassall & Tomlin, *Britannia*, 20 (1989), 343, n. 77; L'Hour, *RAO*, 4 (1987), 120. Cf. Smith, VLRB, p. 905, on LEND- for British *lind-*, and pp. 917 and 940, where he derives *Orivendus* (sic) from *Oriendus*, comparing *Orienda* in CIL vi 28580.

[109] Hassall & Tomlin, *Britannia*, 18 (1987), 360, n. 5.

[110] Holder iii, 157–58.

[111] For *-daga* 'good' (GPN, pp. 188–89) in British *Andagin* see Sims-Williams, in *Gaulois et celtique continental*, and for the possibility of MW *Gwyndaf*, see ‡67. It is not clear whether GVINNDA is the name of a husband or a wife. (The stone is damaged and the published restoration uncertain, omitting moreover the line IADEL[(?), perhaps 'i.e. Æthel[stan]' or similar.) In Middle and Modern Welsh one expects *Gwen-* in female names, usually agreeing with a feminine second element (*Gwenllian, Gwenhwyfar, Gwenfrewi, Gwenda*, etc.), but it is not clear when this arose (cf. SWWF, pp. 27–28 and 454, n. 4). See examples in Lloyd-

odd-looking 1048/Ok 32 FILIA [ ] GVENNCREST or FILI(I)V[S] VENN-
ORCIT (with E for /ɪ/ ?).[112] On the other hand, 3010/M1 HERANNUEN, *if*
female, must correspond to *Isarnowindā*, but the presence of *a*-affection is
not actually proved by the E since Old Breton and Old Cornish also use *e* to
spell /ɪ/.[113] Allan's reading of 1055/Ok3, UAETUENA, could also involve
the 'white' element; Macalister and Thomas, however, prefer to read
TAETUERA, Thomas equating the second element with OB *-uere* (cf.
MW *-wyre* < OW *-uire(g)*, *-ereg*), which is phonetically difficult.[114] One
could perhaps compare OE *Tætwine*.[115] 1030 CERID[WEN UXOR EIUS],
being a conjecture, can be ignored here; in any case, the second element of
Ceridwen was *-fen*.[116] 998/164 HEUTREN, a puzzling form (with merely
orthographical *H*-?), could perhaps be etymologized as *Avi-trina*, with the
element seen in TRINNI on Bath tablet 53 and perhaps in MW *Tringat* and
Tringer (in the unlikely event that their *Trin-* stands for *Tryn-* < *trĭn-*), but
a masculine counterpart *Avitrinos*, spelt with E for /ï/ (i.e. *Eudryn*), is
also possible, and HEUTREN can also be compared with the Dobunnian
name *Trenus*.[117] 1036/360 HAUEN (Macalister's suggested reading) is
obscure, but *awen* 'inspiration', with etymological *e* is a posssibility (‡44
below).

[15] In sum, the only fairly clear examples without *a*-affection are 320/26
ORVVITE and 3025/I6 MELITA, the former being the more significant
since it is less likely to be a conservative Latin spelling. The form SE[V]IRA
on the 'Pillar of Eliseg' (1000/182), referring to the alleged wife of Vortigern

Jones, *Geirfa*, pp. 744–46, and Lloyd, *Cymmrodor*, 9 (1888), 47 (listing male names with *gwen*) and discussion in HPB, p. 288. The spelling with *e* is consistently found in the forms of the male name (with feminine second element) *Guengat* (: Ir. *Findchad*) cited by Lloyd-Jones, *Geirfa*, p. 660, Williams, *Canu Aneirin*, p. 348, and Uhlich, *Morphologie*, p. 252.

[112] Thomas, *Mute Stones*, pp. 290–91; cf. Tedeschi, *Scrittura e civiltà*, 19 (1995), tav. 3: FILIIV GVENNORCIT. If ORCIT- is correct, compare (as does Thomas) the element in GPN, pp. 239–40, and DLG, p. 206, s.v. *Orgeto-*, LEIA O-30, DGVB i, 277, and OW *Cohorget* and *Conhorget*, MW *Kyhoret*, *Kynhoret* (Rhys, *PSAS*, 26 (1892), 326, n. 1, and *AC*, 5th ser. 12 (1895), 33; and LL, pp. xlv and 199). The C instead of G is odd.

[113] HPB, pp. 91–93. The supposition that I is used in masculine and E in feminine forms of 'white' (DGVB i, 192) may be too simplistic; cf. HPB, pp. 96 and 287–88.

[114] Thomas, *Mute Stones*, pp. 287 and 303, n. 53; cf. DGVB i, 161; Sims-Williams, *BBCS*, 38 (1991), 50; SBCHP, p. 222.

[115] Seale, *Onomasticon*, pp. 440–41; note also the element *-wær*, ibid., p. 473.

[116] Lloyd-Jones, *Geirfa*, p. 136.

[117] For both see Tab.Sulis, pp. 180–81 (PRB, p. 102; *Trēnus* in Holder ii, 1911, cited in ‡48n below). For *Tringat* and *Tringer*, see Bromwich & Evans, *Culhwch and Olwen*, p. 147 (also *Ystoria Gereint uab Erbin*, ed. Thomson, l. 604); these cannot be cognate with 353/127/7 TRENACATVS (unless this has E for I) nor with OI *trén*, and are most likely to be based on W. *trin* with original /i:/. See also p. 330 below on *trén*. The Royal Commission compared HEUTREN with 2022/253/984 HU[TR]VM, which is impossible.

(fifth century), is clearly Latin *Severa* (a name attested inter alia on tablets from Uley and Bath).[118] The spelling with I may be a post-*a*-affection hypercorrection, intended to avoid an error comparable with 448/370 NOMENA for *nomina*[119] and 1067 IMAGENEM.[120]

[15] The best examples with *a*-affection may be 394/103 [V]ENEDOTIS, 332/40 [?CVP]ETA and 421/294 R[V]STECE. In 3010/M1 HERANNUEN *a*-affection may be present (if it is referring to a female), as may also be true of 998/164 HEUTREN, but such forms are less significant since they are clearly post-apocope and therefore by definition post-affection. In evaluating the E-spellings, we have to bear in mind that *i* alternated with *e* (and *u* with *o*) in Vulgar Latin, as noted by Jackson.[121] He explains R(O)STECE (as he writes it) for *Rusticae* and 448/370 NOMENA for *nomina* in this way, which begs the question; but he also cites more certain vulgarisms, where *a*-affection cannot be a factor: 445/354 VITALIANI EMERETO for *emeritus* (or *Emeritus?*) and 394/103 CIVE for *civis*, as well as various miswritings of E for /i/ in native names such as 413/272 MONEDORIGI for **Monidorigi* and 374/172 CVNEGNI for **Cunigni*.[122] Vulgar Latin spelling is thus certainly a possible explanation, even though Jackson asserts that it 'appears very rarely in Britain'.[123] On the other hand, R[V]STECE, [?CVP]ETA, NOMENA – and the hypercorrection in SE[V]IRA – could equally well be due to *a*-affection.

‡*16 ū̆ (< IE ū, -ō, and Latin -ō) > ī̆; LHEB §23.2*

This clearly occurred before final *i*-affection (‡19 below) in view of W. *Meilyg < *Maglokū̆*, etc.

---

[118] RIB ii [fasc. 3] 2432.6 and Tab.Sulis no. 51. *Severus* is a very common name in RIB, but there is only one very dubious case of *Sevirus* (RIB ii 2491 [fasc. 5] 108). For examples of *Severa* see Kajanto, pp. 256–57.

[119] Rhys, *AC*, 5th ser. 13 (1896), 106–7, analysed NOMENA as *nomen* + feminine sg. *-a*, which is unlikely; cf. Nash-Williams, ECMW, p. 205 and n. 2; Thomas, *Mute Stones*, pp. 204–5; Swift, *Ogam Stones*, p. 89; Edwards, in Cramp FS, p. 56.

[120] KHJ thought the lettering of 1067 agreed with the seventh-century ('at latest') date proposed by Clapham, *Antiquity*, 8 (1934), 49.

[121] LHEB, p. 191. Rhys mentions examples, but wrongly ascribes them to *Early* Latin in LWP, pp. 209–10.

[122] LHEB, pp. 191–93. Note also that 2020 VERE[could conceivably have E for I in a name like 461/Ok66 VIRICATI (cf. ‡‡ 28 and 34 below on this VIRI-), but for many names in *Vere*- see Holder iii, 205–12. On *emeritus* see Thomas, *Mute Stones*, pp. 74, 86, n. 18, and 106; KHJ suggests 'veteran of Christ'. It can hardly mean 'military veteran', as the feminine *emerita* is even more common in Christian inscriptions than the masculine, but neither does it have to be an epithet since it occurs as an ordinary cognomen in Roman Bath and elsewhere: for example, Kajanto (p. 351) cites an *Emeritianus* son of *Emeritus* in Dalmatia. Cf. OPEL ii, 116–17 and 217. If the nominative -O is taken seriously, we should perhaps consider the ogam inscription as primary, commemorating Vitalianus, and the roman one as secondary, commemorating Emeritus son of Vitalianus.

[123] LHEB, p. 191. But plenty of examples of *e* for *i* in Roman Britain are given by Mann, *Britannia*, 2 (1971), 220 (cf. Hamp, *Britannia*, 6 (1975), 156–57), and Smith, VLRB, pp. 902–11 and 938–39.

[16] Jackson (p. 319) notes no examples of the /ü:/ stage in the inscriptions, explaining the U of 341/71 SALICIDVNI or SALIGIDVNI ('if it contains Celtic *dūno-') and of 457/Ok18 DVNOCATI as Irish /u:/. This view is clearly plausible in both cases.

[16] 341/71 [M]ACCVTRENI + SALICIDVNI (or SALIGIDVNI) starts with a specifically Irish name (*Mak^{w}k^{w}as-Trēnī) and the stone bears an equivalent legend in ogam: **MAQITRENI SALICIDUNI**.[124] We expect an Irish name therefore. But there are two reasons for uncertainty. Firstly, **SALICIDUNI** looks like a place name, 'willow fort' (cf. Ir. *Dún Salach*), and formally this could be either Irish or British.[125] A parallel formation is provided by the place name *Sailchóit*, explained in *Cormac's Glossary* as Brittonic for 'a big wood [cf. W. *coed*?] of willows'.[126] As a resident of Brycheiniog, *Mak^{w}k^{w}as-Trēnī could take his epithet 'of the Willow-town'[127] from a place in Wales rather than Ireland. Secondly, according to Jackson the reading of the Latin text may be SALIGIDVNI, with G abnormally representing British post-lenition /g/ in a British name.[128] Hence, he adds: 'Possibly it is not an Irish name at all, but British (the second element can hardly be regarded as certainly Celtic *dūno- "fort").'[129] His parenthetical remark shows that Jackson was reluctant to accept the natural consequence of identifying the name as British: namely, that U was still being used for /ü:/ or for British /i:/ < /ü:/. Evidently this was because he dated /i:/ < /ü:/ to the 'middle of the fifth century' but the stone as 'end of fifth or beginning of sixth century'.[130] Ignoring these constraints, or allowing for a conservative

---

[124] Nash-Williams's **MAQUTRENI** is a mistake, as noted in LHEB, p. 180, n. 1. On the name see ibid., pp. 140 and 179; Ziegler, pp. 238–39.

[125] LWP, p. 384; Ziegler, p. 230. For *helyg* and *din* in Brittonic place names see also LEIA S-13 and D-222 and CPNE, pp. 128 and 84. To complicate matters, a place in Wales might bear an Irish name. *Helyg* was also a personal name (EANC, p. 149; Pierce, *Place-Names of Dinas Powys*, p. 51) and *Salic-* is an element in Continental Celtic names (Holder ii, 1307; cf. *Saliga* in RIB i 253). The use of -I- as composition vowel in the consonantal-stem **SALICIDUNI** (McManus, *Guide*, p. 118) suggested to KHJ that the ogam was influenced by the roman-letter spelling. Cf. Uhlich, *Morphologie*, pp. 33, n. 25, and 74, n. 60; and below, ‡38 n. 654.

[126] LEIA S-13; Russell, in Evans FS, p. 176. Cf. *Zalesöd* < Alpine Romance (Ladinia submersa) *salicētu* 'region with willow groves' (Anreiter et al., in *Ptolemy*, p. 114).

[127] LWP, p. 384.

[128] LHEB, pp. 179, 180, n. 1, and 707. Note that the ogam **C** *may* transcribe the expected roman C, rather than representing Ir. /x/ as stated in LHEB, p. 179. Bizarrely, the ogam **C** may reflect British spelling habits while the roman G may reflect ogam spelling habits! (See ‡17 below.) The roman G was noted by Macalister as 'perhaps a mere mistake' (CIIC i, 326, n. 2), so evidently Macalister was not *looking* for G. Given the ogam **C**, the roman G is obviously attractive as the *lectio difficilior*. Jackson notes that the G (if present) has been 'obscured by the C which has been painted over it (!)' (LHEB, p. 707; see the suspiciously clear British Museum photograph in Thomas, *Mute Stones*, p. 120, and compare Rhys's difficulty in reading the inscription, LWP, pp. 382–83). The paint has now gone, and what Macalister took to be the tail of a G does seem to be there. The C is, however, accepted on the basis of a rubbing in the new *Corpus*.

[129] LHEB, p. 179. On the date of /ü:/ > /i:/ cf. TRC, pp. 154–55.

[130] LHEB, p. 319.

use of U for /i:/ < /ü:/, the only plausible explanation of SALICIDVNI/ SALIGIDVNI, if it *is* British, is surely that it contains the 'fort' element. But is the roman *V* certain, or could it be an *I*? Rhys, who read SALICIDVNI, stated carefully that:

> the *L* is entirely gone, but its place is there, so I supply it from the Ogam; several of the following letters are doubtful, and as to the *V*, I can only say that I fancied I could trace the first part of that letter standing at the angle to be expected supposing that to be the reading.[131]

If this is correct, **SALICIDINI or **SALIGIDINI can be ruled out as Brittonic equivalents of SALICIDUNI.

[16] The problem with DVNOCATI is that it can be the ancestor of either Irish *Dúnchad* or Brittonic *Din(o)gat*, both well-attested names.[132] Jackson identified this name in 457/Ok18 DVNOCATI HIC IACIT FILI MERCAGNI (or MESCAGNI) as Primitive Irish **Dūnocatōs* [recte **Dūnacatōs*] (with Latin -I replacing the Irish genitive -OS), whereas Okasha quotes O. J. Padel's view that it could be Primitive Welsh/Cornish. Jackson's opinion was based on the patronymic MESCAGNI, which he derived from 'the stem seen in OI. *mescc*, "drunk"'.[133] A problem here is that another possibility is the originally unrelated Irish stem *mesc*- 'mix, agitate, trouble, confuse', which is also attested in Brittonic, as in W. *mysg* 'mixture, confusion; midst', C. *mesk, mysk* 'midst'.[134] Compare OI *Tairmesc* < *tairmesc* 'interdiction', cognate with W. *terfysg* 'trouble'.[135] A better indication of the Irishness of the patronymic is the -AGNI, even though Jackson himself thought that this occurred in British as well as Irish.[136] Even if the patronymic is Irish, however, the name DVNOCATI, with its typically British composition vowel,[137] *could* be Brittonic.

[16] A third form relevant to /ü:/ > /i:/, which Jackson does not mention alongside the Breconshire SALICIDVNI/SALIGIDVNI and Cornish

---

[131] LWP, p. 383. I agree about the V. The editors of the new *Corpus* also detect the left stroke of the V, on the basis of a rubbing.

[132] Uhlich, *Morphologie*, p. 235; EWGT s.n. *Dingad*. We do not need to decide whether this is an inherited 'Insular Celtic' name or a name which had passed from one island to the other before the advent of British /i:/. The element is rare and dubious in Gaulish personal names, although see Holder i, 1377; EPPUDUNOS may be an example (RIG iv, 536). Cf. KGP, pp. 200–1, and Gorrochategui, in Mitxelena FS, pp. 618–19, 623, and 625.

[133] LHEB, pp. 171, 188, and 319, n. 4. (Note that *Mesc*- does not occur as a name element in the ogam corpus.) Actually, a name *Mercán* is noted by O'Brien, *Celtica*, 10 (1973), 221. However, MESCAGNI is probably preferable in view of nearby 458/Ok9 MESGI (or MESCI); cf. Thomas, *Mute Stones*, p. 274, n. 22.

[134] LEIA M-41–42; GPC s.v. *mysg*; Schrijver, *BBCS*, 39 (1992), 2; SBCHP, pp. 415 and 438. The E spelling for original /i/ in CB may have been reached in the first half of the sixth century according to LHEB, p. 285.

[135] CGH, p. 740; LEIA T-14. Cf. ‡14n above.

[136] LHEB, p. 461. See ‡48 below.

[137] The British O may, however, have been substituted for Irish A in bilingual inscriptions; cf. LHEB, p. 644. On O in ogam see ‡38.

DVNOCATI, evidently because he thought it too late for British /ü:/,[138] is DVNOCATI in 327/43 **TURPI[LI MAQI** (or **MOSAC) TRIL]LUNI/ TVRPILLI IC IACIT PVVERI TRILVNI DVNOCATI**, another Breconshire inscription. An Irish context is provided by the use of ogam. On the other hand, *Turpilius/Turpillus* is a Classical Latin name, while no agreement has been reached on the identity of TRILVNI (= **T[RA]LL[O]NI** in the ogam according to Macalister).[139] It is not impossible, then, that DVNOCATI is a Brittonic personal name, or even a place name (functioning like SALICIDVNI/SALIGIDVNI in the other Breconshire inscription): a place in south Wales called *Brehant Din Cat* 'guttur receptaculum pugnae' is mentioned by the ninth-century Breton hagiographer Wrmonoc.[140]

[16] Since only three examples of U-spellings can be cited, all of them more or less under suspicion of being Irish, it might seem that the change of /ü:/ > /i:/ must have antedated the period of the inscriptions. This does not follow, however, for I-spellings are also very rare, evidently because etymological /u:/ was uncommon in personal names. One instance is 984/59 + GURCI BLEDRVS, where GURCI has /i:/ < /ü/ < /u:/. This is obviously a late form, a late compound of *gŵr* 'man' and *ci* 'hound' (cf. OI *Ferchú*), not a descendant of an old compound **Wirokū* comparable with *Meilyg* < **Maglokū*.[141] The only other certain instance in the whole Brittonic corpus, so far as I can discover, is 1019/237/920 ILCI, which is another late compound of *ci*.[142] To GURCI and ILCI we can possibly add 1068/b CONDILICI on the Isle of Man, compared by Ifor Williams with Middle/ Old Welsh *Kyndilic* and *Gurdilic*, if, that is, -DILICI is the Brittonic cognate of the element seen in 83 **DULICCI**(?) and Ziegler is right to equate **DULICCI** with Ir. *dúilech* 'ambitious, voracious'.[143] In Cornwall 1053/Ok1

---

[138] LHEB, p. 184 ('early or mid sixth century').

[139] LHEB, p. 170; Ziegler, pp. 237 and 240. Thomas, *Mute Stones*, p. 124, suggests emending to TRIBUNI, as in 476/Ok45 TRIBVNI. See ‡26n. TVRPILLI has been taken to be *Turpilius*, but *Turpillus* is also well attested (Kajanto, p. 286, Mócsy, p. 297), and is attested in Roman Britain on a graffito on an amphora from London, [FELICI]T[E]R [T]VRPILLV[S], admittedly cut before firing: Hassall & Tomlin, *Britannia* 17 (1986), 445 = RIB ii [fasc. 6] 2493.55.

[140] Jackson, *CMCS*, 3 (1982), 33; cf. Doble, *Lives of the Welsh Saints*, pp. 150–51, who takes *Dincat* as the personal name.

[141] On the name *Gwrgi* (cf. *Gwrgenau*) see EWGT, p. 194, and Uhlich, *Morphologie*, pp. 245–46, and cf. Sims-Williams, in *The Arthur of the Welsh*, p. 42. Welsh names in -*gi* are to be compared with the Irish names with restored -*cú* discussed by Uhlich, *Morphologie*, p. 210, Stüber, *Historical Morphology*, pp. 88–89; and cf. SWWF, pp. 87–88. See ‡19 below. Celtiberian *Uiroku* is unrelated according to MLH v/1, p. 452.

[142] On ILCI see ‡85 below.

[143] Ziegler, p. 174 (no Brittonic cognates are listed in LEIA D-215). But Harvey, *Ériu*, 38 (1987), 52–53, has **L[A]M[A]DULICCI** 'swift-handed' from *dulach* < *dul* (LEIA D-220). A much less likely possibility is *doilig, duilig* 'difficult', which Ó Cuív, *Celtica*, 18 (1986), 167–68, sees in the name *Gilla-duilig* ‘ “hard” (or “intractible”) servant'; compare also OI *Cú-dulig* (Meyer, *Contributions*, p. 539), analysed by O'Brien, *Celtica*, 10 (1973), 228, as *Cú* + adjective. This would have been **DU-LOG-* or **DU-VO-LOG-* (cf. LEIA D-153 and

CILRORON, if that is the correct reading, *may* contain the Brittonic element *cil* 'back' cognate with the Irish *cúl* in 128 **CULIDOVI** (later *Cúldub*),[144] but that is quite uncertain since -RORON is obscure. Again, 462/Ok14 QVENATAVCI IC DINVI [F]I[LI]VS probably does not contain the Brittonic *din-* discussed above since QVENATAVCI is clearly Irish.[145] 320/26 CVLIDOR[I?] is superficially similar to **CULIDOVI** (OI *Cúldub*), but will have had Pr.W. short /u/ if Rhys and Williams are right to compare MW *Kyledyr*.[146] Rhys hinted that CVLIDOR(I)/*Kyledyr* could have been borrowed from an Irish name in *Cú-*, comparing the shortening of /uː/ in MW *Cocholyn* [also *Cychwlynn*] < *Cú Chulainn*.[147] This is improbable, especially as there is no suitable second element. However, it is quite possible that CVLIDOR(I), whether or not it is the source of *Kyledyr*, is an Irish name in *Cúl-*. In these names *Cúl* usually means 'back of the head, hair' and is followed by an adjective or nominal attribute, as in **CULIDOVI** > *Cúldub* 'black-hair'.[148] No suitable adjective or attribute suggests itself for -DOR(I),[149] however, so it may be better to understand CVLIDOR(I) as 'postern-gate' (cf. Mod.Ir. *cúl-doras* 'backdoor'), with the element *dor-* seen in Ir. *Dorchú* 'hound of/at the gate', but here alluding to the bearer's defensive qualities (like *dún* in other personal names).[150] If the Irish name was borrowed with Welsh short /u/ sound-substituted in the post-Irish-apocope form CVLIDOR (which is what seems to occur on the

---

S-202). Lloyd-Jones, *Y Geninen*, 44 (1926), 9–10, thought *Cyndilig* might be 'uchel gyfoethog', and Rhys, *AC*, 6th ser. 7 (1907), 90 and 310, thought *Kindilic mab Corknud*, an *alltud* in *Englynion y Beddau* I.41, a borrowing of '*Cú-duilich*' (sic) son of '*Corco-Nutan*' (cf. Meyer, *Contributions*, p. 489; Rhys, *AC*, 5th ser. 12 (1895), 36; differently Lloyd-Jones, *Geirfa*, p. 164). For the Welsh names see EWGT s.nn. (also *Dilig*) and Williams, *Canu Aneirin*, p. 273. On St Cynddilig see Ó Riain in *Cardiganshire County History*, i, 389. Cf. OC *Ourdylyc*, *Wurôylic*, Bodmin, pp. 94–95; OB *Gurdilec*, Chrest., p. 180. Evans, *Enwau Personol*, p. 278, would connect W. *dil* 'honeycomb'.

[144] Ziegler, p. 157; Uhlich, pp. 40 and 222 (explaining the -I- with reference to OI *Cúilduib*).

[145] LHEB, pp. 140, 171, and 296, n. 2 (and see ‡25n), not mentioning DINVI. Okasha says DINVI is 'Celtic', citing Holder i, 1284, who merely quotes our inscription and various forms in *Dino-* such as *Dino-mogeti-māro* (see n. 275 below); cf. Orel, *BBCS*, 34 (1987), 6. Vendryes, LEIA D-90, connects DINVI, as gen. of *Dinuos, with OI *dín*, gen. *dína* 'protection' (cf. 311 **DINEGLO** > OI *Dínél*, *Díníl*, Ziegler, p. 167). See also below, ‡27, on 454/402 DEN[O]VI (or DENCVI).

[146] Rhys, *Englyn*, p. 13; BWP, p. 22; LHEB, p. 653; see below, ‡17.

[147] Rhys, *Englyn*, p. 13; cf. Sims-Williams, *Celtica*, 21 (1990), 620–33; Jones Pierce, *BBCS*, 5 (1929–31), 63 (*Gocholyn*).

[148] Meyer, *Contributions*, pp. 557–60; DIL, s.v. *cúl*.

[149] Conceivably -DORI could be a spelling of -DOIRI (on the spelling of diphthongs see ‡48) and *dóer could be a variant (by dissimilation or with a different suffix) of *dóel* < **doi-lā-* 'beetle', a common standard of blackness (LEIA D-135). Pokorny has a root **dher-*, **dherə-* 'filth, dirty', with OI *derg* 'red' and Mod.Ir. *drabh* 'husks' as Celtic exponents (IEW, p. 252), but see LEIA D-57–58 and 188.

[150] *Cúldoras* is cited from Keating's *History of Ireland*, Book ii [vol. III] line 2841 in DIL s.v. *cúl*, and *Dorchú* in LEIA D-173; cf. VOTEPO- 'refuge' in names, below, ‡17, and Chapter 5, p. 347.

stone),[151] and before the Welsh change of *-*Vr* > *-*r* (which preceded or was part of Welsh apocope, cf. Latin -*ātor* > MW -*awd(y)r*, Mod.W. -*odr*), CVLIDOR could easily have given MW *Kyledyr*.[152] Nevertheless, all this is uncertain, for one can also segment the name CVLID-O-R(I), as is implied by Ifor Williams's suggested British *Cvlidorix*.[153] In this case, the best etymology I can suggest is *Kö-lliδ-o-rīks < *Kon-slii-, from the root *slī-, *sli-i-, 'take, seize', seen in W. *derllyddu* 'deserve, merit', *cyllid* 'income', and *efrllid* 'merit'.[154] The single -L- of CVLIDOR is not an insuperable objection, as single *l* is often written in Old Welsh too.[155]

[16] Obviously, when there is so little evidence for both U- and I-spellings alike, we cannot assume that the sound change was complete before the period of the inscriptions.

[16] The rarity of etymological /u:/ in early Celtic personal names is borne out by the Gaulish and ogam Irish evidence. Ellis Evans found no clear reflex of IE /u:/ in the Gaulish names he surveyed in *Gaulish Personal Names*,[156] and for Gaulish /-u:/ replacing Latin /-o:/ by sound substitution he noted only a few doubtful examples, of which *Froncu* or *Frontu* < Latin *Fronto* is the best.[157] In Irish, nasal stems with etymological /-(i)o:(n)/ in the nominative must have occurred, but they never appear in the nominative in ogam.[158] This is true even of the popular element *kū* 'hound'.[159] Another popular Irish element, *dūn- (as in *Dúnchath*, *Dúngus*, *Dúnlang*, *Dúnchú*), is strangely absent from the ogam corpus, although the roman-letter examples of DVNOCATI *may* be Irish as we have seen.[160] Rare names with possible /u:/ which occur once each in the ogam inscriptions are 83 **DULICCI**(?) and 128 **CULIDOVI** (both noted above), and an element *drūt-, as in OI

---

[151] The relevant edge was cemented over for a time (Hughes, *AC*, 7th ser. 4 (1924), 46). After it was uncovered Macalister drew the -I, but KHJ, visting the stone in 1947, could not see it, and nor can I: it would have to lie beyond the prepared surface of the stone, which seems unlikely. See Tedeschi, in *Roman, Runes and Ogham*, plate 4

[152] On *-*Vr* > *-*r* see SBCHP, p. 366, and Sims-Williams, in Meid FS, p. 473, n. 2. In this case the MW -*dyr* will represent [ðr], or perhaps [dr] since this cluster probably showed the same variation as [ðl] and [dl] (see SBCHP, pp. 360–65, and below ‡17 on HIROIDIL). The idea that the -*dyr* of *Kyledyr* has a merely epenthetic vowel is supported by the confusion in *Culhwch* with *Kynedyr Wyllt*; see ‡17n below. *Kyledyr* would be a spelling of *Kylydyr*.

[153] BWP, p. 22. See ‡17 below.

[154] GPC, s.vv.; LEIA S-131; and Schumacher, *Historical Morphology*, pp. 45–46.

[155] LHEB, p. 477 (and see p. 540 on IE *-*sl*-).

[156] GPN, p. 395.

[157] GPN, pp. 395, 427 and 450–51. Cf. pp. 104–5 *Nappisetu* (doubtfully Celtic and with /u/), and *Malciu* and *Mommu* (pp. 458–60; further parallels in Stüber, *Historical Morphology*, pp. 108–9). In Roman Britain, names such as *Fronto* were common enough, to judge by RIB, but none of them seems to recur in the Early Christian inscriptions.

[158] Ziegler, pp. 114–15 and references; O'Brien, *Celtica*, 10 (1973), 225.

[159] Ziegler, p. 110; the /u:/ only appeared in the nominative (e.g. *Maglokū* above), not in oblique forms or the composition-form *kuno-* (see Joseph, in Hamp FS, pp. 112–13).

[160] Uhlich, *Morphologie*, pp. 235–36 (cf. names in *Din-* in EWGT s.nn.); Ziegler, p. 175.

drú(i)th 'wanton' and the personal name *Drúith*, may occur in two ogam inscriptions: 87 **DRUTIQULI** and 503 **MAQI DRUTA** (?).[161] Finally, Zeigler compares 304 **CUR[I]T[** with '*Cúrid*' in the genealogies; however O'Brien gives the *u* as short, and OI *Cuirithir* and other *Cur-* names with short *u* also come to mind.[162]

‡17 Lenition; LHEB §142

British lenition involved weakening of consonants, especially inter-vocalically, and can be divided into two types: (1) Voiced spirantization, i.e. /b d g gʷ m/ > /β δ γ γʷ μ/, and (2) Voicing, i.e. /p t k/ > /b d g/. Jackson regarded lenition as a single process, but more recent philologists have swung back to the view, which he rejected, that there was an interval between (1) and (2).[163]

[17] Jackson notes simply that the 'Dark Age inscriptions' provide no evidence for lenition, owing to the spelling system used.[164] While basically correct, this can be qualified slightly.

[17] (i) Firstly, immediately after noting the lack of evidence in the inscriptions, Jackson turns to the 'early written sources' (i.e. manuscript sources), and notes that forms such as *Lovocatus* < *Lugucatus in 509 × 521 and *Mailoc* < *Maglācos in 572 indirectly bear witness to /g/ > /γ/ since they show a subsequent changes of /γ/ > /u̯/ and /γ/ > /i̯/ respectively.[165] If such forms from the 'early written sources' are to be cited as evidence of lenition, it should be added that comparable evidence is to be be found among the inscriptions, for example /γ/ (</g/) > /u̯/ in 365/149 MAVOHENI < *Magusenos[166] and /γ/ (</g/) > /i̯/ in 1024/255/926 ARTHMAIL. The practical usefulness of such forms for establishing the chronology of lenition is, however, very limited. While MAVOHENI clearly shows a later stage than 3016/M7 LAGU,[167] and ARTHMAIL a later stage than 394/103 MAGLI, the contrast is between forms with and without the

---

[161] Ziegler, pp. 101 and 172–73 (but on 503 **DRUTA** cf. ‡65 below). This *druto-* may occur in Gaulish, where the quantity of the vowel is uncertain however (GPN, pp. 293 and 446–47). W. *drud*, which occurs in names like OW *Drutguas*, cannot be cognate with Ir. *drúth*, but could be either an early borrowing from Irish, or else from Romance **drudo-*; see GPN, p. 447, n. 2; LEIA D-205–6; J. E. C. Williams, *Celtica*, 15 (1983), 154; DLG, pp. 126–27.

[162] Ziegler, p. 163; see CGH, pp. 389 and 579. There is nothing comparable in the British corpus, assuming Williams, BWP, pp. 11, 15, 17–18, and Jackson, LHEB, p. 188, are right to compare 971/35 CUURI[S?] with MW *Cyrys*, which implies short /u/; see below, ‡‡ 37n and 54. Cf. *Curita* and *Curitius* in Bordeaux and Breuberg in Holder i, 1202.

[163] LHEB, pp. 544–45. See Sims-Williams, in *Gaulois et celtique continental*, and references.

[164] LHEB, pp. 549–50; also pp. 176–77. The existence of lenition is sometimes revealed by Latin misspellings, e.g. /b/ > /v/ by 1015/233/910 PROPARABIT beside 1027/265/923 and 1022/240/298 PROPARAUIT (*praeparavit*), and /p/ > /b/ by 1012/223/933 APATI for *abati*.

[165] LHEB, p. 550.

[166] LHEB, p. 440.

[167] See below, ‡25.

development to /ụ/ or /ị/, not between post- and pre-lenition forms; the spelling of LAGU and MAGLI is ambiguous between /γ/ and /g/. Therefore forms such as these are best cited in the context of /γ/ > /ụ/ and /γ/ > /ị/ rather than the context of lenition.

[17] (ii) Jackson points out that occasional aberrations in OWCB spelling, such as OW *gubennid* (instead of **gupennid*) and *hendat* (instead of **hentat*), show that lenition had happened.[168] He suggests that the scribes were thinking in terms of the spelling of word-initial /b/ and /d/. Another possibility would be what Jackson terms 'Vulgar Latin . . . scribal habits',[169] and in a case like *hendat* the scribe may well have felt that as *nd* meant /nd/ in Latin it was an acceptable way to spell Welsh /nd/.[170] Whatever the reason for them, there is no reason why such lenition-revealing aberrations should not occur in the inscriptions as well. The best example is 473/b/Ok46 IGNIOC, if I am right to suggest below that it corresponds to OB *agnioc* (cf. W. *egnïol* 'vigorous') < **ad-gnīm-ākos*; the unambiguous use of G for /g/ before /n/ in IGNIOC and *agnioc* may have been made possible by the sound change /γn/ > /ịn/ (see ‡48).[171] A possible further instance is 3020/I1 BELADORE or BELADO RE(*quiescit*), if this is a feminine form of *Belator* or contains the Celtic stem **Belatu-*.[172] Two others are 470/Ok78 MAGARI (beside 403/268/841 MACARITINI (?)[173] and 1212 MACAR[I (?)] CARASIMILIVS) and 519/Scot.6 LOGI (if for Latin *loci* rather than *logii* as Macalister thought); note, however, that Charles Thomas prefers the unremarkable readings MACARI and LOCI.[174] Another example would be 320/26 CVLIDOR(I), if the name of *Kyledyr Wyllt* in *Culhwch ac Olwen* were correctly modernized as *Cyledyr*;[175] the MW *d* is ambiguous, however,

---

[168] LHEB, pp. 69 and 71.

[169] LHEB, p. 549, n. 2.

[170] The most common environment in the inscriptions where medial D = /d/ is in the combination ND; there is no need to list examples (but see ‡22 below), as this spelling is the norm. One can also compare *hendat* with exceptional OI spellings such as *indaas* (GOI, pp. 147 and 478). 456/404 **GENDILI/GE[** does not belong here; if it is Latin *Gentilius* (or *Gentilis*), the **ND** reflects Irish sound substitution of /nd/ for /nt/; see Ziegler, p. 183; cf. Thomas, *Mute Stones*, pp. 73–74 and 86, n. 16. The true Brittonic form (with /nt/ > /nh/) is seen in 988/67 GENILLIN; cf. GPN, p. 205, n. 2; and below, ‡‡27 and 68.

[171] See also below, ‡‡18 and 85.

[172] See IEMB, pp. 79 and 263, and on *Be(l)lator* see Kajanto, pp. 16–17 and Tab.Sulis, p. 177. Various forms in *Bel(l)at-* etc. are cited in Holder i, 367–69, and iii, 823–25 (beside a few *Belad-* names), in VLRB, p. 929, and in OPEL i, 281, 283, and 345.

[173] But on MACARITINI see ‡‡22n and 57.

[174] Thomas, *Mute Stones*, p. 263; *Christian Celts*, pp. 62–63, 72, n. 20, and 122; and *GAJ*, 17 (1991–92), 3, no. 6. (But according to KHJ in 1956 the tail of the G in LOGI 'is quite clear'.) MACARI suggests Latin *Macarius* < Greek *Makarios*, but there was also a Celtic *Macarius, -eus*, etc., with an element possibly cognate with W. *mach* 'surety'; see GPN, p. 365. Note also MICARII (?) at Caersws, RIB ii [fasc. 8] 2502.10. Holder ii, 374 compares 470/Ok78 MAGARI with 'Gabinia Magaria' in CIL ix 119 (*sic leg.*) at Brindisi; for other possible examples of *Magarius* see Anon., *AE*, 1981, p. 191, no. 732, and CIL x 1754.

[175] As even by Jackson, *YB*, 12 (1982), 20–22 (but his *Cyledyr* is presumably due to the translator of his article, for elsewhere KHJ notes that the MW *d* must be *ð* on Ifor

and can denote /ð/, in which case the spelling CVLIDOR[I?] is quite unremarkable, as is implied by Ifor Williams's derivation from *Culidorix rather than **Culitorix.[176] A better example is 341/71 SALIGIDVNI (if that is the reading) beside ogam SALICIDUNI, but here influence from ogam spelling habits is an alternative explanation, as we have seen, even though the accompanying ogam version, SALICIDUNI, ironically fails to show those habits.[177] At first sight a comparable case might be the patronymic CVNOGENI (if = MW *Cyngen*, OW *Concen* < *Kunokennos*) in 342/70 CUNACENNI [A]VI ILVVETO/CVNOCENNI FILIV[S] CVNOGENI HIC IACIT;[178] in fact, however, only the son's name can be equated with OW *Concen* (cf. 1000/182 CONCENN), and the father, CVNOGENI, must be OW *Congen* (MW *Cynien*), as in 1033/287 CINGEN (if that or CUNGEN were the correct reading, rather than CUN BEN).[179] (This is assuming that the names are British; ILVVETO at least may well be Irish.[180]) Another possible instance is provided by a lost inscription from Llanychaer (Fig. 1.2), transcribed as 440/335 MACVDEBETI FILIVS EONOCAN. The first name is Irish (the half-uncial b is surely a miscopying of h for /x/ (*ch*), ‡42 below), but, given the similarity of the transcriber's O and D and the incomprehensibility of the combination EO, the second name probably contains Brittonic EDNO- 'bird' (MW *edn* < *petno-*), cognate with the Irish element (OI *én* < *eθn-*) seen in 488/Ok60 ENABARR/ ENABARRI.[181] If so, the use of medial D for Brittonic /d/ could well be due to ogam spelling habits.

Williams's etymology). Jackson notes the northern connection of the names in the passage. Emendation to *Keleðyr* < *Calidorīx* 'king of ?Calidonia' is therefore tempting – and one could also emend to *Keledyr* < *Caletorīx* 'hard king' – cf. OW *Celetir*, derived by Lloyd-Jones, *BBCS*, 14 (1950–52), 36, from *Caletorīx*, Holder i, 698 and iii, 1047 (*Chaletricus episcopus* at Chartres, AD 573). A point in favour of /d/ is the confusion in *Culhwch* with *Kynedyr Wyllt*, for the latter name certainly had /d/ (cf. LL, p. 277 *Lanncinitir*, Llangynidr, WATU, p. 130 and DEPN s.n. Kenderchurch). See *Culhwch and Olwen*, ed. Bromwich & Evans, pp. 104, 134, and 151–52. However, there may have been variation between [d] and [ð] in both names (see ‡16n above).

[176] BWP, p. 22. See above, ‡16. Both reconstructed forms are unparalleled so far as I know.

[177] Above, ‡16, and see (iii) immediately hereafter.

[178] On the reading see LHEB, p. 185 (where it is also noted that the names may be Irish or British) and McManus, *Guide*, p. 67.

[179] See Rhys, *AC*, 6th ser. 18 (1918), 184, and Morris-Jones, *Cymmrodor*, 28 (1918), 262. Compare LL, pp. 152, 154, and 155, where a careful distinction is made between *Concen abbas Catoci* and *Congen abbas Ilduti*. For the elements *ken-* and *gen-* see GPN, pp. 175–77 and 203–7 (noting a *Congenniccus* in Britain s. *gen-* but wrongly comparing it with CONCENN, p. 205 and n. 1). On *ken-* see also LEIA C-64 and 103, McManus, *Guide*, p. 178, n. 19 (cf. Ziegler, p. 159), and SBCHP, pp. 27 and 36, and on *gen-* see Ziegler, pp. 105–6. For CUN BEN, see BWP, pp. 33–35; cf. ‡38n below.

[180] See below, ‡38 (bis).

[181] 'Bird-head', Ziegler, pp. 176–77; Sims-Williams, *TPS*, 91 (1993), 166 – Schrijver, *Ériu*, 48 (1997), 223, n. 7, is slightly sceptical, but there is no real objection (cf. the epithet of OI *Éis Énchenn*, 'bird head', discussed by Borsje, *CMCS*, 43 (2002), 7; note also the British coin-legend EDN[(De Bernardo Stempel, *ZCP*, 44 (1991), 41) and Gallo-Latin *Etnosus* (Holder

[17] Unfortunately, aberrant spellings such as IGNIOC, BELADORE, MAGARI, LOGI, SALIGIDVNI, and *EDNO- (?) are too rare and uncertain to be useful in arranging the inscriptions in chronological order; they cannot be meaningfully contrasted with inscriptions with regular -T- and -C-. For the sake of completeness, I would add here that while 1032/281 WLEDER does indeed contain D for /d/ (cf. MW *Gwledyr*),[182] this is no doubt because the language is verging on Middle Welsh. On the other hand, 994/125/22 HIROIDIL might be modernized as either *Hirhoedl* or *Hirhoeddl*, and no doubt the latter is to be preferred in view of the normal usage of D for /ð/ in the inscriptions.[183] 1030 [A]MBIGATI would belong here if related to 500 [A]MB[I]CATOS (*sic leg.*); however, the reading of 1030 is very dubious. If Radford was right to reinterpret 980/46a WLIGUE (Nash-Williams's reading) as S(*ignum*) S(*ancti*) (or S(*cribae*)) LIGUE and equate it with Mod.W. *Lligwy*, this would be a further instance of G for /g/; however, LIGUE would more probably represent Mod.W. *Llywy*.[184] Another possibly relevant form is 379/170 CATVRVG(I), if the second element is W. *grug* < *wrūg-* < *wroik-* or *rhug* < *ro-wik-* rather than a mistake for -RIG(I) as has hitherto been assumed. A possible objection is that C is used in the other name in the inscription, LOVERNACI, but conceivably this could be Irish with C for /x/ as opposed to CATVRVG(I) with G for /g/.[185] A final form with D for /d/ may be 979/46 NI(n)ID.[186] 350/116 IAGOBI < *Iacobi* seems to have lenition, like MW *Iago*, but the G rather than C is only attested in one transcript, where C could in fact be read.[187]

---

i, 1481; DGVB i, 168; DLG, p. 141). In 440/335 -CAN may be for -CANI (was the final -I lost or horizontal?), cf. -CANNI below, ‡22n; or, since the N is of different shape from that in 'EONO', -CAN may be a miscopying of (ligatured?) -CAVI, for which element see below, ‡18. See Ch. 1 above, p. 18. For omission of horizonal -I in antiquarian copies cf. 418/283 CVPETIAN(I): LWP, p. 377, and Edwards, *Med. Arch.*, 45 (2001), 26, n. 57.

182   ‡14n.

183   On the svarabhakti vowel see LHEB, p. 337. On /dl/ and /ðl/ (not mentioning this important inscriptional evidence) see WG, p. 185; Russell, *BBCS*, 31 (1984), 104–12; P. W. Thomas, in Evans FS (1995), pp. 219–43, and review by Schrijver, *CMCS*, 34 (1997), 109–10; Schrijver, SBCHP, pp. 360–65, and review by Russell in *JCL*, 6 (1997), 152; and Wmffre, *Language and History*, i, 319, who suggests that 1032/281 ODELEV contains the same element *hoedl* (see ‡80 below); while the D here could be a spirant, it can equally well be a stop in MW spelling in view of WLEDER in the same inscription. A comparable form in Cornish is *Wenceneðel* (Bodmin, p. 86).

184   See below, ‡58.

185   On LOVERNACI see ‡‡ 46 and 84. On CATVRVG(I) see ‡37n below. If the latter is an error for *CATVRIG(I) note that such a form might be equated with the *Caturicus* well attested in Gaul (Holder i, 859) and to be segmented *Catur-icus* according to Lejeune, *ÉC*, 19 (1982), 112, n. 15; in that case G would = /g/, but note that there was also a form *Caturigius* (OPEL ii, 45).

186   See ‡15n (the reading is not certain).

187   Meyrick's drawing has C but Lhuyd's drawing (cf. Fig. 1.2) *seems* to have G (Gruffydd & Owen, *BBCS*, 17 (1956–58), 188, and 19 (1960–62), 231).

[17] (iii) A third point to be made is that the ogam spelling system, which uses its **D** and **G** symbols for /d/ and /g/ irrespective of where they appeared in a name, ought to enable us to distinguish between British /d/ < /t/ and original /t/, and between /g/ < /k/ and original /k/. Examples in Ireland are 265 **AMADU** for Latin *Amatus* with the British (or Vulgar Latin?) pronunciation with /d/,[188] and 256 **T**>**<GANN** (cf. OI *Tecán* [t'ega:n]), which is probably an Irish hypocoristic based on W. *teg* 'fair' with /g/ < /k/.[189] Examples of British and Latin names spelled in this way are, to say the least, uncommon in the ogam inscriptions of Britain. Jackson argues that this was because the ogamists were influenced by British spelling conventions and/or by the way in which Irish cognate names were spelled. Thus in 446/353, **MAGLICUNAS** is written with **C** rather than **G** either to agree with the roman MAGLOCVN[I] (?) or because **C** (= /k/ or /x/ < /k/) would occur in a comparable Irish names such as 126 **VEDACUNA**.[190] Theoretically, however, it is possible that spellings with **T** and **C** occur because the British and Latin names had not yet been fully lenited, as Jackson himself suggests in the case of 445/354 **VITALIANI**, which appeared epigraphically early to him.[191]

[17] The examples of ogam **C** and **T** in British names are 341/71 **SALICIDUNI** (if this *is* a British name),[192] 449/384 **CUNATAMI**,[193] and 446/353 **MAGLICUNAS MAQI CLUTAR[**.[194] In Latin names, the examples of ogam **C** and **T** are 445/354 **VITALIANI** (see above) and 430/306 **ETTERN[I MAQI VIC]TOR**. Jackson suggests that the first contains /t/ but the second /d/, but this opinion is clearly based on his epigraphical datings, since the more natural, though not inevitable, interpretation of the **TT** (and the corresponding TT in the roman-letter ETTERNI FILI VICTOR) is /t/.[195]

---

[188] LHEB, pp. 184–85; Ziegler, pp. 125–26; Swift, *Ogam Stones*, pp. 90 and 95. For a possibly Celtic *Amatu* see Hamp, *Acta Neophilologica*, 9 (1976), 3–4, and OPEL i, 90.

[189] Sims-Williams, *CMCS*, 23 (1992), 51–52; cf. EANC, p. 89; Morgan & Morgan, *Welsh Surnames*, p. 196; Ziegler, pp. 234–35. Note that the reading of 1012/223/933 may be TECAN(I) (Nash-Willliams reads TEC[AI]/N but his drawing seems to show TECA/NI); see below, ‡37. Cf. MW *Tegyr*, Lloyd-Jones, *BBCS*, 14 (1950–52), 36 (if not = *Tyngyr*, cf. ‡14n above). Mócsy cites one example of *Teccus* from Noricum.

[190] Cf. LHEB, pp. 177–79.

[191] LHEB, p. 183.

[192] Cf. LHEB, pp. 179–80 and above, ‡16.

[193] LHEB, pp. 180 and 182–83. The roman SAGRANI beside the conservative ogam spelling **SAGRAGNI** in 449/384 shows that lenition of /g/ had taken place *in Irish*, but this has no bearing on whether or not /t/ had been lenited in British – especially if /t/ > /d/ in British was a later phenomenon than /g/ > /ɣ/.

[194] LHEB, p. 182.

[195] Cf. LHEB, pp. 183–84. *Victor* instead of *Victoris* is not an indication of post-apocope, and therefore post-lenition, date because it may be an example of nominative for genitive, as noted in LHEB, pp. 184 and 620.

[17] In 362/142, **AVITTORIGES** corresponds to AVITORIA, which may be either an Irish or a British name according to Jackson.[196] If it were British, the ogam spelling **TT** would again be notable, especially as Jackson entertains the possibility that the inscription is later than British /t/ > /d/.[197] Compare, however, the TT for Irish /d/ < /nt/ in 318/6 ETTORIGI (if identical with 179 **ETORIGAS** in Ireland),[198] and the CC for Irish /g/ < /nk/ in the second element of 442/346 MACCVDICCL (cf. 256 **DEGLANN** = *Déclán* in Ireland).[199] On the whole, it seems preferable to regard **AVITTORIGES**/AVITORIA as an Irish name (along with 396/104 AVITORI), cognate with OB *Oedri* < **Ai(wi)torīg-*.[200] The diphthong /ai/ would have been monophthongized much earlier in British (‡4 above), giving **E-* (later *Oe-*), but in Irish /ai/ remained and would be spelt **AI** in ogam Irish and later. Even if the element was already **Ait-* in Proto-Celtic,[201] /ai/ might well be spelt **AVI-** under the influence of the prestigious Roman cognomen *Avitus*[202] and/or of uncertainty due to the fact that intervocal /w/ was being lost in Irish (cf. 399/176 **TOVISACI** > OI *toísech*),[203] and might be liable to hypercorrect 'restoration'.

[17] Another name which can be either British (*Cyngen*) or Irish (*Conchen*) appears in 342/70 **CUNACENNI**/CVNOCENNI. The ogamist may be using a **C** rather than a **G** for /g/, contrary to standard ogam usage, but we cannot be sure of this since he may (rightly or wrongly) have been thinking in terms of the preform of Irish *Conchen*.[204] A similar uncertainty obtains in regard to

---

[196] LHEB, pp. 182, 185–86 and 625. See further above, ‡14, also Ziegler, p. 133; Uhlich, *Morphologie*, pp. 24 and 172–73.

[197] LHEB, p. 186.

[198] Assuming my etymology is correct, below, ‡38.

[199] See below, ‡38n.

[200] Fleuriot, *Gramm.*, p. 400; DGVB i, 275–76. See Ziegler, p. 133, citing Motta. Semantically, compare this use of *oed* 'age' with that of *hoedl* 'life' in names. If *Oedri* is separated off, another possibility for AVITO- is **auo-*, **auio-* 'grandfather, etc.' as in Gaulish AVIACOS (RIG iv, 531). Rhys, *AC*, 6th ser. 19 (1919), 204, was of course wrong to connect 396/104 FILI AVITORI with Ir. *Mac Uidhir* > Maguire; see DIL, s.v. *odor*; Uhlich, *Morphologie*, p. 62; NWÄI, p. 451, n. 28.

[201] SBCHP, p. 194. For various opinions, see LEIA A-21, and Uhlich, *Morphologie*, p. 172. Note the name *Aevadia* in Aquitania, discussed by Gorrochategui, in Mitxelena FS, p. 620, and cf. Gaulish names such as *Aetus* in Holder i, 53–54, and iii, 517, and OPEL i, 48–48 – especially *Aetorius* and *Aetoria* at Nîmes (CIL xii 3389).

[202] *Avitus* is attested along with *Avitianus* in Roman Britain and *may* recur on Man in 505 AVITI MONOMENTI. Cf. Hassall & Tomlin, *Britannia*, 18 (1987), 363, and Handley, *EME*, 10 (2001), 195, n. 142. Uhlich, *Morphologie*, p. 172, compares OW *Eguid* (but cf. ‡57 below). We see *Avitus* in a Celtic formation in the name of the emperor Avitus' country seat, *Avitacus* (Lebel, p. 29; Holder i, 315). Attestations of *Avitus* are mapped in OPEL i, 233. Cf. AITI ~ AVITI, Oswald s.n. *Avitus*.

[203] LEIA T-101. It might be suggested that the V of AVITORI is a sub-phonemic glide, as argued by Schrijver, *JIES*, 26 (1998), 425, in the case of 385/89 LOVERNII and 379/170 LOVERNACI. According to Schrijver these have hiatus, however, so they are not comparable to writing a diphthong with a glide.

[204] Cf. LHEB, p. 185. If he was 'translating' the preform of W. *Cyngen* into Irish, cf. Derolez's explanation of *Conchn* for **Concen* in the 'Bamberg cryptogram' (although the error may

380/84 **ICORIGAS**/ICORI FILIVS POTENTINI and 399/176 . . . **[TO]VI-SACI**/SIMILINI TOVISACI, and (in Man) 500 **[A]MBICATOS M[A]Q[I] ROC[A]T[O]S** / AMMECATI FILIVS ROCATI HIC IACIT, where the ogamists may again be thinking in terms of Irish cognates, even if the deceased bore British names, as may well be the case in the two Welsh inscriptions, to judge by the couplings with Latin POTENTINI and SIMILINI rather than with Irish names.[205]

[17] We thus find several instances where ogam **T(T)** and **C** are probably or possibly used for British or Latin /d/ < /t/ and /g/ < /k/. There is even one case in Wales, 409/198/849 **POP[?]**/PVMPEIVS, where a special ogam **P** symbol may be used in British fashion for medial /b/ (assuming the **-P-** = Irish /b/ < /mp/),[206] instead of the conventional **B** symbol. – On the other hand, there is a notable absence of examples in Britain where **D** and **G** are employed (unlike **AMADU** and **T><GANN** in Ireland itself), British influence on the ogam spelling being the most likely explanation. The one exception which proves the rule is the eccentrically located ogam at Silchester, now read as 496 **TEBICATO[S]** (Macalister: **EBICATO[S]**), which I would take to represent the P-Celtic name *Tepikatous* (genitive), possibly at the post-lenition *TebigadōΣ* stage, with **B** for /b/ in the element *teb-* (cf. W. *godeb* 'refuge') < *tep-* < *tek^w-* (the element best known from 358/138 VOTEPORIGIS/**VOTECORIGAS** and Gildas's *Vortipori*).[207] Of

---

be H for E rather than *ch* for *c*); see Sims-Williams, *BBCS*, 29 (1980–82), 603, n. 3, and *WHR*, 17 (1994), 26; Derolez, in Gneuss FS, p. 286.

[205] Cf. LHEB, pp. 173 and 186–87. On **[A]MBICATOS** see McManus, *Guide*, p. 113, and TRC, p. 76; also Uhlich, *Morphologie*, p. 265. For the Latin name *Similinus* (> Pictish *Simul*) see LHEB, p. 483, n. 3; and note *Similina* in RIB etc.

[206] Cf. Charles-Edwards, in *The Celtic World*, pp. 717–18 and references, and *Early Christian Ireland*, pp. 170–71, and below, ‡68. Note, however, that Mann, *Britannia*, 2 (1971), 222, gives Romano-British examples of loss of /m/ before /p/: RIB i 590 SEPR[ONIVS], 686 SEPRONIE, SEPRONIVS, also our 396/104 TEPO[RE]. Cf. VLRB, p. 922. Interestingly, the note on RIB i 686 says: 'the loss of the M is due to the influence of the spoken language, cf. CIL x 7545 (Sardinia) Popeianus.' In fact Rhys, LWP, p. 202, had already compared **POPE[** (his reading) with Latin forms such as *Poponi* and *Seproni* (cf. OPEL iii, 152, and iv, 64). Note also *Popeia* at Leutstetten, in Rhaetia (Anon., *AE*, 1972, 109, no. 359; OPEL iii, 153). On the other hand, in his later 'Goidelic' phase, Rhys suggested that 'the omission of the M of *tempore* argues possibly a Goedelic inscriber' (*AC*, 6th ser. 19 (1919), 203). The layout of 396/104 suggests that no suspension was needed above TE(*m*)PO[RE]. Macalister discusses the reading of 409/198/849 in detail apud Anon., *AC*, 7th ser. 8 (1928), 374–77, preferring **PAMPES** to **POPES** ('the name is so exceedingly foreign that it would hardly be assimilated to such an extent'), and comparing his own reading 421/294 RASTECE for *Rustica* (cf. ‡15); cf. *Pampeius* in Dalmatia (OPEL iii, 150). Loth, *Noms des saints bretons*, p. 107, compares the Breton female saint *Poupaia*.

[207] For the Silchester reading see Fulford et al., *Med. Arch.* 44 (2000), 10–14 (mistakenly thinking the name Irish and wrongly referring to Holder ii, 1779 for *Teb-* as a Celtic name element, when in fact he has nothing relevant). Note the post-500 date for 496 in Wright & Jackson, *AntJ*, 48 (1968), 299; a much earlier date is proposed by Fulford et al., on the basis of a comparison with the ogam material from Orkney (pp. 10 and 15), but on the dating of the latter note the caution expressed by Forsyth, *PSAS*, 125 (1995), 679. Does the name

course, **B** could be an approximation for a still unlenited British /p/ (the ogam **P** symbols may not have been in general currency), and the **C** and **T** could be unlenited British /k/ and /t/. Alternatively, **C** and **T** may be being used in the British fashion for /g/ and /d/, or the British second element may have been equated with the Irish genitive in -**CATO[S]** < *-*katous*.

[17] Whatever the explanation of the rarity of ogam **B, D, G** for British /b, d, g/ in Britain, the impossibility of using the ogam inscriptions to chart the course of British lenition is evident.

‡18 *ā* > *ɔ; LHEB §9*

Lambert has shown that /au/ also merged with /a:/ as /ɔ:/ (see ‡8 above), although it is not clear whether /au/ became /ɔ:/ directly or via /a:/. There are no examples of the /au/ stage in the inscriptions (cf. ‡60).

[18] Jackson lists some twenty-four inscriptions with A- or O-spellings, without of course implying that the change in spelling convention was necessarily contemporary with the change in pronunciation. It is very likely that the A-spelling persisted after /a:/ > /ɔ:/, especially perhaps in the case of Latin names and names with well-known suffixes such as -ACVS and -ANVS. (*Mutatis mutandis*, some of the O-spellings may conceal the subsequent change of /ɔ:/ to a new /au/ in Welsh, on which see ‡60 below.) Jackson argues that the letter A was used into the seventh century,

> but this is not unnatural; the letter *ā* had now come to have the sound-value of *ɔ*, so that there is no reason why engravers should not sometimes use it when they meant *ɔ*, since to them Latin *ō* stood for a different sound, the close *ǫ*, and they had no other *ā*-sound which it would be necessary to keep distinct in writing.[208]

It should be added, however, that a new /a:/ *was* acquired (*a*) by the New Quantity System (‡54) and (*b*) – at least in Irish proper names – when /γ/ was lost with compensatory lengthening (cf. ‡48), as in 449/384 **SAGRAGNI MAQI CUNATAMI/SAGRANI FILI CVNOTAMI**. Here Ir. SAGRANI and arguably W. CVNOTAMI both have /a:/, as does 364/144 QVENVENDANI < *-*agnī*.[209] Such developments may have encouraged the use of O for /ɔ:/.

Tebiawn (ap Cunedda) contain the same element **teb-*? See EWGT, pp. 45 and 49, and references on p. 216 s.n. *Tybion* (the correct standardization?). Of course, a preform **Tapianus* would also give *Tebiawn* (cf. *Tappo* in Tab.Vindol. ii, 393). A curiously similar form is OC *Tethion* (Bodmin, pp. 87–88 and 91), always written with thorn or ð, but here cf. OB *Tethion*, Chrest., p. 167. On VOTEPORIGIS etc. see Sims-Williams, in *Britain 400–600*, p. 226; Hamp, *SC*, 30 (1996), 293; Uhlich, *Morphologie*, p. 308; and below, p. 346.

[208] LHEB, p. 292. As passim, I use the symbol ɔ instead of Jackson's hooked *o*.

[209] Ziegler, p. 221.

[18] There are no inscriptions in which A and O contrast. 408/229/848 BODVOCI . . . PRONEPVS ETERNALI might seem to be an example, but Jackson points out that BODVOC already appears on ancient British coins of the Dubunni, and that *Bodvocus* occurs beside *Bodvacus* in Gaul, where there is 'there is no reason to suppose that *ā* became *ō* . . . . Perhaps it is a question of two different suffixes.'[210] BODVOCI is more likely to contain the /o/ of the stem **bodwo-*[211] than /ɔː/ < /aː/, although the latter is not impossible, in which case the A of ETERNALI might then be due to Latin conservatism. The name *Aeternalis* is attested in Roman Wales, on a lead tag from Caerleon.[212]

[18] (A) The A-spellings listed by Jackson (pp. 290–91) are:

1. 381/87 ELMETIACO
2. 445/354 VITALIANI (in ogam and roman script)
3. 448/370 RINACI[213]
4. 514/Scot.8 CVPITIANI
5. 473/a/Ok46 VITALI
6. 379/170 LOVERNACI
7. 344/73 DERVACI
8. 392/77 VERACIVS
9. 451/401 TVNCCETACE
10. 515/Scot.9 LIBERALI
11. 391/78 SENACVS
12. 424/299 BRIACI[214]
13. 389/97 IOVENALI[215]

---

[210] LHEB, p. 290 and n. 1; Holder i, 460–61, and iii, 896; OPEL i, 306; cf. Nash-Williams on ECMW, no. 229, and contrast BWP, pp. 13–14, and De Bernardo Stempel, *ZCP*, 44 (1991), 40. The same name may appear as [BO]DVACV[S] and BODC in RIB ii [fasc. 5] 2491.82 and [fasc 8] 2503.337. In Gaul compare *Dubnacus* beside *Dubnoco*, also a *Madocus* in Dalmatia (OPEL ii, 110, and iii, 44). Elsewhere, in *JRS*, 37 (1947), 55, Jackson suggests that incipient rounding of /aː/ may be seen in the Romano-British place names *Caunonio* (Peutinger); cf. *Conovio* (Antonine Itinerary), discussed by Jackson apud Rivet, *Britannia*, 1 (1970), 71. In *Thetford Treasure*, p. 47, he derives late fourth-century Romano-British BLOTVGI and (Belgic?) Gaulish *Bloturigi* (dat., KPN, p. 151 = CIL xiii 4350 [La Horgne au Sablon, Gallia Belgica], GPN, p. 246 = DAG, p. 806) < **blāto-* , and refers for /oː/ for /aː/ in late Gaulish to Hubschmied, *RC*, 50 (1933), 261 (cf. also Lambert, in *Ptolemy*, p. 164, on *Ratomagos* > *Rotomagos* 'Rouen'). See also n. 268 below.

[211] GPN, p. 151. Cf. Holder i, 460–61, and iii, 896. Perhaps the /w/ caused rounding of the /aː/?

[212] Tomlin, *Britannia*, 28 (1997), 468.

[213] Presumably an /aːkos/ name; for parallels see below, ‡22. Nash-Williams thought PINACI possible, which is obscure (there is a CVPINACIOS in RIG iv, no. 130, but this is derived from *Cubio-*, p. 535, and there is no CV- on our stone). Nash-Williams takes the name to be **Pinax*, genitive **Pinacis*, and this would have a short /a/ if the same as *pinax, pinacis*, 'picture', which seems unlikely. Edwards, in Cramp FS, p. 56, reads RINACI, as did KHJ in 1947.

[214] BRIACI may be Irish-influenced if not actually Irish; see no. 26 below, and ‡65 below.

[215] Rhys, *AC*, 4th ser. 8 (1877), 142, notes that this develops into OW *Iouanaul* (LL, p. 406; LHEB, p. 385, n. 1). Cf. ‡80.

14. 363/143 CARANTACVS
15. 397/105 CVNACI
16. 408/229/848 ETERNALI
17. 334/54 CATACVS, TEGERNACVS
18. 404/270/843 TEGERNACUS

[18] The quantity of the /a:/ in these is reasonably certain, either from Classical Latin or from later Brittonic reflexes. Forms like 323/32 SATVR-NINVS, and now 2005 S[AT]VRNBIV, are omitted as having /a/ in Vulgar Latin, as W. *Sadwrn* confirms.[216] (What was the current pronunciation of *Macarius*, if that name lies behind 470/Ok78 MACARI/MAGARI etc.? Thomas suggests that this name was 'inspired by incoming Desert Fathers literature', but may it be purely Celtic? [217]) Jackson is also right to omit 1000/182 GERMANUS, which occurs in a passage of Latin narrative, where no other spelling would be appropriate.[218] The most troublesome names are the ones which can also be Irish, especially those which occur in an Irish context. One cannot know whether forms like TIGERNACI or SENACVS or DERVACI[219] are Irish with /a:k/ > /ax/ > /əx/ or Welsh with /a:k/ > /ɔ:g/. Even if they are Irish they may be relevant since we have to reckon with the likelihood that Irish names in Britain may have been naturalized to some extent.[220] On the other hand a late (post-syncope) Irish form like 1038/365 MAIL (or MEIL or MAL) DOMNA[C (cf. Ir. *Máel Domnaig*) clearly has Irish A for /ə/,[221] and can be disregarded. With this caveat about the possibly Irish names, I would, however, add the following items to Jackson's list:

[18]

19.   329/42 CANNTIANI, on the assumption that this the same as the *Cantianus* attested on the Continent and that the latter had the well-known Latin *-ānus* suffix.[222]

---

[216] LHEB, p. 289. For other attestations of OW *Saturnbiu* see Edwards, in Cramp FS, p. 59.
[217] *Christian Celts*, p. 72, n. 20; cf. *Mute Stones*, p. 274, n. 21; OPEL iii, 42 and 175. For MACARI etc. see above, ‡17. Holder ii, 363, suggests that it had /a:/ in Celtic.
[218] The same may apply to 1000/182's ANNAN if from *Ann(i)anus*. See ‡22 below.
[219] On TIGERNACI see below. On DERVACI cf. above, ‡14n.
[220] See ‡65 on 424/299 BRIACI.
[221] This never had /a:/ if *Domnach* is from Latin *dominicus* (well attested as a personal name: OPEL ii, 216; Lebel, pp. 37–38, 52 and 79). Cf. O'Brien, *Celtica*, 10 (1973), 229 (*Máel-Domnaig* = *Máel* + common noun); LEIA D-167; Russell, *Celtic Word-Formation*, p. 52, n. 66. The same etymology has been suggested for 352A/122/5 DOMNICI (W. *Dyfnig*), although this could also be from Celtic *Dumn-; see I. Williams in Fox et al., *AC*, 97 (1942–43), 210–11; Russell, *Celtic Word-Formation*, p. 144. Cf. the problem of OE *Domnoc* in Coates & Breeze, *Celtic Voices*, pp. 234–40.
[222] *Cantianus* is attested in Aquitania (potter's name) and in Germania Superior (Holder i, 748, and iii, 1079; Grauf., p. 265; DAG, pp. 320, 479 and 1115; Evans, *BBCS*, 27 (1976–78), 243; OPEL ii, 32), and Cantianus was the name of one of three celebrated martyrs of Aquileia, the *Cantiani*, along with Cantius and Cantianilla (cf. *Venance Fortunat*, iv, ed. Quesnel, pp. 99 and 170). It is presumably a Latin derivative of the name *Cantius* (Mócsy, p. 65), ultimately from Celtic *kanto- or *kanti- (meanings debated) but formed with the Latin

20. 355/128/8 SILBANDVS, if Jackson is right to suggest that it is a hypercorrection (with nd for nn for n) for Silbanus, a known Vulgar Latin form of Silvānus.[223] W. G. Thomas's alternative reading FILI BANDVS, could be etymologized as MW bann 'noisy, tuneful' < *band-, with short /a/ (see ‡22), but is, however, discounted by Dr Edwards in the new Corpus.

21. 365/149 LVNARI (so read by Lhuyd), which is Lunaris, attested in Roman Britain as well as Gaul.[224]

22. 399/176 [TO]VISACI/TOVISACI has etymological /a:kos/,[225] and is likely to be Irish rather than Welsh in view of the use of ogam. On the other hand a Romanized (therefore British??) context is suggested by the accompanying name SIMILINI, so the preservation of A is perhaps significant. It might be noted that Jackson does include 404/270/843 TEGERNACUS (no. 18 above), which is accompanied by the Romanizing name MARTI, even though he thought that this was a bilingual ogam stone, following Macalister. On the other hand, he deliberately leaves out 432/312 TIGERNACI (see no. 27 below) which is definitely on a bilingual stone.[226] The un-Irish vocalism of TEG- was probably a factor here (see ‡27).

23. 2002/a]AUR[I]ANVS (perhaps Taurianus, or Laurianus).[227]

24. 418/283 SALVIANVS BVRSOCAVI (or BVRGOCAVI) FILIVS CVPETIANI should be included, since 514/Scot.8 CVPITIANI is included (no. 4 above); and Salvianus also had /a:/. The element -CAVI is obscure as to etymology and quantity.[228] Curiously, it recurs nearby in the equally obscure 417/282 CAVO SENIARGII or CAVOSENI ARGII.[229] It may be

---

-(i)ānus suffix (on which see Kajanto, p. 107). It is less likely the rare Latin cognomen Candianus (Kajanto, p. 159, citing CIL iii 2106 (Salona, Dalmatia; OPEL ii, 30)).

[223] LHEB, p. 364, n. 1. One example of Σιλβανος appears in the Lexicon of Greek Personal Names (vol. i, ed. Fraser & Matthews, p. 405), and one in Italy in OPEL iv, 82. For Silbanianus and Σιλβανος in sixth-century Africa and Egypt, see Martindale, Prosopography, iii, 1152, and Kajanto, p. 213. For Silvanus (not Silbanus) and Silvanos see RIB indexes, also Grauf., p. 269 and GPN, p. 470. The name Silvanus was well known from the New Testament. See further, ‡22 below, where I suggest that SILBANDVS could be Hiberno-Latin. KHJ notes that SILBANDVS as a 'perversion' of Silvanus was suggested by Macalister, TCASFC, 15 (1922), 30.

[224] See esp. RIB i 786 (Brougham) and 1521 (Carrawburgh); cf. PRB, p. 113; Aldhouse Green & Raybould, SC, 33 (1999), 107. There is a St Lunaire in Brittany, regarded as a native name (: lun 'image') by Loth, Noms des saints bretons, p. 83.

[225] Ziegler, p. 237; Russell, Celtic Word-Formation, pp. 30–31 and 144.

[226] LHEB, pp. 187 and 291 and n. 1. Macalister's TEGE[ogam on 404/270/843 is not mentioned by Nash-Williams and is specifically denied by the Royal Commission, but this does not affect the point of principle. Incidentally, since Martius gives W. Mawrth, MARTI might also be counted as an example of /a:/.

[227] Tomlin, AC, 124 (1975), 71. Taurianus is recorded by Mócsy, p. 380, along with Gaurianus and Scaurianus.

[228] Cf. LWP, pp. 217, 374, and 377–79.

[229] Cf. LHEB, pp. 521 and 598 (preferring the second segmentation; a possible British parallel to -senos as second element is the Ravenna Cosmography's Leugosena; cf. PNRB 388, and in Irish cf. Finten < *Windo-senos, Uhlich, Morphologie, pp. 43–44 and 255). Rhys's

Latin *cavus* 'hollow, round' (with short *a*), which may be attested in Roman Britain as as a cognomen or epithet, *Ca(v)us*, *Cauua*.[230] Another possibility is a place or tribal name, comparable to Gaulish *Andecavi* (Angers/Anjou).[231] BVRGO- is suggestive of a place name (cf. OB *Burg*, Mod.B. *bourc'h*, 'borough', MW *bwrch* 'rampart'),[232] but it has to be remembered that the reading was already uncertain in the seventeenth century. Anyway, whatever be the case with -CAVI, 418/283 has to be included on the strength of SALVIANVS and CVPETIANI.

25.   419/284 SALVIANI, ONERATI, and [ ]ACI.[233]

26.   426/300 **BRIACI**, if indeed the correct reading in **NETTASAGR[I] MAQI MUCO[I] BRIACI**,[234] should perhaps be included (despite the fact that it is an Irish name in ogam script) alongside the nearby 424/299 BRIACI which *is* in Jackson's list (no. 12), as both forms show British loss of /γ/, as in W. *Briawc*, *Briog* rather than the Irish preservation as in OI *Brígach*.[235] In 424/299, too, the names may also be Irish; whereas Macalister

---

etymology, LWP, pp. 374–76 and 426, SENIARGII > Mod.W. *heinierydd*: heiniar 'crop, payment' (: *âr, iâr* ' ploughing', GPC, < **ar-yelo-*, LEIA A-81) does not explain the G (unless, as Rhys thought, *heiniar*, was from the root **arg-* 'silver'). KHJ explains: 'I think = CAVOSENI ARGII more probable than = CAVO(S) SENIARGII, for one thing because nominatives are so rare, and for another because the second name would be **Senargios*, not **Seniargios*'. (But Rhys, LWP, p. 397, implied that SENI- was < **Senio-*.) KHJ also recorded the mark between CAVOSENI and ARGII, shown by Macalister (interpreted by the latter as 'possibly meant as a symbol for ET'). The comparative evidence is complicated by the probability that some Continental anthroponyms in *Seni-* are proto-Basque: see Gorrochategui, in *Ptolemy*, p. 150.

230   RIB i 94; ii. [fasc. 6] 2492.10 (?) and [fasc. 8] 2503.222; cf. OPEL ii, 46. It is probably not possible to compare CAVVA (RIB i 94) with 401/183 CAVNE; Jackson, LHEB, p. 306, unnecessarily troubled by the survival of /au/ (cf. ‡60), suggests the alternative reading 401/183 CANNE (cf. ‡22 below), though this was denied by J. E. C. Williams, *LlC*, 3 (1954–55), 93 (saying that AV is visible in ECMW), but **CAVVE certainly seems impossible epigraphically. In 1057/Ok54 Macalister read EROCAV[I], but this seems very uncertain. On W. *cau* 'hollow' see LEIA C-258–59. In ‡17 above I suggest that 440/335 EONOCAN may be a mistranscription of *EDNOCAVI.

231   GPN, p. 140; RIG iv, 533 and 547. Holder i, 140, and iii, 612 vacillates over the quantity.

232   See ‡53 below. The only similar form in our corpus is 1050/Ok74, where INBVRGE (an OE female name in -*burh*?) is only one of many dubious antiquarian suggestions.

233   Smith, VLRB, pp. 908 and 912, notes '*Onerata* for *(H)onerata*', the wife of a legionary on a Caerleon (*sic*) tombstone, on which Hassall & Tomlin, *Britannia*, 8 (1977), 429, n. 26, comment: 'Although a cognomen Oneratus is attested, it is very rare compared to the extremely common (H)onoratus/a (two examples of the former, 666 of the latter listed by Kajanto in *The Latin Cognomina*), and it is possible that Honorata is intended.' Cf. OPEL iii, 113 (one example in Pannonia).

234   Macalister read **BRIACI**. For the reading **BRECI** (less likely **SLECI**) see McManus, *Guide*, p. 67, and ‡65 below. Edwards in *Corpus* s. Bridell 1, favours **IA**. KHJ notes that 'everyone but Macalister reads **MUCOI** not **MUCOE**, and even Macalister is doubtful'. KHJ is suspicious of Macalister's **BRIACI**, saying that a British name is not expected with *mocu*; Macalister 'seems to have been influenced to read **BRIACI**, rather than his previous **BRICI** or **BRAICI**, by no. 424'.

235   Ziegler, p. 141 (citing CGH, p. 525, where the length-mark on *Brígach* is editorial; cf. GPN, p. 316); Russell, *Celtic Word-Formation*, pp. 18–20 and 143; Williams, *BBCS*, 16 (1954–56), 28; DP iv, 711; Jackson, *Archaeologia Aeliana*, 5th ser. 10 (1982), 63. See further ‡65 below.

read FILI GLVVOCCI and Nash-Williams FILI [ ]GI, Dr Nancy Edwards thinks that FILI [E]VA[LEN]GI is possible, as suggested by Rhys.[236]

27. 432/312 **DOVAGNI/TIGERNACI DOBAGNI** (although TIGER-NACI could be wholly Irish in phonology, as noted above).

28. 499/Ok77 CARA*N*ACI or CARATACI or CARA*N*TACI, is clearly a Celtic name in /a:kos/.

29. 2029/p.39i CVNIIAC is presumably an /-a:kos/ derivative of the stem seen in Wales in 454/402 CVNIOVENDE (cf. in Ireland 289 **CUNIA** and 286 **CUNEA**).[237]

30. Rhys analysed EVALI in 454/402 EVALI FILI DENCVI CVNIO-VENDE MATER EIVS as *Evo-* as in EVOLENG(G)I (431/308, 436/316, and(?) 424/299 = Irish *Éolang*) plus *-ali* in ETERNALI and VITALI; and he later he compared OI *Éoil*.[238] If there is anything in this comparison with EVOLENG(G)I and *Éolang*, *Evali/Eóil* could perhaps be a hypocoristic form or misanalysis of **Eval-engi*, with the short /a/ of the Irish composition vowel. But it is more likely that EVALI is the 'very rare' Latin name *Aevalis*.[239] The patronymic is presumably Celtic, however. Rhys at one time read DEN[O]VI; if so, it is an adaptation, with British composition vowel, from Irish, as in 279 **DENAVEC[A]** (**dēno-vik-s*), OI *Díanach*,[240] or a else British cognate. If the reading DENCVI is retained, it may be a Welsh name in *-wy* to the Celtic base **denk-* that is seen in 442/346 MACCVDICCL and Ir. *Déclán* < **denk-lo-*.[241]

[18] A perplexing form is 328/44 RVGNIAT(I)O.[242] This may appear to contain the same suffix as Latin names like *Amatius, Curiatius, Egnatius,*

---

[236] *Corpus*, s. Brawdy 4, citing Rhys, *AC,* 5th ser. 14 (1897), 330. KHJ notes that this is 'very conjectural' and says that all that is clear is the V and -CI or -GI (but his drawing seems to show VV). He notes that Lloyd-Jones, *Geirfa*, p. 537, compares GLVVOCCI with *glyw* 'battle, war'. Cf. on *Glywys*, below, ‡58.

[237] See ‡22 below. Could the II be the archaic form of the letter E?

[238] LWP, p. 397; and, *Englyn*, p. 34, comparing Irish *Eoil* in the Book of Leinster, 349e and 352e (*Book of Leinster*, vi, ed. O'Sullivan, pp. 1550 and 1574; cf. CGSH, p. 242, s.n. *Eóil*). For *Éolang* see Uhlich, *Morphologie*, p. 240. Rhys, *AC*, 4th ser. 8 (1877), 144, speculated that EVOLENG(G)I involved 'Celtic equivalents, now lost, of *aevum* and *longus*'.

[239] Kajanto, p. 274, citing CIL xiii 1838 (Lyon: *Augustius Aevalis filius*). Mócsy, p. 8, and OPEL i, 48, add an example of *Evalis* from Cologne (CIL xiii 8422: *Severinio Evali filio*). Thus KHJ rightly queried 'Is there a Latin name *Aevālis*?' EVALI could also be gen. of a derived **Aevalius* (cf. *Gentilis/Gentilius*, ‡27n.).

[240] Ziegler, p. 166; Uhlich, *Morphologie*, p. 225. Rhys, *Englyn*, p. 34, noted that the O 'is imperfect, but the last time I looked at it I thought it too nearly a complete circle to be a C, to which I had been in the habit of giving the preference' (cf. Rhys, *AC*, 5th ser. 14 (1897), 330–31). But his final opinion was that 'the C is practically certain': *AC*, 6th ser. 18 (1918), 188 and n. 1; he equates DENCV–I with Ir. **Dianchú* (cf. ‡54 below). So too Rhys, in Meyer FS, p. 230, where he notes that the genitive *Dianchon* 'swift hound' appears in the Book of Ballymote, fo. 87a, l. 47. In 1947 KHJ recorded: 'The C is *certainly* C, but unusually incurved (not so much as Macalister draws).' In my opinion both C and O are possible. An objection to C is that the C- of CVNIO- is more open. An objection to O is that it is not a full circle – but perhaps the carver was hampered by the indentation in the stone.

[241] See ‡‡ 17 and 38n.

[242] See ‡48 below.

Mercatius, *Munatius*, *Optatius*, and *Paiatius* (all in RIB), that is with /a:/. However, the name is probably acephalous and formed on a Celtic stem such as [D]RVGN- (or [T]RVGN-) or [B]RVGN- with a presumably Celtic suffix, probably the well-attested /-ịato-/ (Thomas prefers the reading]RVGNIATO) or /-ịatịo-/. It is less likely that we have two names here, the second being Latin *Atius*, but if we do, note that the latter had a short /a/.[243]

377/175 AVICAT[VS] may be Welsh *Eugad*, if so with /a/.[244] Macalister's alternative, AMICATI, recalls 500 AMMECATI, again with the element **katus* 'battle'.[245] (Compare Macalister's dubious 1030 [A]MBIGATI.)

444/352]ACATI may well contain the same element (cf. 353/127/7 TREN-ACATVS and 19 **IVACATTOS**), although a Latin name with /a:/ (cf. *Pacatus*, *Pacata*, common in RIB) is also possible. The letters preceding]ACATI are unclear in Lhuyd's and Allen's[246] drawings (S . .L according to Nash-Williams, ST according to Macalister, S(?) . . according to Dr Edwards, *Corpus*, s. Narberth North 1).

1202/Ok2 EVOCATI also seems to contain **katus* (Thomas compares 19 **IVACATTOS**).[247] The alternative reading, EVOCALI looks like a Latin name in *-ālis*, but has not been identified as such.

1024/255/926 was read as NERT*tan* by Macalister (thinking of Ir. *-án*?), but Ifor Williams showed that it is NERTAT, W. *neirth(i)ad*, with /a/.[248]

452/400 PAANI and 451/401 DAARI are at the same location and may reflect a local school of orthography. DAARI in TVNCCETACE VXSOR DAARI HIC IACIT looks like OI *Dá(i)ri*, genitive of *Dáire*, a *io*-stem,[249] in which case the AA may have been intended to distinguish the Irish /a:/ from the British /a:/ > /ɔ:/ in the wife's name.[250] On the other hand, a British cognate **Dārios* is also possible.[251] The P of Lhuyd's VALAVITIVI/PAANI

---

[243] Lewis & Short. GPN, p. 309, mentions various forms such as *Ateano* and *At(t)ianus*. There was also a Germanic diminutive *-iatto*, productive in French (Lebel, p. 47).

[244] LHEB, p. 369. Cf. *Avicada* (?) in Holder iii, 773?

[245] Ziegler, p. 126.

[246] Westwood, *AC*, 4th ser. 13 (1882), 41–42.

[247] *Mute Stones*, pp. 271 and 285. Cf. Ziegler, p. 190: Ir. *Éochaid*. Note, however, an occurrence of EVOCATI (gen.) in Pannonia (OPEL ii, 126, citing CIL iii 4487).

[248] Williams, *Canu Aneirin*, p. 101; and *AC*, 87 (1932), 236; Jackson, *Speculum*, 24 (1949), 600.

[249] O'Brien, *Celtica*, 10 (1973), 223. Note that the Irish ending will have been -I both pre- and post-apocope. Rhys, *Englyn*, p. 86, implausibly equated DAARI with OI *Daigre*. De Bernardo Stempel, NWÄI, p. 207, and in *Ptolemy*, p. 101, links *Dáire* '*Bespringer' with *dairid* 'to bull', v.n. *dáir* (LEIA D-13), and the Irish tribe of *Darinoi* 'leaping ones'; similarly DLG, p. 113.

[250] This would be *Tynghedog*, equivalent in meaning to *Fortunata*, and the NC shows that it is not Irish; cf. LWP, p. 396; LHEB, p. 273; Russell, *Celtic Word-Formation*, pp. 17, 143, and 144; Charles-Edwards, in Evans FS, p. 2; Schumacher, *Ériu*, 46 (1995), 51; Stüber, *Historical Morphology*, p. 139; Luján, in *Ptolemy*, p. 61.

[251] DIL s.n. *Dáire* compares Gaulish *Dariaco* (place name from *Darios*, cf. Holder i, 1241; Grauf., p. 265; DLG, p. 113). Unfortunately we cannot be sure this had /a:/; short /a/, as gives W. *dâr* 'oak', and *(cyn)ddar(edd)* 'rage', is also possible. In fact our DAARI could

(emended by Macalister to VALAVI FILI/PAANI) suggests that it is of non-Irish derivation, and so we may have a British or Latin name with /a:/ spelt AA, perhaps [RI]/PAANI or [VRI]/PAANI.[252] On the other hand the layout suggests that PAANI is a complete name. A possibility, then, is Latin *Pāgānus* 'countryman', an attested personal name; this would probably have developed without the Vulgar Latin shortening of the first *ā* to judge by W. Powys (1000/182 POUOIS) < *pāgenses*, OC *pou* < *pāgus*.[253] In that case both As of PAANI would be relevant to the fate of /a:/ in Brittonic. But this is all doubtful. The best parallel to PAANI, as Rhys and Thomas point out, is *Paan*, son of Brychan, given in the Irish tract on 'The Mothers of Irish Saints' as the eponym of *Cell-Phaain* (Kilfane) in Ossory.[254] *Paan* was presumably borrowed from a British-Latin personal name *Paganus*. If this is the correct explanation of PAANI, then may DAARI also have lost **g*? That would be possible if DAARI shows a Brittonic treatment of Pr.Ir. **Daγarih* < **Dagorīx* (cf. Gaulish *Dagorigis* in Pannonia).[255]

482/Ok71 NEMIANVS might appear to have Latin *-ānus*, but this and the reading (apparently NEMIAVS) are uncertain.[256]

487/Ok10 has been read as DRVSTAVS and DRVSTANVS, inter alia, but here the *-ānus* – *if* that is what is intended – would presumably go back to **-agnas*.[257]

493/Ok58 NEPRANI FILI CONBEVI again looks like *-ānus*, but is unexplained. Could it represent a name **Nebranus* (compare the Roman

---

theoretically be post-New Quantity System W. **Dâr* (cf. *Daron* in *Aberdaron*, Williams, *Enwau Lleoedd*, p. 46).

252 Cf. *Ripanus* in RIB i 1993 and ii [fasc. 7] 2501.471, VRIPPANOS in RIG iv, no. 319 and p. 559 (cf. p. 545 s. *urippo-*), RIPPUS in Grauf., no. 198, *Ripan(i)us* in Holder ii, 1192, Weisgerber, *Rhenania*, p. 469, and OPEL iv, 29–30.

253 LHEB, p. 443.

254 Rhys, *AC*, 5th ser. 15 (1898), 57–59; Thomas, *Mute Stones*, p. 112, n. 50; CGSH, p. 179; EWGT, pp. 33 and 134; Hogan, *Onomasticon*, p. 209. For *Paganus* see Kajanto, p. 311, and OPEL iii, 120; Rhys compared French *Payen*, *Pain*. In July 1947 KHJ thought he could see a small sickle G above and between the AA of PAANI, but Nash-Williams in a letter of October that year wrote that he 'saw no G, but saw what seemed part of a letter on edge of stone opposite P', as in ECMW fig. 400. The latter seems to me to be the base of the V-recorded by Lhuyd. KHJ's G seems possible to me though very uncertain. It would presumably be an addition equating the name with *Paganus*.

255 Holder i, 1215; OPEL ii, 91.

256 It seems to have read NEMIAVS, without ligature (cf. Thomas, *Mute Stones*, pp. 284–85), which recalls *Nemausus* 'Nîmes' (cf. RIG i, p. 208; RIG iv, no. 2 NEMAV(SVS?); GPN, pp. 235–36; Birkhan, *Germanen und Kelten*, p. 216), but in particular the personal name *Nemausus*, [*Ne*]*mauso* (dative): Holder ii, 707; Weisgerber, *Rhenania*, pp. 182, 228, 230 and 236; OPEL iii, 97. There is a name *Nemonius* e.g. in RIB i 1039 (n. 466 below). Okasha compares *Nemanus* in *Vitae Sanctorum Hiberniae*, ed. Plummer, ii, 367 (abbot of Monasterboice); cf. *Neman* in CGH, p. 712, Uhlich, *Morphologie*, p. 285. In Welsh compare *Nyuein* < **Nemaniā*? (EWGT, p. 15; Zimmer, in Evans FS, p. 328: OI *Nemain*, cf. NWÄI, p. 248; also MLH v/1, p. 276, comparing Celtiberian *Namaios*).

257 Cf. Jackson, review of TYP, in *WHR*, 1, special no. (1963), 85; Padel, *CMCS*, 1 (1981), 55, n. 8; Thomas, *Mute Stones*, pp. 279–80, reading -ANVS with ligatured AN followed by V. See also ‡14n above for KHJ's suggestion of an ANV ligature.

name *Nebrus*)? If so, the unlenited /b/ would show that the name is not naturalized. More likely, however, it is Pr.Ir. *Nē-branī*; compare OI gen. *Niad-Brain* (‡42).

1210/Ok5 VALCI FILI V[. . .]ANVS might seem to be a name in Latin *-ānus* (Thomas suggests *Vettanus*), but it is simpler to read -AIVS, with Okasha; a name ECCAIVS cognate with Gaulish ECCAIOS would fit Gough's drawing well, though not explain his V, unless we read VALCI FIL–V ECCAIVS, with a horizontal I as the penultimate letter of FILIV(s), under the influence of the conventional FIL–.[258] The best fit of all would be VERCAIVS, which is especially well attested in Noricum.[259]

403/268/841 BERIA[CI] (also read: BERICCI (?))[260] is an uncertain restoration, but compare the personal name OI *Berach* 'pointed, snouted' or 'armed with the spear' (from OI *bir* : W. *bêr* 'spit').[261] The form could be Irish or British. Compare a French place name *Beraci-aco*.[262]

468/Ok31 RIALOBRANI is compared by Rhys with OC *Riol*, implying **ā*; however, Jackson derives them from **Rīgolo-* (?) and **Rīgālis* respectively, while De Bernardo Stempel more plausibly treats RIALOBRANI under Celtic **-alo-* (with short /a/).[263]

[18] (B) The O-spellings listed by Jackson (p. 291) are as follows (omitting 408/229/848 BODVOCI for the reasons given above):

1. 385/89 ANATEMORI
2. 487/Ok10 CVNOMORI (Cornwall)
3. 490/Ok29 DATUIDOCI and CONHINOCI (Cornwall)[264]

---

[258] Thomas, *Mute Stones*, pp. 281–82 and 301, n. 18 (cf. 510/Scot. 13 VETTA, and ‡42n below); RIG iv, no. 152 and p. 536, suggesting *ec-caio-*. For horizontal I *word-internally* cf. Thomas, *Mute Stones*, pp. 271, 286 and 288. For *-aios* (also a Greek suffix), cf. GPN, p. 459, Alföldy, *Noricum*, p. 231, and RIG i, 140, and see RIB i 159 for a *Mantaius* of the Vettones in Spain. Rhys, *PBA*, 6 (1913–14), 347, compared *Eccaios* with 469/Ok34 GENAIVS (or]ENAIVS?), 1210/Ok5 VECCAIVS (Hübner's reading), and 419/284 VEHIMAIE or VENIMAIE; he linked them to the ogam forms in -AI(S), on which see Ziegler, pp. 55–58. Thomas also suggests *Veddanus*, comparing 211 VEDDONOS; however, the latter had **o* or **u* (Ziegler, p. 243, Hamp, *SC*, 18/19 (1983–84), 129), which should not turn up as A in British or Irish. On VALCI see below, ‡76.

[259] Holder iii, 182–83 and 360; Mócsy, p. 306; Alföldy, *Noricum*, p. 238; Alföldy, *Personennamen*, p. 324. For other names in *V*- see Holder i, 72 and iii, 541–42, s. *-aio-*.

[260] Although Lhuyd's reading is quoted by Macalister and RCAHMW as BERICCI in his drawing in Camden's *Britannia*, col. 620, and in BL Stowe MS 1024, fo. 8r, the fifth letter is *not* a C like the sixth and could be A, making BERIACI.

[261] Meyer, *Contributions*, p. 202; CGH, pp. 518–19; O'Brien, *Celtica*, 10 (1973), 223; GPN, p. 313 and n. 3; LEIA B-52. The Irish personal name may lie behind the river name *Berach* in Carmarthenshire: EANC, p. 3. Westwood, LW, p. 7, quotes an identification of 403/268/841 BERIC(CI?) with Romano-British *Berikos*/VERICA (on which see Sims-Williams, in *Gaulois et celtique continental*). Note that there was an OE name **Berica, Beriga* (DEPN, s.n. Barking; Searle, *Onomasticon*, p. 105). Cf. *Biraco(s)* and *Birac(i)us* in Holder i, 423, and iii, 867, and OPEL i, 295.

[262] Holder iii, 848 (a reconstruction?).

[263] LWP, p. 406; LHEB, pp. 457 and 459; NWÄI, pp. 455–56; Thomas, *Mute Stones*, p. 270. For *Riol* see Bodmin, passim.

[264] The final -I is uncertain in both names.

4. 477/Ok11 CONETOCI (Cornwall)[265]
5. 427/b/301 CATUOCONI

[18] The forms with -MORI are problematic, since this is only relevant when from /ma:ro-/ 'great' rather than /mori-/ 'sea', elements both attested in Gaulish names.[266] Jackson identifies ANATEMORI (name or epithet?) as containing /ma:ro-/, and compares *eneidfawr* ('great soul [?friend]') < *anaṭiomāros*.[267] Although, as Schrijver points out, *eneidfawr* 'magnanimous' is a dubiously attested compound, Schrijver does not actually reject the etymology *Anaṭiomāros*, but simply argues that it would have given *Anadfawr*.[268] In fact, there does not seem to be any other possible etymology. In the case of CVNOMORI Jackson hesitates between 'sea hound' and 'great hound'.[269] The latter is confirmed by *Kynvawr* in Middle Welsh,[270] whereas *Kynuor* seems not to occur during the period when *aw* and *o* contrasted meaningfully in final syllables.[271] Moreover, *Mori-* is always the

---

[265] The first O is also relevant if this is a derivative of *kān-* (and not connected with W. *Cynwyd*, etc.; cf. ‡58). Cf. McManus's review of Thomas, *Mute Stones*, in *CMCS*, 33 (1997), 102; LWP, pp. 403–4 (CONETOCI = 'gloriosus': *gogoniant*); and Lindeman, *BBCS*, 29 (1980–82), 510, and Sims-Williams, *BBCS*, 38 (1991), 39 (on *Conet*). I. Williams, apud Richmond & Crawford, *Archaeologia*, 93 (1949), 27, unsatisfactorily connects CONETOCI not only with *gogoniant* etc. (< *kān-*) but also with *Conetodubnos*, one of a number of ancient Celtic forms which can only have original *o* (see GPN, p. 211, and Birkhan, *Germanen und Kelten*, p. 426). CONETOCI (and *Conet*) belong either with one or with the other (or neither) but not with both. See further below ‡58 on the possible connection with *Cunetio* (which had not occurred to me when writing the *BBCS* article).

[266] GPN, pp. 223–28 and 232–33. The problem that *mōr* and *mawr* are both *Mor-* in Welsh is noted by Lloyd, *Cymmrodor*, 9 (1888), 50–51; Lloyd-Jones, *Y Geninen*, 44 (1926), 13; and Isaac, *LlC*, 24 (2000), 20.

[267] LHEB, pp. 291, 580, 598–99, 610, and 645; cf. already Holder i, 135, Rhys, *Englyn*, p. 58, and *Welsh People*, p. 17.

[268] SBCHP, pp. 272–73. *Eneidfawr* is first attested from Iolo Morganwg in GPC. It is not in Lloyd-Jones, *Geirfa*, nor in the index of names and epithets in EWGT, nor in CBT, nor in SWWF, pp. 191–93. It is difficult to equate ANATEMORI with the (APOLLINI) ANEXTIOMARO inscription from South Shields (RIB ii [fasc. 2] 2415.55, mentioned in another connection in LHEB, p. 407), partly in view of the AT of ANATE- (which would have to be a false archaism due to mistaking /eiθ/ < /ext/ for /eiθ/ by i-affection of /aθ/), and partly because the South Shields inscriber was probably intended to write *Anextlomaro*, which is attested in Gaul (see RIB note, Aldhouse Green & Raybould, *SC*, 33 (1999), 99, n. 17, and GPN, p. 225, citing DAG, pp. 635 and 1108). In any case, /ma:ro-/ 'great' is clearly the element here, although see LHEB, p. 290 and n. 2 on *Vindomora* (differently PNRB, pp. 502–3) for possible early *mōro-* < *māro* (presumably by assimilation, as in cases like OI *mór* < *már* (cf. LEIA M-18) and OW *Morgetiud* < *Margetiud*, OB *Margit-hoiarn* (Williams, *Canu Aneirin*, p. 300; LHEB, p. 346; Wmffre, *Language and History*, i, 351–52)). See also n. 210 above.

[269] LHEB, p. 291.

[270] The earliest and therefore best example in Lloyd-Jones, *Geirfa*, s.n. is *Kenwaur* in *De Situ Brecheniauc* (EWGT, p. 15). Some of Lloyd-Jones's other forms such as *Conmur* and *Conmor* may be distinct; see Sims-Williams, *BBCS*, 38 (1991), 63 and n. 4. KHJ noted that Lloyd-Jones's forms 'can hardly be "sea-hound", which would have to be *Cunomorius* > *Cynfyr*. The high proportion of *Con-* is odd.'

[271] To judge by the texts cited in EWGT, p. 181 s.n. *Cynfor*. On the ambiguity of OW *Conmor* see Sims-Williams, *BBCS*, 38 (1991), 63, n. 4.

first element in the ancient Celtic personal names collected by Ellis Evans, such as *Moricamulus* from St Albans and MORIREGIS from Maryport, to which we can now add *Morivassum* from Bath.[272] Note that 443/349 is probably CAMVLORI < *Camulo-rīx* rather than CAMVMORI (Nash-Williams's alternative suggestion), since CAMV- is an unlikely first element.[273]

[18] Two forms not listed by Jackson are 985/61 MORIDIC and 996/147 MO[RE]DIC, presumably because he regarded them as MORI- names, as Evans does.[274] This is clearly correct. OW *Moridic*, MW *Morid(d)ic*[275] is presumably the same name ('sea-anger'?). The absence of *i*-affection is not an objection. While lack of *i*-affection is typical of words with /o/ < /ɔ/ < /ɔː/ < /aː/,[276] there are also examples of words with original /o/ that lack internal *i*-affection, such as OW *colginn*, and this was not only as a matter of orthographical conservatism, as Mod.W. *colyn* shows.[277] Moreover, in **mori-* we are looking at the environment (nominal compounds) for Jackson's quasi-'final' rather than 'internal' affection, and while Jackson argues that medial /i/ caused this in the case of /a/ (as allegedly in AVI- > *Eu-*), he gives no examples where /o/ was affected.[278] Certainly, /i/ did not cause true final affection of /o/, as W. *môr* 'sea' < **mori-* shows.[279] The affection in OW *Cair Merdin* (> *Caerfyrddin*) < **Moridūnom* is quite different, being due to internal affection, after syncope, by the ultimate /iː/ < /uː/.[280] MORIDIC differs from *Merdin* in lacking syncope (and hence *i*-affection), but this is not problematic, since Jackson notes many exceptions to syncope, for

---

[272] GPN, pp. 232–33 (on *Vindomora*, whence *Vindomoruci*, see n. 268 above); Tyers, *Pottery*, p. 132; RIB i 861; Tab.Sulis, no. 53.

[273] For **Camulorīx* see above, ‡14. If CAMVMORI were correct, it would have an inverted M, as in 487/Ok10 CVNOMORI and 3025/I6 MELITA. If correct, CAMV- must be from **kambo-*, below, ‡22.

[274] GPN, p. 232 and n. 6. Macalister read the [RE] but Nash-Williams puts it in brackets.

[275] See LL, pp. 275–76; and forms in Anglesey and Penllyn genealogies cited in EWGT, p. 205, s.n. *Moriddig: Moruddig, Moriddic, Moreiddic*; also CBT ii, 228 and 246; Pryce, *BBCS*, 33 (1986), 156–57; *St Davids Episcopal Acta*, ed. Barrow, nos. 118 and 120 ([*Ma*]*reduchus* and *Moredicus* [= *Maredudd* according to the editor]); *Merioneth Lay Subsidy*, ed. Williams-Jones, p. 131; *Black Book of St. David's*, ed. Willis-Bund, p. 355. An element DICO (W. *dig* 'anger'?) may be visible in the obscure 2017 DINOCONSVODICOON which Wright, *TCHS*, 23 (1962), 128 and n. 4, analyses as a tripartite *Dinoconsuodico* (plus obscure ON) and compares with CIL xii 4218 *Dinomogetimaro*, a name of Mars in an inscription in Herault (Holder i, 1284; cf. n. 145 above). I will not discuss this obscure inscription further; does it belong in our corpus?

[276] LHEB, p. 293.

[277] LHEB, pp. 589–90 and 607. Cf. OB *Iarnco(g)lin* in Chrest., p. 141?

[278] LHEB, pp. 579–80. In any case, note that his argumentation in connection with AVI- is rejected by Schrijver, SBCHP, pp. 268–76.

[279] SBCHP, pp. 265–66 (rejecting McCone, *Nasal Presents*, p. 77, as does Lindeman in his review in *CMCS*, 26 (1993), 78, n. 6).

[280] LHEB, pp. 605 and 665. Schrijver, SBCHP, p. 275, concurs that internal *i*-affection followed syncope. Isaac, *LlC*, 24 (2001), 13–23, would separate the personal name *Myrddin*.

example OW *Celidon*, MW *Celydon* < *Calidon-*.[281] As in this example, we would expect the first I of MORIDIC to become /ə/, and this may be what is intended by the E which Macalister saw in MO[RE]DIC (clearly a late inscription in view of its Old French MERCI ET GRACE[282] and ELMON FECIT H(an)C CRUCEM – presumably OE *Ælmon*);[283] if so, either the spelling of MW *Moriddic* is archaic, or the second syllable has undergone vowel harmony with the last.

[18] The following can probably be added to Jackson's five inscriptions:

6. 1000/182 POUOIS (W. *Powys* < *pāgenses*) exemplifies /aːγ/ > /ɔːu̯/.[284]

7. 1023/239/927 SCILOC looks like an /aːkos/ name, perhaps the stem seen in Ir. **SCILAGNI** (CIIC 85), *Scellán*, and *Scillíne*, and the common noun *scell(án)* 'kernel'.[285] If the latter has been correctly connected with Ir. *scoilt* and W. *hollt*,[286] SCILOC has to be an Irish name; however, the etymology of *scell(án)* is uncertain, and in view of the I and the O it is easier to regard SCILOC as a Welsh name, cognate with Ir. **Scel(l)ach*. Yet, as SCITOC is also said to be a possible reading, one can compare *Scituc* in a ninth-century charter in the Book of Llandaf.[287] *Scituc* is clearly an /aːkos/ name, although its etymology is obscure – perhaps compare W. *ysgytio* 'to shake' or OI *scíth, scíthech* 'tired', compared by Holder with the Continental name *Scitus*.[288] Since SCI[T?]OC is the 'preparer' of the cross, one might like alternatively to see his name as a hypocoristic based on W. *ysgythru* 'to carve, engrave'; the lack of the /r/ (difficult for children to pronounce) is typical of hypocoristics such as *Iolo* < *Iorwerth*, *Guto* < *Gruffudd*, *Magota* < *Margareta*, and *Katina* < *Katherina*.[289]

8. 473/b/Ok46 IGNIOC is hitherto obscure, and Thomas's new division]IGNI OC 'for "(Stone) of-*Cunignus*" (or similar name), "*oc*" (for *ic* = *hic*

---

[281] LHEB, pp. 582, 605 and 653. See Watson, *Celtic Place-Names of Scotland*, pp. 21 and 71; Clarke, *BBCS*, 23 (1968–70), 191–201.

[282] Not personal names, as noted by Jackson, *Speculum*, 24 (1949), 599, and in ECMW, p. 40.

[283] See Searle, *Onomasticon*, pp. 14 and 30, for **Ælfmann, Ælmanus*, and *Ælmon*, and for *Æl-* < *Æthel-* well before 1066 see Smart, in Dodgson GS, pp. 326–29; also Foster, *Med. Arch.*, 32 (1988), 209. Note, however, an OW(?) *Elmoin* in LL, p. 246.

[284] LHEB, pp. 373 and 443–44. See further below, ‡80.

[285] Ziegler, pp. 230–31; O'Brien, *Celtica*, 10 (1973), 221; CGH, p. 731.

[286] Cf. LEIA S-40; Schrijver, *BBCS*, 39 (1992), 6–7; ADA, pp. 358–59.

[287] There has been doubt about whether the second letter is **T** or **C**, but since Rhys, *AC*, 5th ser. 16 (1899), 159–60, the fourth has generally been read as an L. However, Macalister, quoted by Anon., *AC*, 7th ser. 8 (1928), 369–70, and also cited by Williams, *AC*, 87 (1932), 237, preferred SCITOC to SCILOC or SCROC, partly because of *Scituc* in LL, p. 169. There is no cross-stroke in Lhuyd's drawing (reproduced by RCAHMW) nor in modern photographs, but LW, plate 10, shows traces of one. Mr J. M. Lewis, however, writes: 'I'm sure the reading can't be SCITOC. The stroke curves forward towards the top (making SCICOC just possible), but there is certainly not an angled stroke to make it a T' (letter 25.9.01). In this case, SCITOC can only be saved by supposing that SCICOC is a miscopying of it.

[288] Holder ii, 1398; OPEL iv, 55. Cf. the Latin cognomen *Fessus*, Kajanto, p. 245.

[289] Cane, *Personal Names of Women*, pp. 18 and 34.

"here")' is implausible.[290] I would suggest that it corresponds to OB *agnioc* – and to W. *egnïol* 'vigorous' (15th cent.) which has the more productive *-ol* suffix rather than *-og*.[291] *Agnioc* (< *ad-gnīm-ākos) would develop by internal *i*-affection to *Egnioc, but in Old Breton this would have developed to *Ignioc by 'secondary internal affection' in about the tenth century.[292] This secondary affection is 'apparently not represented in Cornish' according to Jackson,[293] but in view of the sporadic nature of its occurrence in Breton and the closeness of Old Cornish and Old Breton, it cannot be ruled out that IGNIOC is a Cornish example of it (alternatively, IGNIOC could be a Breton in Cornwall). The rest of this inscription, 473/a/Ok46 VITALI FILI TORRICI, is believed to be earlier than IGNIOC, which may explain the A of VITALI, although this could have been maintained under Latin influence. As Jackson lists TORRICI among forms lacking internal *i*-affection, he evidently thought it had original /o/ rather than /ɔ/ < /a:/ which never underwent that affection.[294] If so it is irrelevant here.

9. 489/a/Ok13 FANONI MAQVI RINI in Devon corresponds to ogam SVAQQUCI MAQI QICI, probably an engraver's mistake for SVA[N-N]UCI MAQI [R]I[N]I, and representing the same name as in 455/403 CAMVL(L)ORIGI FILI FANNVCI in Pembrokeshire. The ogam -UCI would seem to reflect the FANNVCI variant rather than the FANONI on

---

[290] *Mute Stones*, pp. 270 and 284. He is wrong in saying that -IGNI is necessarily British, for it is common in Ireland (Ziegler, p. 107).

[291] DGVB i, 56–57; Lambert, *CMCS*, 12 (1986), 107; cf. Russell, *JCL*, 2 (1993), 151–56; GPC s.v. *egni* following Williams, *BBCS*, 2 (1923–25), 302. On the use of G for /g/ in IGNIOC (and *agnioc*) see ‡17 above. If the G of IGNIOC stood for /ɣ/ we would expect the name to develop to an unattested **Iniog, comparable only with W. *Ina* (see LL, p. 405, also the patron of Llanina (see LBS iii, 318, EWGT, p. 20, and Ó Riain, in *Cardiganshire County History*, i, 392)). *Ina* has been compared with the Cornish St Euny, but the spellings do not agree; see Orme, *Dedications*, pp. 96 and 113. We can rule out a link between IGNIOC and the Continental toponym *Igniacus > Igny, Ignac etc. (: Latin personal name *Ignius*), Holder ii, 30.

[292] LHEB, pp. 594–95 and 617; HPB, pp. 299–301. See ‡85 below.

[293] LHEB, p. 594.

[294] LHEB, p. 610. KHJ's notes show that he equated TORRICI with W. *terrig* 'harsh, severe' < **torrīco-* (EANC, p. 197 – without etymology in GPC) and with the Devon river names *Torridge* and *Tory* (DEPN, p. 478) discussed in LHEB, pp. 557 and 612–13. Okasha refers to speculations in LWP, pp. 359 and 405, on TORRICI and to *Vitae Sanctorum Hiberniae*, ed. Plummer, ii, 344, which is an irrelevant reference to To-hypocoristics. Okasha suggests that Jackson thought VITALI Celtic rather than Latin, but he of course regarded it as a Latin name that might be expected to undergo British sound changes (whence OW *Guitaul*, EWGT, p. 193, s.n. *Gwidol*; cf. *Guitolion*, p. 8 < *Vitalianus*; Rhys, LWP, p. 396, and *Englyn*, pp. 72–73; Loth, *Noms des saints bretons*, p. 55). Cf. Jackson in Chadwick GS, pp. 212–13: 'Vitalinus was in use among the early Welsh [Cf. *ad discordiam Guitolini et Ambrosii* in the Exordium to the Annales Cambriae], and Vitalianus was certainly employed by the Irish in Britain' (citing 445/354 **VITALIANI**). Both W. *Gwythelin* and Ir. *Fidlin* have been derived from *Vitalinus*; cf. Rhys, *JRSAI*, 5th ser. 12 (1902), 37 (*Fidlin*); Rhys & Brynmor-Jones, *Welsh People*, p. 66, n. 1. According to Rhys, *PBA*, 1911–12, p. 325, 'it is due to their translating Celtic names [cf. Ir. *béo*, W. *byw*] that the Déssi had such Roman ones as *Vitalis*, *Vitalianus*, and *Vitalinus*'.

the Devonian stone itself – unless, that is, we suppose that -UCI is an error for -UNI.[295] The U of SVA[NN]UCI (or SVA[NN]U[N]I) and FANNVCI evidently reflects the rounding of /ɔ:/ rather than /a:/, and may even be a very early example of the development to -wg rather than -awg typical of south-east Wales (e.g. 333/50 CATVC but also 1061/Dor.iii CATGUG (Macalister: CATTUG) at Wareham, Dorset).[296] The equivalence of FANONI and FANNVCI is most easily explained by supposing that their suffixes are /ɔ:n-/ < /a:n-/ and /ɔ:g-/ < /a:k-/, with the former perhaps being felt to be of higher status because deriving from Latin -ānus,[297] and therefore more appropriate for roman script. In any case, FANONI belongs here as an example of O < /a:/. *Fan(n)ācus or *Fan(n)ānus may be based on Classical Latin Fannius (Fannianus is attested in Spain),[298] and ogam SV- may be substituted for the /f-/, as in the earliest Latin loanwords into Irish (and cf. Februarius > W. Chwefror, fibula > W. hual). On the other hand, the root of the name may be that of W. chwant, chwannog (cf. Old Celtic Suandacca), with SV- and F- both representing Irish renderings of the Brittonic /Σw-/ > /hw-/.[299]

10. 1047/Ok20 RU(n)HOL and 1058/Ok53 RUNHO[L] (?) recall Loth's derivation of MB rouantelez 'royalty' from an Old Breton adjective *roiantol, and his remark that the element roiant became ruant, as in the Cartulary of Landevennec (11th cent.).[300] RUNHOL is close to a hypothetical Breton *Ruantol, but it is difficult to see why the typically Late Old Welsh -nh- should appear instead of -nt- in either Cornish or Breton.[301] It may be better to compare Loth's element roin, ron, run (unrelated to roiant etc., he stresses), as in the personal names Roinoc, Ronhoiarn, and

[295] See ‡60 below. KHJ suggested that -UNI was intended (this would involve the engraver missing a score as well as ignoring the base line) and thought 'it probable the name is Svannucos or Svannonos'.

[296] Ziegler, pp. 90–91, 98–99, and 233; Russell, Celtic Word-Formation, pp. 26–27 and 110–16; and see below ‡60 on -wg. If OI Sannuch is identical with SVA[NN]UCI (GOI, p. 572, Ziegler, p. 233), the loan would be very early, before lenition of /k/ in either language and before the shortening of vowels in unstressed syllables in Irish. This encounters the problem that /a:/ is still intact in the earliest loanwords!

[297] On -acus and -anus see Russell, ÉC, 25 (1988), 131–73.

[298] See Mócsy, p. 124, for Fan(n)ius and Fannianus. Note also FANI (gen.) in RIB i 1445. Holder i, 1492 cites an altar inscription from Gourdan, Haute-Garonne, for which the reading MARTI/DAHO/FANNAC/V.S.L.M., is maintained by Sacaze, BSNAF, 1880, p. 159, but HANNAC as in CIL xiii 87 should be preferred, from an Aquitanian stem.

[299] See below, ‡45. For Suandacca see ‡60 below. On Februarius and fibula see Lewis, Elfen Ladin, p. 17, and Falileyev, in Irland und Europa, pp. 7–9.

[300] Chrest., pp. 162, n. 4, and 163. Cf. Gramm., p. 75; Lambert, in Evans FS, p. 99, n. 4, and review by Schrijver, CMCS, 34 (1997), 108 (MB rouantelez < Latin rēg- plus native *-ant-āl-). RUNHOL was already compared with OW roenhol by Rhys, AC, 4th ser. 6 (1875), 367. When KHJ visited 1058 RUNHO(L) (runhō in Macalister's drawing) in 1951 he found 'there are letters, but they are illegible and certainly not as drawn by Macalister, who is clearly guessing; see his account. His h looks like a b'.

[301] Cf. LHEB, p. 504.

Runhoiarn, and to regard the H as inorganic.[302] Be this as it may, the termination is probably *-ol* < / -a:l-/.[303]

11. 3015/M6 PROSTLON, with B. *-lon* cognate with W. *llawn*.

12. 3019/M10 RIOCUS, clearly the same as OB *Rioc* < *Rīgākos*, and cf. OB *Riocan*, MW *Riogan*.[304]

13. 366/148 ITOCVS if < *(P)itākos*.[305]

14. 993/124/18 DITOC and OCCON (Macalister: UON) have not be satisfactorily explained, but I argue below that the latter name is best read AON with a here irrelevant short /o/.[306] If MADOMNUAC (or, better, MADOMNUACO) on this stone is correctly equated with Ir. *Mo Domnóc* (*Modhomhnóg*),[307] that might seem to support the possibility that -OC and -ON are Irish *-óc* and *-ón*; but then why spell the same Irish vowel in two different ways? If -UAC is an odd spelling, by a Welshman, for OI *-óc* (influenced by W. *-auc* < *-oc*, or less likely by the alternation of *ó* and *úa* in other circumstances in Old Irish), then DITOC is most naturally taken to be a Welsh name. TESQUITUS DITOC, which is given to St *Madomnuac*, probably means 'the hermitage(?) of [a man named] Ditoc'.[308] DITOC could be a hypocoristic/honorific 'thy' form of 366/148 ITOCVS (no. 13 above), although one would normally expect *TITOC.[309]

15. 2028 ARTOGNOV([?]) (cf. OB *Arthnou*) < *-gnāwos*, and similarly:

16. 3006/C1 BODOGNOVS.[310]

17. 1209/Ok12 CAOCI < *Kagiākos* (‡25). If the reading is really CA[ ]OCI, that may also be a relevant name such as *CA[T]OCI or *CA[LI]OCI.[311]

[18] The following are doubtful:

978/49 FLOU may belong here, if from Latin *Flāvus*, but this is not the only possibility.[312]

---

[302] Chrest., p. 163 and n. 2. For inorganic *h* after *n* as in OB *Uuin(h)ic* see Gramm., p. 152.

[303] On Latin *-ālis* and Celtic *-ālos* see Gramm., p. 359.

[304] Gramm., p. 402; *Englynion y Beddau*, I.61, ed. Jones, *PBA*, 53 (1967), 130.

[305] See ‡84 below.

[306] See ‡65 below.

[307] Rhys, *AC*, 5th ser. 13 (1896), 121; Thomas, *Mute Stones*, p. 110, n. 31. (Rhys, *Englyn*, pp. 54–55, redivided *Madomnu ac Occon*, which is obviously unlikely.) *Mo Domnóc* appears in Rhygyfarch's *Life* of St David as *Midunnauc*, varr. *Midumnauc*, etc., i.e. with *-auc* for *-óc*; cf. LBS ii, 353–54; Russell, *Celtic Word-Formation*, pp. 114, n. 296, 144, and 153. W. G. Thomas, in *Cardiganshire County History*, i, 410, read DOMNUACOLLON and compared OW *Dumnagual* and *Dumnguallaun*, which is philologically impossible; the reading must be rejected anyway.

[308] Rhys, *AC*, 5th ser. 13 (1896), 121 and 122, suggests *Dudoch* (cf. LBS iv, 275, n. 4), *Dydoch*, *Didog* or *Dythoch*. Note that MA- instead of MO- /mö/ also suggests a non-Irish writer.

[309] Lewis, *ZCP*, 20 (1936), 142, notes that lenition of *T'* occurs after feminine nouns and through confusion of /t/ and /d/ after /s/. Does the final consonant of *tesquitus* explain the D or was the writer thinking of an underlying Welsh feminine equivalent? On *tesquitus* see Handley, in *Roman, Runes and Ogham*, pp. 26–29.

[310] On the etymology of *-gnou* see Hamp, *Onoma*, 14 (1969), 12, and further references in ‡48n.

[311] For these cf. Russell, *Celtic Word-Formation*, pp. 31 and 144.

[312] See ‡80, also LHEB, pp. 321–22, on Latin *au*.

345/74 **GLUVOCA[** or **GL[U]V[O]C[I]** (Macalister) is the same name as was read by Macalister (alone) on 424/299 BRIAC[I] FILI GLVVOCCI. As the latter has A from /aː/ in BRIACI, it is unlikely to show O < /aː/ in GLVVOCCI, although inconsistency cannot be ruled out. No etymology has been proposed, but a bare possibility (with short /o/) is *kliwoko- 'ridge' (> OI *clíu*, gen. *cliach*), assuming that the /i/ could be coloured by the following /w/; Ziegler finds this element in 86 **CLIUCUNAS** (sic leg.).[313]

997/159 EIUDON is perhaps an odd spelling of *Iudon* (MW *Idon*),[314] or of later Welsh *Eudon*,[315] and if so is irrelevant.

1050/Ok74 CRVX MEVROC, which has also been read IHS UROC or INVROC or IRCVROC, is too uncertain.

1206/Ok4 DOCIDCI or [R]IVGDOCI or [R]IVSDOCI is again too obscure to be considered. If it contains the same -*doc*- element found in various Old Welsh names, note that it is unclear whether this takes its *o* from /aː/ or /o/.[316] The obscure 1001/101 COCOM has been interpreted as an error for COCONI, and the latter has been supposed to be a possible form of W. *Gwgawn*,[317] all of which is incredible.

‡19 Final i-affection; LHEB §169

The number of forms bearing on this is quite small, despite the enormous number of names in genitive -I. Jackson clearly regarded their -I as merely conventional and the ending as 'Latinising' rather than native,[318] and he rightly leaves them out of his lists of names without *i*-affection. Ifor Williams had argued that British genitive forms may have survived as independent names, noting examples such as *Tudri* beside *Tudyr* and *Maelgwn* beside *Meilyg*, but he had not given any *o*-stem examples, and Jackson notes that Williams's splitting into two names occurred in the case of 'British names with oblique cases very different from the nominative',[319] which by

---

[313] Ziegler, p. 150; cf. Uhlich, *Morphologie*, p. 203. For /kl/ ~ /gl/ see Sims-Williams, in Mac Cana FS, pp. 218–19. Rhys, *AC*, 5th ser. 13 (1896), 127–28, read 345/74 as **GLUVOCA/I**, but noted the following alternatives: **GL**; then U or E; then V or S; then **O**, U, E, or I; then **C**; then **A** or another vowel; then **I** on the other side of the stone – maybe *Gleve-cattos* (: OI *glé*, W. *gloyw*), he speculated. KHJ concludes that Macalister's and Nash-Williams's choices of ogam vowels are evidently guesses.

[314] Examples in Sims-Williams, *BBCS*, 38 (1991), 80–84.

[315] *Eudon* in the Dyffryn Clwyd Court Rolls is noticed by Cane, *Personal Names of Women*, p. 44, as a rare Welsh female name, which she derives from the male Norman name *Eudo(n)*, citing Withycombe, *Oxford Dictionary of English Christian Names*, pp. 109–10.

[316] Sims-Williams, *BBCS*, 38 (1991), 67, n. 3. For *Doc(c)*- in Continental names see Holder i, 1297–1300; Weisgerber, *Rhenania*, p. 453; and Evans, *ÉC*, 12 (1968–69), 198, n. 1.

[317] Radford and Hemp, *AC*, 106 (1957), 111; Hemp, *AC*, 107 (1958), 125.

[318] LHEB, p. 623.

[319] BWP, pp. 6–10; LHEB, pp. 623–24. See collection of -*ri*/-*yr* names in Lloyd-Jones, *BBCS*, 14 (1950–52), 36. For a different view, see Dressler, in Pokorny FS, p. 151, deriving names in -*ri* from reformed *nominatives* in *-rīgos*; cf. Lejeune, *ÉC*, 19 (1982), 112 and 116–19, and see Zimmer's suggestion in SWWF, p. 180, n. 18, that *Maglo-cunos* etc. could be nominative (cf. ibid., p. 282, n. 4).

implication excludes the *o*-stems with genitive in -*ī*; and one can add, moreover, that we cannot actually be sure that a form like *Tudri* is from the genitive rather than, say, the accusative.

[19] Incidentally, I would add in passing that it may be an oversimplification to see *Tudyr* (= Gaulish *Toutorix*) versus *Tudri* (= Gaulish *Toutorigis*)[320] as a two-way split of nominative versus oblique. In the case of the 'hound' names, as well as (1) nominative *Meilyg* < *Maglokū and (2) oblique *Maelgwn* < *MaglokunV- (cf. 1027/265/923 GALCU[N], ‡69n.), there are (3) obvious late re-formations such as *Bleddgi* (beside *Bleddyg*) (cf. 984/59 GURCI; 1019/237/920 ILCI).[321] It is quite possible therefore that some names of the *Tudri* type are also late reformations (i.e. *tud* + *rhi*), although there is no way of knowing which, unless the reformation is so late as to escape internal *i*-affection, as perhaps in *Clodri.*[322]

[19] Since forms like **Tudweil or **Tudwyl do not occur beside *Tudwal*,[323] an inscription like 375/166 TOTAVALI (genitive) is really not relevant here (and see ‡12). As a result, Jackson's list of forms where *i*-affection might have occurred but is not visible (pp. 597–98) is short, and confined to names with /iː/ or /i̯/ in the old final syllable of the *nominative* case:

[19] (A)

1. 322/27 CAMVLORIS[324]
2. 320/26 CVLIDORI[325]
3. 446/353 CLVTORI
4. 394/103 CANTIORI
5. 409/198/849 CARANTORIVS (whether for *Carantorix or -*orios*)
6. 380/84 ICORI (whether for *Icorix or -*orios*)
7. 420/289 PORIVS (contrasting with *Piro* in the *Vita sancti Samsonis*, W. *Pyr*)[326]
8. 417/282 CAVOSENIARGII (if cognate with MW *eiry* < **argi̯o*-).

---

[320] Evans, *BBCS*, 24 (1970–72), 420.
[321] See ‡16 above. These correspond to the Irish re-formations like *Glaschú* beside *Glaisiuc* (: W. *Glesyg*), Uhlich, *Morphologie*, pp. 210 and 263; Stüber, *Historical Morphology*, pp. 88–89. A collection of -*gi* names is given by Birkhan, *Germanen und Kelten*, p. 349, n. 824.
[322] On *Clodri* see ‡46n. below.
[323] Cf. Koch, *BBCS*, 30 (1982–83), 211.
[324] Despite the problem of the first vowel, one might compare this with the place name *carn Cymlyr* in LL, p. 145.
[325] The -I is uncertain (see ‡16), but this does not affect the argument, which does however depend on CVLIDOR(I) being an *-*o-rīx* name, which is uncertain (cf. ‡‡ 13 and 16).
[326] Rhys, LWP, p. 376, compared OW *Mainaur Pir* > *Manorbeer*. See Charles, *Place-Names of Pembrokeshire*, p. 698.

[19] I would add the following from my earlier discussion of *-rīx and -rius names:[327]

9.   2006 CVNORIX (admittedly this may be Irish, but the composition vowel is Cambricized and does not show affection)
10. 388/94 DERVORI
11. 396/104 AVITORI
12. 361/140 TALORI
13. 443/349 CAMVLORI (preferable to CAMVMORI)
14. 2001 ORBIORI
15. 516/Scot.1 MAVORIVS.

[19] Note also (assuming the Latin -II reflects a jo-stem like Gaulish Λουερυιος)·
16.   385/89 LOVERNII (cf. MW llewyrn 'fox; ignis fatuus')[328]
It is striking that all these examples except 7, 8, and 16 involve an apparently unaffected composition vowel; conservative spelling may play a part.
325/33 BIVATIS(I) (BIVOTIS?) should also be mentioned here as it could be Brittonic *Biwotīs (< *Gʷiwotūt-s) > W. bywyd 'life', although there are other possibilities.[329]

[19] (B) By contrast, Jackson has only two valid examples where final i-affection is visible (p. 598):[330]

1.   995/133/24   ENEVIRI = Enewyr < *Anaworīks (also with internal i-affection and so definitely late); cf. OB Rianau.[331]
2.   1033/287 CELEN, if it is the ancestor of MW celein 'corpse'; but it may well be the ancestor of MW Celyn 'holly' < *Colino- and so be irrelevant to final i-affection.[332]

---

[327] ‡14 above. I omit 321/25]SORIS and 458/Ok9 RANOCORI or NANOCORI as being too obscure, also 1205/Ok44 MAVORI (Thomas's uncertain reading), and 362/142 AVITORIA (since even if this is a ja-stem, i-affection is not regular, cf. W. myfyr beside B. memor < memoria, cited above, ‡15). With the rest, it is here irrelevant whether they had nominative *-rīx or *-rios/-rius. 397/105 BECCVRI looks like a *-rīx name without i-affection of /u/, but the formation is obscure (see ‡42), as is the reading. Rhys, AC, 4th ser. 13 (1882), 163, thought the following possible: BECCVRI, BECCVBI, BECCVPI; BECLVRI, BECLVBI, BECLVPI. For an obscure BECCDINN in ogam, see Ziegler, p. 136.
[328] SBCHP, pp. 61–62. I assume LOVERNII is British rather than Irish because of the O of ANATEMORI. The name [L]OVERNIVS appears on an altar from Uley, Gloucestershire, and Lovernianus occurs on a platter from Appleford, Oxon.: Hassall & Tomlin, Britannia, 12 (1981), 370 and n. 13.
[329] See ‡14 above and ‡27 below.
[330] I leave out of account 385/89 ANATEMORI (LHEB, pp. 580 and 598) in view of Schrijver's argument that *Anatio- would not be eligible for i-affection (above, ‡18). The same would apply to 1064/Dor.iv AUPRIT, in the unlikely event that AU- is from *Awi- (see ‡57 below).
[331] LHEB, pp. 611 and 621; cf. ‡37 below; Chrest., p. 159.
[332] LHEB, pp. 598, n. 3, and 611, n. 1; BWP, pp. 35–36. Cf. 485/Ok68 COLINI (if correct reading) and 2006 COLINE. For Colinus on the Continent see Holder iii, 1255.

[19] A possible addition to these is:

3. 330/66 CATIRI, which may derive from *Caturīx* (> MW *Cedyr*, or, from the oblique-stem, *Cedri*).³³³ On the obscure dissyllable *kedyr* in the *Gododdin* line 269 (stanza B.11), Ifor Williams noted 'Prin enw priod, o *Caturix* ?', and Koch tentatively translates 'battle leader'.³³⁴ Rhys took CATIRI to be *cadr* (MW *cadyr*) 'powerful', but svarabhakti is extremely rare in the inscriptions.³³⁵ Another possibility is that CATIRI is Irish, OI *Ca(i)thri*, which strikingly has the same form in the nominative and genitive, being either indeclinable or influenced by the *jo*-stems.³³⁶

‡20 *Nasal mutation in West British; LHEB §189*

No inscriptional evidence is cited.

‡21 *Beginning of loss of final syllables; LHEB §182*

For this see below, ‡37, 'Completion of the loss of final syllables'.

‡22 *Beginning of mb > mm, nd > nn, (ng > ŋŋ ?); LHEB §112*

For the completion of these see below, ‡‡ 49 and 56.

I take the first two of these separately (there is no inscriptional evidence bearing on the third).

/mb/

[22] Jackson has no examples of preserved *mb* (p. 509). In 1030, Macalister's reading [A]MBIGATI is, one suspects, inspired by 500 AMMECATI (below) or by Livy's *Ambigatus* (for *Ambicatus*); the stone has long been illegible.³³⁷ The only other occurrence of *mb* in the Brittonic inscriptions is 1051/Ok37 CUMBUIN, and although Macalister and Okasha agree on the MB they also agree that the text is 'impossible to interpret'; Thomas reads Latin ProCUMBU*nt* IN.³³⁸

---

³³³ Macalister speculated on CATVRIGI as the original reading, and KHJ notes 'Perhaps leg. *Caturi* = *Caturix*?'. Evans lists CATIRI alongside ancient forms such as *Caturis* in GPN, pp. 172–73. Cf. Holder i, 859–61 and iii, 1162. The reading and interpretation of 415/278 TARRONERIS is too uncertain to include here as an affected form of *Tarron-o-rīx* or similar; see above, ‡14.

³³⁴ Williams, *Canu Aneirin*, p. 144; Koch, *Gododdin*, p. 39.

³³⁵ LWP, p. 385; cf. GPC, s.v. *cadr* (comparing British *Belatucadros*, although cf. LHEB, pp. 429–31). Cf. OW *Catrgueidan* (LL, p. 166) and OB *Catroc* (Loth, *Noms des saints bretons*, p. 17). Richards, *THSC*, 1965, p. 31, derives W. *Cedrig* and *Cedris* from *cadr*; but how old are these? (Cf. Searle, *Onomasticon*, p. 127: '*Cedric* mistake(?) in Scott's Ivanhoe for *Cerdic*'.) Cf. below, ‡69.

³³⁶ Uhlich, *Morphologie*, p. 190. Cf. Ó Corráin & Maguire, *Gaelic Personal Names*, p. 48.

³³⁷ Cf. *Corpus*, s. Llandrillo (Mer.). For *Ambigatus* see Holder i, 120 and iii, 588.

³³⁸ *Mute Stones*, p. 300, and *Penzance Market Cross*, p. 17. In 1951 KHJ found this panel 'moderately clear', but queried Macalister's CU- in CUMBUIN.

[22] Jackson has two examples where /mb/ > /mm/ has occurred (p. 509): 500 AMMECATI on the Isle of Man (ogam [A]MB[I]CATOS)[339] and, in a Latin word, 427/b/301 AMMULANTIBUS (contrast 2021 MEMBRA, with *mb* preserved). A possible addition is 377/175 AMICATI, if Macalister's reading is preferred to Nash-Williams's AVICAT[VS].[340] In 443/349 CAMVLORI is the more attractive reading, but if CAMVMORI is correct, the only possibility seems to be *cambo-* with /mb/ > /mm/ and a misspelt composition vowel (as in 1028/214/850 VENDVMAGLI), making an opprobrious name *Camfawr* 'great humpback'.[341]

/nd/

[22] (A) Jackson notes (p. 512) that /nd/ is preserved in:

1. 390/96 VENDESETLI
2. 328/44]RVGNIATIO [FI]LI <u>VENDONI</u> ('but this may be Irish; VENDOGNI, no. 422, certainly is', Jackson; [but see below on Latin(?) (*)*Vendonius*])
3. 454/402 EVALI FILI DENCVI (? DEN[O]VI) <u>CVNIOVENDE</u> MATER
4. 368/b/150 <u>BARRIVENDI</u> FILIVS <u>VENDVBARI</u> HIC IACIT (+ unrelated ogam)
5. 1028/214/850 VENDVMAGLI HIC IACIT

[22] Other instances of preserved ND are:
364/144 <u>QVENVENDANI</u> FILI BARCVNI
422/298 **VENDOGNI**/VENDAGNI (Macalister: [U]ENDOGNI) etc.
429/307 SOLINI FILIVS <u>VENDONI</u>
433/313 <u>[A]NDAGELLI</u> MACU CAVE[/<u>ANDAGELLI</u> IACIT FILI CAVETI
441/345 CVRCAGNI FILI <u>ANDAGELLI</u>

[22] One assumes that Jackson omitted these examples of ND because they were Irish, as he says explicitly in the case of 422/298 **VENDOGNI** (quoted above under 2). QVENVENDANI is, as he says elsewhere, 'certainly Irish', and can be compared with CIIC 2 **QENOVENDAGNI** (Gippert's reading), the ancestor of *Cennf(h)innán*;[342] the attested P-Celtic cognates are

---

[339] Cf. above, ‡17n. 496 **EBICATO[S]** (Macalister) is now read **TEBICATO[S]** (see ‡17), and no longer has to be reconciled with these forms.
[340] See above, ‡18.
[341] On 443/349 see above, ‡‡ 14 and 18. For *cambo-* see GPN, pp. 320–22. 'Great stride', from *cam(m)*, is less likely since one might expect *CAMMINO- or *CAMMANO- (cf. LEIA C-55; Lambert, *Langue gauloise*, p. 192).
[342] LHEB, pp. 140–41 and 170; LWP, p. 161; Ziegler, p. 221; Uhlich, *Morphologie*, pp. 199–200 and 290. On 364/144 KHJ noted 'I can see no ogam at all' and 'Note: Preservation of *qv*, not yet *c-*; *vind* spelt *vend*; *gn* > *n*; syncope in both names; *nn*, *rr* > *n*, *r* (ogam-spelling influence, probably)' and later added: 'Motta p. 318 wants to make it British rather than Irish, but in view of *QV-* this is unlikely.'

Πεννοουινδος and MW *Penwyn*.[343] He does not mention 429/307 VENDONI at all in LHEB, even in his discussion of the development of 'British and Latin *g* before *l*, *r*, *n*' (LHEB §84), which suggests that he categorized it as possibly Irish (like 328/44 VENDONI above); certainly one would have expected that British **ogn* would give **oen* (as in *oen* 'lamb' < Celtic **ognos*),[344] and it is most unlikely that VENDONI is the ancestor of a non-existent Welsh **Gwynnoen* with O written for OI/OE.[345] It is also hard to classify VENDONI as Irish because of its composition vowel (cf. ‡‡ 38 and 48). The names appearing with VENDONI are of no help in classifying it: in 429/307, SOLINI is of course Latin, while]RVGNIAT(I)O in 328/44 could be Welsh or Irish.[346] Conceivably there could have been an old British name/theonym **Windōnos* giving W. **Gwynnon*,[347] but if this lies behind VENDONI, the latter cannot be the same name as **VENDOGNI/** VENDAGNI. If we separate VENDONI from **VENDOGNI/**VENDAGNI (or suppose that it was used merely as a vague equivalent of it) – and it seems best to cut the Gordian knot like this – we can follow Holder in regarding VENDONI as a Latin name (*)*Vendonius*, according to him a variant of the more common *Vindonius*, in which case it may indeed go back to Celtic **Windo-*. Holder thought that *Vendonius* was actually attested on a Dalmatian inscription (AVREL. VENDONI), but VENDONI here is almost certainly the common Illyrian female cognomen *Vendo*, which is well attested in Dalmatia, where indeed more than one *Aurelia Vendo/ Aureliae Vendoni* is mentioned in extant inscriptions.[348] Despite the lack of definite support for Holder's view, it is not unreasonable to hypothesize a Latin form **Vendonius*, presumably a variant on *Vindonius*. Whether such a name would be treated in Britain as a native or a Latin name is a moot point.

---

[343] Evans, *BBCS*, 24 (1970–72), 421; RIG iv, 346 and 555; SWWF, pp. 188–89; Jones, *BBCS*, 3 (1926–27), 37; Lloyd-Jones, *BBCS*, 11 (1941–44), 119.

[344] LHEB, p. 461. Jackson does not make this an exception, unlike the doubtful development of -AGN- to W. -*an* (on which see ‡48). On the vocalism of 422/298 **VENDOGNI** see further ‡‡ 38 and 48.

[345] Cf. ogam orthography, where O can be written for OI (Ziegler, pp. 44–46), and see below, ‡48, for similar phenomena in Welsh (OW *mali* for **Maili*, etc.).

[346] See above, ‡18, and below, ‡‡ 46 and 48. On SOLINI note that Westwood, LW, p. 123, quotes Brash's comment that Solinus was a companion of Palladius, according to the *Annals of the Four Masters*, s.a. 432. His name appears as *Solonius* and well as *Solinus*; see *Four Latin Lives of St. Patrick*, ed. Bieler, pp. 10 and 77, and later sources cited by O'Hanlon, *Lives of the Irish Saints*, vii, 73–74, and viii, 294–95; Loth, *Noms des saints bretons*, p. 114.

[347] Rhys, *AC*, 4th ser. 4 (1873), 77, and LWP, p. 381, equated VENDONI with OW *Guennon-oe*, *Guinnon-ui* (LL, p. 402) and MW *Gwenon-wy* (f.) (Lloyd-Jones, *Geirfa*, p. 663), and it has also been equated with Gaulish *Vindona* (LW, p. 123; cf. GPN, p. 387, n. 4).

[348] Holder iii, 157 and 349, citing CIL iii 8321 (cf. 6352); on *Vend-* ~ *Vind-* see below and ‡‡ 15 and 27. On Illyrian *Ven(n)do* see Alföldy, *Personennamen*, p. 323; OPEL iv, 153; Anon., *AE*, 1979, 136–37, nos 455–456 (*Aureliae Vendoni*); Anon., *AE*, 1986, 199, no. 549 (*Aurelia Vendo*).

[22] The remaining omitted names are the two instances of ANDAGELLI. This is probably a preform of OI *Indgall*.[349] The ANDAGELLI of 433/313 is son of CAVETI, which Jackson identifies as Irish *Cawethi* 'with the *th* rendered T in the Latin',[350] and his presumed brother in the same church-yard, COIMAGNI FILI CAVETI in 434/314, bears the definitely Irish name *Cóemán*.[351] The ANDAGELLI of 441/345 is father of CVRCAGNI, a name not discussed in LHEB, presumably because it was clearly Irish (cf. 195 **CURCI**, Ir. *Corcc*).[352]

[22] Thus, the only name with /nd/ that might possibly be added to Jackson's Brittonic list of five is the further VENDONI of 429/307, and even this is highly uncertain. What is striking is that all six inscriptions contain the element VEND-, presumably from **windo-* 'white'. This raises a phonological problem. In Welsh, lowering of /i/ to /e/ occurred in the feminine (> *gwen*), which may explain CVNIOVENDE MATER,[353] whereas the /i/ of **windo-* developed to /ï/ (> *gwyn*). There are sporadic examples of Welsh /ï(:)/ being spelt E,[354] but it is strange that VEND- is *always* written with E. It seems rather unlikely that every example of VEND- is an instance of Vulgar Latin confusion of *e* and *i* or of Celtic confusion of /e/ and /i/ before nasal + stop (comparable with the fourth-century CVNOVENDI at Binchester).[355] Irish influence may provide a better explanation. At first sight any equation of VEND- with OI *find* (m.f.) is ruled out by the standard doctrine that, whereas /e/ could be raised before /nd/ (e.g. *rind* 'star' < **rendu-*), the 'only exception' to lowering 'is *i* before *nd*, which always remains; e.g. *find* "fair", < **windos* **windā*'.[356] However, Ziegler, noting that there is no ogam example of **VIND-** (since **VLATIAMI** is

---

[349] CGH, p. 666 (var. *Fin(d)gall!*). Rhys, *AC*, 5th ser. 10 (1893), 287, compared *Ingel* in the Book of Leinster, 40e, but *Ingell* in the Facsimile was an error for *In Goll*, according to Best et al. (ed.), *Book of Leinster*, i, 190, n. 18. (The name *Ingcél* mentioned by Rhys is distinct (cf. CGH. p. 667), and is derived from OE *Ingeld* by Henry, *Lyric*, pp. 220–21, but from *cél* 'omen' by Charles-Edwards, *Celtica*, 23 (1999), 53, n. 94.) ANDAGELLI has been regarded as British or British influenced (cf. Ziegler, p. 128; Uhlich, *Morphologie*, pp. 162–63); however, the ANDA- is no barrier to its being Irish in view of TRC, p. 78. KHJ regarded [A]NDAGELLI in 433/313 as 'evidently Irish'.

[350] LHEB, p. 181; similarly Ziegler, p. 148 (= *cauuth* 'Wildente').

[351] Lloyd, *History of Wales*, i, 114; Ziegler, p. 152. KHJ: 'no doubt an Irish person, see 433'. W. *Cwyfan* is a borrowing from Ir. *Cóemán*; see ‡48.

[352] Ziegler, p. 162 (but see further below, ‡48). Jackson did not accept Lloyd's view that the two ANDAGELLI are the same person: '441 cannot belong to a son of 433, as it is epigraphically at least fifty years older' (review of CIIC i, in *Speculum*, 21 (1946), 523).

[353] See above, ‡15.

[354] See below, ‡34. (The confusion of *e* and *i* in Cornish and Breton (HPB, pp. 91–93) can be left aside here as our VEND- inscriptions are all in Wales.)

[355] See above, ‡15 and below, ‡27. Another Romano-British instance is COVENTINA/ COVINTINA (LHEB, p. 278). According to Jackson, IE /e/ had become /i/ before nasal + stop, but see Binchy's review, *Celtica*, 4 (1958), 291; Schrijver, *Ériu*, 42 (1991), 19–20; and TRC, p. 55.

[356] GOI, pp. 46–47; TRC, pp. 55 and 110; Schrijver, SBCHP, p. 29, and *Ériu*, 42 (1991), 21.

preferable to **VINDIAMI in CIIC 185),[357] rightly pointed out that *windo- may indeed have been subject to Irish lowering, as also in 2 QENUVEN[(or, according to Gippert, QENOVENDAGNI),[358] and that *wend may later have been subject to raising in auslaut to give OI find (m.f.).[359] This suggestion seems not to have been disproved, or even discussed in fact.

[22] On the basis of their consistent spelling with E, VENDOGNI /VENDAGNI (and possibly VENDONI) may be Irish, and so may VENDVMAGLI (no. 5 above), although both elements of *Windomaglos can be British or Irish. The two elements of BARRIVENDI and VENDV-BARI (no. 4) also occur in names in both branches, but it is significant that the combinations Bairrfhind and Finnbarr are both known Irish names (only Berwyn occurs in Welsh), and that the stone also bears an (unrelated) ogam inscription.[360] The naming pattern of father and son in BARRIVENDI FILIVS VENDVBARI is best paralleled (within Insular Celtic inscriptions) by the Irish names in 378/169 BIVADI FILI (or AVI) BODIBEVE and 428/305 TRENEGUSSI FILI MACUTRENI.[361] The name CVNIO-VENDE is not distinctively British or Irish; the composition with jod is unexpected in a *kuno- ('hound') name, but is paralleled both in Ireland by 289 CUNIA and 286 CUNEA and in Wales by 2029/p.39i

---

[357] KHJ compares GPN, p. 270, and suggests a superlative *Vlati-samos, rejecting the classification as n-stem by O'Brien, Celtica 10 (1973), 225.

[358] Gippert, in Britain 400–600, pp. 303–4, and apud Ziegler, pp. 221 and 253. Macalister (who notes that the second E 'is faint') quotes MacNeill, JRSIA, 39 (1909), 134, for the suggestion QENUVENDI, but MacNeill actually hesitated between 'Qenuvin . . .' and 'Qenuven . . .' and between restoring [di] = Ceannan or 'more probably' [dagni] = Ceanannán. As KHJ notes, MacNeill suggests Qenuvin[dagni] = Cennfindán in PRIA, 27 C (1909), 347.

[359] Ziegler, p. 119. Note OI ind etc. as forms of the article from *sindos, etc. (cf. Schrijver, Studies in the History of Celtic Pronouns and Particles, p. 44).

[360] See Evans, BBCS, 24 (1970–72), 421 for W. Berwyn/Barwyn, but no parallel to Finnbarr. Hughes, Ériu, 44 (1993), 98, writes an asterisk before *Gwynfar, and Rhys, LWP, p. 388, says 'I am not aware that it occurs' – although he is less candid in Englyn, p. 22, and in Welsh People, p. 74. (Any connection with Gwynfor is doubtful.) On Berwyn see also Olson & Padel, CMCS, 12 (1986), 56–57. For Bairrfhind and Finnbarr see most recently Charles-Edwards and Ó Riain, in Mac Cana FS, pp. 18–19, and 189–93. Charles-Edwards takes 368/b/150 VENDVBARI to be British (following Jackson?), and Ó Riain seems to concede this (p. 193, n. 33), but neither gives any justification. Thomas, Mute Stones, pp. 99 and 110, n. 30, favours Irish, while Uhlich, Morphologie, p. 251, lists it as British. For *barro- in ogam inscriptions, see Ziegler, pp. 99–100 (and note also 364/144 BARCVNI, father of the QVENVENDANI discussed above). Brittonic examples are 324/34 CO[N]BARRVS (possibly Irish) with Romano-British parallel CVNOBARRVS (CIL vii 1267 = RIB ii [fasc. 2] 2416.4) incorrectly cited by Nash-Williams (see ‡38n below), 520/Scot.5 BARROVADI, and p. 397/285 BARRECTI. For Barrus etc., on the Continent see OPEL i, 271–72.

[361] Cf. McManus, Guide, p. 113; BWP, p. 24; Evans, BBCS, 24 (1970–72), 421, citing Birkhan, Germanen und Kelten, p. 65 and n. 55, where Finnbarr: Barfind is cited as an example of inversion rather than a patronymic system; SWWF, p. 178. See also Uhlich, Morphologie, pp. 81 and 102. Zimmer, JIES, 27 (1999), 116, notes that BARRIVENDI 'is not simply "head-white", but clearly "white-haired", (probably = "old")'. Cf. MW Penwyn, etc., mentioned above.

CVNIIAC.[362] CVNIOVENDE is connected in the inscription with EVALI FILI DENCVI (or DEN[O]VI ?), which is most easily explained as Latin *Aevalis*, but possibly with an Irish patronymic.[363] Finally, this leaves 390/96 VENDESETLI, which is probably British on account of the un-Irish monophthongization of the second element (**saitlo-* > **sēdl* > W. *hoedl*), and is indeed the same name as that of St Gwyn(h)oedl, who had a cult in the vicinity.[364] While VENDESETLI is certainly not Irish, one may wonder whether the spelling of the first element with an E is not Irish-influenced, and if so whether the ND may not be Irish-influenced as well. All this is of course very uncertain.

On balance, I would only add the following (provisionally) to Jackson's list:

6.   429/307 VENDONI.

[22] (B) Jackson notes (p. 512) that /nn/ < /nd/ has occurred in:

1.   376/174 <u>VENNISETLI</u> FILIVS ERCAGNI
2.   400/177 <u>VINNEMAGLI</u> FILI SENEMAGLI
3.   970/13 CATAMANUS[365]

[22] The first of these is clearly British on account of the -SETLI (see above), even apart from the NN. On the other hand, the name of his father, ERCAGNI, is very probably Irish,[366] and this may explain the use of E in VENN- (although E for /ĭ/ and Vulgar Latin or Celtic confusion of /e/ and /i/ are also possibilities, as we have seen). VINNEMAGLI (cf. OB *Uuinmael* below), on account of its I and its NN, seems to be purely British (and SENEMAGLI *could* be), while CATAMANUS (< **Katumandwos*) is the well-known Welsh king Cadfan.[367]

4.   355/128/8 SILBANDVS is tentatively explained by Jackson as hyper-correction for VL *Silbanus* (= *Silvānus*), after British /nd/ > /nn/.[368] It is conceivable, however, that SILBANDVS is an Irish inscription, and reflects

---

[362] Discussed in ‡18. Rhys, *LWP*, p. 397, compared 394/103 CANTIORI versus Gaulish *Cantorix* (cf. Lambert, *ÉC*, 31 (1995), 118–21). On CVNIO- cf. Birkhan, *Germanen und Kelten*, pp. 348, 365 and 378, n. 943.

[363] See above, ‡18.

[364] *LHEB*, pp. 159, n. 2, 325 and n. 2. Note, however, that Irish *aí/áe* could sometimes be spelt E in Wales according to medieval Latin conventions, e.g. 368/a/150 **DUMELEDONAS**.

[365] The CONVMANI read only by Macalister on 356/132/9 is 'purest fantasy' apart from the C- (KHJ).

[366] On -AGNI names in general and ERCAGNI in particular, see ‡48.

[367] *BWP*, pp. 11–12 and 18–19; *GPN*, p. 223.

[368] *LHEB*, p. 364, n. 1. Cf. Zimmer, *JCL*, 3 (1994), 160. See ‡18 above. According to Macalister, *TCASFC*, 15 (1922), 30, and Thomas, *Mute Stones*, p. 106, it is no coincidence that the stone is at *Silian* (*Sillen*/*Llandasylan* on Rees's map *South Wales and the Border*). The patron is given as Silian by Wade-Evans, *Cymmrodor*, 22 (1910), 61. The preserved S- suggests a Latin or Irish origin. Note that *Silas* (*Sila*) in Acts was identified with *Silvanus* in the Epistles: Wilson, *Means of Naming*, p. 58; Orme, *Saints of Cornwall*, p. 235, and *Dedications*, p. 97.

Middle Irish confusion of *nd* and *nn* and Old Irish gemination of /n/ as, for instance, in *cucann/cucand* < *coquīna* and *persann/persand* < *persōna*. Moreover, although the spelling SILB- may be Vulgar Latin as Jackson suggests, another possibility is that it is an example of the Irish use of *b* for /v/.[369] SILBANDVS could be a translation of Irish *Fidbothach*.[370] Finally, Rhys read BANDVS and W. Gwyn Thomas read FILI BANDVS (nominative for genitive!) and if this were correct (Dr Nancy Edwards rejects it), the name could perhaps be MW *bann* 'noisy, tuneful' < **band-* < **bhn̥d-* with /nd/ preserved – it could not be Irish, as the cognate *Bind* 'melodious' (attested as a feminine name in the *Acallam*) has the wrong vowel.[371]

[22] To these I would add:

5. 1004/260/884 GELUGUIN is presumably a name in OW *-guin* < **-windos* like *Berthguin* (Berthwyn).[372]

6. 2022/253/984 GVLGVEN (Nash-Williams: COVLGVEN)[373] is again likely be a **-windos* name, and is indeed compared by the Royal Commission with GELUGUIN above. The first element may be W. *gwelw* 'pale', dissimilated to **gelw-* in GELUGUIN but assimilated to **gwlw-* in GVLGVEN (although the V may be merely orthographic, as arguably in OW *gundy* for *gwyndy* and *Gunliu* for *Gwynllyw*). Compare OB *Gulugan*, which Loth equated with W. *Gwelwgan*, and a Welsh *Griffinus Welgogh* (= *Gwelwgoch* 'pale-red') in 1284.[374]

7. 3007/C2 VORMVINI is probably to be segmented VORM-VINI (: W. *gwrm* + *gwyn*) rather than VOR-MVINI (: W. *gor-* + *mwyn*, OB *moin*),

---

[369] GOI, pp. 93 (*nd* < *nn* hypercorrection) and 22 and 573 (*b* for /v/); Stüber, *Historical Morphology*, pp. 39 and 43 (/n/ > /nn/ > *nd*). B for /v/ is rare in the Welsh inscriptions, but Charles-Edwards, in *The Celtic World*, p. 719, notes PREPARAUIT (cf. 1012/223/993) spelt PROPE[RA]BIT (?) and PROPARABIT in 1011/220/991 and 1015/233/910. Rhys, *AC*, 5th ser. 16 (1899), 143, compares the confusion of *prae-* and *pro-* here with MI *procept* < *praeceptum* (see VKG i, 213; DIL s.v. *precept*). Cf. 1020/200/921 [P]ROPARARET.

[370] For which see Uhlich, *Morphologie*, p. 249.

[371] LWP, p. 379; Thomas, in *Cardiganshire County History*, i, 414; GPC i, 253b; Schrijver, *Ériu*, 42 (1991), 15; Meyer, *Contributions*, p. 217. Note also the mysterious 'Bende' in the Campbell genealogy discussed by Gillies, *Celtica*, 23 (1999), 88–89 and 94. Rhys, *PBA*, 1905–6, p. 305, mistakenly found a precursor of Ir. *bind* in Gaulish **Binnamos*; see GPN, pp. 310–11, and RIG i, 90. For a possible *Bandius* see Holder iii, 798.

[372] LL, p. 388. Note, however, 1035/303 ETG(uin) i.e. English *Edwin* (if the correct reading; for the name *Etguin* = *Edwin* in Wales, see Sims-Williams, *BBCS*, 38 (1991), 79, n. 3). I leave out Macalister's restoration CERID[WEN] in 1030 (see ‡84 below).

[373] For an etymology of COVL- see ‡80 below.

[374] LL, pp. 120 (*gundy*, cf. DP iv, 426–27) and 252 (*guinnic* ~ *gunnic*); VSB, p. 330 (*Gunliu* etc.); Chrest., p. 134; Jones, *BBCS*, 3 (1926–27), 34. Cf. OB *gudbut*: W. *gwybod* (DGVB i, 184). Further examples of *Gun-* (treated as phonetic and compared with Mod.W. *Gwnnws* < **Windo-gustus*) are given by Rhys, *Cymmrodor*, 21 (1908), 13–14. Note *carn gunstan* in LL, p. 124, perhaps OE *Wynstan* (von Feilitzen, *Pre-Conquest Personal Names*, p. 429).

although the spelling *ui* occasionally occurs in Old Breton, though not in the word *moin*.[375]

8. 3005/F5 VENOMAILI has been plausibly equated with OB *Uuinmael*, *Uuenmael* < *Windomaglos.[376]

9. 3010/M1 HERANNU<u>EN</u>, whether from *Isarnowinda or *-*windos*.[377] In the same inscription RAN HUBRIT is thought to contain the place name element *rann*, which will have /nn/ < /nd/ too, if correctly compared with Gaulish *randa*; however, many scholars prefer an etymology *rasnā.[378] Conceivably the same element appears in 458/Ok9 RANOCORI, but this formation is obscure, and there is an alternative reading NANOCORI.[379]

10. 2021 GVI<u>NN</u>DA < **Windodag-* or **Windotam-* has /nn/ < /nd/.[380]

11. 1048/Ok32, variously read as GVENNCREST (Macalister), VENNORCIT (Thomas),[381] GVENNORCIT (Tedeschi),[382] or [-]NN[AR]L[. .] (Okasha), may contain the 'white' element as well.

[22] Further possible examples of /nd/ > /nn/ are:

12. 398/106 IACONVS FILIVS(?) MINI. Although the A is puzzling, the first name is perhaps *Iucundus* (> Late Latin *Iocundus*, cf. 389/97 IOVE-NALI for *Iuvenalis*) which is common in the inscriptions of Roman Britain.[383] On the other hand, it could be from **i̯akk-* (: W. *iach*, 'healthy':

---

[375] HPB, pp. 189 and 207; DGVB i, 258. The segmentation VORM-VINI is also preferred in IEMB, pp. 84–86 and 151.

[376] See IEMB, p. 135. Note also, however, GPN, pp. 277–79, for VENI-, and MacNeill, *PRIA*, 39 C (1931), 44, and Ziegler, p. 245, for ogam VENNA- in 223 VENNAMMILEA(?) > OI *Fíanamail*.

[377] See above, ‡15.

[378] LEIA R-7; DGVB i, 293; SBCHP, pp. 177 and 456; TRC, pp. 46 and 53; Lambert, *Langue gauloise*, p. 37.

[379] On RANOCORI see ‡‡ 14 and 38. NANOCORI (preferred by Jackson, *Speculum*, 21 (1946), 523) could be compared with Gaulish **Nantu-*, **Nanto-* (W. *nant* 'valley' or OI *néit* 'battle'?, GPN, p. 236; LEIA N-7), maybe *Nantāko-rīx (cf. *Nantiorix* and *Nantiacus > Nancy, Holder ii, 684 and GPN, p. 236), but /nt/ > /nh/ is unexpected in Cornwall, as noted above, ‡18, in connection with RUNHOL. Perhaps the T is suppressed epigraphically, as arguably in 356/132/9 POTEN(t)INA (see above, ‡15, and cf. ‡68 below). For *Nano-* in names, however, see ‡14n.

[380] See above, ‡15, and ‡67 below.

[381] *Mute Stones*, p. 290.

[382] Tedeschi, *Scrittura e civiltà*, 19 (1995), tav. 3. The G- seems to me to be present; at any rate it is not evidently wrong.

[383] MINI could be a masculine equivalent of gen. MINNE (RIB i 694, which Smith, VLRB, p. 918, equates with *Mina* on a fourth-century graffito from Shakenoak Farm villa, Oxfordshire, compared in turn by Wright & Hassall, *Britannia*, 2 (1971), 301, with *Mina* ('Mine fidenti') in Mauretania in *Inscriptiones Latinae Christianae Veteres*, ed. Diehl, i, no. 1598A, compared ibid., iii, 113, with *Menna* (no. 3856, Rome) and *Minna*, gen. *Minne* (no. 2069, Africa). Alternatively, MINI could be gen. of Celtic(?)-Latin *Min(n)(i)us* (see Tab.Sulis, p. 113, n. 7, and Hassall & Tomlin, *Britannia*, 24 (1993), 319, n. 36, and 26 (1995), 376, n. 11, and 379, n. 13). Cf. also British *Adminio* (GPN, p. 130), MW *Mynogan*, ogam 135 MINNACCANNI, etc. (Ziegler, p. 207; TYP, p. 282), and the Irish element *Min*-noted by McManus, *Guide*, p. 178, n. 25, Ziegler, p. 206, and Uhlich, *Ériu*, 40 (1989), 132, n. 11. Cf. below, Ch. 4, §19. For Celtic and non-Celtic names in *Min*- see also Rhys, *AC*, 6th

OI *icc*)[384] with *-on-os* suffix. The best comparison, however, is Rhys's with 48 **IAQINI**, which is now regarded as a hypercorrect spelling (with **Q** for **C**) of a derivative of OI *éo*, gen. *iach* 'salmon' < *esok-*.[385] This fits in with the presence on the stone of 'possible vestiges of ogam' (Nash-Williams).

13. 475/Ok47 IACONIVS would be the same, if genuine, but Thomas and others reject the reading emphatically.[386]

14. 448/370 RINACI and:

15. 489/a/Ok13 RINI if derived from *rind-* 'point' as in OB *gabl rinn*, OI *gabul rind* 'compass, circle';[387] compare the Irish names *Rind* and *Rindach*.[388] On the other hand, there is a series of Old Breton names in *Rin-* (*Rinan*, *Rinuiu*, etc.) and these always have single *n*, which favours Loth's comparison with W. *rhin* 'secret' rather than Fleuriot's with OI *rind*.[389] Note moreover 34 **MUCCOI RINI** > OI *Mocu-Rin* (?), with single **N**; this cannot be cognate with *rhin* (: OI *rún*) but could be related to the Breton names in *Rin-*.[390]

[22] To sum up, NN (and N) < /nd/ is well attested in the inscriptions. By contrast, the only plausible examples of ND appear in names with the element VEND-, all of which are under some suspicion either of being Irish or at least (as in the case of VENDESETLI) of having been influenced by Irish spelling conventions where ND was the norm in this element. It is therefore difficult to use ND versus N(N) as a criterion for arranging the inscriptions chronologically. If ND turns out to cluster in the earlier inscriptions, this may simply be because Irish influence predominated in the earlier period, rather than confirming that ND reflects the /nd/ stage in British.

---

ser. 7 (1907), 95–96, and *PBA*, 6 (1913–14), 39, 93 and 344–45; Holder ii and Oswald, s.nn.; OPEL iii, 82. On IOVENALI see below, ‡80. Cf. *Iocundinus/Iucundinus* in Fleuriot, *Origines de la Bretagne*, p. 146.

[384] Cf. Lambert, *ZCP*, 37 (1979), 210. Rhys, *AC*, 6th ser. 7 (1907), 95, also aired comparisons with W. *iach* and with *Iacobus* (> W. *Iago*).

[385] Ziegler, p. 186. Cf. Gallo-Latin *Exocius*, Holder i, 1489; Schrijver, in Beekes FS, p. 298, n. 12.

[386] *Mute Stones*, p. 282; he reads ADO . . . FILI *on the other face*. KHJ was also 'very suspicious' of Macalister's reading and thought it improbable 'from point of view of arrangement of letters' (1968). He notes that Macalister, *AC*, 84 (1929), 182, had compared his IACONIUS with 398/106 IACONVS.

[387] DGVB i, 173 and 297; ii, 547; LEIA R-32; GPC s.v. *rhyn*.

[388] CGH, p. 724; *Táin Bó Cúailnge: Recension I*, ed. O'Rahilly, line 2325 (noted by Rhys, *AC*, 5th ser. 13 (1896), 107, along with Mod.Ir. *rionnach* 'kind of fish' (*rinnach*, DIL), in his discussion of RINACI, on which see above, ‡18n.).

[389] Chrest., p. 160; DGVB i, 297.

[390] Thomas, *Mute Stones*, p. 268, compared 489/a/Ok13 RINI with 34 **RINI**. The latter has rather dubiously been equated with OI *renn* 'quick', in turn compared with W. *rhyn(n)*: Ziegler, p. 225; LEIA R-20. The name *mocu rin* occurs in MS A of Adomnán's *Life of Columba*, I.20 (ed. Anderson & Anderson, p. 46: *gente mo | curin*), but editors have always preferred MS B's *mocucurin*, Reeves citing *Uí Cuirin* from *Annals of the Four Masters*, s.a. 1196; cf. *Cuirenrige* (CGH, p. 461; Hogan, *Onomasticon*, p. 316).

[22] For the sake of completeness, I mention some other forms with ND and NN which can be eliminated from the discussion.

[22] We can ignore 320/26 SECVNDI as being Latin, and 456/404 **GEN-DILI**/GE[ ] which is probably Latin *Gentilius* (or *Gentilis*) with Ir. /nd/ substituted for /nt/.[391] 325/33 is generally read . . . PAVLINI ANDOCO GNA[TION]E, with ANDOCO taken to refer to the Andecavi, the tribe (*natio*) that gave its name to Angers and Anjou, but L. Olson's reading AVDO (or ANDO) COGNATIONE is preferable.[392] One can compare some of the Gaulish names (or pet names?) such as *Andius*, *Andos*, and *Ando* and *Audio* and *Audo* cited by Evans under *ande-* and *aud-*,[393] but it is impossible to choose. Similar problems arise in the case of 491/Ok55 AVDETI or ANDETI.[394] 2021 GVIN<u>ND</u>A and 1068/b CON-DILICI have /n'd/ or /n'ð/ by syncope and are therefore irrelevant to original /nd/.[395]

[22] A number of forms with NN do not have etymological /nd/, and may indeed have original /n/, as for example do 329/42 CANNTIANI, 3010 /M1 HERANNUEN < *Isarno-*, and 1067 INNSVLI (Latin). 331/41 [A]NNICCI and 465/Ok21 ANNICV are presumably Latin *Annic(i)us*,[396] and 1014/231/908 ENNIAUN is from *Annianus*,[397] a form of which (without *i*) may underlie 1000/182 ANNAN.[398] In 342/70 **CUNACENNI**/CVNOCENNI and 1000/182 CONCENN the second element corresponds to Gaulish *cen(n)-*,[399] while the first element of 3026/I7 GENNOVEUS corresponds to Gaulish *gen(n)-*.[400] 994/125/22 CAROTINN can perhaps be compared with Gaulish *Caratinus*,[401] or perhaps with 403/268/841

---

[391] See ‡17n. But see also ‡68.

[392] Apud Wooding, *Communication and Commerce*, p. 62, and Handley, *EME*, 10 (2001), 194. Cf. RIG iv, 77–78. The '*Andoco* . . . for *Andecavo*' explanation began with Radford, apud Ifor Williams in RCAHMW, *Anglesey*, p. cxiii. Note, however, ANDOC(O) as a personal name on early British coinage and on a graffito at Verulamium (Hassall & Tomlin, *Britannia*, 19 (1988), 501 and n. 66; RIB ii [fasc 8] 2503.138; PRB, p. 122) and *Andoca* in Holder i, 149, and iii, 618.

[393] GPN, pp. 139 and 147. Howlett, *Cambro-Latin Compositions*, p. 27, favours *Audus*.

[394] Thomas, *Mute Stones*, pp. 281 and 301, n. 20, suggests *Auden(t)ius*, comparing RIB i 653 AVDES for AVDENS, 'the loss of -*n* in -*nt*, -*ns* being fairly common'.

[395] On these see above, ‡‡ 15 and 16.

[396] Attested in RIB i 233 and 1618 (with one *n*), and compare Gaulish ANNICCOIOS (RIG iv, no. 29 and p. 530). Cf. Thomas, *Mute Stones*, p. 265. Cf. *An(n)ic(c)(i)us, Annicco(n)* (f.), *Annios, Annius*, in Holder i, 157, and iii, 629–30; Mócsy, pp. 19–20; OPEL i, 118–21; and Weisgerber, *Rhenania*, p. 141, n. 171.

[397] Cf. LHEB, p. 606. Note *Annia[n]o* in Tab.Sulis, no. 98. Lloyd-Jones, *Y Geninen*, 44 (1926), 6, derived *Einiawn < Enniawn < Ann-iawn*.

[398] See above, ‡18, on this name.

[399] See GPN, p. 175, and above, ‡17n.

[400] See commentary for further comparison with OB *Gennai* and 469/Ok34 GENAIVS (or]ENAIVS).

[401] Both are cited in GPN, pp. 164–65; note also *Caraðilonu* (RIG ii/1, 193; Stüber, *Historical Morphology*, p. 108).

CARITINI (Macalister's reading),[402] while 443/349 BRANN[can probably be compared with 468/Ok31 RIALOBRANI, Gaulish BRANOS,[403] W. *Brân*, and the many ogam names in **BRAN**- (always with single N),[404] also 493/Ok58 NEPRANI (‡42). We have already compared 455/403 FANNVCI with Latin *Fannus* and W. *chwant*[405] and noted that 461/Ok66 NONNITA has original /nn/.[406] Finally, 488/Ok60 DOBVNNI has been compared with the Romano-British tribal name *Dobunni* (around Cirencester).[407] On 401/183 CANNE has been read instead of CAVNE, but is uncertain and obscure.[408] If CANNE is correct, a possible comparison is 135 **MINNACCANNI** or **ANNACANNI**, with NN, not ND.[409]

‡*23 ē̆ (< ai [see ‡4]) already > ē̆ⁱ; LHEB §27.3*

There is no inscriptional evidence of course. For the subsequent development see ‡59 below.

‡*24 ē (< ei) already > ēⁱ; LHEB §28.3 [Note I write ē instead of Jackson's ẹ̄]*

There is no inscriptional evidence of course. For the subsequent development see ‡58 below.

‡*25 γ > u̯ in certain circumstances [mostly before /u/]; LHEB §75.8 [Note that I write γ instead of Jackson's ȝ.]*

[25] (A)

1.   A possible example where this change is not yet shown is 3016/M7 LAGU, assuming this is cognate with OB *lau* 'small, mediocre' < *laγu̯os*,[410]

---

[402] The alternative reading 403/268/841 MACARITINI either has hypocoristic MA- (see below, n. 1144, or can be compared (as by KHJ) with 230 **MAQI-CARATTINN** = *Macc Cáerthainn*; McManus, *Guide*, p. 121, and Ziegler, p. 144, equate 230 with 40 **MAQI-CAIRATINI**, i.e. OI *Cáerthann, Cairthenn : cáerthann*, related in some way to W. *cerddin* 'mountain-ash trees' (LEIA C-8; Meid, *Romanze*, pp. 178–79; De Bernardo Stempel, *Sonanten*, pp. 91–92, and NWÄI, pp. 326–27; Coates & Breeze, *Celtic Voices*, pp. 221–22; SWWF, p. 523, n. 26). In the latter case, the name on 403/268/841 would be Irish, as noted by KHJ. For another explanation see ‡57.

[403] RIG iv, no. 334 and p. 532.

[404] Ziegler, p. 100; also Hughes, *CMCS*, 22 (1991), 95–99, and *Ériu*, 44 (1993), 95–98. O'Brien, *Celtica*, 10 (1973), 231, lists *Bran, Brénain(n)*, etc. as 'borrowed names'; cf. Ó Cuív, *Celtica*, 18 (1986), 162–63; Uhlich, *ZCP*, 49/50 (1997), 878–88. 1068/b MALBREN SCRIBA probably belongs here i.e. *Máel Brénaind* (CGH, p. 685; cf. CIIC 540 and 613 MAEL BRENDAIN).

[405] Above, ‡18.

[406] Above, ‡15n.

[407] PNRB, p. 339. Cf. RIB i 621 DOBUNNA 'tribeswoman of the Dobunni'.

[408] See above, ‡18n. There is cleric *Canna* in LL, p. 174 (and cf. ‡36n. on *Tref Canus*). *Canus/Cana* was a Roman cognomen: Kajanto, p. 223.

[409] See also above, ‡17n. However, Ziegler, p. 207, compares *Mincháin* and *Uí Minneccáin*, with a segmentation MINNACC-A-(G)NI, which would rule out comparison with CANNE.

[410] See IEMB, p. 234, and LHEB, p. 440; HPB, p. 256; DGVB i, 237; SBCHP, p. 305. DLG, pp. 164–65 and 176, compares Late Gaulish *lau* 'bad thing' with the personal names

and that a final -S (or -US) has, as often, been lost.[411] It is less likely that GU is comparable to the occasional OW use of -*gu* for post-consonantal /w/, as in *Bodgu* and *Pobdelgu*, since this is not attested in Old Breton.[412] I would compare the Breton LAGU with:

2.   1068/a **LAGUBERI**, an ogam on Man (on the same stone as the Brittonic 1068/b CONDILICI). This *may* be W. *llaw* 'small' + *byr* 'short' – alternatively *Llawfer* or *Llawfyr* 'short arm' or 'short as to his arm' with **GU** for /w/ (< /μ/ in **lāmā*, as in Old Welsh, ‡61).

[25]   As to other examples of GU, 1045/Ok69 AGURED or ÆGVRED etc. is quite obscure,[413] and 407/a/258/846 AVGVS(*to*) is of course Latin, and in any case lies outside the Brittonic corpus proper.

[25]   (B) Jackson's two examples where the change has happened (pp. 440 and 444) are:

1.   408/229/848 VEDOMAVI (Jackson rejects Macalister's VEDOMALI)
2.   365/149 MAVOHE[NI] (MAVOHENI Lhuyd)

Further examples of the same element, **magu-*,[414] appear in:

3.   516/Scot.1 MAVORIVS; cf. Gaulish *Magurix*[415]
4.   1000/182 MAUN (OW *Maun*, MW *Mawn, Mawan*); cf. Gaulish and Romano-British names in *Magun-* and ogam 272 **MAGUNO**.[416] See also 8 below from the same inscription.

5.   1205/Ok44 MAVOUIH (less likely MAVORIH) < **Maguviks*[417]
6.   3002/F2 GALLMAU[418]

Laguaudus (Bordeaux and Autun) and *Lagussa* (Luxeuil), Holder ii, 122; note also *Lagius* in Spain (OPEL iii, 17). Awareness of the etymological **g* may have been kept alive by the superlative OB *laham* 'least', if < earlier **laγ'haμ* (cf. HPB, p. 236, n. 5; SBCHP, p. 305). There is a cognate LAGU- in ogam names, as in the Manx inscription 1068/a **LAGUBERI**(?) below, which *may* be Irish (see Ziegler, pp. 191–92), but an Irish name is not so likely as a Brittonic one in Brittany. LAGU is unlikely to be **Lugus*; *Lagubalium* in the Ravenna Cosmography is probably a scribal error (PNRB, p. 402).

[411] -*o* for -*us* commonly occurs in Late Latin inscriptions: LHEB, p. 192, n. 2; Handley, *EME*, 10 (2001), 194, n. 128. Note, however, the suggestion in IEMB, p. 234, that LAGU is short for a name with medial /w/ like *Laouic*. If this is correct, 3016/M7 cannot be placed under (A).

[412] LHEB, p. 387. Jackson cites no OB examples of -*gu* in LHEB, pp. 388–89, and both he, HPB, p. 466, and Fleuriot, Gramm., p. 93 n., say that it does not occur.

[413] Cf. OE names in *Æg-* and -*red* in Searle, *Onomasticon?*

[414] GPN, pp. 221–22; RIG iv, 539; LHEB, p. 440; HPB, pp. 256–57; GPC, s.v. *meudwy*.

[415] GPN, pp. 100 and 222; RIG i, 158 and iv 554; see above, ‡14.

[416] EWGT, p. 203; EANC, pp. 75–76; GPN, p. 222; OPEL iii, 47; RIB i 2099 and note on *Magunna*; cf. Ziegler, p. 202 (**MAGUNO GATI = MAGU NOGATI**); MacNeill, *PRIA*, 27 C (1909), 363, and *PRIA*, 39 C (1931), 40, n. 9: St Patrick is sometimes called *Magon(i)us* (e.g. *Four Latin Lives of St. Patrick*, ed. Bieler, p. 63) – a name attested in Italy and Spain (OPEL iii, 47) – and this corresponds to *Maun* in the Patrician section of *Historia Brittonum*, §51.

[417] See above, ‡14.

[418] See IEMB, p. 118.

7. 486/Ok56 MAVCI, if a compound of C. *maw* < *magu- and *ci* 'hound'[419]

[25] Further occurrences of the sound change are seen in:

8. 1000/182 POUOIS (*Powys* < *pagenses*).[420] See also 4 above from the same inscription.

9. 978/49 BRIAMAIL FLOU, if = F[ILIVS?] LOU < *Lugus (or an abbreviation for a name like *Loumarch* (*Llywarch*) < *Lugumarkos or *Loubran* < *Lugubranos).[421]

[25] There seem to be no other likely examples. 464/Ok65 MAVISIR recalls Gaulish forms in *Magus*- such as *Magusius*,[422] but can hardly have developed from **Magusorīx in view of the survival of the /s/. *Magesturīx > W. *Meisyr* (compare MW *mäes* < *magest- 'plain')[423] is a more hopeful parallel for MAVISIR, which would then belong in ‡74 below, and would presumably have a glide -V- as a hiatus filler (/w/?) instead of the -*i*- seen in OW *Lann Maies*.[424] At a mere guess, 401/183 CAVNE could presumably come from *Kagunā or *Kagonā from the stem *kag- 'fence?, clasp?' seen in ogam CAGI, Gaulish *Cagius*.[425] This is very doubtful, however, as forms in *Caun*- are attested in antiquity.[426] Compare also CAV- in 417/282 CAVO (or CAVOSENI), 418/283 BVRSOCAVI (or

---

[419] Cf. the re-composition type *Erthgi, Bleiddgi*, Evans, *BBCS*, 24 (1970–72), 423; also 984/59 GURCI (above, ‡19).

[420] LHEB, pp. 91 and 443–44; see below, ‡80.

[421] See below, ‡80; Uhlich, *Morphologie*, p. 273.

[422] GPN, p. 222.

[423] Evans, *Enwau Personol*, p. 424, and Zimmer, in Evans FS, p. 327. Cf. LHEB, p. 445; LEIA M-8. MAVISIR is 'medieval or later?' according to Thomas, *Mute Stones*, p. 328. On 464/Ok65 KHJ notes 'Is it not MAVIGIR?', but he seems not to have visited the stone.

[424] EWGT, p. 14 (*De Situ Brecheniauc*, §2). See also ‡64. Perhaps compare the variation seen in OB *Hoiernin, Houernin* (‡64n below) and in OW *cueeticc*, ModW. *gweëdig, gweuedig*, Falileyev, *Etymological Glossary*, and GPC s.vv.

[425] Ziegler, p. 143, comparing the man's name *Cagius* in Holder i, 682 (beside *Cagirus*, and cf. iii, 1038), for which see GPN, p. 400 (*Caia, Caiaucus, Cagius*, etc.). Rhys, *PBA*, 1911–12, p. 335, explains 47 NETA-CAGI as 'a fence or defence consisting of a warrior, a fighting protector'; cf. the personal name *Caio* (OPEL ii, 21) and Late Gaulish *caio* 'field' (: W. *cae*) < *kagio- (LHEB, pp. 450–51; Lambert, *Langue gauloise*, pp. 203–4; Schrijver, *NOWELE*, 35 (1999), 36–37; Toorians, *Amsterdamer Beiträge zur älteren Germanistik*, 56 (2002), 19–22; Schumacher, *Historical Morphology*, p. 204; Anreiter et al., in *Ptolemy*, p. 117, n. 16). 506 CUGINI in Argyll may be related – Motta, *Studi classici e orientali*, 3 (1982), 299–304, suggests reading CAGI(-). Jackson, in RCAHMS, *Argyll*, i, 97, had preferred COGELI = OI *Coicéle* (CGH, p. 297, var. *Cogēle*); cf. Ziegler, pp. 143, 151, and 157. If CAVNE were from *Kagunā or *Kagonā, one would have to suppose that /u/ > /o/ (‡15) > /u/ (‡26) occurred before ‡25, as Dr Jon Coe points out to me.

[426] Holder i, 868 and iii, 1167; BWP, p. 35, connecting CAVNE with 1033/287 CUN. If the latter reading is correct, as it seems to be (it is supported by Lhuyd's drawing), I would prefer to connect CUN with *Counos* (Holder i, 1150); cf. Lambert, in *Britain 400–600*, p. 209, on W. *Alun* < *Alounā.

BVRGOCAVI), and 1057/Ok54 EROCAV[I],[427] 1404/Ok30 CAVUDI (or CAVVDI).[428] A more likely derivative of *kag- is 1209/Ok12 CAOCI,[429] on which Jackson commented:

> I cannot make anything of CAOCI. In the first place AO as it stands is an impossible collocation of vowels in British or Welsh. It might be a spelling for AU, but an AU diphthong at this date [c. 500 or early 6th cent., Radford], and for long after is extremely rare and is either of Latin origin or arises in quite exceptional circumstances, which are not present here. Nor do I know any Welsh name Cawg or anything like it.[430]

In fact there is a good parallel in the name of a Breton saint, invoked in a litany of c. 900 as Sancte Caoce and in an eleventh-century one as S. Caoc.[431] Despite the spelling, this seems likely to represent *Caioc (< *Kagiākos ?), from the same stem as W. Caeach, Caeo, and OB Caio, as implied by Loth (who in fact misquotes the litanies as giving Caeoce).[432] If this is correct, CAOCI corresponds to OW caiauc, MW kayawc, Mod.W. caeog, probably in the sense 'brooch-wearing one'; MW Kaeawc may occur as a personal name in Canu Heledd.[433]

[25] 438/320 TAVUSI could come from *tagu-, as in Gaulish Tagausus, Prasutagus and Icotagus (British king and potter) and Itotagus (Gaulish gladiator).[434] There is also TAV- in 462/Ok14 QVENATAVCI, but QVENA- implies that that TAVCI- is Irish.[435] (In 1022/240/928 Macalister alone read DO[BI]TAUCI.)

---

[427] According to Thomas, Mute Stones, p. 286, the reading EROCAVI 'is difficult to sustain'. In 1951 KHJ found only LIVS legible in this inscription, which 'might be 6th cent. . . . But if so, it must have been re-used for the cross, which is 8th-12th cent.'

[428] 433/313 **CAVE[TI]** /CAVETI is certainly not Brittonic, however, and comes from Ir. *caw- (Ziegler, p. 148, and above, ‡22).

[429] CAOCI is the reading of Radford, DASP, 27 (1969), 80, quoted by Thomas, Mute Stones, p. 281. The stone is in two parts and Okasha read CA[-]OCI, implying that letter(s) may be missing.

[430] Jackson apud Radford, DASP, 27 (1969), 80. Jackson's **Cawg may suggest the possibility of MW câwc (: OI cúach?) 'cauldron, bowl', used as a personal name, like the synonymous Ketill in Old Norse. Cf. LEIA C-259; Mossé, RC, 50 (1933), 248–53, comparing the use of pair/coire 'cauldron' for 'chief' (e.g. Book of Leinster, v, ed. Best & O'Brien, l. 35341).

[431] Litanies, ed. Lapidge, pp. 84 and 292; d'Arbois de Jubainville, RC, 3 (1876–78), 449; Loth, RC, 11 (1890), 136 and 140.

[432] Noms des saints bretons, pp. 17 and 22. Cf. EANC, pp. 6 and 215–16.

[433] GPC, s.v. caeog; Canu Llywarch Hen, ed. Williams, pp. 36 and 206; Rowland, Saga Poetry, pp. 586–87.

[434] Holder ii, 83, 1041 and 1700; Evans, in Birkhan FS, pp. 100–3; Tyers, Pottery, p. 123.

[435] See ‡16. KHJ queries: 'Is it from q"ennotausācos . . . with tausācos which would give túach "silent"?' Cf. LEIA T-91. Birkhan, Germanen und Kelten, pp. 187, n. 298, 205 and 215, and Weisgerber, Rhenania, p. 473, cite names in Taus-. 438/320 TAVUSI could be an Irish name from the derived stem *tauss- < *taus-t-, as in OI in-tuaisi 'listen', LEIA T-99.

[25] Finally, Jackson comments on 1064/Dor.iv,

[D]ENIEL FI[LIUS
AUPRIT IA[CET

that 'the name Auprit (if the first letter is really A) is unknown, and even with more letters at the beginning it suggests no known name. It looks like a compound in prit, Middle Welsh pryt, "shape", "form".'[436] If Jackson is right, the name could be [M]AUPRIT, a compound of *Mau- < *Magu- and pryd (or possibly bryd 'mind' or 'born'?) – compare the Old Welsh name Meuprit found in the oldest manuscript of the Historia Brittonum, §49, and the Cornish saint's name Meubret.[437] An alternative explanation, however, is suggested by the OW and OB name Albrit, MW Alvryt.[438] This is surely from OE Ælfred (compare OW Gulbrit, Gulfrit, Gulfredus, Gulfridus < OE Wulfrith).[439] It would not be impossible to spell Ælfred as *Alprit in Brittonic (owing to the origin of /lf/ < /lp/ as in Elffin < Latin Alpinus, etc.);[440] on the other hand, the vocalization of /l/ to /u/ is unknown in Brittonic (except for Breton /lt/ > /ut/ in the 'twelfth- to thirteenth-century')[441] and is suggestive of Old French influence. In particular, compare the name or names which appear in early Old Breton documents as Altfrid, -ed, etc. and Alfrit, -et, etc. but in the eleventh century as Aufrid etc. 'which suggests that French influence has somehow entered the

---

[436] Radford & Jackson, in RCHM, Dorset, ii/2, p. 312 (the letter does seem to be an A). Cf. Isaac, SC, 34 (2000), 271–72, on OW Loubrit/Leubrit = LUGUQRIT, and Ziegler, p. 111, on W. prydydd, Gaulish Prittius. For pryd in names, see MW Gwylbrid (Black Book of St. David's, ed. Willis-Bund, p. 286) and note also that Lloyd-Jones, Geirfa, p. 744, on gwynnbryt, cites OB Uuenbrit; however, Loth, Chrest., pp. 111 and 175, gives reason to suppose that brith is the second element. Instead of pryd 'form' (and 'time') or prit 'price, purchase' (Schumacher, Historical Morphology, pp. 45 and 73) an alternative for AUPRIT (implied by McClure, EHR, 22 (1907), 729) is OB brit/W. bryd 'mind, judgement' as perhaps in 1000/182 BRITU (but the modernization Bridw is preferred to Brydw by Rhys, Cymmrodor, 21 (1908), 47, n. 1, and cf. -bryd 'carrying', Schumacher, Historical Morphology, p. 71 and n. 52; 3013/M4 BRIT[and CONBRITI, OB Conbrit, etc. (Chrest., p. 111), OC Britail (Bodmin, p. 83), OW On(n)brit (LL, p. 414, cf. WATU, p. 156: Onfryd), Lunbrit and Sulbrit/Sulurit (LL, pp. 410 and 419), and Romano-British Britivenda in Tab.Sulis, p. 109). For *[M]AU- + radical cf. W. meudwy 'servant of God, hermit' (SBCHP, p. 270; SWWF, p. 6).

[437] Bartrum, EWGT, p. 8, adopts Mepurit from later MSS (a reading unconvincingly preferred by Rhys, Englyn, p. 25) and Dumville, in his edition of the relevant MS, Historia Brittonum, iii, 112, states that Meuprit is 'for (map) Iudnert' (a view rightly rejected by Rhys). For Meubret see LBS iii, 477–78; Loth, Noms des saints bretons, p. 94; Orme, Dedications, p. 73, and Saints of Cornwall, p. 90. (On bryd as in W. hyfryd see Isaac, CMCS, 41 (2001), 73–74, and ‡44n. below.)

[438] LL, p. 386; Chrest., p. 111; Lloyd-Jones, Y Geninen, 44 (1926), 1; Zimmer, JCL, 3 (1994), 160.

[439] LL, p. 402; Davies, Llandaff Charters, p. 168. Similarly Guorfrit and Milfrit (LL, pp. 412–13) are probably from Old English.

[440] LHEB, p. 570 (OW diprotant and OB gurprit have been claimed as examples, cf. Falileyev, Etymological Glossary, s.vv. diprotant and guorfrit); see ‡43 below. Or could there be a palaeographical confusion of B and F? Cf. ‡42 on 3012/M3 PRFTER for PResBYTER.

[441] Piette, French Loanwords, p. 24, n. 2.

picture'.[442] Possibly, then, the father of [D]ENIEL bore an English name
Ælfred (or, less likely, (E)aldfrith) – or a close Germanic cognate – which
was transmitted or inscribed at Wareham in a Continental (Breton?)
environment, leading to AU- < *Al-. This would be understandable in
view of the well-known presence of foreign clerics, including Bretons, in
the Anglo-Saxon church;[443] [D]ENIEL may even have been a Breton. All
this depends, of course, on whether the inscription can be placed late
enough to fit such an historical context, and the catch is that the later it is
put the harder it is to accept that /f/ could still be spelt P.

‡26 ŏ > ŭ before certain consonants in W.Brit.; LHEB §4.1

This principally involved various sequences containing /on/ and /om/;[444] and
according to Schrijver it also happened in SW.Brit. and earlier than
a-affection (views rejected by Jackson).[445] Schrijver argues that it only
occurred (a) after /m/ and (b) (in unstressed syllables) after alveolar
consonants (assuming parallelism with the raising of /e/, cf. ‡27). Russell
comments:

> it is curious that only in (b), and not in (a), do accentual conditions play a
> part. In fact there are only two examples which are preventing us from
> claiming that this is a change that generally occurred in unaccented
> syllable[s], i.e. mwn¹ 'neck' and mwn² 'glove'; all the rest are dissyllabic,
> namely mwnwgl, mynawc, mynw, mynych, mynydd and myfyr.[446]

---

[442] HPB, p. 809; cf. review by Piette, SC, 5 (1970), 160: 'I am inclined to regard Aufret as a Fr.
borrowing; the name is not uncommon as a patronyme, especially in Upper Brittany.' For
OB examples of Alfredus, Alfrid(us), Adalfred, Aldefred, Alurit, etc. see Tanguy, in
Cartulaire de Redon, pp. 57–58 and 62 (and cf. Gaufridus, ibid., pp. 59–60). Tanguy
adopts the view (criticized by Jackson) that Germanic Adalfred merged with a native
Breton Altfrid/Altfred > Alfrid, Alfred, Aufrid. Note VLRB, p. 924: 'In V.L. l before some
consonants vocalized to u, as in alteru > French autre. No British record shows this directly,
but there is one possible hypercorrection, Alfidius for the very common Aufidius in RIB 9
(London). However, this may be a simple error, for the stone bears the H S E formula
typical of the first century, while the V.L. change is usually thought to have begun in the 4th
century at the earliest.'

[443] Little is known about Wareham. Hoskins, The Westward Expansion of Wessex, pp. 20–21,
and Radford, Early Christian Inscriptions of Dumnonia, pp. 13–14, thought it a centre of
surviving Britons, but the Breton possibility was raised by McClure, EHR, 22 (1907),
728–30, and is revived by Dumville, Wessex and England, p. 157. Hinton, PDNHAS, 114
(1992), 260, is doubtful, but thinks it at least possible in the case of 1064/Dor.iv and
1062/Dor.v.

[444] The handbooks cited in LHEB, p. 272 (cf. SBCHP, pp. 52–68), also mention /o/ before *rk,
*rg, *rn, and *ld, but these are not relevant to the inscriptions. We can ignore 1048/Ok32
(G)VENNORCIT (Thomas, Mute Stones, p. 290; Tedeschi, Scrittura e civiltà, 19 (1995),
tav. 3), 1014/231 GUORGORET (merely orthographical -g-), and 1030]OLD. 1060/Ok57
GURGLES, if the correct reading, might be an example of the special treatment of *wor-,
which Schrijver, SBCHP, pp. 58–60, distinguishes from the Pr.B. raising of /o/; but cf. ‡28.
On the second element see ‡58 below.

[445] SBCHP, pp. 27–52 (cf. LHEB, p. 273).

[446] Review of SBCHP in JCL, 6 (1997), 149.

[26] If Russell is right to explain away the two monosyllabic exceptions, as seems plausible, this has important implications for dating because it was the failure of *Monā* to give W. **Mŵn that led Schrijver to argue that raising of /o/ was pre-*a*-affection: *Monā* > * *Munā* > * *Monā* > *Môn*, with *a*-affection reversing the raising of /o/.

[26] Jackson gives two examples from the inscriptions (p. 273): (A) 413/272 MONEDORIGI, 'fifth century', where is has not yet happened and (B) 451/401 TVNCCETACE, 'early or mid sixth century', where it has. While this may well be correct, the different vowel spellings do not provide independent confirmation of the relative dates of these inscriptions. Pretonic /un/ (both original and < /on/) developed to /ön/ > /ən/ in Welsh (cf. *mynydd*, *tyng(h)ed*), and to /ǫn/ in South-Western Brittonic (see ‡28), and Welsh /ön/ and /ən/, and of course Breton and Cornish /ǫn/, could also be spelt ON, as in: 324/34]CO[N]BARRVS CO[N]BURRI (but see (B) no. 6 below); 356/132/9 CONVMANI (Macalister only!);[447] 1000/182 CONCENN and CONMARCH; 1016/234/907 CONBELIN (cf. 1023/239/927 [CO]NBELANI); 490/Ok29 CONHINOC(I); 493/Ok58 CONBEVI; 511/Scot.10 CONINIE; 1048/Ok32 QONFAL (?);[448] 1062/Dor.v GONGORIE (?); 1068/b CONDILICI; 3013/M4 CONBRITI (see below, ‡‡ 28, 46, and 84). In view of these forms, it is clear that a form like MONEDORIGI can only be classified as reflecting the original /on/ stage, rather than the /ön/ < /un/ < /on/ stage, when there is some other evidence which we should already be taking into account in our chronology. In the case of MONEDORIGI it is the lack of syncope. Note that all the above forms with CON- (i.e. W. /kön/ or SW.Brit. /kǫn/) < *kuno- show syncope where applicable (apart from CONVMANI which is completely untrustworthy) – and so does 1033/287 CINGEN.[449] By contrast CVN- (< *kuno-) never occurs with British syncope in the inscriptions:[450] 319/9 CVNOGVS(I); 342/70 CVNOCENNI FILIVS CVNOGENI (and ogam equivalent); 397/105 CVNALIPI CVNACI; 362/142 **CUNIGNI/CVNIGNI**; 374/172 CVNEGNI; 446/353 **MAGLICUNAS/MAGLOCVN(I)** (?); 447/369 CVNISCVS (or, better, CVNIGCVS);[451] 449/384 **CUNATAMI/CVNOTAMI**; 454/402

---

[447] Rejected by I. Williams in his review, *THSC*, 1943–44, pp. 155–56.

[448] Thomas, *Mute Stones*, pp. xxii, 159, n. 29, 290, and 302, n. 52 suggesting Q = /k/ and F = /μ/. Tedeschi, *Scrittura e civiltà*, 19 (1995), tav. 3, reads: + VIR/QONFALI FILIIV/ GVENNORCIT. Macalister read QONFALI the other way up as HADNOB, which seems plausible. Cf. ‡44n.

[449] If it were the correct reading. See above, ‡17. If CUNBEN is preferred, as it should be, it is probably to be segmented CUN BEN rather than treated as a syncopated compound. CUNBEN is deceptively like Gaulish *Cunopennus* and W. *cynben* 'dog-head' (KGP, p. 186; GPC s.v.), but we would expect that to be spelt with -P- (cf. ‡17).

[450] For *kuno- in OW see Sims-Williams, *BBCS*, 38 (1991), 38–47 and 75 (including examples of *Cun*- names with syncope). Obviously, in some of the following examples syncope is not to be expected anyway.

[451] See ‡48 below.

CVNIOVENDE; 468/Ok31 CVNOVALI; 479/Ok16 CVNAIDE or CVNATDO; 487/Ok10 CVNOMORI; 501 **CUNAMAGLI**; 504 **CUNA-VA[LI]**; 2006 CVNORIX. (Some of these may be Irish: 364/144 BARCVNI, which *does* have syncope – Irish syncope presumably – certainly is; but by no means all.)[452] The only possible exception with syncope is the obscure 2018 CVNCUOM – perhaps compare OW *Cuncuman*, *Concuan*, and *Concuu*n.[453]

[26] (A)

1. 413/272 MONEDORIGI, then, on the basis of the lack of syncope can be classed as a genuine example of O for the /o/ that was to become /u/.[454] I can find no other one, unless perhaps it is 419/284 ONERATI (cf. *Honorius* > W. *Ynyr*, with /on/ > /un/ > /ön/ > /ən/), where however the ON-spelling may have been retained under the influence of Latin *Oneratus* or *Honoratus*.[455] I disregard this form. If the first element of 3021/I2 MAONIRN corresponds to W. *maon* 'servants', and if the latter is from **magones*, note that raising would not be expected in the sequence /gonV/ according to Schrijver's rules, which require that the first consonant be /m/ or possibly, in unstressed syllables, an alveolar consonant.[456]

[26] (B) By contrast, I would add to Jackson's single example of U (1. 451/401 TVNCCETACE) as follows:

2. 2019 TVNCCE[(probably a fake, however).[457]
3. 409/198/849 PVMPEIVS < *Pompeius* (the ogam **POP[?]** may reflect the original vocalism of *Pompeius*).[458]
4. 505 MONOMENTI – the second O could be due to post /o/ > /u/ hypercorrection for *Monumenti*, that is, to avoid ****MVNVMENTI**.[459] (Similarly, 398/106 IACONVS could be a post /o/ > /u/ hypercorrection

---

[452] BARCVNI (cf. OI *Barrchú*, Uhlich, *Morphologie*, p. 174) is father of QVENVENDANI, on whom see above, ‡22.
[453] Sims-Williams, *BBCS*, 38 (1991), 38–39 and 46; Hughes, *Ériu*, 44 (1993), 96–97.
[454] It is accepted as such by Schrijver, SBCHP, p. 34.
[455] On these two names see ‡18n. above.
[456] SBCHP, pp. 43–44 (and see p. 39 for **-on-es* in *n*-stems). On MAONIRN see ‡‡ 36, 65, and 74 below.
[457] This is restored as TVNCCE[TATOCVS] by Hemp & Gresham in *AC*, 90 (1961), 154, and similarly by Bowen & Gresham, *History of Merioneth*, i, 289, clearly the result of hesitation between TVNCCE[TACVS] and TVNCCE[TOCVS]. Dr Edwards is certain that it is a fake, inspired by the publication of ECMW no. 401. The CC in both inscriptions is striking.
[458] Hamp, *Britannia*, 6 (1975), 158. Mann, *Britannia*, 2 (1971), 221, had thought that PVMPEIVS has Vulgar Latin *u* for *o* like 408/229 PRONEPVS and 360/139 SERVATVR (Howlett, *Cambro-Latin Compositions*, p. 19, argues that this is a verb, but cf. e.g. *Bellatur* for *Bellator* in OPEL i, 345, and for *seruator* and *cultor* in epitaphs see Sims-Williams, *Britain and Early Christian Europe*, ch. 10, p. 32, nn. 114–15). On the lack of /m/ in the ogam see above ‡17 and below ‡68. In the other half of 409/198/849, **ILLUNA** may have /u:n/ < /o:n/ according to Ziegler, pp. 115 and 188.
[459] On *mynwent*, see SBCHP, pp. 28, 35, and 43; Vallerie, *ÉC*, 23 (1986), 251–53; and Sims-Williams, in *Gaulois et celtique continental*.

for *Iucundus/Iocundus* (and note also 475/Ok47 IACONIVS, *if* that is the correct reading); this cannot be pressed, however, since the etymology is doubtful and Schrijver argues that /o/ was not liable to raising between /k/ and /n/ not followed by stop.[460])

5. 979/46 NI(n)ID (assuming it = MW *Nynnid* < **Nonnitus*)˙ implies /un/ < /on/.[461]

6. 324/34 CO[N]BURRI, assuming that the reading of this lost stone is correct and that the second element is W. *bwrr* (OW *burr*, OC *bor*, MI *borr*) 'fat' < **bhorso-* with /u/ < /o/ by raising, which is uncertain in this environment.[462] Ifor Williams suspected that the original reading was -BARRI with an inverted A;[463] if so the name could be Irish or Welsh and would definitely not belong here.

[26] A few forms can be mentioned only to be excluded. 351/115/2 DVMELVS (whether Irish or British) has original /u/.[464] In 327/43 the variation between T[RA]LL[O]NI (Macalister's reading) and TRILVNI is inexplicable; Thomas suggested that Latin *Tribuni* may be intended in both scripts.[465] In 339/68 the reading is uncertain – N[EMNI]I or N[UMNI]I (Nash-Williams) or NIMRINI (Macalister); NA[*m*]NII (Tedeschi) is adopted in the *Corpus*.[466] In 477/Ok11 CONETOCI both Os may be

---

[460] SBCHP, pp. 43–44 and 50. For alternative etymologies of IACONVS see ‡22 above.

[461] See above, ‡15n., however, on the reading.

[462] See SBCHP, p. 55, and note that Morris-Jones, WG, p. 87, says that raising did not occur before *rr*. Cf. LEIA B-73; Sims-Williams, *BBCS*, 38 (1991), 33, n. 2; DLG, p. 80; MLH v/1, p. 90. Cf. *Burr(i)us* in Holder i, 642–43, and iii, 1008.

[463] BWP, p. 24. See Fig 1.2 above.

[464] Cf. Ziegler, pp. 174–75 on 252 **DUMELI**, 198 **MAQI-DDUMILEAS**, and 368/a/150 **DUMELEDONAS**. I. Williams, rev. of CIIC i, in *THSC*, 1943–44, p. 154, compares MW *Dyfel*, and KHJ notes OW *Dimell* (LL, p. 208). See GPN, p. 196 and n. 5. Rhys, *AC*, 6th ser. 7 (1907), 80–81, had compared Irish names such as *Cluain Domail* (Hogan, *Onomasticon*, p. 261), and this may lie behind Nash-Williams's statement (no. 115) 'Dumelus is an Irish name'. Did DALLVS DVMELVS ('Blind Unlucky') owe his name to congenital blindness? DAILI (RIB i 1620) has been read DALLI (Holder i, 1216).

[465] Macalister explains his reading in *AC*, 77 (1922), 208–9. Nash-Williams and McManus, *Guide*, p. 67, read |LUNI, and Thomas, *Mute Stones*, p. 124, reads |L[.]N[.] He suggests TRILVNI may be a miscopying for TRIBVNI as on 476/Ok45 ('Latin *tribunus* used as a personal name', LWP, p. 403; cf. Thomas, *Mute Stones*, pp. 84 and 269, and *Tribunus*, *Tribonius*, *Trebonius* in OPEL iv, 129), with roman B mistaken for L, and suggests that it is the same name as *Triphun*, as in the Dyfed king-list (McManus is sceptical in his review in *CMCS*, 33 (1997), 102). I think it would be simpler to suppose that TRILVNI is a mistranscription of the ogam, and that the latter's 'L' is in fact a **BB** in ***TRIBBUNI**, with **BB** for /b/ or else for P (cf. Sims-Williams, *CMCS*, 23 (1992), 41). In this way the equation with TRIBVNI and *Triphun* may be correct (though cf. Jones, *ZCP*, 16 (1927), 166, on *Tryffin/Tyrffin*). For a possible explanation of TRILVNI as it stands, however, see below, ‡60. Commenting on Macalister's T[RA]LLONI, KHJ says 'I am not satisfied that the ogam cannot be **TRILLUNI**.'

[466] With *Namnius* (?) compare Latin *Namnis*, 'member of the *Namnetes* (Gaulish tribe from which Nantes is named)' and see GPN, p. 236. Rhys, LWP, p. 381, 'guessed it to be *Nemni*, whence the later form *Nemnivus*' (similarly Rhys, *AC*, 4th ser. 6 (1875), 371). Cf. theonym *Nemnic*[in Holder ii, 713. KHJ notes that Nash-Williams's N[EMNI]I 'if of course a guess', but 'actually in his drawing the NII seems pretty clear'. KHJ's 1947 drawing seems to show

from etymological /a:/; similarly 489/a/Ok13 FANONI.[467] 486/Ok56 CVMREGNI or CVMRECINI[468] is irrelevant if it contains /kü(∶)μ/ < *koimo-.[469] 469/Ok34 CNEGVMI or CLEGUMI is obscure,[470] as is 1051/Ok37 CUMBUIN(?), a very doubtful form.[471] Finally, the /ö/ or /ə/ of 1033/287 CIMALTED (Ifor Williams's reading) is not the end result of /u/ < /o/ (which should not occur in a /komV/ environment according to Schrijver's rules),[472] but is rather the reflex of a much older /ö/ < /o/ in the prefix *kom-.[473]

‡27 ĕ > ĭ before a nasal in W.Brit.; LHEB §6.2

LHEB §6.2 deals with raising of /e/ before single nasal not followed by stop. Jackson thought that this was confined to W.Brit. plus to some extent Devon.[474] Schrijver, on the other hand, argues that it occurred throughout Brittonic, but was confined to position after /m/ and (in unstressed syllables) alveolar consonants.[475] On the analogy of the alleged development of Monā > Môn, where he thought that a-affection reversed the raising of /o/, Schrijver hinted that raising of /e/ might also be pre-a-affection; we have seen, however, that this is doubtful.[476]

---

part of an E after the N-. See also Thomas's suggestion on 2032, quoted in ‡48n. Cf. NEMMONI on a tombstone at Cirencester, which Wright & Hassall, *Britannia*, 3 (1972), 352, compare with *Nemonius* and *Num(m)onius*. Cf. *Nam(m)onius* (OPEL iii, 94–95). Macalister explains his NIMRINI in *AC*, 77 (1922), 199.

[467] See above, ‡‡ 18n. and 18 respectively.

[468] Thomas, *Mute Stones*, p. 278.

[469] KHJ notes: 'I read *Cvmredni*, with reversed D, or perh. *Cvmrecini*. If *Cvmregni* is right, is it for *Coimoregini*, "Dear Stiff One"?' Jackson, *JRS*, 37 (1947), 58, and apud Rivet, *Britannia*, 1 (1970), 78–79, sees this element (OI *rigin*, OW *regin*) in the OW personal name *Regin > Rein* and possibly in the British tribal name *Reg(i)n(o)i*. Cf. GPN, p. 373; LEIA R-30. There was also a Roman name *Regin(i)us, Regin(i)a* (cf. Kajanto, p. 316, and OPEL iv, 25 and 193 – once *Riginus, -a*) and this is attested several times in RIB, also in Hassall & Tomlin, *Britannia*, 27 (1996), 442 ([*centuria*] Ulpi Regini, at Birdoswald). Cf. Jones, *ZCP*, 16 (1927), 166, on ON *Reginn*. Thomas, *Mute Stones*, pp. 278 and 300, n. 4, has 'British *Com-reginos*, perhaps "Very-Proud-one"' from '*regin-* "stiff, proud, tall"', citing Evans, *BBCS*, 24 (1970–72), 419–20, for equative/ intensive *Com-*, but this is unlikely to be present in view of the spelling CVM-. On the second element see further below, ‡‡ 48 and 69.

[470] But KHJ notes that the G is not as drawn by Macalister but is a 3-shaped G. He says the N was invisible in 1951. Thomas, *Mute Stones*, pp. 284 and 302, n. 33, wrongly suggests that CNE- is syncopated from '*Cune-*' (but there is no problem with CN- or CL- in Celtic) and compares -GVMI with OB *Uuorcomet* and *Guorgomed*, in Chrest., p. 178 (where Loth compares the latter with OW *-guomed* = Mod.W. *gomedd* 'refuse').

[471] On CUMBUIN see above, ‡22.

[472] BWP, p. 28; LHEB, p. 668; and ‡63 below. See SBCHP, p. 50.

[473] LHEB, p. 659.

[474] LHEB, pp. 278, n. 3, 279, n. 2, and 681. Note, however, 476/Ok45 BONEMIMORI (below) in Cornwall.

[475] SBCHP, pp. 30 and 43–45.

[476] SBCHP, pp. 38–39 and 45. See ‡26 above.

[27] Jackson (p. 279) lists (A) two forms where the raising is not yet shown, DEMETI and SENACVS, and (B) one where it is shown, CONHINOCI (in Devon).[477] Bearing in mind Schrijver's restrictions (which exclude a host of forms),[478] the following list of possibly significant EN- and EM-forms can be drawn up:

[27] (A)

1. 450/390 DEMETI
2. 391/78 SENACVS
3. 370/157 SENOMAGLI[479]
5. 400/177 SENEMAGLI
6. 417/282 SENIARGII – but not if the reading is CAVOSENI, for in that case /sen/ would be in the tonic syllable and not count (similarly 365/149 MAVOHENI (Lhuyd); and 419/284 RIGOHENE)
7. 483/Ok51 SENILVS (Rhys, Thomas, and Tomlin)[480]
8. 482/Ok71 NEMIANVS or NEMIAVS

[27] The first of these personal names is slightly uncertain, since the old name for Dyfed continued to be spelt *Demetia* etc. in Latin texts.[481] In the same way, most or all of the remaining forms (except NEMIA(N)VS, which is obscure),[482] contain Celtic *sen-* > Brittonic *hen-* 'old' and were obviously open to influence from Latin and Irish *sen-*, Welsh *hen* (although the superlative, OW *hinham*, Mod.W. *hynaf*, might be a counter-influence), and from the /e/ form in tonic syllables, as in MAVOHENI. The modern

---

[477] DEMETI and CONHINOCI are cautiously accepted by Schrijver, SBCHP, p. 31.

[478] 342/70 CVNOCENNI and CVNOGENI (with ogam equivalents), 389/97 IOVENALI, 462/Ok14 QVENATAVCI, 991/113/30]CEN[, 992/120/14 CENLISINI, 993/124/18 ASAITGEN, 1000/182 CONCENN, 1033/287 CINGEN (Nash-Williams), 415/278 IN[G]ENVI (IN[TA]ENVI Macalister), 466/Ok23 INGENVI (or INCENVI)/**IGENAVI**, 362/142 **INIGENA**, 998/164 HEUTREN, 439/319 **INGEN** (Macalister), 364/144 QVEN-VENDANI, 1035/303 RECEN (Macalister – ?cf. 486/Ok56 CVMRECINI (?), above ‡26n, and names like *Ricenus* in Weisgerber, *Rhenania*, p. 469), 436/316 LITOGENI, 445/354 EMERETO, 469/Ok34 (G)ENAIVS, 515/Scot.9 DVMNOGENI (Thomas), 1064/Dor.iv [?D]ENIEL, 1068/b BRENLIER or BREDLIEN, 3026/I7 GENNOVEUS – also 3001/F1 BUDNOUENUS if this contains **gen-* as suggested in IEMB, p. 109 (although a three-element name is unlikely, though not unparalleled; cf. ‡18n above and KGP, pp. 70–72). In any case, some of these are Irish.

[479] Cf. LHEB, p. 518, n. 1: probably Irish in view of the coupling with VLCAGNVS. Note also that Russell, *Celtic Word-Formation*, p. 17, compares SENACVS with Ir. *Senach*, without I think implying that it is Irish – although it certainly could be.

[480] LWP, p. 406; *Mute Stones*, p. 286; Tab.Sulis, p. 228: SELNIVS Macalister, NI SELVS Okasha. Assuming this is Latin *Senilis* (see ‡44n.) it is noteworthy that SINILIS is attested in Roman Britain (L'Hour, *RAO*, 4 (1987), 120); or is this a separate name (cf. *Sinilis* in *Vita Columbani*, equated with OI *Sinell* by Charles-Edwards, in *Literacy in Medieval Celtic Societies*, p. 66)?

[481] Cf. SBCHP, p. 31; Thomas, *Mute Stones*, p. 76 (suggesting nominative **Demetius*). Note, however, *Dimet map Maxim gule[t]ic* in the genealogy of the kings of Dyfed (EWGT, p. 10).

[482] On NEMIA(N)VS see above, ‡18n. Raising occurred in the element **nem-*, e.g. names in *-nimet*, *-nyfed* (LEIA N-9; cf. HPB, p. 91).

name *Nant Henog* (< SENACVS), mentioned by Schrijver, illustrates this – although it should be noted that *Hynog* is also attested, and is probably the regular form.[483] Further problems are Vulgar Latin confusion of *e* and *i*, and that in Old Welsh *en* may sometimes denote /ïn/ (< /in/ < /en/) (a possible example is 1033/287 CELEN if = MW *Celyn*, cf. 485/Ok68 COLINI, 2006 MAQVI COLINE),[484] as well as its later reflex /ǝn/ (MW *yn*). There is similar confusion between *e* and *i* in the spelling of the cognate Old Breton and Cornish vowel [ɪ].[485]

[27] The following are too uncertain to consider: 339/68 N[EMNI]I (N[UMNI]I, NIMRINI, NA[*m*]NII?), 447/369 NEMAGLI or NEMASLI (perhaps acephalous [SE]NEMAGLI or [VIN]NEMAGLI or more likely Pr.Ir. *Nē-maɣlī, ‡42), 1001/181 DETEN (Macalister), 409/198/849 LL[E]NA (Nash-Williams),[486] 450/390 OGTENAS – interestingly beside roman HOGTINIS),[487] 480/Ok19 EMIANCINOINOMINE (?),[488] and 1051/Ok37]ENITHI C[.[489] The prenasal E in 385/89 ANATEMORI and

---

483 SBCHP, p. 31, citing LHEB, p. 518, for *Nant Henog* (Cwm Henog, Brycheiniog?). The *Henocus* in the *Vita Samsonis*, quoted in LHEB, pp. 279 and 518, may be the biblical name *Enoch*, or be influenced by it (Sims-Williams, *BBCS*, 38 (1991), 25), which is a further complicating factor. Although Schrijver writes **Hynog, note the existence of *Bryn Hynog*, Caerns. (Lloyd-Jones, *Enwau Lleoedd Sir Gaernarfon*, p. 36), mentioned by Macalister under no. 392, and also a farm of the same name in Brycheiniog for which I can confirm the pronunciation [hǝnog] (it was my wife's grandparents' farm). Fychan, *Astudiaeth*, p. 633, cites the form *Brinhunog* in 1760, and then mostly *Brynhynog* from 1802 onwards; cf. ibid., p. 654, for *Cwm Henog* spelt with *e* from 1698 onwards. She notes the same alternation in *Llanhynwg*/*Llanhenwg*, Monmouthshire.

484 See above, ‡19, and below, ‡57. In 485/Ok68 the tentative reading COLINI is from Thomas, *Mute Stones*, p. 271. KHJ favoured COCI, and rejected COBI and COGI.

485 HPB, pp. 91–93 (note, however, that Jackson did not believe that raising of /e/ to /ɪ/ occurred before /n/). For confusion of -*in* and -*en* in Old Breton see Gramm., p. 353. An example may be 3001/F1 BUDNOUENUS.

486 Rhys, *AC*, 5th ser. 16 (1899), 134–35, suggested LL-E-N-A on the basis of Ir. *Léan* (e.g. *Martyrology of Gorman*, ed. Stokes, June 5; cf. *Leán* in CGH, p. 671) and Diarmaid *Ua Leanna* (*Annals of the Four Masters*, s.a. 1119) but admitted that he had also read LL-U-S-O, S-E-N-A, etc. KHJ comments that Nash-Williams in giving ROL[IO]N M[AQ]I LL[E]NA is wrong to bracket the Q and 'is evidently following Rhys in desperation'.

487 McManus, *Guide*, p. 65, suggests we should read HOGTINIS (Macalister and Nash-Williams HOGTIVIS; in 1947 KHJ agreed but supposed that 'the IV must be meant for IN' in view of ogam EN). Unfortunately, the name is obscure (hardly *óc* + *tinne*, Ziegler, pp. 217–18). Stüber, *Historical Morphology*, p. 105, argues that OGTENAS has an original *-*on*- or *-*iion*- suffix showing a weakening in pronunciation as in 147 MOINENA (> OI *Moinenn*, Ziegler, p. 209) and 151 BROINIONAS > 120 BROINIENAS (Ziegler, p. 142). In that case OGT- may be a spelling (cf. ‡51) of the stem seen in OI *Ochtach*, *Ochtbran*, etc. (CGH, p. 715; cf. Holder ii, 830–33). If the Irish element is *Ócht*- (so Uhlich, *Morphologie*, p. 184: *Óchtbran*), compare OI *ócht* 'cold' < *oug-tu- (LEIA O-7; ADA, pp. 136–37). Cf. an *Ogrigenus* (: W. *oer* 'cold') at Mainz (CIL xiii 7037; KGP, pp. 59, n. 1, and 250). Dr Edwards rejects Nash-Williams's OGTENLO; cf. ‡38n. I think that OGTENAS is credible, and OGTINAS not impossible.

488 (Okasha). Cf. 482/Ok71 NEMIA(N)VS ? (On INOMINE for IN NOMINE see Jackson, *Antiquity*, 34 (1960), 40–41, and in *St. Ninian's Isle*, i, 167–68.)

489 Latin UENIT HIC according to Thomas, *Mute Stones*, p. 300. In 1951 KHJ seems to have read]EINITHI C[.]

400/177 VINNEMAGLI FILI SENEMAGLI is the reduced composition vowel,[490] and in 3014/M5 HARENBILI it is an epenthetic vowel. 466/Ok23 MEMORIA/**MEMOR** etc. may obviously be Latin/Latinate (cf. 358/138 and 515/Scot.9 MEMORIA), as is the E of 476/Ok45 BONEMIMORI below. 988/67 MENHIR is not an example of /men/ but presumably an early example of MW *mein(h)ir* 'slender-tall' as a personal name.[491]

[27] (B) There are few relevant IN- and IM-forms (most examples of IN being from original /i(:)n/, e.g. 421/294 PATERNINI):

1.   490/Ok29 (Devon) CONHINOCI (CONHINOC Okasha)
2.   476/Ok45 (Cornwall) BONEMIMORI (cf. W. *myfyr* < Latin *memoria*)[492]

[27] A possible example of post- /en/ > /in/ hypercorrection is 448/370 RINACI NOMENA, but Vulgar Latin confusion or British *a*-affection are alternative explanations, as in 1067 IMAGENEM (Man).[493] In 487/Ok10 the readings CIRISINIVS and CIRVSINIUS are too doubtful to be treated as reflexes of **sen*. 462/Ok14 DINVI ought to be Irish (he is father of a QVENATAVCI), but, if it is a (syncopated?) version of an oblique case of 279 **DENAVEC[A]** and 454/402 DEN[O]VI (Rhys's reading instead of DENCVI), its IN cannot be due to raising of /en/ – if these names indeed have /e:/ as in Ir. *Díanach*.[494]

‡27 NOTES (i) and (ii): /e/ > /i/ before nasal + stop, and before /rn/

‡27 NOTE (i) /e/ > /i/ before nasal + stop
When writing LHEB Jackson thought that raising of /e/ before nasal + stop was Common Celtic. This was denied by Binchy and Schrijver,[495] and the latter suggests that in British it 'may be relatively recent, to judge by the *e*-spellings in Romano-British *Gabrosentum*, *Clausentum* and

---

[490]   See ‡38. As noted just above, 447/369 NEMAGLI could be part of one of these names.
[491]   Hardly *maen hir*. See GPC, s.vv. *maen* and *meinir*. MENHIR may have OW *e* for *ei*.
[492]   SBCHP, p. 35. Cf. 466/Ok23 MEMORIA/MEMOR. KHJ notes that it is either a name, *Bonememorius*, or a Gallic-type formula (cf. Le Blant, *Nouveau receuil*, p. 128) *bonememorius* 'of good reputation'. Cf. Thomas, *Mute Stones*, p. 269. To complicate matters, note that there was also an OW name *Mimor*; this is < *My-* + *Môr* according to Lewis, *ZCP*, 20 (1936), 140, but for *Memor* (OPEL iii, 75) and derivatives already in Roman Britain see Tab.Sulis, p. 110, also a MEMOR at Gloucester in RIB ii [fasc. 8] 2503.343, and compare B. *Memor*, Loth, *Noms des saints bretons*, pp. 92, 96–97 and 136.
[493]   See above, ‡15.
[494]   Ziegler, p. 166; Uhlich, *Morphologie*, p. 225. Cf. above, ‡‡ 16n. and 18. Rhys, *Englyn*, p. 34, suggested that DINVI might be for *Dinuvi* = DEN[O]VI. Thomas, *Mute Stones*, pp. 271 and 275, n. 36, suggested that DINVI represented Ir. ***DINAVI**, comparing the situation in 466/Ok23 INGENVI/**INGENAVI**; he took the E in **DENA-** to be short, and compared the rare OI *Dinnu* (CGH, p. 589).
[495]   Binchy, review of LHEB, in *Celtica*, 4 (1956), 291 (hence Jackson's apparent modification of LHEB, p. 278, in HPB, p. 91?); Schrijver, *Ériu* 42 (1991), 19–21, and SBCHP, p. 29. Insofar as this argument depends on OI *find* it may need revising; cf. ‡22 above.

Derventio'.[496] While Schrijver does not suggest a date, his examples imply that it occurred before *a*-affection which reversed the raising in feminine nouns (e.g. *elementum* → **elementā* > W. *elfen* (f.)).[497] This is of course slightly speculative, in that it may have been lack of raising in learned(?) loans like *elfen* and *ffurfafen* that led to them being assimilated to the native *-en* feminine class.

[27 (i)] Be this as it may be, the examples from the inscriptions can be added to the above lists.

[27 (i)] (A) E is generally retained before nasal + stop. Latin spelling (or borrowing after the period of /e/ > /i/) may be responsible in:

9. 380/84 POTENTINI
10. 356/132/9 POTEN(t)INA
11. 361/140 ADVENTI
12. 1000/182 PASCENT
13. 1034/286 PASCENT[I][498]
14. 516/Scot.1 VIVENTIVS
15. 517/Scot.2 FLORENTIVS
16. 2023/Scot.4 VENTIDIVS (?)
17. 505 MONOMENTI (but compare W. *mynwent* too).[499]

[27 (i)] Note also:

18. 454/402 DENCVI may read DEN[O]VI (Rhys), but if correct presumably shows the base **denk-* without raising.[500]

[27 (i)] It has to be admitted that the examples of /e/ without raising before nasal + stop are probably more orthographic than phonetic. As we have seen, the Celtic element **windo-* is frequently written VEND-.[501] This could be merely conventional: because Latin *descendere*, for example, came to be pronounced *discind-* (> W. *disgyn*),[502] END might be felt to be a correct way to write /ind/ (> /ïnd/). But it is also possible to attribute VEND- either to ancient Celtic confusion of /i/ and /e/ in this environment or to lowering in Irish, as suggested earlier.[503]

---

[496] SBCHP, p. 30. Cf. TRC, pp. 55–56, and ‡15 above.
[497] SBCHP, p. 28.
[498] Cf. EWGT, p. 208, *Pascent, Pasgen. Pascentia* occurs in RIB ii (see index), and for *Pascentius* see ECMW, p. 172, n. 4.
[499] On *-ent* here see SBCHP, p. 28, and Sims-Williams, in *Gaulois et celtique continental*. On *mynwent* cf. ‡26n. above.
[500] See above, ‡18.
[501] Note also 376/174 VENNISETLI (versus 400/177 VINNEMAGLI), 1048/Ok32 GVENNCREST/(G)VENNORCIT (Thomas, *Mute Stones*, pp. 290–91; Tedeschi, *Scrittura e civiltà*, 19 (1995), tav. 3), 1055/Ok3 UAETUENA (?), and 3005/F5 VENOMAILI. See above, ‡22.
[502] SBCHP, p. 27.
[503] See above, ‡22.

[27 (i)] 988/67 GENILLIN and 456/404 **GENDILI**/GE[may be loans based on Latin *Gentilius* (or *Gentilis* or *Gentillus*), but are not significant examples of absence of raising since the normal MW form is still *Gen(n)illyn, -in.*[504] Nevertheless, it is interesting to note Rhys's comparison with *Tref Ginhill* (var. *Gynnhill, Gynhil*) in the Book of Llandaf, an unidentified place on the river Ely.[505] 1055/Ok3 T[T]UEN[T] is very doubtful.

[27 (i)] (B) An example of raising before nasal + stop which can be added to the above list is:

3. 359/141 NV[D]INTI, compared to Romano-British NODENTI and NVDENTE.[506]

461/Ok66 ERCILINGI (cf. OI *Erclang/Ercleng*, gen. *Erclaingi*), by comparison with the other Irish names in -LENGI (354/126/6 CORBALENGI; 431/308 EVOLENGI; 436/316 EUOLENGGI (cf. 424/299 [E]VA[LEN]GI (?) (*Corpus*)),[507] may conceivably show British raising, but this cannot be pressed in view of the frequency of the spelling -*l(a)inge* in OI genitive forms.[508] I think it just a confusing coincidence that if 461/Ok66 is segmented 'NONNITA ERCILI VIRICATI TRIS FILI ERCILINGI' (rather than 'NONNITA ERCILIVI RICATI' etc.), it is possible to take -INGI as a patronymic added to the stem of ERCILI.[509]

---

[504] Lloyd-Jones, *Geirfa*, p. 528. See ‡‡ 17n. and 68. For *Gentilis/Gentilius/Gentillus* see Kajanto, p. 303; Mócsy, p. 135; and OPEL ii, 165. The lack of raising (cf. W. *gynt* < *gentem/gentes*, and the OW name element -*gint*, GPC s.v.) could be due to borrowing after /e/ > /i/ had occurred, or perhaps to borrowing via the Irish **GENDILI**.

[505] Rhys, *AC*, 4th ser. 12 (1881), 219. See LL, pp. 32, 43 and 258.

[506] Not discussed as such in LHEB, pp. 278, 306, 316, and 619, though he clearly took the I to be /i/ or /ī/ < /ĭ/, since he thought that it was the Romano-British E in NVDENTE (and NODENTI) that was odd. In RCAMS, *Selkirkshire*, p. 113, Jackson derives *Nudd* from the nominative **Nōdonts*, and says that 'the oblique cases would have yielded **Nuddont* or **Nuddynt*', which is what he takes NV[D]INTI to represent, with the addition of 'epitaphic -I'. (The readings NU[T]INTI or NU[V]INTI are linguistically less probable. According to Rhys, LWP, p. 391, '*Nuvinti*... is otherwise unknown to me, unless we have it in *Ednywain*'. The first element of the latter may be *(H)ed-* according to Williams, *BBCS*, 8 (1935–37), 234; for spellings see Lloyd-Jones, *Geirfa*, pp. 439–40.) In *PBA*, 1903–4, p. 36, Rhys accepted NV[D]INTI and alleged various cognates, including OB *Nodent* (Chrest., p. 155).

[507] For -LENGI see above, ‡14 (also Ziegler, pp. 184–85 and 189). Thomas, *Mute Stones*, p. 283, and Rhys, LWP, p. 404, read ERCILINCI. Even if they are right, it must surely be the same name as *Erclang/Ercleng* in *Patrician Texts*, ed. Bieler, pp. 128 and 140, and *Erclaingi* (gen.) in CGSH, p. 160.

[508] Examples in Uhlich, *Morphologie*, pp. 131 and 236.

[509] This possibility was noted by KHJ: '*Ercili Viricati* seems probable, because *Ricati* would be odd for *Rigocati*, and the termination -*ivi* would be strange (cf. no. 342). This would give **Ercilos* and a patronymic **Ercilingos*.' Rhys, *Englyn*, p. 20, compared LL, p. 159: 'Tref *irgillicg*, id est tref *ircil* antiquo nomine', and *Trem Gyllicg, Tref Gillic*, in LL, pp. 32 and 43. Note that 1051/Ok37 RICATI is a doubtful reading; KHJ found this panel mostly illegible in 1951. On -*ing* see ‡48. For an explanation of ERCILIVI see ‡43n.

‡27 *NOTE (ii) /ern/ > /irn/*

Before /rn/ is the most reliable other environment for raising, although Schrijver notes that examples are 'very scanty indeed', and apparently limited to stressed syllables: *asgwrn* < **-kornV-*; *Edyrn* (beside *Edern*) < *Eternus*; *teyrn* < **tigerno-*; and perhaps *chwyrn* < **su̯ern-*.[510] Schrijver argues that feminine counter-examples such as W. *cern, gwern,* and *orn* imply that raising took place before *a*-affection which reversed it.[511]

[27 (ii)] Of course examples with ERN in the inscriptions are ambiguous, since E can denote /e/ or /ï/; on the other hand, examples with IRN probably do show raising.

[27 (ii)] (A) The following have ERN and can tentatively be added to the above lists (the instances in *unstressed* syllables, which are of doubtful relevance, are bracketed):

(19.   432/312 TIGERNACI)
 20.   1403/Ok25]IGERNI [FIL]I TIGERNI
(21. 334/54 TEGERNACVS)
(22. 404/270/843 TEGERNACUS)[512]
(23. 477/Ok11 TEGERNOMALI)[513]
 24.   389/97 ETERNI
 25.   430/306 **ETTERN[I]**/ETTERNI
(26. 408/229/848 ETERNALI) [dubious in view of (B) 4. CATOTIGIRNI below]
 27.   414/271 AETERN[I] ET AETERN[E]
(28. 421/294 PATERNINI)
 29.   385/89 LOVERNII
(30. 379/170 LOVERNACI)
 31.   2022/253/984 AERERN (Nash-Williams: [B(?)]ERER[ )

[27 (ii)] Most of the above are dubious for one reason or another. In 21–23 the vocalism of TEG- seems to be irregular or late,[514] which casts doubt on the ERN as well. 24–26 may well be influenced by Latin *(A)eternus,* as is MW *Edern* beside *Edyrn*;[515] in 27. the AE is Classicizing, and /e/ would in any case be expected by *a*-affection in the second name if it is feminine *Aeterna,* as suggested. Note also that CATOTIGIRNI appears alongside ETERNALI in 26. PATERNINI (28) is probably also Latinizing, or

---

[510] SBCHP, pp. 65–66 and 68.
[511] SBCHP, pp. 65–66. As noted above (n. 444), there are no good examples relating to /orn/ > /urn/ in the inscriptions.
[512] Plus ogam **TEGE[** according to Macalister only.
[513] Note the early tenth-century OB *Tearnmaile* (voc.) in *Litanies,* ed. Lapidge, pp. 84 and 293; Loth, *RC,* 11 (1890), 150 (not *Tiernmail* as in *Noms des saints bretons,* p. 119).
[514] SBCHP, p. 64.
[515] SBCHP, pp. 58 and 65. Cf. *Edern* in Loth, *Noms des saints bretons,* p. 36. For an AETERNE from Roman Britain see L'Hour, *RAO,* 4 (1987), 120.

conceivably due to internal *i*-affection. The normal Welsh form of *Paternus* is *Padarn*, from a Vulgar Latin form **Patarnus*, but spellings with *ern* are common under the influence of the Classical *Paternus*.[516] The LOVERN-forms are dubious examples of significant non-raising, since some later evidence also points to *llywern* 'fox'.[517] Finally, AERERN, if it is the correct reading, may have *haearn* < **isarno-* as the second element, although a rare adjectival suffix **-erno-* is not impossible: 'pertaining to battle'.[518]

[27 (ii)] (B) The following instances of IRN can be added to the above lists:

4. 408/229/848 CATOTIGIRNI [cf. (A) 26. above]
5. 419/284 TIGIRNICI
6. 3021/I2 MAONIRN[519]

In 990/108/1 both TIGER[N and TIGEIR[N have been read. Jackson read TIGERNI(I) and regarded Macalister's EI as uncertain;[520] but if EI is the reading, as seems probable, it may reflect hesitation between E and I. In 1000/182, the completion of GUARTHI[GIRN] is of course only a guess.

[27 (ii)] 325/33 BIVATIGI(*rni*), while obviously preferable to BIVATI-SI(*rni*), is a dubious expansion in my opinion.[521] Macalister read BIVOTIS (recte BIVATIS?) plus a word divider, while the Ancient Monuments/Nash-Williams drawing shows BIVATISI, which Charles Thomas and David Howlett take as genitive of a name **Bivatisus*.[522] The second part could be the suffix **-tio-*, genitive **-tiī*, either written -TIGI/-TISI with IGI/ISI representing [iι̯i:],[523] or written -TIS (Macalister's reading) with Latinate

---

[516] On /er/ > /ar/ see LHEB, pp. 280–81; SBCHP, pp. 58 and 66; VLRB, p. 900. For /ern/ > /arn/ already in Roman Britain see Tab.Sulis, p. 147, on *Patarnianus* and *Matarnus*. Cf. Loth, *Noms des saints bretons*, p. 101 '*Patern* (saint) . . . prononcez *Pedern* ou *Padern*'. See also BWP, p. 182; Lewis, *Elfen Ladin*, p. 3.

[517] SBCHP, pp. 61–62. *Cruc(ou) Leuyrn/Leuguirn* occurs beside *Louern* in LL (p. 410, cf. Rhys, LWP, p. 390), but these place names may have the plural. Cf. *Laguernnuc*, LL, p. 207 (hypercorrect?).

[518] See below, ‡‡ 48 and 57. For **-erno-* cf. Holder i, 1465; VKG ii, 53; O'Rahilly, *Ériu*, 14 (1943–46), 24–25; Jackson, in *Thetford Treasure*, p. 47; LEIA T-63 s.v. *tigern*; NWÄI, pp. 238, 256, n. 141, and 536; Luján, in *Ptolemy*, pp. 61–62; and Coates & Breeze, *Celtic Voices*, pp. 85 and 351. Another possibility is the element *erno-* ('eagle'?) which appears in Gaulish place names like *Ernodorum* (Holder i, 1465; DLG, pp. 10 and 139–40), i.e. 'battle-eagle'.

[519] See below, ‡74.

[520] LHEB, p. 446 and n. 3.

[521] LHEB, p. 279. This reading originated with Ifor Williams, in RCAHMW, *Anglesey*, p. cxiii. Admittedly *amantissima* is abbreviated drastically as AMATISSI.

[522] Thomas, *Christian Celts*, p. 85; Howlett, *Cambro-Latin Compositions*, pp. 26–27 (reviving Ifor Williams's metrical theory and seeing a rhyme between BIVATISI and PAVLINI). Macalister's BIVOTIS is rejected by Ifor Williams, review of CIIC i, THSC, 1943–44, p. 155, by Nash-Williams, and by Jackson, LHEB, pp. 279 and 446. See further ‡14 above.

[523] For this use of G cf. Szemerényi's explanation, KZ, 88 (1974), 280 and n. 68, of 362/142 AVITTORIGES as '*vr̥kī*-type' genitive **-iyes* < **-iyas* < **-iyos*, cited by Ziegler, p. 132, n. 228; cf. ‡‡ 17 and 65. Since S could mean an /h/ which was in some cases lost, in British and ogam Irish, perhaps ISI could also denote [iι̯i:]? Cf. Ch. 4, p. 302.

third declension -S. The first element is Ir. *BIVA- or W. *biwo- with reduced composition vowel spelt A, or alternatively the A is part of the suffix, since Brittonic is known to have generalized the form *-aṭio-.[524] One way or other, the name may be more or less the same as, or a Welsh cognate of, 246 **BIVITI** > OI *Bithe(us)*.[525] Or BIVATIS(I) (BIVOTIS?) could be a form of Brittonic *Biwotīs* (< *Gʷiwotūt-s*) > W. *bywyd* 'life', or of the cognate element that appears in Old Irish *Mac Bethad*, 'son-of-life', now Mac Beatha, *Macbeth*.[526]

‡28 *u* > *ǫ* in SW.Brit.; LHEB §5.1

In terms of orthography the result of this change looks like that of the W.Brit. pretonic /u/ > /ö/ (‡46 below) – for example *kuno-* becomes CON- in both areas – and a further similarity is that in Cornish it seems that /u/ remained in old tonic syllables.[527] Another complication is that /u/ remained in Breton to some extent; *u* certainly appears in OB and occasionally OC orthography.[528] All this makes it treacherous to build too much on variation between U and O in the inscriptions (hence my label (AB) rather than (A) for the former category). However, the following are possibly significant examples of U (i.e. of /u/ not yet /ǫ/) from the South-West Brittonic area:

[28] (AB)

1. 468/Ok31 CVNOVALI
2. 487/Ok10 CVNOMORI (and DRVST- if the correct reading)
3. 3010/M1 HUBRIT (cf. W. *hyfryd*), although this is not very significant since both *hu-* and *ho-* for the first element appear in Old Breton[529]
4. 479/Ok16 CVNAIDE (Macalister and Thomas; Okasha: CVNATDO): MW *Cynaethwy*[530]

[28] There are many South-Western forms with U which cannot be included:
467/Ok24 (and 472/Ok35) VLCAGNI/**ULCAGNI** is Irish,[531] and 1404/Ok30 CAVUDI or CAVVDI looks like a later form of CAVETI > OI *cauuth*.[532]

---

[524] Lewis & Pedersen, p. 311.
[525] McManus, *Guide*, pp. 108 and 115; Ziegler, pp. 116–17 and 138. Ifor Williams mentions **BIVITI** and *mac Bethad* in RCAMHW, *Anglesey*, p. cxi. Cf. Gaulish *Bivitoni* (gen.), Holder i, 442.
[526] See LEIA B-44–45; SBCHP, pp. 246 and 277; Uhlich, *Ériu*, 46 (1995), 14, n. 19; NWÄI, p. 397.
[527] K. George, cited SBCHP, pp. 28, n. 1, and 44 ('final unstressed syllables' meaning unstressed after the accent shift).
[528] LHEB, p. 274 and n. 2; HPB, pp. 125–27; SBCHP, p. 28.
[529] HPB, p. 148; SBCHP, pp. 162–68.
[530] See ‡58.
[531] Ziegler, p. 241.
[532] On CAVETI and other CAV- names see above, ‡‡18 and 22. LBS ii, 116, and iv, 441–42, saw the saint's name *Cewydd* here, eponym of OW *Lann Ceuid*, OE *Landcawet*, now Lancaut (DP iii, 189).

469/Ok34 CNEGVMI or CLEGUMI, 1051/Ok37 CUMBUIN, and 1045/Ok69 AGURED (etc.), are obscure,[533] as are 480/Ok19 LVRATECVS (Macalister),[534] and 1053/Ok1 ULCUI (etc.). 486/Ok56 CVMREGNI or CVMRECINI probably has CVM- < *koimo-.[535] 484/Ok52 IVSTI/[I]USTI (and 3003/F3) is Latin, and 488/Ok60 DOBVNNI may be Latinate, while both have U in the tonic syllable. 1060/Ok57 GURGLES, if the correct reading, may be from *Wiro-.[536] 1049/Ok33 URITIN, if the correct reading, may have either *Wri- or *Wiri- (as in Gaulish Viretios, Viridovix, etc., and 461/Ok66 VIRICATI if the correct reading), with the same development to *Wri- as is assumed for Viriconium > OW Guricon.[537] Alternatively, it may have an element *urit-.[538] 3022/I3 TVRTOVALDVS is Germanic; if it is OE Torhtweald, as suggested, the V may be hypercorrect, due to the SW.Brit. confusion of o and u.

[28] (B) Jackson notes (p. 274, n. 2) the following possibly significant examples of O:[539]

1. 493/Ok58 CONBEVI

[533] See above, ‡‡ 22 and 25.
[534] Cf. Lurio, said to be Germanic, in RIB i 1483 and 2063, and other names in Lur- in OPEL iii, 39.
[535] See ‡26 above.
[536] Cf. ‡26n., however.
[537] GPN, pp. 125–26; RIG iv, 545; LHEB, p. 601; Jackson apud Rivet, Britannia, 1 (1970), 81; VLRB, p. 907 (reading VRECVNN for Verecunda, on CIL vii 1338.29 = RIB ii [fasc.7] 2501.588); Tab.Sulis, p. 226 (on Uricalus and Urilocolus). See also ‡14n. above on 369/153 and 463/Ok15 VRIVI.
[538] Weisgerber, Rhenania, p. 121, has an element *urit(i)o- in Ateuritus and VriSSulius. Rhys, AC, 5th ser. 12 (1895), 32–33, attempted to isolate an element urit from OW Conurit and Bledciurit, and also compared 155 A><EVRITTI; cf. Ziegler, pp. 122–23, and Uhlich, Morphologie, pp. 158–59, with emendation to AT(T)EVRITTI 'Found again'. See also Holder iii, 454.
[539] There are of course a large number of obscure forms with O which I do not include as there is no reason to suppose that they contain /o/ < /u/. Thus 1048/Ok32 may contain an element QON (see also Thomas, Mute Stones, p. 290: QONFAL, Tedeschi, Scrittura e civiltà, 19 (1995), tav. 3: QONFALI), but the Q suggests that it is Irish. Again, 1062/Dor.v GONGORIE could be a *kuno- name, but the G- is odd (cf. Sims-Williams, BBCS, 38 (1991), 21, n. 1). 3007/C2 VORMVINI, if the first element corresponds to W. gwrm (cf. OE wurma), probably does not show lowering, since u is the more common vowel in Uurm-names in Old Breton. See IEMB, p. 152, also Sims-Williams, BBCS, 29 (1980–82), 223 and n. 6. 1054/Ok43 DONIERT has been identified with the name (and person) of Dumnarth/Dungarth, king of Cornwall, mentioned in the Welsh Annals s.a. 875 (= 876); cf. Brut y Tywysogyon: Peniarth MS. 20 Version, trans. Jones, p. 137; Lloyd-Jones, Geirfa, p. 396. If these names are cognate with W. dwn and the latter is to be compared with Gaulish Dunn- (LEIA D-171), then DONIERT may show /u/ > /o/. However, dwn has also been derived from OE dun (GPC, s.v.), and has been compared with Gaulish Donno- (GPN, p. 194), in which latter case it shows raising of original /o/ (it is not listed in SBCHP, pp. 30–40). Jackson, LHEB, pp. 421–22 (cf. YB, 12 (1982), 21), discusses but does not endorse a derivation Doniert < *Dubnogartos (cf. Rhys, AC, 6th ser. 18 (1918), 193, equating DONIERT with W. Dyfnarth, Ir. Domangart, < *Domnogartos). This is supported by the OW form Dunguallaun (LL, p. 200) < Dumnouellaunus, noted by Lambert, in Britain 400–600, p. 207.

2. 471/Ok39 CLOTUALI[540]
3. 490/Ok29 CONHINOCI (CONHINOC Okasha)
4. 477/Ok11 CONETOCI[541]

[28] To these add only:

5. 3013/M4 CONB[RI?]TI

[28] 1209/Ok12 POPLICI (Radford and Thomas's reading, rejected by Okasha), if correct, is Latin *Public(i)us*; however, /u/ > /o̹/ had already happened in Vulgar Latin *Poblicius, Poplicius*, which probably underlies W. *Peblig* < *Poblig.[542] Similarly CROX for *crux* in two Breton inscriptions (3013/M4 and 3014/M5, cf. 3015/M6 CROUX) reflects a Vulgar Latin change.[543]

‡*29 i > ɪ [I use this symbol for open i instead of Jackson's hooked i] in SW.Brit.; LHEB §7.2*

No inscriptional evidence is cited. But elsewhere Jackson suggests that 493/Ok58 CONBEVI may have E for /ɪ/.[544]

‡*30 Perhaps pretonic W.Brit. ɔ̄ (< ā [and au, ‡18 above]) > ɔ̌; LHEB §10*

No inscriptional evidence can be cited for obvious reasons. There is therefore no need to discuss here Schrijver's suggestion that the shortening also occurred in Cornish and Breton, in closed syllables only.[545]

‡*31 Perhaps ii̯á > əii̯á; LHEB §39*

No inscriptional evidence is cited by Jackson. There are no instances of the /ii̯á/ stage, but the result of this change can probably be seen in the E-spelling of the element **isarno-* > * *hii̯árn-* > **həii̯árn-* in 3010/M1 HERANNUEN

---

[540] Assuming **kluto-* rather than **klouto-*; cf. GPN, p. 180 and n. 6; LEIA C-125. CLOTUALI may easily be Ir. **Cloth(u)al*, with the same termination as *Bres(u)al* (cf. Uhlich, *Morphologie*, pp. 186 and 203–4).

[541] Correct if this is a derivative of the stem seen in Romano-British *Cunētio*, ‡58. But cf. ‡18n. above.

[542] Radford, *DASP*, 27 (1969), 80 (with note by Jackson deriving POPLICI and *Peblig* from VL **Poplic(i)us*, actually attested in OPEL iii, 147); Thomas, *Mute Stones*, p. 281; cf. Richards, *THSC*, 1965, p. 32 (*Peblig*: W. *pabl* '?lively'), and *WHR*, 5 (1971), 349 and n. 29. Loth, *Noms des saints bretons*, p. 102, compares Breton *Pebliau.*

[543] LHEB, p. 274. Derivatives of *crux* are discussed by McManus, *Eriu*, 35 (1984), 152; SBCHP, pp. 222, 229 and 233; and Mac Cana, in *Cymru a'r Cymry 2000*, p. 25, n. 26. RCAHMW read CROS in 1024/255/926.

[544] LHEB, p. 373. See below, ‡34. Note that /ɪ/ is the symbol used in HPB (e.g. p. 91).

[545] SBCHP, pp. 251–52. Cf. Sims-Williams, in *Britain 400–600*, p. 256. In SBCHP, p. 196, n. 1, Schrijver argues from W. *modryb* rather than **medryb that shortening took place after internal *i*-affection (‡57 below), but this can be explained by the supposition that /ɔ/ unlike /o/ was not subject to affection. Note also OW *Guallonir* < *Vellaunorīx, ‡60n. below. Shortening had occurred before *notlaic* 'Christmas' was borrrowed into Irish; see Sims-Williams, in *Britain 400–600*, pp. 251 and 257–58.

FIL' HERA*N*AL (or HERAN*H*AL), 3014/M5 HARENBILI IB FIL HERANHAL.[546] See further ‡47 below.

‡32 *lγ, rγ developing towards lch, rch in SW.Brit.; LHEB §88*

No inscriptional evidence is cited. In fact the combination LCH is absent from the names in the whole Brittonic corpus, and 1000/182 CONMARCH is the only example of RCH (since 365/149 'LUNARCHI' is shown to be LUNARI by Lhuyd's and Lewis Morris's copies). The only South-Western examples of RG (there are none of LG) are irrelevant: 1060/Ok57 GURGLES (if this or similar is the correct reading) probably has RG by syncope,[547] and 1050/Ok74 INBVRGE is an unlikely reading, but presumably is Germanic if correct.[548]

‡33 *Gemination in external sandhi; LHEB §185*

No inscriptional evidence is cited for this development, which is in any case now disputed.[549]

‡34 *i > ï in W. Brit.; LHEB §7.1*

This development is not clear in the inscriptions, since /ï(:)/ continued to be written *i* right down to the Middle Welsh period, in addition to *e* (and *y* which does not appear at all in the inscriptions however).[550] A further difficulty is that, although inscriptions with E for etymological /i/ might be listed as post-/ï/ < /i/, as Jackson does,[551] this cannot be done unless there is some other reason for assigning them a relatively late date because E can also appear for etymological **i* for other reasons, as Jackson shows.[552]

[34] Evidently, Jackson's examples of E for /ï(:)/ – 1025/248/862 ARTBEU and 1011/220/911 RES, SPERETUS, P[ATR]ES (or PA[T]RES) – were selected because these inscriptions are late on other linguistic (and epigraphic) grounds (note also 1022/240/928 SPERI[TUS]). By contrast, inscriptions which seem early, such as 454/402 CVNIOVENDE, have to have their E explained in some other way, such as Vulgar Latin confusion of

---

[546] See IEMB, pp. 179 and 217–18; Sims-Williams, *BBCS*, 38 (1991), 61 and 76; SBCHP, pp. 280–81.

[547] This developed differently: LHEB, p. 469.

[548] See ‡‡ 58 and 18n. respectively.

[549] References in Schrijver, *SC*, 33 (1999), 1.

[550] With the exception of 508 FRYMIA in Scotland (not in Thomas's Brittonic corpus) and]TRY in Macalister's dubious transcription of 1030. MW *e* for /ï/ is already invoked by Rhys, *AC*, 5th ser. 16 (1899), 155, to explain 1011/220/911 RES, SPERETUS, and P[ATR]ES (or PA[T]RES).

[551] LHEB, p. 283, n. 2.

[552] LHEB, p. 191. Note that E corresponds to Latin /iː/ in 418/283 HEC IACET. In 1029, 2028 and 2029/p.39i FICIT may appear for *fecit* but the reading is very doubtful in 1029 and 2029; cf. 508 FICT. For FICIT on the Continent see e.g. Le Blant, *Nouveau recueil*, nos. 54 and 90. Note also 461/Ok66 TRIS for *tres*, and also *iacit* for *iacet* passim (ECMW, pp. 8 and 55; Handley, *EME*, 10 (2001), 188, n. 88, and 190, n. 96).

e and *i*, *a*-affection, or Irish influence.[553] Thus Jackson explains 352A/122/5 BRAVECCI (W. **Brewych*) by VL *e* for *i* (rather than E for /ï/) and similarly 493/Ok58 CONBEVI (OW *Conbiu*, MW *Cynfyw*).[554] In the latter case (in Cornwall) he also suggests that E may denote Pr.C. /ı/ (see ‡29 above), just as in ARTBEU the E may represent Pr.W. /ï/.[555] In 2006, MAQVI COLINE may have E for Pr.Ir. /ī/ < /ĭ/ < /i:/.[556] 397/105 BECCVRI, if it *is* from **Bikkorīx*, may have Vulgar Latin E for I or E for /ï/; but it could be Irish, with lowering as in OI *becc*, ogam **BECC-**, or it may be from ****Bekkorīx**.[557]

[34] In 1035/303 MARGITEUT (OW *Margetiud*) the E denotes /j/.[558] If RESTEUTA(E) is the correct reading of 1401/Ok27, and if it is the same name as W. *Rhystud* in *Llanrhystud*, the spelling may be hypercorrect, influenced by a case like MARGITEUT, where the /j/ became silent (> W. *Maredudd*).[559] In 450/390 DEMETI the Es probably denote original /e/ rather than /ï/.[560]

[34] Since inscriptions with E for etymological **i* are apportioned between the various explanations on the basis of chronological criteria, there is no point in using the presence or absence of E as a chronological indicator. In fact this could be misleading, owing to the continued use of I for /ï(:)/ Neverthless, the following can possibly be added to Jackson's examples:

[34] 1033/287 CELEN, if this is *Celyn*, and TRICET.[561] 1032/281 WLEDER, MW *Gwledyr*,[562] and ODELEV, MW *Hoedlyw* (‡80). 980/46a WLIGUE or S(*ignum*) S(*ancti*) (or S(*cribae*)) LIGUE (Radford) is

---

553 See above, ‡‡ 15 and 22. See ‡48 below on CVNEGNI.
554 LHEB, pp. 191, 566 and 610; EWGT, p. 181.
555 LHEB, pp. 191 and 373. On ARTBEU, OB *Arthbiu*, *Arthueu*, OI *A(i)rtbe*, see Evans, *BBCS*, 24 (1970–72), 427, n. 12, and Uhlich, *Morphologie*, pp. 165–66.
556 McManus, *Guide*, p. 77. Cf. Ch. 4, §22.
557 See ‡43 below.
558 Cf. LHEB, p. 346.
559 Thomas's reading of 1401/Ok27, *Mute Stones*, p. 166 (Okasha: RESGEVT[A(E)]). For *Rhystud*, see Ó Riain, in *Cardiganshire County History*, i, 395, supporting, and Richards, *WHR*, 5 (1971), 349, denying the derivation from *Restitutus* (probably thinking of *Rhys + tud*, with Lloyd-Jones, *Y Geninen*, 44 (1926), 5 and 11; for compounds of *Rhys* < **ret-s-* see Gramm., pp. 96 and 399). A pre-syncope Latin borrowing seems quite possible. But syncope also occurred in Vulgar Latin. Smith, VLRB, p. 909, cites RIB i 566 RESTITAE (dat.), and compares *Restitus, Restutina, Restutianus*, etc. elsewhere. *Restutus, Restuta* are very common in fact: OPEL iv, 27–28 and 193. Thomas, *Mute Stones*, pp. 166 and 180, n. 7, suggests that RESTEUTA (or -AE), though possibly influenced by *Restituta*, is British; he compares Gaulish *Restumarus* (KGP, p. 258, also Holder ii, 1178, and GPN, p. 250) and OB *Restue* (Chrest., p. 159). On loss of /j/ in MARGITEUT etc. see LHEB, pp. 345–47, and ‡81 below.
560 See above, ‡27.
561 BWP, pp. 35–36. Cf. Isaac, *Verb in the Book of Aneirin*, p. 358.
562 Zimmer, in Evans FS, pp. 327 and 332, n. 44.

probably a name in -*wy* – although Macalister read WUMERE or WILMERE or WALMERE (cf. 337/60 VVLMER nearby).[563]

991/113/30]RES[could be another example of RES (*Rhys*) as in 1011/220/911, but is probably an incomplete name or word.[564]

998/164 HEUTREN could represent *Eudryn*, as noted already.[565]

In 2022/253/984, COVLGVEN is read GVLGVEN by the Royal Commission and compared with 1004/260/884 GELUGUIN, which is presumably a name in -*(g)wyn*.[566]

2020 VERE[(for VERED- or VERET-?), *if* comparable with Gaulish *Viretios, Viridorix*, etc. and with 461/Ok66 VIRICATI, may show /i/ > /ɨ/ in the first syllable.[567]

‡35 *ū* (< *ǭ, oi*, Latin *ū* and internal *ǭ*) > *ǖ*; LHEB §22.3

No inscriptional evidence is cited (p. 316), which is only to be expected, as *u* was normally used for both sounds in in OWCB, and examples of *i* for /ü(:)/ are very scarce.[568] Note, however, Jackson's comment that 377/175 CIMESETLI 'is difficult to explain, unless we could emend CVMESETLI (cf. no. 446, MAGLOCVVI for MAGLOCVNI)'. Evidently, he regarded this inscription (CIMESETLI . . . AVICAT[ ) as too early ('fifth or sixth century') to be a possible case of /kü:μ/ (< *koimo-* > W. *cu* 'dear') spelt with I. This is at least questionable since he dated /u:/ > /ü:/ 'first half or middle of the sixth century', and this date and the epigraphic date could probably be manoeuvred to fit.[569] The CIMESETLI stone is in the same churchyard as 376/174 VENNISETLI FILIVS ERCAGNI, and it is reasonable to suppose with Rhys that CIMESETLI and VENNISETLI 'belonged to the same family'.[570] In this case, the patronymic ERCAGNI suggests an Irish

---

[563] See ‡‡ 17, 39, 58, and 68.

[564] Cf. Rhys, *AC*, 5th ser. 13 (1896), 114–15.

[565] Above, ‡15.

[566] Cf. ‡22 above and ‡80 below.

[567] Cf. above, ‡28, on 1049/Ok33 URITIN, for a different treatment. As noted in ‡15n., many names in *Vere*- are given by Holder iii, 205–12.

[568] Sims-Williams, *BBCS*, 38 (1991), 25 and 49 and references.

[569] LHEB, pp. 312 and 696. The problem of dating /u:/ > /ü:/ is noted by Sims-Williams, in *Britain 400–600*, pp. 240–41, and Schrijver, *NOWELE*, 35 (1999), 42, n. 56. 446/353 MAGLOCVVI is read MAGLOCVN (uninflected) by Nash-Williams, but see LHEB, pp. 182, n. 1, and 620, n. 2. KHJ had been sure about the -CVVI in 1947. Rhys, in Meyer FS, p. 230, thought it a Latinised gen. of 'Maglocu', which would have to be Irish in view of the date of British /u:/ > /ɨ:/ (see above, ‡16, and ‡54 below). Cf. Rhys's suggestion, quoted in ‡18n, that 454/402 DENCV–I is Ir. *Dianchú*. McManus, *Guide*, p. 65, gives 'MAGLOCVNI (sic leg.)'. Edwards, *Corpus*, s. Nevern 1, reads MAGLOCVN; she notes that the N is reversed but thinks it unlikely that this could be a NI ligature.

[570] Rhys, *AC*, 6th ser. 7 (1907), 68. On pp. 69–70 and 310 (and apud Jones, *TCASFC*, 2 (1906–7), 174) Rhys links CIMESETLI with OI *cimb* 'silver' and with *cim* in Welsh place names (of Irish derivation according to Lloyd-Jones, *Enwau Lleoedd Sir Gaernarfon*, p. 121, who also notes the Irish personal names *Cimm* and *Cimme*; cf. Meyer, *Contributions*, p. 369). Despite Rhys, it is unlikely that CIMESETLI is Irish (one would expect MB and **-SAITL-, although cf. ‡59 on **E** for **AI** in 368/a/150 **DUMELEDONAS**), and it is also

immigrant background for the family, and this may explain the un-Welsh perception of /ü:/ as a sort of I; compare the Irish loanwords *sciból* 'barn' and *ifern* 'hell' (W. *ysgubor* and *uffern*) and Bede's *Dinoot* for W. *Dunawd*.[571] The change of /u:/ > /ü:/ apparently seen in CIMESETLI must have preceded the completion of /nd/ > /nn/ seen in VENNISETLI (‡‡ 22 and 49) to judge by OE *Lindcylene* (Bede's *Lindocolino*) < *Lindum Colōnia*, where /o:/ > /u:/ > /ü:/ has happened but not /nd/ > /nn/.[572]

[35] One possible further example of confusion between U and I may be 379/170 CATVRVG(I) if this is for the expected *CATVRIGI. Perhaps the V here is a hypercorrection.[573]

‡*36 Σ > h at the beginning of the second element of compounds; LHEB §116*

The symbol /Σ/ denotes a sibilant deriving from IE and Celtic **s*, which remained distinct from Latin *s*, was borrowed as /s/ in loans into Old English, and, unlike Latin *s*, developed into /h/ or zero in Brittonic. See ‡‡ 2–3 above and ‡44 below.

[36] (A) Jackson lists the following inscriptions where S is still written (p. 521):

1. 376/174 VENNISETLI
2. 390/96 VENDESETLI
3. 377/175 CIMESETLI
4. 417/282 CAVOSENI ARGII (probably so divisable, he argues, rather than CAVO SENIARGII)[574]

[36] I have no further relevant examples of S. 992/120/14 CENLISINI is presumably *Cen-lisini* rather than *Cenli-sini*; it may be a diminutive of *Cynlas* (OW *Cinglas*, *Conglas* < *Cuneglase* (Gildas) < **Cunoglastos*), i.e. **Cynlesyn* (with unexpected I for /e/).[575] 407/b/258/846 CANTVSVS is

---

unlikely that CIM- could be the Brittonic cognate of *cimb* (cf. LEIA C-99–100). Rhys, *PBA*, 6 (1913–14), 335, n. 1, unconvincingly explained RIB i 841 DEAE SETLOCENIAE (DLG, p. 230) as having E written for /ai/, and CIMESETLI etc. as Goidelic forms with /ai/ reduced to /e/.

[571] Sims-Williams, *BBCS*, 38 (1991), 25 and n. 1 (cf. Loth, *RC*, 36 (1915–16), 124). On ERCAGNI see ‡48.

[572] Sims-Williams, in *Britain 400–600*, p. 241.

[573] See ‡37n. for another explanation.

[574] For ARGIO- cf. *Arg(i)us* in OPEL i, 167, and cf. e.g. *Argiotalus* ('bright/snowy brow'), GPN, p. 259; KGP, p. 134; LEIA A-88 s.v. *arg*; Sims-Williams, *BBCS*, 29 (1980–82), 219; NWÄI, p. 533. On CAVO- and ARGIO- see above, ‡‡ 18 and 19.

[575] LL, p. 198 (and on *Cynlas* see also Williams, *Canu Aneirin*, p. 382). *Conglis*, LL, p. 205, I take to be OE *Cynegils* or *Coengils* (Searle, *Onomasticon*, pp. 139 and 155; for Welsh metathesis of OE *-gils* cf. *Guictglis* in *Historia Brittonum*, ed. Dumville, iii, 82, §20). There are numerous names in *-lis* in RIB, but not *-lisinus;* the only remotely similar one seems to be *Callisunus* (RIB ii [fasc. 4] 2443.7), clearly derived from the stem *Calli-*. **Cynlys* 'hound-court' is an unlikely explanation of CENLISINI.

obviously not dithematic *Cantu-sus*; Evans compares *Cantus[s]ii* from Vichy (Aquitania), while Tomlin compares *Cantissen(a)e* in the Bath tablets, which is less close.[576] In 447/369 the readings CVNISCVS and NEMASLI are linguistically inferior to CVNIGCVS and NEMAGLI. 464/Ok65 MAVI-SIR is not to be segmented *Mavi-sir* but is probably < *Magestu-rīx*.[577] In 487/Ok10, CIRISINIVS and similar readings are probably inferior to DRVSTA(N)VS or similar.[578] 1212 MACARI[/CARASIMILIVS, read by Thomas in 'west Cornwall', is hardly comparable with Old Breton names in *-hamel*, *-hemel* in view of the vocalism, and may be Latin [*uxor*?] *cara Similius* (nominative for genitive).[579] 426/300 **NETTASAGRI** (Nash-Williams: **NETTASAGRU**) is of course Irish.[580]

[36] (B) Jackson notes (p. 521) that H already appears in:

1. 365/149 MAVOHE[NI] (MAVOHENI Lhuyd)
2. 490/Ok29 CONHINOCI (CONHINO[C(I?)] Okasha)

[36] To these we can add:

3. 979/46 GURHI < *Wirosegos* or *Wersegos*[581]
4. 348/b/110/27 GURHIRT or GURHIRET (either linguistically prefer-able to Macalister's GURHIST) = OW *Gu(o)rhitir*, *Gurhytyr*, OC *Gurheter*, OB *Gurhedr* < *Wiro-sitros*;[582] for the metathesis, compare OB *Gleuhetr*, *Gleuherd*, etc., and OW *Catgulart* for *Cadwaladr*[583]
5. 994/125/22 HIROIDIL (with *-(h)oed(d)l* < *sētlo-*)[584]

---

[576] See Evans, *BBCS*, 27 (1976–78), 243–44, citing CIL xiii 1501 (Cantus[s?]ii) and DAG, §151 Remark (B) (p. 384; cf. p. 374), where Whatmough cites *Cantussius* as a potter's name; Tab.Sulis, p. 196. Cf. *Cantusa* (m.) (Bordeaux) in Holder i, 756, and see iii, 54 for *-uss(i)o-*. Cf. *Melussus* beside normal (NWÄI, p. 293, n. 76) *Melissus*: Hassall & Tomlin, *Britannia*, 18 (1987), 363. (Note that W. *melys*, later also *melus*, is not from Latin *-ōsus*, pace VKG ii, 22; cf. Weisgerber, *Rhenania*, p. 88, n. 5.) Rhys, *AC*, 5th ser. 16 (1899), 146, suggested that *Trem/Tref Canus* in LL, p. 125, may be < *Cannus* < *Cantusus*. Note also Latin *Canus*, above, ‡22n.

[577] See above, ‡25.

[578] See above, ‡14.

[579] Thomas, *Christian Celts*, pp. 62–63 (cf. 'in a cottage fireplace beyond Penzance', letter 1.3.01); cf. Chrest., p. 136; Gramm., p. 368; HPB, p. 291 (*samalio-*); SBCHP, p. 81; GPN, p. 252 (and pp. 162–63 for *Cara-*).

[580] GOI, pp. 197 and 678, n. 73; Ziegler, p. 214. **NETTA-** is probably a compositional form and not for ***NETTAS** (McManus, *Guide*, p. 110).

[581] LHEB, p. 446; Williams, *AC*, 90 (1935), 94; Hamp, *BBCS*, 16 (1954–56), 277.

[582] LL, pp. 148, 176, 191 and 231; GPC s.v. *gwrhydri* 'courage'; LHEB, p. 399; LEIA S-100. Rhys, *AC*, 5th ser. 13 (1896), 119, suggested GURUORET instead of GURHIR . . T. KHJ could not see 'any space for an E' before the T; however, there does seem to be one and Dr Nancy Edwards argues that GURHIRET is the most likely restoration.

[583] Gramm., p. 219; Williams, review of CIIC i, in *THSC*, 1943–44, p. 155; Chrest., pp. 136–37 and 205.

[584] Rhys, *Englyn*, p. 97, explains R instead of RH on the grounds that 'in Old and Medieval Welsh r represented both *r* and *rh*'. (Similarly, LWP, p. 238.) This is plausible in view of the fact that H is not otherwise omitted in the inscriptions. Note, however, the absence of *-h-*, which cannot be so explained, in OW *Rioidyl* beside *Rihedl* and *Rihoithil* in LL, p. 417. Cf. ‡78 below.

6.   1012/223/933 IUTHAHELO (= OW *Iud-hail*, with *h-* < **s-*)[585]
7.   419/284 RIGOHENE[586]

[36] The following names with H are too obscure to include. 1006/197/842, read variously as TEFROIHI, TESROIHI, NEFROIHI, [REFSO]IHI or [REFSD]IHI, could be a name in *-hy* < **-sego-*[587] like GURHI above, but is better explained as Pr.Ir. **Nē-froixī*, ‡42. In 1015/233/910 AHEST or ANEST may be OW *Aches(s)* or MW *Annest*.[588] 1046/Ok8 ARAHI could be etymologized **Ario-segos*,[589] but an alternative reading (rejected by Macalister) is ARTHI (< **Artos* 'bear'); compare ARTI (gen.) on two Roman inscriptions from Llanio-isaf, Cardiganshire,[590] and 2028 ARTO-GNOV([?) at Tintagel. The etymology of 1047/Ok20 RU(*n*)HOL and 1058/Ok53 RUNHO[L ?] (?) is uncertain, and no suitable element in **s-* comes to mind to explain the H.[591] In 3014/M5 HERANHAL there is again no obvious element **sal-* to explain -HAL, and -AL with merely orthographical *h-* is also difficult to explain.[592] HERANHAL is unlikely to be a form of *Iarnuual* with loss of of /w/, as in *Tutuual* > Mod.B. *Tu(d)al*, since /w/ does not start to be lost until the eleventh century, and then only before /o/.[593] I prefer to see HERANHAL as an inverse form of *Talhouarn* (W. *Talhaearn*) 'Iron brow'.[594] The combination of /rn/ + dental was liable to simplification: the /n/ might be lost, as apparently in W. *Haearn + ddur* > 1065/410 HAERDUR (linguistically a preferable reading to HAESDUR), OW *Heardur*, MW *Haeardur, Aeardur*, Mod.W. *Iarddur, Arddur*, and OB *Iarn-* > *Iar-* in *Iardet, Iardrion, Iartiern*,[595] or

---

[585] LHEB, p. 562, n. 1; SBCHP, p. 135. On the second H see ‡48 below.
[586] Listed under REG- etc. in GPN, p. 247.
[587] GPN, pp. 254–57; Hamp, *BBCS*, 16 (1954–56), 277.
[588] On *Annest*, see Cane, *Personal Names of Women*, pp. 15, 38–39, and 98, and on *Aches(s)*, see ‡42 below. Rhys, *AC*, 5th ser. 16 (1899), 142 thought both N and H possible, but chose H in *Englyn*, p. 63, on dubious metrical grounds. Macalister preferred H to N apud Anon., *AC*, 7th ser. 8 (1928), 395.
[589] Assuming non-syncopation of the composition vowel, as occurs sometimes in proper names (see ‡38). For *Ario-* see GPN, pp. 141–42, and Lambert, *ÉC*, 31 (1995), 117. On non-affection by **-io-* see above ‡18 on ANATE-.
[590] RIB i 409–10; Davies, in *Cardiganshire County History*, i, 312 (reconstructing **Artius* as nominative).
[591] Cf. above, ‡18.
[592] **sal-* as in OI *salach* 'dirty', OB *haloc* 'lugubri' (LEIA S-16) is obviously unlikely, though not impossible ('of sombre ironsword'?). I assume that a possible **Isarnālis* (cf. *Isarninus* in Suffolk in RIB ii [fasc. 2] 2417.1218) would have given **HERAN(H)OL. See HPB, p. 558 on inorganic *h*.
[593] Chrest., p. 171; HPB, pp. 445 and 449–50.
[594] Chrest., p. 231 and GPN, p. 259. On inversions see Gramm., pp. 396–97.
[595] Evans, *BBCS*, 24 (1970–72), 423, n. 8, and apud Birkhan, *Germanen und Kelten*, p. 135, n. 110; Williams, *Poems of Taliesin*, p. 127; EANC, p. 217; Chrest., p. 141; CBT ii, 361. On the possibility that HAERDUR contains *haer* rather than *haearn* see ‡47 below. See also above, ‡14, for the possibility that some (or all?) of these forms come from **isar-* 'swift' rather than **isarn-* 'iron'. Note also the French place name *Isarnoduros* > Izernore, Holder ii, 76.

alternatively the dental might be lost, as in *Isarnodatewidos* > OB *Iarndetuuid* > *Iarn(n)etuuid* (846 AD).[596] Compare 3021/I2 MAONIRN < *Maondirn*.[597] Jackson does not cite any examples where the lost dental was from original *t* rather than *d*, assuming that both had merged as /n'd/ after syncope, but it seems possible that original *t* could leave a trace as /h/, as in HERANHAL. Alternatively, the -H- may be merely orthographic.The same name appears in 3010/M1 HERA[ ]AL, where [N] or [NN] or [NH] or [ND] or [NT] must be restored. The final Breton inscription with H is 3011/M2 IRHAEMA * INRI. This is probably for I(*c*) R(*equiescit*) HAEMA (feminine of *Haemus*, a name attested in Gaul and elsewhere) plus the New Testament I.N.R.I. (compare 1057/Ok54 INRI, as reluctantly read by Macalister). It is unlikely that IRHAEMA is a poor or archaic spelling of a Breton name such as *Iarnhoiam* ('au fer très long') < *Isarno-sēsamos*.[598]

‡37 Completion of the loss of final syllables; LHEB §182

I discuss this here together with the evidence for ‡21, 'Beginning of loss of final syllables; LHEB §182'.

It is easy to list inscriptions where final syllables have disappeared. On the other hand, owing to the similarity between British and Latin declensions, it is frequently impossible to distinguish between names where the terminations -VS (and Vulgar Latin -OS, -O), gen. -I, and feminine -A, gen. -(A)E have been artificially tacked on to apocopated British names and those where these terminations represent or replace British terminations. Hence Jackson rightly lists no such names as certain examples of retained final syllables. In fact he has only two examples (pp. 619 and 628) of retained final syllables:

1. 322/27 CAMVLORIS
2. 354/126/6 ORDOVS

[37] Two comparable inscriptions, not known when LHEB was published, are:

3. 2006 CVNORIX
4. 1205/Ok44 MAVOUIH (or MAVORIH?)[599]

[37] It could, of course, be argued that just as most apocopated names were Latinized by adding first or second declension Latin endings, so apocopated names from earlier *-rīks* and *-viks* may have been restored on the pattern of the Latin third declension. Jackson probably disregarded this both on account of the final -S rather than -X of CAMVLORIS and ORDOVS

---

[596] Chrest., pp. 123 and 141; HPB, pp. 328–29 and 790. Cf. Schrijver, *SC*, 33 (1999), 14.
[597] Below, ‡‡ 65 and 74.
[598] Gramm., pp. 251 and 396; cf. LEIA S-116; GPC s.v. *hir*. For *Haemus* see IEMB, p. 190, and OPEL ii, 173.
[599] On 1.-4. see above, ‡14.

(although admitting that -S for -X could be Vulgar Latin) – he thought -S reflected a British change of /-χ^s/ > /-s/ (wrongly, I argued in ‡14 above) – and because of the lack of *i*-affection in CAMVLORIS and the loss of /i/ in ORDOVS.[600] Such arguments apply with less force to the possibly conservative spelling CVNORIX, but with more to MAVOUIH, where -UIH (if the correct reading) probably reflects the true British result of *-*vix* and in any case cannot be Latinate.

[37] Notwithstanding these doubts, the above four forms probably are valid instances of unapocopated forms. By contrast, forms such as 394/103 CANTIORI are quite ambiguous, as the -I may be genitive of Latin *-ius* rather than the remains of British nominative *-*rīx*, as Jackson shows.[601]

[37] There are many definitely apocopated forms, and Jackson does not attempt to list them all. He notes (p. 620 and n. 2) that it is doubtful whether an ending has been lost in 430/306 ETTERNI FILI VICTOR (also [VIC]TOR in the ogam), which may be nominative for genitive, and in 446/353 MAGLOCVN (Nash-Williams's reading), which he argues should be read MAGLOCVNI.[602] Hence, Jackson argues that the first certain examples are 350/116/3 [IV]DNERT (recte IDNERT, Lhuyd), 971/35 VIRNIN FILIUS CUURIS CINI (EREXIT HUNC LAPIDEM), 'where all three names lack endings',[603] 1033/287 CINGEN CELEN etc., and 995/133/24 ENEVIRI, shown by Loth and Ifor Williams to be W. *Enewyr* (: OB *Eneuere* (vocative)) < *Anaworīx* plus 'a factitious Latin genitive ending'.[604]

---

[600] See above, ‡‡ 14 and 19.

[601] See above, ‡14.

[602] See further above, ‡35n.

[603] Jackson's readings (on the first name see ‡66). The apocope is already noted in BWP, pp. 11 and 17–18. Williams compared CUURIS with MW *Cerys* and with *Pwll Ceris*, on which see also Rhys, *AC*, 5th ser. 9 (1892), 67 and n. 1; EANC, p. 30; Pierce, *Place-Names of Dinas Powys*, p. 330; Padel, *Popular Dictionary of Cornish Place-Names*, p. 140; B. L. Jones, *TAAS*, 1984, 102–4; Dumville, *SC*, 10/11 (1975–76), 87; and Clancy, in Anderson FS, p. 90. If *Ceris* originally had *-st*, as indicated by early spellings, it is difficult to equate CUURIS with it. (Theoretically one might equate CUURIS with a pre-apocope dental-stem *Kurit-s* or *Kurid-s*; cf. *koret-s* > OI *cora* 'palisade', OB *coret*, LEIA C-206, which has the wrong vowel, however.) A name *Curisius* is attested in Italy (OPEL ii, 88.) Note that if MW *Cyny* and CINI come from *Cinius* (cf. Holder i, 1020 and iii, 1221; Weisgerber, *Rhenania*, pp. 132 and 141, n. 177), as argued by Williams, CINI could conceivably be a pre-apocope genitive (for nominative; compare 398/106 MINI (above, ‡22n) and 451/401 DAARI. Rhys, *Englyn*, pp. 22–26, read 971/35 CUURIδ, which he equated with MW *Cywryt* (but we would expect -T in the inscription!); in *AC*, 5th ser. 12 (1895), 32, he had noted that *cywryd* appeared as *-cuurit* in OW *Bledcuurit* (LL, p. 388) = MW *Blegywryt* (see Lloyd-Jones, *Geirfa*, s.vv. *kywryt*, *Kywryt*). Note also 304 CURIT[(‡16 above). In Lhuyd's copy of 971/35 in BL Stowe MS 1023 fo. 20r, the reading looks like CUURIL which calls to mind *Gwril* in *Llwyngwril* (WATU, p. 146; cf. *Viril(l)us* etc. in Holder iii, 383–85); the final consonant must be regarded as doubtful, and was probably already damaged in Lhuyd's day.

[604] LHEB, pp. 620–21; Loth, *RC*, 11 (1890), 136 and 141, and *Noms des saints bretons*, p. 38; Williams and Nash-Williams, *AC*, 91 (1936), 15–19; Pierce, *Morgannwg*, 29 (1985), 74–79.

[37] In the following list of inscriptions showing loss of final syllables, forms such as ENEVIRI which include an added Latin termination have been excluded, since this is only identified as such because other features show that the inscription is post-apocope – if the form had been *ANAVORI, the -I would have been quite ambiguous. Since ENEVIRI will in any case be labelled as relatively late on account of its internal *i*-affection, there is no real point in listing it as also post-apocope when that fact is only a deduction from the affection. In the case of inscriptions including several names, I have not always listed every one, but only enough names to show the presence of apocope. When they occur alongside native names, I have ignored biblical names such as *Daniel* and *David*, even though these were 'perhaps regarded as standing for *Danielus*, etc.';[605] note however 35. IOSEPH and 71. MIHAEL, each included here and standing alone.

CIIC etc.	ECMW etc.	Names with apocope
1. 971	35	]VS [ ]NIN, CUURI[S?], CINI (see above)
2. 979	46	GUADAN, NI(n)ID, GURHI
3. 980	46a	(W)LIGUE (Macalister: WUMERE, WILMERE or WALMERE)
4. 978	49	BRIAMAIL FLOU
5. 333	50	CATVC
6. 984	59	GURCI BLEDRUS
7. 337	60	[S]I[U]ERD (?), VVLMER (Old English)
8. 985	61	MORIDIC
9. 986	62	IORUERT, RUALLAUN
10. 988	67	MENHIR, GENILLIN
11. 2018	Caerns.	CVNCUOM SPUO TINM (??)
12. 348/b	110/27	GURHIR(E)T or GURHIST
13. 350	116/3	IDNERT
14. 993	124/18	DITOC, ITGEN (or ASAITGEN)
15. 994	125/22	HIROIDIL, CAROTINN
16. 996	147	MO[RE]DIC, ELMON
17. 997	159	EIUDON
18. 998	164	HEUTREN
19. 1001	181	COCOM[606]

---

[605] LHEB, p. 618. Cf. Harvey, in Mac Cana FS, p. 59. Note two biblical names showing loss of the final consonant: 1061/Dor.iii GIDEO < *Gideon/Gedeon* (Radford & Jackson, in RCHM *Dorset*, ii/2, p. 312; McClure, *EHR*, 22 (1907), 729, comparing OW and OB *Gedeon* – cf. *Gedeaun, Gedianus*, LL, p. 399) and 993/124/18 ASA < *Asaph* (‡65 below).

[606] Accepting the reading of Radford & Hemp, *AC*, 106 (1957), 111, COCOM FILIU EDELSTAN, though not their emendation (on the grounds that 'M is an unlikely ending for a name') to COCONI; see also Hemp, *AC*, 107 (1958), 125.

20.	1000	182	CONCENN, CATTELL, BROHCMAIL, ELISEG, GUOILLAUC, MAUN, ANNAN, CONMARCH, POUOIS
21.	1005	191/886	BRANCUF or BRANCU
22.	1009	193/935	EBISSAR
23.	1008	194/934	EBISAR
24.	1011	220/911	HOUELT, RES
25.	1013	222/912	EBISAR
26.	1014	231/908	ENNIAUN, GUORGORET
27.	1015	233/910	GRUTNE, AHEST or ANEST
28.	1019	237/920	ILCI or]ILCI[607]
29.	1023	239/927	NERTTAN,[608] SCILOC
30.	1025	248/862	ARTBEU
31.	2022	253/984	COVLGVEN or GVLGVEN, [B]ERER[ ] or AERERN, HUHIVM or HU[TR]VM
32.	1024	255/926	ARTHMAIL, GLIGUIS, NERTAT or NERT(tan),[609] FILI[610]
33.	1004	260/884	GELUGUIN or]GELUGUIN
34.	2029	p.39i	ERECOR, CVNIIAC
35.	2031	p.68	IOSEPH[611]
36.	1032	281	WLEDER, ODELEV
37.	1033	287	CINGEN(?) CELEN, TRICET, NITANAM, etc.
38.	1029	Mer.	REU (dubious reading)
39.	1030	Mer.	RHOS (very dubious reading)
40.	1035	303	MARGITEUT
41.	440	335	EOROCAN or EONOCAN or EOPOCAN[612]
42.	1036	360	HAUEN (Macalister; Nash-Williams: HAN EH)[613]

---

[607] Rhys, *AC*, 5th ser. 16 (1899), 138–39, rightly compared OW *Elci* and *Ilci* (see ‡85 below), but mistakenly mentioned OW *Elcu* which has the element *-cu(f)* (cf. OC *Illcum*, Bodmin, p. 86), not Goidelic *cú* as he thought.

[608] Rejected Jackson, *Speculum*, 24 (1949), 600. (Pace Jackson, the reading HERTTAN goes back to Rhys, *AC*, 5th ser. 16 (1899), 159–60; indeed H is already shown in Lhuyd's drawing, reproduced by RCAHMW.) Williams, *AC*, 87 (1932), 238, suggests NERT[(I)ATI].

[609] Rejected Jackson, *Speculum*, 24 (1949), 600.

[610] On the name *Fili* (as in *Caerffili*), OB *Fily* see Loth, *Noms des saints bretons*, pp. 41–42; Williams, *AC*, 87 (1932), 238; Lloyd-Jones, *Geirfa*, p. 95; Olson & Padel, *CMCS*, 12 (1986), 45–46. The reading is rejected (probably wrongly) by RCAHMW.

[611] Although RCAHMW say that Bishop Joseph died in Rome, LL, p. 252, states only that it was at *Agustan* on the *way to* Rome. If this was merely Aust on the Severn crossing (see PNRB, pp. 510–11; Coates & Breeze, *Celtic Voices*, pp. 54–55), it would be possible for Joseph to be buried at Llandaf.

[612] Dubious, since the other name in 440/335 does not show apocope; for possible explanations see ‡17n above.

[613] Cf. OB *Houuen*, *Hewen*, W. *hywen*, Chrest., p. 140, DGVB i, 36, GPC s.v. *hywen*, and W. *Gwên* as personal name? However, the A makes a comparison with W. *awen* preferable; cf. ‡44.

43.	1041	376	GURMARC
44.	1039	382	HED or NED
45.	2005	Pembs.	S[AT]VRNBIV
46.	1065	410	HAESDUR or (better) HAERDUR
47.	2021	Herefs.	GVINNDA
48.	464	Ok65	MAVISIR
49.	473/b	Ok46	IGNIOC
50.	486	Ok56	CVMREGNI or CVMRECINI[614]
51.	1044	Ok7	LEUIUT[615]
52.	1045	Ok69	AGURED or AGUDED or AGUTED or ÆGVRED[616]
53.	1046	Ok8	ARAHI (if not ARTHI)[617]
54.	1047	Ok20	RU(n)HOL
55.	1048	Ok32	GVENNCREST, VIR QONFAL, VENNORCIT (??)[618]
56.	1049	Ok33	URITIN or URITN
57.	1050	Ok74	MEVROC or UROC or INVROC or IRCVROC etc.
58.	1053	Ok1	ALRORON or CILRORON
59.	1054	Ok43	DONIERT
60.	1058	Ok53	RUNHO[L] (?)
61.	1059	Ok64	ÆLRIAT or ÆGRAT or ÆLNAT[619]
62.	1060	Ok57	GURGLES[620]
63.	1061	Dor.iii	CATGUG (Macalister: CATTUG)
64.	1064	Dor.iv	AUPRIT
65.	1066	Manx	GURIAT
66.	1068/b	Manx	MALBREN, BRENLIER or BREDLIEN
67.	1200	Ok42	SPED (obscure)
68.	2038	Manx	BRANHUI (< *Branoụios, ‡58)
69.	3002	F2	GALLMAU
70.	3004	F4	IOCILINX
71.	3009	C4	MIHAEL

---

[614] On the possibility that this has post-apocope -I see below, ‡48.

[615] Assuming this is Cornish (cf. OB *Leu-* 'lion' and *Iud-*, Chrest., pp. 142–44); for another compound of *iud* with fabled beast, cf. OW *Gripp-iud*, OC *Gryfyið/Grifiuð* 'gryphon lord' (‡86 below). Okasha suggests (*Corpus*, p. 83) that LEUIUT may be Old English, noting e.g. *Leuiet* for *Leofgeat* in Domesday Book – hardly a close parallel.

[616] Possibly Old English; see above, ‡25.

[617] See above, ‡36.

[618] Cf. Thomas, *Mute Stones*, p. 290. Tedeschi, *Scrittura e civiltà*, 19 (1995), tav. 3, reads: + VIR/QONFALI FILIIV/GVENNORCIT; see also ‡‡ 44n. and 94.

[619] Old English according to Okasha.

[620] Macalister's reading (see below, ‡58). It is less easy to assess the readings of Okasha and of Thomas, *Mute Stones*, p. 290: GUNGLEI (so Radford, *DASP*, 27 (1969), 81), or GUNIGLEI, GUMGLEI, or GUNGLEL.

72. 3010   M1   HERANNUEN, HERA[N]AL
                    (or HERA[H]AL, etc.), RAN HUBRIT
73. 3014   M5   HARENBILI, HERANHAL
74. 3015   M6   PROSTLON
75. 3021   I2   MAONIRN

76. 2034/871 can be added if it reads BELGINT, as now stated by Knight, rather BELGICU.[621]
77. Finally, 479/Ok16 CVNAIDE (if not CVNATDO) can be added if cognate with W. *Cynaethwy* (‡‡ 51 and 58).

[37] In 319/9 CVNOGVSI the -I seems secure, despite Macalister's doubts. 320/26 CVLIDOR may be CVLIDOR[I] (the reading is debated cf. ‡16) and 1402/Ok26 POTIT[I] is also uncertain. 379/170 CATVRVG, 'uninflected' according to Nash-Williams, was respectively read as or restored to CATVRVGI by Rhys and Macalister.[622] 2007/10 MAILIS must now be read MAILISI with a horizontal -I.[623] Nash-Williams notes that DE[CAB]ARBALOM is 'uninflected' in 372/160 **DECCAIBAR VUGLOB DISI** (Macalister: **[DECCA]IBARVALB [MAQI B]RO[CAGNI]**)/DE[CA-B]ARBALOM FI[L]IVS BROCAGNI, but Jackson regards this interpretation as uncertain.[624] 990/108/1 TIGE(I)R[N may originally have had an inflection. 2001 C (= IC?) [ ]CRET ORBIORI + (or ORBIORIT) *may* contain the element *Ecritu-/Ecretu-* ('ride out, raid'?) that occurs in Gaulish names such as *Inecriturix*, *Ecretumarus*, *Ecrito*, and *Ecritus*,[625] with apocope, but this is of course uncertain, as is the choice between *Orbiorix* and *Orbioritus* as etymologies for the second name. 1006/197/842 NEFROIHI (or the other readings in -HI) may be a name in OW *-hi*, but Pr.Ir. *Nē-froixī* is more likely.[626] In 1007/206/938 Nash-Williams hesitated between IRBICI (so RCAHMW) and IRBIC + (so Macalister).[627] In 1012/223/933 Nash-Williams read TEC[AI]N + (Macalister TECG +, RCAHMW TEC[A]N),

---

[621] See ‡53 below.
[622] LHEB, p. 620, n. 3; Uhlich, *Morphologie*, p. 190. -RVG(I) has not been identified; the identification in LWP, p. 389, and Holder iii, 1164, with OB **rogedou* (and W. *rhewydd*, cf. LWP, p. 426) has to be rejected; see DGVB i, 220 and 298; LHEB, p. 440, n. 2. A possibility, assuming that G stands for /g/ according to ogam conventions (see ‡17), is CAT(V)- + VRVG- > W. *grug* 'heather' < **wrūk-* < **wroik-* (: OI *Fróech*, Ziegler, p. 252). It is curious that the name *Llanrug*, *Lanruc*, appears in Wales and Brittany (Loth, *Noms des saints bretons*, p. 76); can the second element be a personal name rather than the common noun 'heather'? For the association between heather and battle see Vendryes, *ÉC*, 4 (1948), 38–39; Sims-Williams, *SC*, 12/13 (1977–78), 114. A further possibility is CATV- + RVG- < **ro-(w)ik-*; cf. a Pannonian *Vindoroici* (KGP, pp. 100, 261, and 296).
[623] Cf. LHEB, p. 329, n. 1. On the rediscovery of the stone, see ‡14 above.
[624] LHEB, pp. 187 and 620, n. 3. ABSALOM seems impossible. On early readings of the stone see Rhys, *AC*, 6th ser. 7 (1907), 293–309.
[625] GPN, pp. 78–79, 202 and 250; RIG iv, 536; LEIA R-34–35 s.v. *riuth*. Fleuriot, *ÉC*, 20 (1983), 113, compares W. *echryd* 'terror' < *cryd* 'trembling'.
[626] See ‡‡ 36 and 42.
[627] On this name see below, ‡57.

but his drawing seems to show TECANI+.[628] In 1016/234/907 Nash-Williams gives CONBELIN, but the stone is damaged, and the parallel with 1023/239/927 suggests CONBELIN[I] as a possibility. In the eighteenth-century drawing of 1034/286 PASCENT[I] there is no trace of an -I, but horizontal I might have been overlooked.[629] 439/319 **INGEN** (Macalister) is a dubious reading and in any case Irish rather than Brittonic,[630] as are 442/346 [MAC]CVDICCL (MACCVDICCL Lhuyd), 466/Ok23 **MEMOR**,[631] 1038/365 MAIL (or MEIL or MAL) DOMNA[C], 488/Ok60 **ENABARR**, and 507 CRON[*A*]N[.[632] In 490/Ok29 DATUIDOCI CONHINOCI, Macalister's Is are uncertain according to Okasha, and the same applies to 1057/Ok54 EROCAV[I]. 1069/Ok.PictApp.I [B]ETON or [C]ETON or [E]ETON or [T]ETON may be Pictish. 3016/M7 LAGU probably does include the remains of an ending -US (notionally *LAGU-U(S) = *$La\gamma\underline{u}o(\Sigma)$).[633] The same could be true of 2028 ARTOGNOV([?), which is also uncertain because the V is close to the edge of the slate.

‡38 Syncope of composition vowels; LHEB §195

Composition vowels were first reduced and then lost, although there are various exceptions, confined to proper names: for example, MW *Dyfnawal* beside *Dyfnwal* < *Dumnowalos*.[634]

[38] A general exception applies to composition vowels in the stressed penult, for example *Maglo-kū* > W. *Meilyg*.[635] Syncope clearly did not happen here, and presumably the /o/ was intact at the time of its *i*-affection. There is no reason to suppose that such composition vowels were ever liable to reduction in Brittonic. Jackson's citation of 446/353 'MAGLOCVNI (*sic leg.*) FILI CLVTORI' among forms with the 'correct form of the composition vowel . . . preserved',[636] presumably relates to the first name, not to CLVTORI. The relevant examples of stressed composition vowels are: 320/26 CVLIDOR(I);[637] 331/41 TECVRI; 322/27 CAMVLORIS; 443/349

---

[628] This agrees with the inflection of ARTMALI in the same text. Note that the writing of -MALI for -MAILI makes it conceivable that TECANI stands for TECAINI (but what would this be? hardly *Teg + cain*); cf. ‡‡17n. and 48. Rhys, *AC*, 5th ser. 16 (1899), 149, preferred TECANI to TECAIN. Macalister, apud Anon., *AC*, 7th ser. 8 (1928), 406, rejects TECA/+NI and seems to read TECG/+.

[629] LWP, p. 377.

[630] McManus, *Guide*, p. 67, rejects **INGEN**.

[631] LHEB, pp. 140–41, 183, and 620, n. 2.

[632] In 1952 KHJ read '[ ]ACRON ?'

[633] See above, ‡25.

[634] LHEB, p. 648. Cf. Davies, in *Greek Personal Names*, p. 23: 'in a literate society (or for that matter in a society which is rich in oral poetic performances) older forms of words may be recorded in writing or in the poetic tradition. In the case of names, the incentive to resurrect them or to continue them in the original form may be stronger than for other lexical items.'

[635] LHEB, p. 644.

[636] Ibid.

[637] But for a different analysis (CVLI-DOR(I)) see ‡16 above.

CAMVLORI (better than CAMVMORI); 330/66 CATIRI; 380/84 ICORI/
ICORIGAS; 388/94 DERVORI; 394/103 CANTIORI; 396/104 AVITORI;
397/105 BECCVRI; 354/126/6 ORDOVS; 995/133/24 ENEVIRI; 361/140
TALOR[I]; 2001 ORBIORI (but if the reading ORBIORIT[ ] is preferred,
the composition vowel is not in the penult); 409/198/849 CARANTOR-
IVS; 2029/p.39i ERECOR MAGLORI; 415/278 TARRONERIS (Macalister);   1032/281   WLEDER;   446/353   CLVTORI/**CLUTAR[I]**   or
CLUTAR[IGAS];[638]   464/Ok65   MAVISIR;   516/Scot.1   MAVORIVS;
1205/Ok44 MAVOUIH (or MAVORIH?); 2006 CVNORIX; and perhaps
511/Scot.10 CONINIE and [E]RTIRIE (Macalister: [T]VRTIRIE), and
3020/I1 BELADORE. Some of these names, such as 2006 CVNORIX,
may be Irish names with British O substituted for its Irish counterpart, A.
369/153 CVRCAGNVS and 441/345 CVRCAGNI are probably Irish, with
*-a-gnī < *-o-gnī*,[639] however, if British, they would have the composition
vowel in the stressed penult. The same applies to 353/127/7 MAGLAGNI;
357/136 CORBAGNI; 370/157 VLCAGNVS; 372/160 BROCAGNI;
376/174 and 2027 ERCAGNI; 432/312 **DOVAGNI**/DOBAGNI; 434/314
COIMAGNI; 449/384 **SAGRAGNI**/SAGRANI; 457/Ok18 MESCAGNI
or   MERCAGNI;   472/Ok35   VLCAGNI;   478/Ok48   BROCAGNI;
487/Ok10 DRVSTA(G?)NI(??); and (with a later development) 507
CRON[A]N[;[640]   possibly   1012/223/933   TECAN(I)(?);[641]   979/46
GUADAN; 1023/239/927 NERTTAN, also Macalister's NERT*tan* in
1024/255/926;[642] and perhaps 2025/Scot.12 NEITANO. We have already
seen that the instances in 328/44 and 429/307 of VENDONI may
correspond to an ancient name (*)*Vendonius*, but if VENDONI is Irish,
as suggested by Jackson,[643] the O could be due to the initial labial /w/
according to Ziegler's rule,[644] and so too in the ogam, at least, of 422/298
VENDOGNI/VENDAGNI (Macalister: VENDOGNI). VENDONI (if
indeed Irish) might appear to show that this rounding (or retention of
rounding) could lead to a regular Irish phonetic development to /o:/,
distinct from the familiar Irish *-o-gnos > *-a-gnas > -án*.[645] Alternatively,
however, one might attribute **-O-GNI** to British influence or could regard

---

[638] See n. 654 below. Rhys, in Meyer FS, p. 229, would explain the O/A variation starting from
    -ārios (: Latin *-ārius*), but the parallels he cites from Holder ii, 878, *Cluturius* and *Clutoria*
    (unreferenced! cf. *Cluturiacum > Klüsserath*, iii, 1241) are against this. Jackson, LHEB,
    p. 624, plausibly reads **CLUTAR[IGAS]**, with *Irish* composition vowel.
[639] See ‡48 below.
[640] In 1952 KHJ read '[ ]ACRON ?'
[641] See ‡37 above.
[642] Both rejected by Jackson, *Speculum*, 24 (1949), 600.
[643] LHEB, p. 512; cf. ‡22 above.
[644] Ziegler, pp. 63–64. See below.
[645] In connection with 422/298 KHJ compares OI *-ón* in O'Brien, *Celtica*, 10 (1973), 221. The
    VENDAGNI (reading based on Lhuyd) rather than the **VENDOGNI** of 422/298 is
    presumably the ancestor of Ir. *Finnán*. It is difficult to account for the alleged coexistence
    of the two forms on one stone. One is familiar with variation of suffix in Old Irish (e.g.

it as a Latinate(?) genitive of the nominative *-oɣnah which would have arisen by regularly lowering in Irish from an original *-ugnos (see ‡48). 362/142 **CUNIGNI/CVNIGNI** and 374/172 CVNEGNI also have the composition vowel in the penult.[646] Insofar as the above names were British or pronounced with the British accent, their composition vowels were in the stressed penult and hence exempt from reduction and syncope. They are therefore ignored below.

[38] Jackson groups the remaining relevant data in three categories, which we may label (A), (B), and (C):

(A) forms where the etymologically correct vowel appears (p. 644), usually O but also, for example, U in the case of a *u*-stem like CATU-
(B) forms where the vowel is 'wrongly spelt in various ways', presumably owing to the reduction (p. 645)
(C) forms with syncope (p. 646).

There are a few names with unsyncopated composition vowel which cannot be assigned to (A) or (B) because we do not know to which stem class the first element belongs; these may be labelled (BA).

[38] A problem affecting (A) is that presumably in the (B) phase, when various vowels were used almost randomly to denote a *schwa*-like sound, the etymologically 'correct' vowel may occasionally have been written by accident as it were. An extreme example is 477/Ok11 TEGERNOMALI, which appears to have the original composition vowel *o of *Tigernomaglos, yet also shows the loss of /ɣ/ in /ɣl/, a change that is supposed to have taken place after syncope, judging by MW *teilu* < *teɣ'lū̆ɣ* < *tegoslougos.[647] I shall not attempt to distinguish such 'bogus' (A) examples, since wherever they are diagnosable, that will appear anyway in the final analysis under a different heading, for example /ɣl/ > /i̯l/ (‡48) in the case of TEGERNOMALI.

[38] Another chronological problem is that a form such as *DUMNAVALI would not necessarily belong to a stage earlier than (C), seeing that trisyllabic *Dyfnawal* is also attested in Middle Welsh (see above); I shall assign such names, where they can be identified, to a category (BC). A further category (ABC) covers names such as MW *Dinogat* which appears still to preserve the original composition vowel of *Dūnokatus.[648]

[38] A further problem is presented by Irish names, which are not always distinguishable from Brittonic names. The commonest form of the

---

Gabrón ~ *Gabrán*, O'Brien, loc. cit.), but can one really extrapolate an earlier variation between *-oɣnah and *-aɣnah from this?

[646] As would 447/369 CVNISCVS or CVNIGCVS if it were a Celtic name, but see ‡48 below.
[647] Cf. LHEB, pp. 465–66. But see below, Ch. 3, p. 256.
[648] Cf. LHEB, p. 648; Uhlich, *Morphologie*, pp. 15–16.

composition vowel in Primitive Irish, corresponding to the Brittonic /o/, was /a/, normally written **A** in ogam.[649] There is thus a danger that Irish names with original A may be mistaken for Brittonic names with A for the reduced vowel. I have tried to weed out such Irish names from (B) below. Conversely, there is also a danger that Irish names in which O is used for the Primitive Irish reduced vowel may be mistaken for Brittonic names with original /o/. Fortunately, however, **O** seems rarely to have been used for the Irish composition vowel, to judge by the ogam inscriptions from Ireland itself: the main exceptions there, according to Ziegler's data, occur in contact with labial consonants, e.g. 273 **CALUNOVIC[A]** and 186 **EQODDI**, and (once) from /u/ in 95 **MEDDOGENI** (possibly reading **MEDDU-** in any case).[650] She explains 39 **BRANOGENI** and 252 **COBRANOR[IGAS]** by influence from the more distant labials,[651] which if that rule is accepted leaves only 179 **ETORIGAS** unexplained among the ogams in Ireland with **O**; and I suggest below that **ETO-** is another *u*-stem.[652] Leaving aside such instances, it seems most likely that when Irish names in Britain are spelt with O, this is due to British (or Romano-British) influence.[653] Such Irish names presumably belong to the period when O was still the regular British composition vowel. I therefore group them (other than special cases of the **CALUNOVIC[A]** and **MEDDOGENI** types) as a subsection (AI), or (AIBC) as appropriate (I = 'Irish').

[38] (A) Jackson's list of examples of correct composition vowels (p. 644), removing three probable Irish names – CVNOGVSI, DVNOCATI, EUOLENGGI – and adding any ogam equivalents in square brackets, is:

1. 435/315 CLVTORIGI
2. 446/353 MAGLOCVNI (*'sic leg.'*) FILI CLVTORI [ogam **MAGLICUNAS MAQI CLUTAR[I]** or **CLUTAR[IGAS]**][654]

---

[649] On /o/ > /a/ in Irish see Sims-Williams, in *Gaulois et celtique continental* and in Meid FS, pp. 472–73.

[650] Ziegler, pp. 63–64 (cf. MacNeill, *PRIA*, 27 C (1909), 352; Uhlich, *Morphologie*, pp. 33–36). Note that 95 **MEDDOGENI** can also be read with its etymological U: see Harvey, *Ériu*, 38 (1987), 53; McManus, *Guide*, p. 66; and Uhlich, *Morphologie*, pp. 24 and 278, with parallels. Cf. also British Celtic MEDVGENI/MEDIGENI (Jackson, in *Thetford Treasure*, p. 47) and Celtiberian *mesuKenoś* (De Bernardo Stempel, in Meid FS, p. 68; MLH v/1, pp. 251–52). On /a/ > /o/ in 186 **EQODDI** see Harvey, *Ériu*, 38 (1987), 64, and compare LAPIS ECHODI in Iona, published by Steer, *PSAS*, 101 (1968–69), 129 (with etymology by Jackson: *Equodix); cf. Hiberno-Latin *Echodius*: Bergin, *Ériu*, 11 (1930–32), 144 (= *E(o)chuid*, gen. *Echdach*); Swift, *Ogam Stones*, pp. 77–79; and Harvey, in Mac Cana FS, p. 61. On the name(s) *Éochaid* and *Éochu* see O'Brien, *Celtica*, 10 (1973), 220 and n. 13.

[651] This explanation is not entertained by Uhlich, *Morphologie*, p. 34. Another possibility is that the names were British: O'Brien, *Celtica*, 10 (1973), 231.

[652] The other possibilities are: (1) a lost initial labial, since the inscription may be acephalous; (2) **T** < /tw/; (3) British influence, though this seems unlikely in Dingle, Co. Kerry. The name is without a known Irish descendant (Ziegler, p. 181).

[653] Cf. LHEB, p. 644.

[654] The roman-letter patronymic is irrelevant, even if British (it is Irish according to Ziegler, p. 150), since the *o* is in the penult (see above, n. 638). **MAGLI-** rather than ***MAGLA-** may

3. 449/384 CVNOTAMI [ogam **CUNATAMI**][655]
4. 318/6 ETTORIGI – quite likely Irish (see under (AIBC) below)
5. 379/170 CATVRVG(I)[656]
6. 342/70 CVNOCENNI FILIVS CVNOGENI [ogam **CUNACENNI [A]VI ILVVETO**] – although both of these CVNO- names could be Irish;[657] if they are, they belong in the (AI) class, since there is no reason to suppose that the C- retained any of its original labial quality
7. 455/403 CAMVL(L)ORIGI
8. 358/138 VOTEPORIGIS [ogam **VOTECORIGAS**, with **O** either copying the Brittonic form or under the rounding influence of ***Q** > **C**]

[38] The following should be added:

9. 2000 DEVORIGI (though this could be Irish)[658]
10. 349/121/4 BROHO[MAGLI], also perhaps VELVOR[IA][659]
11. 362/142 **AVITTORIGES**/AVITORIA (although this could be Irish)[660]
12. 370/157 SENOMAGLI (possibly Irish)[661]

---

indicate reduction in Irish, although MacNeill (*PRIA*, 27 C (1909), 352) suggested that /i/ may have spread from *i*-stems to other classes, as arguably in Gaulish; cf. Ziegler, pp. 64–65, and above, ‡17, on 496 **TEBICATO[S]**; see also ‡16 n. 125. If MAGLOCVNI is Irish, it cannot be put in (AI) in view of the initial labial.

[655] Although, with regard to classifying this under (A), note the survival of a (reduced) composition vowel in OB *Cunatam* (LHEB, p. 649; Uhlich, *Morphologie*, pp. 209 and 223) as against OW *Condaf*, MW *Cyndaf* (LL, p. 140; EWGT, s.n.). Rhys, *AC*, 4th ser. 4 (1873), 77, quotes OW *Canatam* (expanded as *canataṇ* in LL, p. 239) as the same name; cf. Evander Evans, *AC*, 4th ser. 3 (1872), 312. For OW *Can-* < *Cun-* see Sims-Williams, *BBCS*, 38 (1991), 45 and 47.

[656] But this may be syncopated if it is a compound of W. *cad* and *wrug (> *grug*); see above, n. 622.

[657] See above, ‡‡ 17 and 22. **ILVVETO** may well be Irish, with Irish raising of **elu-*, since British retained *El-* (exceptions such as *Illtud* (cf. 1013/222/912 ILTU[TI(S)]) usually being attributed to Irish influence, although see ‡85 below). See GPN, pp. 347–48; Rhys, *PBA*, 6 (1913–14), 330; Doble, *Lives of the Welsh Saints*, p. 125, n. 85; Evans, *Studies*, 68 (1979), 27; Ó Riain, in *Cardiganshire County History*, i, 378; cf. Ziegler, pp. 108 and 188 (s. **ili-*). See collections of names in *El-* by Rhys, *PBA*, 6 (1913–14), 327–32, Williams, *BBCS*, 5 (1929–31), 136–37, and Thomas, *BBCS*, 8 (1935–37), 30–31, and ‡85 below. **ILVVETO** appears to have syncope, but this may be an illusion; see below, under (C).

[658] It is treated as British in Sims-Williams, *TAAS*, 1999, pp. 146–49, but the -RIGI could be due to British/Latin influence, as may the composition vowel O (and this might be the Irish development seen after labials).

[659] If = /-o-ría/ < /-o-rí:ga:/, rather than /-ó-ria/; see above, ‡14n.

[660] See above, ‡‡14n. and 17. Note also the uncertain accentuation, as indicated in preceding note on VELVOR[IA].

[661] His son is VLCAGNVS, probably an Irish name. SEN- does not occur in the ogam inscriptions and may well be British (W. *hen*), as in 400/177 SENEMAGLI, father of a clearly Welsh VINNEMAGLI (note /nn/ < /nd/). (This is to be distinguished from the *Seno-* < Greek *Xeno-* which appears in Roman Britain, VLRB, p. 928.) Rhys, *AC*, 4th ser. 4 (1873), 197–98, could not find the expected *Henfael < SENEMAGLI, and the *Enfael* which he compares is a ghost name; see LBS ii, 455. Rhys's opponent, Brash (*AC*, 4th ser. 4 (1873), 285–86), correctly pointed out that *Sen-* occurs in (non-ogam) Irish names like *Senach*; but he too failed to find a descendant of SENEMAGLI. Russell, in *Studies in Irish Hagiography*, p. 241, n. 16, notes the lack of compound names in *Sen-*.

13. 401/183 BROHOMAGLI
14. 413/272 MONEDORIGI
15. 419/284 RIGOHENE
16. 454/402 CVNIOVENDE (the accompanying DENCVI or DEN[O]VI does not show syncope either, whichever reading is preferred)[662]
17. 468/Ok31 RIALOBRANI, CVNOVALI
18. 477/Ok11 TEGERNOMALI (on CONETOCI see below)
19. 487/Ok10 CVNOMORI
20. 498/Nb7 BRIGOMAGLOS
21. 515/Scot.9 DVMNOGENI (DIMNOGENI Macalister)[663]
22. 520/Scot.5 BARROVADI (if British)[664]
23. 2028 ARTOGNOV([?)
24. 3005/F5 VENOMAILI (*windo-) and possibly]NOMA(I)LI

[38] (AI) The following item in Jackson's list is probably Irish, but the use of O is still significant as a reflection of British practice (unless due to the rounding influence of the flanking /u/s):

1. 319/9 CVNOGVSI, as Jackson notes, is 'probably Irish rather than British and shows the Irish development of *st* to *ss* in this stem' (Ir. *Congus*, W. *Cynwst*).[665]
A possible further example of British O for Irish A is 2029/p.39i ERECOR (see below).

[38] (AIBC) The following are similar to the (ABC) class:

1. 327/43 DVNOCATI is probably Irish, although this is not quite certain as discussed earlier. Note that the vowel survived in MW *Dinogat* beside OW *Din(a)cat*.[666]
2. 457/Ok18 DVNOCATI is not in Jackson's list, but the same applies.
318/6 ETTORIGI (in Jackson's list, no. 4 under (A) above) may be Irish with Latinized/Brittonicized inflection. I do not list it above under (AI), however, as its O may be an instance of Irish O from /u/ (as in **MEDDO-GENI** above, if that is the correct reading). This depends on the etymology. Jackson compared 'MW *Ethri*', but this hypothetical descendant of

---

[662] See above, ‡18.
[663] Macalister also read O in NVD[OGEN]I, but Radford & Jackson, in RCAMS, *Selkirkshire*, pp. 111 and 113, reject this, reading NVDI and DVMNOGENI, as does Thomas. Rhys, *Englyn*, p. 5, also read DVMNOGENI.
[664] KHJ suggests 'mole-head' (i.e. W. *gwadd*). Cf. 979/46 GUADAN. If BARROVADI is Irish, the O could be due to the labial environment. Thomas, *GAJ*, 17 (1991–92), 6, says it is 'possibly Primitive Irish *Barro-wedas*', but that reconstruction has the wrong vowel.
[665] LHEB, pp. 172, 531, and 533. Williams, BWP, p. 20, suggests that he is the eponym of nearby Pencaernisiog < *Conysiog, and that the names *Cwnws*, *Conws* in the Anglesey pedigrees may also be derived from *Congus*, although here the loss of /t/ may be Welsh. Richards, *THSC*, 1965, p. 38, regards the -*ws* here as a Welsh diminutive, comparing *Einws* < *Einion* and *Iocws* beside *Iocyn*.
[666] Above, ‡16; LHEB, p. 648.

ETTORIGI, postulated by Rhys and quoted by Ifor Williams, is unattested.[667] It is better to compare 179 **ETORIGAS** or]**ETORIGAS** in Dingle, Co. Kerry. Ziegler tentatively connects this with OI *éit* (*i*-stem) 'cattle', unattested in personal names, but a better comparison is *ét* (*o*-stem) 'jealousy, emulation', since the probable Gaulish cognate IANTU- is well attested in names such as *Iantumarus*.[668] *Ianturīx yields **ETORIG**- effortlessly in Irish (although **D** rather than **T** might be expected in ogam), but not in Brittonic, where /i̭/ and /nt/ were retained, as in OB names in *Iant*-.[669] (There is a hypocoristic variant of *Iantu*- without /n/, as in 401/183 IATTI, Old Breton names in *Iat*-, and Gaulish *Iatta* and(?) *Ioturix*,[670] but this could not yield ETTORIGI or **ETORIGAS** regularly). An alternative etymology, however, is Celtic *Aitorīx > OB *Oedri* 'epoch-king', which would have passed through a stage with initial /ε:/ in Brittonic (‡4).[671] In this case, ETTORIGI will of course be Welsh and have the expected Brittonic composition vowel. This justifies retaining it under (A) above, at least provisionally.

[38] A number of forms with O cannot be included under (A) or (AI):

345/74 **GLUVOCA[ ]** (Macalister: **GL(U)V(O)C(I)**) is obscure, but note that the composition vowel appears to follow a labial.

395/102]ORIA does not necessarily contain a composition vowel.[672]

431/308 EVOLENG[I], probably Irish, is not listed under (AI) in view of the labial preceding the O. The accompanying name is **D[O]V[A]TUCEAS** (cf. 37 **DOVATUCI**), with **A** < *o if correctly restored,[673] and DOBTVCI in the roman script perhaps with syncope (so Macalister and the *Corpus*, but Nash-Williams has DOB[I]TVCI).[674]

436/316 EUOLENGGI (in Jackson's list) is similarly omitted from (AI). The accompanying patronymic LITOGENI may contains OI *líth* 'feast', a *u*-stem, as in MI *Líthgen*,[675] in which case the O is for *u. Yet it does not

667 LHEB, pp. 188, 456, n. 1, 566, and 626. See Rhys, LWP, p. 363 ('I do not know it, unless it be the *Etery* of the Cambro-British Saints, p. 101' [really just a misprint for *Et(h)ern*, VSB, p. 148]). Williams, BWP, p. 21, suggests that *Eithir* in the Black Book of Carmarthen *Canu Llywarch Hen* is for *Ethir = *Ethyr < *Ettorix (an alternative would be the attested *Otiorix*, OPEL iii, 117), but this is unlikely in view of the recurrence of the diphthongal spelling *Eithir* elsewhere (Lloyd-Jones, *Geirfa*, s.n.; VSB, pp. 266–68). I would suggest that *Eithir* is for *Eithyr < Latin *Hector* (cf. W. *Gwythyr* < *Victor*, ‡‡ 51n. and 66n.).

668 Ziegler, p. 181; GPN, pp. 45–47 and 211–15; Hamp, *Ériu*, 27 (1976), 1–20; Lambert, ZCP, 37 (1979), 210 and n. 6; ADA, pp. 279–80.

669 Gramm., p. 398.

670 Ibid.; GPN, pp. 214–15; Hamp, *Ériu*, 27 (1976), 2–3 (*Iot*- not connected).

671 On *Oedri* see ‡17.

672 If it does, cf. n. 659 above on VELVOR[IA]. Latin -*o(:)ria* is a possibility. Rhys, *AC*, 6th ser. 19 (1919), 204, suggested [AVIT]ORIA apparently because 396/104 FILI AVITORI also comes from Penmachno.

673 Nash-Williams's reading is preferred by McManus, *Guide*, p. 67, and Ziegler, p. 170, n. 285, to Macalister's **DOVATACIS**. Cf. Uhlich, *Ériu*, 40 (1989), 129, and *Morphologie*, pp. 27 and 233. However, according to KHJ, Macalister's 'seems the correct reading'.

674 KHJ visiting the stone in 1947 noted that there was 'certainly space' for the -I- in DOB[I]TVCI, 'no doubt the correct reading', and also noted the final -I of EVOLENGI.

675 Birkhan, *Germanen und Kelten*, p. 426, n. 1140. Cf. Ziegler, pp. 193–94, on 273 **LIT[ENI]**.

have to be Irish; compare Continental Celtic *Litugen(i)us*, *Litugena*, and Romano-British *Litegenus* and *Litugenus*, and note that both *Litu-* and *Lito-* are attested in Gaul.[676]

1202/Ok2 EVOCATI (or EVOCALI Okasha), with which Thomas compares 19 **IVACATTOS**, is similarly not listed under (AI) in view of the labial.[677]

458/Ok9 RANOCORI or NANOCORI is obscure, but the patronymic MESGI suggests that it is Irish.[678] Restoration to [B]RANOCORI would explain the O by Ziegler's rule.

1057/Ok54 EROCAVI may at first sight have a Brittonicized form of the element *Era-* perhaps seen in 84 **ERACOBI MAQI ERAQETAI**,[679] but more likely these ogam forms are to be segmented **ERACO-BI** (cf. OI *Erccba*) and **ERAQ-ETAI** (cf. OI *Ercaith*) from **Erko-* (with epenthesis).[680] In this case, **ERACOBI** and **EROCAVI** may be the same Irish name (with **-biu̯o-* 'living'), EROC-A-VI having the normal Irish composition vowel -A- and **EROC-O-BI** having -O- before a labial, as noted by MacNeill. 2029/p.39i ERECOR (a 19th-cent. transcript) may a similar Irish name < **Erka-rīx*, but with Brittonicized composition vowel O, or may even be a miscopying of ERECOB(I), in which case the labial B would explain the O.[681]

[38] (B) Jackson's list for reduced composition vowels (p. 645), omitting probable Irish names (CORBALENGI, TRENACATVS, ENABARRI, TRENEGUSSI) and one (BC) name (TOTAVALI – probably Irish anyway) plus CONETOCI (see below), is:

1. 376/174 VENNISETLI
2. 390/96 VENDESETLI
3. 385/89 ANATEMORI[682]
4. 500 AMMECATI[683]

---

[676] Holder ii, 247–48; Grauf., p. 266; GPN, pp. 217–18; DLG, p. 173; Weisgerber, *Rhenania*, p. 460; Alföldy, *Noricum*, p. 235; RIB ii [fasc. 5] 2491.105; Tyers, *Pottery*, p. 227; OPEL iii, 29. KHJ comments on 387/95 LOCVLITI: 'If = **Locculiti* might be "feast-habouring", *llid* and *lloch-* ?' This implies a connection with W. *llochaf* and *llawch*, with an original /a:/, but no element **lākk-* appears elsewhere, so far as I know (132 **LACAVAGNI**, cf. *lachán*, has /a/, Ziegler, p. 191). For a different explanation of LOCVLITI see below (BA) and ‡46. For a 'Celtic' *Locinna* at Bath, see Tab.Sulis, p. 234. Williams, *BBCS*, 5 (1929–31), 6–7, notes that LITU- can be compared either with W. *llydw* 'company' or with OI *lith*, Breton *lid* 'festivity'; DLG, p. 173, favours the latter; cf. MLH v/1, p. 225; ADA, pp. 113–14.

[677] Cf. ‡18n. above.

[678] See ‡‡ 14, 16, 22, and 48.

[679] Ziegler, p. 178, citing Korolev. According to Thomas, *Mute Stones*, p. 286, the reading EROCAVI 'is difficult to sustain'. Cf. ‡25n. above.

[680] MacNeill, *PRIA*, 39 C (1931), 38–39.

[681] See ‡57n. below.

[682] On **Anatio-* here see above, ‡‡18 and 27.

[683] Ogam [E]B[I]CATOS Macalister, but see above, ‡17n.

5. 368/b/150 BARRIVENDI, VENDVBARI (possibly Irish, ‡22)
6. 400/177 VINNEMAGLI FILI SENEMAGLI
7. 397/105 CVNALIPI[684]
8. 408/229/848 CATOTIGIRNI [also VEDOMAVI (or VEDOMALI Macalister), *if* this is another old *u*-stem][685]
9. 1028/214/850 VENDVMAGLI [but this could be Irish, with V for A, especially in a labial environment][686]
10. 970/13 CATAMANUS

[38] To these I would add:

11. 365/149 MAVOHENI (with O for **u* in **magu-*)[687]
12. 377/175 CIMESETLI (the patronymic AVICAT[VS] has the correct composition vowel for **Awi-*, but the reading is uncertain; Macalister reads AMICATI)[688]
13. 447/369 NEMAGLI, known only from Lhuyd's drawing, may – if Brittonic – be for [CV]NEMAGLI, [VIN]NEMAGLI, [TIGER]NEMAGLI, or similar (although a more likely explanation, given the layout of the drawing, is Pr.Ir. **Nē-maɣlī*, ‡42)
13. 496 **TEBICATO[S]**, assuming this new reading is correct, probably has **tepo-* < **tekʷo-* as the first element, as in 358/138 VOTEPORIGIS/**VOTE-CORIGAS**[689]
14. 3006/C1 **BODOGNOVS** (< **bodwo-*, so the composition can hardly be said to be fully intact)

[38] (BA) forms are:

1. 361/140 TALOR[I] (ADVEN[TI] MAQV[ERIGI] FILIV[S]), if a British name either cognate with Continental Celtic names in *Talo-* (*Talu-* ?), i.e. with **o* retained, or with O replacing **u* (if *Tal-* was a *u*-stem as OI *taul* implies) – on the other hand, since MAQV[ERIGI] is

---

[684] Rhys, *AC*, 4th ser. 13 (1882), 163–64, and *Englyn*, pp. 82–83, compares OW *Conlipan* (see LL, p. 393 – note also *Conluip* there), and argues that CVNALIPI would give W. **Cynllib*, comparing OW *Libiau* (LL, p. 410, cf. VSB, p. 236) and *Llanllibio*, Anglesey (cf. LBS iii, 351 and 375). See also GPC s.v. *enllib* (rather than *llibyn*, *llipa*) and DP iv, 606 and 678–79. CVNALIPI is coupled with BECCVRI, on which see ‡42.

[685] LHEB, p. 482; Ziegler, pp. 118 and 242. But Hamp, *SC*, 18/19 (1983–84), 129, argues that *gŵydd* 'wild' was an *o*-stem.

[686] Cf. Ziegler, p. 64. One might consider British raising of /on/ > /un/ (‡26 above), but cf. VENDVBARI above, where this cannot apply.

[687] See above, ‡25.

[688] See above, ‡‡ 18 and 22.

[689] Macalister **EBICATO[S]**. See above, ‡17. But Irish influence could explain the use of **-I-**; see MacNeill, *PRIA*, 27 C (1909), 352; Ziegler, pp. 64–65. For -I- as composition vowel (instead of -U-) in British already in the late fourth century, note MEDVGENI/MEDIGENI (Jackson, in *Thetford Treasure*, p. 47). Another exception is CATAVACVS (instead of **Katu-*, ?through assimilation or under Greek influence, cf. KGP, pp. 166–67) from Shakenoak Farm villa, Oxfordshire: Wright & Hassall, *Britannia*, 4 (1973), 332. For irregular composition vowels in Gaulish see KGP, p. 91. Cf. SENIARGII below.

obviously Q-Celtic, TALOR[I] may be an Irish nominative (or Latinate adaptation of a genitive *TALORIGAS), with O for *u (as in **MEDDO-GENI** above), rather than with O under British influence.[690]

2.   417/282 CAVOSENI – the stem-class of the first element is not known (cf. 1404/Ok30 CAVUDI?) and one should perhaps segment CAVO SENIARGII.[691]

3.   418/283 BURSOCAVI or BVRGOCAVI is similarly uncertain.

4.   387/95 LOCVLITI may contain W. *llwch* 'dust' < *lukk-, but the stem class of *llwch* is uncertain; another possibility is OI *loch* 'dark', an *o*-stem.[692]

5.   325/33 BIVATIGI(RNI) (Jackson; cf. Nash-Williams: BIVATIGI(*rni*) or BIVATISI(*rni*); Macalister: BIVOTIS) may contain a reduced *-o-,[693] but the A may be part of a Brittonic suffix *-atiiī.[694] Yet the name could be be Irish, with an Irish composition vowel; we cannot assume that a priest in Anglesey and 'servant of Paulinus' – VASSO PAVLINI (*gwas Peulin?*) – would have to be British. Rhys thought that all the Welsh *Gwas* names were 'translations of Goidelic names, or . . . made in imitation of Goidelic names'.[695]

6.   436/316 LITOGENI (< *Lito- or *Litu-? cf. above).

[38]   The following are omitted from (B) and (BA) as probably or certainly having an Irish composition vowel:

341/71 **SALICIDUNI/SALICIDVNI** or SALIGIDVNI has the incorrect composition vowel from *o; it may well be an Irish name, or be at any rate influenced by the Irish use of I as the composition vowel[696]

348/a/110/27 **TRENALUGOS** (Macalister)[697]

354/126/6 CORBALENGI[698]

353/127/7 **TRENACCATLO/TRENACATVS**

368/a/150 **DUMELEDONAS**[699]

362/142 **INIGENA**[700]

---

[690]   For *Talo-* (*sic*) see GPN, pp. 259–61; cf. *taul* in LEIA T-182 and for Gaulish *talu-* see Hamp, *ZCP*, 41 (1986), 254–55. Following Holder ii, 1710–11, GPN, pp. 260–61, cites a number of forms in CIL ii from Lusitania: [*T*]*a*[*l*]*ori* 776, *Tal*[*orus*] 413, *Talori*(?) 736, [*T*]*a*[*l*]*orae* 754, and *Oppidani Talori* 760. On the other hand, if TALOR[I] contained the Irish *o*-stem element *tālo-* 'adze' (Ziegler, p. 116) seen in 200 **MAQI-TTAL** (> *Mac Táil*) and 181 **TALAGNI** (> *Tálán*), then its O will probably be due to British influence. Rhys, LWP, p. 375, and *Englyn*, pp. 68–69, compared Pictish *Talorgg*, etc.

[691]   See above, ‡‡ 18, 25, and 36.

[692]   See below, ‡46. Ir. *loch* 'lake' is *u*-stem, but its relationship if any to *llwch* is uncertain; cf. GPC; Sims-Williams, *CMCS*, 32 (1996), 39–40; DLG, p. 174.

[693]   Thus Ifor Williams, in RCAHMW, *Anglesey*, p. cxi, comparing CATAMANVS.

[694]   See ‡27 above. The name is treated as British by Jackson, LHEB, pp. 279 and 446.

[695]   *AC*, 5th ser. 12 (1895), 25 (referring to Irish names in *Máel-*).

[696]   McManus, *Guide*, p. 118, and see above, ‡16 and n. 125. On -I- as composition vowel, see also n. 654 above.

[697]   Macalister explains how he arrived at this reading in *TCASFC*, 15, Part 40 (1922), 30. Even he could not see the **A**.

[698]   See above, ‡14.

[699]   See Ziegler, pp. 174–75, and ‡59 below.

[700]   Ziegler, p. 188.

378/169 BIVADI, BODIBEVE (**BEVV[, BODDIB[** or similar)
2002/b **TARICORO**
424/299 [E]VA[LEN]GI (?) (Edwards; Nash-Williams:]GI; Macalister: GLVVOCCI)
428/305 TRENEGUSSI/**TRENAGUSU** (or **-O** or **-I** Edwards)
433/313 **[A]NDAGELLI**/ANDAGELLI[701]
441/345 ANDAGELLI
461/Ok66 ERCILIVI and ERCILINGI (ERCILINCI Thomas)[702]
462/Ok14 QVENATAVCI[703]
488/Ok60 ENABARRI/**ENABARR**
501 **CUNAMAGLI**
504 **CUNAVA[LI]**
512 QATTIDONA[704]

[38] The following forms are also excluded from (B) for various reasons:
477/Ok11 CONETOCI (in Jackson's list) may be CONET-OCI rather than CONE-TOCI;[705]
2032 [C(?)]AMAGLI could be an example of A for *o in a British name such as *BROCCOMAGLI, but owing to its incomplete state cannot be labelled British rather than Irish;
361/140 MAQV[ERIGI] looks like a Latinized or Brittonicized form of Ir. *MAQI-RIGAS (> *Ma(i)cc-Ríg 'king's son' (probably a name rather than a title). If so, the E read by Lhuyd is not the composition vowel but rather -E from genitive *-ī as in 2006 MAQVI COLINE;[706]
419/284 ONERATI probably does not have E for reduced /o/ in *Honoratus*, treated as if with short /o/ as composition vowel (cf. W. *Ynyr* < *Honorius* with short /o/), since *Onerata* is already attested in Roman Britain, and RIGOHENE in the same inscription has O correctly);[707]
329/42 MACCVTRENI and 425/297 MACCVTRE[NI] (see above) do not have a composition vowel but rather V from Irish nominative *-a(s) < *-os or, more likely, genitive *-ī (coloured by the *k^w) in a loose compound;[708]
341/71 **MAQITRENI** (**MAQUTRENI** Nash-Williams)/[M]ACCVTRENI and 428/305 **MAQITRENI**/MACUTRENI similarly;

[701] Ibid., p. 128.
[702] Thomas, *Mute Stones*, p. 283. See *Erko-* in Ziegler, p. 104. Okasha notes the alternative segmentation ERCILI VIRICATI (cf. LHEB, pp. 456–57, and ‡27 above, rejected by Thomas, *Mute Stones*, p. 301, n. 29); if so, VIRI- *may* have the original vocalism of Gaulish *Viri-* (see ‡15n), but *Wiro-* must also be a possibility.
[703] LHEB, pp. 140, 171, and 296, n. 2. The patronymic DINVI is obscure (see below).
[704] Cf. Ziegler, pp. 146–47 and 222 on **CATTI-** and **QET(T)I-** ?
[705] See above, ‡18. In the same inscription TEGERNOMALI has the correct vowel; see (A) above.
[706] For compound names in MAQI- and *Mac-* see Ziegler, p. 203, O'Brien, *Celtica*, 10 (1973), 227, and CGH, pp. 680–84. Cf. *Meic Rígáin*, CGSH, pp. 158 (§709.208) and 255. On COLINE see ‡34 above.
[707] See above, ‡18n.
[708] Ziegler, pp. 238–39; LHEB, p. 140. See further below, Ch. 4, §30, and Ch. 5, p. 331.

440/335 MACVDEC[C]ETI (Lhuyd: MACVDEbETI for MACVDECETI or MACVDEhETI?), similarly, is *Ma(i)cc-Dechet*.[709] The patronymic, variously read EOROCAN or EONOCAN or EOPOCAN, is obscure and cannot easily be segmented (would it be EO- (= *ewo-?) or EORO- etc.?); it should probably be read EDNO- (: MW *edn* 'bird' < *petno-* ‡48), but, since this is uncertain, I hesitate to include it as a definite example of a correct composition vowel.

326/39 MACCVDECCETI, 336/67A **M[A]Q[I] D[E]C[E]DA**, and 492/Ok59 MACCODECHETI similarly;

442/346 MACCVDICCL (Lhuyd) is similarly explicable.[710] The patronymic CATICVVS is compared by Williams with OB *Catic* and Gaulish *Catica* and by Russell with W. *Cedig*;[711]

2020 VERE[(VERED- or VERET- ?) is unclassifiable;

422/298 [H]OCIDEGNI is obscure;[712]

426/300 **NETTASAGRI** (**NETTASAGRU** Nash-Williams) is a loose compound (cf. OI *Nad Sáir*);[713]

1022/240/928 DO[BI]TAUCI (Macalister only) is a dubious reading;

1046/Ok8 ARAHI could be from *Ariosegos*, but ARTHI has also been read;[714]

1049/Ok33 URITIN (if the correct reading) may have an earlier syncope in the first syllable;[715]

1212 CARASIMILIVS is probably Latin (two words?);[716]

356/132/9 CONVMANI is a very dubious reading;[717]

444/352]LACATI or]STACATI is uncertain;

474/Ok17 CRVARIGI (Macalister) is dubious;

480/Ok19 LVRATECVS (Macalister) is also dubious;

3022/I3 TVRTOVALDVS is probably Germanic, and the O is unlikely to be due to Brittonic spelling habits;

1009/193/935, 1008/194/934(?), and 1013/222/912 EBIS(S)AR is obscure to

---

[709] Ziegler, p. 165; LHEB, p. 140.

[710] LHEB, pp. 140–41 and 620, n. 2. KHJ rejects Williams's equation with Bede's *Dicul* (apud Nash-Williams, *AC*, 92 (1937), 328), on the grounds that that is *Díchuil* 'without sin', which would be *Dīcolis* in the fifth century. Cf. O'Brien, *Celtica*, 10 (1973), 224; Uhlich, *Morphologie*, pp. 131, 134 and 227–28 (< *dí* + *coicell* ='senseless'). Despite the vowel, I take DICCL to be the stem of Ir. *Décl-án* (sic leg.), 256 **DEGLANN** (*degglo-* (sic) < *denklo-* according to Ziegler, p. 165).

[711] Williams, apud Nash-Williams, *AC*, 92 (1937), 328 (citing Chrest., p. 115, and Holder i, 841: 'catica f[ecit]' (Voorburg?); see also iii, 1148, and Weisgerber, *Rhenania*, p. 289, for *Caticcus, Catici*, etc.); Russell, *Celtic Word-Formation*, p. 145 (see EWGT, p. 176).

[712] Could this be a name in Ir. *óc* like 450/390 **OGTENAS** (on which see, however, ‡27n.)?

[713] Ziegler, p. 214.

[714] See above, ‡36.

[715] See above, ‡28.

[716] See above, ‡36.

[717] See above, ‡‡ 22n. and 26n.

me, but perhaps biblical *Abisur* ('father of oxen', I Chron. 2:28–29) or a similar Semitic name.[718]

[38] (BC) The only such name in Jackson's lists is 375/166 TOTAVALI (cf. OW *Tutagual*, MW *Tudwal)*, but as he says elsewhere it 'may very likely be Irish'.[719] The fact that /ǫ:/ has not become /u:/ (‡12 above) certainly supports that. The following more definite (BC) names may be noted:

1. 978/49 BRIAMAIL (< *Brigomaglos*, cf. OW *Briauail*, MW *Briafael)*[720]
2. 996/147 MO[RE]DIC – unless Macalister was wrong about the trace of an E, in which case this belongs with (ABC) below
3. 425/297 CATOMAG[LI] – although this may well be Irish (despite W. *Cad(a)fael*, ‡46), with O from **u*, in view of the pairing with Ir. MACCVTRE[NI].

[38] (ABC)

1. 985/61 MORIDIC preserves the /i/ of **mori-*, but this survived into MW *Moridic*.[721]
2. 1014/231/908 GUORGORET < **wor-wo-ret-* retains the vowel of the second prefix,[722] but this is unlikely to have been syncopated (compare MW *Gwrwaret*, OC *Guruaret*, OB *Uuoruuoret*),[723] partly because /rwr/ would have been a difficult cluster and partly because the structure of the name is clearly [*wor-* + (*wo-* + *ret-*)] 'super-succour (*guoret)*'.[724]

[38] (C) Jackson's list of lost composition vowels (p. 646) is:

1. 493/Ok58 CONBEVI
2. 350/116/3 IDNERT [*sic* Lhuyd]
3. 490/Ok29 DATUIDOCI CONHINOCI
4. 471/Ok39 CLOTUALI

---

[718] *Abisur* is not included in Jerome's *Liber Interpretationis Hebraicorum Nominum.* 1008/194/934 is uninscribed according to the RCAHMW volume, almost certainly wrongly; cf. plates in LW (pl. 23) and ECMW.

[719] LHEB, pp. 648 and 307, n. 2 (cf. Uhlich, *Morphologie*, p. 303). TOTAVALI is son of DOTHORANTI, which is unexplained but perhaps DO-THORANTI (see ‡42n) rather than DOTHO-RANTI.

[720] LL, p. 388 (read *Briauail*); LHEB, pp. 448 and 648; Jackson, *Archaeologia Aeliana*, 5th ser. 10 (1982), 62.

[721] See above, ‡18.

[722] Vowels of prefixes such as **ambi-* are classed by Jackson along with composition vowels, LHEB, p. 643.

[723] Lloyd-Jones, *Geirfa*, p. 721; Chrest., pp. 179–80. Cf. OW *Guoguoret*, VC §55, by scribal error for *Guorguoret* according to Rhys, *AC*, 5th ser. 16 (1899), 139–40 (or by dissimilation?) rather than < ***wo-woret-*. Rhys thinks he may be the GUORGORET of the inscription. Cf. below, p. 278, n. 57.

[724] Cf. DGVB i, 198; GPN, pp. 126–27.

5. 1033/287 CINGEN [a disputed reading][725]
6. 427/b/301 CATUOCONI[726]

[38] The following can be added:

7. 324/34]CO[N]BARRVS CO[N]BURRI (*if* the reading of this lost inscription is correct)[727]
8. 979/46 GURHI
9. 984/59 BLEDRUS (= *Bled'rus*).[728] – This inscription also has GURCI, which is may not be the result of syncope, since it is clearly a late compound.[729] Nevertheless, it may be included as it has either undergone syncope of the first element (< *wiro-) or is a post-syncope formation. On the same grounds we can include the next item:
10. 1019/237/920 ILCI or]ILCI[730]
11. 986/62 IORUERT
12. 2018 CVNCUOM (obscure, but possibly a *kuno- name)[731]
13. 348/b/110/27 GURHIR(E)T (preferable to GURHIST)[732]
14. 992/120/14 CENLISINI (a *kuno- name)[733]
15. 994/125/22 HIROIDIL
16. 997/159 EIUDON (if = *Eu-* < *Awi-)[734]
17. 998/164 HEUTREN (= *Eu-* < *Awi- ?)
18. 1000/182   CONCENN,   BROHCMAIL,   GUARTHI[GIRN], CONMARCH
19. 1005/191/886 BRANCUF or BRANCU
20. 1012/223/933 IUTHAHELO, ARTMALI
21. 1015/233/910 GRUTNE (cf. MW *Grudnei*)[735]

---

[725] Williams, BWP, pp. 34–35, read CUN BEN, while Koch, *SC*, 20/21 (1985–86), 51 and 66, n. 14, prefers CUNGEN(?) with Westwood. The UN ligature and the B are confirmed by Lhuyd's drawing in BL Stowe MS 1023, fo. 160r. CUN is probably < *Counā* f. (‡25 above), assuming that BEN is an unattested cognate of OI *ben* 'wife', although note that British Latin poets affected Hebrew *ben* 'son' (Dumville, *SC*, 10/11 (1975–76), 84, n. 4; Clancy, in Anderson FS, p. 89, n. 2). If 1033/287 CINGEN is discounted, the same inscription's TENGRumUI (‡48) can be counted instead.

[726] It might be suggested that U here denotes /u-w/, i.e. with a surviving composition vowel (cf. LHEB, p. 646, n. 1, on RIB i 1065 *Catuallauna*).

[727] BWP, p. 24 and see ‡26 above. Note the poor quality of the copy reproduced by Hübner, *Inscriptiones Britanniae Christianae*, p. 53, and Westwood, LW, plate 86. See Fig. 1.2 above. On the problems with the reading see Macalister and Nash-Williams. The latter says that *Conbarrus* appears on a Romano-British lead casket from Caistor, citing Anon., *JRS*, 37 (1947), 181, but the form there is correctly CVNOBARRVS! Cf. ‡22n.

[728] See ‡58 below.

[729] See above, ‡19.

[730] Cf. OW *Elci*. See ‡85 below.

[731] See above, ‡26.

[732] See above, ‡36n.

[733] See above, ‡36.

[734] See above, ‡18.

[735] Rhys, *AC*, 5th ser. 16 (1899), 144, identified GRUTNE (where OW *e* = MW *ei*) with the 'man's name *Grudneu* or *Grudnei*', i.e. *Grudnei* in the Triads; see TYP, pp. 39 and 368, where *grudd* 'cheek' is suggested as the first element (*Grudneu* is the inferior reading in MA, p. 389).

22. 1016/234/907 CONBELIN
23. 1023/239/927 [CO]NBELANI
24. 1018/236/919 ILQUICI (if for *Ilguici, OW Iluic (var. Iliuc))[736]
25. 1025/248/862 ARTBEU
26. 2022/253/984 COVLGVEN or GVLGVEN
27. 1024/255/926 ARTHMAIL, also perhaps BRANCIE (Macalister) or BRANTUI (RCAHMW)
28. 1004/260/884 GELUGUIN (< *Welwo-windos ?)[737]
29. 1029 TETQUINI (if, as implied, for *TECQUINI = Tecwyn < *Teko-windos)[738]
30. 1035/303 MARGITEUT
31. 1041/376 GURMARC[739]
32. 2005 S[AT]VRNBIV
33. 1065/410 HAERDUR (preferable to HAESDUR)[740]
34. 2021 GVINNDA
35. 486/Ok56 CVMREGNI (CVMRECINI Thomas) if from *koimo-[741]
36. 1044/Ok7 LEUIUT[742]
37. 1054/Ok43 DONIERT[743]
38. 1060/Ok57 GURGLES (if correct reading)[744]
39. 2036/Dor.i VIDCV[MI ?] (W. Gwyddgu)
40. 1063/Dor.ii IUDNNE[RTH?] (Macalister: IUONA)
41. 1062/Dor.v GONGORIE (?)
42. 1068/b CONDILICI and presumably BRENLIER or BREDLIEN. On the same stone 1068/a **LAGUBERI** may have **GU** written for /u̯/ as in

---

Is the second element *nei* 'nephew' (SBCHP, p. 389) or a cognate of Ir. *nia* 'champion' (< *nei̯H-* 'to lead', Ziegler, p. 114)? Were it not for the spelling in the Triads, one might suggest *grudd + gne* 'cheek-hue, i.e. rosy/ruddy'. *Grut, grud + gne* 'gravel face' is unlikely since *grut* is from ME *grit* < OE *greot*. Cf. ALSNE (= ALGNE ??), one reading of 480/Ok19?

[736] See Williams, *TAAS*, 1939, p. 29, n. 4 (a note cited by RCAHMW, *Glamorgan*, i/3, p. 53 and n. 2, and accepted by Jackson, *Speculum*, 24 (1949), 599, but not reproduced in BWP, p. 4) – his strictures may be directed against Rhys, *AC*, 5th ser. 16 (1899), 137, who remarked on 'the retention of the *qu*'. The first element is presumably *elu- > W. El-* with syncope. The variant in *Il-* (as in *Illtud*, e.g. 1013/222/912 ILTU[TI(S)]) is usually ascribed to Irish influence (see n. 657 above), but in the present case, as in 1019/237/920 ILCI nearby (no. 10 above), a possibility is influence from the following /i:/ (see ‡85 below). If -QUICI is W. *gwig* < Latin *vicus* (cf. C. *gwyk* 'settlement', CPNE, p. 119), ILQUICI/*Iluic* would mean 'possessing many settlements'. For the use of Q cf. 1029 TETQUINI (no. 29 below), *Guedqui* in VC, §60 (Sims-Williams, *BBCS*, 38 (1991), 59), *Quichtrit* beside *Guichtrit* in LL p. 421 s.n. *Uchtrit*, and Falileyev, *Etymological Glossary*, s.v. *quith* = ?*gwyth*.

[737] See above, ‡22.

[738] See WG, p. 184; LBS iv, 225.

[739] Cf. LL, p. 185 (*Gurmarch, Guruarch*). It could be a late compound like GURCI and ILCI at 9 and 10 above.

[740] See above, ‡36.

[741] Thomas, *Mute Stones*, p. 278. See above, ‡26.

[742] See above, ‡37n.

[743] See above, ‡28n.

[744] See ‡‡ 26n. and 58.

Old Welsh rather than being an unsyncopated compound but this is uncertain.[745]

43. 1401/Ok27 RESTEUTA(E) (RESGEVTA(E) Okasha)[746]
44. 3001/F1 BUDNOUENUS
45. 3002/F2 GALLMAU
46. 3007/C2 VORMVINI
47. 3008/C3 MAELDOI (< *maglo-)
48. 3010/M1 HERANNUEN, HERA[N]AL (or HERA[H]AL etc.)
49. 3013/M4 DRILEGO (if dri(ch) + l . . .), CONBRITI
50. 3014/M5 HARENBILI, HERANHAL
51. 3015/M6 PROSTLON
52. 3017/M8 RIMOETE (< *Rīgo-)
53. 3021/I2 MAONIRN

54. 2034/871 BELGINT (Knight's new reading, cited in Corpus) may be added if rightly equated with OW Bledgint below (‡53)
55. 1027/265/923 GALCU[N (Redknap's new reading, ‡69n below)
56. 993/124/18 ITGEN (if the correct reading instead of ASAITGEN)[747]
57. Finally, p. 397/285 BARRECTI (?) is perhaps syncopated from *barro- + *rectu-, *recto-[748]

[38] The following syncopated names are probably Irish:
342/70 ILVVETO (< *Elu-)[749] – but it is not impossible that the VV corresponds to /uw/ (properly written UV), in which case this is not a syncopated form anyway (cf. under (A) above). Moreover, is it possible that ILVVETO is related to the Continental Celtic tribal name Elvetii, Helvetii?[750]

---

[745] See ‡25 above.
[746] If this is from Latin Restituta it may already have been syncopated in Vulgar Latin (Restuta). See above, ‡34n.
[747] See below, ‡65.
[748] GPN, pp. 241–42, and CGH, indexes s. Recht-; Ziegler, p. 225, on 217 and 254 MAQI-RECTA; Koch, Gododdin, p. 221. See also below, Ch. 3, p. 273.
[749] Cf. Ziegler, p. 188; LHEB, p. 185, n. 1, endorsing I. Williams's review of CIIC i, in THSC, 1943–44, p. 155 (< il- + wed- = 'eloquent', as in W. dy-wed-yd 'to say', an etymology due to Rhys, LWP, pp. 384 and 407: 'much-speaking' or 'much-spoken-of'). Celtic also had roots *wed- 'lead' and *wed- 'strike', but really one wants a British root with *t (cf. Hamp, Ériu, 32 (1981), 158–59, Lindeman, BBCS, 31 (1984), 93–94 and 99, nn. 1–2, and Isaac, Verb, p. 327; was British influenced by Ir. in-fét etc.?). Perhaps compare Segovetis (KGP, p. 295). Note that IL- versus W. El- is not in itself a sure sign of Irishness (see ‡85), and that the Irish genitive in -O (cf. Uhlich, Morphologie, p. 134) does not prove the name itself to be Irish. Rhys also compared OI Féth, g. Fétho, which cannot be related to dywedyd (pace Rhys) but could well explain ILVVETO. More than one féth (u-stem) is given in DIL and ADA, pp. 149–50 and 370; Uhlich, Morphologie, pp. 152 and 247, understands it in personal names as 'Ruhe; Glätte; (gesundes) Aussehen'.
[750] Elvetii is cited by Lloyd-Jones, Y Geninen, 44 (1926), 12, as a Gaulish cognate with El-, Elu-, of Welsh names in El-. For this and other etymologies see KGP, pp. 203–4 (cf. GPN, pp. 347–48; Uhlich, CMCS, 39 (2000), 71).

1038/365 MAIL (or MAL or MEIL) DOMNA[C (< *dominicus*)[751]
364/144 QVENVENDANI, BARCVNI[752]
427/a/301 **DUBAR[CUNAS] (DUBR[ACUNAS]** Nash-Williams)[753]
431/308 DOBTVCI (if not DOB[I]TVCI)[754]
450/390 **OGTENAS** (Nash-Williams: **OGTENLO(?))/HOGTIVIS** (recte HOGTINIS ? McManus) – if this is indeed syncopated[755]
462/Ok14 DINVI (very uncertain but father of QVENATAVCI, which *is* Irish)[756]
1068/b LUGNI[757]

[38] The following are not included for various reasons:
1048/Ok32 GVENNCREST and QONFAL(I) have been read in this inscription, but so has (G)VENNORCIT, without syncope.[758]
1064/Dor.iv]AUPRIT may have syncope (e.g. of **Awi-* or **[M]agu-*), but that is uncertain.[759]
1206/Ok4 DOCIDCI or [R]IVGDOCI or [R]IVSDOCI appear syncopated, but the reading and interpretation are uncertain.[760]
352A/122/5 DOMNICI could be syncopated from Latin *Dominicus* but can also come from Celtic **Dumn-*.[761]
1030 [A]MBIGATI is a dubious reading.[762]
483/Ok51 SELNIVS is very doubtful; Rhys, Thomas, and Tomlin read SENILVS.[763]

---

[751] See above, ‡18n.
[752] Above, ‡‡ 22 and 26.
[753] According to Ziegler, p. 202, post-syncope in view of the epenthetic vowel in **dubro-* (if I understand rightly, but this is contradicted by forms like **ERACOBI**, ibid., p. 52, and Ch. 4 below, §41). She ignores Nash-Williams's reading and restoration, which is also that of Rhys, *AC*, 5th ser. 13 (1896), 100. Cf. Fig. 1.1. It depends on whether an indentation between the **B** and **R** is accidental or a letter **A**. An **A** was already read by Haigh, apud Rhys, LWP, pp. 278 and 400. The reading **MAGL[IA(s)] DUBR[ACUNA(s)]**, equated with OI *Máile-Doborchon* (gen. of *Máil-Doborchon*) was first advanced by Rhys his 1896 article, although it conflicts with his reading of 'vowel notches' before the **M**, implying an *unsyncopated* name *ending* in -**AMAGL[I]** or similar (unless the 'notches' belonged to a formula word). It also requires the assumption either that OI *Máil* ('servant of') is being spelt with -**AGL-** for [aïl] under Welsh influence (cf. ‡48 on 353/127/7 MAGLAGNI) or that *Máil* in the OI name replaced earlier *Mál* (Ziegler, pp. 112 and 202; Uhlich, *Morphologie*, p. 229). The official view on Caldey Island is that the ogam refers to a 'servant of St Dubricius'; cf. Doble, *Lives of the Welsh Saints*, p. 59, n. 6.
[754] Ziegler, p. 170, and above, n. 674.
[755] McManus, *Guide*, p. 65 (cf. ‡27n above, and n. 712). Macalister, *TCASFC*, 15, part 40 (1922), 32, argues against **OGTENLO** and for **OGTENAS**. It has been suggested (see Ziegler, pp. 217–18) that this is a syncopated compound of *óc* 'young' (earlier *oäc*) and an element in *t-* as in CIIC 76 **TENAS**, but this is hardly credible.
[756] See above, n. 703.
[757] Cf. OI *Luigne* < **LUGUNI**, Ziegler, pp. 198–99.
[758] Thomas, *Mute Stones*, p. 290; Tedeschi, *Scrittura e civiltà*, 19 (1995), tav. 3.
[759] See ‡‡25 and 57.
[760] Cf. Thomas, *Mute Stones*, pp. 282 and 301, n. 26.
[761] See ‡18n above. Syncope also occurred in Latin: see below, p. 320, n. 125.
[762] See above, ‡22.
[763] LWP, p. 406; *Mute Stones*, p. 286; Tab.Sulis, p. 228.

502]**MAQ LEOG**[(Ir. *Mac-Liac*?) shows apocope of the first element rather than syncope,[764] and the same presumably applies to:
1068/b MALBREN[765]
2038 BRANHUI, if = OW *Brangui* < *Branouios, may not have been subject to syncope.[766]

‡*39 Perhaps loss of γ finally after e; LHEB §79.1*

No inscriptional evidence is cited (p. 455). However, I have argued elsewhere that 1000/182 ELISEG (and OW *Elised*) may be hypercorrect for OW *Elise*.[767] If so ELISEG postdates the loss of /-γ/.

980/46a, which Macalister read WUMERE, WILMERE, or WALMERE, could conceivably contain the Old Welsh name element -*ēreg*, -*uireg* 'arise' as in *Comereg, Cimuireg, Atderreg* (cf. OC *Comoere/Cemoere*),[768] but OE *Wulfmær(e)* seems a better possibility (see also 337/60 VVLMER).[769] This may be a red herring, however, since Nash-Williams read 980/46a as 'WLIGUE (?)', and Radford (quoted in the *Corpus*) has since reinterpreted this as S(*ignum*) S(*ancti*) (or S(*cribae*)) LIGUE.[770]

‡*40 Syncope of other unstressed internal syllables; LHEB §197*

This second type of syncope affected vowels (other than composition vowels, ‡38) immediately before the main stress, but it often failed to occur.[771] According to Jackson 'the only example in the Dark Age inscriptions of a

---

[764] Ziegler, p. 193; cf. below, Ch. 4, §10. Kneen, *Personal Names of the Isle of Man*, pp. 261–62, suggested that **MAQ LEOG** is *Mac Laoghóg, from an unattested diminutive of OI *lóeg* 'calf', whence the Manx surname *Clague* (similarly Kermode, *Manx Crosses*, appendix, p. 3). KHJ compared 169 **MAQI-LIAG**, but confirmed in 1950 that the vowel letters were 'clearly as Macalister has them'. He adds: 'There is a 12th c. record of a *monasterium Sancti Leoc*, usually thought to have been the site of Rushen Abbey, [Basil] Megaw tells me.' This record is a Bull of Eugenius III in 1153 to Furness Abbey granting 'In Man . . . the lands of Carneclet *usque ad monasterium sancti Leoc*' (Oliver, *Monumenta de Insula Manniae*, ii, 10). Oliver's frontispiece map seems to situate this *monasterium* at the place called Lag ny Killey (= *lag na cille* 'hollow of the church') in the north of Kirk Christ, Rushen parish, a ruined church of unknown dedication (cf. Kneen, *Place-Names of the Isle of Man*, i, 43; Broderick, *Placenames of the Isle of Man*, i, 137). Megaw's suggestion is published by him in *Recent Archaeological Research on the Isle of Man*, pp. 262–63: 'parish church of Kirk Malew (St *Ma-Lua): perhaps on the site of the former monastery of "*St Leoc*" (*Lu-óg?).' This is philologically implausible.

[765] See below, ‡‡ 48 and 74.

[766] LHEB, p. 392, n. 2; Thomas, *BBCS*, 7 (1933–35), 126–27; SBCHP, pp. 296–97.

[767] Sims-Williams, *BBCS*, 38 (1991), 51 and n. 1. Differently Koch, *Gododdin*, p. 142.

[768] Sims-Williams, *BBCS*, 38 (1991), 50; SBCHP, p. 222; Bodmin, pp. 96 and 99. See ‡17 above.

[769] Searle, *Onomasticon*, has many examples of *Wulfmær*, but for -*mær[e]* see ibid., p. 345, citing Sweet, *Oldest English Texts*, where names in -*mær*, gen. -*maeri* (*sic*) are given under *mære* 'famous' (p. 600). Cf. von Feilitzen, *Pre-Conquest Personal Names*, pp. 325–26 and 421–22. Note that the font at Defynnog, CIIC 975 (not in ECMW) allegedly reading SIWVRD + GWL[MER] (cf. Moon, *AC*, 127 (1978), 124) is rejected in the *Corpus*.

[770] See ‡58 below.

[771] LHEB, pp. 643 and 651–54. See further Isaac, *SC*, 34 (2000), 105–18.

name where the second type of syncope would occur seems to be' 394/103 VENEDOTIS (W. *Gwyndod*).[772] A case like 994/125/22 CAROTINN, if related to Gaulish *Caratinus*,[773] cannot be cited, since that has a stem where syncope often failed to occur (e.g. OW *Ceretic* beside *Certic*).[774] Some other cases where there is no reason to suppose that syncope should occur are 399/176 TOVISACI (cf. W. *tywysog*), 404/270/843 TEGERNACUS (cf. W. *Teyrnog*), 451/401 TVNCCETACE (cf. W. *tyng(h)edog*),[775] 320/26 CVLIDOR(I) (cf. MW *Kyledyr*) and 995/133/24 ENEVIRI (cf. W. *Enewyr*, B. *Enever*).[776] In instances like 1000/182 GUARTHI[GIRN] (cf. *tigirn*) and 477/Ok11 CONETOCI (cf. OW *Conet*), knowledge of the simpler component may have been a factor.[777] There are also some names which are simply obscure, such as EBIS(S)AR[778] and 415/278 TARRONERIS (Macalister; Nash-Williams: IARRI[ ). All in all, then, it is impossible to see a chronological development in the absence of syncope in these forms. Jackson's lone VENEDOTIS cannot be relied on since it occurs in a Latin context in 394/103; and we know that the vowel was preserved in Latin texts, as in *regio Guenedotae* in *Historia Brittonum*, §62.[779]

[40] The one other form that can now be added is 3021/I2 MAONIRN, which probably shows syncope (rather than simple contraction) of the first syllable of *-diγirn*.[780]

‡41 *Provection; LHEB §143*

No inscriptional evidence is cited, apart from TH in 1012/223/933 IUTHAHELO (cf. OW *Iud-hail*) which Jackson regards as the result of the 'slow process' of the provection of /δ'h/ > /dh/.[781] If one can trust the orthography, one may contrast this form and 1015/233/910 GRUTNE[782]

---

[772] LHEB, p. 655; cf. pp. 188, n. 1, and 551, n. 3; and ‡‡ 13 and 58. Jackson must have regarded 486/Ok56 CVMREGNI or CVMRECINI (below, ‡48) as too uncertain to mention.

[773] Above, ‡22. HIROIDIL in the same inscription shows syncope of composition vowel.

[774] LHEB, pp. 653–54; also Parsons, *CMCS*, 33 (1997), 1–8 (cf. Ch. 4, p. 321). On OE *Cerdic* cf. Ekwall, *River-Names*, p. lxviii, n. 1 (but on *Coroticus* cf. COROTICA in Wiltshire, Wright, *JRS*, 52 (1962), 191). See also 409/198/849 CARANTORIVS, 403/268/841 MACARATINI (CARITINI Macalister), 499/Ok77 CARA*n*ACI, etc. On the relationship between between *carant-* and *carat-* see Hamp, *Ériu*, 27 (1976), 4–6. KHJ rejects Macalister's 499/Ok77 CARA*n*ACI ('what evidence for [*n*-suspension] so early?') and compares the AT ligature in Le Blant, *Inscriptions chrétiennes de la Gaule antérieures au viiie siècle*, i, plate 4, fig. 17, of AD 601, and the same AT ligature in 329/42.

[775] Russell, *Celtic Word-Formation*, p. 144. See below ‡42.

[776] LHEB, p. 653 and above, ‡‡ 19 and 37.

[777] LHEB, p. 653. For *Conet* see above, ‡18n., and below, ‡58.

[778] Above, ‡38.

[779] See also *Venedocia*, etc. in VSB, p. 330, and *Guenedotia*, etc. in LL, p. 401; Pryce, *EHR*, 116 (2001), 783, n. 43.

[780] See ‡74 below.

[781] LHEB, p. 562, n. 1.

[782] See above, ‡38n.

with 350/116/3 IDNERT and 984/59 BLEDRUS, with D for still unprovected /ð/.[783]

‡42 pp, tt, cc > f, th, ch; LHEB §147

Since LHEB was published, Greene's view (not accepted by Jackson) has gained ground, that spirantization involved not /kk/ > /x/ etc., but rather /k/ (< /kk/ and < any /k/ that had escaped lenition at ‡17) > /x/, etc.[784] The Brittonic inscriptions do not cast light on this debate. Variation between C and CC in them cannot be assumed to reflect /k/ versus /kk/, since, for example, CC might well be used for /k/ seeing that C frequently represented /g/, or, again, CC might be used for /x/ under the influence of words with etymological /kk/, such as /ko(:)x/ (W. *coch*) < Latin *coccus*. Again, CH, TH, and PH will not necessarily denote spirants rather than stops, in view of the slow and faltering development of that now familiar spelling convention.[785] The Irish ogam inscriptions may usefully be compared. It has been argued that there is a statistical tendency towards using **CC** for /kk/ and post-lenition /k/ and **C** for /k/ and post-lenition /x/, but this is impossible to apply as a rule in individual instances.[786] Moreover, although additional ogam letters were invented for the voiceless spirants (> < for /x/, etc.) their use is so infrequent that their absence from an ogam inscription is no indication of non-spirantization.[787] Much the same applies to the use of CC, C, CH, etc. in the Brittonic corpus.

[42] The examples of PP, PH, F (excluding FILIUS etc.), TT, TH, CC, and CH (other than those to be cited under ‡‡ 43 and 51) are all listed below, together with forms with H possibly bearing on spirantization.

[42] PP appears only in 1067 EPPS, an abbreviation for *episcopus*.[788] PH only appears in 2031/p.68 IOSEPH.

F appears as a variant of Latin/Greek *ph* in 1000/182 CHIROGRAF(*i*)U(*m*) and 1022/240/928 GREFIUM (*graphium* with internal *i*-affection). In 3012/M3 PRFTER is an odd abbreviation for *presbyter* (Bernier read E rather than F). F has been read in 1006/197/842 TEFROIHI, NEFROIHI, REFSOIHI or REFSDIHI, 470/Ok78 MAFARI and 1048/Ok32 QONFAL(I), but there are other readings in all of these.[789] There are no

---

[783] On BLEDRUS see ‡58 below. IDNERT may be compared with forms such as *Ithnerth* (AD 1242) cited by Wmffre, *Language and History*, i, 319.

[784] See Harvey, *CMCS*, 8 (1984), 87–100, and literature cited by Schrijver in SBCHP, p. 461, and *SC*, 33 (1999), 1.

[785] See Harvey, in Carney FS, pp. 59–64; TRC, p. 29; Sims-Williams, *CMCS*, 23 (1992), 45.

[786] See Harvey, *Ériu*, 38 (1987), 45–71; Ziegler, pp. 4–5, 17–18 and 304–10; TRC, p. 25. Cf. Sims-Williams, *CMCS*, 23 (1992), 46, n. 57.

[787] Ibid., 45–51.

[788] Kermode, *Manx Crosses*, appendix A, p. 5.

[789] In the case of QONFAL, Thomas, *Mute Stones*, p. 302, n. 52, says that the F is 'among the clearer letters', and Tedeschi, *Scrittura e civiltà*, 19 (1995), tav. 3, reads QONFALI. But Macalister was not obviously wrong to read the letters the other way up as HADNOB. NEFROIHI is discussed at the end of this section (‡42).

examples of FF. In 439/319 Nash-Williams gives **EF[E]SS[A]NG[I]**, following Rhys, but the four-stroke ogam letter in question (m4, traditionally **Z**) would not now be transcribed by **F**; in any case, instead of **EF** Macalister and McManus read the vowel **I** followed by the three-stroke letter (m3, traditionally **Ng**) which is now transcribed **G**ʷ.[790] On 2010/272 ITHFUS see below.

[42] TT appears in: 1000/182 CATTELL = *Cadell* with /d/ (note also BRITTANNIAE); 401/183 IATTI (beside BROHOMAGLI), either with etymological * *t* (> /d/) or with 'expressive' alteration of /t/ or /d/ to /tt/ or /t/ or, if earlier, to **tt* > /θ/;[791] 430/306 ETTERNI (and **ETTERNI**) = MW *Edern/Edyrn* with /d/, but paralleled in spelling in third- or fourth-century Roman Britain by *Etterne* for *Aeternae* on a lead *defixio* from Old Harlow, Essex;[792] 471/Ok39 MOBRATTI, which (if Brittonic) may have etymological **t* > /d/ (cf. OW *Bratguenn*, MW *Bratwen*, Mod.W. *Bradwen*) or, again, 'expressive' /tt/ or /t/, or earlier **tt* > /θ/, in a hypocoristic form;[793] 478/Ok48 NADOTTI or RADOTTI, obscure and uncertain readings;[794] and 510/Scot.13 VETTA, which resembles Latin *Vettius* and *Vetto*.[795] In 1061/Dor.iii CATGUG Macalister read CATTUG, arguably wrongly, even though the name may indeed be the same as MW *Cattwg* (cf. 333/50 CATVC).[796] 1035/303 has been read RECETT (= *Rheged*) by Rhys, or simply ETT by Macalister (i.e. Latin *et*), although Nash-Williams has

---

[790] McManus, *Guide*, p. 67; Sims-Williams, *TPS*, 91 (1993), 145–62. The inscription is damaged, but one might suggest something like **[D]IG**ʷ**ESS[A]** ('prayer', 'petition'?, cf. OI *dígde*, Lewis & Pedersen, p. 373), perhaps followed by a name in the genitive case.

[791] See Hamp, *Ériu*, 27 (1976), 2–3, on Gaulish *Iatt-*, and above, ‡38. If the 'expressive' alteration to /tt/ or /t/ took place early enough, it would be subject to spirantization, but not if it occurred subsequently. In general, cf. Evans, *BBCS*, 24 (1970–72), 425–26.

[792] VLRB, p. 919, citing Wright & Hassall, *Britannia*, 4 (1973), 325.

[793] KHJ noted: '*Mobratti* looks like a *Mo-* name with hypocoristic doubling, cf. *Bratwen*, man's name in Book of Aneirin.' See Williams, *Canu Aneirin*, p. 228 (*Bratwen* = *Bradwen*; cf. *Bratguenn*, LL, p. 388). This contains *brad* 'treachery, strategem' (: OI *mrath*, cf. *Dimratae* in Uhlich, *Morphologie*, p. 228, and ‡70 below) in a favourable sense (underlined by *gwen*); see Bromwich & Evans, *Culhwch and Olwen*, p. 72, and cf. *Maelfrad* in Bartrum, *Welsh Genealogies 300–1400*, vi, 384. Okasha assumes that MO is Irish, but this is not clear-cut; cf. Sims-Williams, *TPS*, 91 (1993), 146–47. Pace Thomas, *Mute Stones*, pp. 286 and 302, n. 35, it is unlikely to be a name containing the word for 'judgement' (with /a:/).

[794] Cf. Thomas, *Mute Stones*, pp. 263–64. Okasha's comparison with Irish *Nad-* names is impossible (cf. Ziegler, p. 114), as is that by Rhys, *Englyn*, p. 88, with Ir. *Núada(t)*.

[795] KHJ took VETTA to be masculine *a*-stem. For Latin *Vettius* he cites Tovar, *ZCP*, 34 (1975), 31, who states that it derives from Italy. Cf. Holder iii, 264 (*Vetius*) and 266; Weisgerber, *Rhenania*, p. 476. For attestation in Britain see indices to RIB and Tab.Vindol. ii, also *Vetti* (gen.) on a Carlisle tablet, Tomlin, *Britannia*, 23 (1992), 147. The feminine *Vettia* occurs in Northumberland in RIB i 1789. On Latin *Vetto* see Smith, VLRB, p. 913, who suggests that it occurs in RIB i 2144 BETTO, and compares RIB i 1879 VETTO[N]IANVS. For 1210/Ok5 Thomas, *Mute Stones*, p. 281, suggests V[ETT]ANVS, but see above, ‡18. Rhys, LWP, p. 407, compared OI *Féth* and 342/70 **ILVVETO** (see ‡38 above).

[796] For which see Pierce, *Place-Names of Dinas Powys*, p. 23 (assuming that the *t* and *-wg* are recent dialectal developments, which is not necessarily correct). See ‡60 below.

ETG(*uin*), i.e. *Edwin*, as suggested by Radford.[797] It is preferable, however, to retain RECETT and equate it with W. *rhyged* 'great gift; generous'. This could be an epithet of Maredudd 'the generous', or if the following word is read EIUS the inscription could mean 'Maredudd, his great gift'. Alternatively RECETT could be **Rhyged* as a personal name, perhaps followed by FILIUS or FECIT (a personal name of the same structure as OB *Ro-darch*, OW *Ri-derch*, Mod.W. *Rhy-dderch* 'of great view/appearance').[798]

[42] The following may be Irish names or examples of Irish orthography: 318/6 ETTORIGI, listed by Jackson (p. 566) as the forerunner of a MW **Ethri but in fact possibly Irish with /d/ < /nt/ or with /t/ ~ /θ/ (see above, ‡38); 362/142 **AVITTORIGES**, corresponding to roman-letter AVITORIA; 426/300 **NETTASAGRI** (Nash-Williams -U); 512 QATTIDONA (?).[799]

[42] TH occurs in 375/166 DOTHORANTI and 460/Ok75 VAILATHI (FILI VROCHANI), which Jackson lists as probably Irish, comparing Ir. *Faelad*.[800] The same could apply to 485/Ok68]THI FILI [ ] COLINI, if Thomas's reading is correct,[801] and to 1206/Ok4 DOVITHI, which recalls 128 and 157 **DOVETI** (< **Dubwet(i)i*), ancestor of Ir. *Dubad*, gen. *Duba(i)d*.[802] In 1012/223/933 IUTHAHELO one should segment T-H rather than compare later *Ithel*, and 1051/Ok31]ENITHI is Latin [U]ENIT H[IC] according to Thomas.[803] TH occurs in the biblical MATHEVS in 2013/383 and 1059/Ok64 (contrast 1017/259/867 TOME for *Thomae*). In 2010/272 the Germanic name ITHFUS is supposedly written in runes, using the letter *thorn*.[804]

[42] CC occurs in 352A/122/5 BRAVECCI (> W. **Brewych*), compared by Ifor Williams with W. *brawychu* 'to frighten';[805] and in 397/105 BECCVRI,

[797] Rhys, *AC*, 5th ser. 12 (1895), 187. See discussion in *Corpus*. For ETT = *et* cf. Clancy, *PSAS*, 123 (1993), 346.
[798] Gramm., pp. 37–38.
[799] Cf. Ziegler, pp. 146–47 and 222 on **CATTI-** and **QET(T)I-** ?
[800] LHEB, p. 566. Cf. Rhys, *AC*, 5th ser. 12 (1895), 302 (*faeladh*, gen. of *fáel* 'wolf'); Evans, *BBCS*, 24 (1970–72), 430; O'Brien, *Celtica*, 10 (1973), 226; Birkhan, *Germanen und Kelten*, p. 381. Jackson's 'similarly' in LHEB suggests that he classed DOTHORANTI along with VAILATHI as Irish, but KHJ notes that *nt* appears British. Perhaps we can regard it either as for Ir. *nd* or as part of a Latinate termination. If so, the name is perhaps hypocoristic *Do + Torann* (MI *torand*) 'thunder' (cf. 66 **TURANIAS**, Ziegler, pp. 239–40; W. *Taran* as personal name in *Pedeir Keinc y Mabinogi* and *Culhwch ac Olwen*, Gaulish *Taranis*: LEIA T-113). The development *To > Do* 'took place about the end of the seventh century' according to GOI, p. 111.
[801] *Mute Stones*, p. 271. COLINI could be an Irish or British patronymic. In a letter to me dated 7.11.92 Prof. Thomas was confident about]THI but remarked that]COGNI was more likely than]COLINI.
[802] Ziegler, p. 171. The comparison with W. *dofydd* (Thomas, *Mute Stones*, pp. 158, n. 22, and 282; cf. SWWF, p. 552), is unlikely; cf. ‡55 below.
[803] See above, ‡41, and Thomas, *Mute Stones*, p. 300.
[804] Moon, *AC*, 127 (1978), 126. Cf. Redknap, *Vikings in Wales*, p. 100.
[805] Williams, apud Fox et al., *AC*, 97 (1943), 211, cited in LHEB, pp. 191, 566, and 610.

which recalls W. *bych(an)* 'small' < **bikko-* (with VL E for I or with OW E for /ĭ/?), hence perhaps **Bikkorīx*. It might also be compared with Ir. *be(a)g* 'small', frequently spelt *becc* in Old Irish, and possibly in ogam in **BECCDINN**,[806] but the coupling with CVNALIPI (cf. OW *Conlipan*) is against its being Irish. The best comparison may that of Rhys with the 'Artuir/Artur filio *Bicoir* Pretene/Britone' said in the Irish Annals to have slain Mongán mac Fiachna *c.* 624;[807] the OI *Bicoir* may reflect a pre-spirantization and pre-affection Brittonic **Bikkorī-*. However, one could also start from **bekko-* 'beak' (French *bec*), as in the cognomen *Becco*, French *Becquigny* < **Becconiacum*, and the Italian Celtic tribe of Βεχουνων (gen. pl.) 'the beaked ones'.[808] Holder also records a potter's name *Becuro* from Paris and Rheims.[809] One may further compare the name *Biccus* on a fourth-century *defixio* from Uley, Gloucestershire, which Hassall and Tomlin regard as probably a variant of *Beccus/Becco* 'beak'.[810]

[42] CC also occurs in 2019 TVNCCE[(a fake?), probably the same name as 451/401 TVNCCETACE (cf. W. *Tyng(h)edog*, with original **k*: 172 **TOGITTACC**, OI *Toicthech*).[811] 331/41 [A]NNICCI is Latin *Annic(i)us* (cf. Gaulish ANNICCOIOS).[812] 365/149 COCCI, cited by Jackson as his latest instance of CC,[813] is shown by Lhuyd's transcription merely to be part of Latin HIC OCCISVS (cf. 350/116/3 OCCISV[S F]VIT; 1000/182 OCCIDIT). 403/268/841 BERICCI (so allegedly Lhuyd) is now thought to be BERIA[CI] or similar.[814]

[42] The following are probably all examples of Irish orthography: 326/39 MACCVDECCETI; 329/42 MACCVTRENI; 341/71 [M]ACCVTRENI (**Q** in the ogam); 993/124/18 OCCON (dubious, cf. ‡65); 353/127/7 **TRENACCATLO** (TRENACATVS in the roman letters); 372/160 **DECCAIBAR** (or similar); 425/297 MACCVTRE[NI] (second C apparently inserted, perhaps after flaking of the first); 424/29 GLVVOCCI

---

806 Cf. LEIA B-24; and for **BECCDINN** (not in CIIC) see Ziegler, p. 136, and Uhlich, *Morphologie*, pp. 175–76. Note *Bicanus* in VSB, p. 194.

807 *Englyn*, pp. 83–84 (identifying him with our BECCVRI !). See collation of the Annals by Meyer, *Voyage of Bran*, i, 84; cf. Grabowski and Dumville, *Chronicles and Annals*, p. 143; O'Rahilly, *Ireland and Wales*, pp. 148–49; Barber, *Figure of Arthur*, p. 36.

808 De Bernardo Stempel, in *Ptolemy*, p. 90 (taking the Italian name to refer to distinctive helmets, cf. Jope, *Early Celtic Art: Text*, p. 255); Lambert, *Langue gauloise*, pp. 170 and 188; DLG, p. 60.

809 Holder i, 363 and iii, 821; cf. *Bequro*, p. 848.

810 *Britannia*, 19 (1988), 486, n. 7. They note that *Biccus* is 'already attested' in CIL xiii 5366a (Besançon). See Holder iii, 861.

811 See above, ‡40. Cf. Charles-Edwards, in Evans FS, p. 2; Ziegler, p. 236. Note also the name *Tongeta* ,'fate, luck?', cited by Luján, in *Ptolemy*, p. 61, n. 11, and Schumacher, *Historical Morphology*, p. 98. *Tonget-* names were very common in Hispania: OPEL iv, 126.

812 Above, ‡22n.

813 LHEB, pp. 566–67. Lhuyd is cited by Edwards in the *Corpus*.

814 See ‡18n.

(Macalister's reading, but Edwards suggests [E]VA[LEN]GI); 440/335 MACVDEC[C]ETI (but the second C is doubtful, and MACVDECETI or MACVDEhETI can be deduced from Lhuyd's MACVDEbETI); 442/346 [MAC]CVDICCL; 492/Ok59 MA<u>CC</u>ODECHETI.

[42] CH appears according to Latin (Greek) spelling in 1000/182 CHIROGRAF(i)U(m). CH does not occur in any Brittonic names (excluding those in ‡43 below), although note HC in 1000/182 BROHCMAIL and BROHCMA(i)L (= W. *Brochfael* < **Brokkomaglos*).[815]

[42] H appears in this same element in 349/121/4 BROHO[and 401/183 BROHOMAGLI (beside IATTI with TT, as noted above).[816] 1015/233/910 AHEST (if not ANEST) may be the personal name which appears in twelfth-century contexts in the Book of Llandaf as *Aches* and *Achess*, as Rhys noticed; if this name is *aches* 'sea' < Latin *accessus*, the inscription's -T must be inorganic, due to the well-attested fluctuation between -*st* and -*s*, as in *Conblust*, *Conblus*.[817] The use of H for /x/ is paralleled by 1205/Ok44 MAVOUIH (or MAVORIH?) and, in Ireland, by CIIC 1 MENUEH – unless in the former /-x/ has already developed to /h/. Alternation between H and CH is explained by the equivalence of *h* and *ch* in Late Latin (cf. 3009/C4 MIHAEL).[818] H probably occurs for Ir. /x/ in 322/27 HOI 'here' (cf. ogam > < OI).[819] In 440/335 MACVDEbETI one suspects that the letter transcribed **b** was really an half-uncial **h** for Ir. /x/ (cf. 492/Ok59 MACCO-DECHETI below, and compare the use of half-uncial **h** in 349/121/4 BROhO[ ).[820]

[42] Lastly, it is likely that H for /x/ appears in 1006/197/842 NEFROIHI (also TEFROIHI among other readings), if this contains the Irish name *Fróech*. Macalister quotes MacNeill's suggestion that NEFROIHI is a Latinization of the popular Old Irish name *Nad-Froích*, with H used for /x/. This name occurs in the genitive in the ogam inscriptions 26 **NETTA-VRECC** and 271 **NETA-VROQI**.[821] The form in the inscription, NE, is not a

---

[815] Apart from here the combination HC does not occur, except of course for the common *eta* + *sigma* in IHC = *Iesus*, also IHC for HIC in 478/Ok48.

[816] Jackson notes, LHEB, p. 566, that 478/Ok48 BROCAGNI is probably Ir. *Broccán.*

[817] LL, pp. 32, 44, and 277; Rhys, *Englyn*, pp. 64 (with invalid comparison with OI *éces* 'sage') and 178. Cf. LHEB, p. 531, on *st*. Rhys, *AC*, 5th ser. 12 (1895), 37, suggested that *Maches* (LL, p. 411) is a hypocoristic form of *Aches*; but cf. OPEL iii, s.n. *Maches.*

[818] See above, ‡14, and Sims-Williams, *CMCS*, 23 (1992), 46. On MENUEH see also Uhlich, *Morphologie*, pp. 277–78.

[819] Sims-Williams, *CMCS*, 23 (1992), 49.

[820] A **b** is not otherwise attested alongside capitals, whereas **h** commonly is (ECMW, p. 225). Williams, *AC*, 106 (1957), 121, cites 440/335 as 'MACV-DECETI', along with the other examples of the same name.

[821] CIIC ii, p. 153, n. 1; Ziegler, pp. 215 and 252 (cf. 202 **NIOTT-VRECC**, with the originally distinct element *nia* 'nephew' as in Tírechán's *Nioth Fruich*, *Patrician Texts*, ed. Bieler, p. 162). NEFROIHI certainly seems to be the reading in Lhuyd's drawing published Anon.,

reduced form of NETA- but rather the old nominative < *neit-s, whence OI *nía* 'champion' and the element *Nía*- (less common than the stereotyped oblique *Nad*-) as in OI *Nía-Corb, Nía-Cuilind* and *Nía-Segamain*.[822] IE *neits would develop via Pr.Ir. *nēh*, the /h/ of which would combine with a following /w/ to give Pr.Ir. /f/.[823] Note that whereas the ogam spelling of **NETA-VROQI** < *Nēθa(h)-wroixī* does not reveal whether the /f/ has developed, it is clearly attested in NEFROIHI, probably for the first time. Two other NE- names, which invite similar explanations are 447/369 NEMAGLI (> OI *Nía-Máil* 'champion of a prince') and 493/Ok58 NEPRANI (-P- = [b]) (cf. OI gen. *Niad-Brain* 'champion(?) of a raven').[824]

[42] The following cases of CH are probably examples of Irish orthography: 366/148 ECHADI (so copied in a reply to Lhuyd's *Parochial Queries* and in Lewis Morris's papers);[825] 460/Ok75 VAILATHI FILI VROCHANI (= *Fróechán*, Jackson suggests);[826] and 492/Ok59 MACCODE͟C͟HETI.[827]

‡*43 lp, lc, rp, rt, rc > lf, lch, rf, rth, rch; LHEB §149*

Jackson thought it likely that the development here was /lp/ > /lpp/ > /lf/, etc. (cf. ‡42 above), whereas Russell has argued that /lp/ > /lf/ etc. was rather a matter of the stop being assimilated to the continuant and that it is was essentially the same phenomenon as the 'lenition' in /lb/ > /lv/ etc.[828]

[43] (A) Citing 381/87 ALIORTVS, 386/92 MARTINI, 327/43 TVRPILLI, 461/Ok66 ERCILIVI and ERCILINGI, 404/270/843 MARTI, and 1033/287 MARCIAU, Jackson notes (p. 570) that the (earlier) inscriptions do not use the spellings F, TH, and CH in these combinations, and that this is still frequently the case in Old Welsh.[829] He noted that the reading was uncertain in the one possible exception, 365/149 'LVNAR[C]HI COCCI', saying that Nash-Williams's [C] was more like an [I] – and indeed this is confirmed by

---

AC, 3 (1848), 310, though less clearly so in his drawing in Camden's *Britannia*, col. 616, and BL Stowe MS 1023, fo. 164r.

822 LEIA N-15–16; ADA, pp. 52–53; O'Brien, *Celtica*, 10 (1973), 228; CGH, pp. 712–14. On *niad (niad ?) > nad* see McCone, *Ériu*, 35 (1984), 6, n. 23.

823 See TRC, p. 131, and below, Ch. 4, §§ 20–21. On ogam V see Sims-Williams, *TPS*, 91 (1993), 140–43.

824 CGSH, p. 15.

825 Emery, *AC*, 124 (1975), 108; Owen, *AC*, 5th ser. 13 (1896), 133. For parallels see Ziegler, p. 177, and see ‡38n. above on ECHODI (Iona). The use of CH rather than Q makes Nash-Williams's early date dubious.

826 LHEB, p. 566; for the treatment of the diphthong see Ziegler, pp. 44–46, also Harvey, *Ériu*, 38 (1987), 69–70.

827 LHEB, p. 566.

828 LHEB, p. 565; Russell, *CMCS*, 10 (1985), 53–56.

829 Latin words like 1000/182 PARTA, 1030 PARTEM (> OW *part*, Mod.W. *parth*) and 2013/383 and 1059/Ok64 MARCVS (the Evangelist but equatable with Neo-Brittonic *March*) would have helped to prop up this convention. For OW examples see Watkins, *BBCS*, 21 (1964–66), 139.

Lhuyd's copy, which reads MAVOHENI FILI LVNARI HIC OCCISUS, with the Latin name *Lunaris* (twice attested in RIB).[830]

See ‡15 for the suggestion that 320/26 ORVVITE is a borrowing from Latin *Orfita* earlier than the advent of W. /rf/ < /rp/ and therefore with /rw/ sound-substituted for /rf/.

[43] (B) There are a very few examples of LF/LPH, LCH/LH, RF/RPH, RTH, and RCH/RH in any language in the inscriptions. In Latin words LCH occurs in 986/62 SEPULCHRIS and RCH in 1000/182 MONARCH-IAM, which recalls Harvey's suggestion that if such Latin words underwent the British spirantization, that may have helped the development of the spirant value of *ch* etc.[831] As it happens, 1000/182 also has RCH in a native name in CONMARCH, and RTH in GUARTHI[GIRN]. Another example of RTH is 1024/255/926 ARTHMAIL and possibly]HGERTH (beside NERTAT (Macalister: NERT*tan*), cf. 1023/239/927 NERTTAN),[832] while the 'bear' element may also be spelt with RTH in 1046/Ok8 ARTHI if the correct reading there is not ARAHI.[833] Thus the only certain examples are:

1. 1000/182 CONMARCH, GUARTHI[GIRN]
2. 1024/255/926 ARTHMAIL

[43] RH denotes -R | H- in 979/46 GURHI and 348/b/110/27 GURHIR(E)T and probably 3011/M2 IRHAEMA (see ‡36). It is obscure in 1056/OkAppC RRH, and 1030 RHOS is unlikely to be a correct reading. The only remaining form in the corpus is 3024/I5 BERTHILD*IS*, which is Germanic BERT-HILD-, not a Brittonic name in *Berth-*.[834]

[43] Since only RTH and RCH occur in Brittonic names, it will suffice to list the contrasting examples of RT and RC:

(A) RT
1. 986/62 IORUERT
2. 381/87 ALIORTVS
3. 386/92 MARTINI
4. 350/116/3 [I]DNERT
5. 1012/223/933 ARTMALI

---

[830] LHEB, pp. 570–71 and 571, n. 1; Edwards in *Corpus*. For *Lunaris*, see ‡18 above.
[831] Harvey, in Carney FS, p. 63; cf. TRC, p. 29.
[832] -AN is in both cases rejected Jackson, *Speculum*, 24 (1949), 600. Dr Redknap suggests that 1024/255/926]HGERTH may read]H(I)GERTI.
[833] See above, ‡36.
[834] This is not to imply that Brittonic *Berth-* and Ir. *-bertach* are not, at least in part, of Germanic derivation; cf. LEIA B-43; GPC s.v. *berth*; Uhlich, *Morphologie*, pp. 20, 138, 178 and 256; SWWF, p. 180. Lebel, pp. 44–45, 52, and 129 notes the productivity of *-ber(h)t* in French names, and moreover, that *-hild* was taken over as well (as in the case of *Domnildis* daughter of a *Dominica*). At this rate, BERT-HILD- could be a non-Germanic name recomposed from Germanic elements!

6. 1023/239/927 NERTTAN (ending uncertain)
7. 1025/248/862 ARTBEU
8. 1024/255/926 NERTAT (Macalister: NERT*tan*) [but also ARTH-MAIL as noted above]
9. 404/270/843 MARTI
10. 1054/Ok43 DONIERT
11. 2028 ARTOGNOV([?)

[43] The following may be relevant but are uncertain:
1033/287 M[C]ARTR (?)
1055/Ok3 T[T]UER[T] (?)
511/Scot.10 [E]RTIRIE (Macalister: [T]VRTIRIE)[835]
3023/I4]RTUS
348/b/110/27 GURHIRT or GURHIRET has /r(ə)d/ by metathesis of /dr/ (‡69), and 3022/I3 TVRTOVALDVS and 3024/I5 BERT(-)HILD*IS* are Germanic.

(A) RC
1. 1033/287 MARCIAU
2. 1041/376 GURMARC

[43] The following can be excluded:
2027 ERCAGNI, 376/174 ERCAGNI, and 461/Ok66 ERCILIVI (or ERCILI) and ERCILINGI (or ERCILINCI) probably have Irish *Ercc*-rather than Brittonic *Erch*-.[836]
369/153 CVRCAGNVS and 441/345 CVRCAGNI are also Irish, and so probably is 457/Ok18 MERCAGNI (perhaps better read MESCAGNI anyway).

[43] The RC, being due to post-syncope juncture, is irrelevant in 984/59 GURCI, 364/144 BARCVNI, and 427/a/301 **DUBAR[CUNAS]** (Macalister). Other dubious or irrelevant forms are:
482/Ok71]TRC (?)
1048/Ok32 (G)VENNORCIT (?)[837]
1050/Ok37 IRCVROC (?)
1057/Ok54]RCAS
996/147 MERCI ET GRACE

---

[835] See ‡57.
[836] See ‡48. Thomas, *Mute Stones*, p. 284 compares ERCILIVI with W. *erch* 'speckled' and OC *liu* 'color', but note that OI *lí* is also from **līu̯o-* and may occur in Irish names in -*l(a)e* (GPC, s.v. *lliw*; Uhlich, *Morphologie*, pp. 216 and 268; cf. Gaulish *Liomari*, DLG, p. 173). For a different segmentation see ‡27 above.
[837] So read by Thomas, *Mute Stones*, pp. 290–91, and Tedeschi, *Scrittura e civiltà*, 19 (1995), tav. 3 (with G-); cf. Gaulish names in *Orgeto-*, *Orciti-*, etc. (GPN, pp. 239–40, and DLG, p. 206; and ‡15n. above).

‡44 *Initial Σ- > h-; LHEB §115*

On Σ- < IE *s-* cf. ‡‡ 2–3 and 36 above. Jackson's view was that Σ-
was sufficiently *s*-like to be borrowed as OE *S-* in *Sæfern* (Welsh
Hafren < *Sabrina*) etc., but was nevertheless distinct from Latin *s-* which
rarely became *h-* in Brittonic; Zimmer also argues that British *S-* (Jackson's
Σ-) and Latin *S-* were articulated differently. An alternative view, elaborated
by Schrijver and supported by McCone, is that Brittonic *h-* < **s-* is due to
the generalization of /h/ as a lenited form of /s/ (as if *Hamish* were
generalized at the expense of *Seamus*). In Russell's view this explanation is
not obviously superior to Jackson's.[838] It is not necessary to arbitrate here,
only to note that on either view native names (where *H-* would develop) and
Latin names (where it would not) need to be kept apart.

[44] (A) Jackson notes (pp. 517–18) that only S- appears in the Dark Age
inscriptions, never H-. His two examples are:

1. 400/177 SENEMAGLI[839]
2. 391/78 SENACVS[840]

To these we can probably add:

3. 370/157 SENOMAGLI

[44] Jackson excluded this as probably Irish, because it occurs 'with
VLCAGNVS, which is an Irish name', but this is not conclusive; moreover
note that **SEN-** never appears as first element in the ogam corpus.[841] Jackson
also counted the following forms with S- as Irish, which is certainly true of
SAGRANI, but SALIGIDVNI *may* be Brittonic, as we have seen, so I
tentatively include it (SIMILINI being a Latin name is in any case irrelevant
here):[842]
399/176 SIMILINI (plus ogam version)
449/384 SAGRANI (ogam **SAGRAGNI**)

4. 341/71 SALIGIDVNI [*sic?*] (ogam **SALICIDVNI**).

[44] Other Irish names may be:
426/300 **SLECI** (McManus's tentative alternative to **BRIACI** or **BRECI**)[843]
439/319 **SEGNI** (Macalister, but reading and word-division are unclear)[844]

---

[838] SBCHP, pp. 377–83; TRC, p. 88; Zimmer, *JCL*, 3 (1994), 149–64; Russell, review of
SBCHP, *JCL*, 6 (1997), 148–49, and review of TRC, *CMCS*, 35 (1998), 74.
[839] Rhys, LWP, p. 372, notes that SENEMAGLI should give *Henfael, 'but it does not seem to
occur'; see ‡38n.
[840] This could of course be the common Irish name *Senach* (CGH, pp. 732–33).
[841] LHEB, p. 518, n. 1; and above, ‡36n.
[842] LHEB, p. 518, n. 1. For SALIGIDVNI and SIMILINI see above, ‡‡ 16 and 17.
[843] McManus, *Guide*, p. 67; see further ‡65 below.
[844] Cf. Rhys, in Meyer FS, pp. 236–37; McManus, *Guide*, p. 67; Ziegler, p. 281 and n. 413; and
‡48 below.

489/b/Ok13 SAGRANVI (on 489/a/Ok13 **SVAQQUCI** see ‡45)[845]

[44] Jackson (p. 518, n. 1) notes Latin S- in the following:
373/171 SEVERINI, SEVERI
384 /83 SANCTINVS[846]
472/Ok35 SEVERI
492/Ok59 SABINI[847]

[44] To these add:
320/26 SECVNDI
323/32 SATVRNINVS
355/128/8 SILBANDVS (rejecting FILI BANDUS)
1000/182 SE[V]IRA
418/283 SALVIANVS
419/284 SALVIA[N]I
429/307 SOLINI
483/Ok51 SENILVS (so read by Rhys, Thomas, and Tomlin)[848]
1212 SIMILIVS[849]

[44] Non-Celtic names with S- are:
337/60 SIWERD (or SI[U]ERD)[850]
1013/222/912 SAMSON, SAMUEL[851]
1012/223/933 SAMSONI or SAMSONIS
2005 S[AT]VRNBIV is Brittonic, but no change to /h/ is expected since the name is based on Latin *Saturn-*, W. *Sadwrn-* + W. *byw*). In the following only S- is expected in view of the following consonant (cf. ‡75):
1023/239/927 SCILOC[852]
2018 SPUO (obscure)

---

[845] But for the possibility that they are Brittonic see below, ‡‡ 48 and 60. Even if they are, the spellings with S- and S- may be Irish-influenced.

[846] Against Macalister's SANCE[R]INVS see I. Williams's review, *THSC*, 1942–43, p. 156. He notes that *Sanctinus* is attested on the Continent (see also *San(c)tinius* in Weisgerber, *Rhenania*, pp. 220 and 233) and is the source of MW *seithin* in *Gwawt Llud y mawr* in BT, p. 75.24. Lloyd-Jones, *Geirfa*, p. 177 s.n. Cristin, treats this as a personal name, suggesting emending to *Seith[enh]in*. Cf. Haycock, *Astudiaethau*, p. 479.

[847] But note that S in SABINI developed to /h/ *if* it is the source of W. *Hefin*, as stated in LWP, p. 401. But Rhys's source was 'Hefin ap Gwyndaf Hen o Lydaw' in the *Achau Saint Ynys Prydain* in *Iolo Manuscripts*, ed. Williams, p. 108 (*Hewnin* on p. 132), and seems to be a corruption of *Henwyn, Hywyn*, etc.; see EWGT, p. 57 (*Bonedd y Saint*, §20); LBS iii, 263–65.

[848] Thomas, *Mute Stones*, p. 286; Tab.Sulis, p. 228, comparing *Senilis*, common in RIB (see Indexes, also *Index* to *Britannia*, 1–25, p. 225, and ‡27n. above); Rhys, LWP, p. 406, rejects this identification merely on account of the inflection. Cf. *Senil(i)us, Senillus*, etc., in Holder ii, 1476–77, and OPEL iv, 66.

[849] Thomas, *Christian Celts*, pp. 62–63, reads CARASIMILIVS. Cf. above, ‡36.

[850] Cf. *Siuerd* < OE *Sigefrith* and *Siuuard* < OE *Sigeweard*: von Feilitzen, *Pre-Conquest Personal Names*, pp. 360–61. Differently see Zimmer, *JCL*, 3 (1994), 154.

[851] As noted by Rhys, *AC*, 5th ser. 16 (1899), 152, this gives *Sawyl/Sawel* in Welsh (LBS iv, 175; SBCHP, p. 217).

[852] See above, ‡18.

444/352 STACATI (dubious reading, and possibly acephalous)

1049/Ok33 SN[[853]

1200/Ok42 SPED – but this looks like OE *sped*; the bar over the H in Okasha's plate suggests the restoration [I]HS SPED 'Jesus speed' (cf. Modern English 'God speed').

[44] The following can be noted for completeness:

417/282 CAVO SENIARGII – probably to be divided CAVOSENI ARGII, with Macalister and Jackson[854]

487/Ok10 SIRVSIVS (unlikely to be the correct reading)

[44] (B) When Jackson states that 'there are no inscriptions showing *h-*' (p. 518), this must be because he did not count them as 'Dark Age'. The following have H- < *s-* quite certainly:

1. 994/125/22 HIROIDIL
2. 1011/220/911 HOUELT
3. 1039/382 HED (linguistically preferable to Macalister's NED)[855]
4. 3010/M1 HUBRIT
5. 2022/253/984 HU[TR]VM or HUT[R]VM (RCAHMW and *Corpus*; Nash-Williams: HUHIVM), probably a name in HU- < *Su-* like HUBRIT and HOUELT, perhaps W. *hydrwm* 'positively heavy', or more likely MW *hydrum* 'positively swift, etc.' (cf. B. *trumm* 'swift')[856]

[44] Note also:

6. 1032/281 ODELEV (W. *Hoedlyw*, ‡80)

[44] To these we should possibly add 412/277 FERRVCI (MW *Ferawc*, Mod.B. *le Ferec*) < *ffer* 'ankle' < IE **spher-*, if Jackson is right to suggest that **Σf-* (< **sp-*) > /f-/ may have been simultaneous with **Σ* > /h-/; however, he notes other possible chronologies.[857] If this etymology is not

---

[853] But KHJ noted that this should be SM. . . [judging by Macalister's own plate LXIII]; epigraphically he thought it 'might be very early, say 6th cent.'.

[854] See above, ‡18.

[855] Jackson, *Speculum*, 24 (1949), 599; EWGT, s.n. *Hedd* (presumably W. *hedd* 'peace', though note names like *Hedius* and *Hedo* in OPEL ii, 174 and biblical *Heth*). The H resembles the Insular *autem* symbol and is followed by a raised point. On the river name *Nedd* < **Nidā* see Sims-Williams, in *Britain 400–600*, p. 259.

[856] For **Su-* see GPN, pp. 257–58; RIG iv, 543; Ziegler, p. 233; SBCHP, pp. 162–64; Zimmer, *ZCP*, 47 (1995), 176–200; Wodtko, *Secundäradjektive*, pp. 42–65; and review of Wodtko by Zimmer, *ZCP*, 51 (1999), 295–96; SWWF, pp. 250–70. For *trwm* see LEIA T-151 and DGVB i, 324, and for *hydrum* see GPC s.v., Loth, *RC*, 43 (1926), 409–10, and DGVB i, 322. In a forthcoming review of McKee, *Juvencus*, P.-Y. Lambert argues that the OB *trum* 'inoportune' and OW *trum* 'abrupta' cited in DGVB are 'swift' not 'heavy'. HU[TR]VM is compared by RCAHMW with HEUTREN, but this is philologically impossible. On orthographical grounds HUBRIT presumably corresponds to W. *hyfryd* rather than to W. *hybryd* and OI *sochruth*; on these words see LEIA D-127 (*dochrud*: W. *dybryd*) and S-161; Isaac, *CMCS*, 41 (2001), 73–74; DLG, p. 239.

[857] LHEB, p. 529, §120; SBCHP, pp. 348 and 374. For this and other names containing *Fer-* see Williams, *Canu Aneirin*, p. 172 (preferring *ffêr* 'brave' < ?Latin *ferus*); Russell, *Celtic Word-*

accepted, however, we could perhaps compare FERRVCI with *Ferruciacus*, a place name in France (dép. Creuse) found on Merovingian coins; Holder would derive this from an unattested(?) personal name *Ferrucio*.[858]

[44] The following have H- < $*\Sigma$, but probably from an *internal* $*\text{-}\Sigma\text{-}$ < $*\text{-}s\text{-}$ (in $*isarno\text{-}$) at a much earlier stage (‡2), which came to be in initial position as a result of metathesis – hence they never had initial $*s\text{-}$:[859]

1065/410 HAERDUR (linguistically preferable to HAESDUR)
3010/M1 HERANNUEN; HERA[N]AL or HERA[H]AL (or similar)
3014/M5 HARENBILI; HERANHAL

[44] Obscure forms in H- cannot be given the benefit of the doubt, in view of the possibility of the H- being merely orthographical, the reverse of the frequent IC for HIC. A case in point is 998/164 HEUTREN, which may be a name in OW *Eu-* < $*Awi\text{-}$.[860] Again, 1036/360 HAUEN (Macalister; Nash-Williams: HAN EH) suggests W. *awen* 'inspiration'; the perhaps etymologically related *awel* 'breeze' may occur as a male name *Auel* in Old and Middle Welsh.[861] (Note, however, that there were also Latin names, well-attested in Italy, *Aven(i)us*, *Avena* (m.), *Avenia* – and also *Avel(i)us*.)[862] 1048/Ok32 HADNOBVIS (Macalister)[863] is obscure, as is 1068/b HIPIA or NIPIA. 450/390 HOGTIVIS (McManus: *recte* HOGTINIS (?)) corresponds to ogam **OGTENAS** (Nash-Williams: **OGTENLO**(?)), and may be an Irish name in *Ócht-*;[864] if so the H- is merely orthographical. The same may apply

---

Formation, pp. 45 and 145; LEIA S-73. Cf. Sims-Williams, *Britain and Early Christian Europe*, Ch. II, 33–34 and references, on OW *Fernmail*; note, however, RIB i 1010 *Ferni* and ii [fasc. 7] 2501.181 *Ferna*. The derivation of *Ferawc* from Latin *ferox, ferōc-em* (Koch, *Gododdin*, p. 208) is problematic as the Latin vowel did not normally give *aw*, but there are exceptions (ibid., p. 193; LHEB, pp. 307–8). For *Ferox* (and one *Ferrox*) see OPEL ii, 138.

858 Holder i, 1494.

859 See LHEB, pp. 359–60 and 522.

860 See above, ‡15. Cf. orthographic *h-* in Old Breton: Gramm., pp. 152 and 380 (EU-∼HEU-). I can find no example in the inscriptions where /h-/ is *not* written other than 1032/281 ODELEV and possibly (see ‡68 and p. 258) 1033/287 ANTERUNC.

861 LL, p. 279; *Llandaff Episcopal Acta*, ed. Crouch, p. 19. But *Auel* is also < biblical *Abel*: Haycock, *Blodeugerdd*, p. 88. Jackson, *Speculum*, 24 (1949), 599, notes that HAUEN cannot be *Owein*. W. *awen* and *awel* are connected by Watkins, *Celtica*, 6 (1963), 215–16, but this is denied by him in *How to Kill a Dragon*, p. 117; cf. ADA, p. 57.

862 Holder i, 308 and iii, 769; Mócsy, p. 37; OPEL i, 221–22.

863 Cf. Thomas, *Mute Stones*, p. 290 (reading it the other way up from Macalister). Visiting in bad light in 1951, KHJ could see nothing of FILIA but found the other letters much as given by Macalister, except that he thought his -S was surely R. (This would make HADNOBVIR – cf. Irish names like **CATTUVIR** > *Caither* (Ziegler, p. 148)? – or VIR and HADNOB as separate words, cf. ‡94.) In 1975 KHJ noted Thomas's proposed QONFALI (*sic*) in the programme of the Penzance Celtic Congress, 'but F is very unlikely grammatically, and Q suggests [it] couldn't be *Conval*'. Tedeschi, *Scrittura e civiltà*, 19 (1995), tav. 3, reads: + VIR/QONFALI. Cf. ‡26n.

864 McManus, *Guide*, p. 65. See above, ‡‡ 27n. and 38n. Rhys, LWP, pp. 63 and 277, read N-instead of H-; see ‡51. KHJ notes: 'The H- is of course merely Latin otiose *h-*.'

to 422/298 [H]OCIDEGNI (Macalister), but the H- and indeed the whole reading, is very doubtful (Nash-Williams has V-, following Lhuyd).

[44] 322/27 HOI is Irish, probably with /x/ < *k,[865] and the most plausible explanation of 3011/M2 IRHAEMA is I(c) R(equiescit) plus a non-Celtic name HAEMA.[866]

‡45 *Σu̯* > hw; LHEB §118

No inscriptional evidence is cited for this change, which produced OW hu-, and standard Mod. W. chw-. (Note, too, that a Pictish cluster similar to W. chw- may occur in the inscriptions reading **XEVV** and **HCCVVEVV**.)[867]

[45] It may well be, however, that /Σu̯/ or /hw/ is reflected in ogam script in 489/a/Ok13 FANONI/SVAQQUCI (recte **SVANNUCI** ?or **SVANNUNI**), corresponding to 455/403 FANNVCI (Pembrokeshire). MacNeill derived this name from British *swant- (OB Huant-, W. chwant 'desire', chwannog 'desirous', C. whansek: Old Celtic Suandacca); the F- would probably be the regular Irish development of /hw/.[868]

‡46 Pretonic u, ï̯ (< i) > ö, ι in Pr.W.; LHEB §205 [I use ö in place of Jackson's ə + o digraph.]

The change /ï̯/ > /ι/ is not revealed by the inscriptions, since I and E could probably stand for either, as in Old Welsh.[869]

[46] The change (A) /u/ > (B) /ö/, on the other hand, is revealed when O is used, although, as Jackson points out, the reverse is not necessarily true, because U may denote /ö/ as well as original /u/.[870] Despite this problem, the inscriptions can be arranged in two classes: (AB) those with U for /u/ or possibly /ö/ and (B) those with O for /ö/ (or in some cases its later reflex /ə/, ‡84), and of these the (B) inscriptions *en bloc* should be later than at least some of the (AB) inscriptions.

[46] (AB) Jackson's list (pp. 670–71) of Welsh inscriptions in which /u/ > /ö/ has *apparently* not yet happened (though U *may* = /ö/) is:

1. 320/26 CVLIDOR(I)[871]
2. 374/172 CVNEGNI [probably Irish, however, see ‡48]

---

[865] Sims-Williams, *CMCS*, 23 (1992), 48–49.

[866] See above, ‡38.

[867] Sims-Williams, *CMCS*, 23 (1992), 48, citing Padel.

[868] Mac Neill, *Ériu*, 11 (1930–32), 133–34 (cf. Rhys, in Meyer FS, pp. 239–40); see ‡18 above and ‡60 below. Another possibility is that the F- is due to a rare dialectal development of /h/ or /hw/ in Pr.C.; cf. Falileyev, in *Irland und Europa*, pp. 7–9.

[869] LHEB, p. 666.

[870] LHEB, p. 671. Cf. Sims-Williams, *BBCS*, 38 (1991), 36–47.

[871] This depends on the name having original /u/ rather than /ö/, but both are possible; see above, ‡16.

3. 435/315 CLVTORIGI
4. 446/353 CLVTORI [plus ogam **CLUTAR[I]** or **CLUTAR[IGAS]**[872]
5. 362/142 CVNIGNI [plus ogam **CUNIGNI]** [probably Irish, however, see ‡48]
6. 449/384 CVNOTAMI [plus ogam **CUNATAMI]**
7. 319/9 CVNOGVSI[873]
8. 342/70 CVNOCENNI [plus ogam **CUNACENNI]** FILIVS CVNOGENI [but this could be Irish][874]
9. 455/403 CAMVLORIGI
10. 323/32 SATVRNINVS[875]
11. 397/105 CVNALIPI, CVNACI
12. 971/35 CUURIS
13. 451/401 TVNCCETACE

[46] Further examples, again restricted to Wales (and the borders) and not including the disputed reading 1033/287 CUNGEN (mentioned below) are:

14. 322/27 CAMVLORIS
15. 327/43 TVRPILLI (and ogam equivalent)
16. 387/95 FIGVLINI (with Latin /u/) [probably to be ignored in view of (B) no. 8 below]
17. 351/115/2 DVMELVS (cf. W. *Dyfel* 'not-sweet, bitter', although it could be Irish)[876]
18. 409/198/849 PVMPEIVS (with /um/ < Latin /om/)[877]
19. 2022/253/984 HU[TR]VM or HUT[R]VM (Nash-Williams: HUHIVM(?)), probably W. *hydrum* < *Su-[878]
20. 2029/p.39i CVNIIAC (compare CVNACI above)
21. 418/283 CVPETIAN[I (?)] < Latin *Cupitianus*, with /u/ subject to the

---

[872] This and the preceding item (435/315 CLVTORIGI) have Celtic *kluto-* and *could* be Irish (before the lowering that gave OI *cloth* and *clothri*); but Jackson may well be right in taking them to be Welsh (see above, ‡14). Note in particular that **Clothrí* does not seem to be attested as an Irish personal name (cf. Uhlich, *Morphologie*, p. 204; Ziegler, p. 150). OW *Clotri* is assumed by Jackson in LHEB, p. 607, to have /o/ and to be an exception to internal *i*-affection (if so it may have been influenced by *clod* 'fame' < *klutā*: LEIA C-125). In fact it could have /ö/ < /u/ (cf. *Clydno, Clydog, Clydwyn*). If *Clodri* actually occurs in Middle Welsh (this is how Bartrum modernizes *Clotri* in EWGT s.n.), it may be orthographically conservative or influenced by *clod* – or it may be a post-internal-*i*-affection re-formation (cf. ‡19 above). Cf. Loth, *Noms des saints bretons*, p. 24, and Gramm., p. 239, on CB. *Cleder* < *Klutorīx*.

[873] CVNOGVS(I) is probably Irish, but I let it stand as its vocalism must be influenced by Brittonic orthography. See above, ‡38.

[874] See above, ‡17.

[875] Cf. *Sadyrnin*, Lewis, *Elfen Ladin*, p. 46. Lloyd-Jones, *Y Geninen*, 44 (1926), 3, gives *Sedyrnin*, which is irregular.

[876] See above, ‡26n. A relatively late example of *du-* for *dy-* is OW *dubeneticion*: Falileyev, *Etymological Glossary*, s.v.; Schrijver, *ÉC*, 34 (1998–2000), 154.

[877] See above, ‡26.

[878] See above, ‡44. In the same inscription, GVLGVEN, probably has V for /w/ in *gwelw*; as in 1004/260/884 GELUGUIN; see ‡22.

Welsh change to /ö/, as in Latin *cupidus* > W. *cybydd* and perhaps *Cybi*;[879] also perhaps, in the same inscription, the obscure BVRSOCAVI or BVRGOCAVI

22. 1033/287 DUBUT, if with DU- as in DVMELVS above, plus an uncertain element (hardly *budd* 'profit, victory') – but not if Williams is right to take DU as a modification of the OW preposition *di, dy* 'to'[880]

23. 2019 TVNCCE[(cf. TVNCCETACE above, which may indeed be the model if 2019 is a forgery)

24. 443/349 CAMVLORI (preferable to CAMVMORI)

25. 447/369 CVNISCVS or (better) CVNIGCVS[881]

26. 454/402 CVNIOVENDE

27. 2005 S[AT]VRNBIV

28. 2006 CVNORIX (probably an Irish name, but orthographically Brittonic)

[46] I have attempted to leave out probable Irish names (where V would not in any case be pretonic), and one other foreign name (337/60 VVLMER; cf. Macalister's doubtful WUMERE in 980/46a). Also omitted are names which have V as the pretonic composition vowel; for, while some pretonic composition vowels are known to have survived syncope (‡38), there do not seem to be any examples involving /u/ > /ö/ > MW *y*; 408/229/848 CATOTIGERNI (> OW *Cattegirn*, Pr.B. *Catihernus*) and 425/297 CATOMAGLI (> W. *Cad(a)fael*) < *katu*- clearly participated in the general reduction also manifested in 970/13 CATAMANUS (> MW *Caduan*). If Jackson's suggestion that OW *Catgabail* is a pun on *Catamail* is correct, that confirms that /u/, if it survived, survived as /a/.[882]

[46] I of course omit names in MW *Gwr*- < *Wiro*- (979/46 GURHI;[883] 984/59 GURCI; 348/b/110/27 GURHIR(E)T; 1041/376 GURMARC; and, on the Isle of Man, 1066 GURIAT). The obvious explanation of such names is that the /u/ either developed later than the period of pretonic /u/ > /ö/ or

---

879 Above, ‡18; and Lewis, *Elfen Ladin*, p. 36; EANC, p. 133. *Cupidus* does not occur in RIB i–ii.

880 Cf. BWP, pp. 30 and 32–33. But the editorial comparison with *budd* here (BWP, p. 33, n. 41; cf. GPN, p. 156, n. 8) is orthographically inferior to Williams's comparison with *Boutius* (a possible derivative of which Thomas, *BBCS*, 7 (1933–35), 121, sees in Mod.W. *Budno*). Note also that a name *Butu* appears on a fourth-century *defixio* from Eccles villa, Kent, and is compared by Hassall & Tomlin, *Britannia*, 17 (1986), 428, n. 5, with *Butto* in Pannonia and *Buttus* in Noricum. Cf. Holder i, 645 and iii, 1011 for *Buta* and *Butu*. The fact that OW *di/dy* 'to' ultimately goes back to Celtic *dū* (SBCHP, p. 125) is of course irrelevant to DUBUT. It is unlikely that the latter is an abbreviation or short form of W. *Dyfodwg* (< *Ty-fod-wg*) or Ir. *Dubthach* (cf. Chapter 4, §21n), as suggested by Morris-Jones, *Cymmrodor*, 28 (1918), 265, and Koch, *SC*, 20/21 (1985–86), 51.

881 See ‡48.

882 LHEB, p. 437; and in *Celt and Saxon*, pp. 38–39; TYP, pp. 289–90. In the context of 425/297, CATOMAGLI is likely to be Ir. *Cathmá(e)l* (Uhlich, *Morphologie*, p. 193).

883 *Wer*- rather than *Wiro*- according to Williams, *AC*, 90 (1935), 94.

that it bore some secondary stress. The latter explanation is conceivable in a late compound like GURCI but not in an old formation like GURIAT (MW *Gwriat*), cognate with Gaulish *Viriatus*.[884] But if we then argue that /wïr/ > /wur/ had not happened when pretonic /u/ > /ö/, that leaves us with the problem that /wïr/ > /wɪr/ > **Gwyr*- did not occur either! Schrijver suggests that it did occur, but then /gwər-/ 'reverted to *gwr*- as a result of the general development of *gwə*- to *gw*- in MW'.[885] His Middle Welsh explanation does not explain the inscriptions, nor OW *Guurci*, OC *Wurci*, OB *Gurki* (all cited by him).

[46] 396/104 IVSTI[NI] is not relevant here in view of the way Latin *iu*- developed in Welsh to *i*-.[886] Of course I also omit names with pretonic /ü(:)/ rather than /u/: 346/75 ADIVNETI (Knight's reading); 359/141 NV[D]INTI (cf. Romano-British NODENTI and NVDENTE, Ir. *Núada*, W. *Nudd*); 365/149 LVNARI; 1012/223/933 IUTHAHELO; 1015/233/910 GRUTNE; 2021 (MEMBRA) PVDIC (if = W. *Buddig* < *Boudīkā, -os*; note that if the following word is indeed [MV]LIE[R] or [MV]LIE[RIS] there is hardly room for any case form of Latin *pudicus, -a*).

[46] 328/44, if a Welsh name, should possibly be restored [T]RVGNIATIO (or -ATO);[887] however, the pretonic /u/ in such a sequence would seem to have merged with the following /i̯/ < /γ/ to give a diphthong /ui/ (as in *trwynau*, plural of *trwyn*) earlier than the reduction of /u/ > /ö/. (This suggests that the order of ‡48 below and the present ‡46 should be reversed).[888]

[46] 339/68 the reading N[UMNI]I is too doubtful to include. 2018 CVNCUOM is also very suspicious (and not only for the combination of pretonic V and syncope).

[46] (B) Jackson lists (p. 668) the following cases where /u/ > /ö/ has happened:

1.   1000/182 CONCENN, CONMARCH
2.   1011/220/911 HOUELT
3.   1016/234/907 CONBELIN
4.   1023/239/927 CONBELANI [the CON- is shown by Lhuyd]

---

[884] GPN, p. 287 and n. 5. On GURCI, see above, ‡‡ 16 and 19.

[885] SBCHP, p. 151. On p. 152 he explains *dewr* by internal *i*-affection in *daγwïr*, which would put /wïr/ > /wur/ later than ‡57 below; but he admits that *dagowiros* is a problematic etymology of *dewr*.

[886] Lewis, *Elfen Ladin*, p. 15. IVSTI[NI] is a certain restoration; see Knight, *CMCS*, 29 (1995), 1–10. If 389/97 IOVENALI shows a *Welsh* development of *Iuvenalis* (cf. ‡80 below), it has /uu̯V/ > /ou̯V/ which is not relevant here.

[887] See above, ‡18.

[888] See Ch. 3, p. 256, *re* cols. 15 and 17. A possible counter-example to *trwynau* is MW (and Mod.W. dialectal) *morynyon*, pl. of *morwyn*, but the history of this word is obscure; see LHEB, p. 463, n. 1; SBCHP, pp. 248–49 and 356–57; and ‡48n. below.

[46] Other instances (omitting 356/132/9 CONVMANI, read by Macalister alone)[889] are:

5. 324/34]CO[N]BARRVS CO[N]BURRI[890]
6. 352A/122/5 DOMNICI[891]
7. 1068/b CONDILICI (on the Isle of Man; cf. W. Cynddilig)[892]
8. 387/95 LOCVLITI, compared by Rhys with Lann Mihagel Liclit in the Book of Llandaf.[893] Liclit looks like Mod.W. llychlyd 'dusty, earthy' < llwch, or alternatively *llyglyd 'infested with shrews' (cf. llygodlyd), both with original /u/.[894] LOCVLITI can be the same as llychlyd or *llyglyd if the O represents /ö/ < /u/. A possible objection is that -led is said to be the original form (: OI leth) and -lyd a late and analogical pseudo-masculine on the pattern of gwyn/gwen < *windos/ā, etc.;[895] but this analogy could have arisen at any date after a-affection and apocope (‡‡ 15 and 37 above). In any case, Ifor Williams clearly thought that -lyd was much older and of different etymology, seeing it in Brocoliti 'infested with badgers' in the Ravenna Cosmography.[896] If LOCVLITI is llychlyd 'dusty, earthy', the coupling FIGVLINI FILI LOCVLITI gains added point since Latin figulus (also a name Figulus) meant 'potter' and fig(u)linus meant 'belonging to a potter'; llychlyd would be an appropriate nickname in such a profession, supposing that there still were potters in post-Roman Wales. (For professions in the inscriptions, compare 488/Ok60 DOBVNNI FABRI, 386/92 MELI MEDICI, and 509/Ok.Pict3 MEDICII.) An alternative would be to compare LOCV- with OI loch (o-stem) 'dark, black', as in 170 QENILOCI

---

[889] Cf. I. Williams, review of CIIC i, in THSC, 1942–43, pp. 155–56.
[890] Dubious readings, BWP, p. 24; see ‡‡ 26 and 38 above.
[891] If deriving this from Celtic *Dumno- rather than Latin Dominicus; cf. I. Williams, in Fox et al., AC, 97 (1942–43), 210, and discussion in ‡17n. above.
[892] Above, ‡16.
[893] LWP, pp. 367 and 425; Englyn, p. 85; LL, pp. 32 and 44. In the index to LL (p. 408), this place is equated with the Lann Mihacgel Lichrit of LL p. 244, a place by a ford (rit) on the Troggy, Mon., according to the bounds (p. 380). It is identified by the editors with '? Earlswood Chapel, Mon.', but by Wendy Davies, Welsh Microcosm, p. 185, with '? Llanmelin' (ST 460920), while WATU, p. 121, distinguishes between '[Llanfihangel Llechryd] ?= Llanmelin, Llandegelli' (cf. p. 105, and Rees, South Wales and the Border, SE Sheet (Llanmihangel Lechryd)) and '[Llanfihangel Llyglyd] ?= Earlswood'. Llechryd 'stone ford' is a common Welsh place name (there are three examples in Davies's Rhestr) and could be regarded as the lectio facilior compared to Llychlyd or Llyglyd.
[894] Cf. Sims-Williams, CMCS, 32 (1996), 39–40, on llwch; and GPN, p. 218, on Lucot-. Cf. OW lichou 'palu[de]s', Falileyev, Etymological Glossary, s.v.
[895] Note varying opinions in GPC s.v. -lyd, Lloyd-Jones, Geirfa, pp. 175, 600, and 725, s.vv. creulet, gwaetlyt, and gwyarllyt, and SWWF, p. 524. See also examples of -led in place names given by Wmffre, Language and History, i, 231. For leth < *plet-os see NWÄI, p. 142.
[896] Apud Richmond & Crawford, Archaeologia, 93 (1949), 26 (seemingly equating it with lītu-'feast' via the idea of 'frequented', but the vowel is a problem). Cf. PNRB, p. 284. Cf. brochlyd in SWWF, p. 527. Cf. lech bichlit/bychlyt in LL, pp. 42 and 134, which Dr Jon Coe explains as 'abounding in bucks' (: bwch).

and 192 **QENILOC[A]GNI** > OI *Cellach*, and *Cennlachán*, *Cellachán*.[897] In this case the whole name could be Irish rather than Welsh.

[46] As noted earlier (‡26), a slight problem arises in the case of the combination ON in 413/272 MONEDORIGI which (theoretically) could either be late, the result of /u/ > /ö/, or archaic, antedating the raising of /o/ before nasals. I argued, however, that MONEDORIGI is unlikely to have O for /ö/ because all other relevant cases of ON show syncope; it is thus archaic. I therefore exclude it from (B).

[46] 379/170 LOVERNACI is also problematic, in view of Schrijver's argument that *lop-erno-* developed to *loerno-* and then, by raising in hiatus, to *luerno-*;[898] theoretically our LOVERNACI could reflect either the earlier *loern-* or the later *löern-* from the raised *luern-*. It is only the -ACI rather than -OC(I) that makes the former possibility (*loern-*) more likely.[899]

[46] Of course there are numerous other names with O in pretonic syllables (e.g. 320/26 ORVVITE, 986/62 IORUERT, 1000/182 BROHCMAIL, 401/183 BROHOMAGLI,[900] 408/229/848 BODVOCI) but there is absolutely no reason to suppose that their O is /ö/ (< /u/) > W. *y* rather than original /o/ > W. *o*.

[46] 399/176 TOVISACI/[TO]VISACI is a special case. If it is the preform of W. *tywysog* and the latter derives from *to-wed-tākos*, TOVISACI would have /ö/ < /o/ by Jackson's very early reduction in proclitic preverbs (‡5), and would be irrelevant to /ö/ < from /u/.[901] Schrijver, however, argues that the correct reconstruction of the preverb is *tu* rather than **to*.[902] In this case, it might seem that /tu/ could develop regularly to /tö/; however, this conflicts with evidence that /uu̯/ and /ou̯/ merged as /ou̯/, and leads Schrijver to suggest that '*tou̯iss-* . . . was restored to *tuu̯iss-* by the introduction of

---

[897] MacNeill, *PRIA*, 39 C (1931), 39; Ziegler, pp. 220–21. On LOCVLITI see also KHJ's comment, above, ‡38n. *Locu-* occurs in RIB i 1478 LOCU[(cf. the cognomen *Antilocus* in RIB ii, index). The ΛOCVNILOS in RIG iv, no. 314 is probably for VOCVNILOS (p. 481). An alternative possibility for -LITI is W. *-llid* < *slītu-* as in *cyllid*; see ‡16 above.

[898] SBCHP, p. 61, citing his article in *JIES*, 26 (1998), 421–34. Cf. LHEB, p. 384.

[899] i.e. assuming that the name is Brittonic rather than Irish (cf. OI *Loarn*, latinized as *Loernus* (CGH, p. 673; Uhlich, *Morphologie*, pp. 20 and 269; SBCHP, p. 61)). Tanguy, in *Cartulaire de Redon*, p. 63, notes OB *-loern*, and *-louuernoc* in place names.

[900] The development of W. *Brychan* rather than **Brochan* is problematic (LHEB, p. 665, n. 1, and below, ‡48n.), but there is no evidence for a /u/ > /ö/ stage.

[901] See Ziegler, p. 237; LEIA T-188 (*to-u̯ed-tu-*); cf. LHEB, pp. 658 and 664, n. 1.

[902] SBCHP, pp. 17, n. 2, and 342 (similarly Schumacher, *Historical Morphology*, pp. 33–34 – also pp. 54–55, arguing for *-wid-* 'tell' rather than *-wed-* 'lead'). Schrijver's argument that *to-* would have suffered internal *i*-affection, giving **tewyssawc* depends on rejecting Jackson's early reduction of *to* to unaffectable *tö*, and also arises in the case of *tuu̯iss-* which should have become *tau̯iss-* > **tewïs-* by Schrijver's own rules (although insofar as these depend on *llawer* cf. Uhlich, *Ériu*, 46 (1995), 18, n. 46, and on *llawer* see also Zimmer, in Beekes FS, pp. 354–55); but Schrijver, supported by Schumacher, gives other arguments as well for *tu*.

the normal shape of the preverb'.[903] In that case, we have /tu/ > /to/ →
/tu/ > /tö/ and TOVISACI could theoretically belong to stage 2 /to/ or stage 4
/tö/. A further complication is that it may in any case be Irish (> OI *toísech*)
rather than British.[904]

[46] Similar issues are raised by HOUELT (*Hywel*) in Jackson's list (no. 2
above). The prefix *hy-* is derived from **so-* according to Jackson; however,
*su- is more probable according to Schrijver and others,[905] and /su/ could
presumably develop to /hö/ is in the same way as /tu/ to /tö/.

[46] A stage (C) will be reached when /ö/ passes to /ə/ (see ‡84), and Jackson
sees this first happening in 1033/287 CINGEN (and apparently in
CIMALTED in the same Tywyn inscription, where the I is not from
/ö/ < /u/ however).[906] Yet the correct reading has also been thought to be
CUNGEN or, more likely, CUN BEN.[907] In any case, although stage (C)
forms presuppose stage (B), discussion of them can be deferred to ‡84.

‡47 əii̯á perhaps > W. aia, CB. oia; LHEB §39

[47] (A) No inscriptional evidence is cited. As noted under ‡31 above, the
əii̯á stage is probably represented by E in:

1. 3010/M1 HERANNUEN FIL' HERA*N*AL (or HERAN*H*AL)
2. 3014/M5 (HARENBILI IB FIL) HERANHAL

[47] I am assuming that these names are what Jackson calls 'new and later
coinings on Breton soil' (giving OB partially stressed *Hoiarn-*, *Harn-*) as
opposed to the 'old British compounds' where **Isarno-* gave OB unstressed
Iarn- as a first element.[908] The vowel between the R and N(N), written
indifferently A or E, must be a svarabhakti vowel as in Vannetais *beragn*
'pile' < *bern*.[909]

---

[903] SBCHP, pp. 328 and 342.
[904] Cf. LEIA T-101 and 188; Uhlich, *Ériu*, 46 (1995), 16.
[905] LHEB, pp. 609 and 659; SBCHP, pp. 162–64, cited above ‡44n. Rhys, *AC*, 5th ser. 16
(1899), 155, and again in *Englyn*, p. 30, denied the connection between HOUELT and
Hywel, equating the former with OI *Sualtam* (for which, and *Sualt*, see CGH, p. 738, and
Zimmer, *JCL*, 3 (1994), 160), but this seems to have etymological **alt* (cf. Meyer,
Miscellanea, p. 11, and Uhlich, *Morphologie*, pp. 12 and 113). HOUELT has -T by false
archaism according to Zimmer, *JCL*, 3 (1994), 154; cf. ‡63 below. *Hywel* is 'conspicuous,
easy to see' < **su- + gwel-*, according to Rhys, *PBA*, 1905–6, p. 297 (similarly Lloyd-Jones,
Y Geninen, 44 (1926), 6, and Richards, *THSC*, 1965, p. 32; cf. GPC, s.v. *hywel* 'visible; . . .
keen-eyed'; SWWF, p. 262: 'with good look').
[906] See above, ‡26.
[907] See ‡38n above. For Jackson's interpretation of CINGEN and CIMALTED see LHEB,
pp. 668 and 681. For the reflexes of **kuno-* in 'Archaic Old Welsh', see Sims-Williams,
BBCS, 38 (1991), 36–47.
[908] HPB, p. 230.
[909] See ‡69 below.

[47] (B) The W. *aia* stage may be seen in:

1. 1065/410 HAERDUR (a linguistically preferable reading to the mean-ingless HAESDUR)

[47] In view of the other evidence for OW *Heardur*, MW *(H)aeardur*, where the spellings imply *haearn-* as first element more clearly (see ‡36), I assume that HAERDUR contains *haearn* rather than *haer* 'challenging, firm', although the latter does occur in personal names, such as MW *Haer* (f.), OB *Haer-*, cognate with Gaulish *Sagrus* and the divine name *Ambisagrus* and OI *Sár(án)* (m.).[910] HAER- could be a simplification of *HAEARN-.

[47] Something comparable to the Welsh *aia* seems at first sight to occur in Brittany in 3014/M5 HARENBILI (IB FIL HERANHAL). Here the son might seem to have a more advanced form of the element than his father, unless the variation is accidental, as has been suggested.[911] But a better explanation can start from the fact that HARENBILI is trisyllabic whereas HERANHAL is dissyllabic (discounting the svarabhakti in both cases). There are essentially three forms of the Old Breton 'iron-' element, with decreasing degrees of stress: *Hoiarn-*, *Harn-*, and *Iarn-*. Jackson derives *Harn-* from *Hoiarn-*,[912] but there is no reason why in favourable phonetic circumstances, such as the extreme pretonic position in HARENBILI, it should not have developed from the earlier *Həii̯àr(ə)noβilí* stage and have bypassed the Cornish and Breton rounding to *Hoiarn-*.[913]

[47] It seems impossible to explain HARENBILI by the accent shift, which Jackson dates to the eleventh century. Admittedly, after the accent shift the first element of HARENBILI would still have been pretonic, unlike that of HERANHAL, and this could have encouraged reduction to *Harn-* (=HAREN), as in trisyllables like *Harnguethen* in the Cartulary of Quimperlé.[914] Apart from non-linguistic objections to so late a date, however, it is significant first that 3014/M5 is from Morbihan in the

---

[910] EWGT, p. 196; Chrest., pp. 105 and 212; Loth, *Noms des saints bretons*, p. 62; Holder ii, 1296; GPN, p. 136; LEIA S-26; Ziegler, pp. 115–16; CGH, s.nn. For the suggested *Haear(n)-* > HAER- compare *daear-* > south-eastern Welsh *daer-* etc., WG, p. 100. On the etymology of *haer* and possibility of *sagero-* rather than *sagro-* see SBCHP, p. 134; MLH v/1, p. 328. If HAER- = *haer*, the latter would probably come from *sagero-* since OW *ae* does not normally represent /ai/ < /aγ/ before consonant; see Sims-Williams, *BBCS*, 38 (1991), 61, n. 3 (pace LHEB, p. 460, n. 2).

[911] This was suggested in the draft of IEMB (s. M5: 'Therefore *Haren-* is an aberrant spelling and should be understood as *Heran(n)-*, like the rest'). In the published version, p. 217, a version of my suggestion to the editors is adopted: 'Therefore *Haren-* is the odd spelling and perhaps reflects the unaccented form of the word, OB *Iarn-*.'

[912] HPB, p. 230. Loth, *Noms des saints bretons*, pp. 59–60, claims that *Harn-* occurs in OW *Harn-meini* in LL, but no such form occurs there, as Dr Jon Coe kindly confirms.

[913] On the rounding see Hamp, *CMCS*, 18 (1989), 114 and references. Cf. ‡50 below.

[914] Cf. HPB, p. 230 (cf. p. 80). On the date of the accent shift in Welsh, see however below, p. 289.

Vannetais area which did not participate in the accent shift, and secondly that Jackson notes that the reduction also happened in disyllables, e.g. *Hoiarnscoit > Harscoit*, etc. 'from about the beginning of the 11th century . . . so that this must have taken place before the accent shifted, in those parts of Brittany where this shift did occur'.[915] In other words the advent of *Harn*-predates the eleventh century, by how far we do not know – except in so far as HARENBILI can be dated. HARENBILI and HERANHAL are eccentric spellings in terms of standard Old Breton orthography (as the writing of svarabhakti shows), and so it is not impossible that HARANBILI reveals a phonetic detail not visible in the standard cartulary sources until the eleventh century.

‡*48 γl, γr, γn (>jl, jr, jn) > il̯, ir̯, in̯; LHEB §86*

These groups, whether inherited or arising by syncope (e.g. OC *teilu < *teγlüy*),[916] developed to form a diphthong with the preceding vowel.[917] When the vowel was **i* (by now = [ĭ] or [ɪ], ‡‡ 29 and 34), the normal end-result in Welsh is believed to be *wy*, as in *colwyn* (OC *coloin*, OB *coloinan*: OI *cuilén*) 'puppy' < **kolignos* (cf. Gallo-Latin *Colignii*).[918] If this is correct (a supporting, less well-known example is Latin *Benignus >* MW *Benŵyn*, OI *Benén*), it is puzzling that according to Jackson two further treatments of **ign* can be seen (uniquely) in VL *Nĭgrinus >* W. *(A)neirin* and in British **Kunignos* (cf. 362/142 CVNIGNI) > MW *Cynin*. Schrijver reasonably rejects the *Nigrinus* etymology (VL *Negrinus*, actually attested in Pannonia, would work better) and would dispose of *Cynin* by suggesting that British **Kunignos* may have had a long *i*, which is less convincing, since it would surely run parallel to **kolignos*, as assumed by Thurneysen.[919] One

---

[915] HPB, pp. 230–31.
[916] But see Ch. 3, p. 256.
[917] /ɔːγ/ became /ɔːu̯/ (e.g. /u̯ɔːγn/ > OW *guoun*, MW *gweun*): Hamp, *BBCS,* 26 (1974–76), 30–31 and 139–40; SBCHP, p. 355. There is no example in the inscriptions.
[918] LEIA C-269; Lloyd-Jones, *BBCS,* 11 (1941–44), 119; DLG, p. 101. Schrijver argues that the vowel merged with /i̯/ < /γ/ that gave the long close *e* that was regularly diphthongized in this way (‡58 below): SBCHP, pp. 356–59 (see also below, n. 1059 and ‡51n., on *Nwython*). So far as W. *morwyn* is concerned, note Lambert's derivation from **morugnā*: Gaulish MORVCIN (*Langue gauloise*, p. 125; and cf. ‡46n. above. A problem with the reconstruction **morugnā* is that this should have given **morognā* by *a*-affection; we could avoid this by postulating neuter gender.) In OI *cuilén* the *é* must be due to prior lowering of **-iγnah > *-eγnah* (see TRC, pp. 110 and 122 for the chronology, and O'Brien, *Celtica,* 10 (1973), 221 for *-én < *-ignos*). Thurneysen, GOI, p. 174, argued that *-én* was replaced by *-ín* as in *Baíthín* 'presumably on the model of *Áugustín* ' "Augustinus" and similar forms' (cf. De Bhaldraithe, in Hamp FS, p. 85; NWÄI, pp. 321–23). Influence from the old genitive, from names in *-ine* (NWÄI, pp. 351–52) < **-ignios*, and from British names are also possibilities. Cf. 311 **DINEGLO** giving *Dínél*, gen. *Dínil*, according to Ziegler, p. 167, citing LL 277b24 and 22 [= *Book of Leinster*, v, ed. Best & O'Brien, p. 1218]; cf. *Metrical Dindshenchas*, ed. Gwynn, iv, 304–7, and v, 159: *Dínel*, but DIL: *Dínél*, voc. *Dínéil*, gen. *Dínil*. This name seems to appear borrowed into OW *Lann Diniu(i)l/Dineul*, LL, p. 407, though later equated with *Deiniol*, LBS ii, 330.
[919] LHEB, pp. 461–62; SBCHP, p. 356; GOI, p. 174. *Nigrinus* is common in RIB. The VL variant *Nĕgrinus* (OPEL iii, 102; on *e* for *i* see VLRB, p. 902) would give *(A)neirin*

way round this might be to question the derivation of *colwyn*.[920] It may suffice, however, to note there is no reason to suppose that there ever was a *British* name **Kunignos*. No personal names in *-ignus* or *-icnus* occur in RIB and Tabellae Sulis (aside from Latin *Dignus* and *Benignus*), nor from other Romano-British sources so far as I know, whereas **-IGNI** is very well attested in the ogam corpus.[921] 362/142 CVNIGNI may well be Irish since it appears on a bilingual stone (**INIGENA CUNIGNI AVITTORIGES/ AVITORIA FILIA CVNIGNI**), and the only other certain example of the name in Wales, also in Carmarthenshire, 374/172 CVNEGNI, could well be Irish as well (perhaps intended as genitive of a Latinate *CVNEGNVS). Its E could be explained by regular Irish lowering in the nominative *CVNEGNAS < *CVNIGNAS rather than by the Vulgar Latin spelling influence suggested by Jackson (in Ireland, compare 222]NEGGNI, which may also be based on the nominative).[922] Remarkably, the CVNEGNI stone

---

regularly, as Jackson sees (LHEB, p. 462; cf. Jackson, *BBCS*, 30 (1982–83), 48–49). Note also B. *Nerin* in Loth, *Noms des saints bretons*, p. 97? *Cynin* is the only example of diminutive *-in* in Welsh names cited by Lloyd-Jones, *Y Geninen*, 44 (1926), 7.

[920] Perhaps *colwyn* could come from **kolugnos* (see n. 918 above on *morwyn*), or perhaps **colignus* arrived from Gallo-Latin (cf. DLG, p. 101) and shows a regional *Latin* treatment of *ign* as *ejn* (cf. LHEB, p. 463)?

[921] Ziegler, p. 107; GPN, pp. 209–10; NWÄI, p. 322. The only Continental forms with *-ign-* cited by Evans are *Enignus,* beside *Enigenus* (and perhaps syncopated from it – cf. *Rectugnus* for *Rectugenus* and *Velugn(i)us* for ?**Velugen(i)us,* Holder i, 1096 and 2030, and iii, 19 and 155?), where the first element is a preposition or preverb *eni-* (Rhys, *PBA*, 1911–12, p. 326; KGP, pp. 206–8; Hamp, *Acta Neophilologica*, 9 (1976), 6, and ibid., 11 (1978), 60–61), and *Catavigni Ivomagi f(ilii)* in CIL v 7717 (also listed in GPN s. *Catu-*, p. 172), which is Celtic to judge by *Ivomagi* (KGP, pp. 228 and 235), but dubiously *Continental* Celtic – he is of a *cohors Brittannorum* (cf. ibid., 167 and 219; Untermann, *BzN*, 11 (1960), 302, n. 104; PRB, pp. 103 and 189; cf. Holder i, s.nn. *Catavignus*, *Cattavus*, *Cattaus*). One of the two men called Velugn(i)us came from Chester (OPEL iv, 153; cf. KGP, pp. 287–88). In Continental Celtic *-icn-* is more common and may be connected with Insular *-ign-*, despite GOI, p. 174; see KGP, p. 218, and GPN, pp. 181–83 (also citing the Irish place name *Uenniknion akron* from Ptolemy, as does De Bernardo Stempel, in Meid FS, p. 68, n. 80). Note the alternation between *Tessi-gnius* and *-cnius* in KGP, pp. 219 and 278. The only other forms in *-ign-* listed by Holder i, 2030 s. *-gno-* are two tribes in Tacitus's *Germania*, the *Marsigni* and *Reudigni.* These could be 'offspring' of Tacitus's Germanic *Marsi* tribe or a *Marsus* (Oswald, OPEL) and of an eponymous Celtic **Reud(i)os* 'Red' (cf. KGP, p. 262). A Thracian coin-legend Κασιγνακις is compared by Orel, *BBCS*, 34 (1987), 8, with a non-existent ogam **CASSIGNI. Pelign(os)* (DLG, p. 209 (cf. *P(a)elignus, Pilignus,* OPEL iii, 120 and 141); Fleuriot, *ÉC*, 15 (1976–77), 182–83) is doubtfully Gaulish. These formations in **-gnos* are presumably cognate with Latin *beni-gnus*, etc., Greek *-γνός* (ibid., p. 183; KGP, p. 218).

[922] LHEB, p. 191; cf. ‡34 above. I have not noticed a VL **Benegnus* occurring for *Benignus*. (Rhys was certainly wrong to suppose that CVNEGNI showed raising from *CVNAGNI, LWP, p. 391; but is there merit in the suggestion that MacNeill, *PRIA*, 27 C (1909), 353, that -EGNI may 'represent **-ia-gni** formed on *io-*stems'?) Ziegler, p. 161, compares 222]NEGGNI with OI *Cunníne* (cf. CGH, p. 579), but it is difficult to explain the E starting from **Kunignios.* The descendants of **Kunignos* were already noted as Ir. *Coinín* and W. *Cynin* by Rhys, *Scottish Review*, 16 (1890), 33, cited in DP iv, 422; cf. EANC, p. 198. For the Irish name see *Adomnán's Life of Columba*, ed. Anderson & Anderson, p. 238 (*Conin*); LBS ii, 262; Meyer, *Contributions*, p. 474. Meyer records *Conind* as a female name, e.g.

(374/172) stood at the ruined chapel at Llanfihangel Croesfeini (SN 39402392), at the head of the Nant Hir, a continuation of the river *Cynen*, possibly a dialect form of **Cynein* according to R. J. Thomas; **Cynein* would in fact be the regular result if Ir. **CVNIGNAS* was borrowed at the **CVNEGNAS* [kuneɣnah] stage.[923]

[48] MW *Cynin* (OW *Cynnin*, *Cinin*, *Cunin*) is not necessarily connected with CVNIGNI, for a Romano-British **Cunīnus* would be a possible source; or it may be a Welsh hypocoristic created from *Cyn-* + *-in* < **-īnos*.[924] Or if it does derive from **Kunignos*, it may have been borrowed from the Irish reflex, after *-in* had developed in it.[925] So far as I know, *Cynin* is not attested in the other Brittonic languages,[926] which suits the supposition of borrowing. But if

---

Martyrology of Gorman, ed. Stokes, p. 186 (*Conind chuanna*), and this is clearly Latinized in 511/Scot.10 CONINIE; see MacDonald, *PSAS*, 70 (1935–36), 38. Jackson in RCAHMS, *Peeblesshire*, i, 176, says that the Irish name 'is scarcely likely to be relevant in this geographical context' and prefers British **Cunignia*, a feminine counterpart of *Cynin*; but for problems with *Cynin* < **Kunignos* see above. Jackson, LHEB, p. 174, and McManus, *Guide*, pp. 63 and 113, regard CVNIGNI as British because of the attested Ir. *Conán* < **Kunagnas*; but both suffixes could surely coexist in Irish; see examples of such variation in Ziegler, p. 107.

[923] EANC, p. 110; for the location see Edwards in Corpus. Cf. LWP, p. 391: '*Cynan* enters into the names of no less than three of the neighbouring farms.' In favour of **Cynein* note a 'farm called *Cynéinog* and *Cynéiniog* at the top of the basin of the Eleri in North Cardiganshire' (Rhys, *Cymmrodor*, 21 (1908), 38).

[924] For Welsh names and words in *-in* see EANC, p. 198, and SWWF, pp. 516–23; cf. 384/83 SANCTINVS > *seithin* (above, ‡44n) and 1049/Ok33 URITIN (‡28 above) – the suggestion in BWP, p. 18, that 971/35 may read **VIRNIN* (: W. *gwern*) must be rejected (see ‡‡ 66 and 85). Cf. the OB names in *-in* listed by Fleuriot, Gramm., p. 401, e.g. *Kerentin*: Gallo-Latin *Carantinus* (cf. 994/125/22 CAROTINN, if cognate with Gallo-Latin *Caratinus*, above, ‡22). Williams, BWP, p. 19, suggested that 323/32 SATVRNINVS at Llansadwrn was a diminutive of the eponymous *Saturnus* on the pattern of native names like *Cynin*; the influence could be the other way round. For names in *Cuno-* in the Romano-British period, note *Cunsa*, *Cunsus*, *Cunomolius* and *Cunitius* in Tab.Sulis, nos. 9 and 95; and RIB ii, Index, p. 8, s.nn. *Cunedecanes*, *Cunicatus*, *Cunit(t)us*, *Cunobarrus*, *Cunovendus*, etc. For MW *Cynin* and *Cunin Cof* (possibly the same name, possibly influenced by CVNIGNI in antiquarian tradition – could *Cof* 'memorial' refer to one of the stones?, although cf. *Cov*, Loth, *Noms des saints bretons*, p. 29, and Pierce, *Place-Names of Dinas Powys*, pp. 101–2) see EWGT s.nn. *Cunin* and *Cynin*; LL, p. 210 (*Cinin*); TYP, pp. 313–14 and 548; Bromwich & Evans, *Culhwch and Olwen*, p. 72; EANC, p. 200. In LHEB, pp. 463–64, and *CMCS*, 3 (1982), 31, Jackson suggests that Gildas's *Aureli Canine* (vocative) is a pun on *Cunignos* (cf. Dumville, in *Gildas: New Approaches*, pp. 56–57). However, *Canin(i)us* was a well-attested Roman name (Kajanto, p. 326; OPEL ii, 31 – in Britain note RIB i 1691) and this may be meant. Conceivably *Caninius* (or *Caninus*) developed into *Cynin*, either orally (under the influence of *Cyn-* names?) or orthographically (on OW *Can-* from **kuno-* see Sims-Williams, *BBCS*, 38 (1991), 47).

[925] For the development of Ir. *-in*, see n. 918 above. St Cynin of Llangynin in Carmarthenshire (SN 2519) has sometimes been connected with the CVNIGNI inscription (362/142) at Eglwys Gymyn (SN 2310) 6 miles to the south (LBS ii, 262; EANC, pp. 199–200; ECMW, pp. 109–11), but 6 miles is not close enough to make a connection inevitable.

[926] E. Phillimore, in his 'Persons named "Cynin", and places named after them', in DP iv, 420–22, cites *Tregonning* in Cornwall, but see Padel, *Popular Dictionary of Cornish Place-Names*, p. 166 (*Conan*); cf. Thomas, *Mute Stones*, pp. 250 and 252.

it *is* a borrowed name, there is another, non-Celtic possibility: borrowing from OE *cyning*.

[48] In Pembrokeshire Lhuyd saw a stone reading 447/369 CVNISCVS (or CVNIGCVS) FILI NEMAGLI. Supposing miscopying, this could be another example of Ir. *CVNIGNAS.[927] On the other hand, if the spelling was indeed CVNIGCVS (CVNISCVS is linguistically impossible) this is most likely to represent OW *Conigc*, with -*gc* corresponding to MW -*ng*, as in OW *Ercicg, Gleuissicg* = MW *Ergyng, Glywysing*. *Conigc* is most probably a loan from OE *cyning* 'king', comparable to OI *Conaing*, first attested in 621 and popular for a century afterwards.[928] CVNIGCVS and *Conigc* (name of an abbot of Llancarfan) could indeed be borrowings from Old English into Welsh via Irish, though there is no need to suppose this to be the case. Could this *Conigc* = *Cyning* be the same name as *Cynin*,[929] and indeed be its source? Development of -*n* to -*ng* in Welsh is seen in the name *Ergyng* from Romano-British *Ariconium*,[930] and the reverse change can probably be seen in the many early Welsh personal name-based population names such as *Cyndrwynyn(g)*, -*in(g)*, and *Cynferchyn(g)*.[931] In their collections of such variants Williams and Richards avoid saying whether -*n* or -*ng* is older, but Morris-Jones's and Koch's argument that it derives from the Celtic patronymic suffix -*icn*- seems to support -*ing* as the older one (with metathesis of *-*ygn* according to Morris-Jones).[932] It is a problem, however, that there seems to be little trace of -*icn*- (or -*ign*-) in Britain as opposed to Gaul, and that the -*ing/-yng* type of population names do not seem to occur in Brittany or Ireland. I would therefore suggest that they were in fact borrowed from the similarly used OE -*ingas*[933] in the context of

---

[927] Macalister suggested that CVNIGNVS was the original reading. KHJ interprets Lhuyd's sketch as probably CVNIGCVS. On NEMAGLI see above, ‡42.

[928] O'Brien, *Celtica*, 10 (1973), 231; Ó Corráin & Maguire, *Gaelic Personal Names*, p. 56; Ó Cuív, *Celtica*, 18 (1986), 162; Ó Murchadha, *Annals of Tigernach: Index*, pp. 14–15. Cf. Uhlich's argument, *ZCP*, 49/50 (1997), 878–88, that the preform of W. *brenin* 'king' was twice borrowed into Irish as a personal name. For *Conicg* see VSB, p. 327, Sims-Williams, *BBCS*, 38 (1991), 30, and p. 278 below. For *Ercigc, Gleuissicg* see LL, pp. 398 and 400, and cf. LHEB, p. 513. If NEMAGLI is an Irish name (see above, ‡42) then CVNIGCVS may be a Welsh spelling of OI *Conaing*.

[929] Phillimore, in DP iv, 421.

[930] PNRB, p. 258. Cf. *Kedewein/Kedewyng* in DP iii, 183, n. 3; and Lloyd-Jones, *Geirfa*, p. 120.

[931] Williams, *Canu Llywarch Hen*, p. 207, and *Pedeir Keinc y Mabinogi*, p. 284; CBT, iii, 127; Richards, *JRSAI*, 95 (1965), 206, and ETG, p. 11. See also GMW, p. 8.

[932] Morris-Jones, *Cymmrodor*, 28 (1918), 208–9; Koch, *CMCS*, 14 (1987), 21. W. -*ing* is compared with Gaulish -*icnos* and Germanic -*ing* by Evans, *AC*, 4th ser. 3 (1872), 303, citing Stokes, *Beiträge zur vergleichenden Sprachforschung*, 2 (1861), 111, who however had merely equated (wrongly) Gaulish TRUTIKNI (RIG ii/1, no. E5) with Ir. *Drustice*. Unlike Morris-Jones, Parry-Williams, *English Element in Welsh*, p. 41, did not rule out a connection with OE -*ing*. A Cornish example of -*ng* > -*n* is noted by Padel, CPNE, p. 136. For fairly late examples in Welsh, see Parry-Williams, *English Element*, p. 248, and Wmffre, *Language and History*, i, 89–90.

[933] There is a vast literature, but see e.g. Smith, *English Place-Name Elements*, i, 298–303. These names were also found on the Continent, whence French *Vouflanges*, etc. (Lebel, pp. 56–57).

Anglo-British interaction in sub-Roman Britain, where the existence of
Wulfing(as) etc. on one side might naturally give rise to the appellation
Coiling(as) for the other side.[934] A *possible* example in the inscriptions is
ERCILINGI in 461/Ok66 NONNITA ERCILI VIRICATI TRIS FILI
ERCILINGI, compared by Rhys with OW *Ircil* and *Irgillicg* in the Book
of Llandaf.[935] Be this as it may, it seems clear that the rather isolated Welsh
name *Cynin* can be derived from OW *Conigc*, a borrowing of OE *cyning*
(comparable to, or even borrowed via, OI *Conaing < cyning*), and is not a
unique survival of a British *-ignos* formation. The name *Cynnin* in the Old
Welsh genealogies[936] may thus reflect OE *Cynin(g)*, OI *Conín*, OI *Conaing*,
or possibly Latin *Caninus*, rather than a native British *Kunignos*. In the case
of later persons called *Cynyn* (rather than *Cynin*)[937] a further possibility is
derivation from OW *Congint*, *Cingint*, which would have developed in the
same way as OW *Bledgint* > MW *Bledyn*.[938]

[48] (A) Jackson (p. 463) notes that the loss of /γ/ is not shown in:

1.   446/353 MAGLOCVNI (*sic. leg.*) [note that this is a bilingual stone with
ogam **MAGLICUNAS**, which could theoretically be a factor in writing the
roman-letter GL if the name is British]
2.   394/103 MAGLI [probably the Welsh uncompounded name *Mael* rather
than Ir. *Mál* in view of the title MAGISTRATI and relationship to Brittonic
CANTIORI][939]
3.   425/297 CATOMAG[LI] [but may well be Irish, being paired with
MACCVTRE[NI]][940]
4.   401/183 BROHOMAGLI
5.   1028/214/850 VENDVMAGLI [but quite likely to be Irish][941]

[48] To these he adds only:
362/142 CVNIGNI
478/Ok48 BROCAGNI
but we have already seen that CVNIGNI is probably Irish (OI *Conín*), while

---

[934] And note, from an Irish base (*Éochu*, gen. *Echach*), *Echeching gaer* in *Canu Aneirin*, ed.
Williams, line 140: Anwyl, *THSC*, 1909–10, p. 105. There is no reason, despite Williams
(pp. 113–14) and later commentators, why a Briton, Blaen, should not have been associated
with a Scottish fortress.
[935] Rhys, *Englyn*, pp. 19–20; for a more likely explanation see above, ‡27.
[936] EWGT, p. 181 (HG §23).
[937] Cf. EWGT, p. 182.
[938] See ‡53 below.
[939] Examples in EWGT, p. 202, and Lloyd-Jones, *Enwau Lleoedd Sir Gaernarfon*, pp. 55–56 (cf.
the simplex *Maglius* at Lyon, Holder ii, 380); this casts doubt on the suggestion that
MAGLI MAGISTRATI is Maelgwn Gwynedd (Gruffydd, *SC*, 24/25 (1989–90), 9, and
THSC, 2 (1996), 14–15). For *Mael* in OW see probably + *mali* in ‘Chad 8’, LL, p. xlvii
(although note *Malius* in OPEL iii, 48). For *Mál* see CGH, p. 697.
[940] See above, ‡38.
[941] See above, ‡‡ 22 and 38.

Jackson himself says that BROCAGNI is Cornish or Irish.[942] In fact, I would argue that all -AGNI names are Irish, on four grounds.

[48] First of all, there seem to be no -agn-/-acn- or -ogn-/-ocn- names in Roman Britain (apart from the irrelevant *Magnus* which is very common in RIB),[943] and on the Continent I find in Evans's *Gaulish Personal Names* only]ναϰνος (Apt, Vaucluse), *Deuacnua* and *Diuuogna* (on two arguably Celtic rings from Reims), *Aiciognu(s)*, ?*Celiognis, Sicogninus, Disocno, -i, Mainacnus*, ??*Occocnus/Ociocnus*, and *Ollocnus/Ollognus*, apart from names like *Boduognatus* and *Critognatus* (which are not the same as **-ognos* names, though possibly ultimately related).[944] By contrast, there are over a score of different names in **-AGNI** in the ogam corpus, and over a dozen names in its descendant **-AN(N)**, OI *-án*.[945]

[48] Secondly, it is agreed that the **A** in **-AGNI** is the composition vowel,[946] and since the change of *-o- > -a-* was confined to Irish, instances of A in Britain are most naturally treated as Irish, unless there is good reason to regard the A as a spelling of the Brittonic reduced composition vowel (cf. ‡38).

[48] Thirdly, whereas Irish **-AGN-** has a prolific progeny in the later language in names and words in *-án*, Latin/Brittonic **-agn-* survives among personal names only in MW *Maen*, OB *Main-*, assuming this is from the popular Latin *Magnus* or a native name of similar shape.[947] We do of course have numerous Welsh words and personal names in *-an*, often attached to stems found with *-án* in Irish, but their terminations (insofar as they are neither from an earlier British **-anos* with short /a/ nor borrowed later[948] from Latin *-anus* with long /aː/) was satisfactorily explained by

---

[942] LHEB, p. 665, n. 1.

[943] GPN, p. 182 cites *Biokno* from Roman Britain (cf. KGP, p. 149), but it may have been a fake or read *Biorno* according to RIB ii [fasc. 8] 2504.6. If genuine, cf. Welsh names such as *Bywan, Bywiog, Bywon*, with Evans, *BBCS*, 24 (1970–72), 427–28. GPN, p. 182, also cites the potter's name *Mainacnus* from DAG (pp. 343, 385 (Aquitania), and 840) as possibly Insular Celtic, but only the third DAG reference is under 'British Names', and that with a query (it is not in RIB ii; see *Index*, p. 63 for absence of 'EE ix 1358.23'). Holder ii, 390 cites *Mainacn* from CIL vii 1336.1352 (London); Oswald locates him in France. Cf. KGP, p. 235.

[944] GPN, respectively pp. 461 (cf. RIG i, 135: *-acnos* possibly an isolated equivalent of the common patronymic *-icnos*?), 445, 83–84, 209–10, 181–82, and 208–9 (with references to DAG and KGP); cf. DLG, pp. 149–50 and 153. Holder adds nothing Continental s. *-acn-*, *-agn-*, and *-ocn-*, *-ogn-*, apart from]*ublocnus* in CIL xiii 1646 (Bussy-Albieu(x), Prov. Lugudunensis, Holder iii, 11). Holder i, 2030, s. *-gno-* cites *ocio-gni* (under *Ociocnus*, however, in ii, 828) and *ucio-gni* (not listed in Vol. iii !).

[945] Holder i, 59–60 and iii, 523; McManus, *Guide*, p. 107; Ziegler, p. 107 (*sic*); NWÄI, pp. 323–24; also now **GELAGNI AVI** (Manning & Moore, *Peritia*, 11 (1997), 370–72).

[946] MacNeill, *PRIA*, 27 C (1909), 351; McManus, *Guide*, p. 179, n. 39; Ziegler, p. 107.

[947] *Maen* may be simply the word for 'stone', but this is disputed; cf. BWP, p. 141, n. 52; Gramm., p. 56; Hamp, *PHCC*, 12 (1992), 44.

[948] Post /aː/ > /ɔː/, ‡18 above. For *-an* < **-ăno-* cf. Loth, *RC*, 32 (1911), 407; Gramm, p. 353. Note also that *-an* arose from **-on-* after /w/ as in *breuan* 'quern', Stüber, *Historical Morphology*, pp. 92, 95 and 118.

G. P. Jones, R. J. Thomas, and Pokorny as a borrowing from Ir. -*án* < *-agnas*.[949] While conceding that their explanation makes phonological sense, Jackson and Ellis Evans reject it, while Schrijver notes: 'The type *CVRCAGNI* > OW *Circan* (and other names in W -*an*, e.g. *Cynan*, Ir. *Conán*) as well as W *bychan*, B *bihan* (= OIr. *becán*, ⟨*c*⟩ = [g]) remain unexplained'.[950] Jackson's reasoning is as follows:

> It is strange that a borrowed suffix should have affected *names*, as well as being in general use; one would not expect the natural development of e.g. Brit. **Cunagnos* to have been interfered with by a common-noun suffix, especially a foreign one, yet the result is e.g. *Cynan*, not e.g. **Cynaen*.[951]

[48] The answer to this is surely that there may never have been a British **Cunagnos*, and that *Cynan* may be either wholly Irish in origin or a hypocoristic form of a Welsh *Cyn-* name using a productive Irish-derived suffix -*án*. As Ellis Evans remarks elsewhere, 'Some of the insular suffixes . . . may have had a special vogue resulting in transference from one language to another.'[952] Similarly, Hamp says:

> I do not see a borrowing of the diminutive suffix -*an* from OIr. -*án* . . . as inherently unlikely. . . . It seems to me that precisely in the category of pet names this suffix may have been taken over from Irish contacts. It may have even had a conscious or fashionable effect.[953]

Similarly, according to Ó Maolalaigh, 'it is conceivable that an upsurge in the use of diminutives may come about as a result of contact between two languages'.[954] We can compare the situation in modern Wales where a child called Gwen or Gwenllian is now more likely to be called *Gwennie* with English -*ie* than *Gwenno*. Or compare medieval France, where the popular

---

[949] Jones, *ZCP*, 16 (1927), 162; EANC, p. 34; Pokorny apud Förster, *Themse*, p. 856.

[950] LHEB, p. 461; GPN, p. 182, n. 3; SBCHP, p. 356, n. 2. For OW *Circ(h)an*, *Crican* (first cited by Rhys, LWP, p. 388, and then in VKG ii, 27) see LL, p. 392; EANC, p. 63. This may be borrowed wholesale from Irish (see below), or have the productive Irish-derived -*án* (> -*an*) added to W.(?) *Cyrch*, which is attested in the OW place name *Cilcirch*, noted in EANC. *Cyrch* could be related to W. *cyrch* 'expedition' (: OI *crech*, LEIA C-225 and 235). Hamp, *BBCS*, 27 (1976–78), 215–16, connects *cyrch* with Gaulish *Circos*. On the other hand, I. Williams, apud Richmond & Crawford, *Archaeologia*, 93 (1949), 32, cites an artisan's name *Curcus* (i.e. *Curci .ma[nu]* on a patella in the British Museum, CIL vii 1336.389, cited by Holder i, 1200) and *[C]urcinate* in the Ravenna Cosmography (MS *Durcinate*) (cf. PNRB, p. 351 and review by Coates, *JEPNS*, 13 (1980–81), 65). Continental forms in *Corc-*, of doubtful relevance, are listed by Holder i, 1118.

[951] LHEB, p. 461. Cf. NWÄI, pp. 325–26, nn. 77 and 80.

[952] *BBCS*, 24 (1970–72), 426. Thus Irish borrowed -*óc* from the British reflex of *-ākos*; see Russell, *Celtic Word-Formation*, pp. 112–14. For this reason the occurrence of -*an*, -*ocan*, and -*ican* in Old Breton names (Gramm., pp. 401–2; Hemon, *Celtica*, 11 (1976), 85 and 91–92) cannot be taken to indicate that -*an* is of Common Brittonic origin.

[953] *BBCS*, 26 (1974–76), 31; cf. Mac Cana, in *Cymru a'r Cymry 2000*, p. 25, n. 26; De Bernardo Stempel, in Meid FS, p. 70.

[954] Ó Maolalaigh, in *Uses of Place-Names*, p. 35.

diminutives -*et*, -*ot*, and -*at* (as in *Estevenot*, Stephen) deriving from Gallo-Germanic -*ĭttus* coexisted with Latin-derived -*in* (as in *Estevenin*): 'La finale -*itto*, -*itta* pénétra largement dans l'onomastique et le vocabulaire français.'[955] Compare, too, the spread of Ir. -*ín* in Hiberno-English *girleen*, *ladeen*, and so on.[956]

[48] Fourthly, if we examine all the examples of names in -GN- in our British corpus of inscriptions, we find that all those with -GNI/-GNVS are concentrated in the western areas of Irish settlement, and frequently occur with Irish first elements, or in conjunction with Irish names, or with ogam equivalents:

[48] Anglesey

2027 ERCAGNI

Irish *Erc*- is very productive in personal names, occurring in over a dozen ogam inscriptions, in particular 262 **ERCAGNI** > OI *Erccán*, and this must be why Jackson (unlike Richards) identified ERCAGNI as Irish on its discovery. While there is a native Welsh adjective *erch* 'speckled' occurring lexically and in river names, *Erchan* occurs as a personal name once in the Book of Llandaf and in the place names *carn Erchan* and *Cwm Erchan* in Breconshire (a very Irish area), in a stream name *Erchan* near Aberhafhesb in Montgomershire, in an *Ystrad Gilerchan* in Carmarthenshire, and in a farm name *Rhos Erchan/Rhosferchan* in Cardiganshire.[957] On balance ERCAGNI here and in Carmarthenshire below is probably Irish, although this is the least clear-cut name of all.

[48] Breconshire

328/44 RVGNIATIO (]RVGNIATO Thomas) [FI]LI VENDONI
(+ alleged traces of ogam)
The first name is obscure and very probably acephalous in view of the loss of [FI] in line 2 of the inscription; hence Ziegler's equation with OI *Rónnait* (f.) < **Ro-gnīati- is doubtful, especially as this is clearly one of the many compounds of *Rón* 'seal' (: W. [*moel*]*rhon*), a word which never had *gn.[958]

---

[955] Lebel, pp. 47 and 72–73; Ó Maolalaigh, in *Uses of Place-Names*, p. 51, n. 75.

[956] De Bhaldraithe, in Hamp FS, p. 91.

[957] Ziegler, pp. 104 and 177–180; Jackson and Richards, cited by White, *TAAS*, 1971–72, p. 51 and n. 76; Williams, *Poems of Taliesin*, pp. 57–58; LL, p. 200 (*Erchan* along with a *Talan* < Pr.Ir. *Tālagnas (n. 690 above) in the familia of Bishop Cerenhir; cf. MW *Talan*, Williams, *Canu Llywarch Hen*, p. 96, OC *Talan*, Bodmin, p. 92) and 154 and 370 (*carn Erchan*); EANC, pp. 66–67; DP iii, 212, n. 2; LWP, p. 392 (*Rhos Erchan*, and comparing W. *erchyll*). Dr Jon Coe suggests that *carn Erchan* may be named after the same man as Cwm Erchan. It is doubtful whether the Celtiberian(?) toponym *Ercauica/Ergauica* is related: Holder i, 1458; Curchin, *Emerita*, 65 (1997), 266–67; MLH v/1, p. 119. MW *Keynerch* (Jones Pierce, *BBCS*, 5 (1929–31), 60) is probably a nickname ('freckled back'?), not evidence of *erch* as a personal-name element.

[958] Ziegler, p. 228; CGH, p. 725. Cf. O'Brien, *Celtica*, 10 (1973), 236, s.n. *Rónán*; Ó Corráin & Maguire, *Gaelic Personal Names*, p. 157; Uhlich, *Morphologie*, p. 294; LEIA R-42; Lloyd-Jones, *BBCS*, 15 (1952–54), 202; GPC s.v. *moelrhon*.

]RVGNI- is unlikely to be some *u*-stem with suffixal *-cno-* or *gno-*.[959] As Thomas has seen, it is possible to restore [D]RVGNI- on the analogy of 31 **DRUGNO**, 165 **[D]ROGNO**, and 167 **DROGNO** 'nose' (not 'throng' as Thomas has it) > OI (*Uí*) *Dróna* (gen.) (*u*-stem or *i*-stem),[960] and this would agree with Jackson's (questionable) view that VENDONI may be Irish.[961] On the other hand, we may have a British form, [T]RVGNI- (presumably cognate with Ir. **DRUGNO**), meaning 'nose' > W. *trwyn* (as in MW *Cyndrwyn*?), related to French *trogne*,[962] Galatian δρουγγος 'nose'; for the semantics, compare Latin *Naso* and MW *troyn* and *troynok* 'nosey' as epithets.[963] An alternative is to read [B]RVGN- > OI *brón*, MW *brwyn* 'sorrow', whence the personal names OW and MW *Bruin/Brwyn*, *Brwyno* and *Brunus* (in *Lann Teliau mainaur Brunus* = Llandeilo Rwnws), OB *Broin* and *Broen*, and OI *Brónach*.[964] (In view of the location of the stone it is interesting to note a 'Bruin o Bricheinauc' in *Englynion y Beddau*, I.23.)[965] In either case, the rest of the name, if -IATIO, corresponds to the adjectival suffix that appears in W. *euraid* 'golden',[966] or, if -IATO (Thomas), is probably the suffix *-iatis* that gives W. *-iad* and OI *-ith*, *-id* (*i*-stem), both common in personal names such as 1024/255/926 NERTAT (though neither *Bróinid* nor *Brwyniad* seems to occur).[967] In the ogam inscriptions the genitive of the latter from *-iatōs*, appears as -ITOS, -ETTOS, -ETTO, and

---

[959] Cf. GPN, pp. 181–83 and 209–10 (no examples with preceding *-ru-* cited).

[960] Thomas, *Mute Stones*, pp. 119, 121, and 128, n. 13. See Ziegler, p. 172; O'Brien, *Celtica*, 10 (1973), 224. These and **VENDOGNI** are the only examples of **GN** preceded by **O** or **U** in the ogam corpus.

[961] LHEB, p. 512. But see ‡‡ 22 and 38 above on (*)*Vendonius*. He does not comment on the other name. See also below, under Pembrokeshire, 422/298 **VENDOGNI**.

[962] Cf. SBCHP, p. 442; Lambert, *Langue gauloise*, p. 199; DLG, p. 256. The normal tendency seems to have been /dr/ > /tr/ rather than vice versa; see J. E. C. Williams, *Celtica*, 15 (1983), 152. For *Cyndrwyn* see EWGT, p. 180; Lloyd-Jones, *Y Geninen*, 44 (1926), 9–10: 'ffroen-uchel/ci' (for a different possibility (: Ir. *Trían-*) see n. 1055 below).

[963] Holder i, 1321 and ii, 1745; Ziegler, p. 172; Kajanto, p. 237; Jones, *BBCS*, 3 (1926–27), 38.

[964] LEIA B-96; Lloyd-Jones, *Geirfa*, s.nn.; LL, p. 409; DGVB i, 91; O'Brien, *Celtica*, 10 (1973), 223; Bammesberger, *BBCS*, 27 (1976–78), 552, n. 4. Thurneysen, seems to hint that /ugn/ > *ón* in OI *brón* may not have been regular since he suggests influence from the synonym *broc* (GOI, p. 41). I have checked all the Welsh possibilities under *-rwyn* in Zimmer's *Geiriadur Gwrthdroadol*, p. 107, although *brwyn* is missing there. Note that there is a homonym *brwyn* 'rushes' (OB *broin*), unlikely semantically as a personal name (cf. DGVB i, 90–91), although Dr Jon Coe suggests that the low-lying *mainaur brunus* contains Mod.W. *brwynos*. There is also a rare W. *brwynog*, equated by Fleuriot not with Ir. *brónach* 'sorrowful' (cf. GPC) but with OB *bruinoc* 'rainy', OI *bróen* 'shower' (DGVB i, 91; LEIA B-76). This comparison is difficult unless it is a loanword in one direction or another. Note, however, *Bróen* as an Irish personal name (CGH, p. 526), derived from the noun according to O'Brien, *Celtica*, 10 (1973), 223.

[965] Ed. Jones, *PBA*, 53 (1967), 122.

[966] Lewis & Pedersen, p. 311; Schumacher, *Historical Morphology*, pp. 89 and 110; SWWF, pp. 465–66. It is hardly the *-aid* of *cegaid* etc. (SWWF, pp. 291–94), i.e. 'noseful'!

[967] SWWF, p. 551; NWÁI, pp. 375–80; VKG ii, 36; GOI, pp. 170–71; Gramm., p. 345; Williams, *AC*, 87 (1932), 236; MacNeill, *PRIA*, 39 C (1931), 40; O'Brien, *Celtica*, 10 (1973), 224; Russell, *Celtic Word-Formation*, pp. 105–6. If -IATIO is correct, see GOI, pp. 192–93 (cf. Uhlich, *Morphologie*, pp. 163–64) on 124 **ANAVLAMATTIAS** > ? OI *Anfolmithe* (gen.).

-EOTOS,[968] and one could suppose that just as 172 **SAGARETTOS** was superseded in Old Irish by *Sárach*,[969] so *(B)RVGNIATO(S) was superseded by the attested *Brónach*. What is remarkable is how well the -IAT- is preserved compared to the ogam forms, but this could be due to the writer's familiarity with Brittonic names where the sequence has remained intact to this day (cf. 1066 GURIAT = *Gwriad*).[970] It is also possible, of course, that]RVGNIAT(I)O actually *is* a Welsh name; if it is the -O will probably be the Vulgar Latin or Brittonic nominative ending -O (var. -OS) seen elsewhere in Wales,[971] and not a unique survival of the old *i*-stem genitive. If the name is Welsh, that could explain why the G is retained in this word but lost in the patronymic VENDONI, assuming that the latter is Irish and corresponds to 422/298 **VENDOGNI**. – On the other hand, if both names are Irish, one can argue that /ɣ/ was lost first in Irish unaccented syllables; compare 449/384 SAGRANI in Pembrokeshire below, also 317 **MAGLANI** in Ireland (see below under Cardiganshire).

[48] A less likely possibility is that]RVGNIAT(I)O is two names, the second being Latin *Atto, Attus, Atius* or *Attius* (the last well represented in Roman Britain).[972] This division is at first sight supported by what Nash-Williams calls a 'chisel-picked line' dividing RVGNI | ATIO (but also LIVE | NDONI, impossibly!). Nash-Williams argues, however, that it 'probably marked the limit of the new butt' when the stone was reused and reset upside down.[973]

]RVGNIAT(I)O could thus be either Welsh or Irish. Whichever it is, it is not relevant to the main problem of final -GNI.

[48] Cardiganshire

353/127/7 **TRENACCATLO/TRENACATVS IC IACIT FILIVS MAGLAGNI**
The first name, TRENACATVS, is distinctively Irish and not identical with MW *Tringat* as Rhys thought.[974] There are three examples of **MAILAGNI** > OI *Máelán/Móelán* in the ogam corpus (CIIC 60, 160, 258), and MAGLAGNI could be a Welsh spelling of this, posterior to the change of /aɣ/ > /ai̯/ in Welsh, when -AG- would for a time have meant /ai̯/. Or,

---

[968] GOI, p. 192; McManus, *Guide*, p. 108; Ziegler, p. 108 (*sic*).
[969] Ziegler, p. 229.
[970] See ‡46 above. Cf. Morgan & Morgan, *Welsh Surnames*, p. 115. Rhys apud Jones, *TCASFC*, 2 (1906–7), 177, suggested that 437/317]RIAT[may be the same name.
[971] LHEB, p. 192, n. 2. Cf. ‡25n.
[972] See RIB indexes s.n. *Attius* and s.]*attius*; Tomlin & Hassall, *Britannia*, 32 (2001), 394 and n. 39; VLRB, p. 904; OPEL i, 211–16.
[973] For a different opinion see Macalister, *AC*, 77 (1922), 203.
[974] LWP, p. 380, and *Englyn*, p. 87; on *Tringat* see above, ‡15. In LWP Rhys explains **-LO** as hypocoristic, but it is also suggested that **L** may have been written in error for **O**: Uhlich, *Morphologie*, p. 22; and below, Ch. 5, p. 330. On the **-LO** KHJ notes: 'But cf. no. 450, where Macalister reads **OGTENAS** where others have read **OGTENLO** ?. ∴. **TRENACATAS** ?'. (See Macalister's justification of **OGTENAS** in *TCASFC*, 15, Part 40 (1922), 32.)

more straightforwardly, MAGLAGNI could be an Irish derivative of the well-attested OI *Mál*, giving Ir. **Málán*; I do not have an example, but it is quite likely that Ir. **Málán* would be superseded by the popular *Máelán*, owing to the constant alternation between *Mál* and *Máel* noted by O'Brien, who indeed treats our MAGLAGNI as a form of *Máelán*.[975] Maelan in Welsh place names in Arfon and Merionydd (Rhosmaelan, Garthmaelan, Cefnmaelan) and in Tegeingl (*Caer Faelan*)[976] may well be the Irish personal name.

[48] Carmarthenshire

357/136 CORBAGNI FILIVS AL[

The element **CORB-** is common in the ogam inscriptions but unknown in personal names elsewhere in the roman-letter inscriptions, except for 354/126/6 CORBALENGI, which we have already seen to be Irish.[977] Ifor Williams seems to suggest that CORBAGNI lies behind the Welsh place name *Corfaen* (now *Corwen*), which is exactly what we would expect in an early borrowing from Irish; Richards, however, derives *Corfaen* from W. *maen* 'stone'.[978] *Carfan* in place and river names (e.g. *Llancarfan*, earlier *Nantcarban(ensis)*)) and in the problematic homophone(s) *carfan* can be related only with difficulty in view of the first /a/.[979]

[48] 362/142 **INIGENA CUNIGNI AVITTORIGES**/AVITORIA FILIA CVNIGNI

Note the Irish context provided by the use of ogam and Irish *inigena*, and the Irish nature of the other name (if cognate with OB *Oedri*).[980]

[48] 369/153 IACET CVRCAGNVS [ ]VRIVI FILIVS

This is the ancestor of Ir. *Corcán*, and only possibly of OW *Circ(h)an* (which could rather be based on W. *cyrch* 'expedition'). The first element is less likely to be OI *corc* 'heart' (an obscure glossary word) than *corc* 'purple', a distinctively Irish loanword (with **k^w* for Latin *p*). A less likely etymon is suggested by OB *corcid*, W. *crychydd*, 'heron', Gaulish *Curcio-*; the word for

---

975 O'Brien, *Celtica*, 10 (1973), 229. Ziegler, p. 112, also notes that *mál* and *máel* get confused in Old Irish. Malaen in *Canu Llywarch Hen*, ed. Williams, X.1, is not connected (see Sims-Williams, *CMCS*, 26 (1993), 35, n. 33, and especially SBCHP, pp. 216 and 218).

976 LWP, p. 380 (also citing a *Meurig Maelan* 'vicecomes Merioneth' in Edward III's reign, Wynne, *AC*, 1 (1846), 397); Williams, review of CIIC i, *THSC*, 1943–44, p. 154. For *Caer Faelan* see ‡14n. Loth, *Noms des saints bretons*, p. 84, and Holder ii, 379, speculate that *Maelan* occurs as *Melan* (on *Mael-* > *Mel-* see HPB, p. 162 and n. 94 above).

977 Above, ‡14. KHJ notes that CORBAGNI 'is clearly an Irish name', comparing 98 and 246 **CORBAGNI**. See *Corbbán* in CGH, p. 565.

978 Williams, review of CIIC i, *THSC*, 1943–44, p. 154; ETG, p. 239 (cf. *Torfaen*, ETG, p. 229, and DP iii, 296, n. 6).

979 Cf. LWP, p. 390; Lewis, *BBCS*, 1 (1921–23), 12–14; EANC, pp. 47–50; Pierce, *Place-Names of Dinas Powys*, pp. 69–70; GPC s.n. *carfan*; LEIA C-41.

980 See above, ‡17.

'heron' in Ireland, however, was *corr* (cf. 104 **CORR > <**), which will not explain Ir. *Corcán*.[981]

[48] 370/157 HIC IACIT VLCAGNVS FI(*li*)VS SENOMAGLI

This is OI *Olcán*, either from the specifically Q-Celtic **ulkʷo-* 'wolf', or else from *olc* 'bad', a word without Brittonic cognates (and possibly derived from the 'wolf' word anyway).[982] There are two ogam examples of the name, one in Ireland (100 **ULCCAGNI**) and the other in Cornwall (below). The Welsh names which Rhys compares, *Wlch* in the tale of *Branwen* and *Ylched* in *Llechylched* in Anglesey, may, if relevant, have been borrowed from Irish, since we might expect **Wlff* and **Ylffed* in Welsh (unless there was an early delabialization of **kʷ* as postulated by McCone).[983] Note, however, that Ifor Williams associated *Wlch* with the element **wlch* ('fertile land'?, 'circuit'?) in W. *cyfwlch* and *cyfylchi*.[984]

[48] 372/160 **DECCAIBAR VUGLOB DISI** (Nash-Williams; Macalister: **[DECCA]IBARVALB [MAQI B]RO[CAGNI]**) / DE[CAB]ARBALOM FI[L]IVS BROCAGNI

The ogam establishes an Irish context, even though it is virtually illegible (Nash-Williams's **GL** being in the most intractable part),[985] and BROCAGNI is surely OI *Broccán*, like 316 **BROCAGNI** and 187 **BROCANN**.[986] MW *Brychan* occurs, but as the name of the more or less legendary half-Irish founder of Brycheiniog.[987]

[48] 374/172 CVNEGNI

This is probably genitive (with Latin rather than Irish -I?) of Irish **Kuneγnah*, as already discussed, and possibly the source of the Welsh river name *Cynen* < ?**Cynein*, as we have seen.

---

[981] McManus, *Guide*, p. 107; Ziegler, pp. 156 and 162; LEIA C-208–9 and 212; Ó Corráin & Maguire, *Gaelic Personal Names*, pp. 59–60; NWÄI, p. 505; Gramm., p. 194; DLG, pp. 110–11. *Corr* is not cognate with *crychydd* according to Schrijver, in Beekes FS, p. 297. On OW *Circ(h)an* see n. 950 above.

[982] Ziegler, p. 241; LEIA O-20; McCone, *Ériu*, 36 (1985), 171–76; De Bernardo Stempel, in Meid FS, p. 70, and NWÄI, p. 553, n. 51. It may be worth noting that Vulcan appears as VLK[ANO] in RIB i 899 (cf. Mann, *Britannia*, 2 (1971), 221, Hamp, *Britannia*, 6 (1975), 158 (seeing British influence), and VLRB, pp. 905–6).

[983] Rhys, LWP, pp. 387–88, who also compares *Cefn Amwlch* in Caernarfonshire and *Llanamwlch* in Breconshire (but see Lloyd-Jones, *Enwau Lleoedd Sir Gaernarfon*, p. 86). Williams, *Poems of Taliesin*, p. 83, derives MW *Vlph* from Latin *Ulpius*. On the early delabialization, see further Ch. 5 below, p. 332.

[984] *Pedeir Keinc y Mabinogi*, p. 191; GPC, s.vv., comparing Gallo-Latin *olca*, on which see Holder ii, 842 and Sims-Williams, in *The Indo-European Languages*, p. 355. Cf. MW *Kyvwlch* (Lloyd-Jones, *Geirfa*, s.n.)? Continental forms in *Olc-* and *Ulc-*, of doubtful relevance, are listed by Holder ii, 842–43 and iii, 22–23.

[985] Cf. LHEB, pp. 187 and 620, n. 3.

[986] Ziegler, p. 141.

[987] EWGT, p. 173; Sims-Williams, *CMCS*, 26 (1993), 55–58. The irregular *y* in *Brych-* (see ‡46n. above, cf. SBCHP, pp. 159–60) may be due to contamination with *brych* 'blemish, freckle', possibly with opprobrious intent; cf. the reference to the descendants(?) of a Brochfael as 'Brychuaelyeid (*sic* MS) brychuoelyon', CBT ii, 341).

[48] 376/174 VENNISETLI FILIVS ERCAGNI

For ERCAGNI see Anglesey above. His son VENNISETLI has a British name, but the spelling of VENNI- with E may be due to Irish influence.[988]

[48] Pembrokeshire

422/298 **VENDOGNI/VENDAGNI FILI V[ ]NI** (Macalister: [U]ENDOGNI [F]ILI [H]OCIDEGNI ?)

The ogam provides an Irish context, and the spelling VEND- (rather than VIND-) again may be Irish. VENDAGNI (if that *is* the reading) gives OI *Findán* regularly, though admittedly there are also traces of a MW *Gwynnan* as well.[989] O'Brien compared **VENDOGNI** with 429/307 SOLINI FILIVS VENDONI, also in Pembrokeshire (and note 328/44 VENDONI in Breconshire above), and saw it as the prototype of OI -*ón* diminutives (although he does not actually cite a *Findón).[990] If O'Brien is right (for VENDONI may instead be < (*)*Vendonius*),[991] what may have happened is that the Irish composition vowel /a/ became /o/ in the vicinity of a labial (here /w-/) according to Ziegler's rule and then developed /oγn/ > -*ón*: *Windaγnah > *Wendoγnah > *Wendōn > *Findón.[992] This would be an Irish development, as there is no evidence for such rounding in Welsh, and W. /oγn/ became *oen* as in the word for 'lamb' < Celtic *ognos. Alternatively, and probably preferably, **VENDOGNI** may be influenced by the spelling of the British composition vowel. Another possibility is that **VENDOGNI** has the rare *-*u-gno*- suffix which would develop to *-*o-gna*- by lowering and thence give -*ón*;[993] the spelling of the Latinate(?) genitive might be based on the nominative ***VENDOGNAS**, where the lowering would be regular. In the same way, if Macalister's [H]OCIDEGNI is right, -EGNI may be influenced by the Pr.Ir. nominative *-*eγnah* < *-*ignas*; however, the reading is very doubtful.[994]

---

988 See above, ‡15.
989 Ziegler, p. 244; EWGT, p. 195.
990 *Celtica*, 10 (1973), 221.
991 See ‡‡ 22 and 38.
992 See above, under Breconshire.
993 Cf. MacNeill, *Ériu*, 11 (1930–32), 134, and NWÄI, p. 326, for -*ón* < *-*u-gno*-. Weisgerber, *Rhenania*, pp. 71 and 106, also refers to -*ugno*, citing VKG ii, 27, and Hessen, *ZCP*, 9 (1913), 43, but the direct ogam evidence is questionable. For lowering see below, Ch. 4, §29. MacNeill notes that *-*u-gno*- would have originated in *u*-stems (cf. Holder i, 2030 *Rectug(e)nus*, and iii, 19, 155 and 421 *Velugn(i)us*, *Vlatugni/Vlatucni*; GPN, p. 210), but there is no evidence that *windo- was ever one (though cf. 368/b/150 VENDV-BARI and 1028/214/850 VENDVMAGLI, and a single example of *Vendu*- for *Vindo*- in KGP, p. 296). If it were a *u*-stem, the E of VEND- could not be explained by lowering!
994 KHJ could see only the O and first I of this name in 1947 and was sceptical of Macalister's reading, which is incompatible with Lhuyd's drawing in RCAHMW, *Pembrokeshire*, p. 28.

[48] 432/312 **DOVAGNI/TIGERNACI DOBAGNI**
This is OI *Dubán* (← *Dobán*), and shows the characteristic Irish lowering of /u/ > /o/ in the element *dubwo-* ← *dubu-*.[995] The saint's name *Dyfan* in the place name *Merthyr Dyfan (Dovan)* may be Irish.[996]

[48] 434/314 COIMAGNI FILI CAVETI
The second name is equated with OI *cauuth* and the first, like 71 and 166 **COIMAGNI**, is clearly *Cóemán < cóem* 'dear' < **koimo-* (cognate with W. *cu*).[997] Ifor Williams equated COIMAGNI with W. *Cwyfan*, presumably implying that *Cwyfan* may be a loan from OI *Cóemán*, comparable with MW *Cwyf(i)en* (< OI *Cóemgen*, St Kevin), a name with which *Cwyfan* was often confused.[998]

[48] 439/319 . . . **ASEG[NI]** . . . (Nash-Williams) or . . . **SEGNI** . . . (Macalister)
This stone is too illegible to be confidently interpreted (see ‡‡ 42 and 44 above), but the use of ogam suggests that the **GN** (if present!) is Irish. Rhys conjectured '*Asegni, Osegni, Basegni, Masegni, Dasegni, Lasegni, Gasegni*: it is useless to guess any further.'[999] If the first letter is definitely **G^w** (so McManus), it is difficult to reconstruct a suitable name as stems with this initial sound were rare. If the **G^w** were hypercorrect for **G**, however, a possibility is **G^wUSUGNI** or **G^wUSOGNI** (compare OI *Gussán < *gussu-* 'valour', ogam -**GUSU**).[1000]

[48] 441/345 CVRCAGNI FILI ANDAGELLI
ANDAGELLI is OI *Indgall*, which lacks a Brittonic cognate, but occurs elsewhere in Pembrokeshire (433/313) in ogam script and with the Irish patronymic **CAVE[TI]** discussed above under 434/314 COIMAGNI, which is in the same churchyard; in fact **[A]NDAGELLI** and COIMAGNI were

---

[995] Uhlich, *Ériu,* 40 (1989), 132–33; Ziegler, pp. 102–3 and 169.
[996] Cf. Rhys, *AC,* 5th ser. 14 (1897), 325; LBS ii, 394, n. 2; Loth, *Noms des saints breton,* pp. 31–32 and 131 (distinguishing B. *Devan*); Pierce, *Place-Names of Dinas Powys,* pp. 134–35. The Pembrokeshire river name *Dyfan* may or may not be connected (EANC, pp. 63–64; LHEB, pp. 275–77).
[997] LHEB, p. 312; McManus, *Guide,* p. 107; Ziegler, pp. 148 and 152; LEIA C-4 and 6–7. Possible Continental Celtic parallels, *Koimila* and *Coemoius,* are noted by Rhys, *PBA,* 6 (1913–14), 75, and Hamp, *Acta Neophilologica,* 11 (1978), 59. Cf. Holder i, 1061 and iii, 1252–53; and *Ancoema, Coemea* and *Coemoius* in OPEL i, 108, and ii, 68.
[998] Williams, review of CIIC i, *THSC,* 1943–44, p. 154; LHEB, p. 312, n. 1; LBS ii, 201–2; EWGT, p. 179; Sims-Williams, *Celtica,* 21 (1990), 620, n. 4; cf. *Kwyuyen,* CBT i, 461 and 471. Cf. the generally accepted loan relations between W. *Gwyddel* > OI *Goídel* (Sims-Williams, *BBCS,* 38 (1991), 72, n. 4) and W. *macwy(f)* < OI *maccóem* (LEIA M-3).
[999] Rhys, in Meyer FS, p. 237. None of these occurs in ogam. The nearest are 287 **NISIGNI**, cf. OI *Nessán* and 236 **LOSAGNI**, cf. OI *Loissín* (Ziegler, pp. 215–16 and 196). McManus, *Guide,* p. 67, read the vowel after the **S** as **O**, and Dr Edwards points out the possibility of **U**.
[1000] McManus, *Guide,* p. 67. See O'Brien, *Celtica,* 10 (1973), 221; CGH, p. 664; Ziegler, p. 107. Hypercorrect **Q** for **C** is well evidenced (Ziegler, p. 21).

probably brothers.[1001] In view of his patronymic, CVRCAGNI is again likely to be Irish, as in the Carmarthenshire example discussed earlier.

[48] 449/384 SAGRAGNI MAQI CUNATAMI/SAGRANI FILI CVNOTAMI

While the patronymic is typically Welsh (> *Cyndaf*), *Sagra(g)ni* is generally taken to be OI *Sárán*.[1002] The Brittonic cognate *Haer*(-) is not attested with -*an*, so far as I know,[1003] but that is not conclusive; **Haeran* from native *Haer-* plus borrowed -*an* is quite conceivable. The Irish loss of /γ/ is shown in the second syllable of the roman-letter version SAGRANI, but not in the first syllable – nor in either syllable of the ogam version. Jackson suggests that /γ/ may have been lost sooner in one position than the other, meaning before /n/ sooner than before /r/ rather than in Irish unaccented (or final) syllables sooner than accented (or non-final) syllables, although that is also a possibility and has been suggested by Greene (cf. also 317 **MAGLANI** in Ireland).[1004] In either case we can explain the name of the Welsh saint *Saeran*, who is said to be of Irish parentage in *Bonedd y Saint*, as a *Welsh* development of Ir. SAGRANI (hence the preserved *S*-).[1005] It may be, however, that the writer of SAGRANI was partly thinking of W. *Haer*-, which might still be spelt SAGR-, rather than Ir. *Sár*-, but wrote -ANI for Ir. -*án* because -AGNI would denote a nonexistent Welsh suffix -*aen*. Indeed, a fully naturalized **Haeran* is a distinct possibility, in view of the Welsh patronymic; but this is not to concede that **-agnos* was an inherited British termination.

[48] Cornwall

457/Ok18 DVNOCATI HIC IACIT FILI MERCAGNI (or ME[S]CAGNI) The spelling DVN- rather than DIN- suggests an Irish context (*Dúnchad* rather than MW *Din(o)gat*), as does MESC-, if that is the correct reading, as maintained by Jackson (comparing OI *mescc* 'drunk') and by Ifor Williams (comparing 458/Ok9 MESGI).[1006] If MERCAGNI is right, however, the best comparison is again Irish, *Mercán* (and *Mercón*).[1007]

[1001] See above, ‡22. Cf. Jackson, *Speculum*, 21 (1946), 523: 'these gravestones [433–434] may indeed be those of brothers.'

[1002] LWP, pp. 395–96; Ziegler, pp. 115–16, 160–61, and 229–30.

[1003] See above, ‡47.

[1004] LHEB, pp. 171 and 180; Greene, *Ériu*, 27 (1976), 35, followed by McManus, *Guide*, p. 89.

[1005] Cf. Rhys, *AC*, 6th ser. 18 (1918), 187; LBS iv, 129–30; EWGT, p. 64. However, Richards, *THSC*, 1965, p. 31, derives it from W. *saer* 'artisan' (cf. Ir. *Gobbán*).

[1006] LHEB, pp. 171 and 319, n. 4; Williams, review of CIIC i, in *THSC*, 1943–44, p. 156 (Thomas, *Mute Stones*, p. 265, reads MESGI or MESCI). But see above, ‡16, on *mysg* etc.

[1007] O'Brien, *Celtica*, 10 (1973), 221 and n. 27. This may occur in the Welsh place name *Rhosferchan*, if not a corruption of *Rhos Erchan* (EANC, p. 67). Cf. *Merken* in Cornwall in Domesday Book, ed. Thorn & Thorn, 125a? Names such as *Mercios* and *Merco* are listed by Holder ii, 551–52.

[48] 467/Ok24 [HI]C IACIT VLCAGNI/**ULCAGNI**
Again, OI *Olcán*, as in Carmarthenshire, and here with significant use of ogam.

[48] 472/Ok35 VLCAGNI FILI SEVERI
Similarly Irish, but with a non-diagnostic Latin patronymic.

[48] 478/Ok48 BROCAGNI (Okasha: BR[ ]ACNI) IHC IACIT NADOTTI (Thomas: or RADOTTI) FILIVS
BROCAGNI (the probable reading) is surely Irish, as in Carmarthenshire, although the patronymic has not be identified.[1008]

[48] 487/Ok10 DRVSTAGNI (??) (DRVSTANVS Thomas) HIC IACIT CVNOMORI FILIVS
Okasha notes that first name has also been read CIRISINIVS, CIRV[ ]V[ ]NC, CERVSIVS, CIRUSIUS, SIRVSIVS and CIRVSINIVS, and Rhys himself says 'my *-agni* is rather a guess than a reading'.[1009] According to Jackson and Padel, it is DRVSTAVS with ligatured AV, and Jackson states that W. *Drystan* 'is from *Drustagnos; the interpretation of the Castle Dore stone as DRVSTANVS is doubtful and begs the question'.[1010] If nevertheless DRVSTA(n)VS was intended (compare the Cornish farm name *Tredruston*)[1011] and if this has the Brittonic *-an* suffix, the latter is likely to be Irish-derived in view of the already noted absence of good evidence for Brittonic *-agnos*. One should also note the possibility that *Drystan/Trystan* (late OW *Tristan*) is ultimately a Pictish name (Pictish *Drosten, Drostan*, etc., MI *Drust*) whose limited use in the Brittonic countries is due to the influence of the Tristan legend.[1012]

[48] Irrelevant names with -GN- (added for completeness)

Cornwall

473/b/Ok46 IGNIOC
Despite Thomas's suggested division]IGNI OC, this probably does not belong with -IGNI forms at all, but is a Brittonic form corresponding to OB *agnioc*, W. *egnïog (actually *egnïol*).[1013] The fact that GN rather than CN is

---

[1008] On NADOTTI or RADOTTI (Thomas, *Mute Stones*, p. 263) see above, ‡42.
[1009] LWP, p. 403. Cf. Rhys, *AC*, 4th ser. 6 (1875), 369: 'after poring some time over it, we concluded that it is AGNI, with the N somewhat in the bosom of the G.' No recent writer has accepted this.
[1010] Cf. ‡14 above.
[1011] Padel, *CMCS*, 1 (1981), 73, n. 53. I am grateful to Dr Padel for reminding me of this and for other comments on the name.
[1012] This opinion has frequently been opposed; cf. Thomas, *Mute Stones*, pp. 279–80; TYP, pp. 329–30 and 549; Padel, *CMCS*, 1 (1981), 54–55; Bromwich, in *Arthur of the Welsh*, p. 210; and references.
[1013] See above, ‡18. (Cf. Thomas, *Mute Stones*, pp. 270 and 284.)

used for /gn/ probably implies that /ɣn/ had by now disappeared from Cornish, with the result that GN could be used for /gn/ without ambiguity. Hence IGNIOC is indirect evidence for the *completion* of /ɣn/ > /i̯n/.

[48] 486/Ok56 CVMREGNI (Thomas: CVMRECINI) FILI MAVCI
This is Brittonic, if CVM- is < **koimo-*, but the second element is uncertain as to reading and meaning.[1014] It is tempting to equate it with 359/141 [R]EGIN[I] > OW *Regin* > *Rein*.[1015] On the other hand, Padel has posited a MC **Rigni* to explain the early forms of Tregony (*Trefhrigoni* 1049, *Treligani* 1086, *Trigoni* 1201, *Tregeny* 1214, *Tregny* c. 1540),[1016] and our -REGNI or -RECINI could be a spelling of this (if -RECINI, sharing the svarabhakti of the medieval forms). In this case, the G or C stands for original /k/ > /g/ rather than /g/ > /ɣ/, and is irrelevant to the present investigation.[1017]

[48] 2028 ARTOGNOV([?)
This form seems to have /ɣ/ at the beginning of the second element of a compound, where it would simply disappear without combining with the preceding composition vowel, which would indeed already have been lost (of course the **-agnas* < **-o-gnos* also consisted of composition vowel + second element originally, but it came to be treated as a suffix). We cannot tell whether GN stands for /ɣn/ or is simply an etymological spelling of /n/ < **gn* of the sort familiar in Old Welsh and Old Breton (e.g. OB *Gurgnou* beside *Arthnou*, a cognate of ARTOGNOV[).[1018] The same applies to the following Breton example of GN:

[48] Brittany

3006/C1 BODOGNOVS[1019]

[48] Isle of Man

1068/b LUGNI
This form is clearly Ir. *Luigne*, gen. *Luigni*, with /ɣn/ by syncope; in

---

[1014] For -RECINI see Thomas, *Mute Stones*, pp. 278 and 300, n. 4, and KHJ in ‡26n. above.
[1015] LHEB, p. 445; SBCHP, p. 69. Note that the -I cannot be a surviving Celtic genitive since syncope of **koimo-* implies that apocope has already happened. It can only be a post-apocope termination -*i* (see below) or else a Latinate addition. I cannot see why CVMREGNI is regarded as Latin by Okasha, *Corpus*, p. 46.
[1016] *Popular Dictionary of Cornish Place-Names*, pp. 166 and 210. The first *i* of **Rigni* could be due to internal *i*-affection of /e/.
[1017] Cf. perhaps Ptolemy's Irish island *Ricina* or *Ricena* (EIHM, p. 14), and cf. Holder ii, 1183 and Weisgerber, *Rhenania*, p. 140, n. 151.
[1018] For -*gnou* and -*no(u)* see Chrest., p. 133; Gramm, pp. 80–81; LHEB, p. 383; Hamp, *Onoma*, 14 (1969), 12; SBCHP, p. 300, n. 1; Wmffre, *Language and History*, i, 339 and 347–48.
[1019] See IEMB, p. 142.

Irish, unlike Brittonic, /ɣ/ survived in such clusters when they arose by syncope.[1020]

[48] The conclusion of this long excursus is thus that there are virtually no names with -GN- which are relevant to British /ɣn/. The only one which can be added tentatively to Jackson's list (and it *may* be Irish) is:

6. 328/44 RVGNIATIO ( ]RVGNIATO Thomas), in Breconshire

[48] Further forms, with GL, which I would add are:

7. 400/177 VINNEMAGLI, SENEMAGLI
8. 2029/p.39i MAGLORI
9. 2030/p.39ii MAGLI (if this RCAHMW reading is correct)[1021]
10. 447/369 NEMAGLI (assuming it is Brittonic, perhaps for [VIN]NEMAGLI or similar, although Pr.Ir. *Nē-maɣlī is more likely)[1022]
11. 498/Nb7 BRIGOMAGLOS

[48] The following are ignored as probably or very possibly Irish:
2032]CAMAGLI has the typically Irish composition vowel (e.g. *[ER]CAMAGLI or *[BRO]CAMAGLI) although it *could* be the British reduced vowel A[1023]
372/160 **VUGLOB** (Nash-Williams), a dubious reading
426/300 **NETTASAGRI** (Nash-Williams: **NETTASAGRU**)
427/a/301 **MAGL[I] DUBAR[** (Nash-Williams: **MAGL[IA] DUBR[**)
449/384 **SAGRAGNI/SAGRANI** (see above under 'Pembrokeshire')
501 **CUNAMAGLI MAQ[**

[48] The following are omitted for other reasons:
349/121/4 BROHO[MAGLI] is of course a guess.
474/Ok17]MAGLI is only one possible reading.
1033/287 TENGRUIN has GR- at the start of the second element in a compound, if we accept Ifor Williams's reading and interpretation CENGRUI = **Cein-rwy*; however, Lhuyd's unpublished copy in BL Stowe MS 1023, fo. 160r, reads TENGRUI, with a bar (still visible on the

---

[1020] CGH, p. 680; CGSH, pp. 250 and 296.

[1021] This reading of Lhuyd's drawing is very doubtful. The attested name MATINVS (Holder ii, 460, perhaps < *Matutinus*, Kajanto, pp. 18 and 220, OPEL iii, 65 and 67, and VLRB, p. 909, n. 17) is a possibility, allowing for a NV ligature, and the last part of the inscription could be IBERI, gen. of *Iberius* (see Holder ii, 15 s.n. *Ibertus*). The middle three letters could then be the ogam formula **ANM** 'name', not previously attested in Wales (Ziegler, pp. 128–29). All this is speculation of course.

[1022] See above, ‡‡ 38 and 42.

[1023] Thomas, *Mute Stones*, p. 125, reads the rest of 2032 as '. . . HIC IACIT NIMNI(?)', comparing 339/68 'N(EMNI)I. *Nemni(us)*' (on which see ‡26). His explanation of CAMAGLI as syncopated from *CATAMAGLI is impossible. There is a name *Camalus*, very frequent in Hispania (Mócsy, p. 63), but it seems unlikely that CAMAGLI is a hypercorrect Celtic spelling of this. KHJ dates the lettering of 2032 sixth-century and rejects Webley's comparison of it with 334/54.

stone) over the R, and this was the standard abbreviation for R*um*;[1024] the name should therefore be segmented TENG-R*um*-UI, with *teng-* or *tyng-* ~ *tang* as in MW *tegneved* = *tangnefedd*, and -*rum*- as in OW *Rumceneu* and Old Breton names like *Rumuual*.[1025]

1059/Ok64 ÆGRAT is a dubious alternative to ÆLRIAT or ÆLNAT.

1060/Ok57 GURGLES or GUNGLEI (if correct readings) presumably have GL- at start of the second element of a compound.[1026]

489/b/Ok13 SAGRANVI (on the reverse of an ogam stone) is problematic, although the reading is clear.[1027] It looks like a derivative of OI *Sárán* (compare 449/384 **SAGRAGNI**/SAGRANI), but the ending – hardly a muddle between -VS and -I – looks like an addition to a preform of *Sárán* of the well-known Brittonic -*wy* (OW -*ui*, OB -*oe*, etc.). This may well be the correct explanation; for the same phenomenon in reverse compare the combination of Brittonic and Irish suffixes in OI names in -*uc-án* and -*óc-án*.[1028] Compare also the addition of -*an* (< Ir. -*án* ?) to OB -*oe* in OB *Gan-oe-an* beside *Mad-gan-oe, Mat-gan-et*.[1029] It is less likely that SAGRANVI is a purely Brittonic name **Haeranwy*. While -*on-wy* is a well-attested double suffix in Brittonic (*Mathonwy, Daronwy*),[1030] I do not have examples of -*an-wy* (*My-fan-wy*/*My-ddan-wy*[1031] is *not* one).

[48] (B) As examples of inscriptions where *γl γr γn (> jl jr jn) > i̯l i̯r i̯n* has happened Jackson lists (pp. 463–65):

1.   477/Ok11 TEGERNOMALI
2.   1000/182 BROHCMAIL, BROHCMAL
3.   1012/223/933 ARTMALI [this inscription's IUTHAHELO would be another example if -*hael* is < **saglo*- or similar, but see ‡74 below]
4.   1024/255/926 ARTHMAIL
5.   978/49 BRIAMAIL

[48] As is illustrated by TEGERNOMALI (which Jackson compares with *Tigernomalus* in the *Vita S. Samsonis*), by ARTMALI beside ARTHMAIL,

---

[1024]   Cf. BWP, pp. 29–30; Lindsay, *Early Welsh Script*, pp. 9, 15, etc.

[1025]   GPC s.v. *tangnefedd* and *tangnefaf* (see Evans, GPN, pp. 116 and 261, and in Birkhan FS, p. 101 on *Tanc-* names, and DLG, pp. 244–45, on *tanco-* ~ *tenco-*); VC, §68; Chrest., p. 163 (with uncertain comparison with B. *rumm(ad)* 'group' etc.). Cf. MW *Tyncryn*/*Tyngryn* (‡14n. above)? For the Lhuyd copy see Sims-Williams, *CMCS*, 44 (2002).

[1026]   On GURGLES see below, ‡58.

[1027]   Despite Okasha who reads G[A]G[R]A[NV]I or G[A]G[R]A[SN]I. To judge by his notes, KHJ does not seem to have rejected the reading SAGRANVI (pace Okasha), even if he did not interpret it. The similarity between the S- and the -G- does not prove that they are the same letter. Readers would have been expected to possess some linguistic instinct (as does Okasha in eliminating H instead of N as 'contextually unlikely'). Thomas, *Mute Stones*, p. 268, takes -VI to be genitive of *-uus*.

[1028]   Russell, *Celtic Word-Formation*, pp. 111, n. 283, and 152–54; NWÄI, p. 482.

[1029]   Chrest., p. 131; Gramm., p. 314. Cf. HPB, pp. 210–11.

[1030]   Cf. R. J. Thomas, *BBCS*, 7 (1933–35), 133.

[1031]   Lewis, *ZCP*, 20 (1936), 141–43; Richards, *THSC*, 1965, p. 40.

and in particular by the variation BROHCMAIL/BROHCMAL within one inscription, the I could be omitted from the diphthong /ai̯/, as if it were a mere epenthesis.[1032] A further good example is 3005/F5]NOMALI, where an I seems to have been inserted (?later), beside VENOMAILI in the same Breton inscription.[1033] Note also Macalister's alternative reading VEDOMALI in 408/229/848 (inferior however to VEDOMAVI),[1034] and 1012/223/933 TECAN(I) in the same inscription as ARTMALI, assuming the reading is correct and in the unlikely event that it means *Tecain (see below). One wonders whether the inscribers may have been influenced by Latin names with -AL- such as 389/97 IOVENALI, 408/229/848 ETERNALI, 454/402 EVALI,[1035] 473/a/Ok46 VITALI, and 515/Scot.9 LIBERALI. On the other hand, a similar phenomenon is found in the ogam inscriptions where A and O are sometimes written for the diphthongs AI and OI.[1036] This ogam convention lies behind the following spellings of probable Irish names in Britain:

[48] 1038/365 MAL DOMNA[C] if Macalister is right to read MAL (Nash-Williams has MAIL or ?MEIL)
1068/b (on Man) MALBREN SCRIBA (see below)
460/Ok75 VROCHANI = Ir. Fróechán[1037]
452/400 VALAVI FILI (Macalister's emendation of Lhuyd's VALAVITIVI) may contain OI Fáel- 'wolf', like 460/Ok75 VAILATHI, and be the same as OI Fáelbe/Fáilbe (io-stem), as has been suggested for 302 VALUVI.[1038] Note, however, that there is some evidence that there was also a name Fá(i)lbe without the diphthong.
1048/Ok32 QONFAL(I) (Thomas, Tedeschi)[1039] could conceivably have OI fáel as second element, with silent f written according to OI conventions, but the reading is uncertain and no name *Conf(h)áel seems to be attested.

[1032] LHEB, pp. 463–64. Also in 1000/182, note POUOS twice beside POUOIS. Cf. 1032/281 ODELEV (= Hoedlyw, ‡80); 1011/220/911 EUS for eius. Cf. + mali (gen.) in 'Chad 8', LL, p. xlvii, i.e. MW Mael (though cf. n. 939 above). For Old Cornish examples of omission of i see Olson & Padel, CMCS, 12 (1986), 43, 51, and 59–60.

[1033] IEMB, pp. 61 and 134.

[1034] See above, ‡25.

[1035] Perhaps not Latin; see ‡18.

[1036] Ziegler, pp. 44–46.

[1037] See above, ‡42.

[1038] Ziegler, pp. 39, 241–42 and n. 387 (noting the contrary view of Uhlich, Ériu, 40 (1989), 130–33, where forms of Fá(i)lbe are also cited; cf. Uhlich, Morphologie, pp. 244–45; McManus, Guide, pp. 104 and 122). For Fáelbe see O'Brien, Celtica, 10 (1973), 223, and CGH, pp. 625–26, indicating a diphthong by diacritics in both). KHJ notes that Macalister is wrong to give the impression that Lhuyd's reading was VALAVI FILI, 'though probably the reading really was VALAVI FILI (or FILI–?)'; he also compares 302 VALUVI. One could also emend to VALATI = Fáelad (cf. VAILATHI, on which see above, ‡42).

[1039] Cf. Thomas, Mute Stones, pp. xxii, 159, n. 29, and 290–91, suggesting Q = /k/ and F = /µ/. Cf. ‡44n. above.

[48] To Jackson's Brittonic examples we can add two inscriptions from Brittany with reflexes of *maglos:

6. 3005/F5]NOMALI FILIUS VENOMAILI
7. 3008/C3 MAELDOI

[48] A further likely instance is:

8. 2022/253/984 AERERN (Nash-Williams: [B(?)]ERER[ ), which may be either haer 'challenging, firm' < *sagro- + haearn 'iron' (especially if 1065/410 HAERDUR similarly contains haer + dur 'steel' rather than haearn < *isarno-),[1040] or else 'battle-iron' with Aer- < *agro- 'carnage', as in MW aerdur 'battle-blade, sword', aergi 'battle-hound' (: OI Árchú), etc. and Old Breton personal names in Aer-.[1041]

[48] Finally, we have already seen (under Cardiganshire and Cornwall ['irrelevant names']) that the spelling of the following probably indicates that Brittonic /ɣ/ > /i̯/ had already occurred:

9. 353/127/7 MAGLAGNI (if = OI Máelán)
10. 473/b/Ok46 IGNIOC

[48] A number of names have to be ignored here since they probably show the Irish reflex of /ɣn/:
364/144 QVENVENDANI = Ir. Cennf(h)innán[1042]
429/307 VENDONI (if it has a Celtic *-gn- suffix at all)[1043]
440/335 EOROCAN or EONOCAN or EOPOCAN – obscure, but possibly Irish in view of the coupling with MACVDEbETI. However, the lack of -I coupled with non-syncope is odd, and suggests that British *EDNOCAVI or similar (with ligatured VI) may have been the true reading[1044]
449/384 SAGRANI[1045]
460/Ok75 (VAILATHI FILI) VROCHANI = Ir. Fróechán[1046]
506 MAQ CUGIN[I][1047]
507 CRON[A]N[= OI Crónán[1048]

[1040] For haer and spellings of haearn see above, ‡‡ 36 and 47. If haer comes from *sagero- rather than *sagro- (cf. SBCHP, p. 134, and ‡47n. above), AERERN may belong under ‡74 below rather than here. If its AER- corresponded to MW aer one would rather expect the diphthong to be spelt AI in the Old Welsh period (cf. OW hair 'cladis', Falileyev, Etymological Glossary, s.v.).

[1041] Lloyd-Jones, Geirfa, p. 12; LEIA A-82; Uhlich, Morphologie, p. 164; DGVB i, 58; Chrest., pp. 105 and 212, n. 7.

[1042] See above, ‡22.

[1043] See above, under Breconshire.

[1044] See above, ‡17. The third letter is probably not R or P but the μ form of N (which came in during the sixth century according to Tedeschi, in Roman, Runes and Ogham, pp. 24–25).

[1045] See above, under Pembrokeshire.

[1046] See above, ‡42.

[1047] Uncertain reading. Cf. McManus, Guide, pp. 44–45, and Ziegler, pp. 143, 151 and 157, who compares OI Cúcán, CGH, p. 575, and for Motta's and Jackson's readings see ‡25n.

[1048] In 1952 KHJ read '[ ]ACRON ?'

511/Scot.10 CONINIE = OI *Co(i)nín* + Latin feminine genitive *-i(a)e*[1049]
1068/b MALBREN SCRIBA, either Ir. **Má(e)l-brén* 'stinking prince/bald
one' (cf. OC *Brenci* if 'stink-hound' rather than 'raven-hound), with
n < **gn* < **kn* – unless, of course, MALBREN is an abbreviation of
Mael-Brénaind[1050]
2007/10 MAILISI, if it is *Mael Ísu* or similar.[1051]

[48] Note that McCone suggests that Ir. /Vɣn/ > /V:n/ may have occurred
before syncope while /Vθn/ and /Vxn/ > /V:n/ may have been post-
syncope.[1052] The best example of the latter sound change in the inscriptions in Britain – which does not support this chronology, since it does not
show syncope – is 488/Ok60 ENABARRI/**ENABARR** (cf. OI *én* < **petno-*
: MW *edn* 'bird').[1053] One might also cite the many names like
MACCVTRENI and TRENACATVS (329/42; 341/71; 348/a/110/27
[Macalister!, ‡38n.]; 353/127/7; 425/297; 428/305), assuming that these
contain OI *trén* 'strong' and that this derives from **treksno-* by way of
*trekno-.[1054] Such names also appear with *Trían-* in Old Irish, however, which
is incompatible with any connection with *trén* and points to a preform
*treino-.[1055] (Incidentally, MW *tren(n)* can hardly be borrowed from *trén* in
view of the short /e/,[1056] but could derive from **treksno-* by way of **tresno-* like
pren(n) < **kʷresno-*.[1057] If so, the clearly Welsh 998/164 HEUTREN is
irrelevant to the present discussion of fricative loss, even if it does contain
tren(n).[1058])

[48] 2025/Scot.12 NEITANO (whether British or Pictish) is not
necessarily from or influenced by OI *Nechtan*, but if it is, note that the
latter does *not* have *-án*.[1059] The same is true of OI *Ruan* (cf. *Mael-ruain*),[1060]

[1049] See n. 922 above.
[1050] Cf. O'Brien, *Celtica*, 10 (1973), 229; HPB, p. 157, n. 2; LEIA B-84–85; Hughes, *CMCS*, 22 (1991), 95–99; Coates & Breeze, *Celtic Voices*, pp. 145–46; Uhlich, *ZCP*, 49/50 (1997), 879, n. 6, and 880, n. 8 (and on p. 879 noting *Bren'* as abbreviation for *Brénainn* in the Annals of Ulster, s.a. 752).
[1051] See above, ‡14n.
[1052] TRC, p. 123.
[1053] Ziegler, pp. 176–77. Schrijver, *Ériu*, 48 (1997), 223, n. 7, suggests that the **A** of **ENABARR** is a post-syncope epenthesis; see below, p. 321.
[1054] LEIA T-136; Ziegler, p. 117; cf. De Bernardo Stempel, *IF*, 94 (1989), 226; and OI *Trénmór* = OB *Trechmorus* etc. in Uhlich, *Morphologie*, p. 302. On MW *Tringat* see ‡15 above.
[1055] See Ch. 5, p. 330. Cf. *Trēnus* in Holder ii, 1911 and ‡15 above, and *Trian* in CGH, p. 745. Could MW *Cyndrwyn* contain the Welsh cognate of this *Trian* (cf. n. 962 for a different explanation)?
[1056] Pace VKG i, 296; LEIA T-136. Cf. WG, p. 249.
[1057] LEIA C-223.
[1058] See ‡51.
[1059] Steer, *PSAS*, 101 (1968–69), 128; O'Rahilly, EIHM, pp. 368 and 536; Jackson, in *Problem of the Picts*, pp. 145, 164–65, 173–74 and 176; Jackson, *Gododdin*, p. 48, n. 1; O'Brien, *Celtica*, 10 (1973), 223. See also ‡51. If W. *Nwython* is related (pace O'Rahilly), is a development of /ex/ similar to that of /ïɣ/ in *colwyn* involved (see ‡51)?
[1060] CGH, p. 727; O'Brien, *Celtica*, 10 (1973), 229; cf. LEIA R-49; DIL s.v. *Máel*.

a possible source of 474/Ok17 RVANI (an uncertain reading). 487/Ok10 DRVSTANVS (Thomas), if this is the correct reading or interpretation,[1061] *may* have Ir. *-án* < **-agnas*; although if this name is really derived from Pictish *Drosten, Drostan* it does not seem clear that should have had /a:n/ < **agn* at all.[1062] In any case, the reading may be DRVSTAVS, just possibly implying -VS < **-wiks.*[1063]

[48] 493/Ok58 NEPRANI is probably Pr.Ir. **Nē-branī*; compare OI gen. *Niad-Brain* (‡42).

[48] The following may have the Brittonic suffix *-an* that derives, as we have seen, from Ir. *-án*. (Not every *-an* has this origin; for example, 452/400 PAANI (*Paganus*?) and 1000/182 ANNAN (*Ann(i)anus*?) may have Latin /a:/,[1064] and 468/Ok31 RIALOBRANI and 406/215/844 GVANI have original /a/ (cf. W. *brân, gwân*), while 356/132/9 CONVMANI (Macalister only!) is simply obscure.)

[48] 979/46 GUADAN, a derivative of W. *gwadd* (*gwadden*) 'mole' < **gwodd* as in OW *Guodon*[1065]
1023/239/927 [CO]NBELANI and NERTTAN seem to be the same names, with variant suffix, as 1016/234/907 CONBELIN = OW *Conbelin*, Mod.W. *Cynfelyn* and 1024/255/926 NERTAT = *Neirth(i)ad* (although Macalister would read NERT*tan* here too; cf. his conjecture 59 **[NE]RTAGNI**, MI hapax *nertán*). NERTTAN (if the correct reading!) is the only name in this group of names where -AN attached to a stem that also has *-án* attached to a cognate stem in Irish.[1066]
1033/287 GUADGAN, if a pseudo-etymological spelling of GUADAN above, but Ifor Williams suggests GU[*reic*] | ADGAN, and the latter could be related to MW *adyan* 'lineage', OB *Adgan*, with original /a/.[1067]
1012/223/933 TEC[A]N or TECANI has the Irish or Irish-derived *-án* attached to a Brittonic stem, *teg* 'fair'; this may have happened within Irish since 256 T><**GANN** and OI *Tecán* are agreed to be based on British /teg/ 'fair'.[1068] On the assumption that Nash-Williams's TEC[AI]N is correct, the name has also been analysed as a compound of the synonyms *teg + cain*

[1061] Thomas, *Mute Stones*, pp. 279–80, reading -ANVS with ligatured AN; and see ‡14 for KHJ's suggestion of a ligatured ANV. See also above under Cornwall.
[1062] Pace Jackson, in *Problem of the Picts*, pp. 163–64, who derives *Drosten* from **Drustagnos*.
[1063] See above, ‡14.
[1064] Above, ‡22.
[1065] Williams, *AC*, 90 (1935), 89–90; GPC, s.v.; LL, p. 205.
[1066] The reading NERTTAN is rejected by Jackson, *Speculum*, 24 (1949), 600. OW *Conbelin* is in VC §66.
[1067] BWP, pp. 29–30 and references; also GPC s.v. *adian* (recte *addian* ?); LHEB, pp. 386, n. 1, and 439; Gramm., pp. 111 and 400. (On W. *addiant* see GPN, pp. 211–14.)
[1068] See above, ‡17.

'fair'[1069] (problematical as this was *cein* in Middle Welsh; **kagn-* is more promising).

‡*49 nd > nn probably complete; LHEB §112.2*
See ‡22 above.

‡*50 ɔu (< āu̯, āγ) > ou; LHEB §46.2*
Inevitably, there is no inscriptional evidence to be cited.

Note that Schrijver argues that *pretonically* both native /ău̯/ (whether < /ăγ/ or by syncope of /ău̯i-C/ > /ău̯C/) and Latin *au* became /ou/.[1070] This would obviously have been *after* syncope (‡‡ 38 and 40 above) but *before* subsequent developments of /ou/ (‡‡ 62, 72, 80, and 82 below), so it can reasonably be mentioned here.

[50] (A) The examples of this pretonic /ău̯/ in the inscriptions with /ău̯/ < /ăγ/ (‡25) are:

1. 365/149 MAVOHE[NI]
2. 516/Scot.1 MAVORIVS
3. 1205/Ok44 MAVOUIH (or MAVORIH?)
4. 486/Ok56 MAVCI

[50] There are no examples of AU- < /ău̯i-C/ (unless 1064/Dor.iv]AUPRIT is relevant, which is uncertain),[1071] but examples of pretonic Latin *au* are:

5. 325/33 PAVLINI
6. 360/139 PAVLINVS
7. 410/238/847 PAVLI[NI?]
8. 407/b/258/846 PAVLINVS
9. 435/315 PAVLINI
10. 2002/a]AUR[I]ANVS

[50] (B) There seem to be no examples of Schrijver's /ou/ stage, unless 2022/253/984 COVLGVEN (Nash-Williams) were the correct reading (GVLGVEN is favoured by RCAHMW and the *Corpus*) and had Latin *caula* as its first element (see ‡80 below). This shortage of examples is not wholly surprising, since the development to /ou/, as in OW *Moucan* (> *Meugan*), did not always happen, to judge by the variant *Mawgan*,[1072] and Latin influence may have impeded writing it in cases like *Paulinus* > *Poulin* (> *Peulin*).[1073]

[1069] Evans, *BBCS*, 24 (1970–72), 423. MW *cein* may have been borrowed into OI as *caín* (LEIA C-16; cf. Uhlich, *Morphologie*, p. 135, n. 103).
[1070] SBCHP, pp. 270–72. Cf. HPB, pp. 262–63.
[1071] See ‡‡ 25 and 57.
[1072] See ‡57n. below.
[1073] Cf. SBCHP, p. 272.

‡*51 xt [Jackson's χt] > ịth; LHEB §60*

Jackson is able to cite examples of the traditional CT spelling (pp. 407–8),[1074] but cites no inscriptional evidence for the innovation.

[51] (A) The examples of CT are:

1. 339/68 VICTORINI[1075]
2. 384/83 SANCTINVS (Macalister: SANCE[R]INVS)[1076]
3. 358/138 PROTICTORIS
4. 406/215/844 [?AD]VECTI[1077]
5. 407/a/258/846 INVICTO
6. p. 397/285 BARRECTI[1078]
7. 430/306 **[VIC]TOR/VICTOR**
8. 510/Scot.13 VICTI (or VICTRICIS;[1079] Jackson and Thomas: VICTR[ )

Several of these may well have Latin CT conserved under Latin influence, and there are also various obscure forms: 1016/234/907 RICT[(Corpus reading); 1018/236/919 CTCER (Macalister only; others ACER); 508 FICT.

[51] (B) 1. The innovation probably occurs in 479/Ok16 CVNAIDE (Macalister and Thomas; Okasha: CVNATDO): MW *Cynaethwy*,[1080] assuming that D is used for the voiceless spirant, as occasionally in Old Welsh and Old Cornish (e.g. OW *coueidid* = Mod.W. *cyweithydd* < **ko-ụekt-*),[1081] and that the second element is **ak-t-* 'drive' as in 9 **MAQ-ACTO**, 92 **ACTO**, OI *Achtán*, and in Gaulish *Ambactus* by elision < **Ambi-aktos*.[1082] The presence of this element (cf. W. *aeth* 'went') in *Cynaethwy* is possibly confirmed by the presence of the parallel compounded element (cf. Mod.W. *daeth* 'came'?) in W. **Daethwy* in the place names *Dindaethwy* and *Porth(dd)aethwy*.[1083]

[1074] There are none of XT, for in 413/272 CAELEXTI it represents /st/.

[1075] Source of W. *Gwytherin*: DP iii, 230, n. 1; ETG, p. 203.

[1076] Cited since the /n/ was lost and the name developed as *Seithin*; see Williams, review of CIIC i, in *THSC*, 1943–44, p. 156 (citing BT 75.24 *seithin*, on which see ‡44n. above); LHEB, p. 406; Hamp, *Britannia*, 6 (1975), 155–56 and 160. The alternative treatment was to lose the /k/; cf. 1011/220/911 SANTDI. Smith, VLRB, p. 922, cites *sacto* and *sangto* from Roman Britain. Cf. Macalister's much-derided 189 **SAṇTI** and 439/319 **SANGKTA** (cf. McManus, *Guide*, pp. 61 and 67).

[1077] LWP, p. 387. Cf. Sims-Williams, in Evans FS, pp. 208–9. KHJ noted the bow of what *might* be an open D before VECTI both in the cast and in ECMW plate 10.

[1078] See above, ‡38.

[1079] CIIC ii, p. 202. *Victor, Victorem* gives W. *Gwythyr, Gwythur*: DP iii, 230, n. 1; Lloyd-Jones, *Y Geninen*, 44 (1926), 3, and *BBCS*, 14 (1950–52), 36; Bromwich & Evans, *Culhwch and Olwen*, p. 68.

[1080] See ‡58 below.

[1081] GPC s.v.; BWP, p. 98; LWP, pp. 225–26; Watkins, *BBCS*, 21 (1964–66), 139; Jackson, *SC*, 8/9 (1973–74), 27–28.

[1082] GPN, pp. 128 and 134–35; KGP, pp. 110 and 122; Ziegler, p. 122; ADA, p. 245. Cf. Holder i, 33 and 114, and iii, 498 and 582–83.

[1083] Thomas, *BBCS*, 7 (1933–35), 119; Jones & Roberts, *Enwau Lleoedd Môn*, pp. 40 and 129; cf. CBT v, 208 and 231. But *daeth* is a late development from MW *doeth* < **to-akt-* under the

[51] There are a few names with ITH in the corpus, but there is no reason to suppose them relevant here:

2010/276 ITHFUS (Germanic name, written with *thorn* rune)[1084]

1051/Ok37]ENITHI (= *uenit hic* according to Thomas)[1085]

1206/Ok4 DOVITHI (Okasha: [.O..]I[.]NI or [.O..]I[.]HI); cf. 128 and 157 **DOVETI** < *Dubwet(i)i*)[1086]

[51] While it is possible that some examples of *ith* are lurking behind the spelling IT, I can find no likely examples among, for example, 320/26 ORVVITE; 993/124/18 ASAITGEN (*recte* ASA ITGEN?, ‡65); 366/148 ITOCVS; 436/316 LITOGENI; 509/OkPict3]GRITI; 1049/Ok33 URITIN or URITN; 1064/Dor.iv]AUPRIT; 1205/Ok44 VITO[.[1087] The only other possibly relevant form is 2025/Scot.12 NEITANO when compared with OI *Nechtan*; however, the NEIT- in NEITANO is likely to be a Pictish form (cf. Pictish **NEHHTON** in the Lunnasting inscription, *Naiton* in Bede).[1088] While the name does appear as *Neithon* in OW genealogies relating to northern Britain and Man, the true MW descendant seems to be *Nwython/Nwythyon* (also *Noethon/Noython*), perhaps because the Pictish diphthong was borrowed in Welsh as /ïi̯/ and developed like /ïɣ/ in *kolignos* > *colwyn*.[1089]

[51] It may be worth noting Rhys's remark that 450/390 **OGTENAS** (Nash-Williams: **OGTENLO(?)**, but cf. ‡38n.)/**HOGTIVIS** (*recte* HOGTINIS ? McManus) seemed to read NOGTIVIS with G for the /i̯/ in W. *noeth* 'naked' or *-noeth* 'night' (: Ir. *nocht*).[1090] Rhys subsequently read **OGTENE/ HOGTIVIS**, and suggested that GT represented the cognate OI *cht*, comparing 423/296 **M[A]Q[I] QEGTE**, which he interpreted as the

---

influence of *aeth* (Lloyd-Jones, *BBCS*, 2 (1923–25), 290; cf. GMW, pp. 134–35). Is it possible that the place names really contain *Aethwy* rather than *Daethwy*, coupled with OI *dind* in the case of *Dind-aethwy*? WG, pp. 107 and 114, would derive *Aethwy* from *Octavius*, while Evans, *Enwau Personol*, p. 139, would connect *aeth* (: OI *écht* 'slaughter', which occurs in Ir. *Échtgal*, Uhlich, *Morphologie*, p. 238). A MW *Elaethwy* occurs once (Bartrum, *Welsh Genealogies 300–1400*, v, 110) but is probably a derivative of MW *Elaeth* (pers. comm., M. Cane).

[1084] See above, ‡42.

[1085] *Mute Stones*, p. 300.

[1086] See ‡‡ 42 and 55.

[1087] It is not necessary to derive VITO[from *Victori*; see ‡76n.

[1088] See LHEB, 410–11 and 708; Jackson, in *Problem of the Picts*, pp. 145, 164–65, 173–74, and 176 (citing Watson, *Celtic Place-Names of Scotland*, p. 211, who derives *Abernethy* < *Ne(i)the(a)ch* < *Neithon* and *Ythan* < *Ieithon*); Sims-Williams, *TPS*, 91 (1993), 162–64. Cf. Brigantian *Nectouelius* (RIB i 2142).

[1089] See above, ‡48. For the Welsh forms see EWGT, s.nn. *Neithon*, *Nectan* (Hibernicized, cf. Thomas, *Mute Stones*, p. 178, also p. 182, n. 31 on *Nehtanus*), and *Noethon*; and BWP, pp. 80–81 and n. 44. Jackson, *Gododdin*, p. 48, n. 1, describes *Neithon* and *Nwython* as by-forms of an older Brittonic *Nechton*, but if we regard the name as basically Pictish, that can explain why it is only here that these by-forms from *ekt* arise. Loth, *Noms des saints bretons*, p. 97, connects B. *Neizan(t)*. See also Coates & Breeze, *Celtic Voices*, pp. 97–99.

[1090] LWP, pp. 63–64 and 277; cf. McManus, *Guide*, p. 65; Ziegler, pp. 217–18. See above ‡27n. for the possibility of *Ócht-*. Compare Gaulish *Regtu-* for *Rectu-*, GPN, p. 210.

mythological(?) compound name *Mac Cécht*.[1091] The following year he decided in favour of **QAGTE** in the latter (the reading which Macalister and Nash-Williams adopt) and compared the name *Cacht* (m.f.), given in the Irish genealogies as the name of a legendary daughter of *Cathmand*, a king of Britain (cf. 970/13 **CATAMANVS**).[1092] It is also found as a male name or epithet, and is presumably based on OI *cacht* (: W. *caeth*) 'servant, slave', arguably a Celtic cognate or derivative of Latin *captus, -ā*.[1093] It is presumably masculine here, a patronymic, although if it is feminine **MAQ(I) QAGTE** would have to be a compound name 'son of [the goddess] Cacht' (cf. CIIC 125 **MAQI ERCCIAS**, *Macc Erce* 'son of [the goddess] Erc'). If this name is meant, the ogam **Q** must be a false archaism or hypercorrection for **C**, which is not unparalleled.[1094]

‡*52 Latin xs [= Jackson's χs] > i̯s; LHEB §126*

There seems to be no inscriptional evidence for this (cf. ‡14), unless the mysterious 1022/240/928 COISTO is relevant (cf. Latin *coxa* > W. *coes*), but this could be an acephalous word]CO plus Latin ISTO (Macalister reads LOCO ISTO).

‡*53 lγ, rγ > lj, rj in Pr. W. now or later; LHEB §88*

Cf. ‡‡96–97 below. It seems not to have occurred in post-apocope final position (see LHEB, §§88–89, and ‡97 below). Jackson argues that this development principally applies to the original clusters rather than to /l'γ/ and /r'γ/ by syncope, but that these sometimes developed in the same way, and that in fact in both types the /γ/ could be lost without giving /j/.[1095]

[53] No inscriptional evidence for this is cited; G would have been used for both /γ/ and /j/, as in Old Welsh. There are in any case very few examples of LG and RG in the Welsh corpus.

[1091] *AC*, 5th ser. 12 (1895), 186 (cf. EIHM, pp. 66, 125–26 and 472–73; LEIA C-52); Rhys reverts to the **E** in *AC*, 5th ser. 14 (1897), 328, but it is rejected by Macalister, *TCASFC*, 15, Part 40 (1922), 32.

[1092] *AC*, 5th ser. 13 (1896), 104; *Book of Leinster*, vi, ed. O'Sullivan, p. 1445. Ziegler omits this inscription (p. 280), and McManus, *Guide*, p. 65, reads '. . . AQ . . . QA . . . GTE'. Macalister has **Q . . . QA . . . GTE**, but according to KHJ there is 'No reason for the second gap; Q[ ] QAGTE is clear.' In fact there is a space before the **G**, whether or not it is significant. I agree with McManus about the **AQ**. There is no trace of **M** and there is no damage to the stone where the **I** of **M[A]Q[I]** would be, leaving open the possibility of apocopated **[M]AQ**.

[1093] Meyer, *Contributions*, pp. 295–96; CGH, p. 528; Ó Corráin & Maguire, *Gaelic Personal Names*, p. 40; LEIA C-3–4; Birkhan, *Germanen und Kelten*, p. 562; ADA, pp. 137–39. Cf. *Kaptus* in Holder i, 761.

[1094] e.g. 118 **VEQREQ**, Ziegler, p. 246.

[1095] LHEB, pp. 439 and n. 2 and 466, n. 4. See further ‡96 below and n. 1494.

[53] In 417/282 CAVOSENI ARGII the patronymic(?) *Argiios* is presumed to be the same as MW *eiry* 'snow';[1096] here the -RG- is in post-apocope final position. 418/283 BVRGOCAVI (if not BVRSOCAVI) can be compared with OB *Burg-* and *an uuorhic*, Mod.B. *bourc'h*, 'borough', MW *bwrch* 'rampart' (in *Armes Prydein*), OI *borg*, a Germanic loanword into Celtic which does not consistently conform to the native Brittonic development of **rg*.[1097] 1035/303 MARGITEUT (OW *Morgetiud, Margetiud, Margetud*, MW *Maredud*) and OB *Margit-hoiarn* (possibly related to OB *mergidhaham* 'I grow blunt') is presumably an example of the /rγ/ which gives /rj/, but it belongs to a cluster of Celtic words in *mVrk-/mVrg-* in which analogy and borrowing have confused normal phonetic developments.[1098] On the whole, however, MARGITEUT stands the best chance of being a relevant example. Yet there seem to be no contrasting spellings with LI or RI in the corpus.

[53] In 1014/231/908 GUORGORET < **wor-wo-ret-* the RG is simply orthographic, and the same is true of LG in 2022/253/984 GVLGVEN (or COVLGVEN) FILIVS EIVS, assuming that the second element is *gwyn/gwen* < **windos/-ā*.[1099] 971/35 GVRGUIN (if that is the reading, ‡66) is comparable.

[53] In 2034/871, the Royal Commission's reading B[E]LGICU looks like Latin *Belgicus* 'Belgic', and while this corresponds to Celtic **belg-* and might possibly have developed with /lγ/ > lj/, as in the case of cognates such as MW *boly, bolyon*,[1100] Latin influence might equally well impede this development and still more its representation in writing. More recently, however, Knight (followed in the *Corpus*) has read BELGINT. This is comparable with the Old Welsh names *Bledgint* (> MW *Bledynt* > *Bledyn* (Mod.W. *Bleddyn*)), *Congint/Cingint* (> *Cynyn*?), and *Mirgint*.[1101] According to Ifor Williams, *gynt* 'people' (< Latin *gens, gentis*) is the second element of *Bledgint*, which meant something like 'pertaining to the wolf race'.[1102] The first element of

---

[1096] LHEB, pp. 521 and 598–99 (preferring this segmentation to CAVO SENIARGII). On *argio-* see ‡36n. above.

[1097] DGVB i, 92; Gramm., pp. 126–27; HPB, p. 717; GPC, s.v. *bwrch*; Parry-Williams, *English Element in Welsh*, p. 35; LEIA B-72. According to Rhys, LWP, p. 379, BVRGOCAVI 'would mean "he who watches over, provides for, or takes care of the town"' (presumably Rhys was thinking of Latin *caveo* < **coveo*). Cf. Holder i, 640 and iii, 1005. *Burg-* is a common element in Germanic personal names.

[1098] See LHEB, p. 346; Williams, *Canu Aneirin*, p. 300; Chrest., p. 150; Gramm., pp. 126–27 and 192; DGVB i, 255; HPB, pp. 290, n. 1 (cf. ‡57n. below), 712 and 716 and n. 5. Cf. LEIA M s.vv. *mairg, marcad, marg, margréit, meirc, meircit* and *meirge*; Coates, ZCP, 38 (1981), 255–68.

[1099] See above, ‡‡ 22 and 80.

[1100] Carey, CMCS, 16 (1988), 77–83; Koch, CMCS, 20 (1990), 3–5.

[1101] LL, pp. 388, 392–93, and 413; Lloyd-Jones, *Geirfa*, s.n. *Bleδyn(t)*; and, for *Cynyn*, see ‡48 above. Birkhan, *Germanen und Kelten*, p. 42, compares *Blet-gint* (sic) with OHG *Megin-chint*.

[1102] *Canu Aneirin*, p. xxv; *Pedeir Keinc y Mabinogi*, p. 269; *Armes Prydein*, note on l. 131; BWP, p. 20. For *bled-* names see Lloyd-Jones, Y Geninen, 44 (1926), 12; Birkhan, *Germanen und*

BELGINT is unlikely to be MW *beleu* 'wild beast, wolf, marten', as this is not attested in its root form **bel (< **bhel-* 'bright').[1103] More likely, we have a metathesis *Bleðyïnt > *Belðyïnt > BELGINT /belɣïnt/, with loss of /ð/ in the awkward consonant cluster. If this is correct, BELGINT is not relevant to original /lɣ/ nor even to /l'ɣ/ arising by syncope. Its descendant in later Welsh, if it has one, may be *Belyn* – falling together, that is, with *Belenos* /*Belinos* > OW *Belin*, MW *Belyn*.[1104] 1016/234/907 CONBELIN (cf. 1023/239/927 [CO]NBELANI) cannot be held to contain ***belj-* < **belɣ-* because *Bellinus* is already attested in Roman Britain as a personal name and theonym.[1105]

‡54 The new quantity system; LHEB §35

No inscriptional evidence is cited, which is unsurprising since the use of double vowels is very rare in the corpus. 452/400 PAANI and the adjacent 451/401 DAARI are exceptions, probably Latin *Pa(g)ani* and Ir. *Dáiri*,[1106] while 327/43 PVVERI has VV for British Latin /uu̯/.[1107] In 971/35 CUURI[S] the vowel was always short /u/, according to Ifor Williams's equation with MW *Cerys* (his explanation of the UU spelling is differentiation of /u/ from /ü/, as in Mod.W. *w* versus *u*); and in 442/346 CATICVVS the Latin vowel is obviously short, assuming it *is* the Latin vowel[1108] – given that the other

---

Kelten, pp. 379–80, and Evans, *BBCS*, 24 (1970–72), 430. *Congint* and *Mirgint* will mean 'of the race of hounds' and 'of the race of the seas, the sea-rovers (Vikings?)'.

[1103] GPC, s.v. *belau*.

[1104] On the latter see Schrijver, *ZCP*, 51 (1999), 27–28, and citations in Richards, *THSC*, 1965, p. 37. MW *Bel*, *Bela*, and *Belyn* (Bartrum, *Welsh Genealogies 300–1400*, vii, 520) may all be diminutives of *Bleddyn* (M. Cane, pers. comm.).

[1105] RIB i 611 and 1027; Tab.Sulis, p. 147. See Holder i, 370–73 and iii, 827–28, and Maier, *Dictionary*, pp. 33–34, for *Belinus/Belenus*. A connection with W. *Beli* (LHEB, p. 352) was suggested by Koch, *CMCS*, 14 (1987), 23, but withdrawn by him, *CMCS*, 20 (1990), 6, n. 25, where he derives *Beli* from *Belgios*, with O'Rahilly, EIHM, p. 67. This is in turn rejected (in favour of *Belesos) by Schrijver, *ZCP*, 51 (1999), 31–34. Note moreover that if *Beli* is related to OB *Bili*, as suggested with reference to 3014/M5 HARENBILI in IEMB, pp. 82 and 218, that the latter does not show the Breton *l'ch* reflex of *lg.

[1106] See above, ‡18 for other suggestions as well. On AA cf. LWP, pp. 211 and 396.

[1107] LHEB, pp. 365–66; SBCHP, p. 328. Smith, VLRB, p. 917, notes *poveri* for *pueri* at Pompeii. Corresponding to 327/43 PVVERI the ogam has **MOSAC** (cf. 216 **MOSAC**) according to Macalister; Nash-Williams suggests **MAQI**, but KHJ notes that 'his drawing shows far fewer ogam letters than Macalister's, and he does not justify this reading'. **MOSAC** is obscure and difficult to connect with OI *mosach* 'filthy, stinking' (cf. LHEB, p. 171; LEIA M-65; McManus, *Guide*, pp. 72–73, 104 and 106; Ziegler, pp. 208 and 210). It must be just a coincidence that French *puer* (< *putere*) means 'to stink', as a dental was still present in the ninth century (Pope, *Latin to Modern French*, pp. 137 and 140). Ziegler, p. 202, notes that **MAGU** 'slave, follower' may appear in CIIC 272.

[1108] BWP, pp. 17–18; see ‡‡ 16n. and 37n. above. In CATICVVS we may have hypercorrection to avoid an error like *serus* for *servus* (see above, ‡14). Cf. VLRB, pp. 916 and 928, on RIB i 1534–35 COVVENTINAE. Note also 382/86 MELITVu (but could the last letter be a c-shaped sigma? cf. ECMW, pp. 195 and 227, on use of capital sigma). Double II is frequent (as in FILII etc., not for /i:/), and for examples of EE, with no obvious significance, see 1020/200/921 EE (Macalister); 421/294 R[V]STE{E}CE (presence of second E dubious in

name in 442/346 is Ir. MACCVDICCL (without termination, even in Lhuyd's day), it seems possible that CATICVVS is OI *Cathchú*, with VV for /u:/ and Latin -S (compare Rhys's explanation of 446/353 MAGLOCVVI (ogam **MAGLICUNAS**) and 454/402 DENCVI as Ir. *-cú* plus Latinate -I).[1109]

‡55 $\mu > \tilde{v}$; *LHEB §100*

No inscriptional evidence is cited for this. However, note that 1005/191/886, usually interpreted as BRANCU F[ECIT],[1110] could show the reflex of OW *-cum* < **-koimo-* if read BRANCUF. – Compare OC *Wincuf* and *Bleyðcuf* where Jackson notes that the *-f* is 'due to the influence of AS. spelling habits';[1111] Anglo-Saxon influence might also have been felt at Baglan in Glamorgan. Against this, however, note that the editors of the new *Corpus* see a wide space and colon between the U and F.

399/176 SIMILINI seems to be written with **B** instead of **M** in the ogam version, and while admitting that this is a very easy error in ogam script, Nash-Williams and Ifor Williams suggested that it might reflect a degree of denasalization, comparing + *Sibelini* (gen.) in the Lichfield Gospels ('Chad 8'). Jackson was sceptical, chiefly on the grounds of the early date he assigned to the inscription and to Chad 8's *Sibelini* (which he thought might either be some different name or be contaminated by *Cinbelin*, etc., as Williams and Nash-Williams had conceded).[1112] The main point to note here is probably that the ogam **B** may simply indicate that W. /μ/ was relatively less nasal than Ir. /μ/ to Irish ears.

1206/Ok4 DOVITHI is compared by Thomas with W. *dofydd*, which has been claimed to occur with denasalized spirant already in OW *douid* (better read *domid* !) in the nine Juvencus englynion (stanza 2c); DOVITHI, however, is probably an Irish name.[1113]

1009/193/935 EBISSA[R], 1013/222/912 EBISAR, and 1008/194/934

---

my opinion); 1069/OkPictApp.1 [E]ETON (?). KHJ notes that in ECMW fig. 29(a) Nash-Williams seems to draw 322/27 CAMVVLORIS. On double vowels in Old Cornish and Old Welsh see Olson & Padel, *CMCS*, 12 (1986), 45–46.

[1109] For *Cathchú* see Uhlich, *Morphologie*, p. 193. On DENCVI and MAGLOCVVI see above, ‡‡ 18n. and 35n.

[1110] LHEB, p. 484, n. 1; similarly RCAHMW. Macalister read BRANCU and took the F to be a cross.

[1111] LHEB, p. 486. Cf. Olson & Padel, *CMCS*, 12 (1986), 55.

[1112] Williams & Nash-Williams, *AC*, 92 (1937), 2–3; LHEB, pp. 483 and 484, n. 3; Uhlich, *Morphologie*, p. 22. The Welsh names in 'Chad 8' are assumed to have ceased in the time of 'Wynsi presul' (LL, p. xlvii), i.e. Wynsige, bishop of Lichfield 963 × 964–973 × 975 (on the form *Wynsi* cf. von Feilitzen, *Pre-Conquest Personal Names*, p. 116). If *Sibelini* is unrelated to *Similinus*, it and *Hiubilin* (LL, p. 175), may be composed of **Su-* (see ‡‡ 44n. and 46) or **Sub-*/**Sum-* on which see EANC, pp. 167–68. Note also OC *Sibillon*, discussed by Olson & Padel, *CMCS*, 12 (1986), 47.

[1113] Thomas, *Mute Stones*, pp. 158, n. 22, and 282; BWP, pp. 101 and 107; Haycock, *Blodeugerdd*, p. 10; McKee, *Juvencus*, p. 499; LHEB, pp. 483–44. See above, ‡‡ 42 and 51.

EBISAR (?) were explained by Rhys as Latin *emissarius* 'emissary, spy', with B /v/ for lenited /m/. This seems unlikely, in the absence of any example of *Emissarius* as a personal name.[1114]

‡*56 Completion of mb > mm (ng > ŋŋ ?); LHEB §§ 112.1, 3*
See ‡22 above.

‡*57 Internal i-affection in Pr.W.; LHEB §176*
Three of Jackson's examples of names lacking internal *i*-affection (pp. 610–11) are from the South-West and will be discussed in ‡64 below (473/a/Ok46 TORRICI, 490/Ok29 DATUIDOCI, and 492/Ok59 SABINI). Two other examples have to be excluded since internal *i*-affection is not in fact expected: if 320/26 ORVVITE is related to Mod.W. *Erwyd*, as accepted by Jackson, it would previously have developed – since it is clearly feminine – to *Orwed because of final *a*-affection;[1115] secondly, whereas Jackson expected that the first A of 385/89 ANATEMORI would have suffered internal *i*-affection like the first vowel of MW *eneid* < **anatio-*, Schrijver has shown that it is unlikely that the second A would have suffered final *i*-affection, the necessary condition to lead to **Eneidfawr rather than *Anadfawr.[1116] We must also be doubtful of the following of Jackson's examples since they may well have been regarded as Latin forms in which affection should not be written: 435/315 MARINI (cf. WCB *Merin*),[1117] 386/92 MARTINI (cf. OB *Merthin*, but MW *Marthin*),[1118] and 384/83 SANCTINVS (SANCE[R]INVS Macalister).[1119] I would also omit 1033/287 MARCIAU (> OW *Merchiau*) in view of the likelihood of influence from Latin *Marcianus* (Macalister actually read MARCIAU[N]), especially seing that native CELEN arguably *with* internal *i*-affection appears in the same inscription.[1120]

[1114] Rhys, *AC*, 5th ser. 16 (1899), 165, and *Englyn*, p. 52. For an alternative etymology, see ‡38.
[1115] See above, ‡15.
[1116] See above, ‡18. In the same way, whether the reading in 377/175 is AMICATI (Macalister cf. 500 AMMECATI) > *Amgad or AVICAT[VS ?] (Nash-Williams) > MW *Eugad*, no kind of *i*-affection was involved, according to Schrijver, SBCHP, pp. 268–76. The same applies to 1032/281 EWINI (Macalister: WINI), if this has *Eu-* < *Ou-*, and to 422/298 [H]OCIDEGNI (assuming for the sake of argument that this has a British /hogi-/; but it may have Ir. *Ócht*-like 450/390 HOGTINIS etc. (see above, ‡27n.).
[1117] Loth, *Noms des saints bretons*, p. 93; Williams, *Canu Aneirin*, p. 257; DP iv, 501; TYP, p. 430. Cf. Holder ii, 430. KHJ notes that *merin* 'sea' is probably from Celtic *morīn- rather than Latin *marīn*-, as it is not given in Lewis, *Elfen Ladin*. Cf. *Tremerin/Tremorinus*, etc.: Sims-Williams, *Britain and Early Christian Europe*, ch. 6, 128; Roberts, *BBCS*, 25 (1971–73), 276.
[1118] Loth, *RC*, 40 (1923), 45, n. 1; Chrest., p. 151; *Buchedd Sant Martin*, ed. Jones, passim. Cf. W. *Llanfarthin*, WATU, p. 118 (*Lanmartyn* in LL, pp. 322 and 328).
[1119] See above, ‡‡ 44n. and 50.
[1120] Cf. below and BWP, p. 30; LHEB, p. 611, n. 1; Koch, *SC*, 20/21 (1985–86), 51–52.

[57] To these Latin names we can add: 325/33 PAVLINI (cf. MW
Peulin);[1121] 360/139 PAVLINVS; 410/238/847 PAVLI[NI?]; 407/b/258/846
PAVLINVS; 435/315 PAVLINI (and MARINI above, plus LATIO without
final *i*-affection);[1122] 331/41 [A]NNICCI;[1123] 2002/a [ ]AUR[I]ANVS; 380/84
POTENTINI; 356/132/4 POTEN(t)INA; 350/116/3 DAVID; 418/283
SALVIANVS; 419/284 SALVIA[N]I; 1034/286 PASCENT[I];[1124] 421/294
PATERNINI;[1125] 505 AVITI (> OW *Eguid*??);[1126] 520/Scot.5 LATINVS.[1127]

[57] (A) This leaves the following among the examples listed by Jackson
(pp. 610–11) in which internal *i*-affection is not shown:

1.   381/87 ALIORTVS[1128]
2.   352A/122/5 BRAVECCI [> *Brewych*: *braw* 'terror'][1129]

[1121] Cf. SBCHP, p. 272, for the argument that *eu* is not due to affection anyway.

[1122] LATIO runs up to the present edge of the stone and may be incomplete. The personal name
Lat(t)ius is well attested; see Holder ii, 154 and 156; GPN, p. 216. *Lattio* (f.) occurs in RIB i
936 and *Latio* in Narbonensis and Pannonia (OPEL iii, 20). It is also the second element in
compound names like *Andolatius* and *Segolatius* (GPN, p. 216; ADA, p. 297), so perhaps
MARINILATIO ('sea-warrior'?) should not be divided. The -O could be an example of -*o*
for -*us*. Rhys, *Englyn*, p. 33, translates 'Paulinus Marinus of Latium' but adds: 'in Irish
Latinity the name Latium applied not only to the part of Italy so called, but also to any
place called in Irish Letha and in Welsh Llydaw.' Cf. Hogan, *Onomasticon*, s.n. *letha*;
Falileyev, *Etymological Glossary*, s.v. *litau* 'Latium'. Thomas, *Mute Stones*, p. 66, n. 35,
compares MARINI with RIB i 858 IVLIVS MARINVS (whose tombstone was erected by
MARITI[MA] !). *Marin(i)us* is very common, *Morinus* rare (OPEL iii, 58 and 87).

[1123] [E] does not fit the trace in Nash-Williams's drawing, although [I] would.

[1124] Affection to *Pesgynt* would be expected from *Pascentius*, but not from *Pascentus*.
Pascentia is attested in RIB ii [fasc. 2] 2420.34. Note 1000/182 PASCEN[T].

[1125] If starting from British Latin *Patarninus* (cf. Tab.Sulis, p. 147, *Patarnianus*), PATERNINI
could have affection, though not complete double affection to *Peterninus*.

[1126] Uhlich, *Morphologie*, p. 172. The OW -*d* rather than *-t* in all the forms cited by Uhlich is
troublesome.

[1127] Although on W. *Lledin* see ‡64n. below.

[1128] Foster, in *Prehistoric and Early Wales*, p. 217, comments on ALIORTVS ELMETIACO
that 'this "stranger" had doubtless come from Elmet in south Yorkshire', seemingly
understanding *Aliortus* as a Latin nickname 'stranger' (< Latin *alius + ortus*). This is
attractive, but note that the cognate Celtic element *allo-* (as in W. *alltud*) may also occur
as *alio-* (GPN, p. 133), and that there seems to have been a Celtic element *ortu-* (cf. RIG iv,
no. 219 ORTVBO; Galatian Ὀρτιαγων (*Orgiago* Livy), cited by Weisgerber in Geffcken FS,
p. 155; *Ortus* and *Atortus* in Holder ii, 881, and iii, 727), as well as *vorto-* (GPN, pp. 280–81).
With Foster's 'stranger' theory compare 193 **AILITHIR** (cf. Gippert, *CMCS*, 39 (2000), 93:
ALITHIR), OI *ailithir*, *allmuir*, W. *allfro*, *allmon*, *allmyr*, *alltud* (LEIA A-31 and 33; GPN,
p. 133; Uhlich, *Morphologie*, p. 130; SWWF, pp. 145–47). Ernault, cited by Holder i, 216,
and iii, 565, connected our ALIORTVS and P. AELI[O] ARIORTO (CIL iii 1559, from
Slatina, Dacia) with W. *iorth* 'diligent', but the older form of this was *e(h)orth* (GPC, s.vv.).
But ALIORTVS could be a dissimilated form of *Ariortus*, whatever the latter's etymology
may be.

[1129] See I. Williams, in Fox et al., *AC*, 97 (1942–43), 211; cf. GPN, p. 284. (405/228/845
GRAVICA (Macalister) is a distinct formation according to Ziegler, p. 186.) DOMNICI in
the same inscription (352A/122/5), whether from native *DUMNICI or Latin *Dom(i)nicus*
(with pre-nasal raising of /o/ > /u/), would result in *Dyfnig*, as Williams says, since /ö/ < /u/
was not affected (LHEB, pp. 590–91, although cf. Schrijver, *JIES*, 26 (1998), 425).

[57] The first group of names which can be added to these are ones in which a stressed composition vowel /o/ was in a position to be changed to /i/ (> /ï/) by final *i*-affection (‡19) and was then due to cause internal affection of the type seen in 995/133/24 ENEVIRI < *Anaworīks*. The relevant examples lacking internal affection are:

3. 330/66 CATIRI (> *Cedyr*)[1130]
4. 394/103 CANTIORI (> *Cenhyr*)[1131]
5. 361/140 TALOR[I] (> *Telyr*)[1132]
6. 2001 ORBIORI (> *Erfyr*; or if the reading ORBIORIT[is preferred, something like *Erfryd* would be expected)[1133]
7. 409/198/849 CARANTORIVS (> OW *Cerenhir*, W. *Cerennhyr*)[1134]
8. 2029/p.39i MAGLORI (> *Meilyr*); [also ERECOR rather than *ERECIR][1135]
9. 516/Scot.1 MAVORIVS (> *Mewyr* or *Meuyr* ?)[1136]

[1130] Assuming that this is not OI *Ca(i)thrí*. See above, ‡19.

[1131] Or (if with long *o*) *Cennur*, as argued by Gruffydd, *SC*, 24/25 (1989–90), 9, suggesting an emendation of MW *Cenuur* (but cf. OW *Cinmur, Cinuur*, LL, p. 392).

[1132] Cf. above, ‡38.

[1133] See above, ‡37. I am assuming that while the -IO- would not cause 'final' *i*-affection according to Schrijver's argument (SBCHP, pp. 268–76), its elimination by syncope would make way for internal i-affection by the appropiate following syllable. With *Erfyr* compare OW *Erbic, Eruic*, OC *Erbec* (Olson & Padel, *CMCS*, 12 (1986), 49, and EANC, p. 205), although see also below on IRBIC(I) < *Urbicus*. Cf. perhaps OW and MW *Erbin*, Mod.W. *Erfin* (LL, p. 234; EWGT, p. 188; EANC, p. 205). These could be derived from *Urbinus* if *E* = /ə/, or by an irregular Welsh development to /e/ similar to that in Breton (SBCHP, p. 166), or by an unusual internal *i*-affection (cf. the suggestion in SBCHP, p. 277, that /ə/ < /ï/ could give W. /e/ by internal *i*-affection); on the other hand, an easier starting point may be *Orbi-*, especially in view of the interchange of *Urbi-* and *Orbi-* discussed in GPN, pp. 238–39. If the second element in 2001 is -RIT- cf. GPN, pp. 249–51.

[1134] See ‡14 above. In addition to OW *Cerenhir* etc., Rhys, *AC*, 5th ser. 16 (1899), 136, compares OW *Cerennior* (EWGT, p. 12, HG §24), which is problematic.

[1135] ERECOR looks like another *-rīx* name. If so, -I or even gen. -IGAS should be restored if it is Irish, and if it is Welsh -I must be restored since if the W. -I had already been lost we would expect *ERECIR with final *i*-affection. The first element is probably Celtic *Erko-* 'speckled' with an epenthetic vowel (cf. ‡69). This svarabhakti is rare in Welsh (GMW, p. 12 cites *meirych ~ meirch*, and Morgan & Morgan, *Welsh Surnames*, p. 184, note *Rhydderch* > 'Retherech'; cf. *Llandaff Episcopal Acta*, ed. Crouch, p. 37) but it occurs in ogam in this very stem in the names ERACOBI and ERAQETAI in CIIC 84 (compared by RCAHMW) and in 32 ERACIAS; see Ziegler, pp. 52, 177–78 and 180. Note also *Heric* for *Ercc* in Tírechán, *Patrician Texts*, ed. Bieler, p. 257. As this personal-name element is characteristically Irish (see ‡48) it is probable that ERECOR[is an Irish name ER(E)CAR[I], spelt with the composition vowel O under British influence. A misreading of *ERECOBI is not impossible. 1057/Ok54 EROCAVI may be the same name (see ‡38). The Continental name *Eric(c)os*, discussed by Lejeune, *ÉC*, 31 (1995), 112–13, must be distinct.

[1136] Cf. a *Meuer* in *Black Book of St. David's*, ed. Willis-Bund, p. 314. Schrijver's discussion of *cavitatem* > *ceudod* in SBCHP, p. 271, implies that /au̯/ would normally yield *ew* by internal *i*-affection (unless syncope intervened first as in the case of *ceudod*), but on p. 272 he notes that in theory *Paulinus* > *Peulin* could be attributed to internal *i*-affection 'if this would not have resulted in MW *ew* (as Jackson assumes)'.

[57] In the following, the vowel preceding the composition vowel was not one in which internal *i*-affection would occur or be visible since I, E, and U would be unchanged (if not already syncopated): 320/26 CVLIDOR(I), assuming O is the composition vowel; 331/41 TECVRI; 322/27 CAMVLORIS; 443/349 CAMVLORI (preferable to CAMVMORI); 380/84 ICORI/ **ICORIGAS** (from the latter starting point, the composition vowel might be syncopated, giving **Igri*, again without scope for affection); 388/94 DERVORI; 396/104 AVITORI; 397/105 BECCVRI; 446/353 CLVTORI/**CLUTAR[I]** or **CLUTAR[IGAS]**; 2006 CVNORIX. In 354/126/6 ORDOVS < **Ordoviks* the final syllable probably collapsed too soon to cause final i-affection of the /o/.[1137] 415/278 TARRONERIS (Macalister) is obscure.

[57] Other cases without affection are:

10. 329/42 CANNTIANI (> **Ceiniawn*)
11. 341/71 **SALICIDUNI/SALICIDVNI** (or SALIGIDVNI) (cf. W. *helyg*; but probably Irish)
12. 346/75 ADIVNE *recte* ADIVNETI (Knight) (cf. W. *eiddun(ed)*)[1138]
13. 368/b/150 BARRIVENDI (cf. W. *Berwyn*; but quite possibly Irish)[1139]
14. 442/346 CATICVVS (cf. OB *Catic*, W. *Cedig*)[1140]
15. 514/Scot.8 CARANTI (assuming nom. *Carantius* > W. **Cereint* rather than *Carantus*)[1141]

[57] *If* the following are names of the MW *Berwyn* type (where syncope created the conditions for internal *i*-affection),[1142] note that they have vowels (E (short and long), I, U, O = /ö/) that would not show affection: 318/6 ETTORIGI; 325/33 BIVATIGI(*rni*) (or BIVATISI or similar); 2000 DEVORIGI; 397/105 CVNALIPI; 358/138 VOTEPORIGIS/**VOTE-CORIGAS**; 362/142 AVITORIA/**AVITTORIGES**; 413/272 MONEDORIGI; 435/315 CLVTORIGI;[1143] 1068/b CONDILICI.

[57] The following forms can hardly be included:
403/268/841 MACARITINI (Macalister: CARITINI) may be the Irish 40 **MAQI-CAIRATINI**, 230 **MAQI-CARATTINN** from OI *Cáerthann*, *Cáerthenn* 'Rowan', *Filius Cairt(h)in* (= *Macc Cáerthinn*) in Tírechán.[1144]

[1137] See above, ‡14.
[1138] See above, ‡15n.
[1139] See above, ‡22.
[1140] See above, ‡38. Of course, CATICVVS could be Irish; cf. ‡54.
[1141] Only *Carantus* occurs in RIB, but see both in Holder i, 768–71 and iii, 1093–94, GPN, p. 163, and Weisgerber, *Rhenania*, p. 448.
[1142] Cf. SBCHP, p. 275, n. 3, for reservations about *Berwyn* as a type-model. In 985/61 MORIDIC and 996/147 MO[RE]DIC syncope and hence internal *i*-affection did not occur; see above, ‡38.
[1143] On lack of affection in OW *Clotri*, see above, ‡46n.
[1144] Ziegler, p. 144; LEIA C-8; *Patrician Texts*, ed. Bieler, pp. 253 and 261. The MA could be the hypocoristic 'my' (OI *mo*) with the un-Irish spelling seen in 993/124/18 MADOMNUACO

On the other hand, Rhys, followed by Holder, thought it stood for
*Maceratini, a derivative of an attested Latin name Maceratus.[1145] In the
same inscription the patronymic BERIA[CI] (if that is the reading) may fail
to show affection of /e/, but as ei was often not written in Old Welsh this is
chronologically insignificant; and of course the E could be an affected A,
starting from *Barri̯ākos; the etymology is uncertain.

994/125/22 CAROTINN, while it could be a Welsh cognate of
Gaulish Caratinus (see ‡‡ 22 and 40), could also be the Irish Macc
Cáerthinn.[1146]

1024/255/926 NERTAT (Macalister: NERTtan !) is ambiguous, since even
in Middle Welsh ei was not to be written consistently in ne(i)rth(y)at.[1147]

In 408/229/848 CATOTIGIRNI (> OW Cattegirn) the lack of affection is
expected, due to the fact that the first vowel of the second element must
already have been /e/ as in MW teyrn, despite the frequent spelling
with i.[1148]

In 1035/303 MARGITEUT the absence of affection is not significant, since
this name (Maredudd) appears with a (and o) in Old Welsh.[1149]

1024/255/926 BRANCIE (Macalister) is a dubious reading.

Finally, 2006 MAQVI COLINE is of course Irish, not W. Celyn.

[57] (B) Jackson does not give a full list of examples where internal i-
affection has happened, but simply gives early examples (pp. 598 and
610–11). Leaving aside his suggestion that the second A of 385/89
ANATEMORI stands for /æ/,[1150] his examples are:

1.   1033/287 CELEN (= MW celein 'corpse' < *kolanio-, or, according to
Ifor Williams, Celyn 'holly' < *kolino-) [note also that Williams' ERTRI 'the
three' could be a personal name, *Erthri < *Artorīg-, cognate with OI Artrí
and MW Erthir below][1151]

2.   995/133/24 ENEVIRI (= W. Enewyr < *Anaworīx)[1152]

(see p. 321). MACARITINI or CARITINI can hardly be the W. collective cerddin 'rowan-
trees', e.g. in view of the T, and the same applies to 994/125/22 CAROTINN.

[1145] LWP, pp. 386–87 (it is not in RIB). Evans, GPN, p. 365, n. 1, cites DAG §214 (p. 820), who
in turn cites Holder ii, 363 (our inscription) and 367 (Macerati). For Macerati Rhys and
Holder cite Desjardins, Notice, p. 136, who gives it as a potter's name from Lezoux
(Oswald).

[1146] See Ch. 3, p. 256, n. 11 (re col. 19).

[1147] Williams, AC, 87 (1932), 236, and Canu Aneirin, p. 101; GPC, s.vv. Cf. WG, p. 122.

[1148] Cf. SBCHP, p. 64; NWÄI, p. 535, n. 59. The non-affection in Cattegirn usefully fixes the
date of /ï/ > /e/ here to before internal i-affection. See ‡74n. below. Cf. also OI Ca(i)tchern,
Uhlich, Morphologie, p. 188.

[1149] See above, ‡53. In view of this, it was probably unnecessary for Jackson to explain the lack
of affection in OB Margithoiarn as an archaic spelling, HPB, p. 290, n. 1.

[1150] Cf. SBCHP, p. 273.

[1151] BWP, pp. 35–36 and 39–40; CGH, p. 513. Williams notes that ARTRI is also a possible
reading. See below, on [E]RTIRIE and MW Erthir.

[1152] Misprinted ENEVERI in Nash-Williams. See above, ‡19.

[57] To these we can add:

3. 1009/193/935 EBISSA[R] if < biblical *Abisur* ('father of oxen') or a similar Semitic name, as suggested above[1153]
4. 1008/194/934 EBISAR (?)
5. 1013/222/912 EBISAR
6. 1014/231/908 ENNIAUN[1154]
7. 1022/240/928 GREFIUM < Latin *graphium* (cf. OW *grefiat*)[1155]
8. 1032/281 WLEDER[1156]
9. 1064/Dor.iv [D]ENIEL < *Daniel* (at Wareham in Dorset, so it may count as South-Western and belong in ‡64 below).[1157] AUPRIT, in the same Dorset inscription, shows no trace of the affection one might expect if the second element is W. *pryd*, 'shape, form'.[1158] If the first element is **Awi-*, however, with **Awi-pritu-* giving W. **Eubryd*, note that **Awi- > *Eu-* occurred irrespective of the vowel in the second element of such compounds.[1159] Similarly, if it is acephalous and the first element is [M]AU- < **magu-* (cf. OW *Meuprit*, ‡25), note that this would not necessarily be liable to *i*-affection to ***MEU-*; the development *Meu- < Mou- < Mau-* which occurs in forms like W. *Meugan*, OW *Moucan* (versus OC *Maucan)* is clearly unrelated to such affection.[1160] As it stands, however, AUPRIT can possibly be taken as a Germanic name such as OE *Ælfred* or *(E)aldfrith*, transmitted with the French *Au- < *Al-.*[1161]
10. 2008/82]ESILLIMARIGUELIO (so printed by Nash-Williams but not apparently acephalous in his figure and plate) looks as though it includes a hypercorrect, post-internal-*i*-affection, version of OE *Merewalh*

[1153] ‡38. For another explanation see ‡55 above (*emissarius*).

[1154] See above, ‡22.

[1155] Jenkins & Owen, *CMCS*, 7 (1984), 106.

[1156] See above, ‡14n.

[1157] For the restoration and analysis see Radford & Jackson, in RCHM, *Dorset*, ii/2, p. 312; and ‡59 below. McClure, *EHR*, 22 (1907), 729, had already identified [D]ENIEL with OB *Deniel* in the Cartulary of Redon.

[1158] As suggested by Radford & Jackson, in RCHM, *Dorset*, ii/2, p. 312. See ‡25 above.

[1159] Schrijver, SBCHP, pp. 270 and 275, argues that the development of **Awi- > Eu-* did not involve affection, but rather loss of /i/ at syncope followed by pretonic /au/ > /ou/ > /ëü/ (see ‡80 below). AUPRIT would thus reflect the immediately post-syncope stage. Contrast the non-syncopated **awintros* or **awontīr* > W. *ewythr*, OC *euitor* (GPC, s.v.; Stüber, *Historical Morphology*, p. 110).

[1160] In SBCHP, pp. 270–72, Schrijver argues that /au/ > /ou/ > /ëü/ was regular pretonically (cf. HPB, pp. 251–52 and 262–63). If so, names like OC *Maucan* (> *Mawgan*, Olson & Padel, *CMCS*, 12 (1986), 47) and OW *Caurtam* (EWGT, s.n. *Cawrdaf*, cf. Hamp, *ÉC*, 14 (1974), 188) versus *ceuri* 'giants' have to be explained analogically, presumably from the monosyllabic forms *maw* and *cawr*. (In the case of *Maucan* compare 486/Ok56 MAVCI, presumably a late compound of C. *maw* and *ci* 'hound', ‡25 above.) The variation between *Mawgan* and *Meugan* (< *Moucan*) has also been attributed to variation between **magu-* and **mogu-*; see LHEB, p. 441; Sims-Williams, *JEH*, 43 (1992), 468–69. R. J. Thomas, *BBCS*, 8 (1935–37), 32, suggested that *Meugan* is a hypocoristic in *M'* from *Avicantus*. Cf. in general ‡80 below.

[1161] See ‡25 above.

('famous Welshman'), a name which passed into use in Wales as *Merguall, Mergualdus*.[1162]

[57] A few obscure forms which *may* contain affection are:

1000/182 ELISEG is of uncertain etymology (biblical *Elise*?), but there is no reason to suggest **A-*.[1163]

2022/253/984 [? B]ERER[could be for *Beryr < *Barrorīx, although AERERN is an alternative reading.

1007/206/938 IRBIC or IRBICI can only be derived via OW *Erbic, Eruic*, from **Orbi(o)*- by assuming a Breton-style 'secondary affection' of /e/ > /i/ (‡85), and it is probably easier to start from the Latin name *Urbic(i)us* and assume a regular pretonic development of /u/ > /ö/ > /ə/, with I- (and perhaps some cases of E-) being spellings of the /ə/ of *Yrfyg.[1164]

1068/b (Man) BRENLIER (or BREDLIEN), if < Brittonic *brano-, which is doubtful.[1165]

511/Scot.10 [E]RTIRIE (Macalister: [TV]RTIRIE), with feminine *-i(a)e* (like CONINIE on the same stone for OI *Conind*), looks like an already-affected reflex of *Artorīg- (if not a recomposed *Arth + ri*), cognate with MW *Erthir* (Black Book of Carmarthen = *Erthyr? < *Artorīks), but it has to be remembered that the restoration [+ E]RTIRIE was originally suggested by Ifor Williams on the basis of this MW comparison![1166]

‡58 $ē^i$ > Pr.W. [and Pr.CB.] ui; LHEB §28.3

I include the change in Cornish and Breton here, since Jackson states that it was 'very likely more or less contemporary' with that in Welsh (p. 335). For the development of $ē^i$ (Jackson's $ę̄^i$) from $ē$ (Jackson's $ę̄$) < IE *ei* see ‡24 above.

[1162] Sims-Williams, *Religion and Literature*, pp. 47–48. Cf. MW *Merwallt*: Pierce, *BBCS*, 18 (1958–60), 259.

[1163] Cf. *Alis*- in GPN, pp. 305–7. For *Elise*, see above, ‡39.

[1164] For *Urbic(i)us* see Holder iii, 37–39 and GPN, p. 239, n. 2, and RIB passim, also Tomlin & Hassall, *Britannia*, 31 (2000), 438–39 and 442. For *Urbicus* alongside Celtic names see Weisgerber, *Rhenania*, pp. 90 and 222. Note OW + *urpci.bre*[sbiter?] in 'Chad 8', LL, p. xlvii. The early OC *Erbec* (Olson & Padel, *CMCS*, 12 (1986), 49) is not an objection to derivation from *Urb*-, since this would have become Pr.C. *Orb- and then undergone regular internal *i*-affection to *Erb*-. Note, however, that the complication that OW *Erb* occurs as a simplex in LL, p. 398 (possibly the same as MW *Yrp*, TYP, p. 523, but Jones, *ZCP*, 16 (1927), 166, derives this from ON *Erpr*), possibly < *Orbios, or possibly extracted from *Erbic* etc. Koch, *Gododdin*, p. cxxii, derives OW *Erbic* from Celtic *Orbo-cū. Probably Celtic *Orb(i)(o)*- and Latin *Urbi*- co-existed and maybe sometimes crossed; see GPN, pp. 238–39. A stem *Urbic*- appears in Iberian toponymy: Curchin, *Emerita*, 65 (1997), 276. For *Orbic(i)us* see OPEL iii, 116.

[1165] See ‡57 below for *brano-.

[1166] Apud MacDonald, *PSAS*, 70 (1935–36), 38. [A]RTIRIE is impossible if Jackson, in RCAHMS *Peeblesshire*, i, 176, was right to reject [MA]RTIRIE because 'the fragmentary letter cannot be A'. He rejects TVRTIRIE as 'fanciful, both epigraphically and philologically'.

[58] I have argued elsewhere that the diphthongization in all the Brittonic languages must have preceded the new quantity system (‡54 above), when all long vowels were shortenened before /CC/; and Schrijver has argued that diphthongization probably developed before internal *i*-affection (‡57 above), since that would explain the lack of affection in MW *halwyn* 'salt' < **saleino-*.[1167]

[58] (A) Jackson does not quote the inscriptional evidence for this change, so his allusion (p. 333) to 'the two fifth- and early sixth-century inscriptions quoted' is an uncharacteristic oversight. He was probably referring to the second and third items on the following list (the first being then unknown), for elsewhere he dates them 'end of the fifth century' and 'early sixth century' respectively:[1168]

1. 2000 DEVORIGI (**deiwo-* > OW *duiu*)[1169]
2. 394/103 [V]ENEDOTIS (> MW *Gwyndot*)[1170]
3. 392/77 VERACIVS[1171]
4. 408/229/848 VEDOMAVI (Macalister: or VEDOMALI): W. *gŵydd* 'wild' < **weid-* (ogam VEDA-, VEDDO-)[1172]
5. p. 397/285 CARANTEI (?) (**Karantēios* (or *-ĕios*) > **Carannwy* ?)[1173]

[1167] Sims-Williams, in *Britain 400–600*, pp. 254–55, and *BBCS*, 38 (1991), 48–49 (cf. SBCHP, p. 252); TRC, pp. 158–63; SBCHP, pp. 243 and 359. Note that 374/172 CVNEGNI is not included below as a name which has not yet developed /ui/ since it may well be Irish (see above, ‡48); similarly 2025/Scot.12 NEITANO is not included (despite MW *Nwython*) since it is probably not a purely Brittonic form (see above, ‡51).

[1168] e.g. LHEB, pp. 192 and 291. (On p. 279 CIIC 408 is 'mid to later sixth century', although *c.* 550 is given by Fox & Fox, *Antiquity,* 8 (1934), 401, a reference cited in KHJ's unpublished notes.)

[1169] Sims-Williams, *TAAS*, 1999, p. 147; but DEVORIGI could be Irish, as noted in ‡38 above.

[1170] Cf. *Gwynedd*, with /ui/: LHEB, pp. 188, n. 1, 551, n. 3, and 655; SBCHP, p. 250. Differently Charles-Edwards, *BBCS*, 24 (1970–72), 117–18 (opposed by Hamp, *BBCS*, 28 (1978–80), 215, and *PHCC*, 12 (1992), 46–48, and by Koch, *Gododdin*, p. xcvii, n. 2). Cf ‡‡13 and 42 above.

[1171] KHJ queries whether this is *Vērācius:* W. *gŵyr* 'crooked', as against Rhys's equation (LWP, p. 366) with OW [*villa*] *Guroc* (LL, p. 179) which 'presumably means *Virācius*' (cf. Lewis, *ZCP*, 20 (1936), 139, for *Twrog/Mwrog/Gwrog < *Wirākos*). On the other hand, in LHEB, p. 291, Jackson, like Holder, derives *Warocus* in Gregory of Tours from **Verācius* (actually attested in Italy, Pannonia and Dacia: OPEL iv, 156; Holder iii, 110 and 180, and cf. *Varucius, Veraciacus, Veracus, Verax, Verecius, Vericius, Veruc(c)ius, Viracius,* and *Voracius* s.nn.), so perhaps a late change of mind over the quantity of the /e/ lies behind the oversight mentioned above?

[1172] LHEB, p. 482; Ziegler, pp. 118 and 242; Hamp, *SC*, 18/19 (1983–84), 129.

[1173] No exact parallel is cited in Holder i, 767 or GPN, p. 163, but compare Koch's comparison of *-wy* in Welsh river-names with Romano-British ones in *-eia, SC,* 20/21 (1985–86), 46 (cf. Sims-Williams, *BBCS*, 38 (1991), 53 and 59) and see SBCHP, pp. 289–90. One could perhaps also compare *Cocceius* (OPEL ii, 67, e.g. in RIB ii [fasc. 5] 2491.88 from Clwyd) with OW *Cocboy/Chochui*, MW *Cogwy* (Williams, *BBCS*, 3 (1926–27), 59–62), allowing for some textual corruption. CARANTEI is not included in LHEB. KHJ was doubtful that Macalister's -TEI was ligatured and thought it might be merely -TI. Cf. Nash-Williams,

6. 479/Ok16 CVNAIDE (Macalister and Thomas; Okasha: CVNATDO): MW *Cynaethwy* < **Kun(o)-akt-* (if not **Kintu-* > *Cynh-*)[1174]

7. 477/Ok11 CONETOCI, assuming that this is a derivative (in **-ākos*) of the stem seen in Romano-British *Cunetio* (place name derived from river name), OW *Conet, Conuit*, OB *Conet, Conoit, Chunuett*, OW *arx Cynuit*, W. *Cynwyd* (personal name and place name)[1175]

[58] A further relevant form may be 1063/Dor.ii IUDNNE if it is OW *Iudne*, possibly an archaic form of *Iudnoe* or **Iudnui*; however, IUDNNE[RTH] or even IUDNNO[E] are possible readings (see ‡86). It seems doubtful whether the difficult 3026/I7 GENNOVEUS has *-eus* as more than a Latinate ending. Its *-OV-* may be the common OB hypocoristic *-ou* which seems to come from (or co-exist with?) earlier *-oe*, corresponding to W. *-eu* beside *-wy*, but there is no real reason to derive these from an earlier /-e:/.[1176] A possible further example is 1060/Ok57 GURGLES if the second element is cognate with W. *glwys* 'pleasant' < **glēs-* (cf. Ir. *glésse* 'brightness').[1177] Baring-Gould,

---

who takes the name to be genitive of *Carantus*. Schumacher, *Historical Morphology*, pp. 174–75, argues that the river names in *-eia* (see Holder i, 1410) had short *e* and that **eiiV* (< **eiHV*) developed to *-wy*.

[1174] For *Cynaethwy* see Lloyd-Jones, *Geirfa*, p. 243; BWP (2nd edn only), p. 180, n. 16; Gruffydd, in Mac Cana FS, pp. 40 and 47; Morgan & Morgan, *Welsh Surnames*, pp. 70–71; *St Davids Episcopal Acta*, ed. Barrow, p. 93 (*Gwaret filio Kinhaidi*). I assume that the *h* in forms like *Kanhaethoe* (EWGT, p. 46) is inorganic, though *Cynhaethwy* is the normalization in Bartrum, *Welsh Genealogies 300–1400*. On the *-aeth-* see ‡51. Hitherto CVNAIDE has been regarded as a feminine equivalent, with Latin gen. *-E*, of a Pr.Ir. **Cunaido-* (LHEB, 329, n. 1; Uhlich, *Morphologie*, p. 210; cf. LWP, p. 216; Thomas, *Mute Stones*, pp. 193 and 196, n. 29). As Thomas queries Jackson's evidence, I note that KHJ referred to OI names in *-aed* 'fire' (*u*-stem and *n*-stem), gen. *-AIDONAS*, like *Conaed* (m.) in Meyer, *Contributions*, p. 458. Cf. Birkhan, *Germanen und Kelten*, p. 347; Ziegler, p. 98; Stüber, *Historical Morphology*, pp. 91 and 102. The idea of a female name is due to the *-E* and the old idea that MVL[IER] appeared on the stone (Rhys, *AC*, 4th ser. 6 (1875), 365; Hübner, *Inscriptiones Britanniae Christianae*, no. 7; cf. Macalister, *AC*, 84 (1929), 183: 'the only ancient epigraphic memorial to a woman in Cornwall'). Unfortunately, no Irish female names containing *áed* have yet been cited; if the *-aed* idea is retained, it might be best to regard *-E* as the Latin m. gen. sg. *-i* misspelt owing to Irish confusion of /-i/ and /-e/ (see below, Ch. 4, §22). KHJ probably did not compare *Cynaethwy* (a) because he did not recognize that *-e* was used for later *-ui* (see Sims-Williams, *BBCS*, 38 (1991), 50), and (b) because he dated 479/Ok16 fifth-century, although adding: 'Note that Le Blant treats *hic requiescit in hoc tumulo* etc. as characteristic of his 6th-7th cent. inscriptions' (cf. Knight, in *Early Church in Wales and the West*, p. 48: 454 AD onwards in Gaul). The name *Cunaito* (Alföldy, *Noricum*, p. 234) can hardly be connected.

[1175] For these forms see Williams *apud* Richmond & Crawford, *Archaeologia*, 93 (1949), 30; PNRB, p. 328; Jones, *BBCS*, 25 (1972–74), 109–10; Coates & Breeze, *Celtic Voices*, pp. 126–28, 271, 292 and 337; Loth, *Noms des saints bretons*, p. 25; Olson & Padel, *CMCS*, 12 (1986), 46; Orme, *Devon & Cornwall Notes & Queries*, 37 part 2 (1992), 55–58, and *Dedications*, p. 97 (*Cenewit, Cunetus*). On *Conet* see above, ‡18n.

[1176] Gramm., p. 403; SBCHP, pp. 295 and 303. Perhaps cf. OB *genou* 'mouth' (DGVB i, 175; Gramm., p. 80), as well as 469/Ok34 (G)ENAIVS. Holder i, 2000 has a Spanish estate *Genavia*.

[1177] It may be difficult to reconcile retention of E with the initial GU- (see ‡76). GURGLES cannot be compared with OB *Gurloies* etc., and with Geoffrey of Monmouth's Cornish

Radford and Thomas, however, read GUNGLEI, which Baring-Gould and Rhys thought could be a Latinized form of W. *Gwynllyw* 'or some cognate form': compare *Gundleius, Gundleus, Gunleius*, etc.[1178] This is difficult since no forms with *-g-* are attested or indeed expected since *llyw* is the second element.[1179] Other obscure readings, GUNIGLEI, GUMGLEI, and GUNGLEL, are noted by Okasha.

[58] (B) The change to /ui/ has happened in the following:

1. 980/46a S(*ignum*) S(*ancti*) (or S(*cribae*)) LIGUE (Nash-Williams: WLIGUE; Macalister: WUMERE, WILMERE, or WALMERE), accepting Radford's unpublished reading and interpretation of 'SS' (quoted in *Corpus*). Radford compared the place name *Din Lligwy* (Anglesey), but the problem here is that *Lligwy* seems to derive from earlier *Llugwy*.[1180] It is better to compare *llywy* 'fair, bright, fair one', which occurs as an Old Welsh personal name *Liugui, Legui, Leui*, MW *Llywy*, and also in Old Breton, *Louui, Leugui*.[1181] This is of course assuming that the *-ui* here is from earlier /e:/.[1182]

2. 984/59 BLEDRUS < OW *Bledruis*, also *Bledris*, < ?*-rei-sko-*.[1183]

---

duke *Gorlois*, despite Rhys, *AC*, 6th ser. 18 (1918), 192, since none of the OB forms shows a medial *-g-*: see Hutson, *British Personal Names*, pp. 60–61 and 121, esp. n. 51. On the element *lo(i)es* see HPB, p. 712, n. 2. On the GUR- of GURGLES see ‡‡ 26n and 28 above. Rhys, *AC*, 4th ser. 6 (1875), 362, compared W. *Gwrlais*, citing *Iolo Manuscripts*, ed. Williams, p. 257 (Iolo Morganwg's version of *Englynion y Clywaid*), and MA, p. 461 (*Brut Tysilio*). This is simply Geoffrey's *Gorlois*, and runs up against the same objection; cf. Jones, *BBCS*, 13 (1948–50), 74; Roberts, *BBCS*, 25 (1972–74), 278.

[1178] Baring-Gould, *AC*, 6th ser. 18 (1918), 196 (quoting Rhys); Radford, *DASP*, 27 (1969), 81; Thomas, *Mute Stones*, p. 290; VSB, p. 330; Wmffre, *Language and History*, i, 349. For OW *u* for *ui* cf. *clus* corrected to *cluis* in the Juvencus, BWP, p. 111. Radford's citation is in passing, and is not presented as a correction to Macalister (cf. Thomas, *Mute Stones*, p. 302, n. 47). In 1951 KHJ found **gurgles** 'quite clear and pretty much as [in Macalister's drawing], except that' the shape of the **r** was different, i.e. with a descender at the beginning [hence the readings with **m** or **n**].

[1179] W. *nll* did not develop when /ɣ/ intervened (WG, p. 181), so *glyw* cannot be the second element of *Gwynllyw* – although it could be of GUNGLEI.

[1180] Thomas, *BBCS*, 8 (1935–37), 33–35.

[1181] Ibid., pp. 35–36; Williams, *Canu Aneirin*, pp. 258 and 286; GPC s.v.; LL, pp. 231–32 and 235–36 (probably wrongly equated with biblical *Levi* in Sims-Williams, *BBCS*, 38 (1991), 52; cf. LHEB, p. 442, n. 2); *Englynion y Beddau*, I.70, ed. Jones, *PBA*, 53 (1967), 132 (feminine); BWP, p. 180; Gruffydd, in Mac Cana FS, p. 47; Gramm., p. 66.

[1182] See on river names above, n. 1173; but see also possibilities noted in SBCHP, pp. 294 and 302.

[1183] LL, pp. 185 and 221–22; cf. EWGT, p. 172, s.n. *Bledrus*. The second element may be *rhwys(g)* 'rush, attack', on which see Lloyd-Jones, *BBCS*, 2 (1923–25), 295, GPC, Williams, *Poems of Taliesin*, p. 30, and J. E. C. Williams, *Celtica*, 21 (1990), 678 (< **ro-eisk-*; but perhaps compare instead OI *ríasc* 'marsh' < **rei-* 'flow' (+ **-sko-*) as in *rían* 'sea', LEIA R-27–28, and note *nant Ruisc* in LL, p. 143 – is *Wysg* mis-segmented from e.g. *pont/Caerllion ar *Rwysg* or *Caer *Rwysg*?). Loth, *RC*, 31 (1910), 165, n. 1, has *rhwysc* < **reid-sco-*. A contraction of OW *Bledruis* may be seen in the name *Bledrws* (LW, p. 61), as in the place name *Betws Bledrws*, Ceredigion (WATU, s.n., 13c *Bet(h)us Bledrus*, Wmffre, *Language and History*, i, 327), although this may instead have a Welsh diminutive *-ws* (cf. Richards,

3.   1000/182 GUOILLAUC (= *Gwylog*, OW *Guilauc*) and POUOIS (with -OIS < *-ēs- < *Pagenses),[1184] also BRITU (= *Brydw* or *Britw*) if this is comparable with MW *Gronw* < *Gronwy* and OB *Britou* < (?) *Britoie* and these have original /e:/, which is far from certain.[1185]

4.   1023/239/927 GLIUISSI = W. *Glywys*, if from *Glevensis* 'man of Gloucester' rather than *glyw* 'lord' + -*ys*.[1186]

5.   1024/255/926 GLIGUIS (= *Glywys* again) and possibly the obscure BRANTUI, with NT perhaps for /nd/ < /n'δ/ in *Brandui < *Brano-deiwos 'raven-god'; in Irish compare 288 **DEBRANI** < ?*Deiwo-branos,[1187] and cf. MAELDOI below.

6.   489/b/Ok13   SAGRANVI = **Sa(e)ranwy*,   a   hybrid   Irish-Cornish name?[1188]

7.   2035 (Spoleto, Italy) + GUIL, presumably *gŵyl* 'modest, kind, happy', an element in e.g. OW *Guilbiu*, which occurs alone as a woman's name, MW *Gvyl verch Endavt*.[1189]

8.   3008/C3 MAELDOI < *Maglo-deiwos.

9.   3017/M8 RIMOETE < **Rīgo-meit-* (or -*d*- ??) (: OI *míad*, OB *muoet* [*sic*], *Moet-*).[1190]

10.   1033/287 TENGRUIN was read TENGRUI or, rather, CENGRUI by Ifor Williams, who suggested an element -*grui* (comparing *Creirwy*, which he analysed *Crei-rwy* rather than *Creir-wy*), but the existence and etymology of

---

THSC, 1965, p. 38) – note in particular the OC cognate *Bleðros* in Bodmin, pp. 87, 91, 94. In favour of the equivalence of -*os* and -*ws* note *Gunos* in LL, p. 221, which recalls Mod.W. *Gwnnws* (see ‡22n.), and OW *brunus* = ? Mod.W. *brwynos* in n. 964 above. Apart from *Bledruis* the only other name in -*ruis* in LL is *Athruis* which may be *Athr-uis* (cf. Sims-Williams, *BBCS*, 38 (1991), 52, and CBT i, 169), but with *Bledris* cf. *Eneuris*, *Gu(o)retris*, and *Morcim(b)ris* (*Lifris* is < OE *Leofric* and *Emris/Emrys* is < *Ambrosius*), also OW *Iudris* and MW *Maelrys* (EWGT, s.nn. *Idris* and *Maelrys*); however some of these may be compounds of OW *Ris/Rys* (Lloyd-Jones, *Y Geninen*, 44 (1926), 11, has *Idris* < *iudd-rys* : *Rhys*; cf. Gramm., p. 96). An unlikely Irish etymology of *Bledrus* could involve OI *rús* (cf. *rús con*, LEIA R-54).

[1184] EWGT, p. 195 (and see below on 2035 GUIL); LHEB, pp. 91 and 443–44.

[1185] EWGT, p. 173; IEMB, p. 208 on 3013/M4 BRIT[; cf. SBCHP, pp. 293 and 302.

[1186] Sims-Williams, in Mac Cana FS, p. 220; cf. Williams, *AC*, 87 (1932), 236. On *glyw* see SBCHP, p. 236. On the quantity of the first *e* in *Glevensis* see ‡84n. below.

[1187] Ziegler, p. 164, takes the DE- to be 'two' and compares OI *Dub-dá-braine* (CGH, p. 599; cf. O'Brien, *Celtica*, 10 (1973), 227), but in such names *Da* is generally regarded as a form of *día* 'god': EIHM, pp. 128–29; McCone, *Ériu*, 35 (1984), 6; cf. differently LEIA D-6–7, citing Lambert, in Lejeune et al., *ÉC*, 22 (1985), 168, n. 84: *da* 'fille'. BRANTUI resembles 2038 BRANHUI (considering the late OW use of *nh* for the nasal mutation of /nt/, LHEB, pp. 504–5), but can hardly be related since a segmentation BRANT-UI makes no sense.

[1188] See ‡48 above. This is again assuming that the -VI has an appropriate etymology.

[1189] EANC, pp. 147–48; TYP, pp. 157 and 403. Cf. Ir. *Fial*, also female: CGSH, p. 177; O'Rahilly, *Celtica*, 1 (1950), 365–66. These are to be distinguished from the loans from Latin *velum* and *vigilia* (SBCHP, pp. 225, 234 and 242).

[1190] See IEMB, p. 245, and LEIA, M-47; DGVB i, 62–63; HPB, p. 207, n. 5. The dental is a problem with the Irish cognate.

that element is uncertain.[1191] The probable reading is TENGR*um*UI, as suggested in ‡48 above.

[58] Obscure or rejected forms include:
2038 BRANHUI, which Jackson equates with OW *Brangui* < *Branoụio-.[1192]
2008/82]ESILLIMARIGUELIO, maybe *Esyllt + Mari + Gŵyl* as above, but more likely *Esyllt + Merewalh* (see ‡57).
1018/236/919 ILQUICI may have *gwig* < Latin *vicus* as the second element.[1193]
415/278 IN[G]ENVI (Macalister: IN[TA]ENVI) is probably genitive of Latin *Ingenuus*, as in 466/Ok23 INGENVI /**INGENAVI**.[1194]
434/314 COIMAGNI is not Welsh but is OI *Cóemán*, which can only be related to W. *Cwyfan* as the source from which *Cwyfan* was borrowed.[1195]
480/Ok19 ALSUE CURAVIT is only one possible reading (others are LVRATECVS FECIT and ALSNE CURAVIT) and it has no obvious etymology.
1053/Ok1 ULCUI looks like an (Irish-?)Cornish (hybrid?) name based on (Q-?)Celtic *wlk^{w}o- 'wolf' (as in OI *Olcán* < ULCAGNI), perhaps like *Ylched* in *Llechylched* in Anglesey,[1196] but this is of course uncertain and there are alternative readings.
3007/C2 VORMVINI cannot be included since VORM-VINI (: W. *gwyn*) is equally as likely as VOR-MVINI (: W. *mwyn*, OC *muin*, OB *moin*).[1197]
3005/F5 VENOMAILI may be related to W. *gwyn*[1198] or MW *Gwên* (cf. 400/177 VINNEMAGLI), rather than to *Gwynedd* (cf. 394/103 [V]ENEDOTIS).
454/402 DENCVI appears to be a Welsh -*wy* name (if not the genitive of a Latinate -*uus*), based on the Celtic root *denk- seen in Irish in 442/346 MACCVDICCL (Lhuyd) and Ir. *Déclán* < *denk-lo-.[1199] But if Rhys's suggestion that DENCVI may be DEN[O]VI is correct, the first syllable will have an E that has not been diphthongized; it would probably be Irish (: OI *Dían-*), however, like 279 **DENAVEC[A]** (*dēno-vik-s*).[1200] Compare also 462/Ok14 QVENATAVCI IC DINVI FILIVS, where the Q-Celtic context suggests that DINVI may also be related in some way.[1201]

[1191] BWP, pp. 27–30; cf. TYP, pp. 311 and 547.
[1192] LHEB, p. 392, n. 2; cf. SBCHP, pp. 296–97.
[1193] See above, ‡38n.
[1194] Williams, rev. of CIIC i, *THSC*, 1943–44, p. 156; LHEB, p. 366.
[1195] See above, ‡48.
[1196] Ibid.
[1197] The OB *oi* spelling is no problem: SBCHP, pp. 220–21, 226, 228, and 235.
[1198] As suggested in IEMB, p. 135.
[1199] See Ziegler, p. 165, and above, ‡18.
[1200] See above, ‡18.
[1201] See ‡27 above.

1068/b DIPRUI seems to have the element *prwy (: prynu 'to buy') seen in MW datprwy 'redeem' (: OI taithchricc), dirprwy(aw) 'deputize', Mod.W. g(w)obr(wy) 'reward' (cf. MI tochra 'dowry'). Schrijver has argued that *prwy (: OI -chra(e)) is from *proi̯on, in which case the -UI would not be relevant here.[1202] It would be relevant, however, if *prwy derives directly from *kʷrei̯h-, as argued by Schumacher.[1203]

‡59 $\bar{\varepsilon}^i$ > Pr. W. [and Pr. CB.] ɔi; LHEB §27.3

I include the change in Cornish and Breton here, since Jackson states that it was 'no doubt . . . roughly contemporary' with that in Welsh (p. 330). As noted in ‡58, I have argued elsewhere that the diphthongization in all the Brittonic languages must have preceded the new quantity system (‡54 above). For the development of $\bar{\varepsilon}^i$ < $\bar{\varepsilon}$ < /ai/ see ‡‡ 4 and 23 above.

[59] (A) Jackson notes (p. 325) that the change has not happened in:

1. 390/96 VENDESETLI
2. 376/174 VENNISETLI
3. 377/175 CIMESETLI

[59] A further example (in Dorset, so possibly to be classed with Cornish or Breton rather than Welsh) is:

4. 1064/Dor.iv [D]ENIEL (cf. MW Deinioel < Daniel)[1204]

[59] Note also:

5. 318/6 ETTORIGI, though this is only relevant if < *Aitorīx (> OB Oedri) rather than being an Irish name from *Ianturīx.[1205]

[59] It seems safer not to count 1013/222/912 SAMUEL, since there is no sign that this is being assimilated into Welsh (W. Sawyl),[1206] unlike the i-affected [D]ENIEL above. In 368/a/150 DUMELEDONAS the diphthong of Irish *ai̯d- (> Áed) seems either to have been assimilated to the cognate Welsh /ɛ:(ⁱ)/ < /ai/, or, more likely, to have been spelt with an E under medieval Latin influence.[1207] On the latter basis, ETTORIGI could after all be an Irish derivative of *Aitorīx, albeit with British-influenced composition vowel and inflection.

[1202] See GPC, s.vv. datbrwy, dirprwyaf, gobr, gobrwyaf; SBCHP, pp. 290–91.
[1203] Schumacher, Historical Morphology, pp. 173–75, against the o-grade. Both possibilities are allowed by Schulze-Thulin, Studien, p. 104.
[1204] Restoration and analysis by Radford & Jackson, in RCHM, Dorset, ii/2, p. 312. Cf. LHEB, p. 618. See also ‡‡ 25 and 57 above on the historical context.
[1205] See ‡38 above.
[1206] SBCHP, p. 217; cf. ‡44n. above.
[1207] Ziegler, pp. 91, 98, and 175, n. 294; below, Ch. 4, §21n.

[59] (B) No inscriptional examples of the innovation are cited by Jackson, but note (with the same element as 1–3 above):

1. 994/125/22 HIROIDIL
2. 1032/281 ODELEV (‡80)

[59] Obscure items which I ignore include:
1006/197/842 TEFROIHI, TESROIHI, NEFROIHI, or REFSOIHI, etc. (see ‡42 on NEFROIHI as an Irish name).
508 FRYMIA COESIA FICT is obscure; Macalister compared COISIS on the ancient Todi inscription, which in turn is compared by Lejeune to Lepontic KOIśA.[1208]
2026/RIB i 2331 BEDALTOEDBOS (a dative plural??) also belongs to a more archaic world than Pr.W. /ɔi/.

‡60 Stressed ɔ̄ > au in Pr.W.; LHEB §11

As noted in ‡‡ 58–59, I have argued elsewhere that the diphthongization must have preceded the new quantity system (‡54 above), since otherwise we would have W. **sɔdl instead of sawdl, etc., when two or more consonants followed /ɔ:/.[1209]

[60] The spellings reflecting the /ɔ:/ stage were given in ‡18(B) (/a:/ > /ɔ:/). According to Jackson (pp. 293–94) the latest inscription not to show the change is 427/b/301 CATUOCONI, 'eighth century', and the first to show the innovation, also 'probably eighth century', is:
1. 986/62 R(I)UALLAUN [recte RUALLAUN][1210]

[60] In this and other names in OW -uallaun, the /au/ comes from /ɔ:/ from an earlier /au/,[1211] as in Romano-British Cassiuellaunus > MW Caswallawn,

---

[1208] RIG ii/1, p. 49.

[1209] This argument is accepted by McCone, TRC, p. 163.

[1210] There is no doubt about the reading RUALLAUN (most recently, Thomas, Christian Celts, p. 156). Such a development from *Ri- under the influence of the following /w/ is first found in LL, p. 226 (Ruguallaun, a copy of a ninth-century charter) and in Annales Cambriae, s.a. 1068, ed. Ab Ithel, p. 26: Ruallo var. Ruallaun (= Riwallawn, var. Riallon in Brut y Tywysogyon: Peniarth 20 Version, ed. Jones, p. 20 and n. 8, but Ruallawn in Brut y Tywysogyon: Red Book of Hergest Version, ed. Jones, p. 26). Cf. Llandaff Episcopal Acta, ed. Crouch, pp. 12, 36, 42 and 91: Ruelen, Ruwatlanum, Ruhatlan, Ruathlan. Jackson may have been reluctant to admit this in an 'eighth-century' inscription (or c. 700 according to Thomas, Mute Stones, pp. 322–23). Howlett, Cambro-Latin Compositions, pp. 22–23, scans it Rẏallaun, and his hexameter scansion is accepted in the otherwise critical review by McKee & McKee, CMCS, 39 (2000), 79. In this case RUALLAUN may not be the late form but simply have the /i/ elided for metrical reasons. Loth, Noms des saints bretons, p. 110, notes alternations like Rivalan and Ruellan in Breton; cf. HPB, p. 449, on Ker Rualen. For rhiw > (h)ru in Early Mod.W. place names see Wmffre, Language and History, i, 105–6. See also ‡81n.

[1211] Lambert, in Britain 400–600, pp. 203–15; SBCHP, p. 195, and ‡‡ 8 and 18 above, versus the au > ǭ in LHEB, p. 305. That original /au/ had changed to /ɔ:/ here (rather than simply

and it is perhaps not impossible that knowledge of ancient forms had an influence on the willingness to show AU in the orthography.

[60] Further forms can be added by looking for AV in the stressed syllable. It stands to reason that AV in unstressed syllables cannot be relevant because pretonic /ɔ:/ had already been shortened ($\ddagger$30), whence *sodlau*, plural of *sawdl*. We can therefore ignore forms in Wales and further north such as:

(a) 352A/122/5 BRAVECCI (: W. *braw(ychu)* 'terror(rize)')

(b) 396/104 AVITORI, 362/142 **AVITTORIGES**/AVITORIA, 377/175 AVICAT[VS] (Macalister: AMICATI), 505 (Man) AVITI

(c) 365/149 MAVOHE[NI], 516/Scot.1 MAVORIVS (compare in Cornwall 464/Ok65 MAVISIR, 486/Ok56 MAVCI, and 1205/Ok44 MAVOUIH (or MAVORIH?))

(d) 405/228/845 **GRAVICA** (Macalister)

(e) 433/313 **CAVE[TI]**/CAVETI; 434/314 CAVETI – compare in the South-West 1404/Ok30 CAVUDI or CAVVDI (alliterating with the patronymic FILIVS CIVILI) and 1057/Ok54 EROCAVI[1212]

(f) 438/320 TAVUSI

(g) 1036/360 HAUEN (Macalister (= W. *awen*?); HAN EH Nash-Williams)

[60] Forms from the South-West and Brittany must all be rejected since /au/ < /ɔ:/ is not expected there; in addition to the relevant CAV- and MAV-names just cited:

(h) 491/Ok55 AVDETI (or ANDETI Okasha)

(i) 462/Ok14 QVENATAVCI

(j) 2028 COLIAVI (possibly COLI AVI anyway)

(k) 1064/Dor.iv ( )AUPRIT (in Dorset, though not necessarily a local Briton)[1213]

(l) 3002/F2 GALLMAU

[60] The occurrence of the elements (c & l) (-)MAV-, (e) CAV-, (h) AVD-, (i) -TAVC-, and (j) -IAV- among the above rejected forms makes one suspicious of the following forms from Wales as /au/ < /ɔ:/ candidates, even though their AV is in the stressed syllable:

(c & l)1000/182 MAUN and 408/229/848 VEDOMAVI (preferred to Macalister's VEDOMALI)

(e) 401/183 CAVNE, 417/282 CAVO SENIARGII (which *may* anyway be

---

remaining as /au/ into OW) is proved by the fact that the /ɔ:/ was shortened in pretonic position (cf. $\ddagger$30 above) in OW *Guallonir* < **Vellaunorīx* (Lambert, p. 208).

[1212] According to Thomas, *Mute Stones*, p. 286, the reading 1057/Ok54 EROCAVI 'is difficult to sustain'. Cf. $\ddagger$25n. above. On p. 288 he comments on *Civilis* as a name in fourth-century Britain (see also L'Hour, *RAO*, 4 (1987), 120).

[1213] On AUPRIT see $\ddagger\ddagger$ 25 and 57 above.

CAVOSENI ARGII, with irrelevant pretonic AV); 418/283 BVRGOCAVI
(or BVRSOCAVI)
(h)   325/33 AVDO COGNA[TION]E[1214]
(i)   1022/240/928/ DO[BI]TAUCI, read by Macalister alone, perhaps
partly inspired by 462/Ok14 QVENATAVCI in Cornwall[1215]
(j)   1033/287 MARCIAU

[60] Of these, (c & l) MAUN, etc. are from *magu-,[1216] and (h) AVDO is an
uncertain reading, but could perhaps be Latin or Celtic Latin (cf. *Audo*, a
potter's name in Aquitania, AVDO(S) on coins of the Bituriges Cubi, and
AVDO on an altar from Castlesteads).[1217]

[60] (e) CAV- may have more than one source. **CAVE[TI]** (and CAVUDI)
are probably Irish and may be from *kawit- 'wild bird' (OI *cau(u)th*),[1218]
while CAVO- may be related to Latin *Ca(v)us*, *Cauua*, attested in Roman
Britain, or to Gaulish -*cavo*-.[1219] CAVNE (fem.) has been compared with
Caunus, a Latinized form of OW *Cau* (MW *Caw*), and these could perhaps
contain an element *kagu-;[1220] on the other hand, CAVN- could derive from
*kaw(a)no- and be phonetically comparable to W. *cawr*, B. *kaour*,
'giant' < *kaw(a)ro- < IE *k'euH-ro- (: Sanskrit *śávīra-* 'powerful'), a word
in which /au/ clearly did not become /ɔ:/ since the MW plural is *ceuri*, not
**cori*.[1221]

[60] (i) DO[BI]TAUCI, if present on the Welsh stone at all, can
can hardly have /au/ < /ɔ:/ in view of the Cornish QVENATAVCI,
which Jackson identified as Q-Celtic.[1222] Compare also the clearly Irish
431/308 DOB[I]TVCI or DOBTVCI/D[O]V[A]TUCEAS (Macalister:
DOVATACIS) = OI *Dubthach.*[1223]

[60] For (j), MARCIAU, Macalister's suggestion MARCIAU[N] (= OW
Merciaun < Latin *Marcianus*) is unnecessary, as there was an OW *Merchiau*
(:*march* 'horse'), with the common -*(i)aw* (> -*(i)o*) suffix, which seems to

---

[1214] See above, ‡22. The older readings AVDOCOS or AVDOCOG of course have AVDO- (if
not *recte* ANDO-) in pretonic position.
[1215] DOBITAUCI is rejected by Jackson, *Speculum*, 24 (1949), 599.
[1216] See above, ‡25.
[1217] DAG, p. 345; GPN, p. 147; RIG iv, no. 59; RIB i 1977; cf. Holder i, 285 and iii, 747.
[1218] Ziegler, p. 148; LEIA C-4 and 9.
[1219] See above, ‡18.
[1220] Cf. LHEB, p. 306 and above, ‡‡18n. and 25.
[1221] SBCHP, pp. 98–101; LHEB, p. 582. Weisgerber, *Rhenania*, p. 72, cites Pokorny, *ZCP*, 14
(1923), 291, on *Caunus*, *Caurus*, and *Laurus* as allegro-forms < *Cauannus*, *Cauarus*, and
Lauerus/Lauarus. According to Jackson, *ceuri* is due to internal *i*-affection, but according to
Schrijver to a general development of pretonic /auC/ > /ouC/ > /euC/ (although note the
personal name OW *Caurtam*, MW *Cawrdaf*; cf. ‡‡ 57n. and 80n.). Cf. Isaac, *SC*, 34 (2000),
109, n. 15, and 112, n. 17.
[1222] See above, ‡25.
[1223] See ‡38 above, and below.

come from *-iauos.[1224] 452/400 VALAVI FILI (Lhuyd: VALAVITIVI) PAANI may possibly have a similar suffix, but is in any case probably Irish (: OI Fáel- 'wolf' or Fá(i)l-).[1225]

[60] Leaving out the above dubious cases of AV, we can add only the following to RUALLAUN:

2.   1000/182 GUOILLAUC
3.   1014/231/908 ENNIAUN

[60] I am ignoring Latin(ate) names like 325/33 (etc.) PAVLINI (> MW Peulin), 410/238/847 PAVLI (PAVLI[NI]?); 2002/a]AUR[I]ANVS; 393/101 CARAVSIVS;[1226] 407/a/258/846 AVGVS(to) (> W. Awst); also, 350/116/3 DAVID (> W. Dewi); and, in Cornwall, **IGENAVI**, an ogam equivalent of INGENVI on 466/Ok23. The only other South-Western forms with AV, which should be mentioned for completeness, are the uncertain readings 482/Ok71 NEMIAVS, allegedly for NEMIANVS, and 487/Ok10 DRVSTAVS, possibly for DRVSTANVS, although -VS < *-wiks is a possibility.[1227]

[60] In MW, /au/ < /ɔː/ developed to /o/ in the now unstressed ultimate syllable (e.g. Cadawg > Cadog). This development has not occurred in the witness lists of even the latest charters in the Book of Llandaf,[1228] so it is hardly surprising that it is not reflected in the inscriptions either. The Book of Llandaf (and the Llancarfan charters) do, however, have examples of u (= /u/ rather than /uː/ ?) in final syllables and unstressed monosyllables from /ɔː/ (e.g. Merchiun and trus),[1229] so it seems reasonable to look for this probably dialectal[1230] reflex in the inscriptions. It is not clear whether the u developed directly from /ɔː/ or via /au/, but it cannot be a development from /o/ < /au/ < /ɔː/ since it only occurs as a variant in names like Merchiaun, never in those like Mabon < *Maponos with original /o/. There are three plausible examples in the inscriptions, which can be added to the above examples of /au/ as having roughly the same chronological significance:

[1224] BWP, pp. 30–31; EANC, pp. 215–16; LHEB, p. 383 (Teliau); HPB, p. 256; Koch, SC, 20/21 (1985–86), 51.

[1225] See above, ‡42.

[1226] This may be Celtic, but in any case has ancient -aus(i)us: Birkhan, Germanen und Kelten, p. 216. Cf. ‡79n.

[1227] See above, ‡‡ 14 and 48. Is this possible for NEMIAVS too? Cf. Namiorix as well as Nemausus, etc. in GPN, p. 235.

[1228] SBCHP, p. 195; Sims-Williams, BBCS, 38 (1991), 69.

[1229] Ibid., 63–64 and 70–71 and references; also Rodway, CMCS, 36 (1998), 73, n. 8. The non-appearance of u in non-final syllables is due to pretonic shortening of /ɔː/ (‡30).

[1230] It is interesting to note that seven of the dedications to saints with names in -wg indexed by Wade-Evans, Cymmrodor, 22 (1910), 119–22 (i.e. SS Barrwg, Ciwg, Tanwg, Tyddwg, Tydiwg, and Tyvodwg) are in the southern dioceses and only one (Llandanwg, Mer.) is in the north; note that 412/277 FERRVCI is from as far north as Merioneth.

4. 412/277 FERRVCI (Merionethshire) if this is to be compared with MW *Ferawc*[1231]

5. 333/50 CATVC (Breconshire): cf. MW *Cadawc*, *Cadwc*, and *Cattwc*[1232]

6. 1061/Dor.iii CATGUG (Macalister: CATTUG) (Dorset)

[60] The reason for the disagreement over the reading of 1061/Dor.iii is that, according to Macalister, 'the first G was originally written T and rather clumsily corrected – So it appears to me; though a G corrected to T is also admissible, giving a more plausible reading CATTUG.' Radford and Jackson, on the other hand, conjecture that 'the workman first cut a T, repeating the previous letter, and then corrected to G'.[1233] I think it impossible to choose. Jackson correctly equated CATGUG (his reading) with OW *Catguc* and later Welsh *Cattwg*, and also supposed all these to be the pet form of OW *Catguocaun*, *Catgucaun*, MW *Cadwgan*,[1234] which is more problematic, seeing that MW *Cattwc* undoubtedly occurs as a hypocoristic variant of *Cadawc* (St Cadog), itself a hypocoristic of *Catmail* (Cadfael) according to the *Vita sancti Cadoci* or of *Cadvodus* according to the Cartulary of Quimperlé,[1235] and seeing that *-gu-* is a feasible Old Welsh way of spelling later *-w-*.[1236]

[60] Against the above explanation of FERRVCI etc., we should note the possibility of *-uk-* suffixes in British, as in Romano-British *Mam-uc-io* (Manchester), BLOTVGI (for *BLOTVCI?) on the late fourth-century Thetford treasure, and the English river names Craddock (OE *Craducc*), Ennick (OE *Hennuc*), and Tarnock (OE *Ternuc*).[1237] Such forms are not common, however, and in the case of the river names Ekwall notes a suspicion of derivation from /a:k/, possibly with contamination by an OE diminutive *-uc*. (Note in particular OE *Caducburne* in Somerset, which looks like a derivative of Celtic *Katākos*.)[1238] If FERRVCI were assigned to *-uk-*,

---

[1231] See ‡44 above.

[1232] Russell, *Celtic Word-Formation*, pp. 17–18, 145, and 155; cf. EWGT, pp. 43–44 (*Cattwc*), 59 (*Cadwc*), 69 (*Kattwc*), and 82 (*Cadawc*). Pierce, *Place-Names of Dinas Powys*, p. 23, compares local dialectal *parrwg/perrwg* beside *parrog* < English *paddock*, but in the name *Cattwg* this is clearly older.

[1233] Macalister, *AC*, 84 (1929), 196 and n. 1; Radford & Jackson, in RCHM, *Dorset*, ii/2, p. 311.

[1234] Radford & Jackson, in RCHM, *Dorset*, ii/2, p. 312, citing LL, p. 161; anticipated by McClure, *EHR*, 22 (1907), 729.

[1235] Williams & Nash-Williams, *AC*, 92 (1937), 5; Loth, *Noms des saints bretons*, p. 20. The saint is first attested as *Catoce* (voc.) in a Breton litany of *c*. 900 (*Litanies*, ed. Lapidge, pp. 84 and 293).

[1236] Normally, it has to be admitted, in cases like *Bledgur* (LL, p. xlvii) and *amgucant* (discussed by Schumacher, *Historical Morphology*, p. 199), where the silent *g* has an etymological basis (cf. Lewis, *Disgrifiad o Orgraff Hen Gymraeg*, pp. 63–64 and 680), but note LHEB, pp. 379 and 392, n. 1, on *Mingui*, *Conguoy*, and *Brangui*.

[1237] Jackson apud Rivet, *Britannia*, 1 (1970), 76, and in *Thetford Treasure*, p. 47; Ekwall, *River-Names*, pp. lxxviii, 101, 148, and 392. On the question of an *-uk-* suffix in Irish see Uhlich, *Morphologie*, pp. 195–97. See also *-uco-* in Holder iii, 15.

[1238] Differently Coates & Breeze, *Celtic Voices*, pp. 83–84.

the equation with MW *Ferawc* would have to be abandoned; an alternative connection would be with the French place name *Ferruciacus* (‡44).

[60] There are three other similar forms which cannot be confidently included:
455/403 FANNVCI (Pembrokeshire) resembles 489/a/Ok13 FANONI/ SVAQQUCI in Cornwall (where the ogam is probably a mistake for SVANNUCI ?or SVANNUNI). These names could be British names in *F-*, from **Fannanus* and **Fannacus* (based on Classical Latin *Fannius* ?).[1239] The form with ogam SV- would thus be sound-substituted for British /f/, and could have given rise to OI *Sannuch*, as argued by Thurneysen.[1240] On the other hand, it is simpler, with MacNeill, to start from Brittonic **swant-* (OB *Huant-*, W. *chwant* 'desire' (borrowed into Irish as *sant*)); this is a common element in OB names, and one can compare St David's father, *Sant*, whose name was presumably transmitted via Irish, as well perhaps as *Sannuch*, a British(?) 'monk of St Patrick' listed by Tírechán.[1241] A preform of W. *chwannog* (C. *whansek*, MB *hoantec*), **Ʒwantӡk-* (cf. Old Celtic *Suandacca*), might well appear in Irish as SVA[NN]UCI (with SV = /hw/ for /Ʒw/ and omission of the /t/ owing to the lack of /nt/ in Primitive Irish),[1242] and this would develop regularly *within Irish* to FANNVCI, with the regular Irish change of /hw/ > /f/ (as in *mo fiur* 'my sister'); indeed ogam SV- may actually for a time have meant /f/. FANONI would also be an Irish form (less traditional than SVAQQUCI), but its second N might either be an error for C (mirroring the error QICI in the ogam for RINI) or the result of the provision of a more 'high-class', Roman/British suffix (< Latin *-ānus*).[1243] OI *Sannuch* would either be a 'normalization' (i.e. delenition) of

---

[1239] See above, ‡18.

[1240] GOI, p. 572 (see also Thurneysen, *ZCP*, 12 (1918), 411–12). Cf. McManus, *Guide*, p. 176, n. 44, and *Ériu*, 34 (1983), 53, n. 87, and 37 (1986), 25, n. 36; Sims-Williams, *TPS*, 91 (1993), 159; Schrijver, *Ériu*, 48 (1997), 223.

[1241] Cf. Rhys, in Meyer FS, pp. 239–40; MacNeill, *Ériu*, 11 (1930–32), 133–34; Ziegler, pp. 233–34; Thomas, *Mute Stones*, p. 268; *Patrician Texts*, ed. Bieler, p. 128. Rhys, *Cymmrodor*, 21 (1908), 55, compared FANNVCI and FANONI with the names of *Sannuch* in Tírechán and of Patrick's brother, the deacon *Sannān*, in the notes to Fíacc's Hymn (Stokes, *Tripartite Life*, pp. 305 and 412), but with the important caveat that *Sanuc(i)us* occurs in Continental inscriptions, e.g. CIL v 2080 (SANVCIVS, Feltria) and xiii 5258 (SANVCI, Kaiser-Augst, Basel); see further citations in Holder ii, 1356–57, and iii, 15, and OPEL iv, 48; cf. *Sunuc(i)us* in Holder ii, 1670, and OPEL iv, 100, and Lejeune, *EC*, 17 (1980), 92. On *chwant* etc. see GOI, p. 572; Gramm., p. 144; DGVB i, 214; Sims-Williams, in Evans FS, p. 206; Lambert, *BBCS*, 36 (1989), 114; GPC, s.vv. *chwant* and *chwannog*; LEIA S-25. The expected true cognate in Irish is *sét*; see LEIA S-99; NWÄI, p. 549. For *Suandacca* (CIL v 8773, cf. *Inscriptiones Latinae Christianae Veteres*, ed. Diehl, i, no. 457), see Holder ii, 1649 and Schrijver, in *Kelten in Nederland*, p. 76. Perhaps compare *Sunducca* and *Suniducus* in OPEL iv, 99–100. *Suaducia* etc. (ibid., p. 96) are definitely distinct (GPN, p. 258).

[1242] Cf. ‡68 below.

[1243] See above, ‡18. Alternatively, MacNeill suggested that it was Ir. *-ón* < **-u-gnos*, 'where *-gnos* is added to *u*-stems (see ‡48 above). If it was originally a *u*-stem, that could explain the difference in gender between *chwant* (m.) and *sant* (f.).

Fannuch or the result of a separate borrowing of the same British name, perhaps at the same stage as *sant* was borrowed. If this is correct, the spelling of FANNVCI is properly an *Irish* spelling and does not stand in the Welsh line of orthographic development O > AV > V; it may show an Irish substitution for /ɔ:/ or /au/, comparable with that seen in OI -*uc* beside -*ócán*.[1244] – On the other hand, if the British vocalism is indeed /u:/ and FANONI is an Irish equivalent, for the equivalence of Ir. *ó* and W. /u:/, compare the suggestion that W. *mewn* may be borrowed from Ir. *medón*.[1245]

[60] 431/308 DOB[I]TVCI or DOBTVCI (ogam equivalent D[O]V[A]TUCEAS (Macalister: DOVATACI) = OI *Dubthach*, gen. *Dubthaich/Dubthaige*) clearly shows, if related at all, an *Irish* reduction of the obscure Irish element TAVC- (*a*-stem) seen in 462/Ok14 QVENATAVCI and (according to Macalister alone, implausibly) in 1022/240/928 DO[BI]TAUCI.[1246]

[60] 327/43 [TRIL]LUNI (T[RA]LL[O]NI Macalister) / TRILVNI, which has proved difficult to explain,[1247] could be composed of the well-attested Welsh prefix *Try*-[1248] plus *llawn* 'full' (< *lāno*-), an element denoting plenitude in names like OW *Sciblon* 'sheaf-full', OB *Bodlon* 'content', *Catlon* 'battle-full', and possibly represented by *lano*- in Gaulish personal names.[1249] A Welsh *Trəlʒn*- 'very replete' (known only from Pughe's Dictionary s.v. *trylawn* 'thoroughly full') could well be spelt -LVN- or -LLON- by Irish inscribers. Compare *Sannuch* etc. above and Adomnán's *Cat(h)lon* for *Cadwallawn, -on*.[1250] Another possibility, however, suggested by Pughe's *trylon* 'being thoroughly glad', is *try*- + *llonn* 'strong' (: OI *lond* < *londo*-); this may be attested in MW as *trylonn* (MSS *trytlonn*) 'un

---

1244 Russell, *Celtic Word-Formation*, pp. 111, n. 283, 115–16 and 152–54. For W. /au/ < /ɔ:/ appearing in Irish sources as OI *ó*, see Sims-Williams, *BBCS*, 38 (1991), 49, n. 2. KHJ notes that an objection to seeing OI -*uc*- (as in *Ísucán*, etc.) in 489/a/Ok13 SVAQQUCI and 455/403 FANNVCI is that 'that would be spelt -G- in Ogam. It could easily be -*uc*- suffix as in *Dobituci*' (i.e. 431/308, which I discuss immediately below).

1245 GPC s.v.; cf. NWÄI, p. 326; Koch, *Gododdin*, p. 184.

1246 See ‡25n. for KHJ's comparison with OI *túäch* 'silent' (cf. LEIA T-91) and above. Cf. Ziegler, pp. 170–71; Uhlich, *Morphologie*, pp. 27, 131 and 233–34. Note *Taucius* and *Tauconius* in Holder ii, 1755.

1247 See Ziegler, p. 237, citing Rhys, LWP, pp. 381–82, who thought TRILVNI was for *Trilluni* < *Tris-luni* 'Triformis' (: W. *llun* 'form'); cf. *eilun*?? and note Loth's idea, *Noms des saints bretons*, p. 83, that the name of St *Lunaire* derived from *lun*, W. *llun*). On *eilun* and forms in *tri* see SWWF, pp. 33–34 and 169. Thomas, *Mute Stones*, p. 124, suggested emending to TRIBUNI; see above, ‡26n.

1248 Assuming this had early proclitic reduction (LHEB, p. 659), as against SBCHP, pp. 246–47 and 249. This is supported by Romano-British *Trisantona* (LHEB, p. 525, n. 2; Sims-Williams, *BBCS*, 38 (1991), 74), a form not discussed in SBCHP. See also *Tricasses* etc. in Holder ii, 1940.

1249 Sims-Williams, *BBCS*, 38 (1991), 25, n. 1, 34, and 64; Chrest., pp. 146 and 218; Gramm., p. 369 (cf. Lambert in *Britain 400–600*, p. 206, n. 10); GPN, p. 215; cf. SWWF, pp. 128–29.

1250 Sims-Williams, *BBCS*, 38 (1991), 49, n. 2.

cadarn'.[1251] A further possibility is the element *lun* – perhaps 'moon' as in W. *(Dydd) Llun* 'Monday' < *Dies Lunae* – which occurs in OW *Lunberth, Lunbiu, Lunbrit* and OC *Luncen*.[1252] Could TRILVN- mean 'three moons', perhaps referring to the time of birth like Latin *Lucius* 'prima luce natus'?[1253]

‡*61 Stressed auṽ > auụ̧ (and sometimes > au); LHEB §66.2*

No inscriptional evidence is cited. A possible example is 1068/a **LAGUBERI** on Man, conceivably equivalent to W. *Llawfer* or *Llawfyr* 'short arm' or 'short as to his arm', with **LAGU** for /lauụ̧/ < *lāmā*.[1254]

‡*62 ou (< oụ̧, ɔu) > öü in Pr.W.; LHEB §46.2*

Inevitably, no inscriptional evidence can be cited. Cf. ‡50.

‡*63 lt > ll in W.; LHEB §54.1*

Jackson notes (p. 400) that the change has not yet happened in 1033/287 CIMALTED,[1255] which is his dating criterion (versus *ll* in the OW glosses), but he cites no examples of the change from the inscriptions. It is not impossible that 2008/82]ESILLIMARIGUELIO includes the name *Esyllt* (here masculine?), but if so, it is odd, since loss of /t/ would not be expected in final position. Could there be hypercorrection to avoid the dialectal(?) variation seen in 1011/220/911 HOUELT (~ *Hywel*)[1256] and Mod.W. *dallt ~ deall*, etc.? Or was the Latin -I sufficient to warrant giving /lt/ the internal treatment? Or is it a mistake for T?

‡*64 Internal i-affection in Pr.C. and Pr.B.; LHEB §176*

[64] (A) Jackson cites no South-Western inscriptional evidence for the innovation (cf. ‡57 above for Welsh), but quotes three forms in which the affection is *not* shown (p. 610). One is 492/Ok59 SABINI, which I ignore as

---

[1251] CBT vi, 312 and 320. I am grateful to Mr Gareth Bevan for this reference and for looking at the slips of GPC for the evidence for Pughe's two words.

[1252] LL, p. 410; Bodmin, p. 95. Lloyd, *Cymmrodor*, 9 (1888), 52, compares the use of *Sul* '(Sun[day]')' in names like OW *Sulgen*, although Lloyd-Jones, *Y Geninen*, 44 (1926), 13, regarded the first element as uncertain. Richards, *THSC*, 1965, p. 32, notes also *Tysilio* and *Llandysul*, and cf. St *Sul* in Loth, *Noms des saints bretons*, p. 138.

[1253] Lebel, p. 32. For Celtic *Tri-* 'triple' see LEIA T-140 and CPNE, pp. 233–34. But it can also be Latin, as in *Tricongius* 'qui avait absorbé d'un seul trait trois conges de vin', Lebel, p. 33.

[1254] However, W. *llaw* 'small' is more likely; see ‡25 above.

[1255] That is, following Williams's interpretation, BWP, pp. 28–29; GPC, s.v. *cyfalle(dd)*; Hamp, *Ériu*, 43 (1992), 207–9 (in the context of Celtic *lt* in general). Cf. Koch, *SC*, 20/21 (1985–86), 51. On *comalt* see also HPB, p. 809, n. 5. LT otherwise occurs in: 2026/RIB i 2331 BEDALTOEDBOS; 1013/222/912 ILTU[TI(S)] (now *Illtud*, but formerly with /ld/; see LHEB, p. 400, n. 1; LL, p. 405); 1011/220/911 HOUELT, with clearly inorganic /t/ or /d/ (cf. OB *Houuel*, etc., LHEB, p. 659, and ‡46n); and 1001/181 L(*o*?)TON, interpreted by Radford & Hemp, *AC*, 106 (1957), 109–16, as EDELSTAN.

[1256] See preceding note.

being a Latin form (cf. ‡57 above) and because its alleged descendant W. *Hefin* is of dubious attestation (see ‡44n. above). The other two are:

1. 473/a/Ok46 TORRICI[1257]
2. 490/Ok29 DATUIDOCI cf. W. *Dedwyddog*[1258] [also CONHINOC(I), with /i/ < /e/, which is less significant as affection of the O is not expected to be shown as soon as that of A, cf. nos 9–10 below]

[64] Other forms which can be added are:

3. 485/Ok68 COLINI *if* the correct reading and = OC *kelin* 'holly' (but it may be Irish as in 2006 MAQVI COLINE = OI *Macc Cuilinn*)[1259]
4. 486/Ok56 CVMREGNI or CVMRECINI, which may contain MC **Rigni*, which will then have /e/ > /i/ by *i*-affection like OC and Mod.C. *listri* (: W. *llestri*)[1260]
5. 1044/Ok7 LEUIUT does not show affection of /e/ in *leu* 'lion'; contrast OC and OW *Bleidiud*[1261]
6. 1054/Ok43 DONIERT[1262]
7. 2028 COLIAVI, presumably with *-iauos* suffix,[1263] unless it is read COLI AVI[1264]
8. 3003/F3 ADIVNI (cf. W. *eiddun*)[1265]
9. 3013/M4 CONBRITI, although the lack of visible affection in the first element (< **kuno-*) is non-diagnostic[1266]
10. 493/Ok58 CONBEVI (the same applies)

[64] Latin forms in which affection cannot be expected to be shown are: 461/Ok66 NONNITA;[1267] 465/Ok21 ANNICV; 470/Ok78 LATINI/

[1257] See ‡18 above for KHJ's identification with W. *terrig* (and not with C. *terry*, B. *terri*; versus W. *torri* 'break' which lacks affection, LHEB, p. 590). TORRICI is much less likely to be a derivative of *torr* (cf. OI *ta(i)rr*, originally *i-* or *u-*stem) 'belly'; cf. OI *torrach* 'pregnant', OC and OB *toroc* 'bug' (LEIA T-33–34 and 117; DGVB i, 317 and 334).

[1258] Cf. *Dedwydd* as a Welsh surname (GPC), and OB *Iarndetuuid*, etc. (Gramm, pp. 192 and 200; Schrijver, *SC*, 33 (1999), 14; SWWF, p. 428, n. 6). The final -I is uncertain according to Okasha.

[1259] LHEB, p. 596; Wright & Jackson, *AntJ*, 48 (1968), 298–99; and above, ‡27. On the reading cf. Thomas, *Mute Stones*, p. 271, and Okasha, and n. 1286 below.

[1260] Cf. LHEB, p. 596. On MC **Rigni* see above, ‡48.

[1261] LHEB, pp. 346–47 and 592–93.

[1262] LHEB, p. 422, and above, ‡28n.

[1263] See ‡60n above. But there are cases where OC /o/ is not affected; see LHEB, pp. 590 and 596 (e.g. OC *odion* = W. *eidion*).

[1264] C. Thomas, apud Morris et al., *Med. Arch.*, 43 (1999), 214 segments PATER COLI AVI 'father of a descendant of Coll'. Note the existence of a Latin and OW personal name *Pater*, Oswald and LL, p. 415. Cf. also OI *Coll*, ogam 117 **COLLI** (Macalister: **COLLOS**): McManus, *Guide*, p. 67; Ziegler, p. 153.

[1265] See above, ‡15n.

[1266] See LHEB, pp. 591 and 615–16; HPB, p. 294.

[1267] I = /i:/, so not subject to *a*-affection. On Rhys's suggestion that NONNITA is Ir. *Nannid* rather than Latin see above, ‡15n.

LA[TI]NI (or **LA[DI]NI**)[1268] (MAGIARI is a linguistically unlikely reading here); 483/Ok51 SENILVS;[1269] 1209/Ok12 POPLICI (Thomas);[1270] 1212 CARASIMILIVS (?);[1271] 1400/Ok28 OPTIMI; 1402/Ok26 POTIT[I];[1272] 3025/I6 MELITA (or WELITA?). 1206/Ok4 DOVITHI is probably Irish and so therefore may the same inscription's obscure DOCIDCI or [R]IVGDOCI or [R]IVSDOCI be.[1273] 461/Ok66 ERCILIVI and ERCI-LINGI (ERCILINCI Thomas) are also probably Irish.[1274] 3024/I5 BERTHILD(IS) is Germanic. The reading 475/Ok47 IACONIVS is rejected by Thomas.[1275]

[64] The etymologies (and in most cases) the readings of the following are too uncertain for them to be included: 474/Ok17 CRVARIGI; 1048/Ok32 (G)VENNORCIT and QONFIL(I); 480/Ok19 EMIANCINO (??); 482/Ok31 NEMIA(N)VS. In cases like the last two, there is no way of knowing whether the E is an affected /a/ or an /e/ that has *not* been affected to /i/. 1046/Ok8 ARAHI seems to lack affection by the element *-hi*, but an alternative reading is ARTHI.[1276] 464/Ok65 MAVISIR, even if cognate with W. *Meisyr* < **Magesturīx*, may have a glide that inhibited affection reaching the A although the first I seems to display affection of /e/ (cf. ‡25).

[64] (B) The clear South-Western examples of the innovation (possibly in addition to 1064/Dor.iv [D]ENIEL in ‡57) are:

1.   473/b/Ok46 IGNIOC (cf. OB *agnioc*, W. *egnïol* 'vigorous'), not only with internal *i*-affection but also apparently a Breton-style 'secondary affection' (‡85 below)
2.   3014/M5 HARENBILI (cf. OB *Bili*, MW *Beli*)[1277]

1268   Although Rhys, *JRSAI*, 5th ser. 12 (1902), 15, notes that in Welsh it became *Lledin*; see EANC, p. 209, on *Lledin* as a river name and as MW female name < *Latīnā*. Rhys explains 138 **LADDIGNI** as a hypercorrect form of LATINI (differently Ziegler, p. 191). On the ogam of 470/Ok78 see LHEB, p. 184.

1269   See ‡44n.

1270   *Mute Stones*, p. 281; rejected Okasha. Cf. W. *Peblig*, above, ‡28n.

1271   Thomas, *Christian Celts*, pp. 62–63; cf. ‡36 above.

1272   Thomas, *Mute Stones*, pp. 288 and 302, n. 39, notes that St Patrick's priestly grandfather was called *Potitus* (*Confessio*, §1).

1273   See above, ‡‡ 18 and 42.

1274   See above, ‡43. Cf. Thomas, *Mute Stones*, pp. 283–84; and Okasha, who suggests ERCILI VIRICATI as an alternative; cf. ‡27 on this segmentation.

1275   *Mute Stones*, p. 282.

1276   See above, ‡36.

1277   Gramm., p. 194. On the difference between affection of /e/ in Welsh and Breton see LHEB, pp. 582 and 596. HARENBILI does not show the type of internal affection seen in MW *heyernin* (LHEB, pp. 361 and 582, cf. Ch. 3, below, p. 255), but the first element developed differently in the two languages (cf. OB *Hoiernin, Houernin*, Loth, *RC*, 11 (1890), 144) and affection might well not occur across elements in a dithematic name. See also 3010/M1 HERANNUEN, where the second element may in any case be feminine, with /e/ rather than /ɪ/. It is worth noting that an element *beli/bele/bili* occurs in France outside Brittany: Lebel, p. 62. Gaulish *bili-* (GPN, pp. 149–51; DLG, pp. 64–65) is presumably distinct.

3004/F4 IOCILIN(X) (cf. OB *Goscelin(us)*) is not a pure Brittonic form and the *Di-* of 3006/C1 DISIDERI is paralleled in Late Latin.[1278] There are also a number of forms which are too uncertain and obscure to be included: 487/Ok10 CIRISINIVS (?); 491/Ok55 PRINCIPI and variant readings (Latin?);[1279] 1049/Ok33 URITIN; 1053/Ok1 VILICI, ULLICI, or GU[ ]VILIR, etc.; and 1059/Ok64 ÆLRIAT. 3007/C2 VORMVINI could show a stage in the affection of normal *Uurm-* by /ɪ/ (cf. **kurkito-* > OB *corcid* > Mod.B. *kerc'heiz*), but this is uncertain since the name can also be segmented VOR-MVINI.[1280]

‡65 *γ after ī finally,*[1281] *and before a, o, and after back vowels finally and between them internally, perhaps now lost; LHEB §89*

Note: for /a(:)γu/ and /a:γ/ see ‡25 above and for /-eγ/ see ‡39 above; for /γ/ in other combinations involving front vowel(s) see ‡74 below.

[65] (A) Jackson gives the following examples where the change is *not* shown (pp. 448 and 456 and n. 1):

1. 498/Nb7 BRIGOMAGLOS [also with a second name in -CVS or -GVS]
2. 358/138 VOTEPORIGIS [ogam **VOTECORIGAS**]
3. 318/6 ETTORIGI > MW ****Ethri**[1282]

[65] The last two may be Irish. The same is probably true of most or all of: 348/a/110/27 **TRENALUGOS** (Macalister!); 361/140 MAQV[ERIGI]; 362/142 **AVITTORIGES**/AVITORIA; 428/305 TRENEGUSSI (and ogam equivalent); 502 **|MAQ LEOG|** . Other forms which can be added, however, are:

4. 380/84 **ICORIGAS**/ICORI (though this could be Irish)
5. 2000 DEVORIGI (though this could be Irish)[1283]
6. 379/170 CATVRVG(I) (unless the second element is W. *(g)rug* rather than *rhi* mispelt, ‡37n.)
7. 407/a/258/846 AVGVS(*to*) (> OW *Aust*, MW *Awst*)
8. 413/272 MONEDORIGI
9. 419/284 RIGOHENE

[1278] See IEMB, pp. 87, 130 and 142; OPEL ii, 215; Le Blant, *Inscriptions chrétiennes de la Gaule antérieures au viiie siècle*, i, 77 (DIS(I)DERIVS > *Didier*). Cf. Loth, *Noms des saints bretons*, pp. 32–33: *Disder = Desiderius*.

[1279] Rhys, *AC*, 6th ser. 18 (1918), 191, read PRINCIPI but explained that 'the *pr* at the beginning are only a guess'. Thomas, *Mute Stones*, p. 281, suggests a title or name *Principius*.

[1280] See above, ‡27. On *corcid* see LHEB, pp. 596, 608–9 and 615.

[1281] Including the first half of compounds, LHEB, p. 455.

[1282] LHEB, p. 456, n. 1; but see above, ‡38.

[1283] It is treated as British in Sims-Williams, *TAAS*, 1999, pp. 147–49, but the -RIGI could be due to British/Latin influence, as may be the composition vowel O (and this may be the Irish development seen after labials). In additions to my 1999 references note the Spanish form *Deuorio* discussed by Tovar, *BBCS*, 29 (1980–82), 597.

10. 435/315 CLVTORIGI
11. 444/352]MOGI[1284] (Macalister: ROTI)
12. 455/403 CAMVL(L)ORIGI
13. 474/Ok17 CRVARIGI (also read RVANI or]MAGLI)[1285]

[65] In 325/33 the readings ANDOCOG or AVDOCOG are due to a misunderstanding.[1286] 1030 [A]MBIGATI is extremely dubious, but if genuine would contain /g/ not /γ/, as would 470/Ok78 MAGARI (also read MACARI).[1287] 519/Scot.6 LOGI is also read LOCI (Latin).[1288] 1045/Ok69 AGURED, AGUDED, AGUTED, or ÆGVRED may be Old English.[1289]

[65] (B) Jackson notes (pp. 448, 456–57, and 459) the following examples where the change *has* happened:

1. 978/49 BRIAMAIL
2. 986/62 R(I)UALLAUN [*recte* RUALLAUN][1290]
3. 468/Ok31 RIALOBRANI

[65] The three additions we can make are:

4. 3021/I2 MAONIRN. This looks like a derivative of *Maγon'di-γirn* < *Magono-tigirnos* (: W. *maon* 'host, servants', apparently the plural of *mau* < *magu-*).[1291] Compare, from the singular, OI *Mugthigern*, and Loth's very tentative derivation of B. *Modiern* (probably really *Mordiern*, however, as he says) < *Mawdiern* < *Magutegernos.*[1292]
5. 3017/M8 RIMOETE < *Rīgo-meit-* (‡58)

[1284] But this may be the genitive of *Mogius*, a rare Continental Celtic(?) name: Holder ii, 607 and 610; cf. GPN, p. 222; Mócsy, pp. 191–92.

[1285] KHJ found 474/Ok17 'completely illegible' in 1951.

[1286] See above, ‡22. In 485/Ok68 COGI or [CO]BI have been suggested instead of COLINI and KHJ favoured COCI.

[1287] Thomas, *Mute Stones*, p. 263; for other readings see Rhys, *Englyn*, p. 60, and Okasha.

[1288] See above, ‡17.

[1289] See above, ‡25.

[1290] See above, ‡60.

[1291] In IEMB, pp. 79 and 270, MAONIRN is analysed as *Maguno-?rīxs* or *Maon + -irn* 'of uncertain significance' (cf. *-irn* < *-ern* above, ‡27n?); but for /n'd/ > /nn/ see HPB, p. 790, and cf. ‡36 above on 3014/M5 HERANHAL (however /n'd/ > /nn/ is denied by Schrijver, *SC*, 33 (1999), 14–15). For the vocalism of *tiγirn* in Late British see SBCHP, p. 64 (noted above, ‡57). *Maon* is presumably *n*-stem *magones* replacing *u*-stem *magowes* (> OI *mog(a)e*). (Loth, *RC*, 40 (1923), 342–43, also gives *magones* but derives this from *mag-* 'great; grow', cf. LEIA M-8–9.) See also Koch, *Gododdin*, pp. xxiii and 229. I would suggest that British *magones* may be the source of OE *Magonsætan*, for which see Sims-Williams, *Religion and Literature in Western England*, p. 40. Loth, *Noms des saints bretons*, pp. 76 and 88, notes that *Maon* in *Lan-vaon* is either a personal name or a plural like W. *maon*.

[1292] Uhlich, *Morphologie*, p. 279; Loth, *Noms des saints bretons*, p. 94, whence the garbled account in Smith, *Toponymie bretonne*, pp. 88–89. GPN, p. 100, also refers to Mac Cana, *ÉC*, 7 (1955–56), 110–12, for the Irish sept-names *Mauginrige, Mughanrige*, but Mac Cana derives these from a feminine theonym *Mugain*, not a plural of *mug*.

6. 993/124/18 AON (Macalister: UON; Nash-Williams -CCON; W. G. Thomas: -LLO). According to Rhys, this Llanllŷr inscription reads:

> tesquitus ditoc
> madoMNuaco
> ccon Filius asa
> itgen dedit.[1293]

[65] Rhys separated the -o from *madomnuac* (losing the required dative ending) and created a name *Occon*, which he compared with OI *Ócán*.[1294] I would suggest, however, that **ccon** could be read **aon**, with the 'double-c' form of *a* seen in the same line. *Aon* can be compared with the second element of OW *Auagon*, MW *Adaon/Auaon* (probably with original *Aδ-*) and could derive from **Aγon < *Ag-ŏn-os* (cf. Gaulish *Ago-, Agio*, etc.), presumably from the root **aĝ-* 'drive, lead, go' (although **agh-* 'cattle' is also a possibility).[1295] Note that Aon's name would alliterate with that of his father, which I take to be W. *Asa* rather than Rhys's 'provisional and liable to correction' *Asaitgen*.[1296] ITGEN (a second, secular name or patronymic of *Asa* ?) is a credible compound of *ŷd* 'corn' and *-gen* (i.e. *< *(P)itugenos* 'corn-born'), bearing in mind that the first element of *-gen* compounds 'could be . . . an animal name (as in *Matugenus*), the name of a tree (as in *Vernogenus*) or of a mineral (as in **Isarnogenos* > OBret. *Hoiarngen*)'.[1297] Of course, if a letter is missing there are other possibilities, such as **[L]ITGEN* (cf. 436/316 LITOGENI) or **[R]ITGEN* (OB *Ritgen, Ritien*).[1298]

[1293] *AC*, 5th ser. 13 (1896), 120; cf. unconvincing reading of W. G. Thomas, in *Cardiganshire County History*, i, 416, no. 18.

[1294] *AC*, 5th ser. 13 (1896), 121, and cf. *Englyn*, pp. 54–55 ('Madomnu ac Occon'); similarly Thomas, *Mute Stones*, p. 110, n. 31. Note also *Ochon, Mochon*, Stüber, *Historical Morphology*, p. 104.

[1295] LEIA A-22; Holder iii, 524 (*Agorix, Agosages*); GPN, pp. 300–1 (also 128–31 on *Ad-*); Birkhan, *Germanen und Kelten*, pp. 442–44; DLG, pp. 30–31. For *Auag(g)on* and *Adaon/Auaon* see LL, pp. 232–34; Lloyd-Jones, *Geirfa*, p. 14, s.n. *Afaon*; Williams, *BBCS*, 2 (1924), 118–20, and *Canu Aneirin*, p. 379; TYP, p. 269; cf. Haycock, *Blodeugerdd*, p. 225. The element may also appear in MW *Blathaon* and *Ffaraon* (references in CBT ii, 179 and vi, 488). Rhys, *AC*, 5th ser. 13 (1896), 120, explained ASAITGEN as *As- < *eks-* (cf. GPN, p. 202) plus OI *Aithgen*, as if **Eks-ate-genos*. This is phonetically impossible. Note also that only two names in *As-* are listed in CGH, p. 513: *A(i)ssíd*, gen. *Aissída* (mentioned by Rhys), and *Assiucc* (cf. Ziegler, p. 130, and Uhlich, *Morphologie*, p. 168, on 134 ASSICONA). Thomas, *Mute Stones*, p. 110, n. 31, understands *Asaitgen* as 'parturition born' (cf. *assait*, LEIA A-96 = *asait*, DIL), a tautologous-seeming name (cf. already D'Arbois de Jubainville, *RC*, 17 (1896), 312: 'fils de l'accouchement', and Holder iii, 703). Another possibility is OI **Saithgen* with the obscure element *Saith-* seen in OI *Saithgel* (CGH, p. 729, and Uhlich, *Morphologie*, p. 297; cf. Evans, *ÉC*, 12 (1968–69), 198–200, on Gaulish *Satigenus*), but this leaves an unexplained A-.

[1296] For MW *As(s)a*, equated with (and according to LBS i, 177 derived from) biblical *Asaph*, see EWGT, p. 171; Lloyd-Jones, *Geirfa*, s.nn. *Assa* and *Assaff*.

[1297] GPN, pp. 203–4. For Irish names in *-gen* see O'Brien, *Celtica*, 10 (1973), 222. Cf. below, ‡84, on 366/148 ITOCVS < ?*(p)itu-*.

[1298] See GPN, p. 204, and LHEB, p. 439; and above, ‡38 on LITOGENI. Note also OW *Gueithgen*, LL, p. 401.

[65] Jackson regarded 424/299 BRIAC[I] < *Brīgākos* as dubious, partly because the stone at Brawdy is damaged, but apparently partly because the loss of /γ/ seems here to have preceded the change of /aː/ > /ɔː/ (‡18); he compared fifth- and sixth-century Continental spellings like *Riochatus* and *Riothamus*, where /γ/ may have been regarded as effectively a glide /j/ and not written in Latin.[1299] (Compare in particular the toponym *Villa Briaco* (> Brée, dép. Mayenne) in AD 642.)[1300] While this is possible, it is striking that the other three stones from Brawdy bear obviously *Irish* names (423/296, 425/297, 422/298); if BRIACI is not actually Irish (for OI *Brígach* retains the /γ/), it may have A rather than O under Irish influence. Also in Pembrokeshire, at Bridell, Macalister read 426/300 **BRIACI** (but Nash-Williams has **BRECI**, and McManus judges this or **SLECI** correct, pointing out that the **MUCOI BRECI** may be identical with the *Brecraige*, a subject people of the Uí Néill in Co. Meath).[1301]

[65] Jackson also thought 461/Ok66 RICATI dubious, since the reading might be VIRICATI.[1302] But if RICATI is correct, he notes that it may be explained not with reference to *Riochatus* above but as the result of syncope in the reflex of **Rīgokatus*; if so (as seems plausible) it does not illustrate normal loss of /γ/ rather than a special merger of /γ/ and /g/.[1303] According to Macalister, RICATI also occurs on 1051/Ok37, but this is a doubtful reading.[1304]

[65] Jackson rightly thought 362/142 AVITORIA (with ogam equivalent **AVITTORIGES**) 'very doubtful' evidence of the loss of /γ/, and the same applies to other similar forms where -IA (and -IUS and their genitives) appear in **-rīx* names:[1305] a name like 330/66 CATIRI cannot be assumed to be the preform of **Cedri* < **Katurīg-* rather than of **Cedyr* < **Katurīks*.[1306] So, too, with 380/84 ICORI, 394/103 CANTIORI, 396/104 AVITORI,

---

[1299] LHEB, pp. 454, n. 1, 457 and 459; cf. GPN, p. 400, for *rīgo-* > *rio-* etc., and VLRB, p. 917, on RIB i 1017 RIOCALATI, cf. i 862 RIANORIX. (For a different view – *Rio-* < **Prijo-*: W. *rhydd* 'free' – see KGP, p. 259; Dressler, in Pokorny FS, p. 151; and DLG, pp. 218–19.) Rhys, *Englyn*, p. 8 and n. 2, compared OW *Riacat, Riatam, Riataf, Rioval, Riaual*, and *Riual* in LL, and MW *Riogan*, and also noted a St *Riacatus* [beside a St *Racatus*] in the probably early tenth-century Breton 'Rheims Litany' (*Litanies*, ed. Lapidge, pp. 81 and 261; cf. Loth, *Noms des saints breton*, p. 108; Dumville, *Wessex and England*, p. 155, n. 91). Note that although REO[has been read in 513/Ok.Pict8, KHJ thought it unlikely to be < **Rīgo-*.
[1300] Holder i, 529; cf. iii, 291: *Vidubriaco*.
[1301] *Guide*, pp. 67, 111 and 180, n. 56. In the *Corpus* Edwards, s. Bridell 1, favours **IA**. Rhys, LWP, pp. 274–75, noted that **[BR]ECI** could also be read **[MR]ECI** or **[SL]ECI**, and that 'gr has also been proposed'. Thomas, *Mute Stones*, pp. 71 and 85, n. 11, has **[BR]IECI[I?]**. Cf. Ziegler, pp. 39 and 141. See also above, ‡‡ 18 and 44.
[1302] Thomas, *Mute Stones*, p. 301, n. 29, objects. Cf. above, ‡27.
[1303] LHEB, pp. 456–57, following Rhys, *Englyn*, p. 20.
[1304] KHJ found this part mostly illegible in 1951.
[1305] LHEB, p. 456, n. 1. See ‡‡ 14–15 above.
[1306] See also ‡19 for the possibility that it is OI *Ca(i)thri*. For Welsh names in -*ril/-yr* see Lloyd-Jones, *BBCS*, 14 (1950–52), 36.

397/105 BECCVRI, 995/133/24 ENEVIRI, 361/140 TALOR[I], 2001
ORBIORI (if not ORBIORIT), 446/353 CLVTORI, 458/Ok9 RANOCORI
or NANOCORI, and 1205/Ok44 MAVORI (Thomas, if not MAVOUIH or
MAVORIH).

[65] 452/400 PAANI may be from Latin *Paganus*, possibly in an Irish
context.[1307] 503 **DROATA** is Irish, probably to be read **DRUTA** (OI
Drúith).[1308] 1209/Ok12 CAOCI[1309] could formally come from **Kagākos*,
but *Kagiākos* is more probable, and the reading may be CA[ ]OCI (e.g.
CA[T]OCI).

[65] 2021 GVINNDA, OW *Guinda*, belongs here if the second element is
*dag- 'good' (cf. British *Andagin*, OW *Cunedag*),[1310] but it could equally well
be a form of MW *Gwyndaf* (< **-tam-*) (see ‡67).

‡66 *w already > gw in W.; LHEB §49*

[66] (A) Jackson simply lists (pp. 385–86) one late example *without* this
change in anlaut (his other forms having -U- in inlaut, on which see below):

1.   1028/214/850 VENDVMAGLI

[66] Further examples from Wales and further north (not attempting to
eliminate Irish and Latin names, since these were to some extent subject to
the native Welsh development)[1311] are:

2.   328/44 VENDONI
3.   339/68 VICTORINI
4.   392/77 VERACIVS
5.   390/96 VENDESETLI
6.   394/103 [V]ENEDOTIS [with insufficient room for **[GV]-]
7.   349/121/4 VELVOR[IA]
8.   358/138 **VOTECORIGAS**/VOTEPORIGIS
9.   368/b/150 VENDVBARI
10. 376/174 VENNISETLI
11. 400/177 VINNEMAGLI
12. 2020 VERE[
13. 408/229/848 VEDOMAVI (or VEDOMALI)
14. 419/284 VE[ ]MAIE
15. 422/298 **VENDOGNI**/VENDAGNI FILI V[(?)

[1307] See above, ‡18, where the possibility that **g* has been lost in 451/401 DAARI is also
discussed.
[1308] Ziegler, p. 172. But KHJ rejects this: 'the separate **OA** is clear; visit, Dec. 1950.'
[1309] Radford and Thomas's reading, *Mute Stones*, p. 281. See ‡‡ 18 and 25 above.
[1310] See above, ‡15n.
[1311] e.g. *Victor, Victorem* > W. *Gwythyr, Gwythur*: Lloyd-Jones, *Y Geninen*, 44 (1926), 3, and
BBCS, 14 (1950–52), 36; Bromwich & Evans, *Culhwch and Olwen*, p. 68.

16. 430/306 VICTOR
17. 429/307 VENDONI
18. 445/354 **VITALIANI**/VITALIANI
19. 452/400 VALAVI or VALAVITIVI
20. 506 (Scotland) **VICULA** (dubious reading)
21. 510/Scot.13 VETTA F(*ilius*) VICTI or VICTRICIS[1312] or VICTR[
22. 516/Scot.1 VIVENTIVS[1313]
23. 2023/Scot.4 VENTIDIVS (?)[1314]
24. 2036/Dor.i VIDCV[ ], VIDA[R?][1315]

[66] I ignore the following as very uncertain readings: 993/124/18 UON (Macalister); and 372/160 **VUGLOB** (Nash-Williams). I also ignore various forms with W-, which is a late letter (one that came into use after /gw-/ had arisen):
980/46a WLIGUE (Nash-Williams) or WUMERE, WILMERE, or WALMERE (Macalister) – read S(*ignum*) S(*ancti*) (or S(*cribae*)) LIGUE by Radford (quoted in the *Corpus*)
337/60 VVLMER
1032/281 WLEDER (also WINI according to Macalister, but Nash-Williams has EWINI)

[66] (B) The first of Jackson's examples showing the change in anlaut (pp. 385–86) is 406/215/844 GVANI, but I omit this on the grounds that it has GV- from the labiovelar /g^w/ < IE *g^{w}h, which may have become W. /gw-/ without ever passing through a stage /w/. In the same inscription, Jackson rightly rejects Macalister's [G]VECTI); the reading may have been [AD]VECTI or similar.[1316]

[66] Jackson's remaining examples in anlaut are:

1. 979/46 GUADAN [and GURHI]
2. 1000/182 GUOILLAUC, GUARTHI[GIRN]

[66] To these we can add:

3. 984/59 GURCI

[1312] CIIC ii, p. 202.
[1313] According to Rhys, *Englyn*, p. 36, Latin *Viventius* was probably selected to render an Irish name in *béo*- 'living'. Such names occur throughout Insular Celtic: Evans, *BBCS*, 24 (1970–72), 427–28.
[1314] Handley, *EME*, 10 (2001), 194, n. 132, notes two examples of *Ventidius* in North Africa.
[1315] Radford & Jackson, in RCHM, *Dorset*, ii/2, p. 311, suggest these are *Gwyddgu* and MW *Gwydar*. Cf. *Vidaris*, ‡14.
[1316] Sims-Williams, in Evans FS, pp. 208–9; LHEB, p. 385, n. 4. Cf. Gaulish(?) *Vanus* and *Atvanus* in Holder iii, 101 and 742? For *Advectus* see also Tab.Vindol. ii, p. 390. The trace of [D] or [P] was first noted by Rhys, *AC*, 5th ser. 12 (1895), 181, who suggested *Advectius* or *Advectis* or 'a Celtic form *Duecti*'. He learnt that GVANI, by contrast, was complete and not acephalous before the stone was damaged.

4. 348/b/110/27 GURHIRT or GURHIRET (either linguistically preferable to GURHIST, ‡36)
5. 1014/231/908 GUORGORET
6. 1033/287 GUADGAN (or GU(*reic*), according to Ifor Williams, but this is doubted by Jackson)[1317]
7. 1041/376 GURMARC
8. 2021 GVINNDA
9. 1066 (Man) GURIAT
10. 2035 (Spoleto, Italy) GUIL
11. 971/35 [G]VIRNIN (Ifor Williams and Radford). This reading, inspired by a possible trace of G- in a drawing by Skinner, was rejected by Jackson as too uncertain.[1318] None of these writers was aware of Lhuyd's drawing in BL Stowe MS 1023, fo. 91r, which shows GVRG . . . very clearly. The remaining letters appear at first sight to be NIH or NIN (with two different types of N), but bearing in mind the shapes of U and M elsewhere on the stone, other possibilities are GVRGUIN (cf. OW *Gurguin*) or GVRGUM (cf. OB *Gurcum*, MB *G(u)orcu(n)f*).[1319] Whatever the exact termination, this clearly belongs under (B).

[66] Jackson showed conclusively that once /gw-/ had arisen in anlaut and started to be written GU-, the graph -GU- came to be used by analogy for medial /w/.[1320] It follows from this that inscriptions with medial -GU- can be added to those which postdate the rise of /gw-/. The one cited by Jackson (p. 386), and contrasted with 1023/239/927 GLIUISSI 'of the same date', is:

12. 1024/255/926 GLIGUIS

[66] The following can be added:

13. 980/46a or S(*ignum*) S(*ancti*) (or S(*cribae*)) LIGUE (Radford; cf. WLIGUE Nash-Williams, etc. above)[1321]
14. 2008/82]ESILLIMARIGUELIO (cf. OW *Mergualdus* < OE *Merewalh, Merewald*)[1322]
15. 1014/231/908 GUORGORET (also at 5. above, but cited here for the spelling of medial /(w)o/)[1323]
16. 2022/253/984 COVLGVEN or GVLGVEN

[1317] BWP, pp. 29–30; LHEB, p. 386, n. 1. If GUADGAN is correct, compare 979/46 GUADAN and 520/Scot.5 BARROVADI; see above, ‡38n.
[1318] LHEB, pp. 385–86; cf. Macalister and Nash-Williams's readings, Rhys, *Englyn*, p. 22 (GVRGNIM), and BWP, p. 18.
[1319] LL, p. 186; Chrest., p. 211. The spelling of OW *Gurcum* with -g- rather than -c- would exceptional, however. If GVRGNIN, cf. *Sicogninus* in KGP, pp. 219 and 268.
[1320] LHEB, pp. 391–94. See also Sims-Williams, in Mac Cana FS, pp. 217–18.
[1321] See also ‡‡ 17, 34, 39, and 58.
[1322] Sims-Williams, *Religion and Literature*, p. 48, nn. 162–63.
[1323] See above, ‡38.

17. 1004/260/884 GELUGUIN (possibly with initial G- < /gw-/ < /w-/ too)[1324]

18. 1035/303 ETG(*uin*) (Nash-Williams, following Radford)[1325]

[66] Note also the following, which seem to have QU in place of GU:[1326]

19. 1018/236/919 ILQUICI

20. 1029 TETQUINI

[66] While forms with -GU- indicate that GU- had already begun, the converse is not true: forms with -U- continued in existence after the rise of GU-, as we see, for instance, from 1033/287 with both GUADGAN (or GU(*reic*) ADGAN) and PETUAR. There is therefore no need to add to Jackson's examples of forms with -U- rather than -GU- (p. 386): PETUAR (above); 995/133/24 ENEVIRI; 427/b/301 CATUOCONI; 986/62 IORUERT (cf. ‡90), RUALLAUN; 1023/239/927 GLIUISSI (above); 1011/220/911 HOUELT.

‡*67 Beginning of occasional loss of final -v in polysyllables; LHEB §66.3*

No inscriptional evidence is cited. An example is 1005/191/886 BRAN-CU(:)F, if interpreted as BRANCU F[ECIT] rather than as BRANCUF (cf. OC *Wincuf* etc.).[1327] 2021 GVINNDA, OW *Guinda*, may belong here as a form of MW *Gw(y)nda(f)* (< *-*tam*-),[1328] but the second element could be *dag- 'good' (see ‡65).

‡*68 mp, nt, nc already > m^{p}h, n^{t}h, ŋ^{k}h [in Welsh]; LHEB §108*

I take this with ‡71 below, i.e. the further development to /mh nh ŋh/.[1329]

[68] (A) Jackson notes (p. 502) that this change is not yet shown in:

1. 394/103 CANTIORI

2. 409/198/849 [*sic*, not '514'] CARANTORIVS [also PVMPEIVS, which the ogam seems to render **PoP[**, possibly substituting /p/ for the un-Irish /mp/ or showing a Primitive Irish development to /b/][1330]

[1324] See above, ‡22.

[1325] Doubts about this reading are expressed by Edwards; see p. 279 below.

[1326] See above, ‡38. Another possible example is 1063/Dor.ii QUI[(Macalister: IUI[ ); Radford & Jackson note in RCHM, *Dorset*, ii/2, p. 311, that an Irish name or a Latin name like *Quintus* 'would be quite unexpected at this period'. According to Radford & Jackson QUI[may be preceded by FIL[I] but to my eyes the still raised surface rules out their [I] rather than some other letter; hence QUI[may be the middle not the start of a name.

[1327] See above, ‡55. On loss of /-v/ cf. Olson & Padel, *CMCS*, 12 (1986), 55.

[1328] LL, pp. 235–37 (tenth-century cleric); EWGT, p. 57. Cf. 449/384 **CUNATAMI/ CVNOTAMI**. KHJ notes the collection of -*tam* names in Förster, *Themse*, p. 394. See also Hamp, *ÉC*, 14 (1974), 187–92; NWÄI, p. 428; SWWF, pp. 454 and 459, n. 15.

[1329] On this sound change cf. TRC, pp. 95–96, with the critiques of Russell, *CMCS*, 35 (1998), 75, and Schrijver, *SC*, 33 (1999), 4 and 13.

[1330] Cf. Charles-Edwards, in *The Celtic World*, pp. 717–18, and *Early Christian Ireland*, pp. 170–71. But see also above, ‡17n., on Vulgar Latin.

3. 363/143 CARANTACVS
4. 380/84 POTENTINI
5. 407/b/258/846 CANTVSVS
6. 451/401 TVNCCETACE

[68] 514/Scot.8 CARANTI, of which Jackson gives the number '514' but does not quote (see above), is indeed irrelevant as the /nt/ is, or would be, in irrelevant post-apocope final position where it would be retained.[1331] The same applies to 361/140 ADVEN[TI]; 359/141 NV[D]INTI (or similar); 375/166 DOTHORANTI; 1034/286 PASCENT[I] (cf. 1000/182 PASCEN[T]); 516/Scot.1 VIVENTIVS; 517/Scot.2 FLORENTIVS; also 447/369 CVNIGCVS if GC is the correct reading and represents /ŋk/ (unlikely) rather than /ŋg/.[1332]

[68] Further examples where /nk/ and /nt/ etc. have not changed are:

7. 456/404 **GENDILI**/GE[ ] (see below)
8. 329/42 CANNTIANI
9. 1033/287 ANTERUNC[1333]
11. 2019 TVNCCE[(if genuine a male version of TVNCCETACE above);
12. 2023/Scot.4 VENTIDIVS (?)

[68] I omit 384/83 SANCTINVS owing to the peculiar nature of its cluster.[1334] Obviously forms in which NC and NT seem to denote /n'g/ and /n'd/ arising by syncope are omitted, for example 1000/182 CONCENN and 1024/255/926 BRANTUI. In 415/278 IN[TA]ENVI (Macalister) is less likely that IN[G]ENVI, and 454/402 DENCVI may be DEN[O]VI or similar – although for *denk- compare 442/346 MACCVDICCL (Lhuyd) and Ir. Déclán < *denk-lo-.[1335] 2034/871 BELGINCU might in theory have Pr.Ir. NC as a spelling of /g/ in *Belgicus* (contrasting with G for British-Latin /γ/ in BELG-), rather as a modern Greek might write *Entelbais* for *Edelweis*. Note, however, Knight's new reading BELGINT +, with /nt/ in irrelevant post-apocope final position.[1336] If the reading in 466/Ok23 is INCENVI (ogam **IGENAVI**) rather than INGENVI, the NC may conceivably correspond to Irish **G** /g/ here too.[1337]

[1331] Cf. LHEB, p. 503, n. 1.
[1332] Cf. above, ‡48.
[1333] See BWP, p. 32, where however Williams slightly prefers the (here irrelevant) alternative ANT (= *int*, MW *yn*) + ERUNC 'very near' (cf. Lejeune, *ÉC*, 31 (1995), 113, for *(p)eri-) to ANTER-UNC = *hanner-wnc* 'half-near' (cf. McKee, *Juvencus*, p. 471). But could ANTERUNC be a miscopying of Latin ANTERUNT 'they have gone before, predeceased' (*anteeo*)?
[1334] See above, ‡51.
[1335] See Ziegler, p. 165, and above, ‡18.
[1336] On BELGINT see ‡53 above.
[1337] See further ‡74 below.

[68] (B) No inscriptions where the change has happened are cited by Jackson, and the only likely one[1338] I can find is:

1. 988/67 GENILLIN (MW *Gen(n)illyn*), based on Latin *Gentilius* (or *Gentilis*) – although it is not impossible that this was borrrowed via the Irish form seen in 456/404 **GENDILI/GE[**, especially as this would explain the absence of raising of /ent/ > /int/.[1339] In the latter case, the Welsh sound change would be /nd/ > /nn/ rather than /nt/ > /nh/. If, however, /nh/ is the sound in GENILLIN, there is a clear reason why it may not have been written NH: the same inscription includes an NH of a different description in the name MENHIR = *mein + hir* .[1340] This last is the only example of NH in the entire corpus (apart from 2038 BRANHUI, with silent H),[1341] and MH, NGH, GH, and CGH are completely absent. Note that in 337/60 VVLMER, and 980/46a WUMERE, WILMERE, or WALMERE if Macalister's readings are correct, the H of OE -*here* 'army' may have been omitted after M (perhaps M for /v/ in OE *Wulfhere*?); a more likely Old English comparison, however, is *Wulfmær*.[1342]

[68] Jackson rightly notes (p. 502, n. 1) that 971/35 CINI (OW *Cini*, MW *Cyny*)[1343] and 356/132/9 POTENINA are unlikely to be examples of /nh/, the former because it probably never had *nt. He tends to favour the view of Ifor Williams and Nash-Williams that POTENINA 'is simply the engraver's mistake for *Potentina*'.[1344] Another possibility is Irish influence. Primitive Irish did not have clusters of nasal + voiceless stop like /nt/ (which had become /d/). One way of dealing with them was to substitute a voiced stop, for example /nd/ in 456/404 **GENDILI/GE[** for Latin *Gentilius* (or *Gentilis*).[1345] Another way may be seen in 409/198/849 PVMPEIVS, where the ogam **PoP[** omits the /m/, and possibly also substitutes /b/ for /p/ (although both **P**s may = /p/ and the loss of /m/ may be Vulgar Latin).[1346] 491/Ok55 AVDETI (if the reading is not ANDETI) could conceivably be similar, if it

---

[1338] On 455/403 FANNVCI see below. It seems unlikely that the obscure 1062/Dor.v GONGORIE represents W. *cyng(h)or* (: OI *cocur*) 'council, counsel', although compare *Tangwystl* 'peace-pledge' as a female name. McClure, *EHR*, 22 (1907), 729, read GONGDRIE, and suggested it was a Frankish female name, comparing *Gundric presbyter* in the Cartulary of Redon. Only GON[ ]RIE is clear, and the alleged second O looks like a T to me.

[1339] See above, ‡‡ 17n and 27.

[1340] See above, ‡27.

[1341] LHEB, p. 392, n. 2; see ‡58.

[1342] See forms in von Feilitzen, *Pre-Conquest Personal Names*, pp. 421–22: *Wulmari* (gen.), *Wlmer*, *Vlmar*, etc.

[1343] BWP, p. 17.

[1344] *AC*, 91 (1936), 15.

[1345] See above.

[1346] Rhys, *AC*, 5th ser. 16 (1899), 134, and *PBA*, 6 (1913–14), 63, compared 520/Scot.5 FECERVT for *fecerunt*, but in fact Macalister reads FECERVTN with ligatured TN (KHJ agreed). See ‡17n. above on VL *Popeianus*, *Popeia*, etc.

is for *Audentii*.[1347] A further strategy might be to drop the stop. This seems to occur in 455/403 FANNVCI and 489/a/Ok13 FANONI/**SVAQQUCI** (for **SVANNUCI** ?or **SVANNUNI**), probably representing British *Σwant-*.[1348] POTENINA may be a comparable Irish attempt to deal with the Latin /nt/ by omitting the /t/.

[68] It must be admitted that the attempt by Williams and Nash-Williams to explain POTENINA without reference to /nt/ > /nh/ was probably inspired by the view that the stone was epigraphically early (6th cent. according to Nash-Williams and Jackson). There are no clear *linguistic* pointers to (or against) an early date. One cannot argue that the raising /ent/ > /int/ is not admitted,[1349] as one would expect it to be if /nt/ > /nh/ were admitted, because *theoretically* the E could represent the obscure vowel of a MW ***Pedyn(h)in* < *Podintīn, far-fetched though that seems.

If 1068/b MALBREN is an abbreviation of Ir. *Mael-Brénainn*, it is indirect testimony to W. /nt/ > /nh/ since this Irish name seems to be borrowed from OW *breenhin* < *brigantīnos.[1350]

‡*69 Beginning of svarabhakti in Welsh and Cornish; LHEB §33*

[69] HIROIDIL and ODELEV below can be contrasted with other reflexes of *tl where svarabhakti is *not* shown:[1351]

[69] (A)

1. 390/96 VENDESETLI
2. 376/174 VENNISETLI
3. 377/175 CIMESETLI

[69] Although svarabhakti is not shown in 416/279 EQVESTRI, Latin influence is a possible factor.[1352] 442/346 MACCVDICCL (Lhuyd) is of course Irish,[1353] as is 353/127/7 **TRENACCATLO**, which is hardly to be compared with W. *cathl* 'song'[1354] but rather is an error (by the engraver or

---

[1347] Thomas, *Mute Stones*, pp. 281 and 301, n. 20, suggested *Aude(n)tius*, comparing RIB i 653 AVDES for AVDENS, 'the loss of -*n* in -*nt*, -*ns* being fairly common'.
[1348] See above, ‡‡ 45 and 60. Theoretically, FANNVCI could have British /nt/ → Ir. /nd/ > British /nn/.
[1349] See above, ‡27.
[1350] Cf. Uhlich, *ZCP*, 49/50 (1997), 878–88, and ‡48 above.
[1351] For 1.-3. here see above, ‡36. On HIROIDIL = *Hirhoeddl* see above, ‡17.
[1352] Nash-Williams states that there is no parallel for the use of *Equester*, gen. *Equestris*, in classical or Christian-Roman inscriptions. But see Kajanto, p. 313, OPEL ii, 121, and Tab.Vindol. ii, p. 391.
[1353] See above for comparison with *Décl-án*.
[1354] LHEB, p. 498.

by modern readers?) for **TRENACCATO** in view of the preferable roman-letter reading TRENACATVS.[1355]

[69] (B) Jackson notes (p. 337) that svarabhakti *has* occurred in

1. 994/125/22 HIROIDIL. [CAROTINN in the same inscription is conceivably another example.[1356]]
A further example is:
2. 1032/281 ODELEV (= *Hoedlyw*, ‡80 below), which Iwan Wmffre compares with MW forms such as *Hotheleu* in 1219.[1357]

[69] These seem to be the only certain examples, unless one gives into the temptation of using svarabhakti to explain uncertain forms such as 1027/265/923 GABALA (Macalister only)[1358] by W. *gafl* 'fork', 1018/236/919]ACER (A uncertain; Macalister: CTCER) by Gaulish *Sacro-*, W. *hagr*, MC *hager* 'ugly',[1359] 372/160 DE[CAB]ARBALOM (ogam equivalent **[DECCA]IBARVALB** (Macalister; Nash-Williams: **DECCAIBAR VUGLOB**)) with reference to OI *balb* 'dumb',[1360] 2029/p.39i ERECOR by Old Norse *Erekr*, and so on. If ERECOR has svarabhakti, it is probably *Irish*, as in 84 **ERACOBI MAQI ERAQETAI** and 32 **ERACIAS** < **Erko-* and *Heric* for *Ercc* in Tírechán.[1361] A clear example of svarabhakti *in Irish* is 427/a/301 **DUBAR[CUNAS]** (but **DUBR[ACUNAS]**

[1355] See ‡48n. above.
[1356] Cf. ‡‡ 22 and 57 above, and below, p. 344.
[1357] Wmffre, *Language and History*, i, 319; cf. *St Davids Episcopal Acta*, ed. Barrow, no. 77, pp. 98–99 (*Hothel(en)*), and no. 97, p. 113 (*Hothalum*), wrongly indexed under *Hywel*, p. 186.
[1358] The alternative reading GAI is connected by Rhys (apud Westwood, LW, p. 27) and by Jackson, in *Celt and Saxon*, pp. 36 and 45, with *Gai(i) Campus* (near Leeds) in *Annales Cambriae*, s.a. 656, and *Historia Brittonum*, §64. In all instances it may be the Welsh name *Ceil/Cai* (< Latin *Caius*, TYP, pp. 303, 307, and 547; Loth, *Noms des saints bretons*, p. 20; Orme, *Saints of Cornwall*, pp. 156–58) spelt with *G-* on the pattern of *Caius/Gaius* in Latin. However, Dr Redknap now suggests that the reading may be GALCU[N], comparing *Gallcun* in LL, pp. 212 and 262. Davies, *Llandaff Charters*, p. 164, dates the first to *c.* 862 and the second to the generation before *c.* 1022. This is MW *Gallgwn* (Bartrum, *Welsh Genealogies 300–1400*, v, 111, vi, 254, and vii, 563). Cf. 3002/F2 GALLMAU, connected in IEMB, p. 118, with *Gall-* as ethnonym (cf. Lloyd-Jones, *Geirfa*, s.v. *Gallwyδel*), though note also W. *gallu* etc.
[1359] Lewis & Pedersen, p. 94; KGP, pp. 262–63; Maier, *Celtica*, 19 (1987), 96–97.]ACER could be [S]ACERDOS or Latin *ager* 'field' (if not pronounced with /γ/). Note also Latin *Acer* (OPEL i, 12), and *Acero* and *Aceracus* in Holder i, 17 and iii, 481, compared by him with 124 **A**><**ERAS**> *A(i)cher* (Ziegler, p. 122; McManus, *Guide*, pp. 116 and 180, n. 65). A Welsh cognate would be *Ager* and this may be attested in *Englynion y Beddau*, III.11, ed. Jones, *PBA*, 53 (1967), 136.
[1360] LEIA B-12. Since writing this I note that KHJ wondered whether the Irish name contained **-barrobalvos* 'Dumbhead', with the British -LOM being an attempt to spell the Irish svarabhakti /-lᵊβ/.
[1361] See ‡57n. above.

Nash-Williams).[1362] 330/66 CATIRI could be a precursor of W. *cadr*, with svarabhakti, but on the whole W. **Cedyr* or OI *Ca(i)thrí* is more likely.[1363]

[69] Two other possible examples can be mentioned, one from Wales and the other from Cornwall:
In 348/b/110/27 GURHIRT (Nash-Williams) there has clearly been metathesis (cf. OB *Gleuherd*, etc. versus OW *Gu(o)rhitir*, OC *Gurheter*, OB *Gurhedr* and *Gleuhetr*),[1364] and if the reading GURHIRET is correct (see ‡36n.) svarabhakti presumably has occurred after the metathesis.

[69] The possible example in Cornwall is 486/Ok56 CVMRECINI, if this reading by Thomas is preferred to CVMREGNI and if the second element is MC **Rigni*, seen with svarabhakti in the medieval spellings of Tregony (*Trefhrigoni* 1049, *Treligani* 1086, *Trigoni* 1201, and *Tregeny* 1214).[1365]

[69] Although svarabhakti is not regarded as a feature of Old Breton, note that it occurs in 3010/M1 HERANNUEN and HERA*N*AL (or HERAN-HAL), and 3014/M5 HARENBILI and HERANHAL, which anticipate the svarabhakti noted by Jackson in Vannetais *beragn* 'pile' < *bern*.[1366]

‡70 ṽ already > v before r, fr; LHEB §100

No inscriptional evidence is cited (p. 484). It may be worth noting that alternation between /mr/ and /br/ is quite widespread, as in OI *mrath* versus W. *brad*. Either of these may occur in lenition position in 471/Ok39 MOBRATTI.[1367]

‡71 mᴾh, nᵗh, ŋᵏh already > mh, nh, ŋh [in Welsh]; LHEB §108

See ‡68 above.

‡72 öü falls together with öü and ẹi with ei, in Welsh; LHEB §§ 46.2; 207.5

No inscriptional evidence is cited, inevitably.

‡73 w already > gw in Breton; LHEB §49

There is no inscriptional evidence. The inscriptions cling to U: 3005/F5 VENOMAILI; 3007/C2 VORMVINI; 3010/M1 HERANNUEN; 3022/I3 TVRTOVALDVS. This may be mere convention, as in Old Breton, where a

---

[1362] See Ziegler, p. 202, and Uhlich, *Morphologie*, pp. 49 and 229. But Nash-Williams's reading was also that of Rhys, *AC*, 5th ser. 13 (1896), 100. Cf. ‡38n. **DUBAR[ACUNAS]** is a further possibility. Cf. Fig. 1.1.
[1363] See above, ‡19.
[1364] See above, ‡36.
[1365] Padel, *Popular Dictionary of Cornish Place-Names*, pp. 166 and 210, and above, ‡48.
[1366] LHEB, p. 337 ('not Breton'); HPB, p. 405. This example of svarabhakti is not among those rejected by Piette in his review in *SC*, 5 (1970), 158.
[1367] LEIA s.v *mrath* (> *brath*). See above, ‡42.

name like *Uurmhaelon* is spelt without *Gu-* long after the period when *Gu-* had started to be written for /gw-/. Indeed, the first element *Uurmhaelon* (which may be that of VORM-VINI unless this is VOR-MVINI) *may* (according to the conventional etymology from IE *$g^w her$-*) have an original labiovelar, and this may never have passed through a stage /w/ (compare ‡66 on 406/215/844 GVANI).[1368]

‡74 *Loss of internal γ between front vowels or vowels of different quality, and finally after ī; LHEB §89*

For other positions see ‡‡ 25, 39 and 65 above. Note that 'vowels of different quality' does not include /iːγa/ and /iːγo/ which are covered in ‡65.[1369]

[74] (A) Jackson notes (pp. 445–47) that /γ/ has not been lost in:

1. 359/141 (R)EGIN(I) [> OW *Regin, Rein*]
2. 325/33 BIVATIGI(RNI) [his preferred reading, but cf. ‡27 above]
3. 408/229/848 CATOTIGIRNI
4. 990/108/1 TIGERN(I) [or TIGER[N or TIGEIR[N][1370]
5. 404/270/843 TEGERNACUS [also ogam **TEGE[** according to Macalister alone]
6. 334/54 TEGERNACVS
7. 477/Ok11 TEGERNOMALI

[74] To these can be added:

8. 419/284 TIGIRNICI
9. 1403/Ok25]IGERNI [FIL]I TIGERNI
10. 432/312 TIGERNACI (cf. OI *Tigernach*)
11. 436/316 LITOGENI (cf. 273 **LIT[ENI]** and OI *Lithach*, also Gaulish *Litugenus*, Romano-British *Litugenus/Litegenus*)[1371]
12. 515/Scot.9 DVMNOGENI (DIMNOGENI Macalister)[1372]

[74] It might be objected to the last two items that the /γ/ would not be intervocalic after syncope, and that a cluster like /n'γ/ is not relevant here.[1373]

[1368] Sims-Williams, in Evans FS, p. 208; HPB, pp. 428–29. Whether or not /g^w/ was retained in Brittonic (in which case *Uurm-* would be hypercorrect), there is no doubting the correctness of Jackson's doctrine that OB *Uu-* spellings could be merely conventional, despite IEMB, p. 152.

[1369] Assuming 1209/Ok12 CAOCI is < *$Kagi\bar{a}kos$ (‡25 above), it does not belong here since the velar was lost very early (cf. LHEB, pp. 450–51).

[1370] On the reading see above, ‡27.

[1371] See above, ‡38.

[1372] On the reading see ‡38n.

[1373] /n'γ/ > /ni/ seems to be late orthographically, and Jackson assigned a long time-span to it phonetically (hence it is not in his 'Chronological Table'); see LHEB, pp. 439 and 470 (the form *Unust* from the Lindisfarne *Liber Vitae* cited as Welsh on p. 438 and contrasted with OC *Ungust* (Bodmin, p. 87) is really Pictish; see Sims-Williams, *CMCS*, 32 (1996), 42 and n. 61, and Forsyth, in Anderson FS, pp. 23–26); HPB, p. 719. 1054/Ok43 DONIERT is probably an example. See above, ‡28n. For a collection of OW names like *Cingal* and *Adgar*

However, a similar objection could be made to 498/Nb7 **BRIGOMAGLOS** which Jackson *does* include as a relevant example under /iːɣa/ and /iːɣo/ (see ‡65 above), no doubt because syncope did not occur, as in 978/49 **BRIAMAIL**.[1374] In the same way, we cannot assume that **DVMNOGENI** would develop via syncope to *Dyfnien[1375] rather than *Dyfnöen in view of forms like OW *Dumnagual*, MW *Dyfnawal*, beside OW *Dumngual*, MW *Dyfnwal*, and OW *Urbagen*, MW *Uruöen* beside OW *Urbgen*, MW *Urien*.[1376]

[74] The following, which are not included by Jackson, occur in Irish contexts and are probably all Irish: 362/142 **INIGENA**; 433/313 **[A]NDA-GELLI/ANDAGELLI**; 441/345 **ANDAGELLI** (cf. OI *Indgall*);[1377] 506 (Scotland) **CUGINI**.[1378] 387/95 **FIGULINI** is Latin. 466/Ok23 **IGENAVI** corresponds to roman-letter INGENVI or INCENVI (< *Ingenuus*), and may have **G** for [ŋg] or [ŋk] (perhaps confirming that there was originally no ogam symbol for [ŋ(g)] ?).[1379] Or could it reflect Vulgar Latin, since IGENNVS may occur for *Ingenuus* in Roman Britain, at Cirencester?[1380] If the reading INCENVI is correct, the Irish /g/ may have been substituted for the non-Irish cluster /nk/ = [ŋk], but here again Vulgar Latin may be a factor, since hypercorrect INCENUINA appears for *Ingenuina*, also in Gloucestershire.[1381]

[74] 469/Ok34 **CNEGVMI** or **CLEGUMI** is too obscure to include. 2019 **RIGELLA** (if genuine) could be from *Rīɣo-yellā (with the same second element as ANDAGELLI) and if so have /ɣˈɣ/ > (?) /g/.[1382] On the other hand, it is strikingly like the Old Irish female names *Rigell* (*Rigell*?), *Ricell* and *Ricchell* and could be an Irish name.[1383]

(possibly OE) see Lloyd-Jones, in Torna FS, p. 86, and *Celtica*, 3 (1956), 209–10. Cf. HPB, pp. 720–21.

[1374] On these see Rhys, *Englyn*, pp. 7–8, and Jackson, *Archaeologia Aeliana*, 5th series, 10 (1982), 61–65.

[1375] Jackson, in RCAHMS, *Selkirkshire*, p. 113, notes that *Dumnogenos 'would give Welsh *Dyfnien or *Dynien, but it appears not to occur; the cognate *Domangen* is however found, rarely, in Old Irish.'

[1376] LHEB, p. 648; WG, pp. 190–91; Morgan & Morgan, *Welsh Surnames*, pp. 87–88; Koch, *Gododdin*, pp. cxxii–cxxiii and 134.

[1377] See above, ‡22.

[1378] See above, ‡‡ 25n. and 48n.

[1379] Sims-Williams, *TPS*, 91 (1993), 145–51. See also Thomas, *Mute Stones*, p. 263; and ‡68 above.

[1380] Wright & Hassall, *Britannia*, 3 (1972), 352, cited by Smith, VLRB, pp. 918 and 922. They note, however, that Holder regarded *Ingennus* as Celtic. The popularity of *Ingenuus* and cognates in Britain is noted by Tomlin, *Britannia*, 28 (1997), 459 (cf. 472, n. 77), in connection with a Caerleon tombstone.

[1381] See above, ‡68; and see Smith, VLRB, p. 922, citing RIB i 123 (where it is suggested that the C may be due to nineteenth-century recutting).

[1382] The handbooks do not seem to cover /ɣˈɣ/. See Lewis & Pedersen, p. 125 (on *diwedydd* cf. WG, p. 180); HPB, pp. 326–27. But cf. OB *Ri-ginet*, Chrest., p. 159?

[1383] *Patrician Texts*, ed. Bieler, p. 181; *Tripartite Life*, ed. Stokes, pp. 76, 349 and 432; CGSH, pp. 84 (*Ricchell*) and 127 (*Ricell*, var. *Riagail*).

[74] 3013/M4 DRILEGO could be a compound of OB *Dri((c)h)-* 'face' (or perhaps *tre-*, *dre-* 'through, thorough(ly)-)'[1384] and OB *lei* 'smaller' < /leɣii:h/ < /laɣii:s/. While the /ɣ/ of the latter had probably been absorbed into the /ei̯/ 'before the beginning of the OB. period', there may have been etymological awareness owing to the positive *lau* 'small' (cf. 3016/M7 LAGU) and in particular the superlative OB *laham* < *laɣ'haμ* where the /ɣ/ may have survived longest.[1385] DRILEGO may thus mean 'much smaller' or 'smaller face, of smaller appearance'; compare the MB epithet *Lagat-ley* '(qui a un) œil plus petit?'.[1386]

[74] (B) Jackson (p. 456) cites one inscriptional example where the change has happened:

1. 979/46 GURHI (MW *Gwrhy*, cf. OW *Gelhig* and *Gelhi*, MW *hy* 'bold').[1387]

[74] A further example would be 1046/Ok8 ARAHI, if from **Ariosegos*, but ARTHI has also been read (but rejected by Macalister).[1388] Note also the many readings of 1006/197/842 TEFROIHI, TESROIHI, NEFROIHI, REFSDIHI, and REFSOIHI (but see ‡42 on NEFROIHI). Any comparison of 971/35 CINI with OW *Cinhi* is very uncertain.[1389] We can, however, add two more examples to Jackson's one:
2. 464/Ok65 MAVISIR belongs here, if it is from *Magestu-rīks* 'plain-king' (cf. MW *mäes* < **magest-*), with -V- as a hiatus filler /w/, as suggested above (‡25).
3. 1012/223/993 IUTHAHELO has -HAHEL- = MW *hael* 'generous' as its second element. If *hael* derives from **sag-lo-* or similar, IUTHAHELO would belong in ‡48 above (**ɣl* > *i̯l*); we would have to regard -HAHEL- as an artificial spelling of the diphthong, as Rhys and Jackson do, *Isra(h)el* being an obvious model; Jackson gives OB *Iedicahel* and *Iudicahel* (beside *Iudicael*) as further examples of 'meaningless *h*'.[1390] Schrijver, however, has

---

[1384] Cf. Chrest., pp. 125–26; HPB, pp. 151 and 692–93; SBCHP, pp. 125 and 246–47, and above, ‡60n., on the vocalism.
[1385] See HPB, pp. 159 and 236, n. 5; SBCHP, p. 305. On LAGU see above, ‡25.
[1386] DGVB i, 239. For *Dri((c)h)-* see Gramm., p. 50. MB *le* 'oath' (SBCHP, pp. 310–13) is a less likely etymon, as is *lou*, *leu* 'light', suggested in IEMB, p. 209.
[1387] Williams, *AC*, 90 (1935), 94. On -*hi(g)* < **sego-* see Hamp, *BBCS*, 16 (1954–56), 277; SBCHP, p. 68; GPN, pp. 254–55.
[1388] See above, ‡36.
[1389] BWP, p. 17; LHEB, p. 502, n. 1; and above, ‡37n.
[1390] WG, p. 129; Gramm., p. 56 (**saglo* < **sagilo*); LWP, p. 232; HPB, p. 558 (cf. p. 712). Rhys, *AC*, 5th ser. 16 (1899), 147, compared Bede's *Peanfahel*, but cf. Jackson, in *Problem of the Picts*, pp. 143, 161, and 165. There is rhyme between *hael* and *Israel* in BT, p. 73, l. 25, ed. Haycock, *Blodeugerdd*, p. 68. For intrusive *h* in diphthongs, Lewis, *Disgrifiad o Orgraff Hen Gymraeg*, pp. 662 and 707, notes only *gurehic*, *bahell*, and *delehid*, all from Oxoniensis Posterior, and *luhin* and *cehir* from LL, p. 207 (but Dr Jon Coe regards the latter, also at LL, p. 78, as *cyhyr* 'sinew' with etymological *h*). HPB, p. 558, adds only *Guhir* from LL and *Mahurth* from the Black Book of Chirk (WG, p. 188), neither bona fide Old Welsh.

argued that *hael* derives from **sæg-elo-* < **segh-elo-*, and this is supported not only by Gaulish names like *Deprosagilos* and *Sagill(i)us*, but also by the assonance between *trahäel, ued, gefel*, etc. in *Marwnat Dylan*, a poem in which *mäes* also seems still to be dissyllabic, and by the fact that OW *ae* rarely denotes /ai/.[1391] I put IUTHAHELO here under (B) in view of Jackson's argument that *h* would not be used for /γ/; but see below, p. 280.

[74] 3021/I2 MAONIRN < **Magonotigernos* look as first sight like a case of loss of /γ/ between front vowels; but more likely it has syncope in the element *-(d)įγįrn*. The development may have been to **maγon'nįγįrn* by syncope of composition vowel and /n'd/ > /nn/, and then **maγonn'γįrn* by syncope of the short, immediately pretonic vowel, whence MAONIRN, with the /γ/ absorbed into the /ı/.[1392] If MAONIRN were a case of loss of *intervocalic* /γ/ in **tigernos* it would be unique among the inscriptions, apart of course from 1000/182 GUARTHI[where [GIRN] or similar no doubt occurred at the start of the next line – note that the development of **tïγïrn* > **teγïrn seems* not yet to have occurred or at least to be recognized in writing.[1393]

[74] If 1068/b MALBREN is an abbreviation of Ir. *Mael-Brénainn*, it is indirect testimony to loss of Brittonic /γ/, since this Irish name seems to be borrowed from OW *breenhin* < **brigantīnos*.[1394]

‡*75 Beginning of an on-glide before initial s-groups [in Welsh]; LHEB §119*

See also ‡87 below. The only Old Welsh example of this before the Book of Llandaf is supposed to be *istlinnit* in the Juvencus, but here the *i* may really be miscopied from the abbreviation for *id est*.[1395]

No inscriptional evidence is cited. Only forms without prosthetic vowel occur: 1023/239/927 SCILOC (or SCITOC ??);[1396] 2018 SPUO (obscure); and 444/352 STACATI (dubious reading, and possibly acephalous).

[1391] SBCHP, pp. 135 and 138–41; GPN, pp. 80–81 and 251; MLH v/1, pp. 327–28; BT, p. 67; cf. Gruffydd, *Math vab Mathonwy*, pp. 219–20; Haycock, *YB*, 13 (1985), 33–36.

[1392] On MAONIRN see further above, ‡‡ 36 and 65. On the two types of syncope, see LHEB, pp. 643–56, and above, ‡‡ 38 and 40. For the reconstruction **tïγïrn* < **tigernos* see SBCHP, p. 64. Cf. *Tigernilus* and *Tigorninus* in OPEL iv, 122.

[1393] For **tïγïrn* > **teγïrn* see SBCHP, pp. 63–64 and 69–70. It cannot be used to put the inscriptions in chronological order, since both E and I could be used for /ï/ (note -ERN- as well as -IRN- in the forms cited above, and an interesting hesitation in 990/108/1 TIGEIR[N, probably the correct reading (Rhys, *AC*, 5th ser. 13 (1896), 112, thinks it might be read TEGERRN[, which is linguistically unlikely). As noted above, ‡57n., the lack of affection in OW *Cattegirn* (cf. 408/229/848 CATOTIGIRNI) shows that /ï/ > /e/ occurred before internal *i*-affection (‡57 above),

[1394] Cf. Uhlich, *ZCP*, 49/50 (1997), 878–88, and ‡48 above.

[1395] McKee, *Juvencus*, p. 520.

[1396] See above, ‡18.

‡*76 w already > gw in Cornish; LHEB §49*

[76] (A) No inscriptional evidence is cited (p. 388), but the following relevant examples of V- occur in the South-West:

1. 473/a/Ok46 VITALI
2. 1205/Ok44 VITO[[1397]
3. 1210/Ok5 VALCI FILI V[ETT]ANVS (?)[1398] or V[ ]AIVS

[76] 461/Ok66 VIRICATI is uncertain, as are 463/Ok15 VRIVI (cf. ‡14n), 1048/Ok32 VIR . . . VENNORCIT,[1399] 1049/Ok33 URITIN, URITN or URI, 1050/Ok74 UROC,[1400] 1053/Ok1 VILICI, and 1055/Ok3 UAE-TUENA (in most case there are alternative readings not quoted here). Finally, 460/Ok75 VAILATHI FILI VROCHANI is probably Irish, with V-perhaps for what was already /f/.[1401]

[76] (B) The only plausible examples of the change having happened are:

1. 1060/Ok57 GURGLES or GUNGLEI etc., ‡58 above.
2. 494/Ok79 GOREVS, which looks like the MW superlative *goreu* 'best' (: OI *forg(g)u* < *wor-gous-on*), which occurs in Middle Welsh as the name of a character whose patronymic may associate him with Cornwall: *Goreu mab Custenhin*.[1402] Whether the latinization is GOREV-S or GORE-VS, the *e* rather than *o* is unexpected in the South-West, however; see ‡80 below. (Could GOREVS be intended to avoid the cumbersome sort of latinization apparently visible in 3026/I7 GENNOVEUS (if = GENNOV-EUS or GENNOVE-US) or is it influenced by Latin forms like 1059/Ok64 and 2013/383 MATHEUS?[1403]) It may be better to pursue Holder's comparison of GOREVS with OI *Gúaire*:[1404] GOREVS could be Latinization of *Gúaire*, or reflect its source, presumably something like Pr.Ir. **Gōreah*. Indeed,

---

[1397] Thomas, *CA*, 24 (1985), 174, suggests *Vitori* for *Victori*. Another possibility is a British form of *Vitalis* or similar, with the Brittonic development of /a:/. But *Vitorius* is very well attested (Mócsy, p. 316) and provides the simplest solution.

[1398] Thomas, *Mute Stones*, p. 281. With VALCI = W. *gwalch* cf. LWP, p. 402; Jenkins, *CMCS*, 19 (1990), 55–67. On the second name see above, ‡18.

[1399] Thomas, *Mute Stones*, p. 290. Tedeschi, *Scrittura e civiltà*, 19 (1995), tav. 3, reads: + VIR . . . GVENNORCIT, and I do not think that the G (read by KHJ in 1951) can be ruled out (Macalister read GVENNCREST).

[1400] Cf. *Uroc*[ ]*sius* on a *defixio* from Caistor St Edmund, Norfolk: Hassall & Tomlin, *Britannia*, 13 (1982), 408, comparing an example of *Vrocata*. Ir. *Fróech* is also a possibility.

[1401] See above, ‡48.

[1402] Lewis & Pedersen, p. 186, and *Supplement*, p. 10; Bromwich & Evans, *Culhwch and Olwen*, pp. 114 and 140; TYP, pp. 364–67.

[1403] W. *Mathew*. Cf. LHEB, pp. 367 and 373.

[1404] Holder i, 2032. Rhys, *AC*, 6th ser. 18 (1918), 192, suggested that GOREVS was the ancestor not only of Ir. *Gúaire* but also of W. *Gwair* and perhaps *Gweirydd*. In DP iv, 524, *Gweir* is derived from *Varius* but I. Williams, *BBCS*, 11 (1941–44), 83, suggests **ueĝ-* 'vigilant, etc.'; cf. Lloyd-Jones, *Geirfa*, p. 649. *Gúaire* is listed as a *io*-stem by O'Brien, *Celtica*, 10 (1973), 223, but he gives no etymology. NWÄI, p. 236, equates it with *gúaire* 'hair', a **-io*-derivative of IE **geu-ro-s*.

Goreus is how **Góre* > *Gúaire* is spelt by Adomnán.[1405] If Holder's Irish solution is adopted, the effect on the dating of the stone is significant.[1406]

[76] The other examples of GU- are all dubious readings: 1048/Ok32 GVENNCREST (Macalister) or GVENNORCIT (Tedeschi);[1407] and 1053/Ok1 GU[ ]VILIR.

‡*77 Occasional loss of final -ð in polysyllables already; LHEB §69*

No inscriptional evidence is cited. For what is worth, note 350/116/3 DAVID, in a Latin context.

‡*78 λ, 'ρ probably fully established in Welsh; LHEB §93*

No inscriptional evidence is cited. No HL or HR spellings occur, but 978/49 FLOU conceivably shows an attempt to represent the /λ/ of OW *Lou*, MW *Lleu* (cf. ‡80). It is likely, as Rhys saw, that the omission of H in 994/125/22 HIROIDIL for **HIR-HOIDIL* shows that the letter *r* was already doing duty for *rh* as well as *r*.[1408]

‡*79 5 already > ō in Cornish; LHEB §13*

No inscriptional evidence is cited. Possibly 1061/Dor.iii CATGUG (Macalister: CATTUG) in Dorset is an example, if < **Katākos*, but it could equally well be Welsh; the *u* is paralleled in W. *Cattwg*.[1409] 489/a/Ok13 SVAQQUCI has similar vocalism, but has to be counted an *Irish* form as it stands (cf. OI *Sannuch*?); and note that the roman-letter equivalent FANONI has O, which can easily mean /ɔ:/.[1410] Finally, even with /au/ > /ɔ:/ > /ö:/, it seems phonologically impossible to derive any of the following readings of 487/Ok10, CERVSIVS, CIRUSIUS, SIRVSIVS, or CIRVSINIVS (and there are others!), from *Carausius* (cf. 393/101 CARAVSIVS).[1411]

‡*80 öü > ëü in Welsh; LHEB §46.2*

According to Jackson's scheme, /öü/ has at least ten sources:

(1) British /óụ/ from IE /oụ/ and /eụ/ and British Latin *ov*.

[1405] *Life of Columba*, ed. Anderson & Anderson, I.47. On *-eus* for *-e* see Harvey, in Mac Cana FS, p. 62.

[1406] If Brittonic, the supposed /gw-/ < /w-/ dates GOREVS to periods 22–28; see p. 265 below.

[1407] See n. 1399 above.

[1408] Rhys, LWP, p. 238, and *Englyn*, p. 97; see ‡36 above and cf. WG, p. 25 on MW *araf = a'r haf*.

[1409] See above, ‡60.

[1410] See above, ‡18.

[1411] Rhys, *AC*, 5th ser. 9 (1892), 66–73, and *Celtic Britain*, pp. 286–87, claimed a Celtic origin for *Carausius* (cf. EIHM, pp. 5–6), as does Birkhan, *Germanen und Kelten*, p. 216. He was *Menapiae civis* and this can hardly mean the *Irish* Menapii, as pointed out by Haverfield, *Romanization of Roman Britain*, p. 78, n. 3. Cf. OPEL ii, 58 and 213 for *Cirusius* and *Carusus, -a*.

(2) British /á:u̯/ (with which Latin *au* sometimes fell together).[1412]

(3) British and Latin /a:γ/ (‡25).

(4) /o̯u/ by final *i*-affection (‡19) of /óu̯/ and /áu̯/.

(5) /o̯u/ by quasi-final affection by the composition vowel /i/ in **au̯i*-compounds like AVICATI (> *Eugad*), a point disputed by Schrijver, who argues that **au̯i*- became **au̯*- at syncope (‡38), and then developed to /ou/ (by rounding?) through a regular development of pretonic /au̯/ > /ou̯/ > /ëü/.[1413]

(6) /o̯u/ by internal affection (‡57) of British /au̯/ < /au̯a/ as in MW *ceuri*, plural of *cawr* < **kau̯aros*, also of British /au̯/ < Latin *au* as in *cyngheusaeth* < 'Brit. **concausi̯axtā* (< Lat. *causa*)'; but Schrijver explains the second of these by his rule of pretonic /au̯/ > /ou/.[1414]

(7) /o̯u/ by internal affection (‡57) of British /ou̯/ < Latin *au* as in 'Mod.W. *eurydd* beside *aur*, < *aurum*'; but Schrijver explains *eurydd* etc. by his rule of pretonic /au̯/ (here from Latin *au*) > /ou/.[1415]

(8) British /oγu/ on the basis of MW *meudwy* < **mogu*- (a hypothetical by-form of **magu*-); but Schrijver derives *meudwy* from **magu*- by his rule of pretonic /au̯/ > /ou/.[1416] A problem here is the coexistence of the names *Meugan* (OW *Moucan*) and *Mawgan*, which give some support to Jackson's view.[1417]

(9) British /uγu/ > /ou̯u/ > /ou̯/ on the basis of *Lugus* > MW *Lleu*, and **Lugumarkos* > OW *Loumarch*, *Leumarch*, MW *Llywarch* (with regular pretonic /ou̯/ > /öw/).[1418] According to Schrijver, however, /uγu/ may have

---

[1412] LHEB, p. 322, e.g. *aurum* > OW *our*-, and MW *eur*. Cf. SBCHP, pp. 271–72. I suggest in n. 1415 below that this is valid only for monosyllabic stressed *eur*.

[1413] LHEB, p. 369; SBCHP, pp. 268–72.

[1414] LHEB, pp. 322 and 582; SBCHP, pp. 98–100 and 270 (not explicit about *ceuri*, but this is not covered by his proposed rule of pretonic /au̯/ > /ɔ:/ (pp. 100–1), since the latter was not liable to internal affection). MW *Cawrdaf* raises a slight problem for explaining *ceuri* versus *cawr* simply by stress patterns; see above, ‡57n.

[1415] LHEB, p. 322, and n. 1, and 582; SBCHP, pp. 271–72. Schrijver suggests that MW *eur* (> Mod.W. *aur*) is analogical, and that the original tonic counterpart to *eur*- (OW *our*-) was *awr*. Important evidence for the latter, not noted in LHEB and SBCHP, is provided by the line 'A ryfed *mawr* ac *eur* ac *awr*', *Poems of Taliesin*, ed. Williams, pp. 4 and 52. Note that *awr* could have developed from *aurum* via /ɔ:r/; cf. OI *ór* [ɔ:r] 'gold' (Sims-Williams, *CMCS*, 23 (1992), 60). If Jackson is right about Celtic **du̯au* 'two' > OW *dou*, MW *deu*, Mod. W. *dau* (LHEB, pp. 336 and 373–74), MW *eur* could be the result of a similar treatment of *aurum*; but on *dou* see SBCHP, pp. 328 and 331. Probably *eur* shows the regular development of /á:u̯/ (no. (2) and note above).

[1416] LHEB, p. 441; GPC s.v. *meudwy*; SBCHP, pp. 270–71.

[1417] See above, ‡57n. Cf. **mogu*- in Holder ii, 617.

[1418] LHEB, pp. 441–42 (cf. pp. 384 and 414); cf. OC *Loumarch*, Bodmin, pp. 92 and 94. There do not seem to be any examples of the *Leumarch*, *Llywarch* stage in the inscriptions, unless 1032/281 EWINI is one (see ‡84 below). Note however: 385/89 LOVERNII; 379/170 LOVERNACI = *Llywern(og)* (cf. LHEB, p. 384, and SBCHP, p. 61); 399/176 TOVISACI = *tywysog/toísech* (cf. LHEB, pp. 186–87 and 291, n. 1, SBCHP, p. 342, and ‡‡ 17 and 46 above); 1011/220/911 HOUELT = *Hywel* (if < **suu̯el*- SBCHP, p. 162, n. 1; cf. LHEB, p. 659); 1000/182 POUOIS = *Powys* (LHEB, pp. 443–44; vocalism influenced by preceding bilabial or because the vowel was /ɔ/ < /ɔ:/ < /a:/?).

developed not via /oy̯u/ to /oy̯/ but via /uy̯u/ to /uy̯/; the latter would then have developed in the same way as *klusV- > *kluy̯V- > MW clywet and arogleu 'to hear, smell'.[1419] Note that on either explanation, a tonic development via /oy̯/ is required to explain OW Lou (MW Lleu).[1420]

(10) Immediately pretonic Late British /oy̯/ in some cases, such as *i̯oy̯ánko- > W. ieuanc (: OC iouenc) and *knoy̯énā > W. cneuen (MB cnouenn); but according to Schrijver, British may have had /uy̯/ here too.[1421]

[80] Leaving aside the problematic (5)–(10), of the rest, (2) and (3) developed according to Jackson via (2) /ɔ:y̯/ and (3) /ɔ:γ/ (at ‡18: /a:/ > /ɔ:/) to fall together as (2/3) /ɔ:y̯/ (at ‡25: /γ/ > /y̯/), which then fell together with (1) as (1/2/3) /ou/ (‡50). (1/2/3) /ou/ then developed to Pr.W. (1/2/3) /öü/ (‡62). Pr.W. (1/2/3) /öü/ then fell together with (4) /ou/, later /o̦ü/, in Pr.W. as (1/2/3/4) OW /öü/ (‡72). The latter then became /ëü/ (‡80).[1422]

[80] Jackson cites no inscriptional evidence for /öü/ > /ëü/, but there is a certain amount, especially if all the preforms listed under (1)–(10) above are included.

[80] (A) The following are the three clear cases where OU is retained (leaving out examples like 1000/182 POUOIS = Powys where a development to /ëü/ is not expected):[1423]

1. 978/49 + BRIAMAIL FLOU. Phillimore attractively derived this from Latin flāvus, which is well attested as a cognomen Flavus in Roman Britain.[1424] Alternative interpretations are suggested by the observation that F[L]OU is possibly altered from F[I]OU according to the Corpus. This suggests that the engraver intended FILIVS LOU or FI(li) LOU, i.e. OW Lou (MW Lleu) < *Lugus (cf. (9) above), and that he decided to shorten his task by not writing out fili(us) in full. Compare perhaps 1064/Dor.iv [D]ENIEL . FI[(very probably defective however) and 1005/191/886

1419 SBCHP, pp. 340–44. Cf. Hamp, Britannia, 6 (1975), 157–58, and VLRB, p. 933.

1420 See below. OW Lou is not cited in LHEB or SBCHP, but see Rhys, Cymmrodor, 21 (1908), 5; EWGT, pp. 11 and 127; Sims-Williams, CMCS, 32 (1996), 38 and n. 44 (where OE luh 'pool' > MW lleu is also suggested, pp. 39–41; cf. Coates & Breeze, Celtic Voices, pp. 242–43).

1421 LHEB, p. 384; SBCHP, pp. 330, 333, 338, and 344.

1422 On the date, cf. LHEB, p. 370, n. 1, and Jackson in SEBC, p. 284.

1423 See n. 1418 above.

1424 DP iv, 421, comparing the Brycheiniog inscription with OW Tudual flaui = Tutwal pefir in the Brycheiniog tracts in EWGT, pp. 15 and 18; RIB indexes. The first letter of FLOU now looks like a P or FI ligature, but the F is shown clearly in the Lhuyd drawing in Stowe MS 1023, fo. 166r. There the L seems to have a mark through it, resembling the Latin abbreviation for -lis or -ul- (Lindsay, Early Welsh Script, pp. 25 and 36); however, neither **FLISOU nor **FULOU makes sense. Could the 'bar' be a colon dividing F and LOU? Cf. below on BRANCU:F.

BRANCU(:)F (if = BRANCU F(*ecit*)).[1425] Or FLOU could be a un-Welsh attempt at **Llou*, influenced perhaps by alternations such as *Chlod-*, *Hlod-*, *Lod-*, *Flod-* in Gallo-Germanic names (*Chlodoveus*, *Lodoveus*, *Flotveus*, etc.):[1426] since OE *hr-* was used to represent the OW and OC voiceless *r-*,[1427] it is possible that OE *hl-* was similarly used for voiceless *l-* and then alternated in spelling with *Fl-* under Continental influence. Or, more simply, FLOU could involve sound-substitution for W. /ɬ/ like Shakespeare's *Fluellen* for *Llywelyn*.

2. 389/97 IOVENALI (< Latin *Iuvenalis*) > OW *Iouanaul*, assuming that this would have developed like MW *ieuanc* (: MB *youanc*, Gaulish *Iouincillos*) (cf. (10) above).[1428]

3. 354/126/6 ORDOVS, with OV < composition vowel **o* + **w(iks)* (cf. 1205/Ok44 MAVOUIH if not MAVORI(H)), and 'on its way to OW. **Orðou*'.[1429]

[80] 2022/253/984 COVLGVEN could be a nickname 'white cabbage, broth, seaweed' from W. *cawl* (OC *caul*) < Latin *caula* + *gwen* (or perhaps *gwyn* since *cawl* is now masculine), with the pretonic treatment of Latin *au* seen (according to Schrijver) in *cyngheusaeth* and *eurydd* (nos (6) and (7) above).[1430] Compare the epithet 'soup' of a certain *John Pottes* in 1390.[1431] However, the Royal Commission and the *Corpus* favour a reading GVLGVEN.[1432]

[80] In theory one might include the various names with AU discussed earlier (such as names in MAVO-, CAVO-, AVI-, in ‡‡ 25 and 60), but this is unsafe as we do not know whether they would have developed via /öü/ > /ëü/

[1425] See above, ‡55. According to KHJ and Thomas, 510/Scot.13 has FI(*li*) rather than F as in Macalister. F is used for *filius/filia* in later medieval Wales, e.g. Gresham, *Medieval Stone Carving*, p. 208: FRYN FBLED FMAD (Diserth, *c*. 1400; note that the personal names are abbreviated there as well, which could apply here if LOU = LOU[MARCH] or similar). In 1064/Dor.iv [D]ENIEL . FI the last visible letter may well be plain F rather than FI; I cannot see the drooping cross bar that suggested Radford & Jackson's FI ligature.

[1426] Lebel, p. 55. Cf. ‡78.

[1427] LHEB, pp. 478–79.

[1428] LHEB, p. 384; SBCHP, p. 344. On IOVENALI as a British rather than VL variant see Hamp, *Britannia*, 6 (1975), 158, referring to a discussion elsewhere which I cannot trace. Cf. Gaulish(?) *Ioenalis* (Holder ii, 63; Birkhan, *Germanen und Kelten*, p. 273, n. 576). Rhys, *AC*, 4th ser. 8 (1877), 142, noted the development to OW *Iouanaul* (LL, p. 406); for corrupt MW descendants see EWGT, p. 198 (*Iewanawl*, *Ieuanawl*, etc.). If the general assumption that W. *Iestyn*, B. *Iestin*, is < *Iustinus* is correct (e.g. Loth, *Noms des saints bretons*, p. 64, and Lloyd-Jones, *Y Geninen*, 44 (1926), 4), that must have undergone a similar development to **Iostīnus*; but cf. a *Iestinus* in Italy in OPEL ii, 192.

[1429] LHEB, p. 619. See above, ‡14.

[1430] If so, *cawlen* (singulative) and other derivatives would be influenced by *cawl*: SBCHP, p. 272; cf. LHEB, p. 322. But if the second element is *(g)wyn* and Jackson is right about *i*-affection in *ceuri* and *eurydd*, internal affection could explain the OV. On *cawl gwyn* see GPC s.v.

[1431] Jones, *BBCS*, 3 (1926–27), 48.

[1432] On GVLGVEN see above, ‡22.

in view of exceptions to this like *Mawgan* beside *Meugan* and *Cawrdaf* beside *ceuri*.[1433]

[80] (B) The two clear examples where the change is shown are:

1.   998/164 HEUTREN, apparently a name with **Awi-* as the first element (no. (5) above).[1434] A possibly similar form is 997/159 EIUDON if = MW *Eudon*; but it may be an odd spelling of *Iudon* (MW *Idon*).[1435]

2.   1029 REU DIACON (Anwyl: HELI DIACO(N)I), a highly dubious reading by Macalister, who thought it contained the same Old Welsh name as 1031 REU, to which he refers. Rhys rightly identified the latter with OW *Reu*, but made it dissyllabic *Rëu* for dubious metrical reasons.[1436] Presumably OW *Reu* is not the word for 'frost' (OW *reu-laun* 'frosty' (Juvencus), Mod.W. *rhew*) but MW *reu* 'wealth', as also in *reufedd* 'wealth' and *argyfreu* 'dowry' (: MB *argourou, argobrou*).[1437]

[80] 494/Ok79 GOREVS is a promising-looking form, but cannot be included as it is in Cornwall rather than Wales (see ‡76 above), and the same applies to 1050/Ok74 CRVX MEVROC, a very uncertain reading. In Wales, 968/5 FILIVS EV[is of course uncertain. There remains 1032/281 ODELEV, which at first sight looks like the Continental name *Odilo*.[1438] The -EV is reminiscent of the *eu* [œ ?] < /ɔ:/ which occurs in final syllables of polysyllables in Late Old Breton and Early Middle Breton,[1439] and there might be a connection with this, or with the similar-sounding Middle French *eu* [ö].[1440] Dr Iwan Wmffre, however, convincingly equates ODELEV with the name *Hoedlyw* (OW *Hodliu*, MW *Hoedlew*, etc.) and notes that it is tempting to connect ODELEV with an unlocated *Hendre Hoidliw* nearby in Llanfihangel-y-traethau or Llanfrothen, Merionethshire).[1441]

[1433]   See ‡‡ 57n. and 60 above.

[1434]   See above, ‡15.

[1435]   ‡81 below. See above, ‡18.

[1436]   CIIC 1029 and 1031 are both absent from ECMW, but the former is included in the *Corpus*. Anwyl, *AC*, 6th ser. 6 (1906), 121, read HELI DIACO(N)I in CIIC 1029. Rhys, *Englyn*, p. 46, compared 1031 REU with *Reu* in LL, pp. 169 and 201 (charters 168 and 200), and OB *Rio* in the *Cartulaire de Redon*, ed. de Courson (see 6 citations in index, p. 695). Note also Ir. *Reo* (McManus, *Guide*, p. 173, n. 2; Ziegler, p. 227).

[1437]   Williams, *Poems of Taliesin*, pp. 52 and 109, citing Loth, *RC*, 37 (1917–19), 33–34; GPC, s.vv. *argyfrau, rhau,* and *rheuedd. Cyfrau* is apparently different; cf. DGVB i, 111. Loth equates *reu* with OI *róe* 'field' < **rowi-, *rewi-* (: Latin *rus*); cf. EIHM, p. 6, n. 1, and LEIA R-38–39. Or is *reu* connected with the superlative prefix, OI *rug-*, LEIA R-51?

[1438]   Searle, *Onomasticon*, pp. 362–63, records *Odilo* in England already in the reign of Æthelred II, as the name of a moneyer. The comparison in LW, p. 165, between ODELEV and MW *Edelyvon* (thirteenth-century addition in LL, p. 247) cannot be sustained; the eponym of this commote (*Edeligion* in WATU) was OW *Etelic*: Richards, *JRSAI*, 95 (1965), 209.

[1439]   HPB, pp. 128–29, 134–39 and 825 (cf. SBCHP, pp. 210–11).

[1440]   HPB, p. 128; Pope, *Latin to Modern French*, pp. 201 and 459; Piette, *French Loanwords*, p. 3.

[1441]   Wmffre, *Language and History*, i, 319, citing Mostyn MS 3857 of 1743/44.

‡*81 i̯ü > i-, -ü- in Welsh; LHEB §36.2*

[86] (A) Jackson's example (p. 346) where these changes have not happened is:

1. 1012/223/933 IUTHAHELO

[81] Two others are:

2. 346/75 ADIVNE, now read ADIVNETI (Knight) = W. *eiddun(ed)*[1442]
3. 1035/303 MARGITEUT = OW *Morgetiud, Margetiud, Margetud*, MW *Maredud*[1443]

997/159 EIUDON may represent *Iudon* (MW *Idon*), but MW *Eudon* is also a possibility.[1444] It seems safest not to count the Latin names 344/73 IVSTI and 396/104 IVSTI[NI].[1445]

[81] (B) Jackson notes the one example where the change has happened:

1. 350/116/3 [I]DNERT. (In LHEB, p. 346, n. 2, he restored [IV]DNERT, but subsequently withdrew this when Lhuyd's drawing showing IDNERT was discovered.[1446])

‡*82 Differentiation of ëü and ei towards ēü and ę̈ü, ęi and ęi [in Welsh final syllables]; LHEB §§ 46.2; 207.5*

No inscriptional evidence is cited for this change, which indeed does not manifest itself in normal written Welsh for several centuries (cf. Mod.W. *au* and *ai* < MW *eu* and *ei*).[1447] Jackson's reason for placing it here before the accent shift (‡88 below) is the argument that it was linked to the stress in the final syllables of mono- and polysyllabic words.

‡*83 ɔ > ō̄ in Breton; LHEB §13*

There is no inscriptional evidence, 3015/M6 PROSTLON and 3019/M10 RIOCUS being ambiguous (see ‡18 above).

[1442] See above, ‡15n.
[1443] See above, ‡53.
[1444] ‡80 above. See above, ‡18.
[1445] For *Iustus > Iust* see Olson & Padel, *CMCS*, 12 (1986), 44–45. On *Iustinus > Iestyn* (?) see ‡80n.
[1446] Jackson, *BBCS*, 19 (1960–62), 232–34. Here he also has more discussion of the sound change involved. See further, on *iud-* etc., Sims-Williams, *BBCS*, 38 (1991), 58, and nn. 1–2, and 79–86; Koch, *Gododdin*, p. xlvii (*iud-* < Latin *iudex*); SBCHP, p. 344; Zimmer, *JIES*, 27 (1999), 119–20. Does 986/62 RUALLAUN (‡60 above) exhibit a related sound change /ˈɔiw/ > /ˈɔi̯üw/ > /ˈɔüw/ or simply /ˈɔiw/ > /ˈɔüw/? As mentioned in ‡60n, Howlett, *Cambro-Latin Compositions*, pp. 22–23, scans it *Ru̯allaun*. Note also 1011/220/911 EUS for Latin *eius*.
[1447] LHEB, p. 686; Jackson, *SC*, 10/11 (1975–76), 45 (cf. Watkin, *Ystorya Bown de Hamtwn*, p. civ). Morris-Jones, WG, pp. 31–32, notes an early example in the Juvencus gloss *anutonau.* The differentiation arguably began before **deilγ > deil* i.e. not ***dail* (cf. LHEB, p. 686, n. 1) lost its final consonant at ‡97 below.

‡*84 ö, ι perhaps becoming ə by now [in Welsh]; LHEB §205*

There is inevitably no evidence for pretonic /ι/ > /ə/, both being spelt indifferently E or I (cf. ‡46 above).

Pretonic /ö/ > /ə/ is revealed by the use of E or I for the latter (Y is not used in the inscriptions).

[84] (A) The examples of U and O for the /ö/ stage, when arising from an earlier pretonic /u/, have already been given under (AB) and (B) in ‡46 above. The ones with O, which means /ö/ more certainly than the ambiguous U, were (see ‡46 (B)):

1. 1000/182 CONCENN, CONMARCH (< *kuno-)
2. 1011/220/911 HOUELT (< *su-; cf. W. *Hywel*)
3. 1016/234/907 CONBELIN
4. 1023/239/927 CONBELANI [the CON- is shown by Lhuyd]
5. 324/34]CO[N]BARRVS CO[N]BURRI (if the reading is correct and the names are not Irish)
6. 352A/122/5 DOMNICI (if < *Dumn-* cf. below)
7. 1068/b CONDILICI (on the Isle of Man; cf. W. *Cynddilig*)

[84] For the present purposes we can add the following to these various names with O standing either for an /ö/ that would be expected to develop to /ə/ (Mod.W. *y*) or for an /o/ that would be expected to develop via /ö/ to /ə/ (*y*):

8. 385/89 LOVERNII (comparing W. *Llywern* rather than OI *Loarn*, Hiberno-Latin *Loernus*, in view of the British nature of ANATEMORI in this inscription)
9. 379/170 LOVERNACI (cf. W. *Llywernog* – but conceivably Irish)[1448]
10. 399/176 TOVISACI/[TO]VISACI (cf. W. *tywysog*, if this has /tə/ < /töl < *to-* by the very early reduction in proclitic preverbs (‡5); if the development was /tö/ < *tu-* (‡46) it still belongs here – unless, of course, it is purely Irish > OI *toísech*).[1449] Note that 1000/182 POUOIS cannot be included here, since it developed to W. *Powys*, not **Pywys*.[1450]
11. 413/272 MONEDORIGI (cf. W. *mynydd*) can be also included since even if its O means /o/ (as seems likely), this would have developed /on/ > /un/ > /ön/ > /ən/.[1451] (The same applies to 352A/122/5 DOMNICI > *Dyfnig* above if it is from Latin *Dom(i)nicus* rather than native *Dumno-*).

[84] (B) Jackson notes (pp. 668–69) that /öl > /ə/ has happened in:

1. 1033/287 CINGEN and (according to Ifor Williams's reading) CIMALTED. The former is dubious since the likely reading is CUNGEN

[1448] On *Llywern(og)* see above, ‡80n. On Ir. *Loarn* see ‡46n.
[1449] See above, ‡46.
[1450] See ‡80n above.
[1451] See above, ‡‡ 26 and 46.

or, more probably, CUN BEN, but CIMALTED undoubted derives from *köm- < *kom-.[1452]

[84] Further examples are:

2. 979/46 NI(*n*)ID (> MW *Nynnid*) < *Nonnitus* with /on/ > /un/ > /ön/ > /ən/[1453]

3. 992/120/14 CENLISINI, probably a diminutive of OW *Cinglas* (> *Cynlas*) < *kuno-[1454]

4. 1007/206/938 IRBIC(I) < *Urbic(i)us* (= OW *Erbic, Eruic*?)[1455]

5. 1032/281 EWINI (Macalister: WINI) REGIS (Owain Gwynedd?), MW *Owein/Ywein*, presumably at the stage Jackson represents as *əwein* < *eüyein* (OW *Eugein*) < *öüyein* (OW *Ougein*)[1456]

6. 1030 CERID[WEN] (MW *Cyr(r)ituen, Cer(r)ituen*, Mod.W. *Ceridwen*), if the first element is *cyrr- < cwr(r)*, as proposed by Ifor Williams.[1457] Note, however, that Macalister's CERID[is a dubious reading.

[84] 2019 RIGELLA (if genuine) could be included if the first element is the prefix *(p)ro- > /rö-/ > /'ǫə-/ (*rhy-*),[1458] but the etymology may well be *Rīgo-gellā, and the name may be Irish.[1459]

[84] Many other forms with E or I are of doubtful relevance. 971/35 CINI (MW *Cyny*) can hardly be included as a *kən- < *kuno- name in view of the spelling with U (or rather UU) of CUURI[S] in the same inscription (> MW *Cyrys*); Ifor Williams compared CINI with Gaulish *Cinius*.[1460] Again, 397/105 BECCVRI occurs in the same inscription as CVNALIPI and CVNACI, so can hardly have E for /ə/ < /u/; it may have E for /i/ as in W. *bych* or else etymological /e/ < *bekko-.[1461] In the same way, other more or less obscure names with I or E in the pretonic syllable cannot be assumed to be relevant, for instance: 331/41 TECVRI (cf. W. *teg* 'fair'?); 403/268/841 BERIC(C)[I] (?) or BERIA[CI] (< *Barriākos* ?);[1462] 412/277 FERRVCI (> MW *Ferawc*);[1463] 2029/p. 39i ERECOR; 366/148 ITOCVS, compared

---

[1452] See above, ‡‡ 16 and 26.

[1453] See above, ‡26.

[1454] See ‡36 above.

[1455] See above, ‡57. *Erbic* may alternatively be derived from OW *Erb*.

[1456] In SEBC, p. 284. Cf. LHEB, pp. 323–24 and 370, n. 1 (differently Lewis & Pedersen, *Supplement*, p. 4); EWGT, p. 207; GPN, p. 200, n. 9; TYP, pp. 477–78 and 560; Uhlich, *Morphologie*, p. 240. See also above, ‡57n.

[1457] *Chwedl Taliesin*, p. 3. On *-uen = -fen* see Lloyd-Jones, *Geirfa*, p. 136. See Haycock, in Caerwyn Williams FS (in prep.).

[1458] LHEB, p. 658.

[1459] See above, ‡74.

[1460] BWP, p. 17. See above, ‡‡ 37n and 74, and note W. *cyni* (MW *cyn(h)i*) 'affliction; battle' (GPC).

[1461] See ‡42 above.

[1462] Cf. *Bariacus* and *Barriacum* as place names in Gaul, Holder i, 350 and iii, 809. On the reading BERIA[CI] see ‡18n.

[1463] See ‡44 above.

by Evans with Gaulish names in *It-*;[1464] 436/316 LITOGENI (cf. OI *Líthach*, Gaulish *Litugenus*, Romano-British *Litugenus/Litegenus*);[1465] 448/370 RINACI or PINACI;[1466] and 377/175 CIMESETLI, possibly with CIME- for /kü(:)μə-/ < **koimo-*.[1467] 447/369 NEMAGLI (hardly NEMASLI) is possibly explicable as [SE]NEMAGLI, [VIN]NEMAGLI, [CV]NEMAGLI, [TIGER]NEMAGLI, or similar,[1468] or is more probably explicable as an Irish name in NE-, like 1006/197/842 NEFROIHI (also read TEFROIHI, TESROIHI, [REFSD]IHI, and [REFSO]IHI).[1469] Finally, there is no reason to suppose that the names in 1024/255/926 GLIGUIS and 1023/239/927 GLIUISSI (> *Glywys*), SCILOC, ever had anything but front vowels.[1470]

‡85 Secondary affection by i, i̯ in Breton; LHEB §176

There is no inscriptional evidence from Brittany.

[85] Note that Jackson says that this type of affection is 'apparently not represented in Cornish, and certainly not in Welsh',[1471] which leaves open the possibility of Cornish examples. A probable one is 473/b/Ok46 IGNIOC < **Egnioc* < **ad-gnīm-ākos* (: OB *agnioc*, W. *egnïol* 'vigorous').[1472] The only example in Welsh would be 971/35 VI[RN]IN, compared by Ifor Williams with OW *Guernin* (< *gwern* 'alder'); but the reading is certainly incorrect.[1473]

[85] A related problem is raised by various names in IL- instead of EL- < **(p)elu-* in Welsh inscriptions: 1013/222/912 IL[TUTI] or ILTU[TIS][1474]

[1464] GPN, pp. 356–57; cf. Holder ii, 83–84; PNRB, p. 359; Alföldy, *Noricum*, p. 235 (*Itucus/a*, *Itus*, etc.). Some of these may contain W. *ŷd* 'corn' (OI *ith*, *u*-stem). Cf. GPN, p. 357, n. 3, and ‡65 above on 993/124/18 ITGEN. A derivative of *ŷd* like ITOC- is hypothesized by Coates & Breeze, *Celtic Voices*, pp. 341 and 352, to explain the place name *Pendock* in Worcestershire. W. G. Thomas, apud Emery, *AC*, 124 (1975), 108, n. 23, read 366/148 as CROCUSI. As noted by Lebel, pp. 40 and 46–47, *Crocus* (4c) appears under *Hroc* (cf. OE *Hroc*) in Förstemann, *Altdeutsches Namenbuch*, i, *Personennamen*, col. 712. Lebel regards *Crocus* as a Latinization of *Hroc-*, not as Latin *Crocus* 'saffron'. In either case, one would surely expect gen. *CROCI? For *Crocus* see Holder i, 1173, and for *Croc* see also Searle, *Onomasticon*, p. 144.

[1465] See above, ‡38.

[1466] For various possibilities, see above, ‡‡ 18 and 22.

[1467] LHEB, p. 312, and above, ‡35.

[1468] See above, ‡‡ 27 and 38.

[1469] See ‡42 above.

[1470] See above, ‡‡ 18 and 58. If *Glywys* is from *Glevensis* (rather than: *glyw*), the long vowel of Romano-British *Glevum* (> W. *Caer Loyw*, LHEB, pp. 325–27) must have been shortened at some stage.

[1471] LHEB, p. 594.

[1472] See above, ‡18.

[1473] BWP, pp. 18 and 36; VSB, p. 160; LHEB, pp. 385–86. See ‡66 above.

[1474] This name is treated as second declension in LL, VSB, and in *Vie ancienne*, ed. Flobert; but for the popularity of the third declension for Brittonic names see Harvey, in Mac Cana FS, p. 59.

1019/237/920 ILCI or]ILCI (cf. OW *Elci*)

1018/236/919 ILQUICI, if = *Ilguici*, OW *Iluic* (var. *Iliuc*)[1475]

[85] In the last two the IL- might be attributed to a Welsh version of 'secondary affection', but this will not work with the first (= *Illtud*), where influence from Irish *Il-* (by regular Irish raising before /u/ in **elu-*, as probably in 342/70 **ILVVETO**) is usually invoked.[1476] Would it not be simpler, however, to suppose that [e] was sometimes palatalized to [i] under the influence of a following [l] + high front vowel ([ü(:)] or [i(:)])? In the Book of Llandaf it is noticeable that *Il-* variants tend to occur especially when there is a high front vowel ([ü(:)], [i], [i(:)], [i̥]) in the following syllable: *Eldutus ~ Ildutus*, *Elgui ~ Ilgui/Ylui* (?),[1477] *Eli ~ Ili*, *Elias ~ Ilias*, *Eliuc* (sic) ~ *Iliud* – also, without *El-* variants, *Ilien* and *Iliman*.[1478] In Welsh, there are no minimal pairs distinguished by *el-* and *il-*, so that these alternations may have been allophonic. Note also the alternation in *eili(e)r ~ ilir* 'butterfly', and OW *cilurnn* rather than the expected **celurnn* in the Juvencus glosses.[1479]

‡*86 i̯ü > i-, -ü- in CB.; LHEB §36.2*

No inscriptional evidence is cited. But note the following clear examples of preserved /i̯ü/:

[86] (A)

1. 1044/Ok7 LEUIUT ('lion-lord' cf. OC *Gryfyið/Grifiuð* 'gryphon-lord')[1480]
2. 3003/F3 ADIVNI (and IUSTI) (cf. 346/75 ADIVNE(TI), W. *eiddun(ed)*)[1481]
3. 1063/Dor.ii IUDNNE[RTH?] FIL[I] QUI[(Macalister: IUONA [ ] FILIUS IUI[ ). McClure expands the first name as IUDN[OI], comparing *Iudnoe* in the Book of Llandaf, but if Radford and Jackson are right to assign the 'rounded back' of the last visible letter to an E, rather than to McClure's O with an I above, we should perhaps compare the Book of Llandaf's *Iudne*, possibly an archaic form of *Iudnoe* or **Iudnui*.[1482]

[1475] See above, ‡38.

[1476] See above, ‡38 nn. 657, 736, and 749. For another explanation see Zimmer, in Beekes FS, p. 355.

[1477] The vowel is schwa here, however, according to LHEB, p. 677, supported by the English form *Olway*.

[1478] LL, p. 405. Cf. VSB, p. 331, for *Iltutus ~ Eltutus*. Dr Jon Coe provides a further example from LL: *Ilbri*. Note also variations like *Elec ~ Ilec* in Brittany: Loth, *Noms des saints bretons*, pp. 37, 64 and 149.

[1479] DGVB i, 105, and ii, 414; LEIA C-99; DLG, p. 98. Cf. VLRB, p. 905.

[1480] LHEB, p. 347; Bodmin, p. 91. See ‡37n.

[1481] See above, ‡81.

[1482] McClure, *EHR*, 22 (1907), 729 (not seen by Radford & Jackson?); Sims-Williams, *BBCS*, 38 (1991), 50, n. 3, and 51, and nn. 8–9; Wmffre, *Language and History*, i, 347. To me, only IUDNN[is visible and the third letter could be a squarish O (it is not like a *thorn* as in Radford & Jackson's figure).

[86] A possible further instance is 1206/Ok4, read by Okasha as
[.R]IVGDOCI or [.R]IVSDOCI. Okasha compares the last with *Iuscar* in
the Cartulary of Redon, a variant of *Iudcar* due, according to Jackson, to the
eleventh-century copyist.[1483] Assuming that [.R] belongs to the preceding
line, IVSDOCI could conceivably represent an OC *Iuðdoc*, spelt in a similar
way. Thomas, however, reads FILIVS DOCIDCI (for 'Docidoci').[1484]
Another conceivably relevant but obscure form is 491/Ok55 IVRIVCI
(also read DIRIVI or FILIVS !).

[86] Latin influence is a possible factor in the cases of 3003/F3 IUSTI above
and 484/Ok52 IVSTI/[I]USTI, where one wonders whether the ogam ever
included the un-Irish [i̯] – Macalister says the [I] 'is flaked away'.[1485]

[86] (B)

1. There are no examples of loss of the /i̯/, but I suggested earlier that
1401/Ok27 RESTEUTA(E) (Thomas; RESGEVT[A(E)] Okasha) on Lundy
may be a hypercorrect spelling of *RESTUTA(E) (: W. *Rhystud* < *Rest(i-
t)utus*?), influenced by a case like 1035/303 MARGITEUT > W. *Maredudd*.[1486] If so, the stone would *postdate* /i̯ü/ > /ü/.

‡*87 On-glide before initial s-groups in W. fully established as ə; LHEB
§119*

No inscriptional evidence is cited. See ‡75 above.

‡*88 The accent-shift in W., C., and B.; LHEB §§ 13, 207*

No inscriptional evidence is cited. The position of this change is inferred
from other changes which may be related to the position of the accent (see
‡‡ 75/87; ‡‡ 81/86; and ‡82 above; and ‡91/92 below).[1487]

‡*89 th > s in Breton; LHEB §53*

There is no inscriptional evidence.

‡*90 -lt, -nt > -ls, -ns in Cornish; LHEB §§ 54.1; 110*

No inscriptional evidence is cited. Note that Okasha is confident that
1055/Ok3, formerly read TAETUERA[1488] or UAETUENA, ends with a
(damaged) T, either T[. .] TUENT + or T[. .]TUERT. On etymological
grounds, -UERT (W. *gwerth*, or *berth* as in 986/62 IORUERT = MW

[1483] LHEB, p. 425; HPB, pp. 407, 645 and 673.
[1484] *Mute Stones*, pp. 282–83 and 301, n. 26. For names in *Doc-* see above, ‡18n.
[1485] Hencken, *AC*, 90 (1935), 158, saw 'possible though vague traces of an ogham U'. In 1968
KHJ 'saw no trace of the Ogam U, but the STI are as Macalister draws them'.
[1486] See ‡34 above.
[1487] See further Jackson, *SC*, 10/11 (1975–76), 40–53; Sims-Williams, *BBCS*, 38 (1991), 79;
SBCHP, p. 16; Koch, *Gododdin*, pp. cxxxvii–cxxxviii; and Schrijver, *ÉC*, 34 (1998–2000),
147–55.
[1488] Thomas, *Mute Stones*, p. 287, as well as Macalister.

Iorferth) seems more likely than -UENT (W. *-went*) in a personal name, although Latin *Advent(i)us* is a possibility (cf. 361/140 ADVEN[TI]).[1489]

‡91 *Reduction of au towards ŏ in the now unstressed W. final syllable; LHEB §12*

No inscriptional evidence is cited, which agrees with the absence of evidence for *ŏ* in Old Welsh.[1490]

‡92 *Reduction of ō̆ to ĕ in the now unstressed C. and B. final syllable; LHEB §13*

No inscriptional evidence is cited.

‡93 *Beginning of final -t = [d] > -s = [z] in Cornish; LHEB §52.1*

No inscriptional evidence is cited.

‡94 *Denasalisation of ṽ already complete in W. and C.; LHEB §100*

No inscriptional evidence is cited. Compare ‡55 above on 399/176 S[I]B[I]L[I]NI/SIMILINI, 1005/191/886 BRANCU(:)F, and 1206/Ok4 DOVITHI, all of which are doubtful evidence. In 1048/Ok32, if HADNOB is the correct reading,[1491] one could perhaps compare Gaulish names such as *Adnamo* and *Adnamu(s)*.[1492]

‡95 *δ > z in Breton; LHEB §68*

There is no inscriptional evidence, but cf. ‡86 on 1206/Ok4 IVSDOCI (?).

‡96 *Internal -lj-, -rj- > -li̯-, -ri̯- in W.; LHEB §88*

Cf. ‡53 above. No inscriptional evidence is cited. In a few Welsh words in *gor-* < **wor-* a following **g* is lost altogether (e.g. *goralw*), and an arguable one of these, MW *goreu* 'best' (: OI *forg(g)u*), or a cognate of it, possibly appears in Devon in 494/Ok79 GOREVS.[1493] The date of the loss of **g* is not clear, and it may have occurred at the /rɣ/ rather than the /rj/ stage.[1494]

[1489] Cf. Williams, *BBCS*, 11 (1941–44), 144–45; GPN, pp. 280–81, on *verto-*, also Schrijver, *Ériu*, 47 (1996), 200–1. On -VENT in place names, cf. PNRB, pp. 262–64, and Sims-Williams, in *Gaulois et celtique continental*. In LWP, p. 392, *Adventus* is compared with *Adguen* in LL, p. 167 (but this may have **-windos*, though cf. MW *Adwen(t)* in EWGT, p. 168) and St 'Advent' in Cornwall, who was *Adwen* in Cornish and usually regarded as male; see Orme, *Dedications*, p. 67, and *Saints of Cornwall*, pp. 59–60. *Adventius* is also attested (OPEL i, 28). For other suggestions regarding TAETUERA or UAETUENA see above, ‡15.

[1490] In LHEB, pp. 296–98, Jackson claims that there are examples in LL, but these seem rather to reflect original /ɔː/ (which developed via /au/ > /o/). See Sims-Williams, *BBCS*, 38 (1991), 63–71 and 77; SBCHP, p. 195.

[1491] Macalister HADNOBVIS (recte VIR HADNOB? cf. KHJ cited in ‡44n. above).

[1492] GPN, p. 130.

[1493] See ‡76 above. Cf. LHEB, pp. 439, n. 2, and 466, n. 4, and review by Binchy, *Celtica*, 4 (1958), 291–92; Binchy, *JCS*, 1 (1950), 149; Lewis & Pedersen, *Supplement*, pp. 5 and 10; Uhlich, *Morphologie*, p. 260; Isaac, *SC*, 34 (2000), 108, n. 13.

[1494] Cf. discussion in LHEB, pp. 436–39 (but on *Unust* see ‡74n. above) and HPB, pp. 719–21. The fact mentioned by Binchy, *Celtica*, 4 (1958), 291, and *JCS*, 1 (1950), 149, that *Gwrwst*

‡97 Final -lγ, -rγ > -l°, -r° in W.; LHEB §88

No inscriptional evidence is cited. 417/282 ARGII, if the same as MW *eiry* 'snow', is the only relevant form.[1495]

‡98 s (< th) > z in B.; LHEB §53

There is no inscriptional evidence.

(: OI *Forggus*) is spelt *Gurgust* in OW does not necessarily mean that any trace of the *g* remained, given the habit of spelling the second element of compounds etymologically and analogically.

[1495] See ‡53 above.

BRITTONIC CHRONOLOGY

3.1 CONSTRUCTION OF TABLE 3.1

Extending the procedure explained in Chapter 1, Table 3.1 is constructed on the basis of all the sound changes reflected in the orthography of inscriptions for which we have found evidence of both the earlier (A) and the later (B) stage. The sound changes are dealt with in the order of Jackson's 'Chronological Table' in LHEB, §210,[1] and with reference (by ‡‡) to the discussion in Chapter 2. We shall find that there is sometimes good reason to modify Jackson's order and change the order of some columns in Table 3.1. Of course, this is not done when Jackson's order is linguistically the only logical one. I sometimes quote Jackson's absolute dates simply to show that they present little or no obstacle to the proposed change (see e.g. on col. 5 below).

Sound changes with three stages, such as /a:/ > /ɔ:/ > /au/ (‡‡ 18 and 60), are broken down into two, in this instance: col. 2 A /a:/ > B /ɔ:/ + /au/ (since the presence of /au/ generally implies the occurrence of the preceding stage /ɔ:/); and col. 22 A /a:/ + /ɔ:/ > B /au/ (since the retention of /a:/ implies that the stage /au/ has not been reached).

The columns are assigned as follows:

Col. 1 = 'CIIC' number.

Col. 2

A /a:/ ‡18
B /ɔ:/ ‡‡ 18 and 60 (/au/ < /ɔ:/ < /a:/)

Col. 3

A pre-final *i*-affection
B post-final *i*-affection, ‡19

Col. 4

A /nd/
B /nn/, ‡22 (and ‡49)

---

[1] With the exception of the reduction of composition vowels, which does not appear in his list and is here placed provisionally at col. 11, immediately before the syncope of such vowels (col. 12), logically its latest possible position; see further below, discussion of col. 11.

Col. 5

A /γ/
B /ṳ/, ‡25

Col. 6 (W.Brit.)

A /oN/
B /uN/, ‡26

Col. 7 (here treated as Brittonic in general rather than as W.Brit. as in LHEB; see ‡27)

A /eN/; /eN/ + stop; /ern/
B /iN/; /iN/ + stop; /irn/, ‡27

Col. 8 (SW.Brit.)

A /u/, ‡28 (AB)
B /ọ/, ‡28 (B)

Col. 9

A /-Σ-/
B /-h-/, ‡36

Col. 10

A pre-apocope
B post-apocope, ‡37

Col. 11

A correct composition vowel, ‡38 (A) + (AI)
B wrong composition vowel, ‡38 (B) + (BC)

Col. 12

A unsyncopated composition vowel, ‡38 (A) + (AI) + (B) + (BA)
B syncopated composition vowel, ‡38 (C)

Col. 13

A *rt, rc*
B *rth, rch*, ‡43

Col. 14

A /Σ-/
B /h-/, ‡44

Col. 15 (Pr.W.)

A pretonic /u/, ‡46 (AB)
B pretonic /ö/, ‡46 (B)

Col. 16

A /əii̯/
B W. /ai/, CB. /oi/, ‡47

Col. 17

A /γ/ before /l, r, n/
B /i̯/, ‡48

Col. 18

A /xt/
B /i̯θ/, ‡51

Col. 19

A pre-internal *i*-affection
B post-internal *i*-affection, ‡‡ 57 (Pr.W.) and 64 (Pr.C. and Pr.B.)

Col. 20

A /e:⁽ⁱ⁾/
B /ui/, ‡58

Col. 21

A /ɛ:⁽ⁱ⁾/
B /ɔi/, ‡59

Col. 22 (Pr.W.)

A /ɔ:/, ‡18 (A) and (B) [except (B) no. 6], exx. from Wales, Scotland and Dorset only
B /au/, ‡60

Col. 23

A /γ/
B /∅/, ‡65

Col. 24 (Welsh and Cornish) [not Breton, ‡73]

A /w-/
B /gw-/, ‡‡ 66 (Wales, Scotland, Man, Dorset) and 76 (Cornwall and Devon)

Col. 25 (Welsh)

A /nt/ etc.
B /nᵗh/, /nh/ etc., ‡‡ 68 and 71

Col. 26 (Welsh and Cornish)

A pre-svarabhakti
B post-svarabhakti, ‡69

Col. 27

A /γ/
B /∅/, ‡74

Col. 28 (Welsh)

A /öü/
B /ëü/, ‡80

Col. 29

A /i̯u/
B /i-/ etc., ‡‡ 81 (Welsh) and 86 (Cornish and Breton)

Col. 30 (Welsh)

A /ö/, ‡46 (AB) + (B)
B /ə/, ‡84

Table 3.1 Brittonic sound changes in the inscriptions

col. 1	2	3	4	5	6	7	8	9	10	11	12	13	14	15	16	17	18	19	20	21	22	23	24	25	26	27	28	29	30	31
CIIC																														ECMWetc
p.397											B						A		A												285
318										A̱	A									A		A									6
319										A̱	A			A̱																	9
320		A												A̱																A	26
321																															25
322		A										A		A̱																A	27
323														A̱																A	32
324				B								B		B																A	34
325											A														A						33
326																															39
327														A̱																A	43
328			A												A							A									44
329	A̱																	A		A		A									42
330		B																A													66
331																															41
332																															40
333	B											B								B											50
334	A				A̱															A				A							54
335																															54a
336																															67a
337												B																			60
339																	A					A									68
341													A				A														71
342										A̱	A			A̱																A	70
344	A																			A											73
345																															74
346																		A										A			75
347																															76
348/a																															110/27
348/b							B	B			B														B						110/27
349										A̱	A													A							121/4
350											B		B	A																B	116/3
351													A̱																	A	115/2
352A													Ḇ			A														A	122/5
353																B															127/7
354											A																A				126/6
355	A / b		B																	A											128/8
356								A																							132/9
357																															136
358										A̱	A				A						A	A									138
359					B																					A					141
360																															139
361		A			A					A			A				A														140
362										A̱	A			A̱																A	142
363	A																				A		A								143
364																															144
365	A / b		B			B	B	A												A											149

Table 3.1 *contd.*

col. 1	2	3	4	5	6	7	8	9	10	11	12	13	14	15	16	17	18	19	20	21	22	23	24	25	26	27	28	29	30	31
CIIC																														ECMWetc
366	B																						A							148
368/a																														150
368/b		A									B	A							A					A						150
369																														153
370					A					A	A		A																	157
371																														322
372																														160
373																														171
374															A															A	172
375																														166
376		B					A				B	A								A				A		A				174
377							A				B	A								A				A						175
378																														169
379	A				A					A	A		A								A	A							A	170
380		A			A																A		A							84
381	A													A					A		A									87
382																														86
384																	A													83
385	B	A				A					B	A									A								A	89
386												A																	A	92
387												A	A B																A	95
388		A																												94
389	A				A															A						A				97
390		A					A				B	A								A		A		A						96
391	A				A							A					A			A										78
392	A																		A		A		A							77
393																														101
394		A														A			A		A	A			A	A				103
395																														102
396		A																												104
397	A										B	A			A						A								A	105
398		B																												106
399	A																				A								A	176
400		B				A					B	A		A			A				A									177
401										A	A			A																183
402																														184
403																														268/841
404	A				A							A								A					A					270/843
405																														228/845
406															A					A		A								215/844
407/a															A															258/846
407/b																									A					258/846
408	A *b*	B		A B B	B B	A				B	A		A					A	A		A		A		A				229/848
409	A		B		B									A				A		A			A				A		198/849
410																														238/847
412	B																				A	B								277
413				A						A	A				A	A								A					A	272

Table 3.1 *contd.*

col. 1 / CIIC	2	3	4	5	6	7	8	9	10	11	12	13	14	15	16	17	18	19	20	21	22	23	24	25	26	27	28	29	30	31 / ECMWetc
414						A																								271
415																														278
416																														279
417		A				A		A			A																			282
418	A										A			A						A									A	283
419	A					B		B		A	A										A	A	A		A					
419	b					B		B		b	A										A	A	A		A					284
420		A																												289
421						A																								294
422																						A								298
423																														296
424	A																				A									299
425										B					A															297
426	A																				A									300
427/a																														301
427/b	B										B										A									301
428																														305
429			A												.								A							307
430						A									A								A							306
431																														308
432	A					A															A				A					312
433																														313
434																														314
435										A	A			A								A						A		315
436											A													A						316
437																														317
438																														320
439																														319
440										B																				335
441																														345
442																		A												346
443		A												A														A	349
444																					A									352
445	A																			A		A							354
446		A								A	A			A	A												A	353
447										B	A			A	A												A	369
448	A		B																	A									
448	A		a																	A									370
449									A	A			A														A	384
450			A																										390
451	A			B									A							A		A		A				A	401
452																						A							400
453																													399
454	A	A		A					A	A			A						A								A	402
455									A	A			A								A						A	403
456																							A						404
457																													Ok18
458																													Ok9
459																													Ok63
460																													Ok75
461																													Ok66

Table 3.1 *contd.*

col. 1 / CIIC	2	3	4	5	6	7	8	9	10	11	12	13	14	15	16	17	18	19	20	21	22	23	24	25	26	27	28	29	30	31 / ECMWetc
462																														Ok14
463																														Ok15
464						B																				B				Ok65
465																														Ok21
466																														Ok23
467																														Ok24
468									*A*		*A*	A										*a*								Ok31
469																														Ok34
470																														Ok78
471						B				B																				Ok39
472																														Ok35
473/a	A															A							A							Ok46
473/b	B							B							B	B														Ok46
474																							A							Ok17
475			B																											Ok47
476						B																								Ok45
477	B					*b*	B			*b*	A					B			A							A				Ok11
478																														Ok48
479						*b*	B								B	A														Ok16
480																														Ok19
481																														Ok49
482				A																										Ok71
483				A																										Ok51
484																														Ok52
485																	A													Ok68
486			B					B		B							A													Ok56
487	B					*A*				*b*	A																			Ok10
488																														Ok60
489/a	B		*B*																											Ok13
489/b																			B											Ok13
490	B				B	B	B			B							A													Ok29
491																														Ok55
492																														Ok59
493						B				B							A													Ok58
494																							B							Ok79
496										B	A																			Hants.
497																														409
498										*A*	A			A						A										Nb 7
499	A																													Ok77
500										B	A																			Manx
501																														Manx
502																														Manx
503																														Manx
504																														Manx
505					B	A																								Manx
506																							A							Scot.
507																														Scot.

Table 3.1 *contd.*

col. 1	2	3	4	5	6	7	8	9	10	11	12	13	14	15	16	17	18	19	20	21	22	23	24	25	26	27	28	29	30	31
CIIC																														ECMWetc
508																														Scot.
509																														OkPict3
510															A								A								Scot. 13
511																														Scot. 10
512																														Scot.
513																														OkPict8
514	*A*																		A		A										Scot. 8
515	*A*											*A*	A								A						A				Scot. 9
516		A		B		A													A				A								Scot. 1
517					A																										Scot. 2
518																															Scot. 3
519																															Scot. 6
520												*A*	A																		Scot. 5
968																															5
970			B										B	A																	13
											B			A							B				A						
971											B				*b*							B				A					35
976																															72
978				B								B	B				B					B			A						49
979				B		B			B		B	B	B									B		B					B		46
980												B							A			B									46a
982																															55
984												B	B						B			B									59
985												B																			61
986											B			B	A							B	*B*								62
988												B												B							67
989																															69
990																								A							108/1
991																															113/30
992												B																	B		120/14
993	B									B	B									A	B										124/18
994				B						B	B	B	B							B					B						125/22
995		B														B															133/24
996											B	B																			147
997											B	B																			159
998											B	B														B					164
	B		B		A					B		B	B	B		B		B		B		B		B						A
1000	B				B	*b*				B		B	B	B		B		B		B		B		B						A	182
1001												B																			181
1003																															261/885
1004			B								B	B											B								260/884
1005											B	B																			191/886
1006																															197/842
1007																														B	206/938
1008											B								B												194/934
1009											B								B												193/935
1010																															211/882
1011											B		B	B																A	220/911
1012										B		B	A			B						B					B			A	223/933
1013											B								B												222/912
1014	B										B								B			B		B							231/908

Table 3.1 *contd.*

col. 1	2	3	4	5	6	7	8	9	10	11	12	13	14	15	16	17	18	19	20	21	22	23	24	25	26	27	28	29	30	31
CIIC																														ECMWetc
1015									B		B																			233/910
1016											B		B																A	234/907
1017																														259/867
1018											B												B							236/919
1019									B		B																			237/920
1020																														200/921
1022																			B											240/928
1023	B								B		B	A		B						B		A							A	239/927
1024									B		B	B/A				B			B				B							255/926
1025									B		B	A																		248/862
1027											B																			265/923
1028			A							B	A				A								A							214/850
1029									B		B												B			B				Mer.
1030									B																				B	Mer.
1032		B							B		B	A	A						B	B			B	A					A B	281
1033		B							B		B	A	*b*						B	B			B	*b*					B	287
1034				A																										286
1035									B		B												B						A	303
1036									B																					360
1038																														365
1039									B			B																		382
1040																														379
1041									B		B	A												B						376
1044									B		B					A													A	Ok7
1045									B																					Ok69
1046									B																					Ok8
1047	B								B																					Ok20
1048			B						B																					Ok32
1049									B																					Ok33
1050									B																					Ok74
1051																														Ok37
1052																														Ok38
1053									B																					Ok1
1054									B		B	A				A														Ok43
1055																														Ok3
1056																														OkApC
1057																														Ok54
1058	B								B																					Ok53
1059									B																					Ok64
1060									B		B													B						Ok57
1061	B								B													B								Dor.iii
1062											B																			Dor.v
1063											B																		A	Dor.ii
1064									B											B	A									Dor.iv
1065									B		B				B															410
1066									B															B						Manx
1067																														Manx
1068/a				A																										Manx
1068/b									B		B		B																A	Manx

Table 3.1 *contd.*

col. 1	2	3	4	5	6	7	8	9	10	11	12	13	14	15	16	17	18	19	20	21	22	23	24	25	26	27	28	29	30	31
CIIC																														ECMWetc
1069																														OkPictApp.I
1200										B																				Ok42
1201																														Ok-
1202																														Ok2
1203																														Ok-
1205			B							A													A							Ok44
1206																														Ok4
1207																														Ok-
1208																														Ok6
1209	B																													Ok12
1210																							A							Ok5
1212																														Corn.
1400																														Ok28
1401											B																		B	Ok27
1402																														Ok26
1403					A																				A					Ok25
1404																														Ok30
2000										A	A								A		A									Ang.
2001		A																A												Carms.
2002/a	A																					A								Brec.
2002/b																														Brec.
2003																														Pembs.
2004																														Pembs.
2005										B		B		A															A	Pembs.
										B		B		b															A	
2006		A								A				A															A	Shrops.
2007																														10
2008																		B					B							82
2009																														204/940
2010																														276
2011																														387
2012																														380
2013																														383
2014																														392
2015																														393
2016																														406
2017																														Caerns.
2018										B		B																		Caerns.
2019			B											A										A					A	Mer.
2020																							A							Denb.
2021		B								B		B												B						Herefs.
2022		B			A				B		B		B	A	B								B					A	253/984
		B			b				B		B		B	b	B								B					A	
2023					A																		A	A						Scot.4
2024																														Scot.11
2025																														Scot.12
2026																														RIB 2331
2027																														Ang.
2028	B								A	A	A						A													Corn.
	B								b	A	A						A													

Table 3.1 *contd.*

col. 1	2	3	4	5	6	7	8	9	10	11	12	13	14	15	16	17	18	19	20	21	22	23	24	25	26	27	28	29	30	31
CIIC																															ECMWetc
	A										B			A	A	A		A											A	
2029	A										*a*			A	A	A		A											A	/p.39 i
2030																A															/p.39ii
2031												B																			/p. 68
2032																															Brec.
2033																															Pembs.
2034												B	B																		/871
2035																				B			B								Spoleto
2036													B									A									Dor.i
2037																															Glam.
2038												B																			Manx
3001													B																		F1
3002			B									B	B																		F2
3003																	A													A	F3
3004												B																			F4
		B													A	A			B												
3005		B										*b*				A			B												F5
3006	B														B	A															C1
3007		B													B																C2
3008															B		B		B												C3
3009												B																			C4
		B							A		B		B	B	A															
3010		B									*b*		B	B	B	A														M1
3011																															M2
3012																															M3
3013											B				B				A												M4
3014												B		B			A		B												M5
3015	B											B	B																		M6
3016		A																													M7
3017															B					B		B									M8
3018																															M9
3019	B																														M10
3020																															I1
3021											B	B	B										B								I2
3022																															I3
3023																															I4
3024																															I5
3025																															I6
3026																															I7

3.2 CONSTRUCTION OF TABLE 3.2

The problem inscriptions in Table 3.1 (i.e. instances of 'A . . . B . . .', signifying conservation in the case of an early variable but innovation in the case of a later one) are as follows (in bold and boxed in Table 3.1):

350, 355, 365, 368/b, 376, 377, 385, 387, 390, 397, 400, 408, 409, 419, 448, 451, 468, 477, 479, 516, 971, 986, 993, 1000, 1012, 1023, 1024, 1033, 1041,

2022, 2029, 3005, 3010, and 3014. In addition 487, 2028, and 2005, will be found to present problems (see discussion of cols. 11 and 15 below respectively).

Where changes from A to _b_ etc. are suggested (following the policy suggested in Chapter 1), the emendations are shown in the second boxed row of Table 3.1, which bears the number of the inscription; the unnumbered first row has the original coding. See 355 for an example.

Inspection of Table 3.1 suggests prima facie that the problems lie at the following places:[2]

Col. 2 (A /a:/ > B /ɔ:/, ‡‡ 18 and 60)

is the only problem for:

**355/128/8 SILBANDVS (unless col. 4 is the problem)
**365/149 LVNARI
397/105 CVNACI (unless col. 11 is the problem, q.v.)
**419/284 SALVIANI, ONERATI, [ ]ACI[3]
448/370 RINACI (unless col. 4 is the problem, q.v.)
451/401 TVNCCETACE (unless col. 6 is the problem, q.v.)
2029/p.39i CVNIIAC (unless col. 10 is the problem, q.v.)

and is a contributory problem for **408/229/848 ETERNALI

The problem is probably the conservation of _a_ in Latin names in all four cases marked ** (assuming SILBANDVS is a Welsh hypercorrection for _Silvanus, Silbanus_, which is why it appears in col. 4 at all),[4] and I therefore **change** A to _b_ in these 4 cases.

The retention of A-spellings in Latin names is evidently chronologically unreliable; I indicate this by **changing** 'A' to '_A_' in the other cases in col. 2 where the 'A' code is due to Latin names only: 329/42 CANNTIANI (Latin suffix); 389/97 IOVENALI; 392/77 VERACIVS (Latin?); 418/283 SALVIANVS and CVPETIANI; 445/354 VITALIANI; 454/402 EVALI; 473/a/Ok46 VITALI; 514/Scot.8 CVPITIANI; 515/Scot.9 LIBERALI; 2002/a]AURIANVS (see ‡18).

Col. 3 (A pre-final _i_-affection > B post-final _i_-affection, ‡19)

is the only problem for:

409/198/849 CARANTORIVS (unless col. 6 is the problem, q.v.)
516/Scot.1 MAVORIVS (unless col. 5 is the problem, q.v.)

---

2 Where the probable explanation for an apparent problem in a column lies in another column, this is indicated by 'q.v.'.

3 The last name could be Latin as well; cf. perhaps VERACIVS below (see ‡58). If it is Celtic, note that Celtic names in -_acus_ were very well embedded in the Romano-British onomasticon, e.g. _Sediacus_ and _Petiacus_ in Tab.Sulis, no. 37, and may have been subject to Latinate conservativism to some extent. See also below, n. 27.

4 But see further below, p. 321.

Col. 4 (A /nd/ > B /nn/, ‡22)

is the only problem for:

355/128/8 SILBANDVS (unless col. 2 is the problem, q.v.)
368/b/150 BARRIVENDI, VENDVBARI (unless col. 11 is the problem, q.v.)
448/370 RINACI (unless col. 2 is the problem)

    The easiest explanation of RINACI is probably that it does not derive from *rind-* after all; and this is presumably also true therefore of 489/a/ Ok13 RINI (see ‡22, (B) nos. 14–15). In 448/370, therefore, I **change** B to *a*, and in 489/a/Ok13 I **change** B to *B* to indicate the uncertainty of /nd/ > /nn/ there.

Col. 5 (A /ɣ/ > B /w/, ‡25)

is the only problem for 516/Scot.1 MAVORIVS (unless col. 3 is the problem).

    This can be solved by **moving col. 5** ('beginning of the sixth century') to just before col. 3 ('later fifth to early sixth century').

Col. 6 (A /oN/ > B /uN/, ‡26)

is the only problem for:

409/198/849 PVMPEIVS (unless col. 3 is the problem)
451/401 TVNCCETACE (unless col. 2 is the problem)

The problem of 409/198/849 might be solved either by explaining PVMPEIVS < *Pompeius* as a Vulgar Latin rather than Brittonic development or by attributing the same inscription's unaffected CARANTORIVS (col. 3) to conservatism. However, the neatest solution, which also solves the problem of TVNCCETACE, is to **move col. 6** ('first half of the sixth century') to before col. 2 ('later fifth to early sixth century'); note that, on other grounds, Schrijver has already argued that /oN/ > /uN/ should be placed earlier, earlier indeed than *a*-affection (which was 'first half or middle of the fifth century' according to Jackson). See ‡26.

Col. 7 (A /eN/; /eN/ + stop; /ern/ > B /iN/; /iN/ + stop; /irn/, ‡27)

is the only problem for:

400/177 SENEMAGLI (unless col. 11 is the problem, q.v.)
**1000/182 PASCENT

and is a contributory problem for:

**408/229/848 ETERNALI beside CATOTIGIRNI
2022/253/984 AERERN (Nash-Williams: [B(?)]ERER[ )
477/Ok11 TEGERNOMALI (see below)

The problem is probably the conservation of *e* in Latin names in the two cases marked ** (especially in the case of ETERNALI since CATOTIGIRNI does show the change, and probably so in 1000/182 in view of the Latinate nature of this long inscription); I therefore **change** A to *b* in 1000/182, and **change** AB to B in 408/229/848. A further factor in the case of ETERNALI is that /ern/ is an unstressed syllable, where the change to /irn/ may not have happened (see ‡27, note (ii)). This factor does not apply to AERERN, of course. Here the reading is disputed, and it is possible that the second element is a form of *haearn* and therefore irrelevant (see ‡27, note (ii), (A) no. 31). I therefore **change** A to *b* under 2022/253/984.

A knock-on effect of the changes suggested under col. 17 below is that the A in col. 7 under 477/Ok11 TEGERNOMALI becomes even more clearly anomalous; there is no problem about **changing** it to *b*, however, since /ern/ here again appears in an unstressed syllable. In view of the evident chronological unreliability of /ern/ in ETERNALI and TEGERNOMALI, A must also be **changed** to *A* in all the other inscriptions where /ern/ appears in unstressed syllables: 334/54 TEGERNACVS; 379/170 LOVERNACI; 404/270/843 TEGERNACUS; 421/294 PATERNINI; 432/312 TIGERNACI (cf. ‡27, note (ii)).

Col. 8 (A /u/ > B /o̜/, ‡28)

is the only problem for:

479/Ok16 CVNAIDE (Okasha: CVNATDO) (unless cols. 10 and 18 are the problem)
3010/M1 HUBRIT

In both cases *u* can be a spelling of /o̜/ (see ‡28), so there is no objection to **changing** A to *b* in both cases, this being the neatest solution. I indicate the unreliability of the U-spelling by **changing** A to *A* in col. 8 in the other relevant cases: 468/Ok31 CVNOVALI; 487/Ok10 CVNOMORI (see ‡28).

Col. 9 (A /-Σ-/ > B /-h-/, ‡36)

is the only problem for:

376/174 VENNISETLI (unless col. 11 is the problem, q.v.)
377/175 CIMESETLI (unless col. 11 is the problem, q.v.)

Col. 10 (A pre-apocope > B post-apocope, ‡37)

is the only problem for 2029/p.39i ERECOR, CVNIIAC (unless col. 2 is the problem),
and is a contributory problem for 479/Ok16 CVNAIDE (unless col. 8 is the problem, q.v.).

The obvious explanation in the former is that final syllables (perhaps horizontal -Is) were missed in the 1827 transcription upon which we depend for ERECOR MAGLORI CVNIIAC FICIT. I therefore **change** B to _a_ in the case of 2029/p.39i.

Col. 11 (A correct > B reduced composition vowel, ‡38)

is the only problem for:

368/b/150 BARRIVENDI, VENDVBARI (unless col. 4 is the problem)
376/174 VENNISETLI (unless col. 9 is the problem)
377/175 CIMESETLI (unless col. 9 is the problem)
385/89 ANATEMORI
390/96 VENDESETLI
397/105 CVNALIPI and BECCVRI (unless col. 2 is the problem)
400/177 SENEMAGLI (unless col. 7 is the problem)
3005/F5 VENOMAILI (unless col. 17 is the problem)

Jackson does not include the reduction in his Chronological Table,[5] and it has simply been placed here before col. 12 (syncope) as being its latest possible date. The easiest solution is to **move col. 11** before col. 2 (and to before col. 6 which has already been moved to before col. 2). This solves all the problems except 3005/F5, and the only new one created relates to 419/284 RIGOHENE, 477/Ok11 CONETOCI FILI TEGERNOMALI, 487/Ok10 CVNOMORI, and 2028 ARTOGNOV([?) where the correct composition vowels of *_rīgo-_, *_tigerno-_, *_kuno-_ and *_arto-_ are retained (col. 11) but /ern/ > /irn/ (col. 7) and /Σ/ > /h/ (col. 9) are shown in 419/284 TIGIRNICI . . . RIGOHENE and /a:/ > /ɔ:/ (col. 2) is shown in the other three. This is an unreal problem, because _o_ might be written as it were by accident for the reduced vowel (see ‡38) and might also be retained through a conservative spelling tradition. Indeed, the spelling _Tigernomale_ (voc.) appears in the _Vita Prima S. Samsonis_ (seventh- or eighth-century?), and the -_o_- is also retained, from Gregory of Tours down to the ninth-century Breton hagiographer Wrmonoc, in the name of _Conomorus, Quonomorius,_ a mid-sixth-century ruler who has sometimes been identified with the person named on 487/Ok10.[6] 3005/F5 VENOMAILI may reflect a similar convention. I therefore **change** A to _b_ in col. 11 under 3005/F5, 419/284, 477/Ok11, 487/Ok10, and 2028 and move col. 11 earlier as noted above. _All_ the other cases of A in col. 11 have to be **changed** to _A_ to indicate the

---

[5] But see LHEB, p. 651: 'the high proportion of correct vowels in the inscriptions would show that at least they kept their quality (i.e. chiefly _o_) into the sixth century'. This is not too incompatible with placing col. 11 before col. 2 ('later fifth to early sixth century'). Jackson's argument that the reduction was not completed until after the final _i_-affection of the first element of compounds is undermined in SBCHP, pp. 268–76.

[6] _Vie ancienne,_ ed. Flobert, Prologus, §1 (wrongly emended); TYP, pp. 26 and 444–45.

chronological unreliability of the retention of correct composition vowels in individual cases, even though the overall pattern is surely significant.

Col. 12 (A unsyncopated > B syncopated composition vowel, ‡38)

is the only problem for 387/95 LOCVLITI (unless col. 15 is the problem, q.v.).

Col. 13 (A *rt, rc* > B *rth, rch*, ‡43)

is the only problem for:

350/116/3 [I]DNERT (unless col. 29 is the problem)
986/62 IORUERT
1012/223/933 ARTMALI
1023/239/927 NERTTAN
1024/255/926 NERTAT beside ARTHMAIL
1041/376 GURMARC (unless col. 24 is the problem)

and is a contributory problem for 1033/287 MARCIAU.

Since col. 13 throws up problems in half the relevant inscriptions (7 out of 14), it is of little value in establishing the relative chonology, presumably because the writing of *th* and *ch* came in sporadically (see ‡‡ 42–43); NERTAT beside ARTHMAIL exemplifies the orthographical inconsistency. The obvious solution is to **delete col. 13** entirely. Moving it earlier would create further problems, affecting 1025/248/862 as well as 350/116/3, 986/62, 1012/223/933 and 1023/239/927. It could, however, be moved later: after col. 20 to solve the problem of 1023/239/927, after 23 for that of 986/62, after 24 for 1041/376, after 27 for 1012/223/933, after 29 for 350/116/3, or even after 30 for 1033/287 (although the last move would create a problem with 1000/182 which has B in col. 13 on the strength of CONMARCH and GUARTHI[GIRN] (‡43) but A in col. 30 on the strength of CONCENN and CONMARCH (‡84)). On the whole, deleting col. 13 seems safer than moving it and relying on what is clearly an uncertain orthographical (certainly not phonological) criterion.

Col. 15 (A /u / > B /ö/ pretonically, ‡46)

is the only problem for:

387/95 LOCVLITI beside FIGVLINI (unless col. 12 is the problem)
971/35 CUURI[S] (unless col. 24 is the problem)

and is a contributory problem for:

1033/287 DUBUT (assuming this is a name in *Du-*, which is uncertain: ‡46 (A) no. 22)
2022/253/984 HU[T]RVM

In the last three cases *u* can easily be a spelling of /ö/ or /ə/ (see ‡46), so in them I **change** A to **_b_**. (Note also the evidence of the later change of /ö/ > /ə/ under 1033/287 in col. 30.) In 387/95 the *u* of FIGVLINI is obviously due merely to Latin influence, so I **change** AB to B there. This 'B' is still a problem, which can be solved by **moving col. 15** ('second half of the sixth century') to immediately before col. 12 ('middle of the sixth century').[7] This creates a slight problem for 2005 SATVRNBIV, which has B in col. 12 (syncope) but A in col. 15 on account of the retained U (as if *Sadwrn-* rather than *Sadyrn-*). The vowel is no doubt due to the simplex *Saturn* or to Latin influence, so I **change** A in col. 15 to **_b._**

I **change** all other examples of A in col. 15 to *A̱* to indicate the chronological unreliability of the retention of the U-spelling.

Col. 16 (A /əii̯/ > B /ai/, /oi/, ‡47)

is the only problem for 3014/M5 HERANHAL (unless col. 19 is the problem).

Note that 3014/M5 HARENBILI . . . FIL' HERANHAL is the only problem in both col. 16 and col. 19; the name HERANHAL seems to reflect /əii̯/, hence the A in col. 16, while HARENBILI shows internal *i*-affection of **-beli*, hence the B in col. 19. It would be difficult to solve this by swapping cols. 16 ('second half of the sixth century . . . perhaps') and 19 (in Breton 'eighth century in general'), not least because words like MW *heyernin* and *deyerin* suggest that W. /əi̯/ > /ai/ occurred before internal *i*-affection.[8] A more likely explanation is that B. /əi̯/ > /oi/ did not always occur in unstressed syllables, whence the later OB names in *Harn-* beside *Hoiarn-* (see ‡47). There is no point in changing A to **_b_** in col. 16 under 3014/M5 to take account of this, however, since one would have similarly to discount the 'A' under 3010/M1 HERANNUEN FIL' HERANAL (‡39), leaving no 'A' forms at all to contrast with the solitary 'B' form, 1065/410 HAERDUR (‡47). I therefore **delete col. 16.**

---

[7] Col. 15 cannot be moved so far back as to precede col. 10 without creating a slight problem with 971/35. (Note that col. 11 has already been moved earlier.) A possible reason against moving col. 15 earlier is the argument of Schrijver, *JIES*, 26 (1998), 425–28, that pretonic reduction (= col. 15 = ‡46) was later than internal *i*-affection (= col. 19 = ‡57); he concedes, however, that the reduction had begun earlier on an allophonic level. The only inscription bearing on this (other than 1033/287) is 352A/122/5 DOMNICI IACIT FILIVS BRAVECCI, where BRAVECCI lacks internal affection (‡57) while DOMNICI (> *Dyfnig*) may show /ö/ < /u/ whether it is from Celtic **Dumn-* or from **Duminicus* by pre-nasal raising (col. 6 = ‡26) from Latin *Dominicus* (see ‡57n.). However, the vocalism of DOMNICI could easily be due to Latin influence.

[8] Lewis & Pedersen, p. 108; LHEB, pp. 361 and 582. Breton evidence is scarce (HPB, p. 234), but note that OB *Hoiernin, Houernin* (‡64n) does not show 'double' internal *i*-affection of the *o*. (On 'double' affection see LHEB, pp. 591–92 and 596.) One could argue from this that B. /əi̯/ > /oi/ was later than internal *i*-affection, but equally well analogy could have preserved the /oi/.

Col. 17 (A /γ/ > B /i̯/, ‡48)

is the only problem for 3005/F5 [ ]NOMAILI and VENOMAILI (unless cols. 11–12 are the problem)
and is a contributory problem for 477/Ok11 TEGERNOMALI.

The presence of the unsyncopated composition vowels in 3005/F5 and 477/Ok11 can be solved by **moving col. 17** ('second half of the sixth century') earlier than col. 12 (syncope, 'middle of the sixth century'). Note that col. 11 has already been moved and that col. 15 has already been moved before col. 12. This raises the question of the relative order of cols. 15 and 17 (both 'second half of the sixth century'), which the inscriptions cannot themselves decide. Here a strong argument (as noted in ‡46) can be mounted from forms like W. *trwynau*, plural of *trwyn* < **trugn-*, which imply that /uγ/ had been vocalised (col. 17), creating a diphthong /ui̯/, earlier than than the reduction of pretonic /u/ (col. 15). Hence the order of columns is now . . . 10, 17, 15, 12, 14, 18 . . .

A knock-on effect of moving col. 17 earlier than col. 12 is that the A in col. 7 under 477/Ok11 TEGERNOMALI becomes clearly anomalous and has to be changed to **b** (see col. 7 above).

An objection to moving col. 17 earlier than col. 12, as proposed, is that OC *teilu* < **tego-slougo-* shows that /γl/ > /il̯/ was later than the syncope of composition vowels.[9] If this were proven, one would have to concede that the relative order of the two changes implied by forms like VENOMAILI is a matter of orthographic conventions rather than phonetic change. The conventional etymology for *teilu* is not necessarily correct, however: Schrijver argues that the reconstruction **tegeso-slougo-* is 'a serious alternative'.[10]

Col. 18 (A /xt/ > B /i̯θ/, ‡51)

is a contributory problem for 479/Ok16 CVNAIDE (unless col. 8 is the problem, q.v.).

Col. 19 (A pre-internal *i*-affection > B post-internal *i*-affection, ‡‡ 57 and 64)

is the only problem for 3014/M5 HARENBILI (unless col. 16 is the problem, q.v.).[11]

---

[9] LHEB, pp. 440 n. 1, 462 and 466; Sims-Williams, *BBCS*, 38 (1991), 73 and n. 5. Cf. ‡46n.
[10] SBCHP, p. 71.
[11] Note that if 994/125/22 CAROTINN were assigned A in col. 19 on account of its lack of internal *i*-affection (contrast *Ceredig*, etc.), that would be incompatible with the row of Bs, especially in cols. 21 and 26, which are due to HIROIDIL in the same inscription. The obvious implication is that CAROTINN is an Irish name (see ‡‡ 22 and 57).

Col. 22 (A /ɔ:/ > B /au/, ‡‡ 18 and 60)

is the only problem for 993/124/18 DITOC (unless col. 23 is the problem, q.v.).

Col. 23 (A /ɣ/ > B /∅/, ‡65)

is the only problem for:

468/Ok31 RIALOBRANI
993/124/18 AON (unless col. 22 is the problem)

The second of these presents no difficulty, since the order of cols. 22 and 23 (both 'eighth century in general') can easily be reversed. The problem with 468/Ok31 arises from the *u*-spelling in CVNOVALI (col. 8) and the correct and unsyncopated composition vowels in this and RIALOBRANI (cols. 11 and 12). It would be drastic, though not impossible, to move col. 23 ('eighth century') to before col. 8 ('first half of the sixth century'), but this is hardly necessary in view of the unreliability of the *u*-spelling as a criterion (see on col. 8 above). In the same way, the retention of the correct composition vowel in CVNOVALI and RIALOBRANI is not necessarily significant (see on col. 11 above). The lack of syncope is more of a problem. It is not obvious whether we should think of moving col. 23 to before col. 12 ('middle of the sixth century') or should instead seek to explain away the apparent absence of /ɣ/ in RIALO-, perhaps with reference to the Continental spelling tradition that produced *Riochatus* and *Riothamus* (see ‡65 and n. 1299). The latter seems the better solution, so I **change** B to *a* in 468/Ok31 under col. 23, and indicate the possible unreliability of this feature by **changing** all comparable examples of B in this column to *B*. I also **move col. 23** to before col. 22 to solve the problem of 993/124/18 DITOC . . . AON.

Col. 24 (A /w-/ > B /gw-/, ‡‡ 66 and 76)

is the only problem for:

971/35 GVRG. . . (unless col. 15 is the problem, q.v.)
1041/376 GURMARC (unless col. 13 is the problem, q.v.)

Col. 25 (A /nt/ etc. > B /nh/ etc., ‡‡ 68 and 71)

is a contributory problem for 1033/287 ANTERUNC (if B is preferred to A in col. 30).

One could solve this by moving col. 25 ('late eighth century'/'early ninth century') to after col. 30 ('tenth to eleventh century'). This seems rather a drastic change, however, although of course all it would mean is that the sporadic *writing* of NT continued quite late, which we already know from

Old Welsh sources.[12] However, the relevance of ANTERUNC 'half near, *lled agos*' is questionable, since Ifor Williams preferred to segment ANT ERUNC '*yn agos iawn*'.[13] It seems safer to leave col. 25 in place and **change** A to $\underline{b}$ in this instance in order to indicate that no reliance can be placed on ANTERUNC.

Since the problem with this inscription is a special one, I do not regard the above change of A to $\underline{b}$ as sufficient reason for changing A to $\underline{A}$ generally in col. 25.

Col. 29 (A /i̯u-/ > B /i-/ etc., ‡‡ 81 and 86)

is the only problem for 350/116/3 [I]DNERT (unless col. 13 is the problem, q.v.).

Col. 30 (A /ö/ > B /ə/, ‡‡ 46 and 84)

is a contributory problem for 1033/287 DUBUT beside CIMALTED.

This can be solved by taking the U of DUBUT (if it belongs here at all) to represent /ə/; see col. 15 above, where A has already been changed to $\underline{b}$. I therefore **change** AB in col. 30 to B, preferring the evidence of the innovatory CIMALTED to that of the probably conservative (or simply misinterpreted) DUBUT (see ‡84). Since the problem with 1033/287 may lie with the interpretation of DUBUT rather than the phonology, I do not regard the above change of AB to B as sufficient reason for changing A to $\underline{A}$ generally in col. 30.

3.3 NEW ORDER OF COLUMNS

The new order of columns suggested above, marking the moved ones in **bold**, and duly omitting 13 and 16, is:

11 6 2 **5** 3 4 7 8 9 10 **17 15** 12 14 18 19 20 21 **23** 22 24 25 26 27 28 29 30.

Table 3.2 incorporates these changes in the order of columns and the various changes of A to $\underline{b}$, A to $\underline{A}$, and so on. I have also added a hypothetical 'a' to the right of every A and a hypothetical 'b' to the left of every B for the reasons given in Chapter 1. These letters have then been used to sort the inscriptions into the final column's linguistic periods, which range from Period 1–24 (the very vague periodization of 990/108/1) to Period 28. These periodizations do not take into account the uncertainties signified by the presence of an underlined capital $\underline{A}$ or $\underline{B}$, which can be seen by inspecting the table, nor the problems that certain names are ambiguously Irish or Brittonic and that others may be spelt conservatively.

[12] LHEB, p. 503; McKee, *Juvencus*, p. 471 (OW *anter* = *hanner*).
[13] BWP, p. 32. See ‡68n.

Table 3.2 Brittonic periodization of the inscriptions

§1 PERIODS / §1 COLUMNS		(periods 2–28 grid)	31		
CIIC etc.	epig. date			ECMW etc.	ling. period
321	5-E6			25	?
326	6			39	?
331	6			41	?
332	5-E6			40	?
335	12-13			54a	?
336	5-6?			67a	?
345	5-6			74	?
347	6			76	?
348/a	?			110/27	?
357	5-E6			136	?
360	c.550			139	?
364	6			144	?
368/a	5-E6			150	?
369	5-E6			153	?
371	?			322	?
372	L5-6			160	?
373	5-E6			171	?
375	6			166	?
378	L5-6			169	?
382	5-E6			86	?
386	5-E6			92	?
393	5-E6			101	?
395	5-E6			102	?
402	6			184	?
403	L5-E6			268/841	?
405	5-E6			228/845	?
410	5-E6			238/847	?
415	5-E6			278	?
416	6			279	?
423	5-E6			296	?
427/a	5-6			301	?
428	6			305	?
431	5-E6			308	?
433	5-E6			313	?
434	6			314	?
437	6			317	?
438	5-6?			320	?
439	5-E6			319	?
441	5-E6			345	?
453	5-E6			399	?
457	VI-1			Ok18	?
458				Ok9	?
459				Ok63	?
460	VI-2			Ok75	?
461	VI-2			Ok66	?
462	VI-2			Ok14	?

Table 3.2 *contd.*

periods		§2	§3	§4	§5	§6	§7	§8	§9	§10	§11	§12	§13	§14	§15	§16	§17	§18	§19	§20	§21	§22	§23	§24	§25	§26	§27	§28		
columns		1/1	6	2	5	3	4	7	8	9	10	11	12	13	14	15	16	17	18	19	20	21	22	23	24	25	26	27		
463																													Ok15	?
465	V																												Ok21	?
466	V																												Ok23	?
467	V																												Ok24	?
469	VI-2																												Ok34	?
470	VI-2																												Ok78	?
472	V																												Ok35	?
478	VI-2																												Ok48	?
480																													Ok19	?
481	VI-2																												Ok49	?
484	VI-1																												Ok52	?
488	VI-1																												Ok60	?
491																													Ok55	?
492	VI-2																												Ok59	?
497	6																												409	?
501																													Manx	?
502																													Manx	?
503																													Manx	?
504																													Manx	?
507																													Scot.	?
508																													Scot.	?
509																													OkPict3	?
511	VI-1																												Scot. 10	?
512																													Scot.	?
513																													OkPict8	?
518																													Scot. 3	?
519																													Scot. 6	?
968	12																												5	?
976	7-9?																												72	?
982	7-9																												55	?
989	7-9																												69	?
991	9-10																												113/30	?
1003	9																												261/885	?
1006	7-9																												197/842	?
1010	9																												211/882	?
1017	7-9																												259/867	?
1020	L10-11																												200/921	?
1038	E10																												365	?
1040	10+																												379	?
1051																													Ok37	?
1052																													Ok38	?
1055																													Ok3	?
1056																													OkAppC	?
1057																													Ok54	?
1067																													Manx	?
1069																													OkPictApp.I	?
1201																													Ok-	?
1202	VI-2																												Ok2	?
1203																													Ok-	?
1206	V																												Ok4	?

Table 3.2 *contd.*

periods		§2 §3 §4 §5 §6 §7 §8 §9 §10 §11 §12 §13 §14 §15 §16 §17 §18 §19 §20 §21 §22 §23 §24 §25 §26 §27 §28		
columns		11 6 2 5 3 4 7 8 9 107 117 125 132 148 159 201 213 224 245 267 289 30		
1207			Ok-	?
1208			Ok6	?
1212			Corn.	?
1400			Ok28	?
1402	V		Ok26	?
1404	VI-1		Ok30	?
2002/b	6		Brec.	?
2003	L5-E7?		Pembs.	?
2004	11??		Pembs.	?
2007	5-E6?		10	?
2009	11-12		204/940	?
2010			276	?
2011	7-9		387	?
2012	9-10		380	?
2013	c.1140		383	?
2014	10-11		392	?
2015	10-11		393	?
2016	13?		406	?
2017			Caerns.	?
2024			Scot.11	?
2025			Scot.12	?
2026			RIB 2331	?
2027	V		Ang.	?
2032	6-1		Brec.	?
2033	10-11		Pembs.	?
2037	11-12		Glam.	?
3011			M2	?
3012			M3	?
3018			M9	?
3020			I1	?
3022			I3	?
3023			I4	?
3024			I5	?
3025			I6	?
3026			I7	?
990	7-9	A a a a	108/1	1-24
407/b	6	A a a a a a	258/846	1-22
456	5-E6	A a a a a a a	404	
422	6	A a a a a a a	298	1-21
452	5-E6	A a a a a a a	400	
506		A a a a a a a	Scot.	
1210		A a a a a a a	Ok5	
2020	5-E7	A a a a a a a	Denb.	
444	L6	A a a a a a a a	352	1-19
474		A a a a a a a a	Ok17	
346	5-E6	A a a a a a a a a a A a	75	1-16
442	5-E6	A a a a a a a a a a a	346	
485		A a a a a a a a a a a	Ok68	
3003		A a a a a a a a a a A a	F3	
339	6	A a a a a a a A a a a a a	68	1-15

Table 3.2 *contd.*

periods		§23	§24	§25	§26	§27	§28	§29	§30	§110	§111	§112	§113	§114	§115	§116	§117	§118	§119	§120	§121	§122	§123	§124	§125	§126	§127	§128	§230		
columns		11	6	2	5	3	4	7	8	9	110	107	112	113	114	115	116	117	118	119	201	223	224	225	226	227	228	229	230		
384	5-E6															A	a	a	a	a	a	a	a	a	a	a	a	a	a	83	1-15
406	5-E6															A	a	a	a	a	a	a	a	a	a	a	a	a	a	215/844	
407/a	4															A	a	a	a	A	a	a	a	a	a	a	a	a	a	258/846	
510	V															A	a	a	a	a	a	A	a	a	a	a	a	a	a	Scot. 13	
341	5-E6														A	a	A	a	a	a	a	a	a	a	a	a	a	a	a	71	1-14
325	L6													A	a	a	a	a	a	a	a	a	a	A	a	a	a			33	1-13
436	L6													A	a	a	a	a	a	a	a	a	a	A	a	a	a			316	
323	c.530										A	a	a	a	a	a	a	a	a	a	a	a	a	a	a	a	a	a	A	32	1-12
327	6										A	a	a	a	a	a	a	a	a	a	a	a	a	a	a	a	a	a	A	43	
351	6										A	a	a	a	a	a	a	a	a	a	a	a	a	a	a	a	a	a	A	115/2	
374	5-E6										A	a	a	a	a	a	a	a	a	a	a	a	a	a	a	a	a	a	A	172	
2030	E6									A	a	a	a	a	a	a	a	a	a	a	a	a	a	a	a	a	a	a	a	/p.39 ii	1-11
354	5-E6									A	a	a	a	a	a	a	a	a	a	a	a	a	a	a	a	a	A	a	a	126/6	1-10
356	6			A	a	a	a	a	a	a	a	a	a	a	a	a	a	a	a	a	a	a	a	a	a	a	a	a	a	132/9	1-7
414	5-E6			A	a	a	a	a	a	a	a	a	a	a	a	a	a	a	a	a	a	a	a	a	a	a	a	a	a	271	
421	L5-E6			A	a	a	a	a	a	a	a	a	a	a	a	a	a	a	a	a	a	a	a	a	a	a	a	a	a	294	
430	5-E6			A	a	a	a	a	a	a	a	A	a	a	a	a	a	A	a	a	a	a	a	a	a	a	a	a	a	306	
450	6			A	a	a	a	a	a	a	a	a	a	a	a	a	a	a	a	a	a	a	a	a	a	a	a	a	a	390	
482				A	a	a	a	a	a	a	a	a	a	a	a	a	a	a	a	a	a	a	a	a	a	a	a	a	a	Ok71	
483	V			A	a	a	a	a	a	a	a	a	a	a	a	a	a	a	a	a	a	a	a	a	a	a	a	a	a	Ok51	
517				A	a	a	a	a	a	a	a	a	a	a	a	a	a	a	a	a	a	a	a	a	a	a	a	a	a	Scot. 2	
1034	5-E6			A	a	a	a	a	a	a	a	a	a	a	a	a	a	a	a	a	a	a	a	a	a	a	a	a	a	286	
1403	VI-2			A	a	a	a	a	a	a	a	a	a	a	a	a	a	a	a	a	a	a	A	a	a	a	A	a	a	Ok25	
2023				A	a	a	a	a	a	a	a	a	a	a	a	a	a	a	a	a	a	A	A	a	a	a	a	a	a	Scot.4	
328	5-E6		A	a	a	a	A	a	a	a	a	a	a	a	a	a	A	a	a	a	a	a	a	a	a	a	a	a	a	44	1-6
429	L5-E6		A	a	a	a	a	a	a	a	a	a	a	a	a	a	A	a	a	a	a	a	a	a	a	a	a	a	a	307	
320	5-E6	A	a	a	a	a	a	a	A	a	a	a	a	a	a	a	a	a	a	a	a	a	a	a	a	a	a	a	A	26	1-5
322	5	A	a	a	a	a	A	a	A	a	a	a	a	a	a	a	a	a	a	a	a	a	a	a	a	a	a	a	A	27	
361	6	A	a	A	a	a	a	a	a	A	a	a	a	A	a	a	a	a	a	a	a	a	a	a	a	a	a	a	a	140	
380	6	A	a	A	a	a	a	a	a	a	a	a	a	a	A	a	a	a	A	a	a	a	a	a	a	a	a	a	a	84	
388	5-E6	A	a	a	a	a	a	a	a	a	a	a	a	a	a	a	a	a	a	a	a	a	a	a	a	a	a	a	a	94	
394	5-E6	A	a	a	a	a	a	A	a	a	a	a	a	A	a	a	a	A	A	a	a	a	a	a	a	a	a	a	a	103	
396	c.540	A	a	a	a	a	a	a	a	a	a	a	a	a	a	a	a	a	a	a	a	a	a	a	a	a	a	a	a	104	
417	5-E6	A	a	A	A	a	a	a	a	A	a	a	a	a	a	a	a	a	a	a	a	a	a	a	a	a	a	a	a	282	
420	L5-E6	A	a	a	a	a	a	a	a	a	a	a	a	a	a	a	a	a	a	a	a	a	a	a	a	a	a	a	a	289	
443	5-E6	A	a	a	a	a	a	a	A	a	a	a	a	a	a	a	a	a	a	a	a	a	a	a	a	a	a	a	A	349	
2001	5-7	A	a	a	a	a	a	a	a	a	a	a	A	a	a	a	a	a	a	a	a	a	a	a	a	a	a	a	a	Carms.	
2006	L5	A	a	a	a	a	a	A	a	A	a	a	a	a	a	a	a	a	a	a	a	a	a	a	a	a	a	a	A	Shrops.	
1068/a			A	a	a	a	a	a	a	a	a	a	a	a	a	a	a	a	a	a	a	a	a	a	a	a	a	a	a	Manx	1-4
3016			A	a	a	a	a	a	a	a	a	a	a	a	a	a	a	a	a	a	a	a	a	a	a	a	a	a	a	M7	
329	5-E6	A	a	a	a	a	a	a	a	a	a	a	a	A	a	a	a	A	a	A	a	a	a	a	a	a	a	a	a	42	1-3
*334	L6-E7	A	a	a	a	A	a	a	a	a	a	a	a	a	a	a	A	a	a	a	A	a	a	a	a	a	a	a	a	54	
344	5-E6	A	a	a	a	a	a	a	a	a	a	a	a	a	a	a	a	a	a	a	a	a	a	a	a	a	a	a	a	73	
363	6	A	a	a	a	a	a	a	a	a	a	a	a	a	a	a	a	a	A	a	A	a	a	a	a	a	a	a	a	143	
381	5-E6	A	a	a	a	a	a	a	a	a	a	a	a	a	A	a	a	a	A	a	a	a	a	a	a	a	a	a	a	87	
389	6	A	a	a	a	A	a	a	a	a	a	a	a	a	a	a	a	a	A	a	a	a	a	A	a	a	A	a	a	97	
391	5-E6	A	a	a	a	A	a	a	a	a	a	A	a	a	a	a	A	a	a	a	a	a	a	a	a	a	a	a	a	78	
392	5-E6	A	a	a	a	a	a	a	a	a	a	a	a	a	A	a	a	a	A	A	a	a	a	a	a	a	a	a	a	77	
399	5-E6	A	a	a	a	a	a	a	a	a	a	a	a	a	a	A	a	a	a	a	a	a	a	a	a	a	a	a	A	176	
*404	7	A	a	a	a	A	a	a	a	a	a	a	a	a	a	a	A	a	a	a	A	a	a	a	a	a	a	a	a	270/843	

Table 3.2 *contd.*

periods / columns		grid		
418	5-E6		283	1-3
424	6		299	
426	5-6		300	
432	5-E6		312	
445	5-E6		354	
448	5-E6		370	
473/a	VI-1		Ok46	
499	VI-1		Ok77	
514	VI-1		Scot. 8	
2002/a	5		Brec.	
2029	L5		/p.39 i	
318	L5-E6		6	I
319	5-E6		9	
342	5-E6		70	
349	6		121/4	
358	540-50		138	
362	5-E6		142	
370	5-E6		157	
379	L5-6		170	
401	5-E6		183	
413	5-E6		272	
435	5-E6		315	
446	5-E6		353	
449	5-E6		384	
454	5-E6		402	
455	5-E6		403	
468	VI-2		Ok31	
498	V		Nb 7	
515	VI-2		Scot. 9	
520	V		Scot. 5	
2000			Ang.	
496			Hants.	2-13
500	VI-1		Manx	
425	5-E6		297	2-11
447	6		369	
377	5-E6		175	2-9
368/b	5-E6		150	2-6
390	6		96	
1028	L6-E7		214/850	
397	6		105	2-3
2019	fake?		Mer.	3-12
*505	VII		Manx	3-7
409	6		198/849	3-5
451	6		401	3
1209			Ok12	4-28
3019			M10	
366	L5-6		148	4-20
2028			Corn.	4-13
3006	VI-2		C1	
487	VI-2		Ok10	4-8

Table 3.2 *contd.*

periods		§2	§3	§4	§5	§6	§7	§8	§9	§10	§11	§12	§13	§14	§15	§16	§17	§18	§19	§20	§21	§22	§23	§24	§25	§26	§27	§28		
columns		11	6	2	5	3	4	7	8	9	10	17	15	12	14	18	19	20	21	23	22	24	25	26	27	28	29	30		
385	5-E6	B	b	B		A	a	A	a	a	a	a	a	A	a	a	a	a	a	A	a	a	a	a	a	a	a	A	89	4-5
1205		b	b	b	B						A	a	a	a	a	a	a	a	a	a	A	a	a	a	a	a	a	a	Ok44	5-10
516		b	b	b	B	A	a	A	a	a	a	a	a	a	a	A	a	a	a	a	A	a	a	a	a	a	a	a	Scot. 1	5
330	5-E6	b	b	b	b	B											A	a	a	a	a	a	a	a	a	a	a	a	66	6-16
398	6	b	b	b	b	b	b	B																					106	7-28
475		b	b	b	b	b	b	B																					Ok47	
489/a	VI-2	b	b	B	b	b	b	*B*																					Ok13	
355	5-E6c	b	b	*b*	b	b	b	B												A	a	a	a	a	a	a	a	128/8	7-20
970	c.625	B	b	b	b	b	b	B				A	a	a	a	a	a	a	a	a	a	a	a	a	a	a	a	13	7-13
376	5-E6	B	b	b	b	b	b	B		A	a	a	a	A	a	a	a	a	A	a	a	a	A	a	A	a	a	a	174	7-9
400	5-E6	B	b	b	b	b	b	B	A	a	a	a	A	a	A	A	a	a	a	a	a	a	A	a	a	a	a	a	177	7
*476	V	b	b	b	b	b	b	b	B																				Ok45	8-28
359	6	b	b	b	b	b	b	b	B															A	a	a	a	141	8-24
408	6	B	b	*b*	B	b	b	b	B							A	a	a	a	A	a	a	A	A	a	a	A	a	229/848	8-13
365	L6	B	b	*b*	B	b	b	b	b	B						A	a	a	a	a	a	A	a	a	a	a	a	a	149	10-13
419	6	*b*	b	*b*	b	b	b	b	b	b	B					A	a	a	a	a	a	a	A	A	A	a	a	A	284	
337	11-12	b	b	b	b	b	b	b	b	b	B																		60	11-28
440	6	b	b	b	b	b	b	b	b	b	B																		335	
985	10-11	b	b	b	b	b	b	b	b	b	B																		61	
996	11-E12	B	b	b	b	b	b	b	b	b	B																		147	
1001	9-10	b	b	b	b	b	b	b	b	b	B																		181	
1036	L10-E11	b	b	b	b	b	b	b	b	b	B																		360	
1045		b	b	b	b	b	b	b	b	b	B																		Ok69	
1046		b	b	b	b	b	b	b	b	b	B																		Ok8	
1047		b	b	B	b	b	b	b	b	b	B																		Ok20	
1048	VII	b	b	b	b	b	B	b	b	b	B																		Ok32	
1049		b	b	b	b	b	b	b	b	b	B																		Ok33	
1050		b	b	b	b	b	b	b	b	b	B																		Ok74	
1053		b	b	b	b	b	b	b	b	b	B																		Ok1	
1058		b	b	B	b	b	b	b	b	b	B																		Ok53	
1059		b	b	b	b	b	b	b	b	b	B																		Ok64	
1200		b	b	b	b	b	b	b	b	b	B																		Ok42	
2031	11-12	b	b	b	b	b	b	b	b	b	B																		/p. 68	
3004		b	b	b	b	b	b	b	b	b	B																		F4	
3009		b	b	b	b	b	b	b	b	b	B																		C4	
2038		b	b	b	b	b	b	b	b	b	B																		Manx	
353	5-E6	b	b	b	b	b	b	b	b	b	b	B																	127/7	12-28
477	VI-2	*b*	b	B	b	b	b	*b*	B	b	b	B	A	a	a	a	A	a	a	a	a	a	A	a	a	a			Ok11	12-13
3005		*b*	b	b	b	b	B	b	b	b	b	B	A	a	a	a	a	a	a	a	a	a	a	a	a	a	a		F5	
352A	5-E6	b	b	b	b	b	b	b	b	b	b	b	B	A	a	a	a	a	a	a	a	a	a	a	a	A			122/5	13-16
387	6	b	b	b	b	b	b	b	b	b	b	b	B	A	a	a	a	a	a	a	a	a	a	a	a	a			95	13
471	VI-2	b	b	b	b	b	b	b	B	b	b	b	b	B															Ok39	14-28
997	10	b	b	b	b	b	b	b	b	b	B	b	b	b	B														159	
1005	9	b	b	b	b	b	b	b	b	b	B	b	b	b	B														191/886	
1015	10-11	b	b	b	b	b	b	b	b	b	B	b	b	b	B														233/910	
1019	11	b	b	b	b	b	b	b	b	b	B	b	b	b	B														237/920	
1025	7-9	b	b	b	b	b	b	b	b	b	B	b	b	b	B														248/862	
1027	L10-11	b	b	b	b	b	b	b	b	b	B	b	b	b	B														265/923	
1062		b	b	b	b	b	b	b	b	b	b	b	B																Dor. v	

Table 3.2 *contd.*

periods		§2	§3	§4	§5	§6	§7	§8	§9	§10	§11	§12	§13	§14	§15	§16	§17	§18	§19	§20	§21	§22	§23	§24	§25	§26	§27	§28		
columns		11	6	2	5	3	4	7	8	9	107	115	112	114	189	120	213	224	225	226	227	228	230							
1065	9-10	b	b	b	b	b	b	b	b	b	B	b	b	B															410	14-28
2018		b	b	b	b	b	b	b	b	b	B	b	b	B															Caerns.	
2034	8-9	b	b	b	b	b	b	b	b	b	b	B	b	b	B														/871	
3001		b	b	b	b	b	b	b	b	b	B	b	b	B															F1	
3002	VII	b	b	b	B	b	b	b	b	b	B	b	b	B															F2	
3007	VII	b	b	b	b	b	B	b	b	b	b	b	b	B															C2	
3015		b	b	B	b	b	b	b	b	b	B	b	b	B															M6	
324	6?	b	B	b	b	b	b	b	b	b	b	b	B	B														A	34	14-27
1016	L10-11	b	b	b	b	b	b	b	b	b	b	b	B	B														A	234/907	
1068/b		b	b	b	b	b	b	b	b	b	B	b	B	B														A	Manx	
2005	8-E9	b	b	b	b	b	b	b	b	b	b	b	*b*	B														A	Pembs.	
1063		b	b	b	b	b	b	b	b	b	b	b	b	B													A	a	Dor.ii	14-26
2036		b	b	b	b	b	b	b	b	b	b	b	b	B							A	a	a	a	a	a	a	a	Dor.i	14-21
427/b	E9	b	b	b	B	b	b	b	b	b	B	b	b	B				A	a	a	a	a	a	a	a	a	a	a	301	14-20
486	VI-2	b	b	b	b	b	b	b	b	b	B	b	b	B		A	a	a	a	a	a	a	a	a	a	a	a	a	Ok56	14-16
490	VI-2	b	b	b	B	b	b	b	B	B	b	b	b	B		A	a	a	a	a	a	a	a	a	a	a	a	a	Ok29	
493	VI-1	b	b	b	b	b	b	b	B	b	b	b	B			A	a	a	a	a	a	a	a	a	a	a	a	a	Ok58	
1044		b	b	b	b	b	b	b	b	B	b	b	B			A	a	a	a	a	a	a	a	a	a	a	A	a	Ok7	
1054		b	b	b	b	b	b	b	B	b	b	b	B			A	a	a	a	a	a	a	a	a	a	a	a	a	Ok43	
3013		b	b	b	b	b	b	b	B	b	b	b	B			A	a	a	a	a	a	a	a	a	a	a	a	a	M4	
*p.397	5	b	b	b	b	b	b	b	b	b	b	b	B		A	a	A	a	a	a	a	a	a	a	a	a	a	a	285	14-15
1039	1078-80	b	b	b	b	b	b	b	b	B	b	b	b	B															382	15-28
3010		b	b	b	b	b	B	b	*b*	B	b	b	B	B															M1	
1011	L9	b	b	b	b	b	b	b	b	B	b	b	B															A	220/911	15-27
479		b	b	b	b	b	b	b	*b*	b	B	b	b	b	B		A	a	a	a	a	a	a	a	a	a	a	a	Ok16	16-17
473/b		b	b	B	b	b	b	b	b	b	B	B	b	b	B														Ok46	17-28
995	7-9	b	b	b	b	B	b	b	b	b	b	b	b	b	B														133/24	
1008	11-E12	b	b	b	b	b	b	b	b	B	b	b	b	b	B														194/934	
1009	11	b	b	b	b	b	b	b	b	B	b	b	b	b	B														193/935	
1013	L10	b	b	b	b	b	b	b	b	B	b	b	b	b	B														222/912	
1022	11	b	b	b	b	b	b	b	B	b	b	b	b	b	B														240/928	
3014		b	b	b	b	b	b	b	b	B	b	b	b	b	B														M5	
1064		b	b	b	b	b	b	b	b	B	b	b	b	b	B		A	a	a	a	a	a	a	a	a	a	a	a	Dor.iv	17-18
*489/b	VI-2	b	b	b	b	b	b	b	b	b	b	b	b	b	b	b	B												Ok13	18-28
3008		b	b	b	b	b	b	b	b	B	b	B	b	b	b	B													C3	
1023	11	b	b	B	b	b	b	b	b	B	b	B	B	b	b	B		A	a	a	a	a	a	A				A	239/927	18-20
3017		b	b	b	b	b	b	b	b	b	b	b	b	b	b	*B*	B												M8	20-28
3021		b	b	b	b	b	B	b	b	B	b	b	B	b	b	b	B												I2	
978	L10	B	b	b	B	b	b	b	b	B	B	b	b	b	b	b	*b*										A	a	a	49	20-25
993	7-9	b	b	B	b	b	b	b	b	B	b	B	b	b	b	b	B	A	a	a	a	a	a	a					124/18	20
333	?	b	b	B	b	b	b	b	b	B	b	b	b	b	b	b	B												50	21-28
*412	5-E6	b	b	B	b	b	b	b	b	b	B	b	B	b	b	b	B												277	
986	7-9	b	b	b	b	b	b	b	b	B	b	b	B	b	*b*	B													62	
*1061	VII	b	b	B	b	b	b	b	b	B	b	b	b	b	b	b	B												Dor.iii	
348/b	9-10	b	b	b	b	b	b	b	B	B	b	b	B	b	b	b	b	B											110/27	22-28
494		b	b	b	b	b	b	b	b	b	b	b	b	b	b	b	b	B											Ok79	
980	11-12	b	b	b	b	b	b	b	b	B	b	b	b	b	B	b	b	B											46a	
984	7-9	b	b	b	b	b	b	b	b	B	b	b	B	b	b	B	b	B											59	
1004	7-9	b	b	b	b	b	B	b	b	b	B	b	b	B	b	b	b	b	B										260/884	

Table 3.2 *contd.*

periods	§2 §3 §4 §5 §6 §7 §8 §9 §10 §11 §12 §13 §14 §15 §16 §17 §18 §19 §20 §21 §22 §23 §24 §25 §26 §27 §28		
columns 1/1 6 2 5 3 4 7 8 9 10/7 15/2 14/8 19/0 21/3 22/4 25/6 27/9 23/0			
1014	L9-E10	b b B B b b b b b B b b b b B b b b B B	231/908	22-28
1018	11	b b b b b b b b b b b b B b b b b b b B	236/919	
1024	11	b b b b b b b b b B b B b b b B b b b B	255/926	
1041	9-10	b b b b b b b b b B b b B b b b b b b B	376	
*1060	VII	b b b b b b b b b B b b B b b b b b b B	Ok57	
1066		b b b b b b b b b B b b b b b b b b b B	Manx	
2008	10-11	b b b b b b b b b b b b b b B b b b b B	82	
2021	10-11	b b b b b B b b b B b b b b b b b b b B	Herefs.	
2035		b b b b b b b b b b b b b b b B b b b B	Spoleto	
971	7-9	b b b b b b b b b B b *b* b b b b b b b B	A	35	22-27
1000	9-1	b b B B b b *b* b b B B B b b b B b b B B	A	182	
2022	L11-12	b b b b b B B *b* b b B B B b b b b b b B	A	253/984	
1035	1033-5	b b b b b b b b b B b b B b b b b b b B	A a	303	22-26
988	L11-12	b b b b b b b b b b b b b b b b b b b B	B	67	23-28
994	E9	b b b b b b b b B B b b B B b b b b b b	B	125/22	24-28
464		b b b b b b b b b B b b b b b b b b b b	B	Ok65	25-28
1012	10-11	b b b b b b b B b B b B b b b b b b b b	B	A a	223/933	25-26
998	7-9	b b b b b b b b b B b b B b b b b b b b	B	164	26-28
1029		b b b b b b b b b B b b b b b b b B b b	B	Mer.	
*350	6 [7]	b b b b b b b b b B b b b b b b b b b b	B	116/3	27-28
*1401	V	b b b b b b b b b B b b b b b b b b b b	B	Ok27	
979	9	b B b b b b b B b b B b b B b b b b B b b B b b B b B	46	28
992	7-9	b b b b b b b b b b B b b b b b b b b b b b b b B	120/14	
1007	L10-11	b b b b b b b b b b b b b b b b b b b b b b b b B	206/938	
1030		b b b b b b b b b B b b b b b b b b b b b b b b B	Mer.	
1032	12	b b b b b b b b b B b b b B b B b b b b b B b b b B	281	
1033	7-9	b b b b B b b b b b *b* B b b B B b b b B *b* b b b B	287	

* Marks the 12 anomalous inscriptions underlined in Table 3.3 and listed in Table 3.4

3.4 COMPARISON OF LINGUISTIC AND EPIGRAPHIC RELATIVE DATING: TABLE 3.3

In order to see whether the linguistic relative chronology correlates with the non-linguistic relative chronology suggested by Nash-Williams and others on epigraphic, archaeological, and art-historical grounds, I have added their dates in the column of Table 3.2 headed 'epig. date'. The dates of the Welsh inscriptions are given in arabic numerals, and are taken from Nash-Williams, with a few additions from the new *Corpus*.[14] E = 'early' and L = 'late',[15] and designations like 6–1 and 6–2 mean 'first half of the sixth century' and 'second half of the sixth century'. For non-Welsh inscriptions, I cite the dates in roman numerals given by Tedeschi in 1995:[16] he has four

---

[14] Provisional dates from the new *Corpus* are given for 2001–6, 2020–21, 2029–32, 2034, 2037; the date of 2033 is that of Kay. 350/116/3 is dated 6c in ECMW, but Nash-Williams extends this to early 7c apud LHEB, p. 710, and this is the date quoted here; on this dating see further below.

[15] Or 'later' in the case of 325/33 only.

[16] Tedeschi, *Scrittura e civiltà*, 19 (1995), 119–21, nos 102–49. (Tedeschi also gives dates for 101 Welsh inscriptions (see Ch. 6 below), but these are not collated in Table 3.2.)

epigraphic periods: V; VI-1; VI-2; and VII. (His study did not cover later centuries.) More dates could have been added from the works of other scholars such as Jackson and Thomas,[17] but I have refrained from including these in Table 3.2, partly because Nash-Williams's and Tedeschi's dates are more obviously rooted in a purely typological analysis, and partly because they provide a large enough sample for comparing the linguistic and non-linguistic chronologies.

Our immediate concern is not with the epigraphers' absolute dates, but with their relative chronology, albeit expressed in terms of centuries AD. Is the epigraphic chronology illusory, as has recently been claimed,[18] or does our linguistic progression from Period 1 to Period 28 agree with the epigraphers' typological progression from the fifth century to the twelfth? That it does, broadly, can be seen in **Table 3.3**. This includes all of the 183 inscriptions in Table 3.2 which have both a linguistic periodization and an epigraphic date.

The *horizontal bands* of Table 3.3 are the linguistic periods of Table 3.2, slightly rearranged inasmuch as: (a) The very wide and therefore fairly uninstructive periods like *4–20*, and *14–28* have been removed to the beginning or end and have been put in *italics*. They are not incompatible with the rest of the data, but cannot confirm it significantly. (b) Other bands have been grouped together so as to show the linguistic/epigraphic correspondences for linguistic periods 1–3, 1–7, 1–13, 1–20, 8–28, 10–16, 14–28, 15–28, 21–28, and 24–28. These rearrangements are a matter of convenience; there is no logical order for periods of such disparate size as '2–11' and '4–8'.

The *columns* of Table 3.3 refer to the epigraphic dates, except that these have been slightly simplified to reduce the number of columns; for instance, '5–6' would embrace inscriptions dated 'fifth to early sixth century' as well as 'fifth to sixth century'.

Table 3.3 shows that the two relative chronologies agree broadly, with some obvious exceptions, 12 in number, which I have **embolded and underlined** (and starred in Table 3.2). It is immediately obvious, for example, that the linguistically early inscriptions from Periods 1–7 in the box near the top left are epigraphically early, while those from Periods 21–28 in the box near the bottom right are epigraphically late. Despite such broad agreement, the linguistic/epigraphic agreement involves some fuzzy areas. For example, the discrete linguistic periods 1–13 and 14–28 overlap epigraphically in the sixth and seventh centuries. Thus 970/13 CATAMANUS belongs to the linguistic Period 7–13 (pre-syncope) and is epigraphically early seventh century (indeed it cannot be earlier than King Cadfan's death *c.* 625),[19] whereas 493/Ok58 NEPRANI FILI CONBEVI (if Brittonic!) belongs to the

---

[17] Also Handley in IEMB; see Ch. 6 below.
[18] See Ch. 1 above, p. 5.
[19] On its dating see below, p. 277.

Table 3.3 Comparison of epigraphic and linguistic periodizations

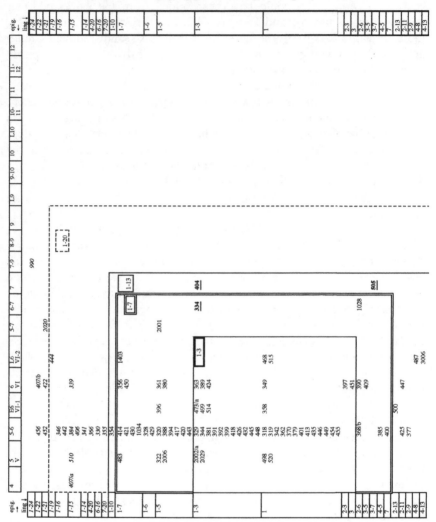

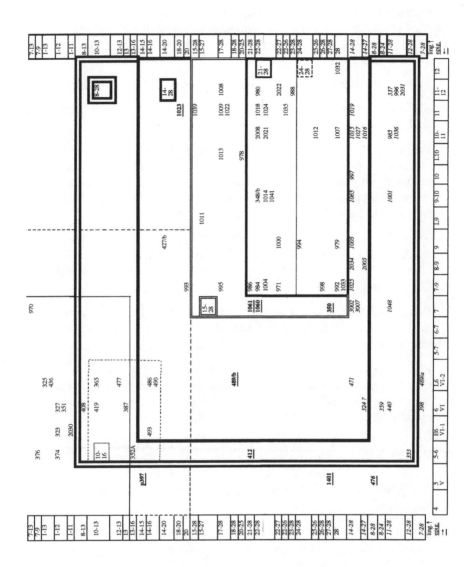

linguistic Period 14–16 (post-syncope) but is dated by Tedeschi to the first half of the sixth century. Such contradictions cannot be resolved without detailed discussion, but the following broad patterns emerge by simple inspection of Table 3.3:

Period 1 inscriptions belong to the epigraphers' fifth or sixth centuries.

The only Period 3 inscription (451/401 TVNCCETACE) is epigraphically sixth-century.

Period 1–3 inscriptions (boxed) are all 5c or 6c centuries, with the exceptions of 334 and 404; the former is 'late 6th–early 7th-century' according to Nash-Williams, which admittedly does allow a 6c date, but VII according to Tedeschi, and conversely 404 is '7th century' according to Nash-Williams, but VI-2 according to Tedeschi.

The only Period 7 inscription (400/177 VINNEMAGLI FILI SENE-MAGLI) is epigraphically 5c to early 6c (a span which of course still allows the possibility of a 6c date slightly later than the above-mentioned Period 3 inscription).

Period 1–7 inscriptions (boxed) can all belong to the epigraphers' 5c or 6c,[20] with the exception of 404 and 505, 7c according to Nash-Williams and Tedeschi respectively (but 404 is VI-2 according to Tedeschi).

Period 1–13 inscriptions (boxed) all belong to the epigraphers' 5c–7c; but note that the only definitely post-6c ones are 404 and 505, already seen to be problematic, and 970/13 CATAMANVS which may well be *early* 7c, if erected immediately after the death of King Cadfan *c.* 625.

The only Period 13 inscription (387/95 FIGVLINI FILI LOCVLITI) is epigraphically said to be 6c (VI-2 according to Tedeschi). It would be neater if it were early 7c, like the CATAMANUS inscription (Period 7–13); obviously Nash-Williams's and Tedeschi's dates were not intended to prevent such fine tuning.

Period 10–16 inscriptions (boxed) can all belong to the 6c, with the exception of p.397 (5c according to Nash-Williams). The sample is small, but it seems surprising that none is epigraphically dated later than the 6c.

Period 8–28 inscriptions can belong to the 6c–12c, with the exceptions of p.397, 1401 and 476, which lie outside the Period 8–28 box.

Inscriptions of Period 14 onwards (boxed) can all be early sixth century

---

[20]   Since 2001's '5–7c' spans 5–6c, and 334's 'late 6–early 7c' (Nash-Williams) allows for a sixth-century date.

onwards,[21] again with the exceptions of p.397 and 476 which are specifically fifth century.

Period 15–28 inscriptions (boxed) belong to the 7c–12c, with the exception of 489/b and 412, as well again of 1401.

The only Period 20 inscription (993/124/18 TESQUITUS DITOC . . .) is epigraphically seventh- to ninth-century. If it were more precisely 9c that would fit in with the ninth-century epigraphic date assigned to the Period 14–20 inscription 427/b/301 AMMULANTIBUS . . . CATUOCONI. Alternatively, both might be 8c (a precise periodization which Nash-Williams avoided for some reason).[22]

Period 1–20 inscriptions (boxed) are all 9c or earlier, with the exception of 1023 (11c).

Period 21–28 inscriptions (boxed) can belong to the 9c–12c centuries, with the exception of 1060, 1061 and 350, as well again of 412 and 1401.

Period 24–28 inscriptions (boxed) can belong to the 9c–12c, again with the exception of 350 and 1401.

Period 28 inscriptions seem to cover a surprisingly wide epigraphical span, from at least the 9c to the 12c, but as there are only five of them they will have to be examined in detail below. In theory, it is conceivable that the linguistic developments up to Period 28 had already been completed by the 9c while the epigraphical developments were still in progress.

Anomalous inscriptions can also be identified by starting from the epigraphical dates. Thus all inscriptions which are epigraphically seventh-century or later (i.e. in or to the right of the 7c column) can belong to the linguistic Period 13 or later,[23] with the familiar exceptions of 404 in Period 1–3 and 505 in Period 3–7. All inscriptions which are epigraphically ninth-century or later can belong to the linguistic Period 14 (or even 20)[24] or later. All inscriptions which are epigraphically tenth-century or later can belong to the linguistic Period 25 or later. All inscriptions which are epigraphically eleventh-century or later can belong to the linguistic Period 26 or later, with the familiar exception of 1023 (Period 18–20).

---

[21] For a suggestion that Tedeschi's dates may be too early here see below, p. 277, in connection with the CATAMANUS stone.

[22] Nash-Williams later conceded that 427/b/301 might be eighth-century epigraphically: LHEB, p. 291, n. 2.

[23] Since e.g. 970/13 CATAMANUS (Period 7–13) could be as late as Period 13.

[24] Since e.g. 427/b/301 AMMULANTIBUS . . . CATUOCONI (Period 14–20) could be as late as Period 20.

3.5 Conflicting epigraphic and linguistic dates: Table 3.4

Table 3.4 The twelve anomalous inscriptions of Table 3.3

§1 Period / CIIC	epig. date	§2	§3	§4	§5	§6	§7	§8	§9	§10	§11	§12	§13	§14	§15	§16	§17	§18	§19	§20	§21	§22	§23	§24	§25	§26	§27	§28	ECMW etc. nos	ling. period
Column		1	6	2	5	3	4	7	8	9	10	17	15	12	14	18	19	20	21	23	22	24	25	26	27	28	30	31		
334	L6-E7		A	a	a	A	a	a	a	a	a	a	a	a	a	a	A	a	a	a	A	a	a	a				54	1-3
404	7		A	a	a	A	a	a	a	a	a	a	a	a	a	a	A	a	a	a	A	a	a	a				270/843	1-3
505	VII	b	B			A	a	a	a	a	a	a	a	a	a	a	a	a	a	a	a	a	a	a				Manx	3-7
476	V	b	b	b	b	b	b	B																				Ok45	8-28
p.397	5	b	b	b	b	b	b	b	b	b	b	b	b	B	A	a	A	a	a	a	a	a	a	a	a	a		285	14-15
489/b	VI-2	b	b	b	b	b	b	b	b	b	b	b	b	b	b	b	B											Ok13	18-28
1023	II	b	b	B	b	b	b	b	b	b	B	b	B	B	b	b	b	B	A	a	a	a	a	a	a	A		239/927	18-20
412	5-E6	b	b	B	b	b	b	b	b	b	b	b	b	b	b	b	b	b	b	b	B	b	B					277	21-28
1061	VII	b	b	B	b	b	b	b	b	b	B	b	b	b	b	b	b	b	b	b	b	b	B					Dor.iii	21-28
1060	VII	b	b	b	b	b	b	b	b	b	B	b	b	b	B	b	b	b	b	b	b	b	b	B				Ok57	22-28
350	6[7]	b	b	b	b	b	b	b	b	b	B	b	b	B	b	b	b	b	b	b	b	b	b	b	b	b	B	116/3	27-28
1401	V	b	b	b	b	b	b	b	b	b	b	b	B	b	b	b	b	b	b	b	b	b	b	b	b	b	B	Ok27	27-28

334/54 CATACVS TEGERNACVS (dated VII by Tedeschi) and 404/270/ 843 TEGERNACUS (dated VI-2 by Tedeschi) are anomalous because of the preservation of A rather than the O for /ɔ:/ expected in Welsh (see ‡18). One obvious explanation is that these names in Breconshire and Glamorgan are in fact Irish (> *Cathach*, *Tigernach*) rather than Welsh (> *Cadog*, *Teyrnog*).[25] If they are regarded as Irish, one also avoids the (much slighter) problem of the absence of W. /ern/ > /irn/, indicated by the _A_ in col. 7. If Irish, these inscriptions have to be removed from the Brittonic chronology. Admittedly, the vocalism of TEG- is an objection, but this could be due to British influence.[26] If this objection is upheld, one could perhaps opt for the earlier epigraphical dates in both cases and move the two inscriptions back into the sixth century with the rest of Period 1–3. Alternatively a conservative British spelling of -*acus* has to be assumed, perhaps due to familiarity with the suffix in Latin contexts.[27]

505 MONOMENTI is placed as early as Period 3–7 on account of the non-raising of /e/ to /i/ before /nt/ (see ‡27, whence the A in col. 7). However, we have already noted that ENT could be due to Latin conservatism and have compared the preservation of /ent/ in the loan-word *mynwent*.[28] Hence 505 should probably be recategorized as Period 3–28, which is compatible with Tedeschi's seventh-century date.

476/Ok45 BONEMIMORI exhibits the reverse problem, being placed after Period 7 on account of the pre-nasal raising (see ‡27). However, this

---

[25] Macalister claimed that 404/270/843 bore ogams (see also LHEB, p. 187), though subsequent scholars have denied this.

[26] See SBCHP, p. 64, and ‡27(ii). In Ireland 214 TEGG[is a possible example of /e/ vocalism (Ziegler, p. 236), but is obviously uncertain.

[27] Cf. -*acus* names listed by Mócsy, p. 345, and n. 3 above.

[28] See ‡27(i) and SBCHP, p. 28.

may be due merely to Vulgar Latin confusion of front vowels (see examples in ‡15), and one should recall Jackson's view that the pre-nasal raising did not occur in Cornwall (see ‡27). If -MIM- is due to Vulgar Latin, there is no objection to reassigning 476/Ok45 to Period 1–28, which is of course compatible with Tedeschi's fifth-century date.

p.397/285 BARRECTI was placed in Period 14 or later because of the presumed syncope of *barro- 'top, head' before *rectu-, *recto- (‡38 (C)). Possibly it could be reanalysed as *barro- + a suffix *-ekt-, perhaps related in some way to the feminine abstract *-ektā (> OI -echt, W. -aeth), or to the suffix of ogam GOSSUCTTIAS, OI Gúassacht.[29] In this case the inscription would be Period 1–15, which is compatible with Nash-Williams's '5th century' date.

It is difficult to avoid putting 489/b/Ok13 SAGRANVI in Period 18 or later, if its -VI represents /ui/ < /e:/.[30] The problem may be that Tedeschi's 'VI-2' date for 489/Ok13 really refers to only 489/a/Ok13 SVAQQUCI MAQI QICI/FANNONI MAQVI RINI. Compare the case of 407/b/258/ 846 where Tedeschi's VI-1 date (his no. 68) obviously refers to the medieval rather than Roman inscription on that stone. Again, 473/a/Ok46 VITALI FILI TORRICI and 473/b/Ok46 IGNIOC are not distinguished in Tedeschi's list (no. 114) – in this case I have assumed that his VI-1 date applies to VITALI FILI TORRICI only.[31]

The problems with 1023/239/927 SCILOC/?SCITOC, 412/277 FERRVCI, and 1061/Dor.iii CATGUG/CATTUG stem from the problem of the fate of /a:/ (see ‡‡ 18 and 60). The A and Bs in col. 22 arise from the view that parallel to the regular Welsh development /a:/ > /ɔ:/ > /au/, there was a dialectal devlopment /a:/ > /ɔ:/ > /u(:)/. SCILOC/?SCITOC would appear to be still at the /ɔ:/ stage (i.e. Period 20 or earlier), and if the art-historical dating of this cross to the eleventh century cannot be moved earlier (it is maintained in the *Corpus*), the -OC is best explained as a conservative spelling. Alternatively, SCILOC/?SCITOC, the carver of the Merthyr Mawr cross, could be a Cornishman or Breton. Conversely, the problem with FERRVCI and CATGUG/CATTUG is that the /u(:)/ stage seems to be occurring too early. However, the 412/277 FERRVCI HIC IACIT stone is known only from an account sent to Lhuyd, and Nash-Williams's '5th–early 6th century (?)' date, presumably based on the HIC IACIT formula and alleged use of capitals, may well be wrong.[32] If it is not, should one suppose that there was an *-ukos suffix as well as the familiar *-ākos, or derive

---

[29] NWÄI, pp. 334–35; SWWF, p. 555; GOI, pp. 167–68 and 452; Ziegler, p. 185. If the stone indeed bore the formula D[is] M[anibus] (see Fig. 1.2), that is in favour of an early date; cf. Handley, *EME*, 10 (2001), 183.

[30] See ‡‡ 48 and 58. Thomas, *Mute Stones*, p. 268, takes -VI to be genitive of *-uus.

[31] Okasha notes that it has been suggested 'many times' that IGNIOC is later than the rest. KHJ exceptionally thought it no later palaeographically than the rest.

[32] Nash-Williams, *BBCS*, 8 (1935–37), 172; Lhuyd, *Parochialia*, iii, 108.

FERRVCI from *Ferrucius (see ‡‡ 44 and 60)? In the case of 1061/Dor.iii CATGUG, while Hinton agrees on the seventh century as 'reasonably assured', Radford and Jackson place it later than Tedeschi, to the '7th to 8th-century'.[33] Such a later epigraphic date fits more easily with CATGUG belonging in Period 21–28, since other Period 21–28 inscriptions begin in the seventh to ninth century (see the box in Table 3.3), and there is one Period 14–20 inscription (427/b/301) dated by Nash-Williams to the early ninth century. If the epigraphic and linguistic dates of CATGUG cannot be reconciled, however, an alternative is to suppose either that /ɔː/ > /u(ː)/ started earlier than /ɔː/ > /au/, or that CATGUG is not after all a derivative of *Katākos but rather a hypocoristic form of Cadwgan, as supposed by McClure and Jackson (see ‡‡ 18, 42, and 60).

1060/Ok57 is dated seventh-century by Tedeschi, as well as by Radford and Thomas, but belongs as late as Period 22–28 on account of the GU-rather than V- (‡76). It could perhaps be moved slightly later than Tedeschi's period; Okasha comments that 'this text uses insular script which suggests a date from the eighth century onwards'.[34]

350/116/3 [I]DNERT is in Period 27–28 on account of the ID- rather than IUD- (‡81), but is epigraphically sixth-century according to Nash-Williams in ECMW; later in correspondence with Jackson he allowed the early seventh century to be possible.[35] At this time Lhuyd's drawing was unknown and it seemed reasonable to restore the extant fragment as [IV]DNERT. However, when Lhuyd's transcription turned up in 1961 (see Fig. 1.2), it was found not only that the name was IDNERT but also that there were more half uncial letters than are now visible at Llanddewibrefi:

> Whereas on the stone itself, as it now is, one in eight of the identifiable letters is half uncial [d e t], in the new drawing the proportion has risen to about one in four [d e t h b m].[36]

Jackson abandoned the restoration [IV]DNERT, but was reluctant to move the inscription later than the seventh century (also Tedeschi's date). Nevertheless, one should surely do so, for the first other evidence for Id- spellings is from the second half of the ninth century, if we rely on charters surviving in twelfth-century copies, or from the second half of the eleventh century if we rely on original manuscripts.[37] Rhys even suggested that the inscription might refer to the plundering of Llanddewibrefi in 1109,[38] which is only possible if an archaic script was practised at Llanddewibrefi then.

---

[33] Hinton, PDNHAS, 114 (1992), 260; Radford & Jackson, in RCHM, Dorset, ii/2, p. 311.

[34] Radford, DASP, 27 (1969), 81; Thomas, Mute Stones, p. 330; Okasha, Corpus, pp. 23 and 270.

[35] LHEB, p. 710.

[36] Jackson, BBCS, 19 (1960–62), 232–33 [my additions in square brackets].

[37] Sims-Williams, BBCS, 38 (1991), 79. Thomas, Peritia, 10 (1996), 157, is prepared to contemplate an early ninth-century dating for the stone.

[38] Englyn, pp. 45–46; see Brut y Tywysogyon, ed. Jones, s.a.

Finally, 1401/Ok27 RESTEUTA(E) is dated to Period 27–28 on the grounds that it may be a hypercorrect, post /i̯ü/ > /ü/, spelling of a cognate of W. *Rhystud* (‡86). This explanation of the EU is incompatible, however, with Tedeschi's fifth-century date and Thomas's early sixth-century date,[39] though not with Okasha's fifth- to eleventh-century date. If Tedeschi and Thomas are anywhere near right (and most evidence broadly supports their dating systems), the identification of the name with *Rhystud* and hence its linguistic dating may have to be abandoned.

If the above twelve exceptions are explained away, the *relative* chronologies implied by epigraphy and philology can be seen broadly to agree. I stress *relative* because up to this point we have been concerned with the epigraphers' centuries and half-centuries more as typological periodizations than as absolute dates.

3.6 ABSOLUTE DATING

Absolute dates can only be assigned to the relative dates for inscriptions implied by the linguistic periods 1–28 insofar as these can be correlated with other sources. In descending order of usefulness these other sources are as follows.

A. *Datable inscriptions*
These are valuable because no allowance has to be made for the use of a different medium or register.

B. *Names and words in Brittonic and British Latin manuscript texts*
These may be more innovative in spelling than the inscriptions,[40] although this cannot be assumed to be the case. It is a real problem that the dates of some of the crucial texts – Gildas; *Vita Prima Sancti Samsonis*; the Llandaf charters – are disputed. Jackson's conventional 'about 540' date for Gildas may yet be vindicated, but a date as early as *c.* 520 (or even earlier) is also possible, and I shall therefore date his work 520 × 540.[41] Jackson and many others date the *Vita Samsonis* to 'the first quarter or first half of the seventh century', but its latest editor favours 735 × 772 (chiefly on the basis of his interpretation of the Prologue and possible echoes of Bede).[42] The Llandaf charters were

---

[39] *Mute Stones*, p. 166. The apparent syncope is less problematical seeing that *Rest(it)uta* already showed this in Latin. Perhaps there was influence from the spelling of *Teuta* and similar names (GPN, p. 267; OPEL iv, 117)?

[40] Cf. Koch, *SC*, 20/21 (1985–86), 43–44; Sims-Williams, *BBCS*, 38 (1991), 20–28; Koch, *Emania*, 13 (1995), 39–50; Sims-Williams, in *Literacy in Medieval Celtic Societies*, p. 29.

[41] LHEB, p. 40; cf. Sims-Williams, *Britain and Early Christian Europe*, chs. 1 and 2 and Addenda; Snyder, *Age of Tyrants*, pp. 45 and 280–81; Stancliffe, in *Columbanus*, pp. 177–81 and 185 (favouring *c.* 530 × 544).

[42] LHEB, p. 40; Flobert, *Vie ancienne*, p. 111 (followed by Orme, *Saints of Cornwall*, p. 7). Cf. Thomas, *Mute Stones*, p. 226.

regarded by Jackson as basically early twelfth-century, and it is certainly true that they (and the comparable Llancarfan charters appended to the *Vita Sancti Cadoci*) have been partially modernized in orthography; nevertheless, it is now clear that various archaisms dating from before our main body of ninth-century Old Welsh glosses have survived the later copyists. The earlier charters cannot be dated precisely, but (perhaps over-cautiously) I have regarded 'Sequence i' of the Llandaf charters as no earlier than roughly seventh-century, and 'Sequence ii' and the contemporary Llancarfan charters as roughly eighth-century; Wendy Davies would put both Sequences half a century earlier than this.[43]

C. *Names and words in non-British Latin texts*
These may well be innovative in orthography, since their writers might not be familiar with Brittonic spelling conventions.[44]

D. *Place names and words borrowed into neighbouring languages (Old English and Old Irish)*
Insofar as the phonology of the borrowing languages permits, these are likely to reveal innovations sooner than native texts. The problem is that the date of the loans can rarely be fixed precisely.[45]

A. Datable inscriptions

Unfortunately, very few inscriptions can be dated absolutely, and those that can be happen to belong to linguistically broad periods (note the length of the oblongs in Table 3.5 below):[46]

(i) 396/104 AVITORI is no earlier than the consulate of Justinus in 540, but could be as late as, say, *c.* 600.[47] Unfortunately it is not a very useful touchstone if the name AVITORI is Irish (**Aitarīs*) rather than British (see ‡17): it is in Period 1–5 on account of the lack of final *i*-affection (see ‡19), but this is of course irrelevant if it is Irish. On the other hand, if it *is* Irish, the use of O for the composition vowel suggests influence from British, probably (but not certainly) at a date when O was still the norm in British, that is, in

---

[43] LHEB, p. 58; Davies, *Llandaff Charters*, pp. 74–76; Sims-Williams, *Britain and Early Christian Europe*, ch. 6; Sims-Williams, *BBCS*, 38 (1991), 20–86.

[44] Sims-Williams, *BBCS*, 38 (1991), 20–21.

[45] Sims-Williams, in *Britain 400–600*, pp. 225–36 and 237–61.

[46] See ibid., pp. 226 and 236–37. Cf. ECMW, p. 1, n. 3. There seem to be no externally datable stones from the south-west; it is very uncertain that 1054/Ok43 DONIERT, which belongs to Period 14–16, commemorates the Cornish king who died in 876, even if the name is the same (see ‡28n.). For Brittany see IEMB, p. 98.

[47] Sims-Williams, in *Britain 400–600*, pp. 236–37; Knight, *CMCS*, 29 (1995), 1–10, and *End of Antiquity*, pp. 169–70; Handley, *EME*, 10 (2001), 192–94.

Period 1 or soon after.[48] (The reason why one cannot be certain about this is that O continued to be used sporadically after Period 1.)[49]

(ii) 970/13 CATAMANUS (linguistically of Period 7–13) is no earlier than the death of King Cadfan *c*. 625. While it could be contemporary, one cannot disprove Jackson's opinion that it was erected later, perhaps by his grandson Cadwaladr.[50] If we accept the straightforward *c*. 625 dating, we might say that 625 fell within Period 7–13 – probably nearer 13 than 7 to judge by Table 3.3 – and that Period 14 (i.e. inscriptional Brittonic showing syncope) probably began after *c*. 625, despite the sixth-century epigraphic dates assigned by Tedeschi to the Period 14ff. inscriptions 493/Ok58, 486/Ok56, 490/Ok29, and 471/Ok39 (see Table 3.3). Note that Jackson dates only the first of these 'mid to later sixth century' and the last two 'seventh century', while the second is compared by Radford with CATAMANUS.[51]

(iii) 1066 GURIAT (on the Isle of Man), which belongs to Period 22–28, may well refer to the father of Merfyn Frych (d. 844),[52] and thus belong to the early ninth century.

(iv) 2005 SATVRNBIV may refer to the bishop who died in 831,[53] though if so this is not very helpful, since it belongs to the broad Period 14–28.

(v) 1012/223/933 IUTHAHELO REX at Llantwit, though at first dated '10th–11th century' by Nash-Williams,[54] which fits our Period 25–26 nicely, has been thought to commemorate *Iudhail/Iuthail, rex Guent*, slain by the men of Brycheiniog in 848 (*Annales Cambriae*); W. Gwyn Thomas in the Royal Commission volume found the style of the shaft and the lettering consistent with such a ninth-century date.[55] Ralegh Radford, on the other

---

[48] The reason why 'A' is not shown for 396/104 in §2/col.11 of Table 3.2 was that if AVITORI was a British form, its composition vowel was probably in the stressed syllable and thus not liable to reduction (see ‡38).

[49] See discusion of col. 11 above, p. 253.

[50] LHEB, p. 161; cf. Lloyd, *History of Wales*, i, 182; Jenkins & Owen, *CMCS*, 5 (1983), 47 and n. 49; Charles-Edwards, in *The Celtic World*, p. 715, n. 65; Dumville, *Palaeographer's Review*, i, 17 (*c.* 620 × 682); Handley, *EME*, 10 (2001), 196 (613 × 629).

[51] LHEB, p. 646; he does not discuss 486/Ok56 in LHEB, but KHJ thought it 'end of 6c or beginning of 7c', later comparing the similar dating by Radford, *Early Christian Inscriptions of Dumnonia*, p. 10.

[52] Sims-Williams, *WHR*, 17 (1994), 14–15.

[53] Cf. Okasha, *AC*, 119 (1970), 69; Edwards, in Cramp FS, p. 59.

[54] In ECMW; but in *BBCS*, 14 (1950–52), 313, Nash-Williams places 1012/223/933 in a 'ninth-and tenth-century' group of crosses.

[55] *Glamorgan*, i/3, p. 31 and no. 933. Note that on this chronology the ARTMALI of 1012/223/933 (Llantwit) cannot be identified with the ARTHMAIL of 1024/255/926 (Ogmore, Per. 22–28) if the latter is art-historically eleventh-century; *Arthfael* was a common name. The Llantwit ARTMALI could, however, be the grandfather of Brochfael ap Meurig ab Arthfael (Harley Genealogies §29, EWGT, p. 12), since Brochfael flourished in the 880s (Asser), and Meurig may be the person of this name who was slain in 849 (although another died in 873). Alternatively he could be the grandfather of Hywel ap Rhys ab Arthfael (Jesus College genealogies §9, EWGT, p. 45), since Hywel also flourished in the 880s (Asser, cf. (viii) below).

hand, dated the epigraphy before 800, making it possible that IUTHA-
HELO is the father (d. c. 750?) of the *Fernmail filius Iudhail* who died in 775
(*Annales Cambriae*).[56] An advantage of Radford's dating is that it makes it
possible to identify the SAMSONI APATI who erected the Llantwit
memorial with the *Samson, abbas altaris sancti Eltuti* (abbot of Llantwit)
who, together with a *Rodri* at the head of the lay witness list, witnesses a
charter of *Conigc, abbas altaris sancti Cadoci* (abbot of Llancarfan)
preserved in *Vita Cadoci*, §55.[57] Of this Llancarfan abbot's three charters
(VC §§ 55, 56, and 66), one (§66) also appears in the Book of Llandaf (charter
210b = Sequence ii no. 57), where the consent of *regis Rotri filius Iudhail* is
noted. This charter is dated c. 765 by Wendy Davies, and in any case belongs
to the second half of the eighth century.[58] The chronologically preceding
charter (Sequence ii.56 = 207) is the final charter of *Fernmail rex filius Iudhail*
(presumably Rhodri's elder brother), who may be the above-mentioned
Fernmail filius Iudhail who died in 775.[59] Radford notes that abbot Samson
may well be the *Samson* who, in pride of place after *Catguoret episcopus*,
witnesses another grant by *rege Rotri filio Iudhail* (ii.58 = 209b) and one by
another brother, *Ris rex filius Iudhail* (ii.59 = 211a), and he notes that the
fourth clerical witness of the latter charter is *Teican*, conceivably the
TECANI whom Abbot Samson commemorated after IUTHAHELO REX
and ARTMALI on 1012/223/933.[60] I would add that ARTMALI may well
be *Arthuail*, the first (and therefore eldest?) son of *Iudhail rex* to be listed in
one of the latter's charters (ii.34 = 191, cf. 179b).[61] These coincidences of
name are certainly suggestive. See further below.

(vi) 1000/182, the Pillar of Eliseg, linguistically Period 22–27, is mid-
ninth-century, since it was erected by King Cyngen (d. 854 or 855). Hence,
Period 22–27 ought to fall on either side of c. 850.

(vii) 3015/M6 PROSTLON may refer to a Breton woman who died
c. 870.[62] It is Period 14–28 on account the syncopated composition vowel.

---

[56] Radford, *AC*, 132 (1983), 109 and 113 (similarly Macalister). B. Davies, *New Welsh Review*,
37 (Summer 1997), 38–51, also rejects Nash-Williams's date, but unfortunately overlooks
Radford's article and adheres to Bartrum's 1948 chronology, disowned by Bartrum in his
Welsh Classical Dictionary, pp. 578–79.

[57] Another lay witness of VC §55 is *Guoguoret*, whom Rhys (see ‡38 n. 723) would identify
with the 1014/231/908 GUORGORET (Period 22–28) at Margam (dated L9–E10c by Nash-
Williams). I do not include this as a dated inscription because of the non-equivalence of the
prefixes *Guo*- and GUOR-.

[58] Davies, *Llandaff Charters*, pp. 52 and 118; Sims-Williams, *BBCS*, 38 (1991), 30 and 34.

[59] He may also may be the *Fernmail map Iudhail* of the Harley Genealogies, §28, EWGT, p. 12.

[60] Radford, *AC*, 132 (1983), 111–12. On the reading TECANI (or similar) see ‡37. Given the
fact that the Book of Llandaf is a late copy, the slight difference between these (rare) name
forms is no obstacle. Macalister (CIIC ii, p. 156) had already made the equation with
Teican.

[61] Davies, *Llandaff Charters*, pp. 113 and 148, thinks *Arthuail* an error for *Fernuail*, but this is
not necessarily the case; for instance, both could have been included and then the two names
could have been run together by haplography. She dates charter 191 c. 730.

[62] IEMB, pp. 98 and 228–29.

(viii) 1011/220/911, erected by HOUELT for the soul of his father RES, probably refers to King Hywel ap Rhys of Glywysing, who flourished in the 880s (Asser, *Life of Alfred*, §80) and died in 886. It belongs to the broad Period 15–27, so is not much use as a touchstone (e.g. it is not particularly helpful to deduce that Period 15 must have begun by *c.* 880).

(ix) 1035/303, the Carew Cross, erected (if Radford's reading of the names is correct)[63] by Maredudd ab Edwin between 1033 and 1035, belongs to Period 22–26.

(x) 3019/M10 RIOCVS ABBA was probably a mid-eleventh-century abbot of Saint-Gildas-de-Rhuys (a companion of the abbot FELIX of 3018/M9, whose Latin name cannot be dated linguistically of course).[64] It is Period 4–28 on account of the change /a:/ > /ɔ:/ having occurred (see ‡18).

(xi) 1039/382, dated AD 1078–80 by Nash-Williams,[65] belongs to Period 15–28.

(xii) 988/67, the Patrishow Font made 'I(*n*) TE(*m*)PORE GENILLIN', which belongs to Period 23–28, is often regarded as coeval with the church of *Merthyr Issiu* in Ystrad Yw dedicated by Bishop Herewald (d. 1104), possibly during the period when Ystrad Yw was dominated by Caradog ap Gruffudd (d. 1081).[66] GENILLIN is usually identified with Genyllyn, son of Rhys Goch of Ystrad Yw, in the 'Pedigrees of the Welsh Tribal Patriarchs'; according to Bartrum, 'the genealogies point to a date of about 1070 for his [Rhys's] birth', and he notes that one version makes Rhys Goch the brother of a Bleddyn ap Maenyrch who was slain in 1093.[67] This would put Genyllyn's floruit in the early twelfth century, perhaps *c.* 1100, when Herewald was still alive.

(xiii) 1032/281, dated *c.* 1150 on the grounds that its EWINI REG(*is*) is Owain Gwynedd (d. 1170), belongs to Period 28.

One *possible* (but of course artificial) sequence of absolute dates which would reconcile the proposed historical dates and linguistic periods for all thirteen inscriptions apart from no. (v) is indicated by the shading on Table 3.5. This at least shows that they are not irreconcilable.

The discrepancy in the case of (v) 1012/223/933 IUTHAHELO REX between the early historical date *c.* 750 and our relatively late linguistic date, Period 25–26, suggests that the latter is erroneous (see the empty box in

---

[63] Radford, *AC*, 100 (1949), 253–55; but the reading is unlikely: see Edwards, *Med. Arch.*, 45 (2001), 34, n. 102. Note that the linguistic periodization of 1035/303 is influenced by the acceptance of Radford's reading ETG(uin) in ‡66 (no. 18 under B), whence the 'B' in col. 24.

[64] IEMB, pp. 98 and 257.

[65] These are the dates of Abraham's episcopate, but the stone could have been erected later than 1080 as noted by Dumville, *Saint David of Wales*, p. 24, n. 106, and Edwards, in Cramp FS, p. 67.

[66] LL, p. 279 (top and bottom of page; on the context cf. Sims-Williams, *CMCS*, 26 (1993), 61–62). There seems to be no basis for dates for the consecration such as 1060 (LW, p. 71) and *c.* 1055 (Haslam, *Powys*, p. 363).

[67] Bartrum, *NLWJ*, 13 (1963), 106 and 130.

Table 3.5). It is due to following Jackson in the opinion that -*h*- never represents /ɣ/ rather than representing hiatus or simply being redundant.[68] If, however, we admit that *h* is ambiguous and *may* represent /ɣ/ or a consonantal reflex of it (as in the form *Catiherno* discussed below and OB *Uuiutihern*), the inscription has to be dated Period 14–26 (as shown by the broken-line box in Table 3.5), quite compatibly with the *c.* 750 date and the rest of Table 3.5. Certainly the Old Welsh glosses imply that /ɣ/ had not been lost in the eighth century. The forms *agit* and *hegit* appear in the Liber Commonei of 817 × 835, and the absence of /ɣ/ in the relevant position is first clearly shown in *cimmaeticion* in the Corpus Martianus Capella (*c.* 850 × *c.* 930, perhaps *c.* 900).[69]

Table 3.5 Inscriptions with absolute dates and linguistic periods (synthesized for argument only)

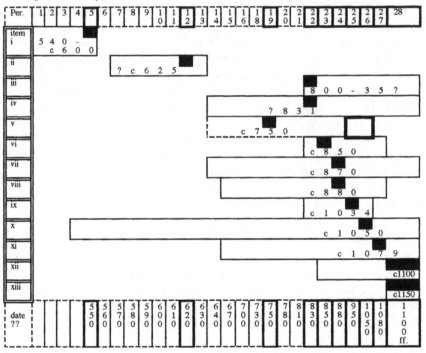

[68] See ‡74 above under (B). In LHEB, p. 454, n. 2, and HPB, pp. 712, 715 and 719, Jackson argues that *h* in forms like OB *mergidhaham* is more likely to indicate hiatus than /ɣ/.

[69] LHEB, p. 460; cf. GPC, s.v. *cyma*; Schrijver, *ÉC*, 34 (1998–2000), 151. Dates from McKee, *Juvencus*, pp. 2–3 and 5, n. 22 (cf. McKee, *CMCS*, 39 (2000), 9, n. 29, implying a date *c.* 900 or a little later for the Martianus).

B–D. Non-epigraphic sources (see above)

These can be considered together as appropriate, in the order of our twenty-eight periods. Cross references are given to the column by column discussion of Table 3.1 above and to the principal ‡‡ of Chapter 2.

Per. 1 = pre Reduction of composition vowels (= A in col. 11 of Table 3.1) ‡38

A correct composition vowel is preserved uniquely in the OE name *Hrofesceaster* < *Durobrivae*, but this could be a very early loan, earlier even than Jackson's 'middle or second half of the fifth century'.[70] The stage of pure composition vowels must already have been long over by 509 × 521 if *Catiherno,* recorded then by a non-Breton scribe, already shows syncope (< *Katutigernos).*[71] Yet native writers may still have written composition vowels, as does *Gonothigernus,* bishop of Senlis, attesting in 556 × 573 (see Per. 14 below). Gildas writes them, but his reduced form *Cuneglase* beside correct *Maglocune,* shows that the Period 1 was over when he wrote *De Excidio Britanniae.*[72] Orally, then, Period 1 was long over by 509 × 521, but native writers may have continued to write correct composition vowels until some time before *c.* 520 × 540 – and indeed occasionally later than that, whether by accident or traditionalism.

Per. 2 = post Reduction of composition vowels (= B in col. 11 of Table 3.1) ‡38

Starting before *c.* 520 × 540; see above.

Per. 3 = post /oN/ > /uN/ in W.Brit. (= B in col. 6 of Table 3.1) ‡26

There is no non-inscriptional evidence to date this orally or in writing.[73] If Schrijver is right to place it earlier than *a*-affection (see ‡26), it will be even earlier than such a presumably early (pre-450?) loan as the name of Dover (OE *Dofras* < *Dubrās)* which shows *a*-affection.[74] However, we do not know when it would have been admitted into native orthography.

Per. 4 = post /aː/ > /ɔː/ (= B in col. 2 of Table 3.1) ‡18

Orally, this change is thought to be later fifth-century on the evidence of Irish loanwords (which reflect both stages) and of place names borrowed

[70] LHEB, p. 647. Cf. Sims-Williams in *Britain 400–600,* pp. 239 and 246–47.
[71] LHEB, pp. 14, 454, and 646–47. Cf. Sims-Williams in *Britain 400–600,* pp. 246 and 248; Tanguy, *BSAF,* 113 (1984), 99 *(Langadiar* (14c) < *Lann-Catihern).*
[72] LHEB, pp. 644–45. In *Vita Samsonis,* note *Penetale monasterium:* Fleuriot, *Origines,* p. 65.
[73] Cf. LHEB, p. 273.
[74] LHEB, pp. 577–78.

into OE (reflecting only the /ɔ:/ stage).[75] In fact it must have happened earlier than 509 × 521 when the *later* change /ɣ/ > /w/ is attested (Per. 5 below). The first non-epigraphic written testimony is the attestation of *Mailoc* at the Council of Braga in 572, but it is uncertain whether this reflects native Brittonic usage, any more than forms like *Chonomorem* in Gregory of Tours.[76] There are no traces of *a*-spellings in the Llandaf charters. Thus Per. 4 cannot be dated, although the absence of *a*-spellings in the charters suggests that it had begun in writing by about 600. Obviously, Latin names were to some extent exempt, a good non-inscriptional example being *Meriano* (< *Mariānus*) in the eighth-century Pelagius colophon.[77]

Per. 5 = post /ɣ/ > /u̯/ (= B in col. 5 of Table 3.1) ‡25

Internal linguistic logic shows that this change was both later than *a*-affection (which had perhaps preceded Period 3 above),[78] and also later than /a:/ > /ɔ:/ (Per. 4 above).[79] The first written evidence is *Lovocatus* < *Lugukatus*, recorded in 509 × 521 by a non-Breton scribe.[80] Again, we do not know whether native writers would have admitted it so early. The only possible trace of a *g*-spelling in the Llandaf charters, so far as I know, is the obscure name *Lugobi* in charter 76b (a Sequence i charter), which looks like a derivative of *Lugu*-.[81] If relevant, this indicates a starting date in the 7c (after *c*. 605 on Wendy Davies's dating of the charter).[82] The termination *-bi* has not been satisfactorily explained, however, and it may be best to regard *Lugobi* as a preform of Ir. *Luigbe*;[83] the charter relates to *Porth Tulon*, on the Gower peninsula, a possible location for an immigrant.

Per. 6 = post Final *i*-affection (= B in col. 3 of Table 3.1) ‡19

Obviously, this preceded apocope (Per. 11 below). Jackson argues that it was later than *a*-affection, since OE *Cantware* 'men of *Cantium*' lacks *i*-affection

[75]   LHEB, pp. 291–92.
[76]   LHEB, p. 291; Sims-Williams, *BBCS*, 38 (1991), 20–21. Gregory's *Chonomorem* appears corruptly as *Commorus* in *Vita Samsonis*, I 59.
[77]   See Per. 17 below for this, and for Latin A in the inscriptions, see on col. 2 above, p. 250.
[78]   LHEB, p. 444 (on Latin *fuga* > *foɣa* before the period of /uɣ/ > /uw/; cf. SBCHP, p. 343). Thomas, in *Christianity in Britain 300–700*, pp. 99 and 115–16, notes that *Luguvallum* etc. gives *Luel* (Carlisle) in Anglo-Saxon.
[79]   See LHEB, pp. 373 and 442–44 on OB *fou*, W. *Powys*, etc.
[80]   LHEB, pp. 442 and 444 (cf. inferior etymology in DLG, p. 176). On this source see Per. 1 above.
[81]   Loth, *RC*, 40 (1923), 25, n. 2 ('pour *Lugovi* = *Lug-ov-io-s*'), countered in LHEB, p. 442, n. 2. For *Lugu*- names see GPN, p. 220; Birkhan, *Germanen und Kelten*, p. 359, n. 864; Ziegler, p. 112; Uhlich, *Morphologie*, pp. 271–74; LHEB, pp. 441–42.
[82]   *Llandaff Charters*, p. 94. A decade or two later on the dating suggested in Sims-Williams, *Britain and Early Christian Europe*, ch. 6, p. 126.
[83]   See Uhlich, *Morphologie*, p. 272, and, for *-bi*, see Ziegler, p. 100, e.g. on **ERACOBI**.

whereas *Dofras* shows *a*-affection (see under Per. 3 above).[84] Outside Kent, however, *i*-affection is universal in place names borrowed by the Anglo-Saxons, which suggests that it was considerably earlier than Jackson's 'later fifth to early sixth century' date.[85] It may not have been admitted into writing until much later, however. Jackson notes that it is absent from Gildas's *Vortipori* but is present in *Piro* (W. *Pyr* < *Porius*) in the *Vita Samsonis*.[86] The uncertain dates of these works mean that the start of Period 6 cannot be dated more precisely than *c.* 520–770! Possible examples in eighth-century Llandaf charters are *Guallonor* (no. 158 = ii.30) and *Gullonar* (no. 145 = ii.17) instead of the normal *Guallonir* < *Vellaunorīx, but they could be mere mis-copyings.[87] Obviously affection occurred before apocope.

Per. 7 = post /nd/ > /nn/ (= B in col. 4 of Table 3.1) ‡22

The fact that post-syncope /n'd/ did not develop in this way implies that /nd/ > /nn/ was earlier than syncope (Per. 14 below).[88] In English place names British /nd/ is more widely preserved in the east than pre-Final *i*-affection forms, but already /nn/ appears in King's *Lynn* in Norfolk, which could well have been borrowed before 500.[89] There seems to be no non-inscriptional evidence for writing *nd*; for instance, there seem to be no *nd* spellings in the Llandaf charters,[90] which suggests that Period 7 had begun by the early seventh century.

Per. 8 = post /e/ > /i/ before nasal or (stressed?) /rn/ (= B in col. 7 of Table 3.1) ‡27

There seems to be little non-inscriptional evidence for the date of this change (or changes).[91] Stressed /ern/ is still intact in *Catihern* in 509 × 521 and *Gonothigernus* in 556 × 573 (see Per. 14 below), and unstressed /ern/ in

---

[84] LHEB, p. 603. See also SBCHP, pp. 259–64, for an internal argument.

[85] LHEB, pp. 600–1 and 695; cf. Sims-Williams in *Britain 400–600*, pp. 238–39 and 247–48.

[86] LHEB, p. 598. At p. 601, n. 1, he rightly disregards Aldhelm's *Geruntius* in 705; such archaic spellings were found in Cornish Latin texts much later; see Olson & Padel, *CMCS*, 12 (1986), 45. For the form GERONTI from Roman Britain see L'Hour, *RAO*, 4 (1987), 120, also PRB, p. 219, and for *Gerontius* elsewhere see OPEL ii, 166 and 221.

[87] Sims-Williams, *BBCS*, 38 (1991), 77 and n. 1.

[88] Cf. Sims-Williams in *Britain 400–600*, p. 239, n. 81, and references. The only way of countering Jackson's argument, quoted there, that if /nd/ > /nn/ had not preceded syncope VENDESETLI would have given **Gwyntoedl rather than *Gwynnhoedl* would be to suppose that /nd/ became /nð/ in the first instance (cf. Russell, *CMCS*, 10 (1985), 53–56, on /rd/) and that /nðVh/ developed > /nðh/ > /nnh/.

[89] Sims-Williams in *Britain 400–600*, pp. 239 and 247. OB *int* (HPB, pp. 344–46) perhaps implies that apocope (at least in proclitics) preceded /nd/ > /nn/.

[90] Sims-Williams, *BBCS*, 38 (1991), 72.

[91] Cf. LHEB, pp. 278–80 (arguing at p. 279, n. 1, that *Demetia* in *Vita Samsonis* is a 'traditional book form').

Tigernomalus in *Vita Samsonis* in 735 × 772 (?), but *Guorthigirnus* appears in the early ninth-century *Historia Brittonum*.[92]

Per. 9 = post SW.Brit. /u/ > /ǫ/ (= B in col. 8 of Table 3.1) ‡28

This is already attested in Gregory of Tours's *Chonomorem* in the late sixth century,[93] but it is unclear when it was admitted by native writers (although *Commorus* in *Vita Samsonis* may be significant); in any case, *u*-spellings never died out completely.[94]

Per. 10 = post /-Σ-/ > /-h-/ (= B in col. 9 of Table 3.1) ‡36

Linguistic logic suggests that this was earlier than syncope (Per. 14 below), but there is no non-inscriptional evidence for the date when *h* started to be written.[95] There are no relevant -*s*- spellings in the Llandaf charters.

Per. 11 = post Apocope (= B in col. 10 of Table 3.1) ‡37

Apocope is recorded in non-native sources in the name *Mailoc* at the Council of Braga in 572 (noted under Per. 4 above), in 'collem qui dicitur Britannica lingua *Cructan*, apud nos Crycbeorh' in an Anglo-Saxon charter of 682, and in Adomnán's *Cat(h)lon* (Cadwallon) *c.* 700, and it is universal when the OWCB glosses begin in the ninth century.[96] The witness lists in the earliest charters in the Book of Llandaf (seventh century onwards?) already show apocope.[97]

Per. 12 = post /γ/ > /i̯/ before /l, r, n/ (= B in col. 17 of Table 3.1) ‡48

Gildas still has *Maglocune*, and Gregory of Tours writes *Macliavus* in the late sixth century. In non-native sources the first sign of change seems to be the just-mentioned *Mailoc* at the Council of Braga in 572, followed in native non-epigraphic sources by *Tigernomalus* in *Vita Samsonis*, although some spellings with *g* continue long after that.[98] Spellings like *Iumail* (no. 162a = i.15) are the norm in the Llandaf charters.[99]

[92] LHEB, p. 280; SBCHP, p. 64.
[93] LHEB, p. 274, n. 2.
[94] Olson & Padel, *CMCS*, 12 (1986), 43–44. For *Commorus* see n. 76 above.
[95] Cf. LHEB, p. 521.
[96] LHEB, pp. 619, 621 and 631; *Adomnán's Life of Columba*, ed. Anderson & Anderson, p. 14.
[97] Sims-Williams, *BBCS*, 38 (1991), 33.
[98] LHEB, pp. 463–65. The forms from the *Anglo-Saxon Chronicle* are of uncertain value (Sims-Williams, *Britain and Early Christian Europe*, ch. 2, esp. pp. 33–34 and 40, n. 177), and it is uncertain that Gildas's *Canine* reflects *Cynin* (see ‡48 n. 924).
[99] Sims-Williams, *BBCS*, 38 (1991), 72–73.

Note that while it is generally supposed that *tego-slougo- > OC/MW *teilu* shows that /ɣ/ > /i̯/ (Per. 12) was *later* than the syncope of composition vowels (Per. 14),[100] non-epigraphic forms like *Tigernomalus* as well as the internal evidence of the inscriptions, show that Per. 12 and Per. 14 have to be placed in the present order at least *as orthographical periods*. This could even be their correct order on the oral level, if Schrijver's alternative derivation of *teilu* < *tegeso-slougo- is correct, since this does not involve /ɣl̥/ > /i̯l̥/.[101]

Per. 13 = post Pr.W. pretonic /u/ > /ö/ (= B in col. 15 of Table 3.1) ‡46

Orally, this cannot be dated more precisely than 'sixth century',[102] but in writing the changeover from *u* to *o* seems to have begun in the earliest Llandaf charters and is completed in the eighth-century ones.[103] *Cunedag* in the early ninth-century *Historia Brittonum* is probably an archaism (complete with reduced composition vowel) derived from an earlier source.[104]

Per. 14 = post Syncope of composition vowels (= B in col. 12 of Table 3.1) ‡38

Orally, syncope may have occurred in the second half of the fifth century, and it is already shown in a non-native source in the above mentioned form *Catihern(o)* from 509 × 521.[105] In native sources, composition vowels are still shown by Gildas in 520 × 540 (?), but syncopated names (*Eltutus, Iudualus* beside *Tigernomalus*) appear by the time of the *Vita Samsonis*,[106] and are the norm in the Llandaf charters (seventh century onwards). The best indication may be the attestation of *Gonotiernus, Gonothigernus* (bishop of Senlis) at the Councils of Orléans and Paris in 549 and 556 × 573.[107] This presumably counts as a native spelling (in view of syncope in the non-native *Catihern(o)* earlier), and suggests that Period 14 began after 556 × 573 and before the seventh century.

[100] VKG i, 522; LHEB, pp. 440, n. 1, 462 and 466; Sims-Williams, *BBCS*, 38 (1991), 73; SBCHP, p. 356.
[101] SBCHP, p. 71. See above on col. 17, p. 256.
[102] Sims-Williams, in *Britain 400–600*, pp. 244–45 and 257.
[103] Sims-Williams, *BBCS*, 38 (1991), 45–47. Schrijver, *JIES*, 26 (1998), 427, puts the reduction later than internal *i*-affection (our Per. 17), at least on the phonemic level, but does not take into account the archaic nature of the relevant LL charters. Cf. n. 7 above.
[104] Isaac, *BBCS*, 38 (1991), 100–1.
[105] Sims-Williams, in *Britain 400–600*, pp. 245–48. This is beside unsyncopated *Lovocatus* in the same text.
[106] LHEB, pp. 645–46.
[107] Sims-Williams, *BBCS*, 38 (1991), 21 and n. 4; Fleuriot, *ÉC*, 24 (1987), 195.

Per. 15 = post /Σ-/ > /h-/ (= B in col. 14 of Table 3.1) ‡44

To judge by Anglo-Saxon river names, this change became perceptible to English-speakers when they reached Staffordshire and Worcestershire, presumably in the sixth century.[108] It appears in native sources in the *Vita Samsonis* (*Henocus, Habrinum*).[109] There are no relevant *S*- or *H*- names in the earliest Llandaf charters (the first are *Haiuoen* and *Hirel* in 150b = ii.15).

Per. 16 = post /xt/ > /i̯θ/ (= B in col. 18 of Table 3.1) ‡45

This pan-Brittonic change does not seem to have been heard by the Anglo-Saxons before they reached Cumberland and West Lothian, presumably in the late sixth or early seventh century.[110] It is first attested in native sources in the OW corpus, including the *Surexit* memorandum (*luidt* = Mod.W. *llwyth*), which is sometimes dated as early as the late eighth century.[111] Even this early dating is too late to be very useful here.

Per. 17 = post Internal *i*-affection (= B in col. 19 of Table 3.1) ‡‡ 57, 64

Jackson shows that logically this must have been later than the changes at Per. 14 and Per. 16, and that it starts to appear in English borrowings in the seventh century.[112] In non-epigraphic native sources it is absent from *Morinus* in *Vita Samsonis*, and from *Catthig* in a Llancarfan charter (VC, §68) of about the end of the seventh century, but it is present in *Meriano* (versus *Papiaui*) in the pre-800 Pelagius colophon.[113] This suggests that Period 17 began in the eighth century (or more precisely 735 × 800 if Flobert is right to date the *Vita Samsonis* to 735 × 772); it was established by the time of the earliest OWCB. Early Cornish evidence is as usual scarce, but *Entenin* < *Antoninus* appears in the Vatican saints' list of c. 900 × 950.[114]

Per. 18 = post /e:^(i)/ > /ui/ (= B in col. 20 of Table 3.1) ‡58

There is little evidence for the date of this diphthongization and those at Pers. 19 and 21, but I have argued elsewhere that they must have preceded the New Quantity System (when remaining long vowels were subject to

[108] LHEB, pp. 518–21; Sims-Williams, in *Britain 400–600*, p. 241; Zimmer, *JCL*, 3 (1994), 155–56.
[109] LHEB, p. 518.
[110] LHEB, pp. 410–11; Sims-Williams, in *Britain 400–600*, p. 242.
[111] LHEB, p. 409. On this dating of 'Chad 2' cf. Sims-Williams, *BBCS*, 38 (1991), 23 and 75, n. 3; Dumville, *Palaeographer's Review*, i, 123, n. 25, and 124, n. 28 (comparing the Stowe Missal, which is 'no earlier than 792', and the Hereford Gospels of ' "viii/ix" or "ix in." ').
[112] LHEB, pp. 409 and 609–13.
[113] LHEB, p. 611; Koch, *SC*, 20/21 (1985–86), 47–48; Sims-Williams, *BBCS*, 38 (1991), 25, 30 and 33 and n. 3; Dumville, *CMCS*, 10 (1985), 41.
[114] Olson & Padel, *CMCS*, 12 (1986), 45.

shortening in heavy syllables) and that the New Quantity System may be early in the first half of the sixth century.[115] In writing, however, the Llandaf and Llancarfan charters indicate that spelling with *ui* took over from *e* in the second half of the eighth century.[116]

Per. 19 = post /ɛ:$^{(i)}$/ > /oi/ (= B in col. 21 of Table 3.1) ‡59

While this may have begun orally in the sixth century (see Per. 18 above), there is some evidence from the charters that *e* was still written in the eighth century.[117] Diphthongal spellings are already well established by the beginning of OWCB (i.e. by *c.* 800, at least in the case of Welsh and Breton).[118]

Per. 20 = post /ɣ/ > /∅/ (= B in col. 23 of Table 3.1) in the environments described in ‡65, i.e. (a) after /i:/ and back vowels finally; (b) after /i:/ and before /a/ and /o/; (c) between back vowels

Jackson shows that (a) has occurred in OWCB, with the exception of the probably archaic *dou rig* and *Cunedag* in the *Historia Brittonum* (early ninth century),[119] that (b) is universal in OWCB,[120] and that (c) has occurred in OWCB with the exception of OW *guragun* in the *Surexit* memorandum.[121] All this suggests that in non-inscriptional sources Per. 20 begins at the end of the eighth century.

Per. 21 = post Pr.W. /ɔ:/ > /au/ (= B in col. 22 of Table 3.1) ‡60

Though this probably began orally before the New Quantity System,[122] there are still occasional examples of *o* being written in OW: *retinoc* in 'Chad 6' ('late ninth or early tenth century'?) and *och* by Scribe E of the Cambridge Juvencus (*c.* 900 or early tenth century).[123] The eighth-century *Vita Cadoci* charters do not favour *au*, but Llandaf charters indicate that *au* was

---

[115] Sims-Williams, in *Britain 400–600*, pp. 254–60; cf. TRC, pp. 161–63. Note also Schrijver's argument from *halwyn*, quoted in ‡58, which would also put Per. 18 before Per. 17 on the oral level.

[116] Sims-Williams, *BBCS*, 38 (1991), 59.

[117] Ibid., pp. 59–63.

[118] LHEB, pp. 329–30; HPB, pp. 184–85.

[119] LHEB, pp. 456 and 458.

[120] LHEB, p. 459.

[121] LHEB, pp. 457–58; on the date of *Surexit* see under Per. 16 above. Jackson rejects e.g. OB *mergidhaham* as evidence for /ɣ/ (cf. p. 280 above).

[122] See reference under Per. 18 above (where I show that Jackson's argument in LHEB, p. 294, for a post-Internal *i*-affection date is wrong). Note that OW *guoun* shows that /ɣn/ > /in/ (Per. 12 above), or rather, in this environment, > /u̯n/, preceded /ɔ:/ > /au/ (Sims-Williams, *BBCS*, 38 (1991), 73).

[123] Sims-Williams, *BBCS*, 38 (1991), 31 and 69. Dates respectively from Jenkins & Owen, *CMCS*, 5 (1983), 56; McKee, *CMCS*, 39 (2000), 9.

becoming popular by *c.* 860 and that *o* had been discontinued by *c.* 910.[124] These non-inscriptional sources suggest that Per. 21 begins *c.* 800 × 850.

Per. 22 = post W.Co. /w-/ > /gw-/ (= B in col. 24 of Table 3.1) ‡‡ 66, 76

There is little evidence for when this sound change occurred.[125] There is some slight evidence for *u-* still being written in the seventh-century charters in the Book of Llandaf, but *gu-* is the norm in Old Welsh when first attested *c.* 800 (and note *guragun* above). Jackson's stray OW example (Bodley MS 572 *uiidimm*) may well be Cornish. In Cornwall *w-* still occurs *c.* 1100, although *gu-* is the norm in the more strictly native Cornish spelling of the Vatican saints' list of *c.* 900 × 950.[126]

Per. 23 = post W. /nt/ etc. > /n^{t}h/, /nh/ etc. (= B in col. 25 of Table 3.1) ‡‡ 68, 71

Orally, this development may have begun in the eighth century, and it is noted in various ways in OW orthography (e.g. by *nn* from *c.* 829 onwards) although *nh* etc. (i.e. with *h*) are not found before the Book of Llandaf (*c.* 1130).[127]

Per. 24 = post W.Co. svarabhakti (= B in col. 26 of Table 3.1) ‡69

There are occasional examples of this being written in Old Welsh, i.e. from *c.* 800 onwards, but it 'is rare before the time of the Book of Llandaff'. (It is very common in Old Cornish (i.e. tenth century onwards), and there may already be an example (*Geuedenoc*) in the Vatican saints' list of *c.* 800 × 850; but this is not strictly relevant here as the only examples of svarabhakti admitted in ‡69 are in Wales.)[128]

Per. 25 = post /γ/ > /∅/ (= B in col. 27 of Table 3.1) in the environments described in ‡74, i.e. (a) between front vowels or (b) vowels of different quality (other than /iːγa/ and /iːγo/ = Per. 20), and (c) finally after *ĭ* (by now > /ïː/ or, after the accent shift, /ï/)

Jackson notes that /γ/ was still audible in position (a) in presumably early-sixth-century loans like *Bregent* (Brent) and 'was also audible, evidently,

[124] Sims-Williams, *BBCS*, 38 (1991), 69.
[125] The discussion in LHEB, p. 390, is bedevilled by the use of 406/215/844 GVANI, which probably has an original labiovelar; see Sims-Williams, in Evans FS, pp. 208–9.
[126] Sims-Williams, *BBCS*, 38 (1991), 71–72 and 78; LHEB, pp. 54–56 and 386–88 (cf. Dumville, *Palaeographer's Review*, i, 125, n. 31, on Bodley 572 = 'Ox.2'); Olson & Padel, *CMCS*, 12 (1986), 39, 42, 44, 49, and 59.
[127] LHEB, pp. 502–6. See further Rowland, *BBCS*, 29 (1980–82), 513–20. Cf. Sims-Williams, *BBCS*, 38 (1991), 39 and n. 3.
[128] LHEB, pp. 337–38; Olson & Padel, *CMCS*, 12 (1986), 53.

much later in the *Cundiȝeorn* of DLV., *c.* 840'. The latter is dubious evidence, since many of the names in the Durham *Liber Vitae* were transcribed from earlier sources.[129] Old Welsh sources regularly write *g*, but it is already omitted occasionally in the glosses, starting with *cueeticc* etc. in the Martianus Capella, *c.* 900,[130] and is arguably always absent in Old Breton, and also in Old Cornish when a relevant form is first attested in 959 × 993; hence it seems reasonable to give *c.* 900 as the approximate start of Per. 25 in native non-inscriptional written sources for position (a).[131] The same seems to apply to positions (b) and (c), although the evidence is scanty.[132]

Per. 26 = post W. /öü/ > /ëü/ (= B in col. 28 of Table 3.1) ‡80

There is no evidence for this having happened in English place names, and in non-inscriptional written Old Welsh there is only one example before *c.* 1100: *guorennieu* in *De Mensuris et Ponderibus* in the Liber Commonei of 817 × 835.[133] Presumably Per. 26 was just beginning *c.* 820 so far as non-inscriptional written Welsh was concerned. Orally, /ëü/ was already in existence and developing via /ëü/ in final, stressed position in the direction of Mod.W. *-au* before the accent shift (‡‡ 82 and 88). The accent shift had already occurred when the Corpus Martianus Capella was glossed *c.* 900, but *-ou* is still written in that source, evidently being regarded as the correct way of writing /ëü/.[134]

Per. 27 = post /i̯u-/ > /i-/ etc. (= B in col. 29 of Table 3.1) ‡‡ 81, 86

Orally, this too preceded the accent shift (‡88). The first Old Welsh manuscript to attest to it (*Ithael*) is TCD A.iv.20 in 1064 × 1082, but this hardly marks the beginning of Period 27 in non-inscriptional native sources, since Jackson rightly stresses the lack of evidence either way for the preceding period, *c.* 950–1050. The Llandaf charters suggest a start by *c.* 860 or at any rate *c.* 1030.[135] A similar *c.* 850 date is possible for Old Breton as well, if

---

[129] LHEB, pp. 447 and 453; cf. SBCHP, pp. 70 and 262; Sims-Williams, *CMCS*, 32 (1996), 41–42.

[130] LHEB, p. 453, but with date from n. 69 above.

[131] Cf. LHEB, pp. 454–55. Note that Jackson's pre-ninth-century date for Breton in LHEB entails explaining away OB *Uuiutihern* (821), *Elegium* (*c.* 880), and *egit*; cf. HPB, pp. 712–13 and 847.

[132] LHEB, pp. 460 and 455–56 respectively. On p. 460 he argues that *Brehant* in Wrmonoc in 884 has merely hiatus-filling *h*; cf. HPB, pp. 846–47, and p. 280 above.

[133] LHEB, pp. 47, 370, n. 1, and 371, n. 2; cf. Jackson, in SEBC, p. 284. On the date of Liber Commonei see Dumville, *Palaeographer's Review*, i, 123. Forms in *eu* beside *ou* in the Llandaf charters (Davies, *BBCS*, 28 (1978–80), 557) may well be due to copyists.

[134] See Schrijver, *ÉC*, 34 (1998–2000), 147–55 (for date see n. 69 above). Note Ekwall's suggestion, *English River-Names*, pp. 458–59, that Asser *c.* 894 wrote *Guilou* for OE *Wīl-ēa* (cf. Sims-Williams, in *Britain 400–600*, p. 258).

[135] LHEB, p. 346; Sims-Williams, *BBCS*, 38 (1991), 79.

Ied- spellings then are significant, or *c.* 1050 if *Id-* spellings are insisted on, while Cornish spelling seems not to change until after *c.* 975.[136]

Per. 28 = post W. /ö/ > /ə/ (= B in col. 30 of Table 3.1) ‡84

In non-inscriptional written sources, this is already attested by spellings in *i* and *e* (alongside *o* and *u*) in Old Welsh sources from the ninth century onwards (or late eighth, if the *Surexit* with its *Cinda* is so early).[137] The Llandaf charters suggest that the change was starting to be shown in spelling (as *i*) in the late eighth century and was dominant by the second half of the ninth century, and that the rounding was not shown after *c.* 960.[138] In such sources, then, Per. 28 begins in earnest *c.* 850 and is completely established by *c.* 960.

3.7 SUMMARY OF ABSOLUTE DATING FROM NON-INSCRIPTIONAL SOURCES

On the working assumption that each period starts no earlier than the preceding period (a simplification, no doubt),[139] approximate dates for the periods in native, non-inscriptional sources are as follows, on the basis that the above argumentation is correct.[140]

- Per. 1 ends before *c.* 540 at the latest.
- Per. 2 begins by *c.* 540 at the latest.
- Per. 3 is undated but presumably begins after Per. 2, i.e. by *c.* 540 at latest.
- Per. 4 begins by *c.* 600 at latest.
- Per. 5 begins during 7c (if *Lugobi* is relevant), and presumably (since it is earlier than Per. 7) in *early* 7c. Note that if 396/104 AVITORI really does belong to Per. 1–5 (see item (i) in Table 3.5), a date 540 × *c.* 600 for it is compatible with the present periodization.
- Per. 6 begins *c.* 520 × 770, but presumably (since it is between Per. 5 and Per. 7), during early 7c (assuming *Lugobi* was relevant to Per. 5).
- Pers. 7–12 begin *by* the 7c at the latest, and presumably *in* the early 7c since they are after Per. 5 (again assuming *Lugobi* was relevant to dating Per. 5).
- Per. 12 begins before 735 × 772(?).

[136] LHEB, p. 347; HPB, pp. 407–8.
[137] LHEB, pp. 668–69. On the date of *Surexit* see above under Per. 16.
[138] Sims-Williams, *BBCS*, 38 (1991), 45 and 47.
[139] See below on Periods 27–28.
[140] If it is not, adjustments will be needed and can easily be made. Note, for instance, that the validity of the form *Lugobi* affects the dating not only of Per. 5 but also of subsequent periods dated in relation to Per. 5.

- Per. 13 begins in 7c (and probably no earlier since some *u*-spellings still occur in 8c).
- Per. 14 (post-syncope) begins between 553 × 573 and before the 7c Llandaf charters (except *Lugobi*), but if the inscriptional evidence is taken into account this can be narrowed down to soon after *c.* 625 (since the pre-Per. 14 CATAMANUS stone cannot be earlier than *c.* 625). This would accord with a late synchronism between Iddon ab Ynyr Gwent, the grantor of what are probably the earliest Sequence i charters, and Cadwallon of Gwynedd (d. 634).[141]
- Pers. 15–16 begin after *c.* 625 (since they follow Per. 14).
- Per. 17 begins in 8c, possibly in the first half if it is before Per. 18.[142]
- Per. 18 begins *c.* 750.
- Per. 19 begins during 8c, perhaps *c.* 750 × 800.[143]
- Per. 20 begins *c.* 800.
- Per. 21 begins *c.* 800 × 850, presumably *c.* 800 since it is before Per. 22.
- Per. 22 begins by *c.* 800. Note that this is compatible with dating 1066 GURIAT (item (iii) in Table 3.5) to *c.* 800–35.
- Per. 23 begins by *c.* 800.
- Per. 24 begins by *c.* 800.
- Per. 25 begins *c.* 900.
- Per. 26 begins 817 × 835, but is not well established until later.
- Per. 27 may begin *c.* 850, but is not well established until *c.* 950 × *c.* 1050. Hence there is no *linguistic* objection to the Carew Cross (1035/303 MARGITEUT), belonging to Per. 22–26 and being dated AD 1033–35 (item (ix) in Table 3.5).
- Per. 28 begins by *c.* 800, and is fully established by *c.* 960. This Period thus spans the time when Per. 27 was establishing itself,[144] which would help to explain the apparent problem that the Carew Cross, which is Per. 22–26 (i.e. pre-Per. 28), is dated AD 1033–35. Note, moreover, that the Cross provides no evidence either way on the criterion for Per. 28 – the 'a' in the final column of Table 3.2 is merely inferential – and that the orders of Pers. 27 and 28 (= cols. 29–30 of Table 3.1) could be easily be reversed. If, however, the Carew Cross has been misread as 'REX ETGuin' and so misdated,[145] no special pleading is required. If RECETT = *rhyged* is the true reading and interpretation (as argued in ‡42), note that Carew must belong to Per. 28 (/ö/ > /ə/). This does not seriously conflict with the failure of its MARGITEUT to have become

---

[141] Sims-Williams, *Britain and Early Christian Europe*, ch. 6, p. 126. The synchronism is found in *Buchedd Beuno*, on the early sources of which see Sims-Williams, in *150 Jahre 'Mabinogion'*, pp. 122–24.

[142] Orally the order of Per. 17 and Per. 18 may have been different; see above, n. 115.

[143] That is, if after Per. 18, but their relative ordering is uncertain.

[144] Cf. the dates in LHEB, p. 698: 'later tenth century' for the beginning in Welsh of my Per. 27, and 'tenth to eleventh century . . . perhaps' for my Period 28.

[145] See above, n. 63.

*MARGITUT at Per. 27, since Pers. 27 and 28 seem to have over-lapped, and their order could indeed be reversed, as just noted.

3.8 SYNTHESIS OF EPIGRAPHIC AND LINGUISTIC DATES

It is notable that the *externally datable* inscriptions (Table 3.5) are quite compatible with the above scheme. This encourages one to see whether the *epigraphically dated* ones can also be reconciled with it, in which case one would have to conclude that inscriptional and non-inscriptional ortho-graphies were not as distinct as has sometimes been supposed.[146] The *epigraphical dates* for linguistic periods suggested by Table 3.3 (excluding the underlined exceptions) are listed below.

- Pers. 1–3 = 5c–6c epigraphically, quite compatible with the linguistic date of *c.* 540–*c.* 600 as the latest dates for Per. 3. The *c.* 600 terminus depends on Sequence i in the Book of Llandaf beginning roughly *c.* 600.[147] If Sequence i begins *c.* 585, as suggested by Wendy Davies,[148] the resulting *c.* 540–*c.* 585 is equally compatible with the 5c–6c epigraphic date for Pers. 1–3. Handley's suggestion that some of the inscriptions may be earlier than the 5c cannot be confirmed from the linguistic evidence because of the complete absence of external evidence for British sound changes which can be securely dated to the 4c.[149] In theory the use of Latin memorial formulae might help us to test the linguistic and epigraphic datings, but here too there are problems. Thus while Thomas describes HIC IACET/IACIT as 'a mid-to-late fifth century borrowing from the Continent', Knight emphasizes that it was in use in Italy much earlier, and argues that it is the use of HIC in *initial* position that is distinctive in the Lyon inscriptions of 422 and later, while Handley rejects any attempt to use the Lyon inscriptions to date the British ones.[150] HIC IACIT and variants appear in several of the Per. 1 inscriptions of Table 3.2 (318/6, 319/9, 342/70, 370/157, 401/183, 498/Nb7, and 515/Scot.9) but in none of these is it in initial

---

[146] See n. 40 above.

[147] Or a little later; cf. n. 141 above. Iddon's charter, 166, which I regard as the earliest of Sequence i, is witnessed by a *Biuoc* < **Biu̯ākos.*

[148] *Llandaff Charters*, pp. 35 and 93 (her date for 73a which contains the names *Arcon* and *Guodcon*).

[149] LHEB, p. 694. Cf. Handley, *EME*, 10 (2001), 197–98. (Of course early strays like 2002/a and 2026 are not in question here.) A case could be made for moving *a*-affection and /ü:/ > /i:/ back to the fourth century, but even if this were done, the evidence for inscriptions not showing these changes is poor (see ‡‡ 15–16). A further question, which cannot be considered here, is whether the prevalence of Irish names in our linguistically earliest inscriptions is compatible with a pre-410 date. Tedeschi, in *Roman, Runes and Ogham*, p. 24, rejects a pre-fifth-century *terminus post quem* on palaeographical grounds.

[150] Thomas, *Mute Stones*, p. 204; Knight, *End of Antiquity*, p. 107; Handley, *EME*, 10 (2001), 186–88.

position, and in every case there is only a weak linguistic case for a very early date for the inscriptions (as indicated by the underlining of the _A_s in Table 3.2). Among the inscriptions placed in the early Pers. 1–3, 2–3, 3, 4–5 and 5 in Table 3.2 the HIC IACIT formula appears in 334/54, 344/73, 381/87, 391/78, 418/283, 397/105, 451/401 and 516/Scot.1, but the only ones in which it is initial position are 418/283 HEC IACET SALVIANVS BVRGOCAVI FILIVS CVPETIANI and 516/Scot.1 A ET ω HIC IACENT SANCTI ET PRAECIPVI SACERDOTES ID EST VIVENTIVS ET MAVORIVS. The first of these (418/283) is only dated as early as Per. 1–3 on the basis of the retention of Latin _ā_, which is not a reliable criterion. The second (516/Scot.1) is as early as Per. 5 on the strength of the lack of final _i_-affection in MAVORIVS, and here conservative spelling may be at work (as noted in ‡19). In short, the use of HIC IACIT casts no light on the linguistic dating. If we had found that the formula initiated a large number of Per. 1–3 inscriptions, that might have indicated that Per. 1–3 began later than _c._ 422 on Knight's argument; but the near-absence of the initial formula proves nothing.

• Pers. 1–7 = 5c–6c epigraphically, or possibly 5c–6/7c (in view of Nash-Williams's dating of 1028/214/850 VENDVMAGLI); the linguistic date of ‘early 7c’ for the start of Per. 7 is compatible with the later epigraphic bracket, but again depends on the dating of Sequence i charters – if these begin _c._ 585, Pers. 1–7 can be epigraphically _and_ linguistically 5–6c. VENDVMAGLI could be Irish (see p. 310 below).

• Pers. 8ff. = 5c/6c ff. epigraphically (including some specifically E6). This E6 start is incompatible with the linguistic dating of Pers. 8ff. to the 7c onwards, even if this terminus is pushed back to _c._ 585 ff. The most troublesome inscription is the one dated E6 (493/Ok58 NEPRANI FILI CONBEVI, Per. 14–16), since this specifically _early_ 6c date is incompatible even with _c._ 585 ff. Maybe this inscription should be dated later – Jackson dates it ‘mid to later sixth century’ – or be regarded as wholly Irish.[151] Alternatively, the 7c linguistic terminus a quo for Pers. 6–12 inclusive, which is based on _Lugobi_ being pre-Per. 5, could be revised if _Lugobi_ is explained away in some way (e.g. as an Irish name, _Luigbe_, as noted earlier).

• Pers. 10–16 = 5/6c epigraphically. At first sight one might expect some to be 7c epigraphically in view of the linguistic dating of Pers. 16–17. Note, however, that none of these eight inscriptions (in dotted box in Table 3.3) _need_ be later than Per. 14, and that only five must be Per. 13 or later. Per. 13 is characterized by pretonic _u_ /u/ > _o_ /ö/. In 352A/122/5 DOMNICI, the name may be Latin _Dom(i)nicus_ rather than from

---

[151] LHEB, p. 646 (cited above, p. 277). Note that since NEPRANI is probably Irish, so may CONBEVI be; see Ch. 4 below, §§ 21, 29, 41, and pp. 294 and 346.

Celtic *Dumnīkos (‡46), and 387/95 LOCVLITI could perhaps be Irish (‡46). On the three 'Per. 14–16' inscriptions see next paragraph. The remaining three 'Per. 10–16' inscriptions (419/284, 365/149, 477/Ok11) may all belong to Pers. 10, 11, or 12, and these Periods could in fact start in the 6c if Lugobi is explained away.

- Pers. 14ff. = E6ff. epigraphically, an earlier starting point than the linguistic starting date of c. 625. There are two possibilities. The non-syncope in 970/13 CATAMANUS (contrasting with the regular syncope in the Llandaf charters apart from Lugobi) could be archaizing,[152] in which case the epigraphic dates may be allowed to stand. Alternatively, the epigraphic dates in the 6c (493/Ok58 [possibly Irish]; 324/34 [dubious anyway]; 486/Ok56; 490/Ok29; and 471/Ok39) – mostly in the later sixth – could be moved into the 7c. (See comments above, p. 277, on item (ii) of Table 3.5.)

- Pers. 15ff. = 7c ff. epigraphically, compatible with the linguistic dating.

- Pers. 1–20 = up to and including 9c epigraphically, compatible with the linguistic dating, since linguistically Per. 20 begins c. 800.

- Pers. 21ff. = 7/9c ff. epigraphically and Pers. 24ff. = 7/9c ff. epigraphically, are all compatible with the linguistic datings (c. 800ff.) if Nash-Williams '7/9c' in the cases of 995/133/24, 986/62, 984/59, 1004/260/884, 971/35, 998/164, 992/120/14, and 1033/287 is interpreted as '9c'. This redating is more satifactory linguistically, since otherwise Pers. 21–28 would be spread over many centuries. The established mid-9c dating of the Pillar of Eliseg (1000/182, item (vi) in Table 3.5), linguistically Per. 22–27, is quite compatible with this, as is the early ninth-century dating of 1066 GURIAT (Per. 22–28). Note that a product of redating '7/9c' inscriptions to the 9c is that the famous Tywyn vernacular inscription (1033/287) now becomes 9c. This is not unreasonable, in view of the rather dubious palaeographic grounds on which Tywyn was originally dated earlier than 800, and the palaeographic advantages of a 9c date.[153] As Tywyn is a Per. 28 inscription, it might be supposed that it, and the other epigraphically earlyish Per. 28 inscriptions (992/120/14 CENLISINI and 979/46 GUADAN . . .) should be moved even later than the 9c. However, as we have seen, Per. 28 probably began slowly as early as c. 800. Moreover, Tywyn includes the form

---

[152] Jackson, LHEB, p. 621, n. 2, thought 971/35 CUURIS CINI roughly contemporary with 970/13 CATAMANUS (which he dated later than 625). They are also compared by Hughes, AC, 7th ser. 4 (1924), 55–57, and Radford, in RCAHMW, Anglesey, pp. civ-cvi. If this is correct, CATAMANUS is surely linguistically archaizing (cf. Tigernomalus in Vita Samsonis) since 971/35 belongs to Per. 22–27.

[153] See Sims-Williams, BBCS, 38 (1991), 22–23, on Morris-Jones's misinterpretation of Lindsay. I argued for a date 'nearer 800 than 700' on the basis of the o2 form of or in MORTCIC. Dumville, Palaeographer's Review, i, 124–25 and n. 33, cites this 'ultimately majuscule O + R monogram' as a characteristic of the 'Welsh Reformed minuscule' that arose 'perhaps around the middle of the ninth century'.

CIMALTED (> *cyfalledd*), not yet showing the loss of /t/ that is normal in the Old Welsh glosses, such as *mellhionou* 'violas' (Martianus Capella).[154] There is in fact no *linguistic* criterion by which post-800 inscriptions can be periodized, definitely late features like prosthetic vowels (‡‡ 75 and 87) being notably absent. The linguistic features of Pers. 24–28 may have been more typical of the 10c and 11c but nevertheless have begun to appear in the 9c.

---

[154] ‡63; cf. GPC s.v. *meillion*; VKG i, 137 (noting however 'durch Analogiebildungen kann c. -llt- auch ins Innere des Wortes dringen'; *lt* is also preserved in loanwords like OW *altaur*, *cultel* and *cultir*: Falileyev, *Etymological Glossary*, s.vv). This feature does not appear in my tables, since the inscriptions include no clear contrasting example where LT does *not* appear; see ‡63.

4

IRISH PHONOLOGY (§§ 1–43)

As yet there is no systematic chronology of Primitive Irish sound changes comparable to the Brittonic one in LHEB. In LHEB, pp. 142–43, Jackson gave a tentative chronology of the main Primitive Irish sound changes, and this skeleton has been fleshed out by Greene, Cowgill, McManus, Kortlandt, McCone, Schrijver, and others. Many points, however, are still uncertain or disputed. In what follows I refer especially to Kim McCone's 1996 monograph *Towards a Relative Chronology of Ancient and Medieval Celtic Sound Change* (TRC), but it should be stressed that TRC does not include a complete relative chronology, but rather various discrete sequences and isolated observations, which McCone and others might well not arrange quite in the order presented below. In other words, there is an element of personal preference in my presentation, despite the frequent reference to TRC.

As in Chapter 2, we can start from a Common Celtic phonological system with the following phonemes:

Vowels: a e i o u   a: e: ($< *ei$) i: u:
Semi-vowels: i̯ u̯
Short diphthongs:[1] ai oi au ou ($< *eu$ and $*ou$).
Consonants: m n r l s (with allophone z) t k^w k (with allophone x) b d g g^w ($< *g^wh$).

McCone regards various combinatory changes, mostly involving /s/, as arguably Proto-Celtic or 'Insular Celtic' (the hypothetical common ancestor of Brittonic and Irish).[2] He also argues for the existence of the allophones [ɪ] < /e/ and [æ] < /a/ by raising and fronting before nasals, which must have occurred earlier than Common Celtic *rannā < *rasnā.[3] Another important feature was the existence (before lenition) of positional allophones of consonants, e.g. /b/ = both [b] and either [B] or [bb]. McCone does not commit himself as to the original realization of this lenis/fortis system, but

---

[1] On the long diphthongs see TRC, p. 64.
[2] TRC, pp. 48 and 98–100 (note also p. 45 for /sp/ > /sw/). The validity of 'Insular Celtic' except as a geographical term is debatable; cf. Sims-Williams, in *Gaulois et celtique continental*, where the early phonology (e.g. /ns/ > /s/) is also discussed in more detail than is required here.
[3] TRC, pp. 46, 79 and 106. Pre-nasal raising seems to have been a recurrent phenomenon; see further Sims-Williams, in *Gaulois et celtique continental*, and below.

quotes with approval Greene's view that /nt/ and /nd/ were realized as [nT] and [Nd].[4]

It is commonly supposed that /i̯/ had a post-consonantal allophone [i̯i̯] from an early date, e.g. /omi̯on/ = [omi̯i̯on] (> OI *umae* 'copper, bronze'); however, McCone regards this as a Primitive Irish development in TRC (p. 109), and has since assigned a late date (= §27 below) to it.[5] Some of the first few changes listed below are regarded by McCone as 'Insular Celtic' or earlier.

1. -m > -n (apparently before /m/ > /μ̯/).[6]
2. Voiced or first lenition: [b d g gʷ m] > [v δ γ γʷ μ]. This presumably preceded /nt/ > /d/ (6. below), which phonemicized /δ/; unless, that is, one maintains the older view that /nt/ gave geminate /dd/ (thus allowing /d/ > /δ/ and /dd/ > /d/ to be later).[7]
3. z > δ, presumably after the advent of /δ/ by lenition at 2., as noted by Watkins.[8] If the ogam inscription 28 **TASEGAGNI** is OI *Tadcán* (with epenthetic vowel)[9] a later position in this sequence must be assigned to z > δ.
4. o > a in final syllables[10] and in composition vowels.
5. -i > -∅.[11]
6. nt > d, nk > g, nkʷ > gʷ, ns (< nts) > s, nxt > xt. A preceding /e/ or /a/ (= [ɪ] and [æ]) > /ɛː/, perhaps only in stressed syllables, except before /s/ or /x/ where lengthening was unconditional and applied to all vowels (cf. *karæns (< *karants) > OI *car(a)e*, *ænxtu- > OI *écht*).[12] Similarly *wēdans (< IE *wei̯donts) > *wēdās > Early OI *féda*, which fixes this stage later than 4. /o/ > /a/ above.[13] Note that the forms *Andros* and Ἔδρου (< *Antros) in Pliny and Ptolemy respectively suggest that /nt/ > /nd/ > /d/ had occurred by AD 150.[14]

---

[4] TRC, pp. 82, 91, and 107. This explains why they did not fall together when /nt/ > /nd/ > /d/ occurred.
[5] In Ó Cléirigh FS, p. 312. Cf. Sims-Williams, *BBCS*, 29 (1980–82), 211–13; SBCHP, p. 110; Lindeman, *ZCP*, 52 (2001), 227.
[6] Cf. TRC, p. 87.
[7] See TRC, pp. 81–87 and 90–91. The /k/ of the name *Reculver* < Romano-British *Regulbio* is an objection to voiced lenition being Insular Celtic; see Sims-Williams, in *Gaulois et celtique continental*.
[8] Insular Celtic according to TRC, p. 98, but see Watkins, in Meid FS, p. 541, and Sims-Williams, in *Gaulois et celtique continental*.
[9] Ziegler, p. 234.
[10] Conceivably Insular Celtic according to TRC, p. 109, but see Sims-Williams, in *Gaulois et celtique continental*, and GOI, p. 59, for composition vowels. CVNARIS at Housesteads (‡14) may be the first example.
[11] Insular Celtic according to TRC, p. 102, but see Sims-Williams, in Meid FS, p. 473, where it is argued that it is posterior to Irish /o/ > /a/ at 4., hence *-onti and *-mori > Early OI -ot and -mor rather than -at and -mar.
[12] TRC, pp. 74–75 and 106–7.
[13] Sims-Williams, in Meid FS, p. 473.
[14] Ibid., pp. 472–73.

7. ou ($<$ au/ou) $>$ /o:/ (completed before the extant ogam inscriptions, which show only **O**).[15]
8. ænn (including ænn $<$ ændn) $>$ enn; -æn $>$ -en.[16]
9. -xs(-) $>$ -ss(-) (and probably then -ss $>$ -s in auslaut).[17]
10. e $>$ i(i̯) in hiatus before back vowel, e.g. *neotas $>$ *niotas ($>$ ogam **NIOTTA**).[18]
11. Voiceless or second lenition: [t k kʷ] $>$ [θ x xʷ]. This evidently occurred after the borrowing of the first stratum of British Latin loanwords, which were affected by it (e.g. puteus $>$ OI cuithe), but the date of these loans is unknown.[19]
12. s $>$ h in lenition position, ambiguously written with the **S** symbol in the ogam inscriptions which are therefore no help in dating the change.[20]
13. In a final syllable following another unstressed syllable, a short vowel is lost by syncope between pairs of δ/θ, of s, or of r; then -δ'θ $>$ -θθ and -θθ $>$ -t.[21]
14. -θ, -δ, -x (also -s $<$ -ss) $>$ -h.[22]
15. Unstressed long vowels shortened except before -h, e.g. māθīr $>$ māθir ($>$ máthair) and wirī $>$ wiri ($>$ fir nom.pl.), unlike wirūh ($>$ firu, acc. pl.).[23]
16. h ($<$ s) $>$ i̯ in certain intervocalic environments, e.g. /iha/ and /ihi/.[24]
17. Stressed e lowered to æ ($>$ OI a) before γ(ʷ)i or γ(ʷ)e unless following syllable contained i̯ including i̯ $<$ s.[25] Also a $>$ æ before x + r/l/n.[26]
18. Perhaps /Vi̯V/ $>$ /VV/; /i̯V-/ $>$ /V-/; /-ii̯i/ ($<$ /-ii̯i:/) $>$ /-i:/ (written -**I** on

---

[15] /ou $>$ /o:/ is possibly but not necessarily an Insular Celtic development according to TRC, p. 103. The fact that /au/ remained distinct from /ou/ in Brittonic (Lambert, in Britain 400–600, pp. 203–15) is against this. De Bernardo Stempel, in Ptolemy, pp. 104 and 107, argues from Ptolemy's Irish river Mōdonos that monophthongization had already occurred by c. AD 150.

[16] TRC, pp. 50 and 106. The chronological position of this is unclear.

[17] TRC, p. 105. CVNARIS as Housesteads may be the first example; see ‡14.

[18] TRC, p. 109; GOI, pp. 50 and 207; McManus, Guide, pp. 109–10 and 120. See however Greene, Ériu, 23 (1972), 232 (raising in hiatus post-syncope). It might be argued that this raising should occur later than lowering at 29. below since otherwise this would have reversed it. Note, however, that lowering seems not to have been effective in this environment, to judge by 156 **MAQQI-IARI** and 415/278 IARRI ($<$ *isarī) $>$ Mac-Iair (see ‡14).

[19] They must have been borrowed before British /t/ $>$ /d/ etc., but the date of this voicing is also uncertain. See Sims-Williams, in Britain 400–600, pp. 223–36, 238, and 248; cf. TRC, pp. 89 and 91.

[20] According to TRC, p. 89, /s/ $>$ /h/ is Insular Celtic; but see Sims-Williams, in Gaulois et celtique continental.

[21] TRC, pp. 105–6.

[22] TRC, p. 105.

[23] TRC, p. 110.

[24] Examples given in TRC, pp. 100, 111, and 131–32, are *nemesa $>$ *neṽiha $>$ *niṽiya $>$ OI nime (pl.), *tegisos $>$ *teγiyah, *-āsisi $>$ *-āhihi $>$ *-āiyi.

[25] TRC, p. 111; for a critique cf. SBCHP, p. 140, n. 1.

[26] TRC, p. 111.

ogam stones), e.g. kēli̯ī̯ > kēlī > *céili* (nom.pl.).[27] But more recently McCone has implied that the development was /-(i)i̯i:/ > /-i̯i(:)/ > /i:/, and that /i̯/ was still in place at 27. below.[28]

19. Raising (rarely across voiceless consonant or group of consonants): stressed e and o were often raised to i and u when the next syllable contained i(:) or u(:),[29] e.g. melis > melih > milih > *mil* 'honey' (contrast ek^wī > *eich)*; omi̯on > oμ(i)i̯an > uμ(i)i̯an > *umae*; kogīnā > kogina > kugina > kugena > *cucann* 'kitchen'.

20. rw > rv, lw > lv, δw > δv, nw > nv, and hw > f.[30]

21. Loss of -h and -n, unless already transferred to following word beginning with vowel etc.[31]

22. -e and -i may have merged as an (in due course palatalizing) schwa sound (-ĭ).[32]

23. Stressed a > au before u(:) in following syllable, e.g. 273 **CALUNO-** > Caulun- > *Caulann*.[33]

24. e i o > eu iu ou before *short* u in next syllable, except in the case of stressed /e/ across /ss/, e. g. wirū > wiru > wiuru > *fiur* (dat. sg.) unlike wirūh > wirū > *firu* (acc. pl.) and messuh > *mes*.[34]

25. æmb/ænd > amb/and before back vowels, but > ımb/ınd before front vowels, while æng(^w) was always raised.[35]

26. First palatalization: intervocalic single consonants (and mb, nd, ng (and ng^w ?)) palatalized **both before** i(:) [and /i̯/], *except* when the consonant(s) was preceded by a: [or o: and not followed by /i̯/] (e.g. māθir > *máthair*) and *also except*, in the case of labial and guttural consonants and clusters (i.e. mb, ng), when preceded by stressed o(:) or u(:); **and before** e(:), except when the consonant was preceded by a(:), o(:) or u(:).[36] All consonants and clusters (except /xt/) were palatalized by -ĭ.[37] I would suggest that palatalization of -ir > -ir' occurred at this stage (as in OI *máthair*).[38]

[27] TRC, p. 113.
[28] In Ó Cléirigh FS, pp. 311–12.
[29] TRC, pp. 110–11. If post-consonantal /i̯/ was not already /ii̯/, /i̯/ must be added to the causes of raising.
[30] TRC, pp. 120 and 130.
[31] TRC, p. 120. Garrett, *Ériu*, 50 (1999), 155–57, suggests that -/n/ and any preceding /e/ or /i/ may have been lost earlier than 15., but notes various objections.
[32] TRC, pp. 115–16.
[33] TRC, p. 111.
[34] TRC, p. 112. Does /i/ > /u/ in the case of *tīxtiyū (TRC, p. 106) > tíchtu, or should one suppose /iu/ > /u/ and link this with unstressed short eu > u at 42. below?
[35] TRC, pp. 78 and 112. On Latin *ancora* > *ingor* 'anchor' cf. Schrijver, *Ériu*, 44 (1993), 50.
[36] TRC, p. 116, with revisions in square brackets from McCone in Ó Cleirigh FS, pp. 308 and 312.
[37] TRC, p. 117.
[38] This palatalization is usually denied, but see Sims-Williams, in *Gaulois et celtique continental*.

27. -C(′)i̯V(-) > -C(′)i̯i̯V-.[39]

28. k^w > k, g^w > g [presumably along with their lenited equivalents] before
     u(:), o(:) and a.[40]

29. Lowering of i (and /ɪ/) to e, and of u to o, when next syllable contained
     a(:) or o(:), e.g. wiros > wirah > wera > *fer* 'man'; kluton >
     kluθan > kloθa > *cloth* 'fame'; kuginā > kugena > *cucann* – with the
     alleged exception that i was not lowered before nd, e.g. windah > *find*
     'white'; but here Ziegler argues for lowering too on the basis of ogam
     VEND-.[41] Palatalization was now partially phonemic, i.e. not simply
     predictable from the flanking vowels, since al′ei̯a (< al′i̯i̯ah < ali̯os: W.
     ail) > *aile* now contrasted with kaleθa (< kaletos: W. *caled*) > *calad*.[42]

30. Rounding after k^w and g^w of i > u and a > o.[43] Also k^wri- > k^wru-, and
     k^wɛ:g^w- > k^wɔ:g^w-.[44]

31. k^w > k, g^w > g [and presumably their lenited equivalents] in all
     remaining positions.

32. æ (< stressed e before γ(^{w})i or γ(^{w})e, see 17. above) > a.[45]

33. Second palatalization of initial consonant(s) by following stressed i(:)
     or e(:) [and ɛ: and ɪ:].[46]

34. In internal unstressed syllables later liable to syncope: u > ü before i or
     e in following syllable.[47]

35. In internal unstressed syllables later liable to syncope: ü, i, and e merge
     as palatalizing schwa (ï), and i or e > non-palatalizing schwa /ŭ/ before
     non-palatal -h-.[48]

36. Third palatalization of consonants followed by palatalizing schwa (ï).

37. u̯′ > i̯.[49]

---

[39] McCone in Ó Cleirigh FS, p. 312; cf. 18. above. This seems to rule out the explanation of
     -*guid* by early i̯e > i in TRC, pp. 42 and 49. Note that the latter does not work with the voc.
     sg. of *io*-stems. On the other hand, early ei̯e > ī (TRC, p. 49) is less problematic.

[40] TRC, p. 24 (although a 'rounded back vowel' is specified, unstressed /a/ seems to be
     included here since 2006 MACVS < *mak^w*k*^{w}*as* is cited). On stressed /a/ see 30. below.

[41] TRC, p. 110 (and p. 112 for /ɪ/). On **VEND-** see ‡22.

[42] TRC, pp. 121–22; Greene, *TPS* (1973), 131. Thurneysen, GOI, p. 46, refers only to lowering
     in *stressed* syllables, but on p. 47 he mentions Pokorny's article in *ZCP*, 12 (1918), 415–26,
     which covers unstressed syllables as well and is followed in LHEB, pp. 137 and 143. Greene,
     Ériu, 23 (1972), 233, implies it was later in unstressed syllables.

[43] TRC, pp. 24 and 118. McCone does not restrict this to stressed syllables, and indeed in the
     case of unstressed /i/ it seems to be the easiest way of explaining the occurrences of
     MACCV-/MACCO- < **MAQQI-DECEDA** etc., with /u/ (or /ŭ/ or /ü/?) < /ĭ/ < /i/ < /iː/.
     Jackson's explanation in Chadwick GS, pp. 211–12, and LHEB, p. 140 (cf. McManus,
     Guide, pp. 90 and 98), is more complicated: *mak^w*k*^{w}*i(ː)* apocopated to **mak′k′u̯*, and then
     vocalized in British to **mak′k′u*.

[44] GOI, pp. 137 and 246; Schrijver, *Ériu*, 50 (1999), 133–37.

[45] TRC, p. 118.

[46] Ibid.

[47] TRC, p. 119.

[48] Ibid.

[49] This is placed post-syncope in TRC, p. 131, but, in the study to which McCone refers,
     Uhlich, *Ériu*, 46 (1995), 15, is non-committal as to whether it was u̯′ 'or its reflex' which
     survived syncope. OI *bí* (following note) supports placing 37. before 38.

38. Apocope of short unstressed final vowels [and any remaining trace of preceding /i̯/].[50] Palatalization of preceding consonants was now phonemic. This made way for the later shortening of long final vowels.[51]

39. Loss of γ [and δ] before r/l/n with compensatory lengthening of preceding vowel (note o > ɔ: [or o:?], e > ɛ:, i > i:u) or diphthong eu (> ɛ:u), and with diphthongization (e > ɛ:u) before palatal consonant.[52] The comparable loss of x and θ before r/l/n with compensatory lengthening, e.g. k'en'eθl > k'en'ɛ:l, can provisionally be regarded as contemporary.[53]

40. Dissimilatory loss of first of two homorganic consonants in the environment: stressed vowel + consonant + i (or e) + consonant.[54]

41. Syncope of every second non-final syllable in words of three or more syllables.[55]

42. Unstressed short eu > u, e.g. tomessus > toμeusuh > OI *tomus*.[56]

43. An epenthetic vowel breaks up final consonant clusters and some clusters arising at syncope, e.g. araθr > araθər.[57]

We can now examine the Irish, or possibly Irish, names and words in the inscriptions in the light of the above chronology. The probably Irish names are **DOUBLE UNDERLINED** and the possible ones are <u>SINGLE UNDERLINED</u>. These names are mostly given in the simplified forms found in the Index; in other words, doubtful letters are often not marked and it is not implied that the forms cited are necessarily the best readings. Needless to say, the dates based on the <u>SINGLE UNDERLINED</u> category will be more hypothetical and often merely alternative to the dates based on the assumption that the names are Brittonic.

The inscriptions will be dealt with under each sound change roughly from north to south in Wales and then, for the other countries, in Macalister's order – but I often depart from this in order to place similar names together.

None of the possibly Irish inscriptions *fail* to show any of the changes before raising (§19), and even the examples of non-raising are all dubious in one way or another (see below, p. 303). Only a few of the prior changes require comment:

---

[50] TRC, pp. 121–22; dated *c.* 500 on p. 127. Note that /i̯/ < /u̯'/ merged with preceding /i/ to give /i:/ e.g. in *bí* pl. of *béo*, TRC, p. 131.

[51] TRC, p. 132.

[52] TRC, pp. 112 and 122–24. On [ɔ:] cf. TRC, pp. 153–54, and Sims-Williams, *CMCS*, 23 (1992), 59.

[53] As by Greene, *TPS* (1973), 133–34. In TRC, p. 123, it is placed after syncope, but McCone is hesitant about this, and note the apparent lack of syncope in 488/Ok60 **ENABARR**. For further discussion, see ‡48 and below, p. 330.

[54] TRC, p. 124.

[55] This marks the end of Primitive Irish *c.* 550 according to TRC, pp. 124–27.

[56] TRC, p. 112. Cf. n. 34 above on *tíchtu*.

[57] TRC, pp. 124 and 127.

§4 Occurrences of the composition vowel **O** rather than **A** in the ogam inscriptions are not exceptions to earlier /o/ > /a/ but are secondary, mostly due to the vicinity of labials (see ‡38).

§7 The ogam inscriptions show no exceptions to §7 (ou > o:) and a further example from our roman-letter corpus is 375/166 **TOTAVALI** (‡12).

§9 I assume that xs > s(s) had been completed before all the extant inscriptions, as in **CVNARIS** at Housesteads on Hadrian's Wall, if it is Irish, and that the -X of 2006 **CVNORIX** at Wroxeter is merely Latinizing (see ‡14).

§10 The ogam inscriptions show no exceptions to e > i(i̯) in hiatus, and a further example from our roman-letter corpus is 398/106 **IACONVS** (also Macalister's dubious 475/Ok47 **IACONIVS**) < *esok- (‡22).[58] 502]**MAQ LEOG[** cannot be taken seriously as an exception to §10, especially since **MAQ** shows the much later apocope (§38). If it does correspond to OI *Macc-Liac* (cf. ‡38 and n. 764), note that OI *lie*, gen. *liac* (*c* = [g]), seems anyway to have original Celtic /i:/ (< IE *$\bar{e}$).[59]

§11 Ogam spelling disguises whether or not voiceless lenition has occurred, except where the *forfeda* >< and <-> are used, but the roman-letter inscription 322/27 CAMVLORIS **HOI** shows /k/ > /x/ quite clearly.[60] Note also 375/166 **DOTHORANTI** (‡42n.) and 1006/197/842 **NEFROIHI** (‡42).

§14 Reflexes of final dentals and changes such as -x > -h and -s(s) > -h are unlikely to show up in inscriptions.

§15 506 **COGELI**, if = OI *Coicéle* (‡25n.), is clearly a later formation than §15 (but the reading is doubtful).

§16 Possible indirect testimony to §16 (ihi > ii̯i) is provided by 325/33 BIVATISI if this is the correct reading and represents *Biwatii̯i*, g.sg. of a *io*-stem: ISI (the traditional ogam way of writing /ihi/) would be a hypercorrect spelling of /ii̯i/. There are other readings and interpretations however (see ‡27).

§17 These sequences happen not to appear in our corpus, unless]**ACRON** is read instead of 507 **CRONAN**.[61]

---

[58] The /s/ had been lost very early in such forms according to Greene, *Ériu*, 27 (1976), 27, although note McCone's assumption of /h/ as at §16.
[59] VKG, i, 251, and ii, 100; NWÄI, pp. 178, n. 10, and 259, n. 163. On the forms of this word see Bergin, *Ériu*, 12 (1934–38), 217–18.
[60] Sims-Williams, *CMCS*, 23 (1992), 45–51.
[61] KHJ's reading, noted in ‡‡ 37n., 38n., and 48n. But **dakron* (> OI *dér* 'tear') is an unlikely name, and -**ON** rather than -**A(N)** is not expected in ogam.

§19 Raising

[19] (A) The following forms appear not to show raising:

1. 2006 MAQVI COLINE > OI *Maicc Chuilinn* (cf. §22) and similarly
2. 485/Ok68 COLINI (if this reading is correct; cf. ‡64).
3. 403/268/841 BERIA[CI] seems not to show raising of BER- (OI *bir* 'spit, spear' < *beru-*) before the I, but the reading and language are uncertain (‡18). If the name is Irish, note that the *attested* Old Irish parallel (which may have been intended) is *Berach* (< *Berākos* without yod), and that there may be influence from the British cognate (W. *bêr*).
4. 482/Ok71 NEMIANVS (?better read NEMIAVS) presents a similar situation: NEM- is not raised by the I, but in fact the closest parallel in Irish is OI *Neman* without trace of the I and without raising (‡18n.).
5. 461/Ok66 NONNITA (if < *Nonnitas*, ‡15n.).

[19] 386/92 MELI and 453/399 MELI may be related to OI *mil* < *melis*, gen. *melo* < *melous*),[62] but may have the unraised vocalism of the genitive singular (with merely Latinate -I); alternatively, if MELI is the genitive of an *o*-stem, it may have the vocalism of the nominative *MELAS – the existence of such a name is implied by OI *Mel* (without raising), ‡15n. One also has to bear in mind the possible analogy in spelling from the non-raising in names with this element in unstressed position, such as 351/115/2 DVMELVS and 368/a/150 **DUMELEDONAS**.[63] Note further that there seems to have been a Latin/Latinate name *Melus* current in Ireland (‡15n.). (An alternative reading of 453/399 is NESI which, if correct, might be a Latinization of Irish *Ness* or *Neissi*.[64])

[19] 439/319 **(A)SEGNI** is obscure – and **INGEN** (*with* raising) is said (dubiously!) to occur in the same inscription. 456/404 **GENDILI/** GE[NDILI] does not show raising across /nd/, but this may be due to influence from the Latin source of the name, *Gentili(u)s* (‡‡ 17n., 22, 27 and 68). 399/176 [TO]VISACI/TOVISACI may be a pre-raising form, but this depends on whether the original vowel was /o/ rather than /u/, which is disputed (see ‡46).[65]

---

62 Ziegler, p. 175. Cf. TRC, p. 110.
63 See further McManus, *Guide*, p. 180, n. 50, and Ziegler, p. 175, comparing OI *Duimle* (cf. *Daimle*, Mahon, *PHCC*, 8 (1988), 13) with 198 -**DDUMILEAS** (probably a *ia*-stem). Note that the **I** of the latter cannot be explained by raising (Ziegler, p. 40), since this is specifically restricted to stressed syllables (TRC, p. 110). In 252, **DUMELI** (an *o*-stem, Ziegler, p. 175, comparing Gaulish *Sumeli*) occurs alongside **GLASICONAS** which is clearly post-lowering and therefore post-raising.
64 On which see Sims-Williams, *BBCS*, 29 (1980–82), 610, n. 4.
65 Cf. Uhlich, *Ériu*, 46 (1995), 16, and SBCHP, pp. 17, n. 2, and 342.

[19] (B) The following forms show raising:

1. 342/70 **ILVVETO** < *elu- (‡‡ 38 and 85)
2. 362/142 **INIGENA** = OI ingen < *enigenā[66] [I ignore the very dubious 439/319 **INGEN**]
3. 398/106 **MINI**, assuming it is the same as OI min 'small' and that the latter is < *menu-;[67] but there are other possibilities (see ‡22n.)

[19] Little reliance can be placed on 409/198/849 **ILLUNA** (> OI Illann, a derivative of ela 'swan' (with etymological *e), like 79 **ELUNA**[68] since the vowel symbols are unclear.[69] 327/43 **TRILLUNI/TRILVNI** cannot be included as its etymology is obscure (‡‡ 26 and 60).

§20 rw > rv, lw > lv, δw > δv, nw > nv, and hw > f

[20] (A) Forms with /w/ (spelt V):

1. 388/94 DERVORI and
2. 344/73 DERVACI (both from *derwo-, ‡14n.)

On 489/a/Ok13 **SVAQQUCI** (for *SVANNUCI) beside innovative FANONI see below.

[20] (B) Forms with /v/ (spelt B) or with /f/ (spelt F):

1. 372/160 **BARVALB/BARBALOM** if < *Barrobalvos (: OI balb), with ogam -B and roman -M both spelling /v/ (‡69). (The medial -RV- reflects a post-syncope /rv/ and is strictly irrelevant here; but it casts some doubt on -RV- spellings as always meaning /rw/.)
2. 455/403 FANNVCI and
3. 489/a/Ok13 **FANONI** beside conservative **SVAQQUCI** (for *SVANNUCI), which must be disregarded as an archaism (‡‡ 18, 22, 45, 60, 68, and 79).
4. 355/128/8 SILBANDVS may be an Irish spelling of Silvanus, reflecting the Irish use of LB that arose after /lw/ > /lv/; however, Silbanus is attested in Vulgar Latin (‡‡ 18 and 22).
5. 1006/197/842 NEFROIHI, if the first element is nía < *neits (‡42).

[20] Note that the RB in 354/126/6 CORBALENGI (> OI Corbleng) and 357/136 CORBAGNI (> OI Corbbán) is not relevant here, assuming, as seems likely, that it is connected with Latin corbis rather than corvis.[70] 439/

---

[66] Ziegler, pp. 188–89.
[67] Ziegler, p. 206, n. 331. Cf. LEIA M-53.
[68] Ziegler, pp. 176 and 188; cf. SBCHP, p. 76.
[69] McManus, *Guide*, p. 67. Macalister may have wrongly borrowed the I- from the preceding M[A]Q[I].
[70] ‡14. Cf. Ziegler, pp. 109–10.

319 **EFESSANGI** is irrelevant, as Nash-Williams wrongly transcribed **IG^W** as **EF** (‡42).

§21 Loss of -h (and -n), unless already transferred to following word beginning with vowel etc.

Preserved or lost -h (< -s and -ss, etc. see §14) is manifested in the inscriptions by the presence or absence of -S; however, the many forms where this may be due to Latin influence e.g. 324/34 CONBARRVS (Latin -*us*?), 388/94 DERVORI (= Latin gen. sg. -*i(i)*?) have to be ignored. In 426/300 **NETTASAGRU** or **NETTASAGRI** one cannot really say whether **Nētas Sagrī > Nad Sáir* has lost the -S or not, or, as is more likely, whether **NETTA-** is a compositional form without -S. Obviously I also omit defective inscriptions where the -S is editorial (e.g. 427/a/301 and 378/169).

[21] (A)

1.   322/27 CAMVLORIS (Hibernicized form of British *Camulorīx*, at time when Irish still had **-RIS**; ‡14), and similarly perhaps
2.   321/25]SORIS (if = *Vassorix or similar, ‡14)
3.   380/84 **ICORIGAS/ICORI**
4.   2006 CVNORIX (if reflecting Ir. **Kunari(:)s*, ‡14)
5.   354/126/6 ORDOVS (Hibernicized form of British *Ordovix, at a time when Irish still had -S; ‡14)
6.   358/138 **VOTECORIGAS/VOTEPORIGIS**
7.   362/142 **AVITTORIGES/AVITORIA** (with **-ES** = -><S = **-IAS**? ‡14n.)
8.   368/a/150 **DUMELEDONAS** (= *-*aidonas*)[71]
9.   431/308 **DOVATUCEAS** or **DOVATACIS/DOBITVCI** or DOBTVCI[72]
10. 446/353 **MAGLICUNAS** / MAGLOCVNI (or -CVVI)
11. 496 **TEBICATOS**[73]
12. 500 **ROC[A]T[O]S** and **[AM]B[I]CATOS**[74]
13. 504 **BIVAIDONAS** (< *-*aidonas*)[75]

[21] There are also some uncertain forms in -S:
348/a/110/27 **TRENALUGOS** (a dubious reading)
450/390 **OGTENAS** also read **OGTENLO/HOGTIVIS** or HOGTINIS – an obscure name (cf. ‡27n.)

---

[71]   Ibid., pp. 91 and 175. I take the writing of **E** for *ai/ae* to be a Latinism, whereas Ziegler thinks of the ancient British monophthongization of /ai/ (‡‡ 4, 23 and 59). The Welsh name *Aeddon* (BWP, p. 180 and n. 16) may be borrowed from this oblique stem **Aiðon-* of the popular Irish name *Áed*.
[72]   It not clear if this is OI *Dubthach* (< **Dubu̯otākos*, Ziegler, p. 170) or a gen. of a form in *-*taukā* (‡60).
[73]   An Irish treatment of a British name. One stroke of the -S survives: Fulford et al., *Med. Arch.*, 44 (2000), 10.
[74]   Ziegler, p. 227; ‡17.
[75]   Ibid., pp. 98 and 138.

[21] (B)

1. 342/70 **ILVVETO**
2. 336/67a **[M]AQ[I] D[E]C[E]DA**
3. 405/28/845 **GRAVICA** (Nash-Williams:]LICA)[76]
4. 461/Ok66 **NONNITA** (if < *Nonnitas, ‡15n.)
5. 503 **DOVAIDONA** (Dubáed < *Dubu̯aidonas), also **DRUTA** (or **DROATA**), which is more obscure[77]
6. 1006/197/842 **NEFROIHI**, if the first element is nía < *neits (‡42), and similarly
7. 447/369 **NEMAGLI**
8. 493/Ok58 **NEPRANI**

[21] Obviously, I have excluded damaged inscriptions which may have lost -S (e.g. 345/74).

428/305 **TRENAGUSU** never had such an -S, but may originally have read **TRENAGUSI** with Latin -I as in the roman **TRENEGUSSI**.[78] 512 **QATTIDONA** and 2002/b **TARICORO** are omitted as being obscure. 454/402 **DENOVI** and 462/Ok14 **DINVI** are too uncertain as examples of *-u̯iks names to be included (see ‡‡ 18, 27, and 58).

§22 -e and -i may have merged as an (in due course palatalizing) schwa sound (-ĭ)

[22] (A) All examples of -I are fatally ambiguous, since they may be conservative or due to the influence of Latin gen. sg. -I.

[22] (B) The possibly significant examples of -E are as follows (cf. §38n. below):

1. 2006 **MAQVI COLINE** < *Kolini(:)[79]
2. 378/169 **BODIBEVE**, perhaps with -E for Irish *i(:) (Buaidbéo being an o-stem) or for Latin(ate) -I[80]
3. 423/296 **QAGTE** (if masculine, cf. ‡51 – The fact that cht could not be palatalized may have hastened loss of awareness of the historical -ī.)
4. 479/Ok16 **CVNAIDE**, perhaps a Latinized form of Ir. *Kunaidonas (gen. of OI Conaed), with -E for Latin -I (cf. ‡58n.)[81]

---

[76] Cf. 150 **GRAVICAS**, Ziegler, p. 186.
[77] Ibid., pp. 98, 101 and 170. If this is Drúith as i-stem (cf. ‡65), the ending -A rather than -O(S) would be very late (cf. GOI, p. 192).
[78] CIIC i, 409, n. 1; LHEB, p. 181, n. 1. KHJ notes that MacNeill [PRIA, 27 C (1909), 361] took the -U to represent -O.
[79] Cf. McManus, Guide, p. 180, n. 62.
[80] On the ogam see LHEB, pp. 180–81 and n. 3 (apparently taking it as ā-stem, cf. Orel, BBCS, 34 (1987), 7, and Ziegler, pp. 100 and 139). BEV- rather than BIV- may be due to lowering in the nominative *-beu̯a- < *-biu̯o-.
[81] But Okasha notes that the earliest transcripts have -O rather than -E. The inscription is now (in 2000) obliterated by lichen.

5. 361/140 <u>MAQVERIGI</u> < *$Mak^wk^w\bar{\iota}$-$R\bar{\iota}gos$ (‡38)

§23 Stressed a > au before u(:) in following syllable

No relevant examples of AU occur in the corpus. 1068/a **LAGUBERI** fails to show the diphthongization of OI *laugu* < *$lagi\underset{.}{u}s$*, but it is not certain that this is its etymon.[82]

§24 e i o > eu iu ou before short /u/ in next syllable

No examples of these diphthongs occur.

§25 æmb > ɪmb etc.

[25] (A)

1. 500 [AM]BICATOS (> OI *Imchad*, ‡17 and n. 205 on the [A]);
2. 433/313 [A]NDAGELLI/ANDAGELLI (cf. OI *Indgall*, ‡‡15, 22, 48, and 74 – despite Nash-Williams the [A] is not in doubt), and similarly
3. 441/345 <u>ANDAGELLI</u>

[25] (B) – no examples.

§26 First palatalization

Not visible orthographically.

§27 $\underset{.}{i} > i\underset{.}{i}$

The only possibly significant example of II is 2029/p.39i <u>CVNIIAC[I?]</u> < *$Kuni\underset{.}{a}k\bar{\iota}$ (‡‡ 18 and 22; cf. §29 below).

§28 $k^w > k$, $g^w > g$ before u(:), o(:) or a

[28] (A) There are no examples of labiovelars being retained in this position.

[28] (B)

1. 358/138 **VOTECORIGAS**/VOTEPORIGIS < *$Votek^wor\bar{\iota}gos$*[83]
2. 366/148 <u>ECHADI</u> < *$Ek^wodi\underset{.}{o}s$*[84]
3. 2006 <u>MACVS</u> < *mak^wah*
4. 369/153 <u>CVRCAGNVS</u> (> OI *Corcán*) and
5. 441/345 <u>CVRCAGNI</u>, if the first element of these is *k^wurk^w*- < Latin *purpura*, although this is not the only possibility (‡‡ 22 and 48)
6. 1048/Ok32 <u>QONFAL</u>, if a hypercorrect (post /k^w/ > /k/) spelling of OI

---

[82] Ziegler, p. 191; cf. ‡‡ 25, 38 and 61.
[83] LHEB, p. 139. The composition vowel may have been /a/ < *o but this may have been coloured to /o/ by the labial environment (‡38). The reading given by Charles-Edwards, *Early Christian Ireland*, p. 166, n. 88, and fig. 4.2, appears to be **VOTECORIG"AS**, with hypercorrect /g^w/, but see Rhys, *AC*, 5th ser. 12 (1895), 313.
[84] Ziegler, p. 177; ‡42.

Con(u)al < **Kunoualos*; but there are problems with this reading and interpretation (‡‡ 26n., 28n., 44n., and 48)

§29 Lowering by a(:) and o(:)

[29] (A)

1. 319/9 CVNOGVS(I)
2. 325/33 BIVATIGI or BIVATISI
3. 380/84 **ICORIGAS/ICORI**
4. 2006 CVNORIX
5. 342/70 **CUNACENNI/CVNOCENNI** (if = OI *Conchenn*, ‡17 bis)
6. 358/138 **VOTECORIGAS/VOTEPORIGIS**[85]
7. 369/153 CVRCAGNVS (> OI *Corcán*)
8. 370/157 VLCAGNVS (> OI *Olcán*)
9. 405/228/845 **GRAVICA** or |LICA[86]
10. 403/268/841 BERIACI
11. 2029/p.39i CVNIIAC[87]
12. 454/402 CVNIOVENDE (f.)
13. 426/300 **MUCOI** (or **MUCOE**)[88]
14. 427/a/301 **DUBRA|CUNAS|** or **DUBAR|CUNAS|** (> *Doborchon*), also **MAGL|IA|** if that reading could be substantiated
15. 428/305 **TRENAGUSU** (or **-O** or **-I**)/**TRENEGUSSI**[89]
16. 435/315 CLVTORIGI (cf. OI *clothrí*, ‡46n.)
17. 441/345 CVRCAGNI
18. 446/353 **MAGLICUNAS/MAGLOCVN(I)**; **CLUTARI|GAS|/ CLVTORI**
19. 447/369 CVNIGCVS – *if* this is a loan from OI *Conaing* < OE *cyning* (‡48), note that it does not show the Irish (analogical?) /o/
20. 448/370 RINACI (‡22)
21. 461/Ok66 NONNITA (if < **Nonnitas*, ‡15n.)
22. 467/Ok24 **ULCAGNI/VLCAGNI**
23. 468/Ok31 CVNOVALI (if = OI *Con(u)al*)
24. 472/Ok35 VLCAGNI
25. 479/Ok16 CVNAIDE
26. 482/Ok71 NEMIANVS, although if it is a spelling of OI *Neman* (‡18n.), it cannot be expected to have become **NEMEANVS
27. 487/Ok10 DRVSTAGNI (if = OI **Drostán*) – but the reading is unlikely (‡48)

---

[85] McManus, *Guide*, p. 99, notes the non-lowering of /i/ (< /i:/) here.
[86] Cf. 150 **GRAVICAS**, Ziegler, p. 186.
[87] Cf. 289 **CUNIA**, 286 **CUNEA**, Ziegler, p. 161. Could the II be the old form of the letter E?
[88] Lowered **MOCOI** occurs elsewhere: McManus, *Guide*, p. 94.
[89] The OI *Tréngusso* (rather than *-*gosso*) quoted from Korolev by Ziegler, p. 238 shows the well-attested OI confusion of *o* and *u* in this position (cf. below, Ch. 5, n. 13).

28. 501 **CUNAMAGLI**
29. 504 **BIVAIDONAS** and **CUNAVALI**
30. 364/144 BARCVNI < *Barrakunas* (‡‡ 22n. and 26)
31. 449/384 **CUNATAMI/CVNOTAMI**

[29] There are also some forms apparently with unlowered composition vowels, but I hesitate to include them since it is unclear whether composition vowels were affected by lowering:[90]

320/26 CVLIDOR(I)
2002/b **TARICORO**
1022/240/928 DOBITAUCI (dubious)
496 **TEBICATO[**
500 **[AM]BICATOS**[91]
512 QATTIDONA
1028/214/850 VENDVMAGLI < *u̯indo-* (hypercorrect -V-?; note that E *is* lowered, cf. below)

[29] Other forms not included are:
415/278 IARRI[(> *(Mac-)Iair*); hiatus seems to have impeded lowering (see n. 18 above).
348/a/110/27 **TRENALUGOS** (> *Trénlogo*)[92] is too dubious a reading to include.
328/44]RVGNIAT(I)O does not show the lowering of OI *Brón-* and *Dróna*, but on the other hand the I would have impeded this (cf. ‡‡ 18, 22, and 48); moreover, VENDONI in the same inscription may show lowering.
345/74 **GLUVOCA** or **GLUVOCI** and 424/299 GLVVOCCI may be special cases with /iw/ > /uw/ (‡18). Note that 424/299 *does* show lowering if EVALENGI (see below) is the correct reading (cf. ‡‡ 14 and 18).
378/169 **BIVVAIDONA(S)/BIVADI** (OI *Béoáed*)[93] do not show lowering of I, but this appears in the same inscription in **BODDI(BA)BEVVA(S)/BODIBEVE** (see below).

[29] (B)

1. 324/34 CONBARRVS
2. 362/142 **AVITTORIGES** if -ES = -><S = -EAS < *-i̯ās*, ‡14n.)
3. 378/169 **BODDI(BA)BEVVA(S)**/BODIBEVE (< *-biu̯as*)[94]
4. 374/172 CVNEGNI (if based on nom. *Kunegnah* < *Kunignas*, ‡48)
5. 409/198/849 **POPIAS** (if the correct reading) for Latin *Pompeius* may be a hypercorrect spelling after /ia/ > /ea/ (was -AS substituted for the

---

[90] Cf. Ziegler, pp. 62–65.
[91] The roman equivalent AMMECATI shows British reduction according to LHEB, p. 645.
[92] Ziegler, p. 238.
[93] Ibid., p. 138. Is BIVAD-I based on the nominative?
[94] Ziegler, p. 139 (cf. §22n. above); forms with BIV- in the same inscription are presumably conservative.

corresponding Latin nominative -*us*?); and the same inscription's **[I]LLUNA** < **elonas* 'swan'[95] could also be hypercorrection from the period after /una/ > /ona/

6. 424/299 <u>EVALENGI</u> (> OI *Éolang* < **Iu̯o*-; but reading is uncertain, ‡18n.)
7. 436/316 <u>EUOLENGGI</u>
8. 471/Ok39 <u>CLOTUALI</u> (if OI **Cloth(u)al*)[96]
9. 493/Ok58 <u>CONBEVI</u> < **Kunobiwas*
10. 494/Ok79 <u>GOREVS</u> if = OI *Gúaire*, *io*-stem, ‡76)
11. 511/Scot.10 <u>CONINIE</u> (= OI *Co(i)nín* or *Conind*, ‡48n., presumably with *Con*- by analogy with other forms with *Con*- < **kuno*-)
12. 1048/Ok32 <u>QONFAL</u> if = OI *Con(u)al*, which is problematic (cf. §28 above)
13. 1202/Ok2 <u>EVOCATI</u> (if correct reading cf. 19 **IVACATTOS** > *Éochaid*, ‡‡ 18 and 38)

[29] The following forms in DOV- must all belong to the period after lowering, when the graph DOV(A)- < **dubu̯o*- probably established itself:[97]

14. 431/308 **D[O]VATUCEAS** [note also **-EAS**] or (less likely) **DOVATACIS/DOB(I)TVCI** (and <u>EVOLENGI</u>)
15. 432/312 **DOVAGNI/DOBAGNI** (cf. OI *Dubán*, with restored /u/, ‡48)
16. 503 **DOVAIDONA** (cf. OI *Dubáed*)[98]
17. 1206/Ok4 <u>DOVITHI</u> (cf. OI *Duba(i)d* = ogam **DOVETI**, ‡‡ 42, 51 and 55)

Some or all of the following have VEND- < **Winda*- < **Windo*-, in which the E may be due to lowering (‡22):

18. 328/44 <u>VENDONI</u>
19. 368/b/150 <u>BARRIVENDI</u> and <u>VENDVBARI</u>
20. 1028/214/850 <u>VENDVMAGLI</u>
21. 422/298 **VENDOGNI/VENDAGNI**
22. 429/307 <u>VENDONI</u>

The O in 18, 21, and 22 may reflect lowering of /u/ in a nominative **-ugnas*, unless there is British influence or the name is (?Celtic-)Latin (*)*Vendonius* (‡‡ 22, 38, and 48).

[29] I exclude some uncertain forms:
450/390 **OGTENAS** (or **OGTENLO** (!))/<u>HOGTINIS</u> (or <u>HOGTIVIS</u>); we

---

[95] Cf. ibid., p. 188. The **I**- (if correct!) would be due to raising in the nominative before /u:/ < **ō*.
[96] Cf. e.g. OI *Bres(u)al*, Uhlich, *Morphologie*, p. 186.
[97] Cf. Ziegler, p. 102.
[98] Ibid., pp. 98, 102 and 170.

do not know what the segmentation should be nor whether it contains an element *ten- or *tin- or indeed *-on-.[99]

454/402 EVALI (cf. OI *Eóil*?), if Irish, may have EVA < *$I\underset{\sim}{u}o$-, but the formation, if Irish, is obscure and CVNIOVENDE (f.) in the same inscription does not show lowering of CVNIO- to *CVNEO-/CVNEA-. EVALI is probably Latin *Aevalis* (‡18).

2019 RIGELLA (assuming it is not a fake) cannot be included, even if identical with OI *Rígell* since we do not know whether it is from *$R\bar{\imath}g$-*illā* or *$R\bar{\imath}g$-*ellā* or similar (‡‡ 15 and 74).

§30 Rounding after k^w etc.

[30] (A)

1. 361/140 MAQVERIGI < *$Mak^wk^w\bar{\imath}$-Rīgos* (‡38)
2. 2006 MA[Q]VI COLINE < *$Mak^wk^w\bar{\imath}$-Kolinī* (‡64)
3. 368/a/150 **MAQI** (reading uncertain?)
4. 426/300 **MAQI**
5. 446/353 **MAQI**
6. 449/384 **MAQI**
7. 489/a/Ok13 **MAQI/MAQVI**
8. 500 **M[A]QI**
9. 504 **MAQI**

[30] 341/71 **MAQITRENI** (rejecting Nash-Williams's **MAQUTRENI**) and 428/305 **MAQI MAQITRENI** must be archaizing/conservative since roman MACCVTRENI and MACUTRENI < *$Mak^wk^w\bar{\imath}$-Trēni* occur in the same inscriptions (see B below). This casts doubt on the other unrounded forms above: **MAQI** was a formula word.

[30] Examples like 336/67a **[M]AQ[I]D[E]C[E]DA** where the [I] is a restoration are of course excluded above.

[30] (B)

1. 326/39 MACCVDECCETI < *$Mak^wk^w\bar{\imath}$-Dekantos*[100]
2. 440/335 MACVDE[H]ETI (‡‡ 17, 28, 42)
3. 492/Ok59 MACCODECHETI
4. 329/42 MACCVTRENI < *$Mak^wk^w\bar{\imath}$-Trēnī*[101]
5. 341/71 MACCVTRENI (beside **MAQITRENI**)
6. 428/305 MACUTRENI (beside **MAQI MAQITRENI**)
7. 425/297 MACCVTRENI

---

[99]   See ‡27n.; cf. discussion of 76 **TENAS** and 148 **TENAC[I]** in Ziegler, p. 235.
[100]   Cf. LHEB, p. 181. See also Motta, in Szemerényi FS iii, pp. 293–303.
[101]   LHEB, p. 140.

8. 442/346 MACCVDICCL (‡38; beside trace of hypercorrect(?) ogam **Q** on the other side of the stone)
9. 433/313 **MACU**

§31 $k^w > k$, $g^w > g$ in all remaining positions

[31] (A)
1. 361/140 MAQVERIGI
2. 2006 MA[Q]VI COLINE;
3. 336/67a [M]AQ[I?]D[E]C[E]DA (cf. §30)
4. 364/144 QVENVENDANI (*K^wennouindagnī> Cennfhinnán, ‡22)
5. 462/Ok14 QVENATAVCI (< *K^wenno-, ‡25n.)
6. 368/a/150 **MAQI** (reading uncertain?)
7. 426/300 **MAQI**
8. 446/353 **MAQI**
9. 449/384 **MAQI**
10. 489/a/Ok13 **MAQI/MAQVI**
11. 500 **M[A]QI**
12. 409/198/849 **M[A]Q[I]**[102]
13. 501 **MAQ[I]**
14. 504 **MAQI**
15. 439/319 **IG^w[** (possibly with following **E**, ‡42)

[31] 341/71 **MAQITRENI** and 428/305 **MAQI MAQITRENI** must be archaizing/conservative since roman MACCVTRENI and MACUTRENI < *$Mak^wk^w\bar{\imath}$-Trēni occur in the same inscriptions (see (B) below). This casts doubt on the value of the Q(V) spellings in the above as well. So do 502 **]MAQ LEOG[** and 506 **MAQ ?CUGINI** which are post-apocope and must be archaizing. In 423/296 **M[A]Q[I] QAGTE** the **Q** of **QAGTE** may be hypercorrect (see below), which makes the **Q** of **M[A]Q[I]** suspicious (possibly to be read **[M]AQ**, ‡51n). 512 QATTIDONA is obscure (‡‡ 15, 38, and 42).

[31] (B)

1. 326/39 MACCVDECCETI
2. 440/335 MACVDE[h?]ETI
3. 492/Ok59 MACCODECHETI
4. 329/42 MACCVTRENI
5. 341/71 MACCVTRENI (beside **MAQITRENI**)
6. 428/305 MACUTRENI (beside **MAQITRENI**)
7. 425/297 MACCVTRENI

---

[102] The **Q** was read by Macalister and is shown in ECMW, plate 3. Cf. ‡27n. and McManus, *Guide*, p. 67. The editors of the *Corpus* note that the gap for the supposed **A** is unusually wide.

8. 442/346 <u>MACCVDICCL</u>
9. 423/296 **QAGTE** (hypercorrect **Q**, ‡51)
10. 467/Ok24 <u>ULCAGNI/VLCAGNI</u> (assuming < *ulk^w- 'wolf', ‡48)
11. 472/Ok35 <u>VLCAGNI</u> (similarly)
12. 370/157 <u>VLCAGNVS</u> (similarly)
13. 1048/Ok32 <u>QONFAL</u>, if a hypercorrect spelling of OI *Con(u)al* < *Kunoụalos*, which is problematic (§28 above)
14. 403/268/841 <u>MACARITINI</u> (if the same as 230 **MAQI-CARATTINN** and OI *Macc Cáerthinn*, ‡‡ 22n. and 57)
15. 433/313 **MACU**

§32 æ > a; §33 Second palatalization; §34 u > ü etc.

There is no evidence for these in our corpus.

§35 In internal unstressed syllables later liable to syncope, ü, i, and e > ĭ

The only one of these likely to show up orthographically is ü (< u) > ĭ, for example (A) **LUGUNI**[103] might pass through a stage (B) ***LUGINI** or ***LUGENI** on the way to 1068/b <u>LUGNI</u> (OI *Luigni*). In fact, however, only the (A) stage seems to occur:

[35] (A)

1. 318/6 <u>ETTORIGI</u> (cf. 179 (])**ETORIGAS**?) if < *Ianturīgos* (‡‡17, 38 and 59)
2. 361/140 <u>TALORI</u> if < *Talurīks* (‡38)
3. 408/229/848 <u>CATOTIGIRNI</u> if > OI *Caitchern, Catigern*[104]

342/70 **ILVVETO** may stand for /ilüụe(:)θo(:)/, but if normal ogam conventions are observed, the **VV** should represent /ụ/ (‡38).

§36 Third palatalization

There is no inscriptional evidence for this.

§37 ụ' > ị

[37] (A)

1. 399/176 **TOVISACI/TOVISACI** (if > OI *toísech* rather than W. *tywysog* ‡‡ 17, 18, 46 and 84)
2. 342/70 **ILVVETO** < *Ilu-ụe(:)θ-* (‡38)
3. 405/228/845 **GRAVICA** (see §40 below)
4. 461/Ok66 <u>ERCILIVI</u> if the second element is Ir. gen. sg. *līụī* (‡43n.) and not a Latin genitive based on the nominative < *-līụos*. (493/Ok48

---

[103] Ziegler, pp. 198–99.
[104] Uhlich, *Morphologie*, p. 188.

CONBEVI is clearly based on the nominative in view of the lowering /i/ > /e/, §29.)

[37] (B)

1. 396/104 AVITORI if a hypercorrect spelling of *Aiθ(a)ri < *Aitorīx (see ‡17 – with other possibilities)
2. 362/142 AVITTORIGES/AVITORIA (similarly, *mutatis mutandis*)

§38 Apocope

As in the case of the Brittonic names (‡37), one cannot rely on the presence of -VS and -I, or of (feminine) -A (and of course genitive -(A)E), as these may be Latin. This leaves only a few fairly certainly unapocopated forms:

[38] (A)

1. 322/26 CAMVLORIS (with Hibernicizing *-rīs*, ‡14)
2. 321/25]SORIS (cf. §21)
3. 380/84 ICORIGAS/ICORI
4. 2006 CVNORIX (with British -RIX for Ir. *-rīs*, ‡14)
5. 354/126/6 ORDOVS (Hibernicized -VS < British *-ṵiks*, ‡14)
6. 336/67a DECEDA (< *Dekantos*)[105]
7. 342/70 ILVVETO (< *-ous*, ‡38n.)
8. 2002/b TARICORO (? obscure)
9. 358/138 VOTECORIGAS/VOTEPORIGIS
10. 362/142 AVITTORIGES/AVITORIA
11. 368/a/150 DUMELEDONAS
12. 405/228/845 (GRA)VICA (cf. 150 GRAVICAS)[106] or]LICA (‡15n.)
13. 426/300 MUCOI (or MUCOE)[107]
14. 431/308 DOVATUCEAS (or, less likely, DOVATACIS)/DOB(I)TVCI
15. 446/353 MAGLICUNAS/MAGLOCVN(I)
16. 450/390 OGTENAS (or OGTENLO)/HOGTINIS (or HOGTIVIS)
17. 461/Ok66 NONNITA (if < *Nonnitas* ‡15n.)
18. 496 TEBICATO[
19. 500 ROC[A]T[O]S/ROCATI and [AM]BICATOS
20. 503 DOVAIDONA and DROATA or DRUTA
21. 504 BIVAIDONAS
22. 512 QATTIDONA (obscure)

[38] 345/74 GLUVOCA cannot be included as it may have read GLUVOCI, and similarly 428/305 TRENAGUSU may have read TRENAGUSI like its roman-letter TRENEGUSSI. I also exclude readings where the ending is

---

[105] See §30n. above.
[106] Ziegler, p. 186.
[107] Cf. McManus, *Guide*, pp. 119–20. If MUCOE were correct it would show *-ī > ĭ (§22 above).

conjectural (e.g. 378/169). 348/110/27 **TRENALUGOS** is too uncertain a reading to include.

[38] (B)

1. 320/26 <u>CVLIDOR</u> (apparently without -I; possibly Ir. *Cúldor*, ‡‡ 16, 19n., and 37)
2. 327/43 **MOSAC** (obscure, but seemingly apocopated, ‡54n.)
3. 372/160 **BARVALB/BARBALOM** (? OI *Barrbalb*, ‡69)
4. 409/198/849 **ROLACUN** (or **RO[LI]ON**) < ? *Ro-ola-kun-* and possibly **M[A]Q**[108]
5. 430/306 **VICTOR**/VICTOR (cf. ‡37)
6. 442/346 MACCVDICCL
7. 466/Ok23 **MEMOR**/MEMORIA (if = OI *mebuir*)[109]
8. 488/Ok60 **ENABARR/ENABARRI**
9. 502 **MAQ**
10. 506 **MAQ**
11. 1048/Ok32 QONFAL (but -I has also been read, ‡26n.)
12. 1068/b MALBREN (‡48)
13. 403/268/841 MACARITINI (if = *MAC CARITINI, cf. §31 above)
14. 994/125/22 CAROTINN

[38] I do not include 2029/p.39i <u>CVNIIAC</u> as a final -I may well be missing,[110] nor 439/319 **INGEN**, a dubious reading (‡37). Apart from <u>MACCVDICCL</u> I do not include names such as <u>MACCV-TRENI</u> since it is not clear, despite Jackson,[111] that the -V reflects /u̯/ in a post-apocope /k'u̯'/ < /kʷi:/ rather than the rounding at §30 of /ĭ/ < /ĭ/ < /i:/. Indeed, on the present chronology one would have expected such a /u̯/ to have been palatalized and have become /i̯/ at §37.

§39 Loss before r/ll/n of γ (cf. ‡48 on most of these forms – there are no examples of /δ/), also of voiceless fricatives

[39] (A)

1. 2027 <u>ERCAGNI</u> (> OI *Erccán*)
2. 353/127/7 **MAGLAGNI** (= OI *Málán* or *Máelán*, beside **TRENACCATLO/TRENACATVS**, see (B) below)

---

[108] Ziegler, p. 85; Macalister, apud Anon., *AC*, 7th ser. 8 (1928), 377, compares a (hypothetical) Ir. *Rolchu*. While **M[A]Q[I]** is possible, note that Macalister takes the **I** to be part of the following name.

[109] LHEB, p. 141; but cf. ‡27n. on OB *memor*.

[110] See above, Ch. 3, p. 253.

[111] LHEB, pp. 140–41. See n. 43 above. The non-apocope of the -V in <u>MACCV-DICCL</u> could be due to a fairly close compounding of the two elements along the lines discussed by Garrett, *Ériu*, 50 (1999), 139–60. Macalister's restoration MACCVDICCL[I] is conjectural (CIIC ii, p. 200) and unsupported by Lhuyd's sketches.

3. 2032 ?]CAMAGLI
4. 357/136 CORBAGNI (> *Corbbán*)
5. 362/142 **CUNIGNI/CVNIGNI**
6. 369/153 CVRCAGNVS (> OI *Corcán*)
7. 370/157 VLCAGNVS (> OI *Olcán*) and SENOMAGLI[112]
8. 372/160 **[B]RO[CAGNI]/BROCAGNI** (> *Broccán*), also perhaps the dubious **VUGLOB**
9. 374/172 CVNEGNI
10. 376/174 ERCAGNI (> *Erccán*)
11. 1028/214/850 VENDVMAGLI (if Ir. *Finn + mál*)
12. 2029/p.39i MAGLORI
13. 2030/p.39ii MAGL(I)
14. 425/297 CATOMAG[LI] (beside MACCVTRE[NI], see (B) below)
15. 422/298 **VENDOGNI/VENDAGNI** (> *Finnán*) and HOCIDEGNI
16. 426/300 **NETTASAGRU** or **NETTASAGRI** (> *Nad Sáir*)
17. 427/a/301 **MAGL[IA]** or **MAGL[I]**
18. 432/312 **DOVAGNI/DOBAGNI** (> *Dubán*)
19. 434/314 COIMAGNI (> *Cóemán*)
20. 439/319 **ASEGNI** or **SEGNI** (dubious)[113]
21. 441/345 CVRCAGNI (> *Corcán*)
22. 446/353 **MAGLICUNAS/MAGLOCVN(I)** or MAGLOCVVI
23. 447/369 NEMAGLI
24. 457/Ok18 MERCAGNI (> *Mercán*) or MESCAGNI (> **Mescán*)
25. 467/Ok24 **VLCAGNI/ULCAGNI** (> *Olcán*)
26. 472/Ok35 VLCAGNI
27. 474/Ok17]MAGLI
28. 478/Ok48 BROCAGNI (> *Broccán*)
29. 487/Ok10 DRVSTAGNI (in the unlikely event that this is the correct reading)
30. 501 **CUNAMAGLI**

[39] In some of the above it is very likely that the writing of G is conservative (although there is no evidence such as hypercorrect spellings to indicate that it is ever merely an orthographic device to denote a long vowel). It is particularly significant that 449/384 **SAGRAGNI** (cf. OI *Sárán*) is accompanied by roman-letter SAGRANI, suggesting that the ogam **GN** is old-fashioned – also perhaps that /γr/ lasted longer than /γn/, although the variation may instead be due to the differing stress in the two syllables (cf. 489/b/Ok13 SAGRANVI, ‡‡ 48 and 58).[114] Another significant form is 328/44]RVGNIAT(I)O; if this is OI *Brón-* or *Drón-*, note that VENDONI < **Windognī* appears in the same inscription, with loss of /γ/

---

[112] Probably Irish according to LHEB, p. 518, n. 1.
[113] See ‡48 (p. 167).
[114] See ‡48 (p. 168).

shown (if this etymology is correct). All these inscriptions are listed under (B) only.

[39] (B)

1. 398/106 I̲A̲C̲O̲N̲V̲S̲ (if < *Esokognos, parallel to 48 **IAQINI** < *Esokignos)[115]
2. 475/Ok47 I̲A̲C̲O̲N̲I̲V̲S̲ (dubious reading)
3. 328/44 V̲E̲N̲D̲O̲N̲I̲ (‡‡ 22 and 48) (beside ?]R̲V̲G̲N̲I̲A̲T̲(̲I̲)̲O̲, see (A) above)
4. 364/144 Q̲V̲E̲N̲V̲E̲N̲D̲A̲N̲I̲ (> Cennfhinnán)
5. 429/307 V̲E̲N̲D̲O̲N̲I̲
6. 449/384 S̲A̲G̲R̲A̲N̲I̲ (beside **SAGRAGNI**, see above)
7. 460/Ok75 V̲R̲O̲C̲H̲A̲N̲I̲ (> Fróechán)
8. 489/b/Ok13 S̲A̲G̲R̲A̲N̲V̲I̲ (see above)
9. 506 **CUGINI** (if = *Cúcín, a form parallel to Cúcán – but the reading is doubtful)[116]
10. 507 **CRON[A]N[** (> Crónán)
11. 511/Scot.10 C̲O̲N̲I̲N̲I̲E̲ (if = OI Coinín, §29 above)

[39] Examples with lost voiceless fricatives:[117]

12. 488/Ok60 **ENABARR/ENABARRI** (if Én- < *(p)etno-)
13. 1068/b M̲A̲L̲B̲R̲E̲N̲ (if *Máel-brén < *brekn-, ‡48)

[39] Also, with TREN- (only relevant if it *is* the same as OI trén):

14. 353/127/7 **TRENACCATLO/TRENACATVS** (beside M̲A̲G̲L̲A̲G̲N̲I̲, see (A) above);
15. 329/42 M̲A̲C̲C̲V̲T̲R̲E̲N̲I̲
16. 341/71 **MAQITRENI/MACCVTRENI**
17. 425/297 M̲A̲C̲C̲V̲T̲R̲E̲[̲N̲I̲]̲ (beside C̲A̲T̲O̲M̲A̲G̲[̲L̲I̲]̲, see (A) above)
18. 428/305 **TRENAGUSO** (or **-O** or **-I**) / T̲R̲E̲N̲E̲G̲U̲S̲S̲I̲ and **MAQITRENI/MACUTRENI**.

There is also 348/a/110/27 **TRENALUGOS**, but this is a dubious reading.

---

[115] Ziegler, p. 186. The development of -ón rather than -án (via *-agnas) in such cases is a problem, but one arguably already found in VENDONI etc.; see above, ‡48 (pp. 163 and 166).

[116] Ziegler, p. 157; ‡48n. **COGELI** (= Coicéle) and **CAGI(-)** have also been read, ‡25n.

[117] Cf. above, ‡48, and De Bernardo Stempel, NWÄI, p. 258 (deriving trén < *treg(s)no- but implying that this passed via *trek(s)no- to *trekno-, as she kindly confirmed orally). On the problem of TREN- names see below, p. 330.

§40 Dissimilation

No examples appear in the corpus. A distinct type of dissimilation may occur in 405/228/845 **(GRA)VICA** (cf. 150 **GRAVICAS**) if this is < **GRAVA-VIKAS*.[118]

§41 Syncope

[41] (A)

1. 318/6 ETTORIGI
2. 319/9 CVNOGVS(I) (> OI *Congus*)
3. 321/25]SORIS (*if* < **Vassorīks* or similar)
4. 320/26 CVLIDOR(I) (*if* > **Cúldor*, also ORVVITE if this should be read ORINITE = *Órnait* (‡15), although then the first I could well be epenthetic)
5. 322/27 CAMVLORIS (*Camulorīx* hibernicized, ‡14n.)
6. 325/33 BIVATIGI or BIVATIS(I) if = **Biwatii̯i* or similar (see §16 above)
7. 2000 DEVORIGI
8. 380/84 **ICORIGAS/ICORI** (> *Echrí* ?)[119]
9. 388/94 DERVORI
10. 396/104 AVITORI
11. 399/176 **TOVISACI/TOVISACI** and **SIBILINI/SIMILINI**
12. 2006 CVNORIX
13. 354/126/6 CORBALENGI (> OI *Corbleng*)
14. 353/127/7 **TRENACCATLO/TRENACATVS**
15. 327/43 DVNOCATI (if > OI *Dúnchad*)
16. 328/44]RVGNIAT(I)O
17. 330/66 CATIRI (if > OI *Caithrí*)
18. 342/70 **CUNACENNIVI** or **CUNACENNI [A]VI/CVNOCENNI**
19. 341/71 **SALICIDUNI/SALICIDVNI** or SALIGIDVNI
20. 2002/b **TARICORO**
21. 2032]CAMAGLI
22. 358/138 **VOTECORIGAS/**VOTEPORIGIS
23. 361/140 TALORI
24. 362/142 **INIGENA** and **AVITTORIGES/AVITORIA**
25. 366/148 ECHADI (> OI *Echde*)[120]
26. 368/a/150 **DUMELEDONAS** (< **Du-mel-aidonas*)[121]
27. 368/b/150 BARRIVENDI and VENDVBARI (if > OI *Bairrfhind* and *Findbairr*)

---

[118] Ziegler, p. 186.
[119] Cf. ibid., p. 187.
[120] Cf. ibid., p. 177.
[121] Cf. ibid., p. 175.

28. 370/157 <u>SENOMAGLI</u>
29. 375/166 <u>TOTAVALI</u> (> OI *Túathal*)
30. 378/169 **BODDIBEVVA(S)** or **BODDIBABEVE/BODIBEVE** (> *Búaidbéo*);[122]
31. 379/170 <u>CATVRVG(I)</u>
32. 409/198/849 **ROLACUN** (if not **ROLION**) (if < *Ro-ola-kun-*, §38 above)
33. 1028/214/850 <u>VENDVMAGLI</u>
34. 408/229/848 <u>CATOTIGERNI</u> (if > OI *Caitchern, Catigern*)[123]
35. 1022/240/928 <u>DOBITAUCI</u> (dubious reading)
36. 403/268/841 <u>MACARITINI</u> (if = 230 **MAQI-CARATTINN** > *Macc Cáerthinn*, see §31 above)
37. 2029/p.39i <u>MAGLORI</u>, <u>CVNIIAC[I?]</u>, <u>ERECOR[I?]</u>
38. 425/297 <u>CATOMAGLI</u>
39. 422/298 <u>HOCIDEGNI</u> (dubious reading)
40. 424/299 <u>EVALENGI</u> (if correct reading, > OI *Éolang*)
41. 428/305 **TRENAGUSU** (or **-O** or **-I**)/**TRENEGUSSI** (> OI *Tréngusso*)
42. 431/308 **DOVATUCEAS** or **DOVATACIS/DOBITVCI** or <u>DOBTVCI</u>; and <u>EVOLENGI</u> (assuming that DOBTVCI is not the right reading, ‡38n.)
43. 433/313 **ANDAGELLI/ANDAGELLI** (> OI *Indgall*)
44. 442/346 <u>CATICVVS</u> (> *Cathchú* ?, ‡54)
45. 435/315 <u>CLVTORIGI</u> (if = OI *Clothrí*)
46. 436/316 <u>EUOLENGGI</u> (> *Éolang*) and <u>LITOGENI</u> (> *Líthgen*)
47. 441/345 <u>ANDAGELLI</u> (> *Indgall*)
48. 446/353 **MAGLICUNAS/MAGLOCVN(I)** and **CLUTAR[IGAS]/** <u>CLVTORI</u>
49. 449/384 **CUNATAMI/CVNOTAMI**
50. 452/400 <u>VALAVI</u> or <u>VALAVITIVI</u> (> *Fáelbe* or *Fá(i)lbe*, ‡48)
51. 457/Ok18 <u>DVNOCATI</u>
52. 458/Ok9 <u>RANOCORI</u> or <u>NANOCORI</u>
53. 461/Ok66 <u>ERCILIVI</u> (if not <u>ERCILI</u>) and <u>ERCILINGI</u> or <u>ERCILINCI</u>
54. 462/Ok14 <u>QVENATAVCI</u>[124]
55. 468/Ok31 <u>CVNOVALI</u> (> OI *Con(u)al*)
56. 488/Ok60 <u>ENABARRI/**ENABARR**</u> (but see §43)
57. 496 **TEBICATO[**

---

[122] Ibid., p. 139. In the other name in this inscription, **BIVVAIDONA(S)**/BIVADI (OI *Béoáed*), syncope of the diphthong is not predictable; cf. Ziegler, pp. 45, 138, and 197, and McManus, *Guide*, p. 96, on OI *Lug(u)a(e)don*. The same applies to 503 **DOVAIDONA** and 504 **BIVAIDONAS**. Ziegler, p. 137, suggests that BIVADI corresponds to OI *béodae* 'living'; if this were so we might like to restore **BIVVA[DI]** rather than **BIVVA[IDONA(S)]** or similar in the ogam, but that seems to be ruled out by the presence of vowel notches after the **A**.

[123] Uhlich, *Morphologie*, p. 188.

[124] Although <u>DINVI</u>, if < *Dēnovik-* (‡‡ 16, 27, 38, and 58), would have syncope.

58. 500 **AMBICATOS**/AMMECATI
59. 501 **CUNAMAGLI**
60. 504 **CUNAVALI** (> OI *Conual*)
61. 512 **QATTIDONA**
62. 520/Scot.5 **BARROVADI**
63. 1068/a **LAGUBERI**
64. 1202/Ok2 **EVOCATI** (or EVOCALI) (cf. 19 **IVACATTOS** > *Éochaid*)
65. 994/125/22 **CAROTINN** (but see §43)

[41] I omit 348/110/27 **TRENALUGOS** (> OI *Trénlogo*), as the reading is dubious.

[41] (B)

1. 324/34 **CONBARRVS**
2. 993/124/18 **MADOMNUAC(O)** = *Mo Domnóc* (if based on Latin *Dominus*, *Dominicus* rather than Celtic **dumno-*, cf. ‡18n.)[125]
3. 1038/365 **MAIL DOMNA[C** = *Máel Domnaig* (similarly, cf. ‡38)
4. 364/144 **QVENVENDANI** (> *Cennfhinnán*) and **BARCVNI** (‡‡ 22, 26, and 38)
5. 372/160 **BARVALB/BARBALOM** (< *? *Barrobalvos* , ‡69)
6. 471/Ok39 **CLOTUALI** (if = **Cloth(u)al*, see §29 above)
7. 493/Ok58 **CONBEVI**
8. 1048/Ok32 **QONFAL** (if = OI *Con(u)al*, cf. §28)
9. 1068/b **LUGNI** (> OI *Luigni*)

[41] I omit four problem cases. First, in 427/a/301, **DUBR[ACUNAS]** would not have syncope, but **DUBAR[CUNAS]** would have syncope and epenthesis; unfortunately the reading is disputed (‡‡ 38n. and 69; cf. §43 below). Secondly, in 454/402, **DENCVI** (if > **Díanchú*) does have syncope, unlike **CVNIOVENDE**, but an alternative reading is **DENOVI** (< **Dēnouiks*) without syncope (‡‡18 and 27). Thirdly, the reading of 1057/Ok54 **ERO-CAVI** is dubious, but if this is OI *Erccba* (‡‡ 38 and 57n.), the epenthesis between the R and C might suggest that syncope had occurred, despite the writing of the composition vowel A; this is unlikely to be the case, however, since epenthetic and composition vowels appear side by side in what is probably the same stem **erko-* in 84 **ERACOBI** and **ERAQETAI** and in 2029/p.39i ERECOR[?I] (see ‡‡ 57n. and 69). Fourthly, 450/390 **OGTENLO** or **OGTENAS/HOGTIVIS** or **HOGTINIS** will show syncope if segmented **OG-TEN-** etc., but that is debatable (see ‡27n.).

[125] But note in any case that *Dom(i)nus*, *Dom(i)nicus* were often syncopated already in Christian Latin: Kajanto, pp. 135 and 362.

§42 Unstressed eu > u

There are no examples in the corpus.

§43 Epenthesis

Possible examples are:

320/26 ORVVITE if read ORINITE = *Órnait* (‡15)
372/160 **BARVALB/BARBALOM** (if: OI *balb*, ‡69)
427/a/301 **DUBAR[CUNAS]** (but see §41 above; and note that **DUBAR[ACUNAS]** is also possible, with epenthesis but without syncope, as in 84 **ERACOBI**)
2029/p.39i ERECOR[I] (see ‡‡ 57n. and 69)
1057/Ok54 EROCAVI (see §41 above)

[43] 994/125/22 FILIUS CAROTINN, in HIROIDIL FILIUS CAROTINN, if it is the Irish patronymic *Macc Cáerthinn* (cf. 40 **MAQI- CAIRATINI**, 230 **MAQI-CARATTINN**, *Filius Cairtin* (Book of Armagh) in Ireland, and possibly 403/268/841 MACARITINI in Wales),[126] has an unexpected composition vowel which it is tempting to explain as an epenthetic vowel introduced by a Welsh scribe, like the third I of HIROIDIL (cf. ‡69). In this case, CAROTINN should not have been listed as an example of a pre-syncope form under §41. Compare also Schrijver's suggestion that the second vowel of 488/Ok60 **ENABARRI/ENABARR** is epenthetic and not the old composition vowel.[127]

[43] Later sound changes need not be dealt with systematically, as very few inscriptions seem to show them. Note, however, that 375/166 DOTHORANTI may show the late seventh-century or later *do* (rather than *to*) form of the second person singular possessive pronoun (see ‡42n.), and that 993/124/18 MADOMNUACO seems to show late vocalism (/ə/) in the first person (OI *mo*) as well as a possible reflection of the Old Irish graph *úa* which would not be expected before the late seventh century (see ‡18 and n. 308). Finally, 355/128/8 SILBANDVS (§20), if an Irish form of *Silvanus*, would seem to show Middle Irish *nd*.[128]

---

126 Ziegler, p. 144. Cf. ‡57.
127 Schrijver, *Ériu*, 48 (1997), 223, n. 7. Cf. ‡48n. For svarabhakti in ogam see MacNeill, *PRIA*, 39 C (1931), 37–40.
128 This is incompatible with the alleged early epigraphic date, however, which is in favour of regarding it as a British form of *Silvanus, Silbanus*: ‡‡ 18 and 22.

5

IRISH CHRONOLOGY

5.1 Construction of Table 5.1

Data for the more secure items cited in the preceding chapter (the numbered ones under A and B in each §) are summarized in Table 5.1. This differs from the similar table in the 'Brittonic Chronology' chapter in that I have included sound changes for which only the stage A is recorded, or only the stage B.[1] For some inscriptions, relevant sound changes neither occur nor fail to occur (e.g. 351/115/2 DALLVS DVMELVS). I have not entered any data for 348/a/110/27 **TRENALUGOS**, since this reading by Macalister is so extremely dubious. At the right I have listed all the forms present (or claimed to be present) in the inscriptions that have been included in my Index, irrespective of whether or not they are relevant to the Irish phonology.

---

[1] One reason for doing this is that the data for periodizing the Irish would otherwise be too scanty. Another is that in the Brittonic chapters, but not here (see below), I was attempting to refine the order of the sound changes, and for this contrasting A and B stages were needed.

Table 5.1 Irish sound changes in the inscriptions

col. 1	2	3	4	5	6	7	8	9	10	11	12	13	14	15	Index entries
§§	19	20	21	22	25	28	29	30	31	35	37	38	39	41	
318/6									A					A	ETTORIGI
319/9							A							A	CVNOGVS(I)
320/26												B		A	CVLIDOR(I) ORVVITE SECVNDI
321/25		A										A		A	ISORIS
322/27		A										A		A	CAMVLORIS HOI
324/34						B								B	CONBARRVS CONBVRRI
325/33							A							A	JIVA JINA BIVATIGIrni? BIVATISI BIVOTIS VASSO PAVLINI ANDO COGNATIONE AVDO
326/39							B	B¡							MACCVDECCETI
327/43												B		A	**TURPILI / TVRPILLI** **MOSAC** **TRILLVNI** or **TRALLONI /** TRILVNI PVVERI DVNOCATI
328/44						B							B	A	RVGNIATIO VENDONI
329/42							B	B¡					B		CANNTIANI PATER MACCVTRENI
330/66														A	JTIRI TIBE[ ]VS CATIRI
334/54															CATACVS TEGERNACVS
336/67a		B						A¡		A					**MAQI DECEDA**
341/71							B	B¡					B	A	**MAQITRENI** MACCVTRENI **SALICIDVNI /** SALICIDVNI or SALIGIDVNI
342/70	B	B			A						A	A		A	**CUNACENNIVI** or **CUNACENNI [A]VI** CVNOCENNI **ILVVETO** CVNOGENI
344/73		A													DERVACI IVSTI
345/74															**GLVVOCA** or **GLVVOCI**
348/a/110/27															**TRENALVGOS**
351/115/2															DALLVS DVMELVS
353/127/7												B A / A	A / A	**TRENACCATLO /** TRENACATVS MAGLAGNI
354/126/6		A										A		A	CORBALENGI ORDOVS
355/128/8		B													SILBANDVS BANDVS

Table 5.1 *contd.*

col. 1	2	3	4	5	6	7	8	9	10	11	12	13	14	15	Index entries
§§	19	20	21	22	25	28	29	30	31	35	37	38	39	41	
357/136														A	CORBAGNI / ALI{
358/138		A			B	A				A				A	MEMORIA **VOTECORIGAS** VOTEPORIGIS PROTICTORIS
		b			B	A				A				A	
361/140			B				A	A	A					A	TALORI ADVENTI MAQVERIGI
362/142	B	A			B				B	A	A			A	**INGENA** **CUNIGNI** / CVNIGNI **AVITTORIGES** / AVITORIA
	B	*b*			B				B	A	A			A	
364/144					A		A					B	B		**QVENVENDANI** BARCVNI
					b		*b*					B	B		
366/148				B										A	ECHADI ITOCVS CROCUSI
368/a/150		A				A	A			A				A	**DUMELEDONAS** **MAQI**
368/b/150					B									A	BARRIVENDI VENDVBARI
369/153					B	A				A				A	CVRCAGNVS IVRIVI
370/157					A	B				A	A			A	VLCAGNVS SENOMAGLI
					A	*a*				A	A			A	
372/160	B								B	A	B			B	**DECCAIBAR** or **DECCAIBARVALB** **VUGLOB** DECABARBALOM **BROCAGNI** / BROCAGNI DISI
	B								B	*b*	B			B	
374/172					B									A	CVNEGNI
375/166														A	TOTAVALI DOTHORANTI
376/174														A	VENNISETLI ERCAGNI
378/169			B		B									A	**BIVVAIDONAS** **BODDIBEVVAS** or **BODDIBABEVE** BIVADI BODIBEVE
379/170														A	CATVRVGI LOVERNACI
380/84		A			A					A				A	**ICORIGAS** / ICORI POTENTINI
386/92															MELI MEDICI MARTINI
388/94	A													A	DERVORI
391/78															SENACVS
396/104										B				A	AVITORI TEPORE IVSTINI
398/106	B												B		IACONVS MINI

Table 5.1 *contd.*

col. 1	2/19	3/20	4/21	5/22	6/25	7/28	8/29	9/30	10/31	11/35	12/37	13/38	14/39	15/41	Index entries
399/176									A					A	**SIBILINI** / SIMILINI / **TOVISACI** / TOVISACI
	A					A	B				B			A	
403/268/841	*b*					*b*	B				B			A	**MACARITINI** / CARITINI / BERICCI / BERIACI
404/270/843															**TEGEI**-/TEGERNACUS / MARTI
405/228/845		B				A			A	A					**GRAVICA** or]**VICA** /]LICA
408/229/848							A							A	**BODVOCI** / CATOTIGERNI / ETERNALI / VEDOMAVI or / VEDOMALI / PRONEPVS
					B	A					B			A	
409/198/849					B	*b*					B			A	**POPIAS** / **PAMPES** / **ROLION** or / **ROLACUN** / **LLENA** / **ILLUNA** / **M[A]Q[I]** / PVMPEIVS / CARANTORIVS
415/278															IN[G]ENVI / INT[AE]NVI / IARRI[/ TARRONERIS
422/298					B								A	A	**VENDOGNI** / VENDAGNI / HOCIDEGNI
423/296			B			B									**QAGTE**
424/299					B									A	BRIACI / GLVVOCCI / EVALENGI ?
					B	B							A	A/B	
425/297					B	B							A	A	MACCVTRENI / CATOMAGLI
426/300					A	A	A						A	A	**NETTASAGRU** or / **NETTASAGRI** / **MUCOE** or **MUCOI** / **BRECI** / **BRIACI** / **SLECI** / **MAQI**
427/a/301					A									A	**MAGL[IA]** or / **MAGL[I]** / **DUBRACUNAS** / **DUBARCUNAS**
					A	B	B					B	A		
428/305					*b*	B	B					B	A		**TRENAGUSU** or -O / or -**I** / TRENEGUSSI / **MAQITRENI** / MACUTRENI
429/307					B							B			SOLINI / VENDONI
430/306											B				**ETTERNI** / ETTERNI / **VICTOR** / VICTOR

Table 5.1 *contd.*

col. 1	2	3	4	5	6	7	8	9	10	11	12	13	14	15	Index entries
§§	19	20	21	22	25	28	29	30	31	35	37	38	39	41	
			A				B						A	A	
431/308			*b*				B						A	A	DOVATUCEAS DOVATACIS DOBITVCI DOBTVCI EVOLENGI
432/312							B							A	DOVAGNI DOBAGNI TIGERNACI
				A			B	B						A	
433/313				*b*			B	B						A	ANDAGELLI / ANDAGELLI CAVETI / CAVETI MACU
434/314														A	COIMAGNI CAVETI
435/315							A							A	CLVTORIGI PAVLINI MARINI LATIO
436/316							B							A	EUOLENGGI LITOGENI
438/320															TAVUSI
439/319								A						A	EFESSANGI ASEGNI INGEN SANGKTA SEGNI IG"I
440/335							B	B							MACVDECETI MACVDEBETI MACVDEHETI EOROCAN EONOCAN EOPOCAN
				A	B	A							A	A	
441/345				*b*	B	A							A	A	CVRCAGNI ANDAGELLI
442/346							B	B				B		A	MACCVDICCL CATICVVS
445/354															VITALIANI / VITALIANI EMERETO
446/353		A					A	A	A				A	A	A	MAGLICUNAS / MAGLOCVNI MAGLOCVVI CLUTARI or CLUTARI[GAS] CLVTORI MAQI
447/369		B					A							A	CVNISCVS CVNIGCVS NEMAGLI or NEMASLI
448/370							A								RINACI PINACI NOMENA
							A	A	A				B	A	
449/384								*b*	*b*				B		SAGRAGNI SAGRANI CUNATAMI CVNOTAMI MAQI

Table 5.1 *contd.*

col. 1	2	3	4	5	6	7	8	9	10	11	12	13	14	15	Index entries
§§	19	20	21	22	25	28	29	30	31	35	37	38	39	41	
450/390													A		OGTENLO OGTENAS HOGTIVIS or HOGTINIS DEMETI
451/401															TVNCCETACE VXSOR DAARI
452/400													A		PAANI VALAVI or VALAVITIVI
453/399															MELI NESI
454/402				A											EVALI DENCVI DENOVI CVNIOVENDE
455/403	B														CAMVLLORIGI FANNVCI
456/404															GENDILI / GENDILI
457/Ok18													A	A	DVNOCATI MERCAGNI MESCAGNI
458/Ok9														A	RANOCORI NANOCORI MESGI or MESCI
460/Ok75														B	VAILATHI VROCHANI
	A	B			A						A	A		A	
461/Ok66	*b*	B			A						A	A		A	NONNITA ERCILIVI or ERCILI RICATI VIRICATI TRIS ERCILINGI ERCILNCI
462/Ok14							A_1							A	QVENATAVCI DINVI
466/Ok23												B			INGENVI or INCENVI **IGENAVI** MEMORIA **MEMOR**
					A		B					A			
467/Ok24					A		*a*					A			VLCAGNI / ULCAGNI
468/Ok31					A									A	RIALOBRANI CVNOVALI
471/Ok39						B								B	CLOTUALI MOBRATTI
					A		B					A			
472/Ok35					A		*a*					A			VLCAGNI SEVERI
474/Ok17														A	CRVARIGI RVANI]MAGLI
475/Ok47														B	IACONIVS ADO
478/Ok48														A	BROCAGNI NADOTTI RADOTTI
479/Ok16			B_1		A										CVNAIDE CVNATDO
482/Ok71	A				A										NEMIANVS NEMAVS]TRC

Table 5.1 *contd.*

col. 1	2/19	3/20	4/21	5/22	6/25	7/28	8/29	9/30	10/31	11/35	12/37	13/38	14/39	15/41	Index entries
485/Ok68	A														JTHI COLINI JCOBI COGI
487/Ok10							A							A	CIRISINVS DRUSTANUS CERVSIVS DRVSTAVS CIRUSIUS DRVSTAGNI CIRVSINIVS SIRVSIVS CVNOMORI
488/Ok60												B	B	A	DOBVNNI FABRI ENABARRI / ENABARR
489/a/Ok13		B					A	A							SVAQQVCI QICI FANONI RINI MAQI MAQVI
489/b/Ok13													B		SAGRANVI
492/Ok59							B	B							SABINI MACCODECHETI
493/Ok58			B			B								B	NEPRANI CONBEVI
494/Ok79							B								GOREVS
496		A								A				A	EBICATO[S] TEBICATO[
500		A		A			A	A		A				A	AMMECATI ROCATI /ROC[A]T[O]S EBICATOS AMBICATOS MAQI
501							A	A					A	A	CUNAMAGLI MAQI
502											B				MAQ LEOG
503			B			B				A					DOVAIDONA DROATA DRUTA
504		A				A	A	A		A				A	BIVAIDONAS MAQI CUNAVALI
506											B	B			VICULA CUGINI COGELI MAQ
507													B		CRONAN[JACRON
510/Scot.13															VETTA VICTI VICTRICIS F or FILI
511/Scot.10						B								B	CONINIE TVRTIRIE ERTIRIE
512											A			A	QATTIDONA
520/Scot.5														A	LATINVS FECERVTN BARROVADI
990/108/1															TIGEIRNI or TIGERNI

Table 5.1 *contd.*

col. 1	2	3	4	5	6	7	8	9	10	11	12	13	14	15	Index entries
§§	19	20	21	22	25	28	29	30	31	35	37	38	39	41	
993/124/18														B	DITOC MADOMNUACO OCCON UON AON ASAITGEN ITGEN ASA
994/125/22												B	A		HIROIDIL CAROTINN
1006/197/842		B	B												TEFROIHI TESROIHI NEFROIHI REFSOIHI REFSDIHI
1022/240/928														A	DOBITAUCI PROPARAUIT GREFIUM COISTO SPERITUS
1028/214/850						B							A	A	VENDVMAGLI
1038/365														B	MAIL DOMNAC MEIL DOMNAC MAL DOMNAC
1048/Ok32					B	B	B					B		B	GVENNCREST HADNOBVIS QONFAL(I) or QONFILI VIR (G)VENNORCIT
1057/Ok54															EROCAVI INRI IRCAS
1068/a														A	**LAGUBERI**
1068/b												B	B	B	LUGNI HIPIA NIPIA DIPRUI CONDILICI MALBREN BRENLIER BREDLIEN
1202/Ok2						B								A	EVOCATI EVOCALI
1206/Ok4						B									DOVITHI DOCIDCI RIVGDOCI RIVSDOCI
1210/Ok5															VALCI VEITANVS V[ ]AIVS VECCAIUS
1403/Ok25															IIGERNI TIGERNI
1404/Ok30															CAVUDI or CAVVDI CIVILI
2000														A	DEVORIGI
2002/b													A	A	**TARICORO**
	A		A	B		B	A	A	A				A	A	
2006	*b*		*b*	B		B	A	A	A				A	A	CVNORIX MAQVI COLINE MACVS
2007/10															MAILIS(I)
2019															RIGELLA TVNCCE[
2027														A	ERCAGNI
2029/p.39i								A					A	A	ERECOR MAGLORI CVNIIAC

Table 5.1 *contd.*

col. 1	2	3	4	5	6	7	8	9	1 0	1 1	1 2	1 3	1 4	1 5	Index entries
§§	1 9	2 0	2 1	2 2	2 5	2 8	2 9	3 0	3 1	3 5	3 7	3 8	3 9	4 1	
2030/p.39ii														A	MAGLI MATIM JINMIBERI
2032													A	A	ICAMAGLI NIMNI(?)

5.2 Problems in Table 5.1

Since the inscriptions of Ireland have not been examined, it is obviously inappropriate to seek to reorder the sound changes on the basis of this limited sample of possible Irish names from Britain. However, the following comments can be made on the eighteen boxed problem cases in Table 5.1 where 'A' occurs before 'B'.

In 353/127/7 the problem under §39 is that MAGLAGNI shows retained voiced velars (= A) whereas TRENACATVS and TRENACCATLO (probably a scribal error for TRENACCATO)[2] seems to show a lost voiceless velar (= B), if the first element is Irish *trén* and this derives from **trekno-* < **treks-no-*. A possible way round this would be to suppose that voiceless velars were lost before /n/ etc. earlier than the voiced ones were (the opposite of the order contemplated by McCone in TRC).[3] It is certainly striking that, whereas medial combinations like **GR** and **GN** are common in the ogam corpus, there are no relevant and certain examples of medial **CN**, **CL**, **CR**, **TN**, **TL**, and **TR**.[4] An alternative approach is to separate TREN- from *trén*; here McManus makes the valuable observation that the diphthongization to *ia* in OI *(Úa) Trianlugo* implies that 120 **TTRENALUGOS** does not have *é* by compensatory lengthening since this *é* was not subject to diphthongization.[5] Tentatively I regard 353/127/7 **TREN-** as somehow an exception to §39 and retain only 'A' in this column. The same probably applies to 425/297 MACCVTRE[NI] beside CATOMAG[LI], which is treated similarly by retaining only the 'A', although another possibility in

---

2 ‡‡ 48n. and 69; Ziegler, pp. 23 and 237 and n. 382.

3 See Ch. 4, n. 53 above. It would be phonetically natural for the voiceless spirant to be lost first; on the other hand, the voiced ones were of longer standing (cf. §§ 2 and 11) and had had longer to weaken, so to speak.

4 29 **DUCR[I/E]DDA** and 227 **VECR[EC]** are irrelevant (Ziegler, pp. 174 and 246), and 62 **DOCRANORI** was doubted by Macalister himself and is not mentioned by Ziegler and McManus. They also omit 238 **JQNETN[.]** The reading 223 **VINNAGITLEAT** is not accepted by Ziegler (pp. 244–45), and, finally, 353/127/7 **TRENACCATLO** is probably a scribal error, as noted above.

5 McManus, *Guide*, pp. 103, 107, 177, nn. 12–13, and 179, n. 35 (contrast Ziegler, p. 117). Nominative *Trianlug* is cited without reference by MacNeill, *PRIA*, 27 C (1909), 361; for further documentation see Grosjean, *Celtica*, 5 (1960), 45–51. British *Trenus* and MW *Cyndrwyn* may be related; cf. ‡48 n. 1055.

this case might be to regard CATOMAG[LI] as Welsh (i.e. with the velar being retained longer in Welsh than in Irish). All this means that 329/42 MACCVTRENI, 341/71 **MAQITRENI/MACCVTRENI**, 428/305 **TRENAGUS(U)/TRENEGUSSI**, and **MAQITRENI/MACUTRENI** are all dubious evidence, which I indicate by underlining the 'B' under §39 in each case.

The problem in 358/138 is either the 'A' under §21, due to the preservation of -S in **VOTECORIGAS**, or the 'B' under §28, due to the delabialization of $C < *k^w$. Since innovations are more significant that conservations,[6] I assume that the -S is an archaism, perhaps influenced by the (semi-Latinized?) British equivalent VOTEPORIGIS, or based on preservations in sandhi (e.g. before ***AVI**?), and accordingly change the A under §21 to ***b.*** The same applies both to 362/142 **AVITTORIGES/AVITORIA**, which shows 'A' under §21 but 'B's under §§29 and 37, and also to 431/308 **D[OV[A]TUCEAS** (or -**TACIS**)/DOB(I)TVCI, which shows 'A' under §21 but 'B' under §29; in both cases I change the 'A' under §21 to ***b***. All this in turn casts doubt on all the other 'A's under §21 that are due to retained -S in genitives: 368/a/150 **DUMELEDONAS**; 380/84 **ICORIGAS/ICORI**; 446/353 **MAGLICUNAS/MAGLOCVNI** (or -**CVVI**); 496 **TEBICATOS**; 500 **[AM[B[I]CATOS**/AMMECATI and **ROCATOS/ROCATI**; 504 **BIVAIDONAS**. I indicate the uncertainty by underlining the 'A' in these cases. I allow the 'A' under 322/27, for example, to stand, however, on the grounds that CAMVLORIS is a Hibernicization of nominative *Camulorīx* presumably at a time when Ir. -S < *-gs was still current.

The problem shared by 364/144 QVENVENDANI and 409/198/849 M[A[Q[I] or **MAQ** is the retained labiovelar (§31) despite later changes, but this is easily explained as conservative or archaizing, seeing that in ogam **Q** continued to be written for delabialized velars and even, by hypercorrection, for other velars.[7] I therefore change 'A' to ***b*** under §31 in both cases, and indicate the uncertain value of retained Q by underlining 'A' in the other relevant examples: 336/67a, 368/a/150, 446/353, 500, 504 **MAQI**; 462/Ok14 QVENATAVCI. (On 449/384 **MAQI** see below.) In 489/a/Ok13 I have allowed the 'A' to stand as **MAQI** is supported by the roman MAQVI, and similarly in the cases of 361/140 MAQVERIGI (a non-conventional spelling) and 2006 MA[Q]VI which contrasts with MACVS in the same inscription (§28) so that there is unlikely to be conservatism or archaicization. Note that in 341/71 and 428/305 the evidence of MACCVTRENI and MACUTRENI has already been preferred to that of the ogam **MAQITRENI** (see §31).

A further problem with 364/144 is the non-lowering (§29) in BARCVNI of the Irish genitive *kunas* > *konah*; here, however, -CVN-, like -I, may be

---

[6]   Sims-Williams, in *Britain 400–600*, p. 237; endorsed by McCone, TRC, p. 147, and Uhlich, *ZCP*, 49/50 (1997), 891, n. 44.

[7]   LHEB, p. 141, nn. 1–2; Ziegler, p. 21. Cf. §31 above on 502 and 506 **MAQ**.

part of the conventional British-Latin spelling. I therefore change the 'A' under §29 to _b_.

In 370/157 VLCAGNVS, 467/Ok24 ULCAGNI/VLCAGNI, and 472/ Ok35 VLCAGNI (: *$Ulk^w ognos$ > OI _Olcán_) lowering is absent (§29) but delabialization is shown (§31). The simplest explanation is that this name, which is never spelt with a *Q, and never shows A < *_o_ rounded to *O as one might expect after a labiovelar, had undergone a precocious delabialization by dissimilation in the vicinity of /u/ as proposed by McCone. (An alternative would be to connect it with OI _olc_ 'bad' and disassociate this from the 'wolf' word.)[8] I therefore change 'B' to _a_ under §31 in all three cases.

The problem with 372/160 DE[CA]BARBALOM FI[L]IVS BROCAGNI is that it preserves the velar in BROCAGNI (§39) but shows syncope (§40) and epenthesis (§43) in BARBALOM (ogam ?**BARVALB** 'dumb-head, _Dummkopf_: OI _balb_, ‡69), apparently the epithet of DE[CA] (which is perhaps a modern miscopying of *DEGA, the (early eighth-century?) Old Irish descendant of ogam **DEGO(S)**).[9] The only solution seems to be to regard BROCAGNI rather than *BROCANN as a conservative spelling or archaism in this very well-known name,[10] and hence to change the 'A' under §39 to _b_. There are three parallels in ogam inscriptions for -AGNI being written alongside apocope: 75 **ANM . . . RODAGNI**;[11] 166 **COIMAGNI . . . VITALIN** (Latin name); 202 **NIOTT-VRECC MAQI . . .]GNI.**[12]

403/268/841 BERIA[CI] is a problem because it does not show raising of E (§19) or lowering of the I (§29). The reading is uncertain, however, and perhaps one should regard it as British. Provisionally I disregard this name and change the 'A' to _b_ in both columns. As 482/Ok71 NEMIANVS presents similar problems (see §§ 19 and 29) I indicate the uncertainty by underlining A under §§ 19 and 29.

Lowering is also absent in 428/305 **TRENAGUSU** (or -O or -I)/ TRENEGUSSI, but here there may be influence from the nominative in *-_gussus_ where lowering did not occur; indeed, the roman form (and possibly the ogam, §38) may actually be based on the nominative. Note also that in

---

[8] McCone, _Ériu_, 36 (1985), 172; LEIA O-20; Ziegler, p. 241. Cf. ‡48.

[9] For **DEGO(S)** and OI _Daig_, gen. _Daig/Dega_ see Ziegler, p. 165, and TRC, pp. 23–24 (and p. 139 for -_o_ > -_a_, although on _feda_ see Sims-Williams, in Meid FS, pp. 471–72). An objection to my suggestion of G miscopied as C is that the inscription would then have included two different shaped forms of G; note, however, that ECMW, pp. 224–25, groups 'short or long tail' Gs together as variants of a single type. The ogam equivalent is too uncertain to be useful here.

[10] Examples in Ziegler, p. 141. A Broccán was eponym of the neighbouring kingdom of Brycheiniog.

[11] Note, however, the argument of Garrett, _Ériu_, 50 (1999), 154–57, that *_anmen_ underwent a precocious apocope (but see MacWhite, _ZCP_, 28 (1960–61), 298 and 307, and Stüber, _Historical Morphology_, p. 21).

[12] Cf. Ziegler, pp. 128, n. 221, 249, and 252.

Old Irish -*gusalo* occurs beside -*gosalo*.[13] I therefore change 'A' under §29 to *b*.

433/313 fails to show /æ/ > /ɪ/ in [A]NDAGELLI/ANDAGELLI (§25) but shows innovations in MACU (§§30–31). The same problem arises with 441/345 ANDAGELLI beside CVRCAGNI with delabialization (§28). The simplest explanation[14] is that the name, if not actually a Welsh cognate of OI *Indgall*, is influenced by Welsh. I therefore change 'A' under §25 to *b* in both cases, and indicate the doubtful nature of the criterion by underlining 'A' under §25 in the case of 500 [AM]BICATOS/AMMECATI.

449/384 MAQI fails to show rounding to *U and delabialization to *C (§§30–31), but we have already seen that these do not always appear in this conventional formula word (especially in ogam script), so I therefore change the 'A's under §§30–31 to *b*. I underline the 'A's in the other comparable examples under §30[15] to indicate the uncertain value of the -I of MAQI/ MAQVI: 368/a/150; 446/353; 489/a/Ok13; 500; 504; 2006. Note that in 341/71 and 428/305 the evidence of MACCVTRENI and MACUTRENI has already been preferred to that of MAQITRENI (§§30–31).

A further problem with 449/384 is the absence of lowering (§29) in CUNATAMI/CVNOTAMI, despite the later /n/ < *gn in SAGRANI (§38). The obvious explanation is that whereas SAGRANI may be Irish, CUNATAMI is British, as stated by Jackson and McManus.[16] I therefore delete the 'A' under §29, and similarly delete the 'A' under §41 which was due to the hypothetical absence of *Irish* syncope in the same name.

461/Ok66 NONNITA is a problem because of the lack of raising of the /o/ > /u/ (§19). This could be due to Latin influence, assuming that **Nonnitus* is the ultimate source of the name; hence I change A to *b* under §19. Of course, all problems would vanish if we discarded the theory that NONNITA (one of 'TRIS FILI') is an Irish masculine name **Nonnitas* (‡15n.) and supposed that 'FILI' could be used to refer to children of either sex.

2006 CVNORIX seems to show a trace of the old nominative case-ending (with -X reflecting Irish -S = /-h/, ‡14), hence the 'A' under §21, but this conflicts with the 'B's under §§22 and 28 on account of the -E of MAQVI COLINE and the C of MACVS. The simplest solution is to suppose that CVNORIX is after all a Latinization of Irish *CUNARI; hence I change 'A' under §21 to *b*. In the same inscription the non-raising of /o/ in MAQVI

---

13 Examples in MacNeill, *PRIA*, 27 (1909), 361; Ziegler, pp. 107, 159, 238, and 246–47; Uhlich, *Morphologie*, pp. 246–47 (*sic*).

14 It would be difficult to solve 433/313 by reordering the sound changes if McCone is right to argue in TRC, pp. 112 and 118, that /æ/ > /ɪ/ (our §25) preceded lowering (our §29), and that lowering preceded delabialization (our §30).

15 The 'A's under §31 have already been dealt with above. Various explanations of the apparent fossilization of MAQI are discussed by Garrett, *Ériu*, 50 (1999), 146–47.

16 LHEB, pp. 182–83; McManus, *Guide*, p. 113. On CUNATAMI see further ‡‡38n. and 67n.

COLINE (> OI *Maicc Chuilinn*) also appears anachronistic (§19) in view of the later changes shown;[17] the explanation of the O may be orthographical conservatism or influence from the cognate British **kolin-* (> W. *celyn*). I therefore change 'A' under §19 to *b*. In turn, this casts doubt on the validity of the 'A' under §19 in the case of 485/Ok68 COLINI (even assuming that this reading is correct, cf. ‡64, and that it is the ancestor of Ir. *cuilenn* rather than OC *kelin*). I indicate this doubt by underlining this 'A' too.

Finally, although 994/125/22 CAROTINN and 488/Ok60 ENABARRI/ ENABARR do not appear among the eighteen problem cases, we should underline the As under §41 to reflect the doubts about whether these really are pre-syncope forms (see §43).

5.3 Periodization of the Irish or possibly Irish names: Table 5.2

The data in Table 5.1 can be sorted as in Table 5.2 so as to group the inscriptions in periods ranging from 1 to 15. The validity of these periods is of course only as good as the data and chronology on which they are based, and two further caveats must be made. First, the periodization is only valid insofar as the names are Irish, hence it is more reliable when based on names that were double-underlined. Second, it may be unreliable wherever it depends on 'A's and 'B's that we have underlined to indicate the uncertainty of the criteria concerned (A; B).

5.4 Comparison of linguistic and epigraphic relative dating

Before attempting to map these periods onto an absolute chronology for Irish, we can compare them broadly with the epigraphic dates (from Chapter 6) suggested by Nash-Williams, Jackson, and others for the relevant roman-letter inscriptions, to see whether our 'early' and 'late' periods match their 'early' and 'late' epigraphic dates. A similar analysis has already been undertaken by McManus in respect of a sample of twenty-two Irish inscriptions in Britain and Man which Jackson had dated epigraphically between the fifth and the seventh centuries; in his tentative conclusion McManus noted a number of discrepancies and unresolved contradictions, and Harvey and Swift have since used these as ammunition in a thoroughgoing attack on the value of Jackson's epigraphic dating.[18] When

---

[17] Cf. McManus, *Guide*, p. 180, n. 62. Since /-i/ caused raising but /-e/ did not, they cannot have fallen together until after raising (cf. the attempt to get round this by Garrett, *Ériu*, 50 (1999), 156–57).

[18] McManus, *Guide*, pp. 97–99; Harvey, *Éigse*, 26 (1992), 189, and in *Roman, Runes and Ogham*, pp. 41–42 and 44; Swift, *Ogam Stones*, pp. 55–56 and 62. The importance of the roman-letter inscriptions for dating is noted by McManus, *Guide*, p. 62, 'Ogam "palaeography" being relatively useless in this regard'.

Table 5.2 Irish periodization of the inscriptions

col. 1	2	3	4	5	6	7	8	9	10	11	12	13	14	15	Per	Index entries	Suggested epigraphic dates
§§	19	20	21	22	25	28	29	30	31	35	37	38	39	41			
334/54																?	CATACVS TEGERNACVS	ECMW: late 6-early 7c; Ted: VII; LHEB: 7c
345/74																?	GLUVOCA or GLUVOCI	ECMW: 5-6c
348/a/110/27																?	TRENALUGOS	ECMW: ogam = dubious/'vestiges only'
351/115/2																?	DALLVS DVMELVS	ECMW: 6c; Ted: VI-1; KHJ: mid to later 6c, or later?
386/92																?	MELI MEDICI MARTINI	ECMW: 5-early 6c; Ted: VI-1; LHEB: beg. 6c
391/78																?	SENACVS	ECMW: 5-early 6c; Ted: VI-1; LHEB: early or mid 6c
404/270/843																?	TEGE[-TEGERNACUS MARTI	ECMW: 7c; Ted: VI-2; LHEB: 7c
415/278																?	IN[G]ENVI INT[AE]NVI IARRI[TARRONERIS	ECMW: 5-early 6c
438/320																?	TAVUSI	ECMW: 5-6c?
445/354																?	VITALIANI / VITALIANI EMERETO	ECMW: 5-early 6c; Ted: V; LHEB: 5c
451/401																?	TVNCCETACE VXSOR DAARI	ECMW: 6c; Ted: VI-1; LHEB: early or mid 6c
453/399																?	MELI NESI	ECMW: 5-early 6c; Ted: VI-1; KHJ: 5c
456/404																?	GENDILI / GENDILI	ECMW: 5-early 6c; KHJ: 8c, but ogams and horizontal I are odd so late
510/Scot.13																?	VETTA VICTI VICTRICIS F or FILI	Ted: V; LHEB: early 6c
990/108/1																?	TIGEIRN[or TIGERNI	ECMW: 7-9c; LHEB: 7c
1057/Ok54																?	EROCAVI INRI IRCAS	Th: 6c; KHJ: 6c?
1210/Ok5																?	VALCI VEITANVS V[ ]AIVS VECCAIUS	Th: pre-700
1403/Ok25																?	JIGERNI TIGERNI	Ted: VI-2; Th: c.600
1404/Ok30																?	CAVVDI or CAVVDI CIVILI	Ted: VI-1; Th: VI.3
2007/10																?	MAILIS(I)	ECMW: 5-early 6c?; Ted: V; LHEB p. 239 n.1: 5c
2019																?	RIGELLA TVNCCE[	fake? (Corpus)
330/66																A 1-14	]TIRI TIBE[ ]VS CATIRI	ECMW: 5-early 6c; KHJ: no reason why not 5c
375/166																A	TOTAVALI DOTHORANTI	ECMW: 6c; Ted: VI-2; LHEB: mid to later 6c
379/170																A	CATVRVGI LOVERNACI	ECMW: late 5-6c; Ted: V; LHEB: end 5c or beg. 6c
452/400																A	PAANI VALAVI or VALAVITIVI	ECMW: 5-early 6c; Ted: VI-1; KHJ: early to mid 6c
458/Ok9																A	RANOCORI NANOCORI MESGI or MESCI	Th: VI.3; KHJ: end 6c?
520/Scot.5																A	LATINVS FECERVTN BARROVADI	Ted: V; LHEB: beg. 6c

Table 5.2 *contd.*

Ref											Cols	Range	Inscription	Dating
*1022/240/928											A		DOBITAUCI PROPARAUIT GREFIUM COISTO SPERITUS	ECMW: 11c
1068/ a											A		LAGUBERI	
2000											A		DEVORIGI	
353/127/7									A	A		1-13	TRENACCATLO / TRENACATVS MAGLAGNI	ECMW: 5-early 6c; Ted: V; LHEB: end 5c or beg. 6c
357/136									A	a			CORBAGNI ALI	ECMW: 5-early 6c; KHJ: early 6c
376/174									A	a			VENNISETLI ERCAGNI	ECMW: 5-early 6c; Ted: VI-1; LHEB: 5c
434/314									A	a			COIMAGNI CAVETI	ECMW: 6c; Ted: VI-2; LHEB: late 6c
457/Ok18									A	A			DVNOCATI MERCAGNI MESCAGNI	Ted: VI-1; LHEB: early 6c; Th: VI.2
474/Ok17									A	a			CRVARIGI RVANI]MAGLI	Th: c.600; KHJ: too illegible to date
478/Ok48									A	a			BROCAGNI NADOTTI RADOTTI	Ted: VI-2; LHEB: mid 6c; Th: VI.3? c.600?
2027									A	a			ERCAGNI	Ted: V
2030/p.39li									A	a			MAGLI MATIM]INMIBERI	early 6c, *Corpus*
2032									A	A			]CAMAGLI NIMNI(?)	1st half 6c, *Corpus*; KHJ: 6c, rejecting Webley's 5-6c
450/390								A	a	a		1-12	OGTENLO OGTENAS HOGTIVIS or HOGTINIS DEMETI	ECMW: 6c; Ted: V; LHEB: early 6c
512								A	a	A			QATTIDONA	
2002/b								A	a	A			TARICORO	6c, *Corpus*
399/176							A	a	a	A		1-11	SIBILINI SIMILINI TOVISACI TOVISACI	ECMW: 5-early 6c; Ted: V; LHEB: end 5c
318/6						A	a	a	a	A		1-10	ETTORIGI	ECMW: late 5-early 6c; Ted: VI-1; LHEB: beg. 6c
408/229/848						A	a	a	a	A			BODVOCI CATOTIGERNI ETERNALI VEDOMAVI or VEDOMALI PRONEPVS	ECMW: 6c; Ted: VI-2; LHEB: mid or later 6c
439/319						A	a	a	a	A	a	1-9	EFESSANGI ASEGNI INGEN SANGKTA SEGNI IG"[	ECMW: 5-early 6c
462/Ok14					A	a	a	a	a	A			QVENATAVCI DINVI	Ted: VI-2; LHEB: mid to later 6c; Th: VI.2/VI.3
319/9				A	a	a	a	a	a	A		1-7	CVNOGVS(I)	ECMW: 5-early 6c; Ted: V; LHEB: beg. 6c
325/33				A	a	a	a	a	a	A			]IVA]INA BIVATIGIrni? BIVATISI BIVOTIS VASSO PAVLINI ANDO COGNATIONE AVDO	ECMW: later 6c; Ted: VI-2; LHEB: early 6c
370/157				A	a	a	a	a	A	A			VLCAGNVS SENOMAGLI	ECMW: 5-early 6c; Ted: VI-1; LHEB: 5c

Table 5.2 *contd.*

Ref.	Columns	Reading	Notes
426/300	A A A a a A A a	NETTASAGRU or / NETTASAGRI / MUCOE or MUCOI / BRECI / BRIACI / SLECI / MAQI	ECMW: 5-6c
427/a/301	A a a a a a A a	MAGL[IA] or / MAGL[I] / DUBRACUNAS / DUBARCUNAS	ECMW: 5-6c
435/315	A a a a a a a A	CLVTORIGI / PAVLINI / MARINI / LATIO	ECMW: 5-early 6c; Ted: VI-1; LHEB: later 5c
448/370	A a a a a a a a	RINACI / PINACI / NOMENA	ECMW: 5-early 6c; Ted: V; LHEB: 5c
454/402	A a a a a a a a	EVALI / DENCVI / DENOVI / CVNIOVENDE	ECMW: 5-early 6c; Ted: V; LHEB: end 5c
467/Ok24	A a a a a a A a	VLCAGNI / ULCAGNI	Ted: V; LHEB: 5c; Th: late VI.1 or early VI.2
468/Ok31	A a a a a a a A	RIALOBRANI / CVNOVALI	Ted: VI-2; LHEB: early or mid 6c; Th: VI.2
472/Ok35	A a a a a a A a	VLCAGNI / SEVERI	Ted: V; LHEB: end 5c; Th: c.500 or VI.1
487/Ok10	A a a a a a A a	CIRISINIVS / DRUSTANUS / CERVSIVS / DRVSTAVS / CIRUSIUS / DRVSTAGNI / CIRVSINIVS / SIRVSIVS / CVNOMORI	Ted: VI-2; LHEB: end 5c; Th: VI.2 or VI.3
501	A a A a a a A A	CUNAMAGLI / MAQI	
2029/p.39i	A a a a a a A A	ERECOR / MAGLORI / CVNIIAC	late 5c, *Corpus*
321/25	A a a a a a a a a A a A 1-3	ISORIS	ECMW: 5-early 6c; KHJ: beg. 6c?
322/27	A a a a a a a a a A a A	CAMVLORIS / HOI	ECMW: 5c; LHEB: early 5c
354/126/6	A a a a a a a a a A a A	CORBALENGI / ORDOVS	ECMW: 5-early 6c; Ted: VI-1; LHEB: 5c
368/a/150	A a a a a A A a a A a A	DUMELEDONAS / MAQI	ECMW: 5-early 6c
*380/84	A a a a A a a a a A a A	ICORIGAS / ICORI / POTENTINI	ECMW: 6c; Ted: V; LHEB: mid or later 6c
446/353	A a a a a A A A a A A A	MAGLICUNAS / MAGLOCVNI / MAGLOCVVI / CLUTARI or / CLUTARI[GAS] / CLVTORI / MAQI	ECMW: 5-early 6c; Ted: VI-1; LHEB: mid or later 5c
*496	A a a a a a a a a a A a A	EBICATO[S] / TEBICATO[	Jackson in Wright&Jackson 1968: not earlier than c.500
500	A a a A a a A A a a A a A	AMMECATI / ROCATI / /ROC[A]T[O]S / EBICATOS / AMBICATOS / MAQI	Ted: VI-1; LHEB: end 5c
504	A a a a a A A A a a A a A	BIVAIDONAS / MAQI / CUNAVALI	

Table 5.2 *contd.*

Ref	Letters	No.	Inscription	Dating
*344/73	A a a a a a a a a a a a	1-2	DERVACI IVSTI	ECMW: 5-early 6c; Ted: VI-1; LHEB: early 6c
388/94	A a a a a a a a a a a a A		DERVORI	ECMW: 5-early 6c
*482/Ok71	A a a a a a A a a a a a a a	1	NEMIAVS NEMIAVS JTRC	Th: VI.2 or VI.3; KHJ: may have been as old as 6c
*485/Ok68	A a a a a a a a a a a a a a		JTHI COLINI JCOBI COGI	Th: VI.2/VI.3; KHJ: 6c??
355/128/8	b B	3-15	SILBANDVS BANDVS	ECMW: 5-early 6c; LHEB: beg. 6c
455/403	b B		CAMVLLORIGI FANNVCI	ECMW: 5-early 6c; Ted: VI-1; LHEB: early or mid 6c
489/a/Ok13	b B ... A A a a a a a	3-8	SVAQQUCI QICI FANONI RINI **MAQI** MAQVI	Ted: VI-2; LHEB: end 6c; Th: VI.1 or early VI.2
1006/197/842	b B B	4-15	TEFROIHI TESROIHI NEFROIHI REFSOIHI REFSDIHI	ECMW: 7-9c
336/67a	b b B ... A a a A a a	4-9	**MAQI DECEDA**	ECMW: 5-6c?
342/70	B b B ... A a a a A A a A	4-7	**CUNACENNIVI** or **CUNACENNI [A]VI** CVNOCENNI **ILVVETO** CVNOGENI	ECMW: 5-early 6c; Ted: VI-1; LHEB: early 6c
405/228/845	b b B ... A a a a A A a a		**GRAVICA or JVICA** JLICA	ECMW: 5-early 6c
447/369	b b B ... A a a a a a A a		CVNISCVS CVNIGCVS NEMAGLI or NEMASLI	ECMW: 6c; KHJ: early to mid 6c?
*461/Ok66	*b* b B ... A a a a A A a A		NONNITA ERCILIVI or ERCILI RICATI VIRICATI TRIS ERCILINGI ERCILINCI	Ted: VI-2; LHEB: mid 6c; Th: not pre VI.3
361/140	b b b B ... A A A a a a A	5-8	TALORI ADVENTI MAQVERIGI	ECMW: 6c; Ted: VI-1
479/Ok16	b b b B ... A a a a a a a a	5-7	CVNAIDE CVNATDO	LHEB: 5c; Th: 5c, prob. not post 450-75
366/148	b b b b b B ... A	7-14	ECHADI ITOCVS CROCUSI	ECMW: late 5-6c
*358/138	b b *b* b b B A a a a a A a A	7	MEMORIA **VOTECORIGAS** VOTEPORIGIS PROTICTORIS	ECMW: 'AD 540-50'; Ted: V; LHEB: c. 550
369/153	b b b b b B A a a a a a A a		CVRCAGNVS JVRIVI	ECMW: 5-early 6c; KHJ: 5c, but then seems to accept ECMW date
*441/345	b b b b *b* B A a a a a a A A		CVRCAGNI ANDAGELLI	ECMW: 5-early 6c; Ted: VI-1; KHJ: 5c
*2006	*b* b *b* B b B A A A a a a a A		CVNORIX MAQVI COLINE MACVS	5c, Jackson in Wright & Jackson, although Jackson says purely epigraphically it could be c.400-550
494/Ok79	b b b b b b B	8-15	GOREVS	KHJ: late 6c or early 7c
1206/Ok4	b b b b b b B		DOVITHI DOCIDCI RIVGDOCI RIVSDOCI	Ted: V; Th: pre-700
368/b/150	b b b b b b B ... A	8-14	BARRIVENDI VENDVBARI	ECMW: 5-early 6c; Ted: VI-1; LHEB: end 5c or beg. 6c
378/169	b b b B b b B ... A		BIVVAIDONAS BODDIBEVVAS or	ECMW: late5-6c; Ted: VI-1; LHEB: early 6c

Table 5.2 *contd.*

Code	markers	range	Names	Notes
			BODDIBABEVE / BIVADI / BODIBEVE	
424/299	b b b b b b B — A		BRIACI / GLVVOCCI / EVALENGI ?	ECMW: 6c; Ted: VI-1; LHEB: early or mid 6c
436/316	b b b b b b B — A		EUOLENGGI / LITOGENI	ECMW: late 6c; Ted: VI-2; LHEB: end of 6c
1202/Ok2	b b b b b b B — A		EVOCATI / EVOCALI	Ted: VI-2; Th: late VI.2/VI.3
*374/172	b b b b b b B — A a	8-13	CVNEGNI	ECMW: 5-early 6c; Ted: V; LHEB: 5c
422/298	b b b b b b B — A A		VENDOGNI / VENDAGNI / HOCIDEGNI	ECMW: 6c; KHJ: too feint to date
432/312	b b b b b b B — A a		DOVAGNI / DOBAGNI / TIGERNACI	ECMW: 5-early 6c; Ted: V; LHEB: late 5c or early 6c
1028/214/850	b b b b b b B — A A		VENDVMAGLI	ECMW: late 6-early 7c; Ted: VII; LHEB: late 6c or early 7c
431/308	b b b _b_ b b B — A a A	8-12	**DOVATUCEAS** / **DOVATACIS** / DOBITVCI / DOBTVCI / EVOLENGI	ECMW: 5-early 6c; Ted: V; LHEB: early or mid 6c
503	b b B b b b B — A a a		**DOVAIDONA** / **DROATA** / **DRUTA**	
326/39	b b b b b b b B B	10-15	MACCVDECCETI	ECMW: 6c; Ted: VI-1; LHEB: early or mid 6c
423/296	b b b B b b b b B		**QAGTE**	ECMW: 5-early 6c
440/335	b b b b b b b B B		MACVDECETI / MACVDEBETI / MACVDEHETI / EOROCAN / EONOCAN / EOPOCAN	ECMW: 6c; LHEB: 6c?
492/Ok59	b b b b b b b B B		SABINI / MACCODECHETI	Ted: VI-2; LHEB: late 6c or early 7c; Th: VI.2
433/313	b b b b _b_ b b B B — A	10-14	**ANDAGELLI /** / **ANDAGELLI** / **CAVETI / CAVETI** / **MACU**	ECMW: 5-early 6c; Ted: VI-1; LHEB: early or mid 6c
425/297	b b b b b b b B B — A A	10-13	MACCVTRENI / CATOMAGLI	ECMW: 5-early 6c; Ted: VI-1; LHEB: early or mid 6c
396/104	b b b b b b b b b b B — A	12-14	AVITORI / TEPORE / IVSTINI	ECMW: 'c. 540AD'; Ted: VI-1; LHEB: 540
*362/142	B b _b_ b b B b b b B A A A	12	**INIGENA** / **CUNIGNI /** / **CVNIGNI** / **AVITTORIGES /** / **AVITORIA**	ECMW: 5-early 6c; Ted: V; LHEB: end 5c
*320/26	b b b b b b b b b b B — A	13-14	CVLIDOR(I) / ORVVITE / SECVNDI	ECMW: 5-early 6c; Ted: V; LHEB: 5c
327/43	b b b b b b b b b b B — A		TURPILI / TVRPILLI / MOSAC / **TRILLUNI** or **TRALLONI /** / TRILVNI / PVVERI / DVNOCATI	ECMW: 6c; Ted: VI-1; LHEB: early to mid 6c
403/268/841	_b_ b b b b b _b_ b B b b B — A		MACARITINI / CARITINI / BERICCI / BERIACI	ECMW: late 5-early 6c; Ted: VI-1; KHJ: hardly older than early to mid 6c
409/198/849	b b b b b b B b _b_ b b B — A		**POPIAS**	ECMW: 6c; Ted: VI-1; LHEB: early or mid 6c

Table 5.2 *contd.*

													A	No.		
															PAMPES ROLION or ROLACUN LLENA ILLUNA M[A]Q[I] PVMPEIVS CARANTORIVS	
*994/125/22	b	b	b	b	b	b	b	b	b	b	b	B		A		HIROIDIL CAROTINN	ECMW: early 9c; LHEB: 1st half 9c
442/346	b	b	b	b	b	b	b	B	B	b	b	B		A		MACCVDICCL CATICVVS	ECMW: 5-early 6c; Ted: V; LHEB: end 5c or beg. 6c
430/306	b	b	b	b	b	b	b	b	b	b	b	B			13-15	ETTERNI / ETTERNI VICTOR / VICTOR	ECMW: 5-early 6c; Ted: VI-1; LHEB: end 5c or beg. 6c
466/Ok23	b	b	b	b	b	b	b	b	b	b	b	B				INGENVI or INCENVI IGENAVI MEMORIA MEMOR	Ted: V; LHEB: early 6c/end 5c or early 6c; Th: VI.1, c.500?
502	b	b	b	b	b	b	b	b	b	b	b	B				MAQ LEOG	
329/42	b	b	b	b	b	b	B	B	b	b	b	B			14-15	CANNTIANI PATER MACCVTRENI	ECMW: 5-early 6c
398/106	B	b	b	b	b	b	b	b	b	b	b	B				IACONVS MINI	ECMW: 6c— 'possible vestiges of Ogam', Ted: VI-1; KHJ: mid 6c?
429/307	b	b	b	b	b	b	B	b	b	b	b	B				SOLINI VENDONI	ECMW: late 5-early 6c; Ted: VI-1; KHJ: perhaps early 6c?
449/384	b	b	b	b	b	b	b	*b*	*b*	b	b	B				SAGRAGNI SAGRANI CUNATAMI CVNOTAMI MAQI	ECMW: 5-early 6c; LHEB: early 6c
460/Ok75	b	b	b	b	b	b	b	b	b	b	b	B				VAILATHI VROCHANI	Ted: VI-2; LHEB: mid 6c
475/Ok47	b	b	b	b	b	b	b	b	b	b	b	B				IACONVS ADO	KHJ: might be 7c, but Macalister's arrangement of letters very suspicious
489/b/Ok13	b	b	b	b	b	b	b	b	b	b	b	B				SAGRANVI	Ted: VI-2 but perhaps meaning 489/a only?; this part not cited in LHEB; Th: VI.2 or VL3; KHJ: earlier [*recte* later?? PS-W] than 489/a
506	b	b	b	b	b	b	b	b	b	b	b	B	B			VICULA CUGINI COGELI MAQ	
507	b	b	b	b	b	b	b	b	b	b	b	B				CRONAN[ ]ACRON	
511/Scot.10	b	b	b	b	b	b	B	b	b	b	b	B				CONINIE TVRTIRIE ERTIRIE	Ted: VI-1; Nash-Williams apud Macdonald 1935-36: pre 550; Jackson apud RC *Peeblesshire* i, 176: lettering early part of 6c, language ?later
*328/44	b	b	b	b	b	b	B	b	b	b	b	B	A		14	RVGNIATIO VENDONI	ECMW: 5-early 6c; Ted: V; LHEB: 5c
341/71	b	b	b	b	b	b	B	B	b	b	b	B	A			MAQITRENI MACCVTRENI SALICIDUNI / SALICIDVNI or SALIGIDVNI	ECMW: 5-early 6c; Ted: V; LHEB: end 5c or beg. 6c
*428/305	b	b	b	b	b	*b*	B	B	b	b	b	B	A			TRENAGUSU or -O or -I / TRENEGUSSI MAQITRENI / MACUTRENI	ECMW: 6c; Ted: VI-2; LHEB: early 7c
488/Ok60	b	b	b	b	b	b	b	b	b	b	B	B	A			DOBVNNI FABRI ENABARRI / ENABARR	Ted: VI-1; LHEB: early or mid 6c; Th: ogam VI.1, after 500; roman VI.2
324/34	b	b	b	b	b	B	B	b	b	b	b	B			15	CONBARRVS CONBURRI	ECMW: 6c ?
364/144	b	b	b	b	b	*b*	b	*b*	b	b	b	B	B			QVENVENDANI	ECMW: 6c; Ted: VI-2; LHEB:

Table 5.2 *contd.*

372/160	b	B	b	b	b	b	b	b	b	b	b	B	*b*	B

BARCVNI — mid 6c
DECCAIBAR or [DECCA]IBARVAL — BCMW: late 5-6c; Ted: VI-1; LHEB: early 6c
B̄
VUGLOB
DECABARBALOM
BROCAGNI /
BROCAGNI
DISI

471/Ok39	b	b	b	b	b	b	B	b	b	b	b	b	B

CLOTUALI / MOBRATTI — Ted: VI-2; LHEB: 7c; Th: VI.3 or VII.1

493/Ok58	b	b	B	b	b	b	B	b	b	b	b	b	B

NEPRANI / CONBEVI — Ted: VI-1; LHEB: mid to later 6c; Th: VI.3

993/124/18	b	b	b	b	b	b	b	b	b	b	b	b	B

DITOC / MADOMNUACO / OCCON / UON / AON / ASAITGEN / ITGEN / ASA — BCMW: 7-9c

1038/365	b	b	b	b	b	b	b	b	b	b	b	b	B

MAIL DOMNAC / MEIL DOMNAC / MAL DOMNAC — BCMW: early 10c

1048/Ok32	b	b	b	b	b	B	B	b	B	b	B	b	B

GVENNCREST / HADNOBVIS / QONFAL(I) or QONFILI / VIR / (G)VENNORCIT — Ted: VII; Th: VII.1?

1068/b	b	b	b	b	b	b	b	b	b	b	b	B	B	B

LUGNI / HIPIA / NIPIA / DIPRUI / CONDILICI / MALBREN / BRENLIER / BREDLIEN

* Marks the 16 anomalous inscriptions discussed under (a)–(g).

the whole corpus is examined, however, Jackson's dates – regarded for the time being as a *relative* chronology – stand up quite well (the sixteen problem cases discussed below are marked * on Table 5.2: 320, 328, 344, 358, 362, 374, 380, 428, 441, 461, 482, 485, 496, 994, 1022, 2006).

(a) None of the ninety-two pre-Period 15 (i.e. pre-syncope) inscriptions need be post-sixth century on Jackson's epigraphical dating (or, failing that, other scholars' dating, as cited in the last column of Table 5.2), with the three exceptions of 1022/240/928 (eleventh century!, Per. 1–14), where Macalister's reading DOBITAUCI is universally unacceptable, 994/125/22 CAROTINN (first half of ninth century, Per. 13–14), where the under-lined '<u>A</u>' in the last column indicates that CAROTINN could possibly be included in Period 15 after all, with the -O- being attributed to svarabhakti (§43), and 428/305 TRENEGUSSI (early seventh century, Per. 14), where Nash-Williams and Tedeschi both offer sixth-century dates (see (g) below).

(b) All of the nine Period 15 (i.e. post-syncope) inscriptions can be sixth-century or later.

(c) All of the thirty-six inscriptions of Period 7 and earlier (i.e.

pre-lowering) may be epigraphically fifth-century or *early* sixth-century,[19] with the following three exceptions:

- 358/138 **VOTECORIGAS**/VOTEPORIGIS (Per. 7), dated *c.* 550 by Jackson and 540–50 by Nash-Williams. These dates were based on an insecure identification of the subject of the inscription with Gildas's *Vortipori* and on an insecure dating of Gildas to *c.* 540 (see p. 346 below). Note that Tedeschi, using epigraphic criteria only, dates the inscription to the 5c.[20]

- 380/84 **ICORIGAS**/ICORI (Per. 1–3, or Per. 1–7 if the '**A**' is ignored), dated mid- or later 6c by Jackson, but simply 6c by Nash-Williams and V by Tedeschi. The epigraphic dating seems to depend on the nature of the half-uncial S of FILIVS, which is not at all clear.[21] If the late epigraphic date is insisted on, an easy way out of the impasse would be to suppose that the name is British and that the British vocalism has impeded lowering in the ogam equivalent.[22]

- 461/Ok66 **NONNITA** (Per. 4–7), dated mid-6c by Jackson. This may be the female Latin name, however, rather than from Pr.Ir. *Nonnitas (<? Latin *Nonnitus, ‡15n.), in which case one would not expect to see lowering of the I. Even if **NONNITA** is Irish, the pronunciation or spelling may be influenced by Latin (as already posited to explain the lack of raising of the O (§19), above p. 333).

- [Jackson does not date 485/Ok68 **COLINI** (Per. 1) so precisely as to exclude the early 6c (whereas Thomas has the last two thirds), but in any case we have seen (a) that **COLINI** may be British and (b) that the non-raising is an uncertain criterion, hence the '**A**' (see p. 334 above). Rather similarly Thomas's identical date for 482/Ok71 **NEMIANVS** (Per. 1) is no great problem in view of the uncertainties denoted by the '**A**'s here: NEMIAVS may be a better reading, ‡18n.]

(d) All of the fifty-three inscriptions of Period 8 onwards (i.e. post-lowering) may be *early* 6c or later, with the following four exceptions:[23]

- 374/172 **CVNEGNI** (Per. 8–13), dated 5c by Jackson (and Tedeschi), is in Period 8 or later on account of the E rather than I, which is attributed to lowering in the nominative *Kuneγnah (§29). It has also, however, been explained away by Vulgar Latin confusion of E and I (‡15).

[19] In making such statements I regard dates such as 'early to mid 6c' as allowing the possibility of a narrower dating to 'early 6c', and so on.

[20] *Scrittura e civiltà*, 19 (1995), 103–4 and 115.

[21] Nash-Williams only refers to this S. KHJ noted that it ('if certain' – he was doubtful in 1947) and the (first?) N were both 6c, and gave the date 'Mid–later 6c' with a question mark that he omitted in LHEB.

[22] Cf. Ziegler, p. 187; and ‡‡ 14, 17, and 19.

[23] Note, however, that Tedeschi dates rather more of these to the fifth century, earlier than other authorities.

Alternatively one might adopt Nash-Williams's broader 5c–early 6c date.

- 362/142 **AVITTORIGES** (Per. 12), dated end 5c by Jackson; if this early date is correct, possibly I am wrong to explain -**ES** as a spelling of -**EAS** lowered from *-**IAS** (§29) and **V** as a hypercorrect spelling of /i̯/ (§37). However, Nash-Williams's date is broader: 5c–early 6c.

- 320/26 **CVLIDOR(I)** (Per. 13–14), dated 5c by Jackson (and Tedeschi). This is placed in a late period solely on account of the apparent apocope (§38), which, if the stone is so early, is a problem whether the name is British or Irish. Possibly the -I has simply been obliterated (cf. ‡16n.), which is why it was not counted as an example of British apocope in ‡37. Again, Nash-Williams's date is broader – 5c–early 6c – which could alleviate the problem a different way. On the other hand ORVVITE without *a*-affection (‡15) supports an early date.

- 328/44 **VENDONI** (Per. 14), dated 5c by Jackson (and Tedeschi). This is placed in a late period because of the apparent lowering in VEND- (§29) – for which Vulgar Latin confusion of E and I could provide an alternative explanation (‡22) – and because of the N rather than GN (§39). This is a puzling inscription, since]RVGNIAT(I)O with GN preserved also appears in it; the easiest solution is to suppose that the name with GN is British and that only **VENDONI** is Irish (or else is (?Celtic-)Latin (*)*Vendonius*, ‡22). Nash-Williams's date is again the broader 5c–early 6c, which would would fit better.

(e) All of the thirteen pre-Period 4 (i.e. pre-loss of -S) inscriptions may be epigraphically 5c, with the following five exceptions:[24]

- 380/84 **ICORIGAS/ICORI** (Per. 1–3), dated mid- or later 6c by Jackson, perhaps too late (see (c) above).

- 496 **TEBICATO[S]** (Per. 1–3, on account of a visible trace of -S), dated not earlier than *c.* 500 by Jackson, but on the grounds of *ogam* epigraphy (and language).[25] But note that earlier dates have been advocated,[26] and that the writing of -S is a doubtful criterion, as indicated by the '**A**' under §21. The name is apparently British (based on **Tep-* < **Tek^w-*) and -**ICATOS** rather than **-**OCATI** or **-**OCADOS** may be part of an attempt to Hibernicize the name – an attempt that could well have involved some archaicization (cf. ‡‡ 17 and 38n.).

---

[24] KHJ's date for 321/25 was clearly not intended to exclude the fifth century and is therefore not discussed here.

[25] Wright & Jackson, *AntJ*, 48 (1968), 299.

[26] Fulford et al., *Med. Arch.*, 44 (2000), 15. But the early date of the ogam from Pool, Orkney, which they compare, cannot yet be relied upon according to Forsyth, *PSAS*, 125 (1995), 679.

- 344/73 <u>DERVACI</u> (Per. 1–2), dated early 6c by Jackson (and Tedeschi). Possibly the writing of RV rather than *RB is not significant (cf. §20), or the name may simply be British.
- 485/Ok68 <u>COLINI</u> (Per. 1), dated 6c(??) by KHJ; this has been discussed under (c) above: if Irish it may be conservative in spelling; but it may be British.
- 482/Ok71 <u>NEMIANVS</u> (Per. 1) has not been dated earlier than 6c; but the linguistic evidence for its dating and even its Irishness is weak (see (c) above).

(f) Another revealing approach is to list the inscriptions which Jackson dates specifically to the 5c (i.e. rather than '5–early 6c' etc.) (see Table 5.3). The first fifteen of these '5c' inscriptions could all be linguistically early and belong, say, to Periods 1–5. The problem of the last four has been discussed above, where it was suggested that the epigraphic dates or my Irish periodization may be wrong. This leaves the two '5c' inscriptions in Period 7. In both cases Jackson's date may be too early. 441/345 is dated VI-1 by Tedeschi, a possibility allowed for by Nash-Williams.[27] Jackson himself admits that 2006 (at Wroxeter) could be *c.* 400–550 epigraphically; Swift correctly dismisses his historical argument that it has to be fifth-century.[28]

(g) A similar table (Table 5.4) can be constructed for the inscriptions which Jackson (or, in this case, others, failing Jackson) assign epigraphically to the seventh century or later.

The first of these (Macalister's dubious <u>DOBITAUCI</u> on an 11c stone!) can be disregarded, and the second (<u>CAROTINN</u>) *may* be Period 15 (post-syncope) if svarabhakti is allowed for, as noted at (a) above. The others too can all be Period 15 (post-syncope) apart from 428/305 **TRENEGUSU (-O, -I) MAQI MAQITRENI/TRENEGUSSI FILI MACUTRENI**. Jackson dated this 'early seventh century', a date which McManus found particularly awkward in view particularly of the post-syncope character of the Irish poems generally dated to the end of the sixth century.[29] In fact, Jackson's epigraphic date may be incorrect here, for both Nash-Williams and Tedeschi assign 428/305 to the sixth century.[30] In that case, the epigraphers' seventh century onwards corresponds neatly with Period 15.

---

[27] KHJ's date was due to the use of pure capitals.

[28] Wright & Jackson, *AntJ*, 48 (1968), 299; Swift, *Ogam Stones*, pp. 55 and 68. Cf. McManus, *Guide*, pp. 76–77.

[29] McManus, *Guide*, pp. 98–99. One could, however, compare the survival of the composition vowel in 970/13 CATAMANUS, which cannot be earlier than *c.* 625, despite the sixth-century dates often assigned to the earliest Welsh poetry, and the early evidence for Brittonic syncope such as the early sixth-century form *Catihernus* (see above, p. 285)

[30] KHJ admitted that the individual 'late' letter forms **s, t, g, h, u** all occurred in the 6c, but felt that the combination of them pointed to a date later than Nash-Williams's 6c; 'the names were by now *Trēnʒuso* and *Maᶦcc Thrēᶦn.*'

Table 5.3 Jackson's epigraphically '5c' inscriptions

No.	Our period	Comment
330/66	1–14	These periodizations
376/174	1–13	are compatible with
399/176	1–11	e.g. Periods 1–5.
370/157	1–7	
435/315	1–7	
448/370	1–7	
454/402	1–7	
467/Ok24	1–7	
472/Ok35	1–7	
487/Ok10	1–7	
322/27	1–3	
354/126/6	1–3	
446/353	1–3	
500	1–3	
479/Ok16	5–7	
441/345	7 ⎫	See (f).
2006	7 ⎭	
374/172	8–13 ⎫	
362/142	12 ⎬ See (d) above.	
320/26	13–14 ⎪	
328/44	14 ⎭	

Table 5.4 Epigraphically '7c or later' inscriptions

No.	Our period	Comment
1022/240/928	1–14 ⎫	See (a) above.
994/125/22	13–14 ⎭	
475/Ok47	14–15 ⎫	Compatible with Per. 15.
1006/197/842	4–15 ⎭	
428/305	14	See (a) above and (g).
471/Ok39	15	
993/124/18	15	
1038/365	15	
1048/Ok32	15	

Period 15 would seem to have *begun* during the sixth century, however, to judge by the epigraphic dates for the last nine inscriptions in Table 5.2. Some of the 'sixth-century' ones may be British or present other problems of reading or interpretation. Nevertheless 364/144 <u>QVENVENDANI FILI BARCVNI</u>, at least, is readable and is linguistically clearly Irish, and this is dated mid-sixth century by Jackson[31] (VI-2 by Tedeschi). 493/Ok58

---

[31]   LHEB, pp. 140, 141, n. 3, and 170; not later 6c as quoted by McManus, *Guide*, p. 98.

NEPRANI FILI CONBEVI is also agreed to be sixth-century, and can more easily be regarded as Irish than Brittonic.[32] More puzzling is 372/160 DE[CAB]ARBALOM FI[L]IVS BROCAGNI, which seems to show syncope of *Barrobalvos and epenthesis, and possibly even the late genitive Dega (see p. 332 above), even though it is dated epigraphically to the early sixth century or before.[33] If this is correct, Irish syncope must have begun earlier than has previously been thought. Possibly, however, the linguistic or epigraphic assessment is incorrect.

5.5 SUMMARY

Putting the above together, we find that our Irish linguistic Periods and the epigraphers' centuries progress broadly in tandem:

Periods 1–5 = '5c'
Periods 6–7 = 'early 6c'
Periods 8–14 = 'early to mid-6c'
Period 15 = 'mid-6c onwards'.

5.6 ABSOLUTE DATING OF IRISH PERIODS

It is impossible to be precise, but the above absolute dates quoted with inverted commas may well be roughly correct. Note in particular Swift's argument that the Irish ogam tradition starts with Irish Christianity,[34] and the general opinion that syncope (the hallmark of Period 15) occurred in the mid to later sixth century.[35]

The only fixed date, however, is provided by 396/104 AVITORI (Per. 12–14) which cannot of course be earlier than 540, the date of the consul Justinus referred to in its 'post-consular' dating clause, but could be some decades later than 540.[36] It is often supposed, as mentioned above (p. 342), that 358/138 VOTECORIGAS/MEMORIA VOTEPORIGIS PROTICTORIS (Per. 7), from Castelldwyran in the heart of Dyfed, 'a

---

[32]   See above, Ch. 3, p. 293.
[33]   Thomas, Mute Stones, p. 135 has 'end of V or VI.1 [= first third]'.
[34]   See Ogam Stones (but note her caution about 'the fifth century' on p. 126) and review by Gippert, CMCS, 39 (2000), 90 and 93. Harvey, in Roman, Runes and Ogham, pp. 44–50, is the best recent advocate for an early date.
[35]   See above and LHEB, p. 143, n. 2; McManus, Guide, p. 92; TRC, p. 127. Carney's dating, discussed by Sims-Williams in Britain 400–600, p. 225, n. 31, was modified by him in Early Irish Literature: Media and Communication, pp. 54–55 (cf. also review by Breatnach, CMCS, 23 (1992), 120).
[36]   See p. 276 above.

bare three miles from Narberth, the Arberth which was the principal court of
the chiefs of Dyfed according to the Mabinogion',[37] refers to the ageing
tyrant of Dyfed, named *Vortipori* in Gildas's *De Excidio Britanniae* and
Guortepir or similar in the genealogies. These sources always have an /r/,
however, and since the elements **u̯o* 'under' and **u̯or* 'over' are quite
distinct, I have suggested that the two men were 'rather two members of
the same dynasty'.[38] (As has often been noted, 'people liked to have one
element in the name of the son identical with an element in his father's
name'.)[39] Since the name *Guotepauc* and the word *godeb* 'refuge' (< **u̯otepo-*)
are attested elsewhere,[40] and since a progression **u̯or* 'over' → **u̯o* 'under'
rather than vice versa would be bathetic, I would guess that VOTEPORIGIS
flourished earlier than Gildas's tyrant, that is, before *c.* 540 on the conventional dating of Gildas but perhaps before *c.* 520 according to some
more recent datings.[41] This is quite compatible with an early sixth-century
date for Period 7. Beyond this one cannot go in absolute dating.

5.7 BRITTONIC AND IRISH CHRONOLOGY COMPARED

Having periodized the Brittonic and Irish names separately, it ought to be
possible to use the inscriptions which combine British and Irish names to
correlate the two sets of periodizations. In practice this is not easy. In the
first place, it is often not entirely certain which language some names belong
to (as indicated by the **SINGLE UNDERLINING** in Chapters 4 and 5 for
possibly Irish names). In the second place, some inscriptions are not assigned
to periods in both of Table 3.2 (Brittonic) and Table 5.2 (Irish), for example
451/401 TVNCCETACE VXSOR DAARI HIC IACIT, where the wife's
name belongs precisely to the Brittonic Period 3 but the husband's probably
Irish (cf. ‡18) name **DAARI** cannot be periodized.

   Table 5.5 lists all the inscriptions which contain names which can be fairly
certainly assigned to the two languages and periodized in both. Note that
449/384 **CVNOTAMI/CUNATAMI** and 328/44]RVGNIAT(I)O are both
assigned to British for the reasons given above,[42] while 994/125/22
CAROTINN is assigned to Irish, as argued in Chapter 3.[43] The 'narrow'

---

[37]   Richards, *JRSAI*, 90 (1960), 146. On the siting see further Edwards, *Med. Arch.*, 45 (2001),
       27.
[38]   In *Britain 400–600*, p. 226, with further references; endorsed by Dumville, *EHR*, 116 (2001),
       406, and by Harvey, in *Roman, Runes and Ogham*, pp. 43–44; and cf. Charles-Edwards,
       Early Christian Ireland, p. 168: 'Voteporix might conceivably have been a kinsman of
       Vortiporius . . . of a slightly earlier generation.' A further instance of the -*r*- form is the
       territorial name *Gurthebir-iuc* in LL, p. 201 (assuming *b* = /b/). On **u̯o* and **u̯or* see Sims-
       Williams, in *Gaulois et Celtique Continental*, and SWWF, pp. 229–30.
[39]   BWP, p. 24; cf. McManus, *Guide*, pp. 112–13; SWWF, p. 176.
[40]   Mac Cana, *BBCS*, 19 (1960–62), 116; Hamp, *SC*, 30 (1996), 293.
[41]   On the dating of Gildas, see above, Ch. 3, p. 275.
[42]   See above, pp. 333 and 343.
[43]   See above, Ch. 3, n. 11 (*re* col. 19).

Table 5.5 Inscriptions with periodized Brittonic and Irish names

Nos.	Brittonic names	Brittonic periods			Irish periods			Irish names	Epigraphic dates
		Narrow	Broad	?	?	Narrow	Broad		
500	AMMECATI	2-13		2	2	1-3	1-12	**AMBICATOS** **ROCATOS**	L5
358/138	VOTEPORIGIS	1	*1-13*	5	7	7		**VOTECORIGAS**	[V]
376/174	VENNISETLI	7-9		9	*13*	1-13		ERCAGNI	5
366/148	ITOCVS	4-20		9	*13*	7-14		ECHADI	L5-6
328/44	]RVGNIAT(I)O	[1-6]	*1-11*	10	*14*	14		VENDONI	[5-E6]
329/42	CANNTIANI	1-3	*1-16*	10	*14*	14-15		MACCVTRENI	5-E6
449/384	CVNOTAMI CUNA-TAMI	1	*1-13*	10	*14*	14-15	*10-15*	SAGRANI **SAGRAGNI**	E6
455/403	CAMVLLORIGI	1	*1-13*	10	*14*	3-15		FANNVCI	E-mid6
409/198/849	PVMPEIVS CARAN-TORIVS	3-5	*3-13*	10	*14*	13-14		**POPIAS ROLACUN**	E-mid6
440/335	E[D]NOCAN	11-28*		11	*15*	10-15		MACVDE[h]ETI	E-mid6
1068/b	DIPRUI CONDILICI	*14-27*		*14*	*15*	15		LUGNI MALBREN	
993/124/18	DITOC AON ITGEN	20		20	*15*	15		MADOMNUACO	7-9
994/125/22	HIROIDIL	24-28		25	*15*	13-14	*13-15*	CAROTINN	E9

* 440/335 was assigned to Period 11 or later on account of the apparent apocope in 'EOROCAN', but this does not apply if the real reading was 'EDNOCAVI' or similar (see ‡‡ 17n. and 48). In the latter case, it would have the correct composition vowel (< *petno-, cf. ‡38) and should belong to Per. 1 or, more broadly, Per. 1–13 (i.e. pre-Syncope).

periodization is given as in Tables 3.2 and 5.2. The alternative 'broad' periodizations take into account uncertainties mostly indicated by underlining of '<u>A</u>' or '<u>B</u>' in those tables. For example, VOTEPORIGIS, CVNOTAMI, and CAMVL(L)ORIGI belong in Brittonic Period 1 (the narrow periodization) on account of their correct composition vowel O, but as this is an unreliable criterion they may belong to Period 1–13 (the broad periodization). 329/42 CANNTIANI is in Period 1–3 on account of the retention of a in the -$\bar{a}nus$ suffix, but since retention of a has been shown to be unreliable in traditional Latin names,[44] of which CANNTIANI may have been felt to be one (cf. ‡18 for the occurrence of the name in Roman Gaul and as a saint's name), the broader periodization 1–16 may be preferable. The same inscription's <u>MACCVTRENI</u> may belong to the Irish Period 10–15 in view of the great uncertainty attaching to the validity of TREN < *$trekn$-, which was the reason for the narrow periodization.[45] 328/44 should certainly be placed in the broader Brittonic Period 1–11 (i.e. up to loss of GN in -VGN-); for the periodization 1–6 was based on counting <u>VENDONI</u> as British (‡22), which we have seen to be unlikely – if not Irish it may in fact be a (?Celtic-)Latin (*)$Vendonius$.[46] Finally, the lack of i-affection in CARANTORIVS and the raising of /o/ in PVMPEIVS suggested Period 3–5, but if the latter is attributed to Vulgar Latin influence,[47] 409/198/849 belongs to British Period 3–13 or even 3–16.

This sample contains a surprising proportion of inscriptions where broader periods are possible than those given in Tables 3.2 and 5.2. It is obvious (for example from the incompatibility of 500 with 358/138) that the narrower Brittonic periods cannot always be correlated with the Irish ones, but if the broader periods are taken into account as necessary, the Brittonic and Irish periods *are* compatible; this is indicated by the (completely hypothetical!) periods included in the central columns (headed '?') merely to demonstrate this point. The fact that it is necessary to use the broader periodizations is a warning against accepting the narrower periodizations in Tables 3.2 and 5.2 without regard for any possible broader periodizations indicated there by underlined <u>A</u>s and <u>B</u>s.

In the final column I have given preference to epigraphical dates from Jackson (where available), with the exception of 358/138 <u>VOTECORIGAS</u>, where we have already noted that Jackson's 'historically' based $c.$ 550 date is unsatisfactory, and 328/44 <u>VENDONI</u>, where we have already found his fifth-century date problematical (pp. 342 and 343). In these two cases I quote the dates of Tedeschi and Nash-Williams respectively.

---

[44] See ibid., p. 250 (*re* col. 2).
[45] See above, p. 330.
[46] See above, p. 343, (d).
[47] See above, Ch. 3, p. 251 (*re* col. 6).

Again, the epigraphic dates are broadly compatible with the linguistic period-ization.

The data summarized in Table 5.5 is clearly not good enough to allow us to match up periods in the two languages beyond the generalization that the fifteen Irish periods seem to have run their course over *roughly* the same period as the first fifteen or so Brittonic periods – with Period 15 in each case starting in about the late sixth or early seventh century, if the epigraphic dates are reliable.

6

CONCLUSION AND LIST OF PROPOSED DATES

6.1 CONCLUSION

The principal conclusion of this study is that a comprehensive examination of the phonology of the Brittonic inscriptions broadly vindicates the relative chronologies that have been suggested for them on epigraphic and typological grounds. This is contrary to the gloomy recent assessments quoted in Chapter 1. It suggests that future studies could refine the chronology by combining the linguistic and non-linguistic approaches.

The history of Celtic philology shows that the relative chronology of the Brittonic sound changes was mainly worked out on internal grounds before Jackson consolidated it in *Language and History in Early Britain* and attempted to fix the absolute chronology, for example on the basis of the epigraphy of the inscriptions.[1] Hence the relative chronology based on phonology provides a genuinely independent check on the non-linguistic relative chronologies based on epigraphy, typology, and so on.[2]

I have not simply taken the standard historical phonology on trust, but have attempted to take account of all relevant modifications that have been proposed in the half-century since Jackson's great work was published, and have proposed some further refinements myself, based on internal linguistic logic rather than the evidence of the inscriptions; see, for example, Chapter 2, ‡58, where diphthongization is placed before the new quantity system and internal *i*-affection.

It has also been possible to refine Jackson's relative chronology by discovering the order of sound changes which provides the best fit with the corpus of inscriptions as a whole (see Chapter 3). This involved deciding that some features, mainly innovations, were more significant than others, such as conservations in Latin names; the decisions taken are clearly set out in Table 3.1. Although this merely formalizes the sort of choices that philologists always have to make, the presentation in the table is intended to make the procedure explicit and so enable others to test the data for themselves – and to reformat it if new data comes to light. The most significant differences from the order in LHEB are shown in Table 6.1

---

[1] J. E. C. Williams, *LlC*, 3 (1954–55), 82. See Ch. 1 above.
[2] Handley, *EME*, 10 (2001), 197, is too pessimistic: 'At best we can hope for a relative chronology, but exactly what this chronology might be based on is, as yet, uncertain.'

below. This shows the optimum order for the appearance of the relevant sound changes in the inscriptions, and can be compared with the order in which they appear in LHEB §210 as indicated by the column numbers in the second column (these refer to Chapter 3, Tables 3.1 and 3.2) and by the section numbers (‡‡) of Chapter 2, for that chapter followed the order in which the sound changes are listed in LHEB §210. The final column includes Jackson's absolute dates for comparison.[3] It can be seen from the absolute dates that the revised order does not conflict wildly with Jackson's scheme. Where there is a conflict, I have argued that my order is compatible with the internal linguistic logic of the sound changes. For example, whereas Jackson argues that reduction of composition vowels postdated final i-affection in view of *Au̯i- > W. Eu-, this need not be so in view of Schrijver's demonstration that Eu- arose independently of i-affection.[4] Again, words like Welsh trwynau 'noses' < *trugn- imply that the development /ɣ/ > /i̯/ before /n/, which produced the diphthong wy, occurred before pretonic /u/ could become reduced to /ö/ (see ‡46). And, to give a final example, /ɣ/ > /i̯/ before /l/ need not have occurred after syncope, as usually argued on the basis of OC teilu < *tego-slougo- 'house-troop' since the etymology may rather be *tegeso-slougo- as suggested by Schrijver.[5]

On the basis of the revised order of Brittonic sound changes, the inscriptions have been placed in twenty-eight linguistic periods, as set

Table 6.1 Main revisions to conventional order of the Brittonic sound changes which are seen in the inscriptions

Sound change	Table cols.	‡‡	LHEB date
Composition vowels reduced	11	38	6c
W.Brit. oN > uN	6	26	1st half 6c
a: > ɔ:	2	18	later 5–early 6c
ɣ > u̯ before u etc.	5	25	beg. of 6c
Final i-affection	3	19	later 5–early 6c
nd > nn	4	22/49	end 5c–2nd half 6c
ɣ > i̯ before l, r, n	17	48	2nd half 6c
Pr.W. pretonic u > ö	15	46	2nd half 6c
Syncope of composition vowels	12	38	mid 6c
Σ - > h-	14	44	mid or later 6c
ɣ > ∅ in various environments	23	65	8c
Pr.W. ɔ: > au	22	60	8c

---

[3] Dates from LHEB §210 (cf. Appendix 3 below) except for reduction of composition vowels, dated in LHEB, p. 651.
[4] LHEB, pp. 580 and 651; SBCHP, p. 272.
[5] SBCHP, p. 71. See above, p. 256.

out in Table 3.2 and summarized at the end of this Chapter. Few inscriptions can be assigned to a precise linguistic period as opposed to a span of several periods. In some cases a choice is provided between a narrow and a broad periodization depending on what weight is attached to certain linguistic features. It is hoped that this procedure will be transparent and robust enough to be used and revised in future scholarship as the need arises.

Absolute dates are difficult to attach to these twenty-eight periods, owing to the scarcity of datable sources before the ninth century – obviously dates derived from epigraphic typologies could not be used – but a cautious scheme is given in Section 3.7 above, based on comparison with dated texts and manuscripts and on the few stones with absolute dates.[6]

Many of the inscriptions contain Irish names, owing to the well-known Irish settlements in western Britain. Most of these names were identified in Chapter 2, with a view to eliminating them from the Brittonic data; for example, in ‡14 the accepted Brittonic sound law -*x* > -*s* is rejected on the grounds that the two inscriptions supposed to demonstrate it are both Irish. In Chapters 4 and 5 the definite or possible Irish forms are dealt with more systematically, with a view to arranging the Irish inscriptions of Britain in linguistic periods. Like the Brittonic periods, the Irish ones correlate broadly with the epigraphic dates suggested for the roman-letter inscriptions, contrary to the fears expressed in recent scholarship.[7] Since some inscriptions contain both Irish and Brittonic names, it proved possible to correlate the fifteen Irish linguistic periods with the earlier Brittonic ones, at least in broad terms. This correlation gives some help in dating the Irish sound changes and in some cases helps to decide which names are likely to be Irish rather than Brittonic.

Since nearly all the names in the inscriptions are discussed somewhere in this book, it is hoped that it will be useful to students of comparative Celtic onomastics,[8] and to scholars interested in particular stones; references can be located via the Index of Forms Discussed. Nevertheless, the main aim has been to establish the linguistic chronology of the inscriptions in comparison with the chronologies suggested by non-epigraphic evidence, so it is appropriate to conclude with a list of proposed dates.

6.2 LIST OF PROPOSED DATES

In the following list, epigraphic dates are given from a variety of sources. For Welsh stones they are given from ECMW mostly, but from the draft

---

[6] On the dating of sound changes not occurring in the inscriptions see Sims-Williams, in *Britain 400–600*, pp. 217–61.

[7] Section 5.4 above.

[8] See further my article in *CMCS*, 44 (2002).

Corpus and elsewhere for a few Welsh stones not in ECMW. Other frequently cited sources are: Ted = dates (in roman) from Tedeschi 1995; RC = dates from Royal Commission volumes (Glamorgan, Dorset and Peeblesshire stones); LHEB = dates from LHEB (for LHEB page references, cf. Index to CIIC references in LHEB, pp. 751–52); Th = dates (in roman) for South-Western stones from Thomas, *Mute Stones* (see his Index, pp. 352–53, for the page references, and p. xxiv for Thomas's system of dating by thirds of centuries); Han = dates by Mark Handley from IEMB; KHJ = unpublished notes by Jackson (see p. 5 above).

The linguistic periods are given so as to refer the reader to the relevant section of Table 3.2 in all instances (= 'Brittonic Period') and then to Table 5.2 (= 'Irish Period') in the case of the inscriptions containing possibly Irish names. Generally the choice between 'Brittonic Period' and 'Irish Period' is left open, as being too complex to discuss here; further discussion must be sought via the references to individual names and forms in the Index. Note that in many – though not all – cases 'Brittonic Period ?' will mean that an inscription is really Irish.

Where the underlined 'A's and 'B's in Tables 3.2 and 5.2 allow a broader periodization than is given in those tables, this is indicated below, for example: '318/6 **Brittonic Period** 1 (if presumably correct composition vowel is significant) or (if not) 1–13'. I have noted a few cases where there is a clear incompatibility between the linguistic periodization and other indicators, and have given cross-references to discussions in Chapters 3 and 5. The list is not a substitute for the detailed discussion elsewhere in this book, but may be useful for a general overview and for statistical purposes; for instance, an archaeologist wishing to generalize about the distribution or layout of linguistically 'early' or 'late' inscriptions might select the inscriptions assigned to a particular range of periods as appropriate.

p.397/285 (ECMW: 5c; KHJ: rather early 5c if the E is really only T) **Brittonic Period** 14–15. This assumes that BARRECTI shows syncope; otherwise it is 1–15, which is more compatible with the suggested 5c date; see Ch. 1 and Section 3.5.

318/6 (ECMW: late 5–early 6c; Ted: VI-1; LHEB: beg. 6c) **Brittonic Period** 1 (if presumably correct composition vowel is significant) or (if not) 1–13 **Irish Period** 1–10.

319/9 (ECMW: 5–early 6c; Ted: V; LHEB: beg. 6c) **Brittonic Period** 1 (if correct composition vowel is significant) or (if not) 1–12 (if lack of CVNO- > CONO- is significant) or (if not) 1–13 (pre-syncope) **Irish Period** 1–7.

320/26 (ECMW: 5–early 6c; Ted: V; LHEB: 5c) **Brittonic Period** 1–5 **Irish Period** 13–14 (if there is Irish apocope in CVLIDOR(I?), otherwise 1–14; see Section 5.4).

321/25 (ECMW: 5–early 6c; KHJ: beg. 6c?) **Brittonic Period** ? **Irish Period** 1–3.

322/27 (ECMW: 5c; LHEB: early 5c) **Brittonic Period** 1–5 **Irish Period** 1–3.

323/32 (ECMW: c. 530 AD; Ted: VI-1; LHEB: c. 525) **Brittonic Period** 1–12 (if the U for pretonic /u/ > /ö/ in SATVRNINVS is significant) or (if not) 1–27.

324/34 (ECMW: 6c (?)) **Brittonic Period** 14–27 **Irish Period** 15. See Ch. 1 and Section 3.8.

325/33 (ECMW: later 6c; Ted: VI-2; LHEB: early 6c) **Brittonic Period** 1–13 **Irish Period** 1–7.

326/39 (ECMW: 6c; Ted: VI-1; LHEB: early or mid-6c) **Brittonic Period** ? **Irish Period** 10–15.

327/43 (ECMW: 6c; Ted: VI-1; LHEB: early to mid-6c) **Brittonic Period** 1–12 (if writing of U for /u/ > /ö/ in TVRPILLI is significant) or (if not) 1–27. (All this is assuming that the name DVNOCATI is Irish; if it were not, the inscription would be very early, ‡16, and probably incompatible with the epigraphic date.) **Irish Period** 13–14.

328/44 (ECMW: 5–early 6c; Ted: V; LHEB: 5c) **Brittonic Period** 1–6 (in the unlikely event that VENDONI, which does not show /nd/ > /nn/, is Brittonic) or (if it is not) 1–11 (i.e. on the basis of the preserved G in RVGN-) **Irish Period** 14 (if VENDONI is Irish, but it may well be an old Celtic(?)-Latin name (*)*Vendonius*). See Sections 5.4 and 5.7.

329/42 (ECMW: 5–early 6c) **Brittonic Period** (the name CANNTIANI) 1–3 (if retention of Latin *ā* is significant) or (if not) 1–16. **Irish Period** (the name MACCVTRENI) 14–15 (if -TRENI is OI *trén* i.e. with loss of fricative) or (if = OI *Trian*-, as is more likely) 10–15. See Section 5.7.

330/66 (ECMW: 5–early 6c; KHJ: no reason why not 5c) **Brittonic Period** 6–16 **Irish Period** 1–14.

331/41 (ECMW: 6c; Ted: VI-1; KHJ: early to mid-6c) **Brittonic Period** ?

332/40 (ECMW: 5–early 6c) **Brittonic Period** ?

333/50 (ECMW: 'uncertain date') **Brittonic Period** 21–28.

334/54 (ECMW: late 6–early 7c; Ted: VII; LHEB: 7c) **Brittonic Period** 1–3 **Irish Period** ? See Section 3.5.

335/54a (ECMW: 12–13c) **Brittonic Period** ?

336/67a (ECMW: 5–6c?) **Brittonic Period** ? **Irish Period** 4–9 (if preservation of Q in formula M[A]Q[I] is significant) or (if not) 4–12.

337/60 (ECMW: 11–12c) **Brittonic Period** 11–28.

339/68 (ECMW: 6c; Ted: VI-1; LHEB: mid- or later 6c) **Brittonic Period** 1–15.

341/71 (ECMW: 5–early 6c; Ted: V; LHEB: end 5c or beg. 6c) **Brittonic Period** 1–14 (but very early if the reading -DVNI is correct and the name is Brittonic, ‡16) **Irish Period** 14 (if -TRENI is OI *trén* with loss of fricative) or (if = OI *Trian*-, as is more likely) 10–14.

342/70 (ECMW: 5–early 6c; Ted: VI-1; LHEB: early 6c) **Brittonic Period** 1 (if the correct composition vowel is significant) or (if not) 1–12 (if writing of U for /u/ > /ö/ is significant) or (if not) 1–13 **Irish Period 4–7**.

344/73 (ECMW: 5–early 6c; Ted: VI-1; LHEB: early 6c) **Brittonic Period 1–3 Irish Period 1–2**. See Section 5.4.

345/74 (ECMW: 5–6c) **Brittonic Period ? Irish Period ?**

346/75 (ECMW: 5–early 6c; Ted: V; KHJ: 5c) **Brittonic Period 1–16**.

347/76 (ECMW: 6c; Ted: VI-1; KHJ: 6c) **Brittonic Period ?**

348/a/110/27 (ECMW: ogam = dubious/'vestiges only') **Brittonic Period ? Irish Period ?** (not periodized as the reading is dubious; see Section 5.1.).

348/b/110/27 (ECMW: 9–10c; KHJ: 8c) **Brittonic Period 22–28**.

349/121/4 (ECMW: 6c; Ted: VI-2; LHEB: mid-6c) **Brittonic Period 1** (if correct composition vowel is significant) or (if not) 1–13.

350/116/3 (ECMW: 6c [> 1st half 7c apud Gruffydd & Owen 1960–62]; Ted: VII; LHEB: 1st half 7c; Thomas, *Peritia*, 10 (1996), 157: AD 806) **Brittonic Period 27–28**. See Ch. 1 and Section 3.5.

351/115/2 (ECMW: 6c; Ted: VI-1; KHJ: mid- to later 6c, or later?) **Brittonic Period 1–12** (if writing of U for /u/ > /ö/ is significant) or (if not) 1–27 **Irish Period ?** See Section 5.1.

352A/122/5 (ECMW: 5–early 6c; Ted: VI-1; LHEB: end 5c or beg. 6c) **Brittonic Period 13–16**. See Section 3.8.

353/127/7 (ECMW: 5–early 6c; Ted: V; LHEB: end 5c or beg. 6c) **Brittonic Period 12–28 Irish Period 1–13**. It is probably Irish, which suits the epigraphic date better.

354/126/6 (ECMW: 5–early 6c; Ted: VI-1; LHEB: 5c) **Brittonic Period 1–10 Irish Period 1–3**.

355/128/8 (ECMW: 5–early 6c; LHEB: beg. 6c) **Brittonic Period 7–20 Irish Period 3–15**. If Irish it would be well on in Period 15 if SILBANDVS has Middle Irish hypercorrect *nd*, so the name is probably British-Latin if the epigraphic dates are correct. See §43n.

356/132/9 (ECMW: 6c; Ted: VI-1; LHEB: end 6c) **Brittonic Period 1–7**.

357/136 (ECMW: 5–early 6c; KHJ: early 6c) **Brittonic Period ? Irish Period 1–13**.

358/138 (ECMW: 'AD 540–50'; Ted: V; LHEB: *c.* 550, but cf. Sections 5.4, 5.6, and 5.7) **Brittonic Period 1** (if correct composition vowel in VOTEPORIGIS is significant) or (if not) 1–13 **Irish Period 7**. See Section 5.7.

359/141 (ECMW: 6c; Ted: VI-1; LHEB: mid- or later 6c) **Brittonic Period 8–24**.

360/139 (ECMW: '*c.* 550'; Ted: V; LHEB: early or mid-6c) **Brittonic Period ?**

361/140 (ECMW: 6c; Ted: VI-1) **Brittonic Period 1–5 Irish Period 5–8**.

362/142 (ECMW: 5–early 6c; Ted: V; LHEB: end 5c) **Brittonic Period 1** (if apparently correct composition vowel is significant) or (if not) 1–12 (if U for pretonic /u/ > /ö/ is significant) or (if not) 1–13. **Irish Period 12**. See Section 5.4.

363/143 (ECMW: 6c; LHEB: mid- or later 6c) **Brittonic Period** 1–3.

364/144 (ECMW: 6c; Ted: VI-2; LHEB: mid-6c) **Brittonic Period** ? **Irish Period** 15. See Section 5.4.

365/149 (ECMW: late 6c; Ted: VI-2; LHEB: end 6c) **Brittonic Period** 10–13.

366/148 (ECMW: late 5–6c) **Brittonic Period** 4–20 **Irish Period** 7–14. See Section 5.7.

368/a/150 (ECMW: 5–early 6c) **Brittonic Period** ? **Irish Period** 1–3 (if retention of **-S** is significant) or (if not) 1–8 (if the lack of rounding after **Q** in **MAQI**(?) is significant) or (if not) 1–9 (if the retention of **Q** in **MAQI**(?) is significant) or (if not) 1–12.

368/b/150 (ECMW: 5–early 6c; Ted: VI-1; LHEB: end 5c or beg. 6c) **Brittonic Period** 2–6 **Irish Period** 8–14.

369/153 (ECMW: 5–early 6c; KHJ: 5c, but then seems to accept ECMW date) **Brittonic Period** ? **Irish Period** 7.

370/157 (ECMW: 5–early 6c; Ted: VI-1; LHEB: 5c) **Brittonic Period** 1 (if correct composition vowel is significant) or (if not) 1–7 **Irish Period** 1–7.

371/322 (ECMW: Early Christian?) [fake?] **Brittonic Period** ?

372/160 (ECMW: late 5–6c; Ted: VI-1; LHEB: early 6c) **Brittonic Period** ? **Irish Period** 15. See Sections 5.2 and 5.4.

373/171 (ECMW: 5–early 6c; Ted: VI-1; KHJ: beg. 6c) **Brittonic Period** ?

374/172 (ECMW: 5–early 6c; Ted: V; LHEB: 5c) **Brittonic Period** 1–12 (if U for pretonic /u/ > /ö/ is significant) or (if not) 1–27 **Irish Period** 8–13. See Section 5.4.

375/166 (ECMW: 6c; Ted: VI-2; LHEB: mid- to later 6c) **Brittonic Period** ? **Irish Period** 1–14. DO- rather than *TO- in DOTHORANTI might suggest a late 7c Irish date (§43), but this conflicts with the epigraphic dating as well as the non-syncope in TOTAVALI.

376/174 (ECMW: 5–early 6c; Ted: VI-1; LHEB: 5c) **Brittonic Period** 7–9 **Irish Period** 1–13. See Section 5.7.

377/175 (ECMW: 5–early 6c; Ted: VI-1; LHEB: 5c(?)) **Brittonic Period** 2–9.

378/169 (ECMW: late 5–6c; Ted: VI-1; LHEB: early 6c) **Brittonic Period** ? **Irish Period** 8–14.

379/170 (ECMW: late 5–6c; Ted: V; LHEB: end 5c or beg. 6c) **Brittonic Period** 1 (if correct composition vowel is significant) or (if not) 1–3 **Irish Period** 1–14.

380/84 (ECMW: 6c; Ted: V; LHEB: mid- or later 6c) **Brittonic Period** 1–5 **Irish Period** 1–3 (if the preservation of **-S** is significant) or (if not) 1–7. See Section 5.4.

381/87 (ECMW: 5–early 6c; Ted: V; LHEB: late 5c) **Brittonic Period** 1–3.

382/86 (ECMW: 5–early 6c; Ted: V; KHJ: no reason why not 5c) **Brittonic Period** ?

384/83 (ECMW: 5–early 6c; Ted: V; LHEB: early 6c) **Brittonic Period** 1–15.

385/89 (ECMW: 5–early 6c; Ted: V; LHEB: end 5c) **Brittonic Period** 4–5.

386/92 (ECMW: 5–early 6c; Ted: VI-1; LHEB: beg. 6c) **Brittonic Period** ? **Irish Period** ?

387/95 (ECMW: 6c; Ted: VI-2; KHJ: mid- to later 6c) **Brittonic Period** 13. See Section 3.8.

388/94 (ECMW: 5–early 6c) **Brittonic Period** 1–5 **Irish Period** 1–2.

389/97 (ECMW: 6c; Ted: V; LHEB: mid-6c) **Brittonic Period** 1–3 (if writing of A for /a:/ > /ɔ:/ is significant) or (if not) 1–7 (if the retention of ERN in ETERNI is significant, which is not certain) or (if not) 1–20.

390/96 (ECMW: 6c; Ted: V; LHEB: 5c) **Brittonic Period** 2–6.

391/78 (ECMW: 5–early 6c; Ted: VI-1; LHEB: early or mid-6c) **Brittonic Period** 1–3 **Irish Period** ?

392/77 (ECMW: 5–early 6c; Ted: VI-1; LHEB: early 6c) **Brittonic Period** 1–3 (if writing of A in VERACIVS for /a:/ > /ɔ:/ is significant) or (if not) 1–17 (assuming that E = /e:/ > /ui/).

393/101 (ECMW: 5–early 6c; Ted: V; LHEB: end 5c) **Brittonic Period** ?

394/103 (ECMW: 5–early 6c; Ted: V; LHEB: end 5c) **Brittonic Period** 1–5.

395/102 (ECMW: 5–early 6c; Ted: V; KHJ: nothing against 5c except perhaps the R) **Brittonic Period** ?

396/104 (ECMW: 'c. 540 AD'; Ted: VI-1; LHEB: 540, but see Sections 3.6 and 5.6) **Brittonic Period** 1–5 **Irish Period** 12–14. See Section 3.6.

397/105 (ECMW: 6c; Ted: VI-1; LHEB: mid- or later 6c) **Brittonic Period** 2–3.

398/106 (ECMW: 6c – and 'possible vestiges of Ogam'; Ted: VI-1; KHJ: mid-6c(?)) **Brittonic Period** 7–28 **Irish Period** 14–15.

399/176 (ECMW: 5–early 6c; Ted: V; LHEB: end 5c) **Brittonic Period** 1–3 **Irish Period** 1–11.

400/177 (ECMW: 5–early 6c; Ted: V; LHEB: beg. 6c) **Brittonic Period** 7.

401/183 (ECMW: 5–early 6c; Ted: VI-1; LHEB: mid-6c) **Brittonic Period** 1 (if correct composition vowel is significant) or (if not) 1–11.

402/184 (ECMW: 6c; Ted: VI-2; LHEB: mid- or later 6c) **Brittonic Period** ?

403/268/841 (ECMW: late 5–early 6c; Ted: VI-1; KHJ: hardly older than early to mid-6c) **Brittonic Period** ? **Irish Period** 13–14. See Section 5.2.

404/270/843 (ECMW: 7c; Ted: VI-2; LHEB: 7c) **Brittonic Period** 1–3 **Irish Period** ? See Ch. 1 and Section 3.5.

405/228/845 (ECMW: 5–early 6c) **Brittonic Period** ? **Irish Period** 4–7.

406/215/844 (ECMW: 5–early 6c; Ted: VI-1; LHEB: beg. of 6c(?)) **Brittonic Period** 1–15.

407/a/258/846 (ECMW: 4c) **Brittonic Period** 1–15.

407/b/258/846 (ECMW: 6c; Ted: VI-1; LHEB: mid- or later 6c) **Brittonic Period** 1–22.

408/229/848 (ECMW: 6c; Ted: VI-2; LHEB: mid- or later 6c) **Brittonic Period** 8–13 **Irish Period** 1–10.

409/198/849 (ECMW: 6c; Ted: VI-1; LHEB: early or mid-6c) **Brittonic Period** 3–5 **Irish Period** 13–14. See Section 5.7.

410/238/847 (ECMW: 5–early 6c; Ted: V; LHEB: 5c) **Brittonic Period** ?

412/277 (ECMW: 5–early 6c) **Brittonic Period** 21–28. See Section 3.5.

413/272 (ECMW: 5–early 6c; Ted: V; LHEB: 5c) **Brittonic Period** 1 (if correct composition vowel is significant) or (if not) 1–2.

414/271 (ECMW: 5–early 6c; Ted: V; KHJ: beg. 6c(?)) **Brittonic Period** 1–7.

415/278 (ECMW: 5–early 6c) **Brittonic Period** ? **Irish Period** ?

416/279 (ECMW: 6c; Ted: VI-1; LHEB: mid- or later 6c) **Brittonic Period** ?

417/282 (ECMW: 5–early 6c; Ted: VI-1; LHEB: early or mid-6c) **Brittonic Period** 1–5.

418/283 (ECMW: 5–early 6c) **Brittonic Period** 1–3 (if writing of A for /aː/ > /ɔː/ is significant) or (if not) 1–12 (if writing of U for /u/ > /ö/ is significant, ‡46) or (if not) 1–13.

419/284 (ECMW: 6c; KHJ: mid- to later 6c) **Brittonic Period** 10–13.

420/289 (ECMW: late 5–early 6c; Ted: V; LHEB: beg. 6c) **Brittonic Period** 1–5.

421/294 (ECMW: late 5–early 6c; Ted: V; LHEB: 5c) **Brittonic Period** 1–7 (if lack of ERN > IRN in PATERNINI is significant) or (if not) ?

422/298 (ECMW: 6c; KHJ: too feint to date) **Brittonic Period** 1–21 **Irish Period** 8–13.

423/296 (ECMW: 5–early 6c) **Brittonic Period** ? **Irish Period** 10–15.

424/299 (ECMW: 6c; Ted: VI-1; LHEB: early or mid-6c) **Brittonic Period** 1–3 **Irish Period** 8–14.

425/297 (ECMW: 5–early 6c; Ted: VI-1; LHEB: early or mid-6c) **Brittonic Period** 2–11 **Irish Period** 10–13.

426/300 (ECMW: 5–6c) **Brittonic Period** 1–3 **Irish Period** 1–7.

427/a/301 (ECMW: 5–6c) **Brittonic Period** ? **Irish Period** 1–7.

427/b/301 (ECMW: early 9c; LHEB: 8c; cf. Ch. 1) **Brittonic Period** 14–20.

428/305 (ECMW: 6c; Ted: VI-2; LHEB: early 7c) **Brittonic Period** ? **Irish Period** 14 (if **TRENA**- is OI *trén* with loss of fricative) or (if = OI *Trian*-, as is more likely) 10–14. See Section 5.4.

429/307 (ECMW: late 5–early 6c; Ted: VI-1; KHJ: perhaps early 6c?) **Brittonic Period** 1–6 **Irish Period** 14–15.

430/306 (ECMW: 5–early 6c; Ted: VI-1; LHEB: end 5c or beg. 6c) **Brittonic Period** 1–7 **Irish Period** 13–15.

431/308 (ECMW: 5–early 6c; Ted: V; LHEB: early or mid-6c) **Brittonic Period** ? **Irish Period** 8–12.

432/312 (ECMW: 5–early 6c; Ted: V; LHEB: late 5c or early 6c) **Brittonic Period** 1–3 **Irish Period** 8–13.

433/313 (ECMW: 5–early 6c; Ted: VI-1; LHEB: early or mid-6c) **Brittonic Period** ? **Irish Period** 10–14.

434/314 (ECMW: 6c; Ted: VI-2; LHEB: late 6c) **Brittonic Period** ? **Irish Period** 1–13.

435/315 (ECMW: 5–early 6c; Ted: VI-1; LHEB: later 5c) **Brittonic Period** 1 (if correct composition vowel is significant) or (if not) 1–12 (if U for pretonic /u/ > /ü/ is significant) or (if not) 1–13 **Irish Period** 1–7.

436/316 (ECMW: late 6c; Ted: VI-2; LHEB: end of 6c) **Brittonic Period** 1–13 **Irish Period** 8–14.

437/317 (ECMW: 6c; KHJ: early to mid-6c?) **Brittonic Period** ?

438/320 (ECMW: 5–6c?) **Brittonic Period** ? **Irish Period** ?

439/319 (ECMW: 5–early 6c) **Brittonic Period** ? **Irish Period** 1–9.

440/335 (ECMW: 6c; LHEB: 6c(?)) **Brittonic Period** 11–28 **Irish Period** 10–15. See Ch. 1 and Section 5.7.

441/345 (ECMW: 5–early 6c; Ted: VI-1; KHJ: 5c) **Brittonic Period** ? **Irish Period** 7. See Section 5.4.

442/346 (ECMW: 5–early 6c; Ted: V; LHEB: end 5c or beg. 6c) **Brittonic Period** 1–16 **Irish Period** 13–14.

443/349 (ECMW: 5–early 6c) **Brittonic Period** 1–5 (periodization based on reading CAMVLORI).

444/352 (ECMW: late 6c) **Brittonic Period** 1–19.

445/354 (ECMW: 5–early 6c; Ted: V; LHEB: 5c) **Brittonic Period** 1–3 (if preservation of Latin $\bar{a}$ is significant) or (if not) 1–20 **Irish Period** ?

446/353 (ECMW: 5–early 6c; Ted: VI-1; LHEB: mid- or later 5c) **Brittonic Period** 1 (if correct composition vowel is significant) or (if not) 1–5 **Irish Period** 1–3 (if retention of -S is significant) or (if not) 1–7.

447/369 (ECMW: 6c; KHJ: early to mid-6c?) **Brittonic Period** 2–11 **Irish Period** 1–7.

448/370 (ECMW: 5–early 6c; Ted: V; LHEB: 5c) **Brittonic Period** 1–3 **Irish Period** 1–7.

449/384 (ECMW: 5–early 6c; LHEB: early 6c) **Brittonic Period** 1 (if correct composition vowel is significant) or (if not) 1–12 (if U for pretonic /u/ > ö/ is significant) or (if not) 1–13 **Irish Period** 14–15. See Ch. 5.2 and 5.7.

450/390 (ECMW: 6c; Ted: V; LHEB: early 6c)[9] **Brittonic Period** 1–7 **Irish Period** 1–12.

451/401 (ECMW: 6c; Ted: VI-1; LHEB: early or mid-6c) **Brittonic Period** 3 **Irish Period** ?

452/400 (ECMW: 5–early 6c; Ted: VI-1; KHJ: early to mid-6c) **Brittonic Period** 1–21 **Irish Period** 1–14.

453/399 (ECMW: 5–early 6c; Ted: VI-1; KHJ: 5c) **Brittonic Period** ? **Irish Period** ?

454/402 (ECMW: 5–early 6c; Ted: V; LHEB: end 5c) **Brittonic Period** 1 (if correct composition vowel is significant) or (if not) 1–3 (if retention of Latin $\bar{a}$ is significant) or (if not) 1–6 **Irish Period** 1–7.

---

[9]   In July 1947 KHJ dated this inscription in 'pure capitals' to the fifth century, but in October moved it later under the influence of a letter from Nash-Williams claiming that his tracing showed a half uncial h. To me it seems to be a capital H. Note that the stone is at St Dogwells, not St Dogmaels as stated in ECMW.

455/403 (ECMW: 5–early 6c; Ted: VI-1; LHEB: early or mid-6c) **Brittonic Period** 1 (if correct composition vowel is significant) or (if not) 1–12 (if U for pretonic /u/ > /ö/ is significant) or (if not) 1–13 **Irish Period** 3–15. See Section 5.7.

456/404 (ECMW: 5–early 6c; KHJ: 8c, but ogams and horizontal **I** are odd so late) **Brittonic Period** 1–22 **Irish Period** ?

457/Ok18 (Ted: VI-1; LHEB: early 6c; Th: VI.2) **Brittonic Period** ? **Irish Period** 1–13.

458/Ok9 (Th: VI.3; KHJ: end 6c?) **Brittonic Period** ? **Irish Period** 1–14.

459/Ok63 (Th: long post-700; KHJ: not older than 8c, prob. not older than 9c) **Brittonic Period** ?

460/Ok75 (Ted: VI-2; LHEB: mid-6c) **Brittonic Period** ? **Irish Period** 14–15.

461/Ok66 (Ted: VI-2; LHEB: mid-6c; Th: not pre VI.3) **Brittonic Period** ? **Irish Period** 4–7. See Sections 5.2 and 5.4.

462/Ok14 (Ted: VI-2; LHEB: mid- to later 6c; Th: VI.2/VI.3) **Brittonic Period** ? **Irish Period** 1–9 (if retention of Q in QVENATAVCI is significant) or (if not) 1–14.

463/Ok15 (Th: 10–11c; KHJ: not enough to date, esp. if **RI** *is* N) **Brittonic Period** ?

464/Ok65 (Th: medieval or later?; KHJ: early to mid-6c) **Brittonic Period** 25–28.

465/Ok21 (Ted: V; Th: VI.2; KHJ: no reason why not 5c) **Brittonic Period** ?

466/Ok23 (Ted: V; LHEB: early 6c/end 5c or early 6c; Th: VI.1, *c.* 500?) **Brittonic Period** ? **Irish Period** 13–15.

467/Ok24 (Ted: V; LHEB: 5c; Th: late VI.1 or early VI.2) **Brittonic Period** ? **Irish Period** 1–7.

468/Ok31 (Ted: VI-2; LHEB: early or mid-6c; Th: VI.2) **Brittonic Period** 1 (if correct composition vowel is significant) or (if not) 1–8 (if U for /u/ > /ọ/ is significant) or (if not) 1–13 **Irish Period** 1–7.

469/Ok34 (Ted: VI-2; Th: VI.3; KHJ: end 6c or early 7c?) **Brittonic Period** ?

470/Ok78 (Ted: VI-2; LHEB: late 6c; Th: VI.2) **Brittonic Period** ?

471/Ok39 (Ted: VI-2; LHEB: 7c; Th: VI.3 or VII.1) **Brittonic Period** 14–28 **Irish Period** 15. See Section 3.8.

472/Ok35 (Ted: V; LHEB: end 5c; Th: *c.* 500 or VI.1) **Brittonic Period** ? **Irish Period** 1–7.

473/a/Ok46 (Ted: VI-1; LHEB: late 5c or early 6c; Th: VI.1 or early VI.2) **Brittonic Period** 1–3 (if retention of Latin *ā* is significant) or (if not) 1–16.

473/b/Ok46 (I assume Tedeschi's VI-1 date applies to 473/a only (above, p. 273); Th: after 473/a, prob. before 600; KHJ: no reason to take any later, palaeographically, than 473/a, and cannot accept Radford's view in *Early Christian Inscriptions of Dumnonia*, p. 10, that it is 200+ years later, if Macalister's drawing is right) **Brittonic Period** 17–28.

474/Ok17 (Th: *c.* 600; KHJ: too illegible to date) **Brittonic Period** 1–19 **Irish Period** 1–13.

475/Ok47 (KHJ: might be 7c, but Macalister's arrangement of letters very suspicious) **Brittonic Period** 7–28 **Irish Period** 14–15.

476/Ok45 (Ted: V; Th: VI.1; KHJ: no reason why not 5c) **Brittonic Period** 8–28 (better 1–28; cf. Section 3.5).

477/Ok11 (Ted: VI-2; LHEB: 7c; Th: VI.3) **Brittonic Period** 12–13.

478/Ok48 (Ted: VI-2; LHEB: mid-6c; Th: VI.3? *c.* 600?) **Brittonic Period** ? **Irish Period** 1–13.

479/Ok16 (LHEB: 5c; Th: 5c, prob. not post-450–75) **Brittonic Period** 16–17 **Irish Period** 5–7. The Irish identification fits the epigraphic dates better.

480/Ok19 (Th: 11–12c?; KHJ: 9c or even later) **Brittonic Period** ?

481/Ok49 (Ted: VI-2; Th: VII; KHJ: perhaps late 7c or early 8c?) **Brittonic Period** ?

482/Ok71 (Th: VI.2 or VI.3; KHJ: may have been as old as 6c) **Brittonic Period** 1–7 **Irish Period** 1 (if non-raising in NEMIA(N)VS is significant) or (if not) 1–7 (if non-lowering in -IANVS is significant) or (if not) 1–15. See Sections 5.2 and 5.4.

483/Ok51 (Ted: V; KHJ: E suggests 6c, perhaps latish) **Brittonic Period** 1–7.

484/Ok52 (Ted: VI-1; LHEB: end 6c or beg. 7c; Th: VI.2) **Brittonic Period** ?

485/Ok68 (Th: VI.2/VI.3; KHJ: 6c??) **Brittonic Period** 1–16 **Irish Period** 1 (if non-raising in COLINI is significant) or (if not) 1–15. See Sections 5.2 and 5.4.

486/Ok56 (Ted: VI-2; Th: late VI.2 or VI.3; KHJ: end 6c or beg. 7c) **Brittonic Period** 14–16. See Section 3.8.

487/Ok10 (Ted: VI-2; LHEB: end 5c; Th: VI.2 or VI.3) **Brittonic Period** 4–8 (if U for /u/ > /o̜/ in DRVST- and CVNO- is significant) or (if not) 4–13 **Irish Period** 1–7 (in the unlikely event that DRVSTAGNI is the correct reading).

488/Ok60 (Ted: VI-1; LHEB: early or mid-6c; Th: ogam VI.1, after 500; roman VI.2) **Brittonic Period** ? **Irish Period** 14 (if ENABARRI/ ENABARR has unsyncopated composition vowel) or 15 (if it has post-syncope epenthesis). See Section 5.2.

489/a/Ok13 (Ted: VI-2; LHEB: end 6c; Th: VI.1 or early VI.2) **Brittonic Period** 7–28 (if RINI shows /nd/ > /nn/) or (if not) 4–28 **Irish Period** 3–8 (if lack of rounding after /kʷ/ in the formula **MAQI** / MAQVI is significant) or (if not) 3–9.

489/b/Ok13 (Ted: VI-2 (but perhaps meaning 489/a only?); this part not cited in LHEB; Th: VI.2 or VI.3; KHJ: earlier [*recte* later? PS-W] than 489/a) **Brittonic Period** 18–28 **Irish Period** 14–15. See Section 3.5.

490/Ok29 (Ted: VI-2; LHEB: early 7c; Th: VI.3 or just post 600) **Brittonic Period** 14–16. See Section 3.8.

491/Ok55 (Th: VI.3; KHJ: mid-6c?) **Brittonic Period** ?

492/Ok59 (Ted: VI-2; LHEB: late 6c or early 7c; Th: VI.2) **Brittonic Period** ? **Irish Period** 10–15.

493/Ok58 (Ted: VI-1; LHEB: mid- to later 6c; Th: VI.3) **Brittonic Period** 14–16 **Irish Period** 15. See Sections 3.8 and 5.4.

494/Ok79 (KHJ: late 6c or early 7c) **Brittonic Period** 22–28 **Irish Period** 8–15.

496 (Jackson, in Wright & Jackson 1968: not earlier than *c.* 500; cf. ‡17n.) **Brittonic Period** 2–13 **Irish Period** 1–3 (if retention of -S is significant) or (if not) 1–12. See Section 5.4.

497/409 (ECMW: 6c) **Brittonic Period** ?

498/Nb7 (Ted: V; LHEB: late 5c or early 6c) **Brittonic Period** 1 (if correct composition vowel is significant) or (if not) 1–11.

499/Ok77 (Ted: VI-1; KHJ: possibly late 5c) **Brittonic Period** 1–3.

500 (Ted: VI-1; LHEB: end 5c) **Brittonic Period** 2–13 **Irish Period** 1–3 (if retention of -S is significant) or (if not) 1–5 (if lack of /æmb/ > /mb/ is significant) or (if not) 1–8 (if lack of rounding after /k^w/ in formula **MAQI** is significant) or (if not) 1–9 (if retention of **Q** in **MAQI** is significant) or (if not) 1–12. See Section 5.7.

501 **Brittonic Period** ? **Irish Period** 1–7.

502 **Brittonic Period** ? **Irish Period** 13–15.

503 **Brittonic Period** ? **Irish Period** 8–12.

504 **Brittonic Period** ? **Irish Period** 1–3 (if retention of -S is significant) or (if not) 1–7.

505 (Ted: VII; KHJ: early 7c) **Brittonic Period** 3–7 (better 3–28; see Section 3.5).

506 **Brittonic Period** 1–21 **Irish Period** 14–15.

507 **Brittonic Period** ? **Irish Period** 14–15.

508 **Brittonic Period** ?

509/Ok.Pict3 (KHJ: Stevenson, Nat. Mus. Scot., dates 1st half 9c) **Brittonic Period** ?

510/Scot.13 (Ted: V; LHEB: early 6c) **Brittonic Period** 1–15 **Irish Period** ?

511/Scot.10 (Ted: VI-1; Nash-Williams apud Macdonald (1935–36): pre 550; Jackson in RC *Peeblesshire* i, 176: lettering early part of 6c, language ?later) **Brittonic Period** ? **Irish Period** 14–15.

512 **Brittonic Period** ? **Irish Period** 1–12.

513/Ok.Pict8 **Brittonic Period** ?

514/Scot. 8 (Ted: VI-1; LHEB: late 5c or early 6c) **Brittonic Period** 1–3 (if retention of Latin *ā* is significant) or (if not) 1–16.

515/Scot.9 (Ted: VI-2; LHEB: early to mid-6c) **Brittonic Period** 1 (if correct composition vowel is significant) or (if not) 1–3 (if retention of Latin *ā* is significant) or (if not) 1–13.

516/Scot.1 (KHJ: beg. to mid-6c) **Brittonic Period** 5.

517/Scot.2 (KHJ: may be earlier than no. 516) **Brittonic Period** 1–7.

518/Scot.3 (KHJ: early 7c or later) **Brittonic Period** ?

519/Scot.6 (Jackson, in *St. Ninian's Isle*, i, 172, n. 1: late 6c or early 7c) **Brittonic Period** ?

520/Scot.5 (Ted: V; LHEB: beg. 6c) **Brittonic Period** 1 (if correct composition vowel is significant) or (if not) 1–13 **Irish Period** 1–14.

968/5 (ECMW: 12c) **Brittonic Period** ?

970/13 (ECMW: *c.* 625 AD; Ted: VII; LHEB: mid-7c; cf. Section 3.6) **Brittonic Period** 7–13. See Section 3.8.

971/35 (ECMW: 7–9c; LHEB: mid-7c) **Brittonic Period** 22–27. See Section 3.8.

976/72 (ECMW: 7–9c? Jackson, in *St. Ninian's Isle*, i, 167: 7–8c) **Brittonic Period** ?

978/49 (ECMW: late 10c; LHEB: 10c to 11c) **Brittonic Period** 20–25 (if loss of G in BRIA- is significant) or (if not) 12–25.

979/46 (ECMW: 9c; LHEB: 9c) **Brittonic Period** 28.

980/46a (ECMW: 11–12c) **Brittonic Period** 22–28.

982/55 (ECMW: 7–9c) **Brittonic Period** ?

984/59 (ECMW: 7–9c) **Brittonic Period** 22–28. See Section 3.8.

985/61 (ECMW: 10–11c) **Brittonic Period** 11–28.

986/62 (ECMW: 7–9c; LHEB: prob. 8c, cf. Ch. 1) **Brittonic Period** 21–28. See Section 3.8.

988/67 (ECMW: late 11–12c, cf. Section 3.6) **Brittonic Period** 23–28.

989/69 (ECMW: 7–9c) **Brittonic Period** ?

990/108/1 (ECMW: 7–9c; LHEB: 7c) **Brittonic Period** 1–24 **Irish Period** ?

991/113/30 (ECMW: 9–10c) **Brittonic Period** ?

992/120/14 (ECMW: 7–9c) **Brittonic Period** 28. See Section 3.8.

993/124/18 (ECMW: 7–9c; Edwards, *Med. Arch.*, 45 (2001), 32: before 800) **Brittonic Period** 20 **Irish Period** (the name MADOMNUAC(O)) 15. See §43 and Section 5.7.

994/125/22 (ECMW: early 9c; LHEB: 1st half 9c) **Brittonic Period** 24–28 (the name HIROIDIL) **Irish Period** 13–14 – but 15 if the -O- of CAROTINN is explained by svarabhakti, as is likely, rather than by non-syncope; see Sections 5.2, 5.3, 5.4, and 5.7.

995/133/24 (ECMW: 7–9c; LHEB: 7c or 8c) **Brittonic Period** 17–28. See Section 3.8.

996/147 (ECMW: 11–early 12c) **Brittonic Period** 11–28.

997/159 (ECMW: 10c) **Brittonic Period** 14–28.

998/164 (ECMW: 7–9c; Ted: VII) **Brittonic Period** 26–28. See Ch. 3.8.

1000/182 (ECMW: 1st half 9c; LHEB: 9c, cf. Section 3.6) **Brittonic Period** 22–27.

1001/181 (ECMW: 9–10c) **Brittonic Period** 11–28.

1003/261/885 (ECMW: 9c) **Brittonic Period** ?

1004/260/884 (ECMW: 7–9c) **Brittonic Period** 22–28. See Section 3.8.

1005/191/886 (ECMW: 9c; LHEB: 9c) **Brittonic Period** 14–28.

1006/197/842 (ECMW: 7–9c) **Brittonic Period** ? **Irish Period** 4–15.

1007/206/938 (ECMW: late 10–11c) **Brittonic Period** 28.

1008/194/934 (ECMW: 11–early 12c) **Brittonic Period** 17–28.

1009/193/935 (ECMW: 11c) **Brittonic Period** 17–28

1010/211/882 (ECMW: 9c) **Brittonic Period** ?

1011/220/911 (ECMW: late 9c; LHEB: 9c, cf. Section 3.6) **Brittonic Period** 15–27.

1012/223/933 (ECMW: 10–11c; LHEB: 10c to 11c, but cf. Section 3.6) **Brittonic Period** 25–26 (but see Section 3.6: 14–26?).

1013/222/912 (ECMW: late 10c; LHEB: 10c) **Brittonic Period** 17–28.

1014/231/908 (ECMW: late 9–early 10c) **Brittonic Period** 22–28.

1015/233/910 (ECMW: 10–11c) **Brittonic Period** 14–28.

1016/234/907 (ECMW: late 10–11c; LHEB: 10c to 11c) **Brittonic Period** 14–27.

1017/259/867 (ECMW: 7–9c) **Brittonic Period** ?

1018/236/919 (ECMW: 11c) **Brittonic Period** 22–28.

1019/237/920 (ECMW: 11c) **Brittonic Period** 14–28.

1020/200/921 (ECMW: late 10–11c) **Brittonic Period** ?

1022/240/928 (ECMW: 11c) **Brittonic Period** 17–28 **Irish Period** 1–14 (only on basis of Macalister's highly dubious DOBITAUCI, cf. Section 5.4).

1023/239/927 (ECMW: 11c; LHEB: *c.*1000 AD) **Brittonic Period** 18–20. See Section 3.5.

1024/255/926 (ECMW: 11c; LHEB: *c.*1000 AD) **Brittonic Period** 22–28.

1025/248/862 (ECMW: 7–9c; LHEB: 8–9c) **Brittonic Period** 14–28.

1027/265/923 (ECMW: late 10–11c) **Brittonic Period** 14–28.

1028/214/850 (ECMW: late 6–early 7c; Ted: VII; LHEB: late 6c or early 7c) **Brittonic Period** 2–6 **Irish Period** 8–13. See Section 3.8.

1029 **Brittonic Period** 26–28.

1030 **Brittonic Period** 28.

1032/281 (ECMW: 12c, cf. Section 3.6) **Brittonic Period** 28.

1033/287 (ECMW: 7–9c; LHEB: 7–8c) **Brittonic Period** 28. See Section 3.8.

1034/286 (ECMW: 5–early 6c) **Brittonic Period** 1–7.

1035/303 (ECMW: '1033–5 AD'; LHEB: 1033–35; but cf. Section 3.6) **Brittonic Period** 22–26 (but cf. Section 3.7).

1036/360 (ECMW: late 10–early 11c) **Brittonic Period** 11–28.

1038/365 (ECMW: early 10c) **Brittonic Period** ? **Irish Period** 15.

1039/382 (ECMW: '1078–80 AD', but cf. Section 3.6) **Brittonic Period** 15–28.

1040/379 (ECMW: not pre-10c) **Brittonic Period** ?

1041/376 (ECMW: 9–10c) **Brittonic Period** 22–28.

1044/Ok7 (Th: mid 10c? late 10c?) **Brittonic Period** 14–16.

1045/Ok69 (Th: 11c?) **Brittonic Period** 11–28.

1046/Ok8 (Th: 10–11c) **Brittonic Period** 11–28.

1047/Ok20 (Th: late 10c) **Brittonic Period** 11–28.

1048/Ok32 (Ted: VII; Th: VII.1?) **Brittonic Period** 11–28 **Irish Period** 15.

1049/Ok33 (KHJ: 6c?) **Brittonic Period** 11–28.

1050/Ok74 (Th: 11c) **Brittonic Period** 11–28.

1051/Ok37 (Th: *c.* 1050) **Brittonic Period** ?

1052/Ok38 **Brittonic Period** ?
1053/Ok1 (Th: 11c) **Brittonic Period** 11–28.
1054/Ok43 (Th: 9c) **Brittonic Period** 14–16.
1055/Ok3 (Th: VII.1 or VII.2; or later 7c; or *c.* 700) **Brittonic Period** ?
1056/OkAppC **Brittonic Period** ?
1057/Ok54 (Th: 6c; KHJ: 6c?) **Brittonic Period** ? **Irish Period** ?
1058/Ok53 (Th: late 10c) **Brittonic Period** 11–28.
1059/Ok64 (Th: 11c) **Brittonic Period** 11–28.
1060/Ok57 (Ted: VII; Th: 7c; Radford (1969): 7c) **Brittonic Period** 22–28. See Section 3.5.
1061/Dor.iii (Ted: VII; RC: 7–8c) **Brittonic Period** 21–28. See Section 3.5.
1062/Dor.v (RC: 8–9c) **Brittonic Period** 14–28.
1063/Dor.ii (RC: late 7c) **Brittonic Period** 14–26.
1064/Dor.iv (RC: late 8c) **Brittonic Period** 17–18.
1065/410 (ECMW: 9–10c) **Brittonic Period** 14–28.
1066 (LHEB: 8–9c cf. Ch. 3.6) **Brittonic Period** 22–28.
1067 (see p. 42, n. 120) **Brittonic Period** ?
1068/a **Brittonic Period** 1–4 **Irish Period** 1–14.
1068/b **Brittonic Period** 14–27 **Irish Period** 15. See Section 5.7.
1069/Ok.PictApp.I **Brittonic Period** ?
1200/Ok42 (Th: pre-700) **Brittonic Period** 11–28.
1201/Ok- (Th: pre-700) **Brittonic Period** ?
1202/Ok2 (Ted: VI-2; Th: late VI.2/VI.3) **Brittonic Period** ? **Irish Period** 8–14.
1203/Ok- (Th: pre-700) **Brittonic Period** ?
1205/Ok44 (Th: pre-700) **Brittonic Period** 5–10.
1206/Ok4 (Ted: V; Th: pre-700) **Brittonic Period** ? **Irish Period** 8–15.
1207/Ok- (ogam damaged) (Th: pre-700) **Brittonic Period** ?
1208/Ok6 (Th: pre-700) **Brittonic Period** ?
1209/Ok12 (Th: VI.3 ?or late VI.2; Radford (1969): *c.* 500 or early 6c) **Brittonic Period** 4–28.
1210/Ok5 (Th: pre-700) **Brittonic Period** 1–21 **Irish Period** ?
1212 **Brittonic Period** ?
1400/Ok28 (Th: pre-*c.* 500) **Brittonic Period** ?
1401/Ok27 (Ted: V; Th: a little after *c.* 500) **Brittonic Period** 27–28 (but see Section 3.5).
1402/Ok26 (Ted: V; Th. *c.* 550) **Brittonic Period** ?
1403/Ok25 (Ted: VI-2; Th: *c.* 600) **Brittonic Period** 1–7 **Irish Period** ?
1404/Ok30 (Ted: VI-1; Th: VI.3) **Brittonic Period** ? **Irish Period** ?
2000 (Sims-Williams, *TAAS*, 1999, 147: 6c?) **Brittonic Period** 1 (if the correct composition vowel is significant) or (if not) 1–13 **Irish Period** 1–14.
2001 (5–7c, *Corpus*) **Brittonic Period** 1–5.
2002/a (5c, *Corpus*) **Brittonic Period** 1–3 (if the retention of Latin *ā* is significant, which is unlikely) or (if not) 1–20 (before /ɔ:/ (< /a:/) > /au/).
2002/b (6c, *Corpus*) **Brittonic Period** ? **Irish Period** 1–12.

2003 (late 5–early 7c?, *Corpus*) **Brittonic Period** ?

2004 (11c?, *Corpus*) **Brittonic Period** ?

2005 (8–early 9c, *Corpus*, cf. Section 3.6) **Brittonic Period** 14–27.

2006 (late 5c, *Corpus*; 5c, Jackson in Wright & Jackson 1968, although Jackson says purely epigraphically it could be *c.* 400–550) **Brittonic Period** 1–5 **Irish Period** 7. See Sections 5.2 and 5.4.

2007/10 (ECMW: 5–early 6c?; Ted: V; LHEB (p. 239, n. 1): 5c) **Brittonic Period** ? **Irish Period** ? Unlikely to be Brittonic with MAIL- < **maglo-* if the epigraphic dates are correct.

2008/82 (ECMW: 10–11c) **Brittonic Period** 22–28.

2009/204/940 (ECMW: 11–12c) **Brittonic Period** ?

2010/276 **Brittonic Period** ?

2011/387 (ECMW: 7–9c) **Brittonic Period** ?

2012/380 (ECMW: 9–10c) **Brittonic Period** ?

2013/383 (ECMW: 'c. 1140') **Brittonic Period** ?

2014/392 (ECMW: 10–11c) **Brittonic Period** ?

2015/393 (ECMW: 10–11c) **Brittonic Period** ?

2016/406 (ECMW: '13c?') **Brittonic Period** ?

2017 **Brittonic Period** ?

2018 **Brittonic Period** 14–28.

2019 (fake?) **Brittonic Period** 3–12 (if writing of U for /u/ > /ö/ is significant) or (if not) 3–22 **Irish Period** ?

2020 (5–early 7c, *Corpus*) **Brittonic Period** 1–21.

2021 (10–11c, *Corpus*) **Brittonic Period** 22–28.

2022/253/984 (ECMW: late 11–12c) **Brittonic Period** 22–27.

2023/Scot.4 **Brittonic Period** 1–7.

2024/Scot.11 **Brittonic Period** ?

2025/Scot.12 (Steer (1968–69): late 7c or early 8c) **Brittonic Period** ?

2026/RIB i 2331 **Brittonic Period** ?

2027 (Ted: V) **Brittonic Period** ? **Irish Period** 1–13.

2028 **Brittonic Period** 4–13.

2029/p.39i (late 5c, *Corpus*) **Brittonic Period** 1–3 **Irish Period** 1–7.

2030/p.39ii (early 6c, *Corpus*) **Brittonic Period** 1–11 **Irish Period** 1–13.

2031/p.68 (RC: 11–12c) **Brittonic Period** 11–28.

2032 (1st half 6c, *Corpus*; KHJ: 6c, rejecting Webley's 5–6c) **Brittonic Period** ? **Irish Period** 1–13.

2033 (10–11c, Kay) **Brittonic Period** ?

2034/871 (8–9c, *Corpus*) **Brittonic Period** 14–28.

2035 (Tedeschi 2000: 8–10c) **Brittonic Period** 22–28.

2036/Dor.i (RC: 7c) **Brittonic Period** 14–21.

2037 (11–12c, *Corpus*) **Brittonic Period** ?

2038 (LHEB, p. 392, n. 2: 9c; Megaw (1946–50): *c.* 820 [similarly Radford cited KHJ]) **Brittonic Period** 11–28.

3001/F1 (Han: 8–10c) **Brittonic Period** 14–28.

3002/F2 (Ted: VII; Han: late 7–8c) **Brittonic Period** 14–28.
3003/F3 (Han: 9–11c) **Brittonic Period** 1–16.
3004/F4 (Han: 5–12c) **Brittonic Period** 11–28.
3005/F5 (Han: late 5–early 7c) **Brittonic Period** 12–13.
3006/C1 (Ted: VI-2; Han: 6c) **Brittonic Period** 4–13.
3007/C2 (Ted: VII; Han: late 6-mid-7c) **Brittonic Period** 14–28.
3008/C3 (Han: late 6–7c) **Brittonic Period** 18–28.
3009/C4 (Han: 8–10c) **Brittonic Period** 11–28.
3010/M1 (Han: 7–8c) **Brittonic Period** 15–28.
3011/M2 (Han: 5–6c) **Brittonic Period** ?
3012/M3 (Han: 6c) **Brittonic Period** ?
3013/M4 (Han: 8–9c) **Brittonic Period** 14–16.
3014/M5 (Han: 7–8c) **Brittonic Period** 17–28.
3015/M6 (Han: 7–10c, cf. Section 3.6) **Brittonic Period** 14–28.
3016/M7 (Han: 8–9c?) **Brittonic Period** 1–4.
3017/M8 (non-Gaulish part) (Han: late 7–10c) **Brittonic Period** 20–28 (if
  non-writing of /γ/ in RIMOETE is significant) or (if not) 18–28.
3018/M9 (Han: 11c, cf. Section 3.6) **Brittonic Period** ?
3019/M10 (Han: 11c, cf. Section 3.6) **Brittonic Period** 4–28.
3020/I1 (Han: 6–7c) **Brittonic Period** ?
3021/I2 (Han: 7c) **Brittonic Period** 20–28.
3022/I3 (Han: 6–7c) **Brittonic Period** ?
3023/I4 (Han: 6–early 7c) **Brittonic Period** ?
3024/I5 (Han: ?) **Brittonic Period** ?
3025/I6 (Han: late 5–early 7c) **Brittonic Period** ?
3026/I7 (Han: 6–7c) **Brittonic Period** ?

APPENDIX 1

SIMPLIFIED TEXTS OF INSCRIPTIONS

On the purpose and status of this appendix see Section 1.2 above.

CIIC etc.	ECMW etc.	Readings from ECMW, Mac[alister, CIIC], McM[anus, *Guide to Ogam*], Ok[asha, *Corpus*], Th[omas, *Mute Stones* and 1991–92], the new Welsh *Corpus* [*of Early Medieval Inscribed Stones and Stone Sculpture in Wales*] (see Preface), etc., but slightly simplified for the purpose of electronic searching after global deletion of square and round brackets: i.e. capitals within square brackets are italicized; Nash-Williams's 'corrected' inflexions etc., whether right or wrong, are shown after = between { }; spaces are added between end of words and {?}; (?) within words is moved to before or after the word or is paraphrased 'letter *x* uncertain' etc.
p.397	285	D(*is*) M(*anibus*) BARRECTI {?} CARANTEI {?}
318	6	ETTORIGI {-i = -is} H[*IC IACIT*]
319	9	CVNOGVSI < Mac: -I dubious > HIC IACIT
320	26	CVLIDOR {or CVLIDOR[*I*] ?} IACIT ET ORVVITE {-e = -ae} MVLIERI {-i = -is} SECVNDI [*FILIVS* {?}]
321	25	[*HIC I*]ACIT [ ]SORIS
322	27	A W CAMVLORIS HOI {= hic ossa iacent?} // C- ⊃ { = theta?} CAMVLORIS
323	32	HIC BEA[*TV*]S [ ] SATVRNINVS SE[*PVLTVS* {?} *I*]ACIT ET SVA SA[*NCTA* {?}] CONIV(*n*)X PA[*X VOBISCVM SIT* {?}]
324	34	]CO[*N*]BARRVS CO[*N*]BVRRI IC {= hic?} IACIT
325	33	]IVA {or]INA} SANCTISSIMA MVLIER HIC IACIT QVE {= quae} FVIT AMA(*n*)TISSI(*ma*) CONIV(*n*)X BIVATIGI(*rni*) {or BIVATISI(*rni*)} < Mac: BIVOTIS > [*F*]AMVLVS [D](e)I SACERDOS ET VASSO PAVLINI ANDOCOG {or AVDOCOS or ANDOCOS or AVDOCOG } NA[*TION*]E {Wooding, *Communication and Commerce*, p. 62: AVDO COGNATIONE } ET OMNIVM CIVIVM ADQVAE {= atque} PARENTVM EXEMPL[*VM* {?}] ET MORIBVS DISCIPLINA AC SAPIENTIAE AVRO E[*T* {?}] LAPIDIBVS
326	39	HIC IACIT MACCVDECCETI

327	43	**TURPI[***LI MAQI*** {?}** ***TRIL***]**LUNI** < Mac: **MOSAC TRALLONI** > {McM p. 67: **TURPiLli [**]**LUNI** } < *Corpus* **TURP[***o***]L[***li* **. . .]** L[*u*]N[*i*] > // TVRPILLI IC {=hic} IACIT PVVERI TRILVNI DVNOCATI
328	44	RVGNIATIO {-o = -os} [*FI*]LI VENDONI
329	42	CANNTIANI ET PATER ILLIVS MACCVTRENI HIC IACIT < PSW: IACIVNT >
330	66	]TIR[*I* {?} *FILI*]VS CATIRI < *Corpus*: TIBE[ ]VS CATIRI >
331	41	[(?) *A*]NNICCI FILIVS [*H*]IC IACIT TECVRI IN HOC TVMVLO
332	40	[*P*]ETA FIL[*IA* < Mac: or [*M*]ETA > {*Corpus*: [-]PETA }
333	50	CATVC
334	54	CATACVS HIC IACIT FILIVS TEGERNACVS
335	54a	*H*]IC IACE[*T* {*Corpus*: = 12–13c addition}
336	67a	Q[ ]T[ ]C[ ]D {Webley and Williams, *AC*, 106 (1957), 118–21: M[*A*]Q[*I*] D[*E*]C[*E*]DA } < *Corpus*: [*M*]AQ[*I*] D[*E*]C[*E*]DA >
337	60	HIC IACET [*S*]I[*U*]ERD < *U* uncertain, *W* acc. to Mac and *Corpus*, i.e.: SIWERD > [*F*]ILIVS VVLMER
339	68	N[*EMNI*]I {or N[*UMNI*]I ? < Mac: NIMRINI > < *Corpus*:NA[*M*]NII > } FILIVS VICTORINI
341	71	**MAQUTRENI** < Mac & *Corpus*: **MAQITRENI** > **SALICIDUNI** // [*M*]ACCVTRENI + SALICIDVNI (or SALIGIDVNI) < *Corpus*: SALIC[*I*]D[*V*]NI >
342	70	**CVNACENNIVI** < McM p. 67 & *Corpus*: **CUNACENNI [***A***]VI** > **ILVVETO** // CVNOCENNI FILIV[*S*] CVNOGENI HIC IACIT
344	73	DERVACI FILIVS IVSTI IC {=hic} IACIT
345	74	**GLUVOCA[**] **I[** < Mac: **GL(***U***)V(***O***)C(***I***)** > < *Corpus*: **GL[***alolu***]V[***alolu***]C[***alolu*** >
346	75	ADIVNE < Knight, *Merthyr Historian*, 2 (1978), 110, n. 24, and *Corpus*: ADIVNETI >
347	76	HIC IACIT
348/a	110/27	< **TRENALUGOS** {?} {Mac, doubted W. G. Thomas } >
348/b	110/27	GURHIRT or GURHIST { W. G. Thomas: GURHIRT } < *Corpus*: GURHIRET {?} >
349	121/4	VELVOR[*IA*] FILIA BROHO[*MAGLI*]
350	116/3	[+ *HI*]C IACET // [*I*]DNERT FILIVS IA[*QVI*] OCCISV[*S F*]VIT PROPTER PR[*AEDIVM SANCTI*]

{ W. G. Thomas: IDNERT and IACOBI < IAGOBI
? > and PREDAM SANCTI DAVID (Lhuyd) }

351	115/2	*D*]ALLVS DVMELVS { W. G. Thomas: DALLVS }
352A	122/5	DOMNICI IACIT FILIVS BRAVECCI
353	127/7	**TRENACCATLO** // TRENACATVS IC {= hic} IACIT FILIVS MAGLAGNI
354	126/6	CORBALENGI IACIT ORDOVS
355	128/8	SILBANDVS IACIT < Mac adds HIC – rejected *Corpus* > { W. G. Thomas < rejected *Corpus* > :] FILI BANDUS IACIT }
356	132/9	POTENINA {or POTEN(*t*)INA} MVLIIER < Mac adds CONVMANI {?} , rejected *Corpus* >
357	136	CORBAGNI FILIVS AL[
358	138	**VOTECORIGAS** // MEMORIA VOTEPORIGIS PROTICTORIS
359	141	[*R*]EGIN[*I*] FILIVS NV[*D*]INTI < Mac: or NU[*T*]INTI or NU[*V*]INTI >
360	139	SERVATVR FIDAEI PATRIEQ(*ue*) {-e- = -ae-} SEMPER AMATOR HIC PAVLINVS IACIT CVL[*T*]OR PIENT[*I*]SIM[*VS* {-s- = -ss-} *AEQVI*]
361	140	TALOR[*I*] {-i = -ix ?} ADVEN[*TI*] MAQV[*ERIGI*] FILIV[*S*]
362	142	**INIGENA CUNIGNI AVITTORIGES** // AVITORIA FILIA CVNIGNI
363	143	CARANTACVS
364	144	QVENVENDANI FILI BARCVNI
365	149	MAVOHE[*NI*] FILI LVNAR[*C*]HI {*C* uncertain} COCCI {*Corpus*: MAVOHENI FILI LVNARI HIC OCCISUS Lhuyd}
366	148	ECHADI FI(*li*) {?} ITOCVS {?} {CROCUSI {?} Emery, *AC*, 124 (1975), 108, n. 23; cf. *Corpus* on MSS}
368/a	150	**DUMELEDONAS MAQI M[*UCOI*]** < Mac & McM p. 65 transpose. **D** uncertain acc. to McM >
368/b	150	BARRIVENDI FILIVS VENDVBARI HIC IACIT
369	153	[*HIC* {?}] IACET CVRCAGNVS [ ]VRIVI FILIVS
370	157	HIC IACIT VLCAGNVS FI(*li*)VS SENOMAGLI
371	322	CANV {*Corpus*: fake}
372	160	**DECCAIBAR VUGLOB DISI** < Mac: [*DECCA*]**IBARVALB [***MAQI* *B*]**RO**[*CAGNI*] > {*Corpus*: only **IBA** certain}// DE[*CAB*]ARBALOM FI[*L*]IVS BROCAGNI
373	171	SEVERINI FILI SEVERI
374	172	CVNEGNI
375	166	TOTAVALI FILIVS DOTHORANTI

376	174	VENNISETLI FILIVS ERCAGNI
377	175	CIMESETLI [*FILIVS* {?} < Mac: *FILI* >] AVICAT[*VS* {?} < Mac: AMICATI >]
378	169	**BIVVA[*IDONA*]** {or **BIVVA[*IDONA(s)*]** McM p. 67: **BEVVu** for * **BIVV** - *Corpus*: either **BEVV** or **BIVV** possible } **AVVI BODDIB[*EVVA*]** {or **BODDIB[*EVVA(s)*]** < Mac: **BODDI[*BA*]BEVE** > } // BIVADI FILI < Mac & *Corpus*: AVI > BODIBEVE {-e + -ae ?}
379	170	CATVRVG < Mac: CATVRVGI > FILI LOVERNACI
380	84	**ICORIGAS** // ICORI {-i = -ix} FILIVS POTENTINI
381	87	ALIORTVS ELMETIACO {-o = -os} HIC IACET
382	86	MELITVu {-u intended for -s, or mere graffito acc. to Mac.}
384	83	SANCTINVS {?} < Mac: SANCE[*R*]INVS > SACER(*dos*) {?} I[*N*] P(*ace*)
385	89	FILI LOVERNII ANATEMORI
386	92	MELI MEDICI FILI MARTINI I[*A*]CIT
387	95	FIGVLINI FILI LOCVLITI HIC IACIT
388	94	DERVORI HIC IACET < Mac: IACIT, correctly, Edwards, *Med. Arch.*, 45 (2001), 19, n. 18 >
389	97	IOVENALI {-i = -is} FILI ETERNI HIC IACIT { CIIC ii p. 201: IACET }
390	96	VENDESETLI
391	78	SENACVS PR(*e*)SB(*yte*)R HIC IACIT CVM MULTITVD(*i*)NEM FRATRUM // PRESB[*IT*]E[*R* {?}]
392	77	VERACIVS P(*res*)B(*yte*)R HIC IACIT
393	101	CARAVSIVS HIC IACIT IN HOC CONGERIES LAPIDVM
394	103	CANTIORI {-i = -ix} HIC IACIT [*V*]ENEDOTIS CIVE {-e = -es} FVIT [*C*]ONSOBRINO {-o = -os} MA[*G*]LI MAGISTRATI
395	102	]ORIA IC {= hic} IACIT
396	104	]FILI AVITORI // IN TE(*m*)PO[*RE*] IVSTI[*NI*] CON[SVLI(*s*)]
397	105	FILI CVNALIPI CVNACI [*HIC* {?}] IACIT [ ] BECCVRI
398	106	IACONVS FILIVS {?} MINI IACIT
399	176	**S[*I*]B[*I*]L[*I*]N[*I*]** < or **SIMILINI** McM p. 65 > **[*TO*]VISACI** // SIMILINI TOVISACI
400	177	VINNEMAGLI FILI SENEMAGLI

401	183	BROHOMAGLI IATTI IC {=hic} IACIT ET VXOR EIVS CAVNE
402	184	HIC IACIT MVLIER BONA NOBILI {-i = -is}
403	268/841	MACARITINI < Mac: CARITINI > FILI BERIC[*I* *HIC IACIT* {?}] < Mac: BERIC[*CI* . . .]CAL[> < RCAHMW: BERIA[*CI*] >
404	270/843	< Mac: **TEGE[** {rejected *Corpus*} > // TEGERNACUS FILI[*U*]S < Mac: FILI > MARTI HIC IACIT
405	228/845	[*L*]LICA < Mac: **GRAVICA** > < *Corpus*:]L[ ]VICA or]L[ ]LICA >
406	215/844	[{?} *AD*]VECTI < RCAHMW: *D*]VECTI or *G*]VECTI or *P*]VECTI {?} > FILIVS [ ]GVANI < Mac: GVANI not acephalous, cf. RCAHMW and *Corpus* > HIC IACIT
407/a	258/846	IM[*P*(*eratore*) *C*(*aesare*)] FLA(*vio*) [*VA*]L(*erio*) M[*AXI*]MINO INVICTO AVGVS(*to*)
407/b	258/846	HIC IACIT CANTVSVS PATER PAVLINVS
408	229/848	BODVOCI HIC IACIT FILIVS CATOTIGIRNI PRONEPVS ETERNALI {-i = -is} VEDOMAVI < Mac: or VEDOMALI >
409	198/849	**POPIA[*S*] ROL[*IO*]N M[*AQ*]I LL[*E*]NA** < Mac: **PAMPES** // **ROL[*ACU*]N M[*A*]Q** {*Corpus*: gap big enough for [*U*] rather than [*A*] } **ILLUNA** > { McM p. 67: **PoP[** or **PaP[** } < RCAHMW: **POP[*IAS*** {?} or **PAP[*IAS*** {?} // **R[*O*]L[** . . .]N[. . .]M[. . .]Q[ ]LLUNA > {*Corpus*: P[*o*]P[*IAS*] R[*O*]L[.]]N[.]]M[.]]Q[.]]LLUNA } // PVMPEIVS CARANTORIVS
410	238/847	PAVLI < RCAHMW and *Corpus*: or PAVLI[*NI*] > FILI M[*A* {?} < RCAHMW: M[A or M[E >
412	277	FERRVCI HIC IACIT
413	272	CAELEXTI {-i = -is} MONEDORIGI {-i = -is}
414	271	AETERN[*I* {?}] ET AETERN[*E* {?} {-e = -ae}]
415	278	IN[*G*]ENVI {g uncertain; Mac: IN[*TA*]ENVI } IARRI[< Mac: TARRONERIS > *HI*]C IA[*CIT*]
416	279	EQVESTRI {-i = -is} NOMINE
417	282	CAVO SENIARGII < Mac:]CAVOSENI ARGII >
418	283	HEC {=hic} IACET SALVIANVS BVRSOCAVI {-i = -is} {or BVRGOCAVI {-i = -is} } FILIVS CVPETIAN[*I* {?}] < Mac: CVPITIANI >
419	284	FILIAE SALVIA[*N*]I HIC IACIT VE[ ]MAIE UXOR TIGIRNICI ET FILIE {-e = -ae} EIUS

ONERATI [*UXSOR* {?} *IA*]CIT RIGOHENE
[ ]OCETI [ ]ACI

| 420 | 289 | PORIVS HIC IN TVMVLO IACIT HOMO PLANVS < Mac. & Gresham, *BBCS*, 32 (1985), 386–92: XPIANVS > FVIT |

| 421 | 294 | HIC [*IN*] TVM[*V*]LO IACIT R[*O*]STEECE < Mac: R[*A*]STECE > FILIA PATERNINI AN(*n*)I(*s*) XIII IN PA(*ce*) |

| 422 | 298 | **VENDOGNI** // VENDAGNI FILI V[ ]NI {?} < Mac: [*U*]ENDOGNI [*F*]ILI [*H*]OCIDEGNI > {*Corpus*: V[*G*]NI possible in Lhuyd} |

| 423 | 296 | **M[*A*]Q[*I*] QAGTE** { cf. McM p. 65 } |

| 424 | 299 | BRIAC[*I*] FILI [ ]GI < Mac: GLVVOCCI > {*Corpus*: [*E*]VA[*LEN*]GI {?} } |

| 425 | 297 | MACCVTRE[*NI*] FILI CATOMAG[*LI* |

| 426 | 300 | **NETTASAGRU MAQI MUCOI BRECI** {?} < Mac: **NETTASAGRI MAQI MUCOE BRIACI** > < McM p. 67: or **SLECI** > |

| 427/a | 301 | **MAGL[*IA* {?}] DUBR[*ACUNAS* {?} *MAQI*]INB** < Mac: **MAGL[*I*] DUBAR[*CUNAS MAQI*]QI** > |

| 427/b | 301 | ET SINGNO {= signo} CRUCIS IN ILLAM FINGSI {= finxi} ROGO OMNIBUS AMMULANTIBUS {= ambulantibus} IBI EXORENT PRO ANIMAE CATUOCONI |

| 428 | 305 | **TRENAGUSU** {*Corpus*: or **TRENAGUSO** or **TRENAGUSI** } **MAQI MAQITRENI** // TRENEGUSSI FILI MACUTRENI HIC IACIT |

| 429 | 307 | SOLINI FILIVS VENDONI |

| 430 | 306 | **ETTERN[*I MAQI VIC*]TOR** // ETTERNI FILI VICTOR {= -is} |

| 431 | 308 | **D[*O*]V[*A*]TUCEAS** < also McM p. 67; Mac: **DOVATACIS** > // DOB[*I*]TVCI {Mac & *Corpus*: DOBTVCI} FILIVS EVOLENG[*I*] |

| 432 | 312 | **DOVAGNI** // TIGERNACI DOBAGNI |

| 433 | 313 | [*A*]NDAGELLI MACU < Mac: **MACV** > CAV[*ETI* {?}] {Mac & *Corpus* **CAVE[*TI*** } // ANDAGELLI IACIT FILI CAVETI { cf. McM p. 67 } |

| 434 | 314 | COIMAGNI FILI CAVETI |

| 435 | 315 | CLVTORIGI {-i = -is} FIL[*I*] PAVLINI MARINI LATIO |

| 436 | 316 | EUOLENGGI FILI LITOGENI HIC IACIT |

| 437 | 317 |]RIAT[|

| 438 | 320 | TAVUSI F[. .]LI < Mac: FI[*L*]I > |

| 439 | 319 | **EF[*E*]SS[*A*]NGI ASEG[*NI*]** < Mac: **INGEN** |

SANGKTA SEGNI {?} > {McM p. 67: **IG^w[ ] SSG^w[**
{second G^W uncertain} **]ASOG[** or **]ASOV[** or **]ASOS[**
or **]ASON[** }

440 335 MACVDEC[*C*]ETI {*Corpus*: MACVDEBETI for
MACVDECETI Lhuyd} FILIVS EOROCAN {r
uncertain} < Mac: EONOCAN > {*Corpus*: Lhuyd also
EOPOCAN }

441 345 CVRCAGNI FILI ANDAGELLI

442 346 [*MAC*]CVDICCL FILIVS CATICVVS {cf. CIIC ii,
p. 200; *Corpus*: MACCVDICCL Lhuyd} // ogam,
denied in CIIC ii, p. 200, and 'reading uncertain'
according to ECMW, but see Nash-Williams, *AC*, 92
(1937), 326, and *Corpus*.

443 349 [ ] FILI {or HIC IACIT} CAMVMORI {-i = -ix or -is}
{or CAMVLORI {-i = -ix or -is}} BRANN[*I*] {or
BRANN[*VS*] }

444 352]MOGI FILIVS [ ]S[ ]LACATI < Mac: ROTI FILIVS
[ ]STACATI >

445 354 **VITALIANI** // VITALIANI EMERETO

446 353 **MAGLICUNAS MAQI CLUTA[*RI*]** < Mac & *Corpus*:
CLUTAR[*I*] > // MAGLOCVN {uninflected = -*i*}
< Mac: MAGLOCVVI; McM p. 65: MAGLOCVNI
(sic leg. but cf. *Corpus*) > FILI CLVTORI

447 369 CVNISCVS < *Corpus* also Lhuyd, or CVNIGCVS
{Mac: = Cvnignus ?} > FILI NEMAGLI < *Corpus*: or
NEMASLI >

448 370 RINACI {or PINACI {-i = -is?}} NOMENA
{= nomina}

449 384 **SAGRAGNI MAQI CUNATAMI** // SAGRANI FILI
CVNOTAMI

450 390 **OGTENLO** {?} < Mac: **OGTENAS** {*Corpus*:
OGTEN[*A*]S (?)} > // HOGTIVIS < McM p. 65 leg:
HOGTINIS ? > FILI DEMETI

451 401 TVNCCETACE VXSOR DAARI HIC IACIT

452 400 PAANI < Mac: VALAVI FILI PAANI > {*Corpus*:
Lhuyd VALAVITIVI PAANI }

453 399 MELI < Mac: NESI rejected *Corpus* >

454 402 EVALI FILI DENCVI < *Corpus*: or DEN[*O*]-
VI > CVNIOVENDE MATER EIVS

455 403 CAMVLORIGI {recte CAMVLLORIGI < PSW > }
FILI FANNVCI

456 404 **GENDILI** // GE[*NDILI*] // N {?} A H Q {?} // K {?} S
{?}

457	Ok 18	DVNOCATI HIC IACIT FILI MERCAGNI < or ME[S]CAGNI Ok >
458	Ok 9	RANOCORI < or NANOCORI Ok > FILI MESGI {or MESCI Th p. 265}
459	Ok 63	Orate Pro EPiscopuS TITUS
460	Ok 75	VAILATHI FILI VROCHANI
461	Ok 66	NONNITA ERCILIVI RICATI < Ok: or ERCILI VIRICATI > TRIS FILI ERCILINGI {Th p. 283 ERCILINCI}
462	Ok 14	QVENATAVCI IC DINVI FILIVS
463	Ok 15	VRIVI < or VN VI Ok >
464	Ok 65	MAVISIR
465	Ok 21	ANNICV FIL[I
466	Ok 23	INGENVI < or INCENVI Ok > MEMORIA // **IGENAVI MEMOR**
467	Ok 24	[HI]C IACIT VLCAGNI // **ULCAGNI**
468	Ok 31	RIALOBRANI CVNOVALI FILI
469	Ok 34	CNEGVMI < or CLEGUMI > FILI GENAIVS < or]ENAIVS >
470	Ok 78	LATINI IC IACIT FILIUS MAGARI {Th p. 263 MACARI < Ok: or MAGIARI or MAFARI > } // **LA[TI]NI**
471	Ok 39	CLOTUALI FILI {Th p. 285 & Ok: no FILI} MOBRATTI
472	Ok 35	VLCAGNI FILI SEVERI
473/a	Ok 46	VITALI FILI TORRICI
473/b	Ok 46	IGNIOC {Th pp. 270 & 284:]IGNI OC }
474	Ok 17	CRVARIGI HI[C IACIT] < or RVANI HIC IACIT or]MAGLI HIC[Ok >
475	Ok 47	IACONIVS {rejected Th p. 282, who has ADO . . . FILI }
476	Ok 45	BONEMIMORI [F]ILLI TRIBVNI < Ok rejects [F]ILLI >
477	Ok 11	CONETOCI FILI TEGERNOMALI
478	Ok 48	BROCAGNI < Ok: BR[ ]ACNI > IHC IACIT NADOTTI {Th p. 263: or RADOTTI} FILIVS
479	Ok 16	HIC IN TVMVLO {Th p. 193: HIC PACE NUP(er) } REQVIEVIT [ ] CVNAIDE < Ok: CVNATDO > HIC IN TVMVLO IACIT VIXIT ANNOS XXXIII
480	Ok 19	LVRATECVS FECIT < or ALSUE CURAVIT or ALSNE CURAVIT Ok > CRUCEM + PRO ANIMA SVA < also: EMIANCINOINOMINE + Ok >
481	Ok 49	N[ ] NOTI [ ] NOTI
482	Ok 71	] FILIVS {?} NEMIANVS {?} {Th p. 285: N[} FILI

{?} IC {?} NEMIANVS } < Ok: NL[ ]L[*I*]TRC
NEMIAVS >

483	Ok 51	SELNIVS {Th p. 286 SENILVS < Ok: NI SELVS > } IC IACIT
484	Ok 52	IVSTI // [*I*]USTI
485	Ok 68	THI FILI [ ] COLINI {? Th p. 271} < Ok:]HI FILI [*CO*]BI { or COGI {?} } >
486	Ok 56	CVMREGNI { Th p. 278: CVMRECINI } FILI MAVCI
487	Ok 10	CIRISINIVS { DRUSTANUS Th p. 279 < or CIRV[ ]V[ ]NC or CERVSIVS or CIRUSIUS or SIRVSIVS or DRVSTAGNI or CIRVSINIVS Ok > } HIC IACIT CVNOMORI FILIVS
488	Ok 60	DOBVNNI FABRI FILII ENABARRI // **ENABARR** {Ok: dubious}
489/a	Ok 13	**SVAQQUCI MAQI QICI** // FANONI MAQVI RINI
489/b	Ok 13	SAGRANVI < rejected Ok: G[*A*]G[*R*]A[*NV*]I or G[*A*]G[*R*]A[*SN*]I >
490	Ok 29	DATUIDOCI CONHINOCI < DATUIDOC[{or CATUIDOC } CONHINO[C] Ok > FILIVS { Th p. 281: FILI; Ok: nil }
491	Ok 55	PRINCIPI < Ok: ChiRho + [*R*]INCIP[*I*] > IVRIVCI < Ok: or DIRIVI or FILIVS > AVDETI < Ok: or ANDETI >
492	Ok 59	SABINI FILI MACCODECHETI
493	Ok 58	NEPRANI FILI CONBEVI
494	Ok 79	GOREVS
496	Hants	**EBICATO[*S MAQ*]I MUCO[** {Fulford et al., *Med. Arch.*, 44 (2000), 11: **TEBICATO[*S MAQ*]I MUCO[*I*--]** }
497	409	*IA*]CIT IN HOC TVMVLO [< *Corpus*: thus far = guess >]LLII PARENT[*I*]S {?} < *Corpus*: PARENT[*IS*] >
498	Nb 7	BRIGOMAGLOS HIC IACIT [ ]ECVS {Th:]CVS or]GVS }
499	Ok 77	[ ]S [ ] CARA*n*ACI {Th p. 288: CARATACI < Ok: or CARANTACI > } NEPVS
500	Manx	AMMECATI FILIVS ROCATI HIC IACIT // **[*E*]B[*I*]CATOS M[*A*]QI ROC[*A*]T[*O*]S**
501	Manx	**CUNAMAGLI MAQ[**
502	Manx	**]MAQ LEOG[**
503	Manx	**DOVAIDONA MA[ ]QI DROATA**
504	Manx	**BIVAIDONAS MAQI MUCOI CUNAVA[*LI***
505	Manx	AVITI MONOMENTI

506	Scot.	**VICULA MAQ CUGINI** { dub. cf. McM pp. 44–45 }
507	Scot.	**CRON[A]N[**
508	Scot.	FRYMIA COESIA FICT
509	Ok.Pict3	]GRITI FILII MEDICII
510	Scot. 13	IN OC TVMVLO IACIT VETTA F*ilius* VICTI {or VICTRICIS CIIC ii p. 202; Th: VICTR[}
511	Scot. 10	CONINIE // [*T*]VRTIRIE {Th: [*E*]RTIRIE }
512	Scot.	QATTIDONA
513	Ok.Pict8	[*I*]N NOM[*IN*]E IHU X[*PI CR*]UX XP[*I IN*] COMM[*E*]MORAT[*I*]ONE REO[? *E*]TII [*R*]EQUIESC[*AT* ?]
514	Scot. 8	HIC IACIT CARANTI FILI CVPITIANI
515	Scot. 9	HIC MEMORIA PerETVA {sic} IN LOCO INSIGNI {Th: INSIGNISIMI } PIIQVE PRI {Th: PRINCIPES } NVD[*OGEN*]I {Th: NVDI DVMNOGENI } // PRINCI {not Th } DIMNOGENI {not Th } HIC IACENT IN TVMVLO DVO FILII LIBERALI
516	Scot. 1	A ET W HIC IACENT SanCtI ET PRAECIPVI SACERDOTES ID EST VIVENTIVS ET MAVORIVS
517	Scot. 2	IST*T*]S {Th: TITVS ? } ET FLORENTIVS
518	Scot. 3	INITIVM ET FINIS
519	Scot. 6	LOGI {Th: LOCI } T PETRI APVSTOLI
520	Scot. 5	TE DOMINVM LAVDAMVS LATINVS ANNORUM XXXV ET FILIA SVA ANNI V {Th: ANN(*orum*) IV } IC SINVM FECERVTN [Th: recte -nt} NEPVS BARROVADI
968	5	]FILIVS EV[*CVIVS A*]NIMA REQVIES[*CAT IN PAC*]E
970	13	CATAMANUS REX SAPIENTISIMUS {-s- = -ss-} OPINATISIMUS {-s- = -ss-} OMNIUM REGUM
971	35	]VS [ ]NIN FILIU[*S*] CUURI[*S* {?}] CINI EREXIT HUNC LAPIDEM
976	72	+ IN NOMINE D(*e*)I SUM(*m*)I [ ]ILUS < *Corpus*: = miscopying of 339/68 >
978	49	+ BRIAMAIL FLOU < *Corpus*: F[*L*]OU altered from F[*I*]OU ? >
979	46	+GUADAN SACERDOS // FECIT CRUX P(*ro*) AN(*ima*) NI(*n*)ID & ANI(*ma*) GURHI // GUADAN
980	46a	WLIGUE {?} < Mac: WUMERE or WILMERE or WALMERE > < C. A. R. Radford apud *Corpus*: S(*ignum*) S(*ancti*) { or S(*cribae*) } LIGUE >
982	55	+CO {?}
984	59	+GURCI BLEDRUS

985	61	[*I*]OHANNIS // MORIDIC SUREXIT {r= rr} HUNC LAPIDEM
986	62	[*I(n)* *S*]IN[*D*]ONE MUTI IORUERT RUALLAUNQ(*ue*) SEPULCHRIS + IUDICII ADU[*E*]NTUM SPECTA(*n*)T I(*n*) PACE TREM(*en*)DUM
988	67	MENHIR ME FECIT I(*n*) TE(*m*)PORE GENILLIN
989	69	HIC IACI[*T* {?}
990	108/1	TIGER[*N* or TIGEIR[*N* {W. G. Thomas: TIGERN[. . . } < *Corpus*: TIGEIR[>
991	113/30	]LO[ ]OL[ ]QU[ ]ANI[ ]RES[ ]CEN[//]R {?} [ ]RU[ ]D [ ]N {or S[ ] UAT {U uncertain} [ ]AR [ ]S {?} [ ]O [ ]A [{W. G. Thomas: ANI[*MA*] and [*C*]RU[*X*] or [*C*]RU[*CEM*] ? }
992	120/14	CENLISINI BT {= benedicat ?} D[*eu*]S
993	124/18	TESQUITUS DITOC MADOMNUAC OCCON < Mac: MADOMNUACO UON { W. G. Thomas: QUA(*m*) DOMNUACOLLO } > FILIUS ASAITGEN DEDIT
994	125/22	+ IHS XPS // Q(*u*)ICUNQ(*ue*) EXPLICAU(*er*)IT H(*oc*) N(*omen*) DET BENEDIXIONEM PRO ANIMA HIROIDIL FILIUS CAROTINN
995	133/24	ENEVIRI { ENEVERI in ECMW is misprint, cf. Plate }
996	147	+ MERCI ET GRACE // MOR[*ED*]IC ELMON [*F*]ECIT H(*an*)C CRUCEM
997	159	EIUDON
998	164	HEUTREN
1000	182	+ CONCENN FILIUS CATTELL CATTELL FILUS BROHCMAIL BROHCMA(*i*)L FILIUS ELISEG ELISEG FILIUS GUOILLAUC + CONCENN ITAQUE PRONEPOS ELISEG EDIFICAUIT HUNC LAPIDEM PRO AUO SUO ELISEG + IPSE EST ELISEG QUI NECXIT {c uncertain} HEREDITATEM POUO(*i*)S[ ] PER VIII [*ANNOS* {?}] E POTESTATE ANGLORUM IN GLADIO SUO PARTA IN IGNE [+*QUIC*]UMQUE RECIT[*A*]UERIT MANESCRIP[*TUM LAPID*]EM DET BENEDICTIONEM SUPE[*R ANIMA*]M ELISEG + IPSE EST CONCENN [ ] MANU [ ]AD REGNUM SUUM POUO(*i*)S [ ] ET QUOD [ ] [ ]MONTEM [ ] MONARCHIAM [ ] MAXIMUS BRITTANNIAE [*CONCE*]NN PASCEN[*T*] MAUN ANNAN [+] BRITU A[*U*]T[*E*]M FILIUS

GUARTHI[*GIRN*] QUE(*m*) BENED[*IXIT*]
GERMANUS QUE(*m*)[*QU*]E PEPERIT EI SE[*V*]IRA
FILIA MAXIMI R[*EG*]IS QUI OCCIDIT REGEM
ROMANORUM + CONMARCH PINXIT HOC
CHIROGRAF(*i*)U(*m*) REGE SUO POSCENTE
CONCENN + BENEDICTIO D(*omi*)NI IN
CONCENN ET S(*uo*)S I(*n*) TOTA FAMILIA EIUS
ET IN TOTA(*m*) [*RE*]GIONE(*m*) POUOIS USQUE
IN [*DIEM IUDICII AMEN* {?}] < N.B. Mac not
collated in detail >

1001	181	+ XR[*I*] CON {*o* uncertain} FILIUS LTON {letter between l and t? *o* uncertain < Mac: DETEN > } {*Corpus*: [*CO*]COM FILIU ED[*ELS*]T[*AN*] {?} cf. Radford & Hemp, *AC*, 106 (1957), 109–16}
1003	261/885	FEC[*IT*] C[*RUX* {?}]UT
1004	260/884	CRUX XPI // GELUGUIN < RCAHMW: or]GELUGUIN >
1005	191/886	+ BRANCUF < Mac: BRANCU with no -f >< RCAHMW: BRANCU · F[*ECIT*] >< *Corpus*: BRANCU:F >
1006	197/842	TEFROIHI or TESROIHI < Mac: NEFROIHI >< RCAHMW: [*REFSO*]IHI or [*REFSD*]IHI >
1007	206/938	IRBIC[*I*] or IRBIC [+] < RCAHMW and *Corpus*: IRBICI]NUR[{?} >
1008	194/934	EBISAR
1009	193/935	EBISSAR [*S* {?}] < RCAHMW: EBISSA[*R* {?}] P[(?) QVE[*SCIT* {?} >
1010	211/882	CRUX XPI
1011	220/911	NI {= in} NOMINE < RCAHMW and *Corpus*: [*I*]N INOMINE {sic} > D(*e*)I PATRIS ET F(*ili*) < om. RCAHMW and *Corpus* > [*ET* {?} *S*]PERETUS SANTDI {= sancti} ANC {= hanc} [*CR*]UCEM HOUELT PROPE[*RA*]BIT < RCAHMW: PROPE[*R*]ABIT > PRO ANIMA RES P[*ATR*]ES {= patris < RCAHMW: PA[*T*]RES > *Corpus*: P[*A*][*TR*]ES } E(*i*)US
1012	223/933	IN NOMINE D(*e*)I SUMMI INCIPIT CRUX SALUATORIS QUAE PREPARAUIT SAMSONI < RCAHMW and *Corpus*: SAMSO-NIS > APATI PRO ANIMA SUA [*ET*] PRO ANIMA IUTHAHELO REX ET ARTMALI ET TEC[*AI*]N + {ECMW drawing seems to show TECANI +} < Mac: TECG + >< RCAHMW: TEC[*A*]N >

1013	222/912	+ SAMSON POSUIT HANC C[R]UCEM + PRO ANMIA {=anima < RCAHMW and *Corpus*: ANIMA >} EIUS // ++ ILT[*UTI* {? < RCAHMW: sic drawings > < *Corpus*: ILTU[*TIS*] >] SAMSON REGIS // SAMUEL + // EBISAR +
1014	231/908	CRUX XPI + ENNIAUN P(*ro*) ANIMA GUORGORET FECIT
1015	233/910	I(*n*) NOMINE D(*e*)I SUM(*m*)I CRUX CRIZDI {or CRIZDI} {= Christi} PROPARABIT {= praeparavit} GRUTNE PRO AN(*i*)MA AHEST < RCAHMW: ANEST >
1016	234/907	CONBELIN [*PO*]SUIT [*H*]A[*NC* < Mac adds: CRUCEM PRO ANIMA EIUS ET PRO ANIMA PATRIS EIUS > < RCAHMW: P[*O*]SUIT [.]AC [{?} *C*]RUCEM P(*ro*) [*A*]NIMA RI[*C*] {?} T[{?} > < *Corpus*: RICT[>
1017	259/867	TOME {= Thomae}
1018	236/919	[ ] PETRI ILQUICI [ ]ACER {a uncertain, Mac: CTCER } [ ]ER {? Mac: ICR } [ ]C HAN[*C CRUCEM*]T [ ] < RCAHMW: H[*E* {?}] [ ]PETRI ILQUICI [ ]E[. . . .]ACER [{?}]CE[.]]C HANC [. . . .]U[.]]T > {*Corpus*:]CHANC [ ]T }
1019	237/920	ILCI < RCAHMW: or]ILCI > [*FE*]CIT [*HANC*] CRUCEM I[*N*] N[*OM*]INE D(*e*)I SUMMI
1020	200/921	Mac: I[*N*] NOMINE < rejected RCAHMW and *Corpus* >]FCA[ ]CAT FECIT HANC [PRO] ANIMA]EE[< RCAHMW: O . . OP { or O . . AP ?} [*HA*]EC CR[*UC*]AM [*P*]ROPARARET [*P*]R[*O*] ANIMA E { or C } U {or I } >
1022	240/928	I(*n*)NOMINE D(*e*)I PATRIS ET FILI {*et*} SPERI[*TUS SAN(c)TI* < Mac adds: DO[*BI*]TAUCI PROPARAUIT HANC CRUCEM PRO ANIMA EIUS, ET PATRIS O . . . . . LI, FIL[*I* . . . .]P D . . . SEPULTI. POSUIT [*CRUCEM*] LOCO ISTO IN GREFIUM, etc. >]IMA[ ]M[ ]I PA[ ] CA {?} ISTO IN GREFIUM {= graphium} IN PROPRIUM USQ(*ue*) IN DIEM IUDICI(*i*) > < But RCAHMW adds: FI [ ]MA[ ]IN[I PA[ ]E {*Corpus*: I.PA[} COISTO IN GREFIUM INPROPRIUM USQ IN DIEM IUDICI >
1023	239/927	[*CO*]NBELANI [*P*]OSSUIT HANC CRUCEM PRO ANIMA EIUS SCI {= sancti} GLIUISSI {g uncertain} NERTTAN ET FRATRIS EIUS ET PATER EIUS A ME PREPARATUS + SCILOC

1024	255/926	[*SCIENDUM*] EST [*OMNIB(us)*] QUOD DE[*DIT*] {*Corpus*: DED[IT] } ARTHMAIL AGRUM D(e)O ET GLIGUIS ET NERTAT < Mac: NERT*tan* > ET FILI EPI {= episcopo < Mac: EPILI > } < RCAHMW: ET FILIE SU[*A*] > // [*I(n) NOMINE* {?}] D(e)I SUM(m)I [ ]RO SI[ ]H GESTI < RCAHMW: CROSI [{?} *R*] HGERTH > {*Corpus*: CROS[*IR*]H(I)GERTI } BRANTUI [ ]US[ ] < RCAHMW: [*P*]RUS > {*Corpus*: BRANTUI [*B*]RUS[*FE*] } < Mac adds: BRANCIE >
1025	248/862	ARTBEU
1027	265/923	PROPARAUIT {= praeparavit} GAI CI[{?} < Mac: GABALA > < RCAHMW: GAI C[>
1028	214/850	VENDVMAGLI HIC IACIT
1029	Mer.	SANCTE {?} TETQUINI PR // REU DIACON ME FICIT + A B C D E F +
1030	Mer.	]R DEDICAVIT REG[*NUM DE*]TRY ET CERID[*WEN UXOR EIVS*]IMAM PARTEM [*TERRAE*]OLD DIM RHOS [ ] DEO IN NOMINE [*FILI EORUM A*]MBIGATI + O +
1032	281	+ HI(c) EST SEPVLCRV(m) WLEDER MAT(r)IS ODELEV Q(u)I P(r)IMV(m) EDIFICAV(it) HANC EC(c)L(esi)A(m) IN TE(m)P(o)R(e) EWINI < Mac: WINI > REG(is)
1033	287	+ CINGEN CELEN TRICET NITANAM + TENGRUIN MALTE[*C* {?}] < Mac: MALTE[*D*] > GUADGAN ANTERUNC DUBUT MARCIAU < Mac: MARCIAU[*N*] > // MOLT CIC {?} PETUAR // M[*C*]ARTR {?}
1034	286	PASCENT[*I*
1035	303	MARGITEUT REX ETG(uin) FILIUS < Mac: MARGITEUT ETT RECEN > {*Corpus*: MARGITEUT RECETT F?X? }
1036	360	HAN EH < Mac: HAUEN {?} > // DNS {= dominus ?}
1038	365	HEC {= haec} EST CRUX QUAM AEDIFICAUIT MAIL {?or MEIL} < Mac: MAL > DOMNA[*C* < Mac adds: H . . GUI[>
1039	382	A W // IHS XPS // + PONTIFICIS ABRAHAM FILII HIC HED < Mac: NED > 7 {= et} ISAC QUIESCUNT
1040	379	]AU {?} [ ]X[ ]CN[ ]BT[ ]TD[ ]D[{*Corpus*: CA not CN } < I ignore Mac's conjecture: + DAUID[*US ERE*]XIT [*HANC A*]RCA[*M Pro OSSI*]Bus T[*HOME E*]T D[*A*]UIDI >

1041	376	A 7 {= et} W I[*H*]S XPS // GURMARC
1044	Ok 7	+ LEUIUT IUSIT HEC ALTARE PRO ANIMA SUA
1045	Ok 69	AGURED < Ok: or AGUDED or AGUTED or ÆGVRED >
1046	Ok 8	ARAHI + < Ok: or ARTHI + {rejected Mac} or [ ]R[*A*]H + >
1047	Ok 20	+ BeatuS ID ET IMAH < or BREID ET [*I*]MAH Ok > // RU(*n*)HOL
1048	Ok 32	FILIA [ ] GVENNCREST // HADNOBVIS {?} {Th p. 290: VIR QONFAL FILIV (-u = -us) VENNORCIT} < Ok: NR QON[*FI*]LI [ ]NN[*AR*]L[ ] QON[*FI*]LI >
1049	Ok 33	URITIN FILI SN[< Ok: or URITN FILI M[or URI + N FILI M[>
1050	Ok 74	CRVX MEVROC < Ok: or IHS UROC or INVROC or IRCVROC or INBVRGE >
1051	Ok 37	REGIS RICATI CRUX < rejected Ok > //]CUMBUIN FO [ ]UICUMG; P[ ]ENITHI C[{ Th p. 300: Procumbu*nt* in fo[*ris*] quicumq(*ue*) pa[*ce*] uenit hic o[*ret* < cf. Ok > }
1052	Ok 38	] RN[ ]F {or S }
1053	Ok 1	+ ALRORON < or CILRORON Ok > // ULCUI < or VILICI or ULLICI or GU[ ]VILIR + CUS Ok > + FILIVS
1054	Ok 43	DONIERT ROGAVIT PRO ANIMA
1055	Ok 3	TAETUERA {Th p. 287} < Ok: T[*T*]UEN[*T*] + or T[*T*]UER[*T*] + or UAETUENA + >
1056	Ok AppC	RRH
1057	Ok 54	]RCAS [ ] O {rejected Ok} // EROCAV[*I*] FILIVS IC // INRI or IACIT {rejected Ok}
1058	Ok 53	RUNHO[*L*]
1059	Ok 64	MATHEUS MARCVS LVCAS IOHA[*NNES*] // ÆLRIAT < Ok: or ÆGRAT or ÆLNAT > FECIT HA(*n*)C CRVCEM P(*ro*) A(*n*)IMA SUA
1060	Ok 57	GURGLES { Th p. 290: GUNGLEI } < Ok: or GUNIGLEI or GUMGLEI or GUNGLEL >
1061	Dor.iii	CATGUG < Mac: CATTUG > C [ ]LIUS GIDEO
1062	Dor.v	GONGORIE
1063	Dor.ii	IUDNNE[FIL[*I*] QUI[< Mac: IUONA [ ] FILIUS IUI[>
1064	Dor.iv	[*D*]ENIEL FI[*LIUS* [ ]AUPRIT IA[*CET*] < Mac: ENIEL F[ ] AUPRIT I[>

1065	410	[*A*] W IHS XPC // HAESDUR {or HAERDUR < *Corpus*: HAERDUR > } FECIT CRUCEM ISTAM
1066	Manx	CRUX GURIAT
1067	Manx	XPI NOmiNE ITSPLI EPPS DE INNSVLI // CBPAT & G // IN IHU XPI NOMINE, CRVCIS XPI IMAGENEM
1068/a	Manx	**LAGUBERI** {?}
1068/b	Manx	LUGNI // HIPIA or NIPIA // DIPRUI // CONDILICI // MALBREN SCRIBA // BRENLIER or BREDLIEN
1069	Ok.Pict App.I	[*X*]RI [*B*]ETON {or [*C*]ETON or [*E*]ETON or [*T*]ETON }
1200	Ok 42	]IUS SPED {? or]HS SPED Th p. 289 }}
1201	Ok -	]IUMI[ ]PI[{?}
1202	Ok 2	EVOCATI CA[*I* {?} < or EVOCALI CAT[Ok >
1203	Ok -	]US[{Th p. 279 }
1205	Ok 44	MAVORI FI[*LI*] VITO[< Ok: MAVOUIH VITO[>
1206	Ok 4	DOVITHI IC FILIVS DOCIDCI < Ok: [*O*]I[ ]NI [{?} *R*]IVGDOCI or [*O*]I[ ]HI [{?} *R*]IVSDOCI >
1207	Ok -	< ogam damaged Th p. 331 >
1208	Ok 6	[*D*]AP[*NICI*]N[ ]SC[*I*]
1209	Ok 12	CAOCI FILI POPLICI {Th p. 281 < rejected Ok >}
1210	Ok 5	VALCI FILI V[*ETT*]ANVS {?} {Th p. 281} < V[ ]AIVS Ok >
1212	Corn.	MACARI[{?} CARASIMILIVS {Thomas, *Christian Celts*, pp. 62–63}
1400	Ok 28	OPTIMI < Ok: TIMI >
1401	Ok 27	RESTEUTA or RESTEUTAE {Th p. 166} < Ok: RESGEVT[*A*] or RESGEVT[*AE*] >
1402	Ok 26	POTITI < Ok: [*PO*]TIT >
1403	Ok 25	]IGERNI [*FIL*]I TIGERNI
1404	Ok 30	CAVUDI < Ok: CAVVDI > FILIVS CIVILI {Th p. 288 }
2000	Ang.	DEVORIGI {Sims-Williams, *TAAS* 1999, 146–49}
2001	Carms.	C {?} CRET ORBIORI + {or ORBIORIT } {*Corpus*, Laugharne-2, BL MS Stowe 1023, fo. 178}
2002/a	Brec.	[*LV*]CIVS {or [*DE*]CIVS or [*IC*]CIUS etc.} [*FILI*]VS [*T*]AUR[*I*]ANVS {or [*L*]AUR[*I*]ANVS etc.} {Tomlin, *AC*, 124 (1975), 68–72}
2002/b	Brec.	**TARICORO** < *Corpus*: **TARI[*C*]OR[*O*]** > {Tomlin, *AC*, 124 (1975), 68–72}
2003	Pembs.	AWAOS or AVVAOS (*Corpus* St Brides-1; BL Stowe MS 1023, fo. 23)
2004	Pembs.	[*X*]PC // AW {Craster, *AC*, 106 (1957), 118}

2005	Pembs.	S[*AT*]VRNBIV {Okasha, *AC*, 119 (1970), 68–70}
2006	Shrops.	CVNORIX MACVS MA[*Q*]VI CO[*L*]I[*N*]E {Wright & Jackson, *AntJ*, 48 (1968), 295–300}
2007	10	MAILIS
2008	82	]ESILLIMARIGUELIO
2009	204/940	[ ]MSCEP[*T P*]S {?} [< RCAHMW:]MSCEP[*I* {?}] P[ ]SES·C[>
2010	276	ithfus {th = runic thorn, Moon, *AC*, 127 (1978), 126}
2011	387	]D[ ]I[
2012	380	A W // IHC XPC
2013	383	MATHEVS MARCVS LVC[*AS*] [*I*]OHAN(*n*)ES
2014	392	A W // IHC XPC
2015	393	[*A*] W // [*XP*]C [*IH*]C
2016	406	]IAH;[< *Corpus*: illegible, ?13c. >
2017	Caerns	DINOCONSVODICOON (?) {Wright, *TCHS*, 23 (1962), 127–28 }
2018	Caerns	CVNCUOM SPUO TINM {??} {*Corpus*, s. Llandegai: L. Morris, BL Add. 14907, fo. 189}
2019	Mer.	RIGELLA HI[*C IACET*] FILIA TVNCCE[*TATOCVS*] {Hemp & Gresham, *AC*, 110 (1961), 154–55; *Corpus*: fake?}
2020	Denb.	VERE[{for VERED- or VERET- ?} {Edwards, *Archaeology in Wales*, 27 (1987), 58}
2021	Herefs.	HOC TVMVLVM RETINE[*T*] MEMBRA PUDIC[*E*] [*MVL*]IE[*RIS*] GVINNDA CAR[*AE*] { *Corpus*: CAR[*A*] } CONIU[*GIS*] { *Corpus*: CONIVNX } QVE FVIT IPSA [*IB*]IDEM {C. A. R. Radford and A. R. Dufty, apud Anon., *TWNFC*, 36 (1958–60), 239 and 262}
2022	253/984	[{?} *D*]IC [*ET* {?}] COVLGVEN. < RCAHMW: HIC I[*AC*]E[*T*] {*Corpus*: IAC[*E*]T } GVLGVEN > FILIVS EIVS // [{?} *B*]ERER[ ] < RCAHMW and *Corpus*: AERERN > FECIT LAPIDEM // EMIT HUHIVM {?} < RCAHMW: HU[TR]VM {*Corpus*: HUT[*R*]VM } > LAPIDEM
2023	Scot.4	H {?} V {?} VENTIDIVS {?} SVBDIACONVS {?}
2024	Scot.11	LOCVS SANCTI NICOLAI { NINIANI ? } EPISCOPI
2025	Scot.12	NEITANO SACERDOS
2026	Cumb.	BEDALTOEDBOS { RIB i 2331; cf. Thomas, *GAJ*, 17 (1991–92), 4}
2027	Ang.	ERCAGNI {White, *TAAS*, 1971–72, 19–51}
2028	Corn.	PATER COLIAVIFICIT ARTOGNOV[{*The Times* 7.8.1998; Morris et al., *Med. Arch.*, 43 (1999), 213 –

		N.B. their plate seems to show 2 more lines: COL[ ] FICIT }
2029	/p.39 i	ERECOR MAGLORI CVNIIAC FICIT < or FILI or HIC {?} > < *Corpus*: or HIC IACIT or FILI IACIT >
2030	/p.39 ii	MAGLI {?} {*Corpus*: MAGL[(?)} < PSW: MATIM [ ]INMIBERI >
2031	/p. 68	EPISCOPI IOSEPH
2032	Brec.	[(?) *C*]AMAGLI {Webley, *AC*, 107 (1958), 123–24} < *Corpus*: CAMAGLI HIC IACIT N[L *or* I.] FI[>
2033	Pembs.	A W IHC XPC {Kay, *AC*, 107 (1958), 123}
2034	/871	B[*E*]LGICU < *Corpus* {1st draft}: + BELGINCU CE[// + BELGIN[*G*] > < *Corpus* {2nd draft, following Knight}: + BELGINT + [FE[*CIT*]] // + BELGIN[*T* >
2035	Spoleto	+ GUIL {Tedeschi, *Scrittura e civiltà*, 24 (2000), 417–18}
2036	Dor.i	VIDCV[ ] FILIVS VIDA[
2037	Glam.	] bEN[*E*]DICIT[*E*] ANIMA[{*Corpus*, s. Llandaff Cathedral 5}
2038	Manx	IHS XPS BRANHUI HUC AQUA DIRIVAVIT {Cubbon, in *The Early Church in Western Britain and Ireland*, p. 262}
3001	F1	+ HEC CRUX BUDNOUENUS ABAX IUBSIT FACERE ISTAM
3002	F2	+ GALLMAU
3003	F3	HIC IACENT [ ] ADIVNI F*RAT*RI HI*C* VNA FIL*I* IUSTI
3004	F4	IOCILINX
3005	F5	?]NOMA*I*LI FILIUS VENOMAILI
3006	C1	DISIDERI FILI BODOGNOVS
3007	C2	+ VORMVINI
3008	C3	MAELDOI IA*CIT* P*lus* M*invs* L A*nnos*
3009	C4	CRUX MIHAEL
3010	M1	LAPIDEM HERANNUEN FIL*ia* HERA[*N*]AL (*or* HERA[*H*]AL) A*nnum* M*enses* S*eptem* RAN HUBRIT
3011	M2	IRHAEMA * INRI
3012	M3	TEC[ ]TI HIC IACIT FILI[ ]VS PRFTER
3013	M4	CROX BRIT[ ] ET MULIER*IS* [ ] DRILEGO [ ] F*I*LI CONB*RI*TI HOC OPU*S E*ORUM QUICUMQUE LIGAVIRIT
3014	M5	CROX HARENBILI IB FIL*II* HERANHAL
3015	M6	CROUX PROSTLON
3016	M7	LAGU
3017	M8	{omitting Gaulish = M8a} // RIMOETE {= M8b}

3018	M9	+ II Id*uum* FEBR*uarii* OBIIT FELIX ABB*as* ISTIUS LOCI
3019	M10	RIOCUS ABBA
3020	I1	BELADORE *or* BELADO R*Equiescit*
3021	I2	MAONIRN
3022	I3	TVRTOVALDVS
3023	I4	]RTUS+
3024	I5	HIC REQUIESCIT BERTHILD*IS*
3025	I6	WELITA *or* MELITA
3026	I7	+ GENNOVEUS HIC R*E*QUIISCIT

APPENDIX 2

CONCORDANCE TO ECMW and CIIC NUMBERING[1]

	ECMW nos.	CIIC etc. nos.
Anglesey	5	968
	6	318
	9	319
	10	2007
	13	970
	25	321
	26	320
	27	322
	32	323
	33	325
	34	324
	35	971
	39	326
	–	2000
	–	2027
Breconshire	40	332
	41	331
	42	329
	43	327
	44	328
	46	979
	46a	980
	49	978
	50	333
	54	334
	54a	335
	55	982
	59	984
	60	337

[1] This is included because Nash-Williams, unlike Thomas and Okasha (see Ch. 1 above), did not include such a concordance in his corpus. The list also locates the inscriptions of Wales and the border by the names of the (old) counties. Where no number is given in the ECMW column, bibliographical details may be found in Appendix 1 above.

	61	985
	62	986
	66	330
	67	988
	67a	336
	68	339
	69	989
	70	342
	71	341
	72	976
	73	344
	74	345
	75	346
	76	347
	–	2002/a
	–	2002/b
	–	2032
Caernarfonshire	77	392
	78	391
	82	2008
	83	384
	84	380
	86	382
	87	381
	89	385
	92	386
	94	388
	95	387
	96	390
	97	389
	101	393
	102	395
	103	394
	104	396
	105	397
	106	398
	–	2017
	–	2018
Cardiganshire[2]	108/1	990
	110/27	348/a
	110/27	348/b

[2] Nos. after slashes refer to W. G. Thomas, in *Cardiganshire County History*, i.

	113/30	991
	115/2	351
	116/3	350
	120/14	992
	121/4	349
	122/5	352A
	124/18	993
	125/22	994
	126/6	354
	127/7	353
	128/8	355
	132/9	356
	133/24	995
Carmarthenshire	136	357
	138	358
	139	360
	140	361
	141	359
	142	362
	143	363
	144	364
	147	996
	148	366
	149	365
	150	368/a
	150	368/b
	153	369
	157	370
	159	997
	160	372
	164	998
	166	375
	169	378
	170	379
	171	373
	172	374
	174	376
	175	377
	–	2001
Denbighshire	176	399
	177	400
	181	1001
	182	1000

	183	401
	–	2020
Flintshire	184	402
Glamorganshire[3]	191/886	1005
	193/935	1009
	194/934	1008
	197/842	1006
	198/849	409
	200/921	1020
	204/940	2009
	206/938	1007
	211/882	1010
	214/850	1028
	215/844	406
	220/911	1011
	222/912	1013
	223/933	1012
	228/845	405
	229/848	408
	231/908	1014
	233/910	1015
	234/907	1016
	236/919	1018
	237/920	1019
	238/847	410
	239/927	1023
	240/928	1022
	248/862	1025
	253/984	2022
	255/926	1024
	258/846	407/a
	258/846	407/b
	259/867	1017
	260/884	1004
	261/885	1003
	265/923	1027
	268/841	403
	270/843	404
	–/p.39 i	2029
	–/p.39 ii	2030

[3]   Nos. after slashes refer to W. G. Thomas, in RCAHMW, *Glamorgan*, i/3.

	–/p. 68	2031
	–/871	2034
Merionethshire	271	414
	272	413
	276	2010
	277	412
	278	415
	279	416
	281	1032
	282	417
	283	418
	284	419
	285	p.397
	286	1034
	287	1033
	289	420
	–	1029
	–	1030
	–	2019
Montgomeryshire	294	421
Pembrokeshire	296	423
	297	425
	298	422
	299	424
	300	426
	301	427/a
	301	427/b
	303	1035
	305	428
	306	430
	307	429
	308	431
	312	432
	313	433
	314	434
	315	435
	316	436
	317	437
	319	439
	320	438
	322	371
	335	440

	345	441
	346	442
	349	443
	352	444
	353	446
	354	445
	360	1036
	365	1038
	369	447
	370	448
	376	1041
	379	1040
	380	2012
	382	1039
	383	2013
	384	449
	387	2011
	390	450
	392	2014
	393	2015
	399	453
	400	452
	401	451
	402	454
	403	455
	404	456
	–	2003
	–	2004
	–	2005
	–	2033
Radnorshire	406	2016
Herefordshire	409	497
(England)	410	1065
	–	2021
Shropshire	–	2006
(England)		

APPENDIX 3

ABSOLUTE DATES IN LHEB FOR SOUND CHANGES ‡‡ 1–98

In his 'Chronological Table' in LHEB §210 Jackson arranges nearly a hundred unnumbered Brittonic sound changes (numbered ‡‡ 1–98 in Chapter 2 above) under periods ranging from 'FIRST CENTURY B.C.' to 'TWELFTH CENTURY'. In a few cases he indicates a specific order within a period by labelling them (1) and (2) (see e.g. ‡‡ 2–3 below). The list below is intended to enable easy cross-reference between Jackson's list of sound changes and the numbering system used in the present work, especially in Chapters 2–3.

First century BC ‡1
Second half of the first century AD (1) ‡2, (2) ‡3
Late first century ‡‡ 4–11
End of the third century ‡12
Fourth to early fifth century ‡13
First half or middle of the fifth century ‡‡ 14–15
Middle of the fifth century ‡16
Second half of the fifth century ‡17
Later fifth to early sixth century ‡‡ 18–20
End of the fifth century ‡‡ 21–22
Sixth century ‡‡ 23–24
Beginning of the sixth century ‡25
First half of the sixth century ‡‡ 26–33
First half or middle of the sixth century ‡‡ 34–36
Middle of the sixth century ‡‡ 37–39
Mid or later sixth century (1) ‡40, (2) ‡41; ‡‡ 42–45
Second half of the sixth century ‡‡ 46–49
Late sixth to early seventh century ‡‡ 50–53
About 600 ‡54
Seventh century ‡‡ 55–57
Second half of the seventh century ‡58
Early to mid eighth century ‡59
Eighth century in general (1) ‡60, (2) ‡61; ‡‡ 62–65
Late eighth century ‡‡ 66–68
Early ninth century ‡‡ 69–71

---

[1] For Breton compare the dates in HPB, pp. 846–48. I discussed the validity of the LHEB dates in *Britain 400–600*, pp. 217–61; and see further Ch. 3 above.

The ninth century in general ‡‡ 72–75
Tenth century ‡‡ 76–78
Later tenth century ‡‡ 79–81
Late tenth to early eleventh century ‡‡ 82–83
Tenth to eleventh century ‡‡ 84–85
Early eleventh century ‡86
Eleventh century (1) ‡87, (2) ‡88; ‡89
Second half of the eleventh century ‡90
Late eleventh century ‡‡ 91–92
About 1100 ‡93
Early twelfth century ‡‡ 94–95
Twelfth century ‡‡ 96–98

ABBREVIATIONS AND BIBLIOGRAPHY

ABBREVIATIONS

Linguistic abbreviations

B.	Breton
BC.	Breton and Cornish
C.	Cornish
CB.	Cornish and Breton
Ir.	Irish
MB	Middle Breton
MC	Middle Cornish
ME	Middle English
MI	Middle Irish
Mod.C.	Modern Cornish
Mod.Ir.	Modern Irish
Mod.W.	Modern Welsh
MW	Middle Welsh
OB	Old Breton
OC	Old Cornish
OE	Old English
OI	Old Irish
OW	Old Welsh
OWCB	Old Welsh, Old Cornish, and Old Breton
Pr.B.	Primitive Breton
Pr.C.	Primitive Cornish
Pr.Ir.	Primitive Irish
Pr.W.	Primitive Welsh
SW.Brit.	South-West Brittonic
VL	Vulgar Latin
W.	Welsh
W.Brit.	West Brittonic
W.Co.	Welsh and Cornish
WCB	Welsh, Cornish, and Breton

Bibliographic abbreviations

Journals are in *italics*. Abbreviations for collections (e.g. Beekes FS) are only included in cases where the titles are abbreviated in citations in the Bibliography. Throughout this work references like 'RIB i 123' refer to inscriptions by number, whereas those like 'RIG i, 123', refer to pages.

AC	*Archaeologia Cambrensis.*
ADA	Irslinger, Britta Sofie, 2002. *Abstrakta mit Dentalsuffixen im Altirischen*, Heidelberg: Winter.
AE	*L'Année épigraphique.*
Annales Cambriae	Phillimore, Egerton (ed.), 1888. The *Annales Cambriae* and Old-Welsh genealogies from Harleian MS. 3859. *Cymmrodor* 9, 141–83.
AntJ	*Antiquaries Journal.*
ArchJ	*Archaeological Journal.*
BBCS	*Bulletin of the Board of Celtic Studies.*
Beekes FS	Lubotsky, Alexander (ed.), 1997. *Sound Law and Analogy: Papers in Honor of Robert S. P. Beekes*, Amsterdam: Rodopi.
Bodmin	Förster, Max (ed.), 1930. Die Freilassungsurkunden des Bodmin-Evangeliars. In *A Grammatical Miscellany offered to Otto Jespersen*, Copenhagen: Levin & Munksgaard, 77–99.
BSAF	*Bulletin de la Société Archéologique de Finistère.*
BSNAF	*Bulletin de la Société Nationale des Antiquaires de France.*
BT	Evans, J. Gwenogvryn (ed.), 1910. *Facsimile and Text of the Book of Taliesin*, Llanbedrog: J. G. Evans.
BWP	Williams, Ifor, 1980. *The Beginnings of Welsh Poetry*, 2nd edn, Cardiff: University of Wales Press.
BzN	*Beiträge zur Namenforschung.*
CA	*Cornish Archaeology.*
CBT	Gruffydd, R. Geraint (ed.), 1991–99. Cyfres Beirdd y Tywysogion, 7 vols, Cardiff: University of Wales Press.
CGH	O'Brien, M. A. (ed.), 1962. *Corpus Genealogiarum Hiberniae*, i, Dublin: Dublin Institute for Advanced Studies.
CGSH	Ó Riain, Pádraig (ed.), 1985. *Corpus Genealogiarum Sanctorum Hiberniae*, Dublin: Dublin Institute for Advanced Studies.

Chad   'Extracts from the Book of St. Chad', in LL,
              pp. xliii–xlviii.
Chrest.   Loth, J., 1890. *Chrestomathie bretonne*, Paris:
              Bouillon.
CIIC   Macalister, R. A. S. (ed.), 1945–49. *Corpus
              Inscriptionum Insularum Celticarum*, 2 vols, Dublin:
              Stationery Office.
CIL   Corpus Inscriptionum Latinarum, Berlin 1863–.
CMCS   *Cambrian* [up to 1993 *Cambridge*] *Medieval Celtic
              Studies.*
Corpus   Edwards, Nancy, Redknap, Mark, & Lewis, John
              (ed.), *Corpus of Early Medieval Inscribed Stones and
              Stone Sculpture in Wales*, 3 vols (draft version).
CPNE   Padel, O. J., 1985. *Cornish Place-Name Elements*,
              Nottingham: English Place-Name Society.
Cymmrodor   *Y Cymmrodor.*
DAG   Whatmough, Joshua, 1970. *The Dialects of Ancient
              Gaul*, Cambridge, MA: Harvard University Press.
DASP   *Devon Archaeological Society Proceedings.*
DEPN   Ekwall, Eilert, 1960. *The Concise Oxford Dictionary
              of English Place-Names*, 4th edn, Oxford: Clarendon
              Press.
DGVB   Fleuriot, Léon, & Evans, Claude, 1985. *A Dictionary
              of Old Breton: Dictionnaire du vieux breton (Diction-
              naire des gloses en vieux breton)*, 2 vols, Toronto:
              Prepcorp.
DIL   *Dictionary of the Irish Language*, 1913–76. Dublin:
              Royal Irish Academy.
DLG   Delamarre, Xavier, 2001. *Dictionnaire de la langue
              gauloise*, Paris: Errance.
Dor.   see p. 2.
DP   Owen, Henry (ed.), 1892–1936. *The Description of
              Penbrokshire by George Owen of Henllys*, 4 parts,
              London: Honourable Socety of Cymmrodorion.
EANC   Thomas, R. J., 1938. *Enwau Afonydd a Nentydd
              Cymru*, i, Cardiff: University of Wales Press.
ÉC   *Études celtiques.*
ECMW   Nash-Williams, V. E., 1950. *The Early Christian
              Monuments of Wales,* Cardiff: University of Wales
              Press.
EHR   *English Historical Review.*
EIHM   O'Rahilly, Thomas F., 1946. *Early Irish History and
              Mythology*, Dublin: Dublin Institute for Advanced
              Studies.

EME	*Early Medieval Europe.*
ETG	Richards, Melville, 1998. *Enwau Tir a Gwlad*, Caernarfon: Gwasg Gwynedd.
Evans FS	Eska, Joseph F., et al. (ed.), 1995. *Hispano-Gallo-Brittonica: Essays in Honour of D. Ellis Evans*, Cardiff: University of Wales Press.
EWGT	Bartrum, P. C. (ed.), 1966. *Early Welsh Genealogical Tracts*, Cardiff: University of Wales Press.
FS	Festschrift.
GAJ	*Glasgow Archaeological Journal.*
GMW	Evans, D. Simon, 1964. *A Grammar of Middle Welsh*, Dublin: Dublin Institute for Advanced Studies.
GOI	Thurneysen, Rudolf, 1946. *A Grammar of Old Irish*, Dublin: Dublin Institute for Advanced Studies.
GPC	*Geiriadur Prifysgol Cymru: A Dictionary of the Welsh Language*, 1950–. Cardiff: University of Wales Press.
GPN	Evans, D. Ellis, 1967. *Gaulish Personal Names*, Oxford: Clarendon Press.
Gramm.	Fleuriot, Léon, 1964. *Le Vieux Breton: éléments d'une grammaire*, Paris: Klincksieck.
Grauf.	Marichal, Robert, 1988. *Les Graffites de La Graufesenque*, Paris: CNRS.
GS	Gedenkschrift.
Hamp FS	Matonis, A. T. E., & Melia, Daniel F. (ed.), 1990. *Celtic Language, Celtic Culture: A Festschrift for Eric P. Hamp*, Van Nuys, CA: Ford & Bailie.
Holder	Holder, Alfred, 1896–1913. *Alt-celtischer Sprachschatz*, Leipzig: Teubner.
HPB	Jackson, Kenneth Hurlstone, 1967. *A Historical Phonology of Breton*, Dublin: Dublin Institute for Advanced Studies.
IEMB	Davies, Wendy, et al., 2000. *The Inscriptions of Early Medieval Brittany: Les inscriptions de la Bretagne du Haut Moyen Âge*, Oakville, CT and Aberystwyth: Celtic Studies Publications.
IEW	Pokorny, Julius, 1959. *Indogermanisches etymologisches Wörterbuch*, Bern: Francke.
IF	*Indogermanische Forschungen.*
JCL	*Journal of Celtic Linguistics.*
JCS	*Journal of Celtic Studies.*
JEH	*Journal of Ecclesiastical History.*
JEPNS	*Journal of the English Place-Name Society.*
JIES	*Journal of Indo-European Studies.*
JRS	*Journal of Roman Studies.*

JRSAI	*Journal of the Royal Socety of Antiquaries of Ireland.*
Kajanto	Kajanto, Iiro, 1965. *The Latin Cognomina*, Helsinki: Societas Scientiarum Fennica.
KGP	Schmidt, Karl Horst, 1957. *Die Komposition in gallischen Personennamen*, Tübingen: Niemeyer.
KHJ	see p. 5.
KZ	*Zeitschrift für vergleichende Sprachforschung.*
LBS	Baring-Gould, S., & Fisher, John, 1907–13. *The Lives of the British Saints*, 4 vols, London: Honourable Society of Cymmrodorion.
Lebel	Lebel, Paul, 1949. *Les Noms de personnes en France*, 2nd edn, Paris: Presses Universitaires de France.
LEIA	Vendryes, J., et al., 1959–. *Lexique étymologique de l'irlandais ancien*, Dublin: Dublin Institute for Advanced Studies, and Paris: CNRS.
Lewis & Pedersen	Lewis, Henry, & Pedersen, Holger, 1961. *A Concise Comparative Celtic Grammar*, 2nd edn with *Supplement*, Göttingen: Vandenhoeck & Ruprecht.
Lewis & Short	Lewis, Charlton T., & Short, Charles, 1879. *A Latin Dictionary*, Oxford: Clarendon Press.
LHEB	Jackson, Kenneth, 1953. *Language and History in Early Britain*, Edinburgh: Edinburgh University Press.
LL	Evans, J. Gwenogvryn, & Rhys, John (ed.), 1893. *The Text of the Book of Llan Dâv*, Oxford: J. G. Evans.
LlC	*Llên Cymru.*
LW	Westwood, J. O., 1876–79. *Lapidarium Walliae*, Oxford: Cambrian Archaeological Association.
LWP	Rhys, John, 1879. *Lectures on Welsh Philology*, 2nd edn, London: Trübner.
MA	Jones, Owen, et al. (ed.), 1870. *The Myvyrian Archaiology of Wales*, 2nd edn, Denbigh: Gee.
Mac Cana FS	Carey, John, et al. (ed.), 1999. *Ildánach, Ildírech: A Festschrift for Proinsias Mac Cana*, Andover, MA and Aberystwyth: Celtic Studies Publications.
Med. Arch.	*Medieval Archaeology.*
Meid FS	Anreiter, Peter, & Jerem, Erzsébet (ed.), 1999. *Studia Celtica et Indogermanica: Festschrift für Wolfgang Meid*, Budapest: Archaeolingua.
MLH v/1	Wodtko, Dagmar S., 2000. *Wörterbuch der keltiberischen Inschriften*, vol. v, Part 1, of Untermann, Jürgen (ed.), *Monumenta Linguarum Hispanicarum*, Wiesbaden: Reichert.

Mócsy	Mócsy, András, et al., 1983. *Nomenclator provinciarum Europae Latinarum et Galliae Cisalpinae cum indice inverso*, Budapest: Dissertationes Pannonicae ex Instituto Archaeologico Universitatis de Rolando Eötvös nominatae Budapestinensis provenientes.
Nb	see p. 2.
NLWJ	*National Library of Wales Journal.*
NWÄI	De Bernardo Stempel, Patrizia, 1999. *Nominale Wortbildung des älteren Irischen*, Tübingen: Niemeyer.
Ok	see p. 2.
OPEL	Lörincz, Barnabás, & Redö, Ferenc (ed.), 1994–2002. *Onomasticon Provinciarum Europae Latinarum*, 4 vols, Budapest: Archaeolingua (vol. i); Vienna: Forschungsgesellschaft Wiener Stadtarchäologie (vols. ii–iv).
Oswald	Oswald, Felix, 1931. *Index of Potters' Stamps on Terra Sigillata*, East Bridgford: privately ptd.
PBA	*Proceedings of the British Academy.*
PDAS	*Proceedings of the Devon Archaeological Society.*
PDNHAS	*Proceedings of the Dorset Natural History and Archaeological Society.*
PHCC	*Proceedings of the Harvard Celtic Colloquium.*
PNRB	Rivet, A. L. F., & Smith, Colin, 1979. *The Place-Names of Roman Britain*, London: Batsford.
PRB	Birley, Anthony, 1979. *The People of Roman Britain*, London: Batsford.
PRIA	*Proceedings of the Royal Irish Academy.*
PSAS	*Proceedings of the Society of Antiquaries of Scotland.*
RAO	*Revue archéologique de l'Ouest.*
RC	*Revue celtique.*
RCA(H)MS	Royal Commission on the Ancient (and Historical) Monuments of Scotland.
RCAHMW	Royal Commission on the Ancient and Historical Monuments of Wales.
RCHM	Royal Commission on Historical Monuments (England).
RIB	Collingwood, R. G., et al., 1990–95. *The Roman Inscriptions of Britain*, 2 vols, Stroud: Sutton.
RIG	Recueil des Inscriptions Gauloises, 1985–. Paris: CNRS.
SBCHP	Schrijver, Peter, 1995. *Studies in British Celtic Historical Phonology*, Amsterdam: Rodopi.
SC	*Studia Celtica.*

Scot.   see p. 2.

SEBC   Chadwick, Nora K. (ed.), 1958. *Studies in the Early British Church*, Cambridge: Cambridge University Press.

SWWF   Zimmer, Stefan, 2000. *Studies in Welsh Word-Formation*, Dublin: Dublin Institute for Advanced Studies.

TAAS   *Transactions of the Anglesey Antiquarian Society.*

Tab.Luguval.   Tomlin, R. S. O. (ed.), 1998. Roman manuscripts from Carlisle: the ink-written tablets, *Britannia* 29, 31–84.

Tab.Sulis   Tomlin, R. S. O. (ed.), 1988. *Tabellae Sulis: Roman Inscribed Tablets of Tin and Lead from the Sacred Spring at Bath*, Oxford: Oxford University Committee for Archaeology.

Tab.Vindol. ii   Bowman, Alan K., & Thomas, J. David, 1994. *The Vindolanda Writing-Tablets (Tabulae Vindolandenses II)*, London: British Museum Press.

TCASFC   *Transactions of the Carmarthenshire Antiquarian Society and Field Club.*

TCHS   *Transactions of the Caernarvonshire Historical Society.*

THSC   *Transactions of the Honourable Society of Cymmrodorion.*

TPS   *Transactions of the Philological Society.*

TRC   McCone, Kim, 1996. *Towards a Relative Chronology of Ancient and Medieval Celtic Sound Change*, Maynooth: Department of Old and Middle Irish, St. Patrick's College.

TWNFC   *Transactions of the Woolhope Naturalists' Field Club.*

TYP   Bromwich, Rachel, 1978. *Trioedd Ynys Prydein*, 2nd edn, Cardiff: University of Wales Press.

VC   *Vita Sancti Cadoci*, in VSB, pp. 24–141.

VKG   Pedersen, Holger, 1909–13. *Vergleichende Grammatik der keltischen Sprachen*, 2 vols, Göttingen: Vandenhoeck & Ruprecht.

VLRB   Smith, Colin, 1983. Vulgar Latin in Roman Britain: epigraphic and other evidence. In Temporini, Hildegard, & Haase, Wolfgang (ed.), *Aufstieg und Niedergang der römischen Welt*, Teil ii, Band 29, ii, Berlin: de Gruyter, 893–948.

VSB   Wade-Evans, A. W. (ed.), 1944. *Vitae Sanctorum Britanniae et Genealogiae*, Cardiff: University of Wales Press.

WATU	Richards, Melville, 1969. *Welsh Administrative and Territorial Units*, Cardiff: University of Wales Press.
WG	Morris Jones, J., 1913. *A Welsh Grammar, Historical and Comparative*, Oxford: Clarendon Press.
WHR	*Welsh History Review.*
YB	*Ysgrifau Beirniadol.*
ZCP	*Zeitschrift für celtische Philologie.*
Ziegler	Ziegler, Sabine, 1994. *Die Sprache der altirischen Ogam-Inschriften*, Göttingen: Vandenhoeck & Ruprecht.

BIBLIOGRAPHY

Ab Ithel, John Williams (ed.), 1860. *Annales Cambriae*, London: Longman, Green, Longman, & Roberts.

Alcock, Leslie, 1973. *Arthur's Britain*, rev. edn, Harmondsworth: Penguin.

Aldhouse Green, M. J., & Raybould, M. E., 1999. Deities with Gallo-Roman names recorded in inscriptions from Roman Britain. *SC* 33, 91–135.

Alföldy, Géza, 1969. *Die Personennamen in der römischen Provinz Dalmatia*, Heidelberg: Winter.

Alföldy, Géza, 1974. *Noricum*, London: Routledge & Kegan Paul.

Allmer, A. & Dissard, P., 1888–93. *Musée de Lyon, Inscriptions antiques*, 5 vols, Lyon: Léon Delaroche.

Anderson, Alan Orr, & Anderson, Marjorie Ogilvie (ed.), 1991. *Adomnán's Life of Columba*, Oxford: Clarendon Press.

Anon., 1848. Letters of E. Lhwyd no. II. *AC* 3, 309–13.

Anon., 1928. Report of the 82nd Annual Meeting held at Aberafan. *AC* 7th ser. 8, 363–421.

Anon., 1947. Roman Britain in 1946. *JRS* 37, 165–82.

Anon., 1958–60. A ninth century tombstone from Clodock. *TWNFC* 36, 239 and 262.

Anon., 1972. Rhétie. *AE*, 109.

Anon., 1979. Dalmatie. *AE*, 133–37.

Anon., 1981. Mésie. *AE*, 189–98.

Anon., 1986. Dalmatie. *AE*, 198–200.

Anreiter, Peter, Haslinger, Marialuise, & Roider, Ulrike, 2000. The names of the Eastern Alpine region mentioned in Ptolemy. In Parsons & Sims-Williams (ed.), *Ptolemy*, 113–42.

Anwyl E., 1906. The Llandecwyn inscribed stone. *AC* 6th ser. 6, 121–24.

Anwyl E., 1909–10. The Book of Aneirin. *THSC*, 95–136.

Bammesberger, Alfred, 1976–78. Old English *broc* and Middle Irish *broc(c)*. *BBCS* 27, 552–54.

Bammesberger, Alfred & Wollmann, Alfred (ed.), 1990. *Britain 400–600: Language and History*, Heidelberg: Winter.

Barber, Richard, 1972. *The Figure of Arthur*, London: Longman.

Baring-Gould, S., 1918. Two inscribed stones in Devon. *AC* 6th ser. 18, 195–98.

Barrow, Julia (ed.), 1998. *St Davids Episcopal Acta, 1085–1280*, Cardiff: South Wales Record Society.

Bartrum, Peter C., 1963. Pedigrees of the Welsh tribal patriarchs. *NLWJ* 13, 93–146.

Bartrum, Peter C. (ed.), 1974. *Welsh Genealogies* AD *300–1400*, 8 vols, Cardiff: University of Wales Press.

Bartrum, Peter C., 1993. *A Welsh Classical Dictionary*, Aberystwyth: National Library of Wales.

Bergin, Osborn, 1930–32. Eochu, Eochuid. *Ériu* 11, 140–46.

Bergin, Osborn, 1934–38. *Lie, lia*, 'stone'. *Ériu* 12, 217–18.

Best, R. I., Bergin, Osborn, & O'Brien, M. A. (ed.), 1954. *The Book of Leinster*, i, Dublin: Dublin Institute for Advanced Studies.

Best, R. I. & O'Brien, M. A. (ed.), 1967. *The Book of Leinster*, v, Dublin: Dublin Institute for Advanced Studies.

Bieler, Ludwig (ed.), 1971. *Four Latin Lives of St. Patrick*, Dublin: Dublin Institute for Advanced Studies.

Bieler, Ludwig (ed.), 1979. *The Patrician Texts in the Book of Armagh*, Dublin: Dublin Institute for Advanced Studies.

Binchy, D. A., 1950. Ir. *forggu* (W *goreu* ?), *digu. JCS* 1, 148–51.

Binchy, D. A., 1958. Review of LHEB. *Celtica* 4, 288–92.

Birkhan, Helmut, 1970. *Germanen und Kelten bis zum Ausgang der Römerzeit*, Vienna: Österreichische Akademie der Wissenchaften.

Bodel, John (ed.), 2001. *Epigraphic Evidence: Ancient History from Inscriptions*, London: Routledge.

Bonser, Wilfrid, 1957. *An Anglo-Saxon and Celtic Bibliography (450–1087)*, 2 vols, Oxford: Blackwell.

Borsje, Jacqueline, 2002. The meaning of *túathcháech* in early Irish texts. *CMCS* 43, 1–24.

Bowen, E. G., & Gresham, C. A., 1967. *History of Merioneth*, i, Dolgellau: Merioneth Historical and Record Society

Brash, Richard Rolt, 1873. Inscribed stones of Wales. *AC* 4th ser. 4, 285–87.

Breatnach, Liam, 1992. Review of Carney 1989. *CMCS* 23, 120.

Broderick, George, 1994–. *Placenames of the Isle of Man*, Tübingen: Niemeyer.

Bromwich, Rachel, 1991. The *Tristan* of the Welsh. In Bromwich et al. (ed.), *Arthur of the Welsh*, 209–28.

Bromwich, Rachel, & Evans, D. Simon, 1992. *Culhwch and Olwen: An Edition and Study of the Oldest Arthurian Tale*, Cardiff: University of Wales Press.

Bromwich, Rachel, Jarman A. O. H., & Roberts, Brynley F. (ed.), 1991. *The Arthur of the Welsh*, Cardiff: University of Wales Press.

Camden, William, ed. Gibson, Edmund, 1695, *Britannia*, repr. 1971: *Camden's Britannia 1695*, ed. Piggott, Stuart, & Walters, Gwyn, Newton Abbot: David & Charles.

Cane, Meredith, 1999. *Personal Names of Women in Wales, Cornwall and Brittany, 400–1400 AD*, M.Phil., University of Wales, Aberystwyth.

Carey, John, 1988. *Fir Bolg*: a native etymology revisited. *CMCS* 16, 77–83.

Carney, James, 1989. The dating of archaic Irish verse. In Tranter, Stephen N., & Tristram, Hildegard L. C. (ed.), *Early Irish Literature – Media and Communication*, Tübingen: Gunter Narr, 39–55.

Charles B. G., 1992. *The Place-Names of Pembrokeshire*, 2 vols (one pagination), Aberystwyth: National Library of Wales.

Charles-Edwards, T. M., 1970–72. Some Celtic kinship terms. *BBCS* 24, 105–22.

Charles-Edwards, T. M., 1995. *Mi a dynghaf dynghed* and related problems. In Evans FS, 1–15.

Charles-Edwards, T. M., 1995. Language and society among the Insular Celts AD 400–1000. In Green, Miranda J. (ed.), *The Celtic World*, London: Routledge, 703–36.

Charles-Edwards, T. M., 1998. The context and uses of literacy in early Christian Ireland. In Pryce, Huw (ed.), *Literacy in Medieval Celtic Societies*, Cambridge: Cambridge University Press, 62–82.

Charles-Edwards, T. M., 1999. Britons in Ireland, *c.* 550–800. In Mac Cana FS, 15–26.

Charles-Edwards, T. M., 1999. Geis, prophecy, omen, and oath. *Celtica* 23, 38–59.

Charles-Edwards, T. M., 2000. *Early Christian Ireland*, Cambridge: Cambridge University Press.

Clancy, Thomas Owen, 1993. The Drosten Stone: a new reading. *PSAS* 123, 345–53.

Clancy, Thomas Owen, 2000. Scotland, the 'Nennian' recension of the *Historia Brittonum*, and the *Lebor Bretnach*. In Taylor, Simon (ed.), *Kings, Clerics and Chronicles in Scotland 500–1297: Essays in Honour of Marjorie Ogilvie Anderson*, Dublin: Four Courts, 87–107.

Clapham, A. W., 1934. Notes on the origins of Hiberno-Saxon art. *Antiquity* 8, 43–57.

Clarke, Basil, 1968–70. Calidon and the Caledonian Forest. *BBCS* 23, 191–201.

Coates, Richard, 1980–81. Review of PNRB. *JEPNS* 13, 59–71.

Coates, Richard, 1981. Margidunum. *ZCP* 38, 255–68.

Coates, Richard, & Breeze, Andrew, 2000. *Celtic Voices, English Places: Studies of the Celtic Impact on Place-Names in England*, Stamford: Shaun Tyas.

Coe, Jonathan Baron, 2001. *The Place-Names of the Book of Llandaf*, Ph.D., University of Wales, Aberystwyth.

Craster, O. E., 1957. Early Christian stone found at the Bishop's Palace, St. David's. *AC* 106, 118.

Crouch, David (ed.), 1988. *Llandaff Episcopal Acta, 1140–1287*, Cardiff: South Wales Record Society.

Cubbon, A. M., 1982. The early Church in the Isle of Man. In Susan M. Pearce (ed.), *The Early Church in Western Britain and Ireland: Studies presented to C. A. Ralegh Radford*, British Archaeological Reports British Series 102, Oxford: BAR, 257–82.

Curchin, Leonard A., 1997. Celticization and Romanization of toponymy in Central Spain. *Emerita* 65, 257–79.

d'Arbois de Jubainville, H., 1876–78. Quelques noms de saints bretons dans un texte du XIᵉ siècle. *RC* 3, 449–50.

d'Arbois de Jubainville, H., 1896. Review of Rhys, Epigraphic notes (1895). *RC* 17, 311–12.

Dark, Ken, 1992. Epigraphic, art-historical, and historical approaches to the chronology of Class I inscribed stones. In Edwards & Lane (ed.), *Early Church in Wales and the West*, 51–61.

Davies, Alun Eirug, 1969. Sir Ifor Williams: a bibliography. *SC* 4, 1–55.

Davies, Anna Morpurgo, 2000. Greek personal names and linguistic continuity. In Hornblower, Simon, & Matthews, Elaine (ed.), *Greek Personal Names: Their Value as Evidence*, Oxford: Oxford University Press, 15–39.

Davies, Brian, 1997 (Summer). Archaeology and ideology, or how Wales was robbed of its early history. *New Welsh Review* 37, 38–51.

Davies, Elwyn, 1967. *Rhestr o Enwau Lleoedd: A Gazetteer of Welsh Place-Names*, Cardiff: University of Wales Press.

Davies, J. L., 1994. The Roman period. In Davies & Kirby (ed.), *Cardiganshire County History*, i, 275–317.

Davies, J. L., & Kirby, D. P. (ed.), 1994. *Cardiganshire County History*, i, Cardiff: University of Wales Press.

Davies, Wendy, 1978. *An Early Welsh Microcosm: Studies in the Llandaff Charters*, London: Royal Historical Society.

Davies, Wendy, 1978–80. The orthography of personal names in the charters of *Liber Landavensis*. *BBCS* 28, 553–57.

Davies, Wendy, 1979. *The Llandaff Charters*, Aberystwyth: National Library of Wales.

Davies, Wendy, 1990. *Patterns of Power in Early Wales*, Oxford: Clarendon Press.

De Bernardo Stempel, Patrizia, 1987. *Die Vertretung der indogermanischen liquiden und nasalen Sonanten im Keltischen*, Innsbruck: Innsbrucker Beiträge zur Sprachwissenschaft.

De Bernardo Stempel, Patrizia, 1989. Britannischer Komparativ und Konsonantenverdoppelung. *IF* 94, 207–33

De Bernardo Stempel, Patrizia, 1991. Die Sprache altbritannischer Münzlegenden. *ZCP* 44, 36–55.

De Bernardo Stempel, Patrizia, 1999. Zur Methode der Wortbildungsanalyse von Korpussprachen (anhand keltischen Materials). In Meid FS, 61–77.

De Bernardo Stempel, Patrizia, 2000. Ptolemy's Celtic Italy and Ireland: a linguistic analysis. In Parsons & Sims-Williams (ed.), *Ptolemy*, 83–112.

De Bhaldraithe, Tomás, 1990. Notes on the diminutive suffix *-ín* in Modern Irish. In Hamp FS, 85–95.

De Courson, Aurélien (ed.), 1863. *Cartulaire de l'Abbaye de Redon*, Paris: Imprimerie Impériale.

Derolez, René, 1992. Language problems in Anglo-Saxon England: *barbara loquella* and *barbarismus*. In Korhammer, Michael (ed.), *Words, Texts and Manuscripts: Studies in Anglo-Saxon Culture presented to Helmut Gneuss*, Cambridge: Brewer, 285–92.

Desjardins, Ernest, 1873. *Notice sur les monuments épigraphiques de Bavai et du Musée de Douai*, Douai: Crépin and Paris: Dumoulin.

Diehl, Ernest (ed.), 1925–31. *Inscriptiones Latinae Christianae Veteres*, 3 vols, Berlin: Weidmann.

Dobbs, Margaret E., 1938–39. Miscellany from H.2.7 (T.C.D.). *ZCP* 21, 307–18.

Doble, G. H., ed. Evans, D. Simon, 1971. *Lives of the Welsh Saints*, Cardiff: University of Wales Press.

Dressler, Wolfgang, 1967. Galatisches. In Meid, Wolfgang (ed.), *Beiträge zur Indogermanistik und Keltologie Julius Pokorny gewidmet*, Innsbruck: Sprachwissenschaftliche Institut, 147–54.
Dumville, David N., 1975–76. 'Nennius' and the *Historia Brittonum*. *SC* 10/11, 78–95.
Dumville, David N., 1984. Gildas and Maelgwn: problems of dating. In Lapidge, Michael, & Dumville, David (ed.), *Gildas: New Approaches*, Woodbridge: Boydell Press, 51–59.
Dumville, David N. (ed.), 1985. *The Historia Brittonum, iii, The 'Vatican' Recension*, Cambridge: Brewer.
Dumville, David N., 1985. Seventh- or eighth-century evidence for the British transmission of Pelagius. *CMCS* 10, 39–52.
Dumville, David N., 1992. *Wessex and England from Alfred to Edgar*, Woodbridge: Boydell Press.
Dumville, David N., 1999. *A Palaeographer's Review: The Insular System of Scripts in the Early Middle Ages*, i, Osaka: Kansai University Press.
Dumville, David N., 2001. Review of Howlett 1998. *EHR* 116, 405–8.
Dumville, David N., 2001. *Saint David of Wales*, Cambridge: Hughes Hall and Department of Anglo-Saxon, Norse, and Celtic.
Edwards, Nancy, 1987. Bryn Gwylan, Llangernyw. *Archaeology in Wales* 27, 58.
Edwards, Nancy, 1997. Two carved stone pillars from Trefollwyn, Anglesey. *ArchJ* 154, 108–17.
Edwards, Nancy, 1999. Viking-influenced sculpture in north Wales, its ornament and context. *Church Archaeology* 3, 5–16.
Edwards, Nancy, 2001. Early-medieval inscribed stones and stone sculpture in Wales: context and function. *Med. Arch.* 45, 15–39.
Edwards, Nancy, 2001. Monuments in a landscape: the early medieval sculpture of St David's. In Hamerow, Helena, & MacGregor, Arthur (ed.), *Image and Power in the Archaeology of Early Medieval Britain: Essays in Honour of Rosemary Cramp*, Oxford: Oxbow, 53–77.
Edwards, Nancy, & Lane, Alan (ed.), 1992. *The Early Church in Wales and the West*, Oxford: Oxbow.
Ekwall, Eilert, 1928. *English River-Names*, Oxford: Clarendon Press.
Emery, F. V., 1975. A new reply to Lhuyd's *Queries* (1696): Llanboidy, Carmarthenshire. *AC* 124, 102–10.
Evans, D. Ellis, 1968–69. Nomina Celtica I: Catamantaloedis, Docnimarus, Satigenus. *ÉC* 12, 195–200.
Evans, D. Ellis, 1970–72. A comparison of the formation of some Continental and early Insular Celtic personal names. *BBCS* 24, 415–34.
Evans, D. Ellis, 1976–78. Some Celtic forms in *cant-*. *BBCS* 27, 235–45.
Evans, D. Ellis, 1998. Rex Icenorum Prasutagus. In Tuczay, Christa, et al. (ed.), *Ir sult sprechen willekomen: Grenzenlose Mediävistik – Festschrift für Helmut Birkhan*, Bern etc.: Peter Lang, 99–106.
Evans, D. Simon, 1979. Irish and the languages of Post-Roman Wales. *Studies* 68, 19–32.
Evans, Elwyn, 1964. *Yr Enwau Personol mewn Saith o Destunau Detholedig*, MA, University of Wales, Bangor.
Evans, Evander, 1872. Studies in Cymric philology. *AC* 4th ser. 3, 297–314.
Falileyev, Alexander, 2000. *Etymological Glossary of Old Welsh*, Tübingen: Niemeyer.
Falileyev, Alexander, 2001. Beyond historical linguistics: a case for multilingualism in early Wales. In Ní Chatháin, Próinséas, & Richter, Michael (ed.), *Irland und Europa im früheren Mittelalter: Texte und Überlieferung*, Dublin: Four Courts, 6–13.
Fleuriot, Léon, 1976–77. Le vocabulaire de l'inscription gauloise de Chamalières. *ÉC* 15, 173–90.
Fleuriot, Léon, 1980. *Les origines de la Bretagne*, Paris: Payot.
Fleuriot, Léon, 1983. Brittonica. *ÉC* 20, 101–18.
Fleuriot, Léon, 1987. *Samsoni, Uurgonezlo*, noms de saints bretons dans les reliques de Chelles. *ÉC* 24, 194–97.
Flobert, Pierre (ed.), 1997. *La Vie ancienne de saint Samson de Dol*, Paris: CNRS.
Förstemann, Ernst, 1856. *Altdeutsches Namenbuch*, i, *Personennamen*, Nordhausen: F. Förstemann.
Förster, Max, 1941. *Der Flussname Themse und seine Sippe*, Munich: Bayerische Akademie der Wissenschaften.

Forsyth, Katherine, 1995. The ogham-inscribed spindle-whorl from Buckquoy: evidence for the Irish language in pre-Viking Orkney? *PSAS* 125, 677–96.

Forsyth, Katherine, 2000. Evidence of a lost Pictish source in the *Historia Regum Anglorum* of Symeon of Durham. In Taylor, Simon (ed.), *Kings, Clerics and Chronicles in Scotland 500–1297: Essays in Honour of Marjorie Ogilvie Anderson*, Dublin: Four Courts, 19–34.

Forsyth, Katherine, 2000. The Ogham inscription at Dunadd. In Lane, Alan, & Campbell, Ewan, *Dunadd: An Early Dalriadic Capital*, Oxford: Oxbow, 264–72.

Foster, I. Ll., 1965. The emergence of Wales. In Foster, I. Ll., & Daniel, G. E. (ed.), *Prehistoric and Early Wales*, London: Routledge & Kegan Paul, 213–35.

Foster, Sally M., 1988. Early medieval inscription at Holcombe, Somerset. *Med. Arch.* 32, 208–11.

Fox, Cyril, et al., 1942–43. The Domnic inscribed slab, Llangwyryfon, Cardiganshire. *AC* 97, 205–12.

Fox, Cyril, & Fox, Aileen, 1934. Forts and farms on Margam Mountain, Glamorgan. *Antiquity*, 395–413.

Fraser, P. M., & Matthews, E. M. (ed.), 1987. *A Lexicon of Greek Personal Names*, i, *The Aegean Islands, Cyprus, Cyrenaica*, Oxford: Clarendon Press.

Frere, S. S., 1977. Roman Britain in 1976: sites explored. *Britannia* 8, 356–425.

Fulford, Michael, Handley, Mark, & Clarke, Amanda, 2000. An early date for ogham: the Silchester ogham stone rehabilitated. *Med. Arch.* 44, 1–23.

Fychan, Gwerful Angharad, 2001. *Astudiaeth o Enwau Lleoedd Gogledd Cantref Buellt*, Ph.D., University of Wales, Aberystwyth.

García Alonso, Juan Luis, 1995. *La geografía de Claudio Ptolomeo y la Península Ibérica*, microfiche edition, Salamanca: Ediciones Universidad de Salamanca.

Garrett, Andrew, 1999. On the prosodic phonology of ogam Irish. *Ériu* 50, 139–60.

Gillies, William, 1999. The 'British' genealogy of the Campbells. *Celtica* 23, 82–95.

Gippert, Jost, 1990. Präliminarien zu einer Neuausgabe der Ogaminschriften. In Bammesberger & Wollmann (ed.), *Britain 400–600*, 291–304.

Gippert, Jost, 2000. Review of Swift 1997. *CMCS* 39, 90–93.

Gorrochategui, Joaquín, 1985. Lengua aquitana y lengua gala en la Aquitania etnográfica. In Melena, José L. (ed.), *Symbolae Ludovico Mitxelena Septuagenario Oblatae*, Vitoria: Facultad de Filología y de Geografía e Historia, 613–28.

Gorrochategui, Joaquín, 2000. Ptolemy's Aquitania and the Ebro valley. In Parsons & Sims-Williams (ed.), *Ptolemy*, 143–57.

Grabowski, Kathryn, & Dumville, David, 1984. *Chronicles and Annals of Mediaeval Ireland and Wales*, Woodbridge: Boydell.

Greene, David, 1972. A detail of syncope. *Ériu* 23, 232–34.

Greene, David, 1973. The growth of palatalization in Irish. *TPS* 127–36.

Greene, David, 1976. The diphthongs of Old Irish. *Ériu* 27, 26–45.

Gresham, Colin A., 1968. *Medieval Stone Carving in North Wales*, Cardiff: University of Wales Press.

Gresham, Colin A., 1985. Bedd Porius. *BBCS* 32, 386–92.

Grosjean, Paul, 1960. Espoic Branduibh aui Trenloco anchoritae. *Celtica* 5, 45–51.

Gruffydd, R. Geraint, 1989–90. From Gododdin to Gwynedd: reflections on the story of Cunedda. *SC* 24/25, 1–14.

Gruffydd, R. Geraint, 1996. Why Cors Fochno? *THSC* 2, 5–19.

Gruffydd, R. Geraint, 1999. A Welsh 'Dark Age' court poem. In Mac Cana FS, 39–48.

Gruffydd, R. Geraint, & Owen, Huw Parri, 1956–58. The earliest mention of St. David? *BBCS* 17, 185–93.

Gruffydd, R. Geraint, & Owen, Huw Parri, 1960–62. The earliest mention of St. David? an addendum. *BBCS* 19, 231–32.

Gruffydd, W. J., 1928. *Math vab Mathonwy*, Cardiff: University of Wales Press.

Gwynn, Edward (ed.), 1924–35. *The Metrical Dindshenchas*, iv and v, Dublin: Royal Irish Academy.

Hamp, Eric P., 1954–56. Proto-British *-eg-*. *BBCS* 16, 277–79.

Hamp, Eric P., 1969. Early Welsh names, suffixes, and phonology. *Onoma* 14, 7–13.

Hamp, Eric P., 1974. The element *-tamo-*. *ÉC* 14, 187–92.

Hamp, Eric P., 1974–76. On the rounded character of British ǭ. *BBCS* 26, 30–31.

Hamp, Eric P., 1974–76. Vagniacis. *BBCS* 26, 139–40.

Hamp, Eric P., 1975. Social gradience in British spoken Latin. *Britannia* 6, 150–62.

Hamp, Eric P., 1976. On some Gaulish names in -*ant*- and Celtic verbal nouns. *Ériu* 27, 1–20.

Hamp, Eric P., 1976. On the Celtic names of Ig. *Acta Neophilologica* 9, 3–8.

Hamp, Eric P., 1976–78. La Graufesenque *Circos*. *BBCS* 27, 215–16.

Hamp, Eric P., 1978. Further remarks on the Celtic names of Ig. *Acta Neophilologica* 11, 57–63.

Hamp, Eric P., 1978–80. Notulae etymologicae Cymricae. *BBCS* 28, 213–17.

Hamp, Eric P., 1981. Old Irish *in·fét*, Welsh *dywedwyt*. *Ériu* 32, 158–59.

Hamp, Eric P., 1983–84. Miscellanea Celtica. *SC* 18/19, 128–34.

Hamp, Eric P., 1986. Notulae praeromanicae. *ZCP* 41, 251–55.

Hamp, Eric P., 1989. Breton *bern* 'tas'. *ÉC* 26, 64.

Hamp, Eric P., 1989. The Laud Herbal Glossary and English–Celtic contacts. *CMCS* 18, 113–16.

Hamp, Eric P., 1992. Goidelic *alt* and *allt*. *Ériu* 43, 207–9.

Hamp, Eric P., 1992. *Goídil, Féni, Gŵynedd*. *PHCC* 12, 43–50.

Hamp, Eric P., 1996. Voteporigis Protictoris. *SC* 30, 293.

Handley, Mark A., 2001. The origins of Christian commemoration in late antique Britain. *EME* 10, 177–99.

Handley, Mark A., 2001. Isidore of Seville and 'Hisperic Latin' in early medieval Wales: the epigraphic culture of Llanllyr and Llanddewi-brefi. In Higgitt et al. (ed.), *Roman, Runes and Ogham*, 26–36.

Harvey, Anthony, 1984. Aspects of lenition and spirantization. *CMCS* 8, 87–100.

Harvey, Anthony, 1987. The ogam inscriptions and their geminate consonant symbols. *Ériu* 38, 45–71.

Harvey, Anthony, 1989. Some significant points of early Insular Celtic orthography. In Ó Corráin, Donnchadh et al. (ed.), *Sages, Saints and Storytellers: Celtic Studies in Honour of Professor James Carney*, Maynooth: An Sagart, 56–66.

Harvey, Anthony, 1992. Review of McManus 1991. *Éigse* 26, 188–90.

Harvey, Anthony, 1999. Some observations on Celtic-Latin name formation. In Mac Cana FS, 53–62.

Harvey, Anthony, 2001. Problems in dating the origin of the ogham script. In Higgitt et al. (ed.), *Roman, Runes and Ogham*, 37–50.

Haslam, Richard, 1979. *Powys*, The Buildings of Wales, Harmondsworth and Cardiff: Penguin Books and University of Wales Press.

Hassall, M. W. C., & Tomlin, R. S. O., 1977. Roman Britain in 1976: inscriptions. *Britannia* 8, 426–49.

Hassall, M. W. C., & Tomlin, R. S. O., 1981. Roman Britain in 1980: inscriptions. *Britannia* 12, 369–96.

Hassall, M. W. C., & Tomlin, R. S. O., 1982. Roman Britain in 1981: inscriptions. *Britannia* 13, 396–422

Hassall, M. W. C., & Tomlin, R. S. O., 1986. Roman Britain in 1985: inscriptions. *Britannia* 17, 428–54.

Hassall, M. W. C., & Tomlin, R. S. O., 1987. Roman Britain in 1986: inscriptions. *Britannia* 18, 360–77.

Hassall, M. W. C., & Tomlin, R. S. O., 1988. Roman Britain in 1987: inscriptions. *Britannia* 19, 485–508.

Hassall, M. W. C., & Tomlin, R. S. O., 1989. Roman Britain in 1988: inscriptions. *Britannia* 20, 327–45.

Hassall, M. W. C., & Tomlin, R. S. O., 1993. Roman Britain in 1992: inscriptions. *Britannia* 24, 310–22.

Hassall, M. W. C., & Tomlin, R. S. O., 1995. Roman Britain in 1994: inscriptions. *Britannia* 26, 371–90.

Hassall, M. W. C., & Tomlin, R. S. O., 1996. Roman Britain in 1995: inscriptions. *Britannia* 27, 439–57.

Haverfield, F., 1923. *The Romanization of Roman Britain*, 4th edn, Oxford: Clarendon Press.

Haycock, Marged, 1982. *Llyfr Taliesin: Astudiaethau ar Rai Agweddau*, Ph.D., University of Wales, Aberystwyth.

Haycock, Marged, 1985. Dylan ail Ton. *YB* 13, 26–38.

Haycock, Marged (ed.), 1994. *Blodeugerdd Barddas o Ganu Crefyddol Cynnar*, [Swansea:] Cyhoeddiadau Barddas.

Hemon, Roparz, 1976. Diminutive suffixes in Breton. *Celtica* 11, 85–93.

Hemp, W. J., 1958. The cross of Gwgan at Llanrhaiadr ym Mochnant. *AC* 107, 125.

Hemp, W. J., & Gresham, C. A., 1961. A new Early Christian inscribed stone from Trawsfynydd, Merioneth. *AC* 110, 154–55.

Hencken, H. O'Neill, 1935. Inscribed stones at St. Kew and Lanteglos by Fowey, Cornwall. *AC* 90, 156–59.

Henry, P. L., 1966. *Early English and Celtic Lyric*, London: Allen & Unwin.

Hessen H., 1913. Zu den Umfärbungen der Vokale im Altirischen. *ZCP* 9, 1–86.

Higgitt, John, Forsyth, Katherine, & Parsons, David N. (ed.), 2001. *Roman, Runes and Ogham: Medieval Inscriptions in the Insular World and on the Continent*, Donington: Shaun Tyas.

Hinton, David A., 1992. The inscribed stones in Lady St. Mary Church, Wareham. *PDNHAS* 114, 260.

Hogan, Edmund, 1910. *Onomasticon Goedelicum*, Dublin: Hodges & Figgis.

Holder, Nick, & Wardle, Peter, 1999. A disputed early-medieval inscribed stone from Barry, Vale of Glamorgan. *Med. Arch.* 43, 216–22.

Hoskins, W. G., 1970. *The Westward Expansion of Wessex*, Leicester: Leicester University Press.

Howlett, David, 1998. *Cambro-Latin Compositions: Their Competence and Craftsmanship*, Dublin: Four Courts.

Hübner, Aemilius (ed.), 1876. *Inscriptiones Britanniae Christianae*, Berlin: Reimer and London: Williams & Norgate.

Hubschmied, J. U., 1933. *Bāgāko-*, **Bāgon(o)*- 'forêt de hêtres': étude de toponymie suisse. *RC* 50, 254–71.

Hughes, A. J., 1991. The Old Cornish personal name *Brenci* and Middle Welsh *Brengi/Bryngi*. *CMCS* 22, 95–99.

Hughes, A. J., 1993. Old Welsh *Cunbran/Conbran* < *Kunobranos 'wolf-raven', in the light of Old Irish *Conbran(n)*. *Ériu* 44, 95–98.

Hughes, H. Harold, 1924. Early Christian decorative art in Anglesey. *AC*, 7th ser. 4, 39–58.

Hughes, Marian Beech, & Williams, J. E. Caerwyn, 1988. *Llyfryddiaeth yr Iaith Gymraeg*, Cardiff: University of Wales Press.

Hutson, Arthur E., 1940. *British Personal Names in the Historia Regum Britanniae*, Berkeley: University of California Press.

Isaac, Graham R., 1991. *Cunedag*. *BBCS* 38, 100–1.

Isaac, Graham R., 1996. *The Verb in the Book of Aneirin*, Tübingen: Niemeyer.

Isaac, Graham R., 2000. Colli sillafau mewn Brythoneg. *SC* 34, 105–18.

Isaac, Graham R., 2000. Leubrit, Loubrit. *SC* 34, 271–72.

Isaac, Graham R., 2001. Myrddin, proffwyd diwedd y byd: ystyriaethau newydd ar ddatblygiad ei chwedl. *LlC* 24, 13–23.

Isaac, Graham R., 2001. Review of SWWF. *CMCS* 41, 73–76.

Jackson, Kenneth H., 1946. Review of CIIC i. *Speculum* 21, 521–23.

Jackson, Kenneth H., 1947. On some Romano-British place-names. *JRS* 37, 54–58.

Jackson, Kenneth H., 1949. Review of CIIC ii. *Speculum* 24, 598–601.

Jackson, Kenneth H., 1950. Notes on the ogam inscriptions of southern Britain. In Fox, Cyril, & Dickins, Bruce (ed.), *The Early Cultures of North-West Europe (H. M. Chadwick Memorial Studies)*, Cambridge: Cambridge University Press, 199–213.

Jackson, Kenneth H., 1957. The names in the Yarrow Stone inscription. In RCAMS, *Selkirkshire*, 113.

Jackson, Kenneth H., 1958. The sources for the Life of St Kentigern. In Chadwick, Nora K. (ed.), *Studies in the Early British Church*, Cambridge: Cambridge University Press, 273–357.

Jackson, Kenneth H., 1960. The St Ninian's Isle inscription: a re-appraisal. *Antiquity* 34, 38–42.

Jackson, Kenneth H., 1960–62. The Idnert inscription: date, and significance of Id-. *BBCS* 19, 232–34.

Jackson, Kenneth H., 1963. Review of TYP. *WHR* 1, Special Number, 82–87.

Jackson, Kenneth H., 1964. On the Northern British section in Nennius. In Chadwick, Nora K. (ed.), *Celt and Saxon: Studies in the Early British Border*, Cambridge: Cambridge University Press, 20–62.

Jackson, Kenneth H., 1967. Early Christian inscribed stone, Manor Water (Site). In RCAHMS, *Peeblesshire: An Inventory of the Ancient Monuments*, i, Edinburgh: HMSO, 176.
Jackson, Kenneth H., 1969. *The Gododdin*, Edinburgh: Edinburgh University Press.
Jackson, Kenneth H., 1971. Ogam stone, Cnoc na Carraigh, Gigha. In RCAHMS, *Argyll: An Inventory of the Ancient Monuments*, i, *Kintyre*, Edinburgh: HMSO, 96–97.
Jackson, Kenneth H., 1973. The inscriptions. In Small, Alan, et al., *St. Ninian's Isle and its Treasure*, i, *Text*, Oxford: Oxford University Press, 167–73.
Jackson, Kenneth H., 1973–74. Some questions in dispute about early Welsh literature and language. *SC* 8/9, 1–32.
Jackson, Kenneth H., 1975–76. The date of the Old Welsh accent shift. *SC* 10/11, 40–53.
Jackson, Kenneth H., 1980. The Pictish language. In Wainwright, F. T. (ed.), *The Problem of the Picts*, 2nd edn, Perth: Melven Press, 129–66 and 173–76.
Jackson, Kenneth H., 1982. Brigomaglos and St. Briog. *Archaeologia Aeliana*, 5th ser. 10, 61–65.
Jackson, Kenneth H., 1982. Rhai sylwadau ar 'Kulhwch ac Olwen'. *YB* 12, 12–23.
Jackson, Kenneth H., 1982. *Varia*: II. Gildas and the names of the British princes. *CMCS* 3, 30–40.
Jackson, Kenneth H., 1982–83. Prosthetic vowels before *n-* in Early Middle Welsh. *BBCS* 30, 45–49.
Jackson, Kenneth H., 1983. The inscriptions on the silver spoons. In Johns, Catherine, & Potter, Timothy, *The Thetford Treasure*, London: British Museum, 46–48.
Jenkins, Dafydd, 1990. Gwalch: Welsh. *CMCS* 19, 55–67.
Jenkins, Dafydd, & Owen, Morfydd E., 1983. The Welsh marginalia in the Lichfield Gospels, part I. *CMCS* 5, 37–66.
Jenkins, Dafydd, & Owen, Morfydd E., 1984. The Welsh marginalia in the Lichfield Gospels, part II: The 'Surexit' memorandum. *CMCS* 7, 91–120.
Jones, Bedwyr Lewis, 1984. Pwll Ceris or the Swillies: a hydronymic note. *TAAS*, 102–4.
Jones, Evan John (ed.), 1945. *Buchedd Sant Martin*, Cardiff: University of Wales Press.
Jones, Glyn E., 1972–74. Brân Galed: Brân fab Ymellyrn. *BBCS* 25, 105–12.
Jones, Gwilym Peredur, 1926–27. A list of epithets from Welsh pedigrees. *BBCS* 3, 31–48.
Jones, Gwilym Peredur, 1927. The Scandinavian element in Welsh. *ZCP* 16, 162–66.
Jones, Gwilym T., & Roberts, Tomos, 1996. *Enwau Lleoedd Môn: The Place-Names of Anglesey*, Bangor: Isle of Anglesey County Council and Research Centre Wales, University of Wales, Bangor.
Jones, M. H., 1906–7. Principal John Rhys' lecture on inscribed stones. *TCASFC* 2, 173–75 and 177.
Jones, Thomas (ed.), 1941. *Brut y Tywysogyon: Peniarth MS. 20*, Cardiff: University of Wales Press.
Jones, Thomas, 1948–50. Anorlos. *BBCS* 13, 74–75.
Jones, Thomas (trans.), 1952. *Brut y Tywysogyon: Peniarth MS. 20 Version*, Cardiff: University of Wales Press.
Jones, Thomas, 1967. The Black Book of Carmarthen 'Stanzas of the Graves'. *PBA* 53, 97–137.
Jones, Thomas (ed.), 1973. *Brut y Tywysogyon: Red Book of Hergest Version*, 2nd edn, Cardiff: University of Wales Press.
Jones Pierce, T., 1929–31. A Lleyn lay subsidy account. *BBCS* 5, 54–71.
Jope, E. M., 2000. *Early Celtic Art in the British Isles: Text*, Oxford: Clarendon Press.
Joseph, Lionel, 1990. Old Irish cú: a naïve reinterpretation. In Hamp FS, 110–30.
Kay, R. E., 1958. An Early Christian monument from Walton West (Pembs.). *AC* 107, 122–23.
Kermode, P. M. C., 1994. *Manx Crosses*, Balgavies: Pinkfoot Press.
Kneen, J. J., 1925–27. *The Place-Names of the Isle of Man*, 2 vols, Douglas: Manx Society.
Kneen, J. J., 1937. *The Personal Names of the Isle of Man*, Oxford: Oxford University Press.
Knight, Jeremy K., 1978. Early Christian origins and society in south Wales. *Merthyr Historian* 2, 101–10.
Knight, Jeremy K., 1992. The Early Christian Latin inscriptions of Britain and Gaul: chronology and context. In Edwards & Lane (ed.), *Early Church in Wales and the West*, 45–50.
Knight, Jeremy K., 1995. Penmachno revisited: the consular inscription and its context. *CMCS* 29, 1–10.

Knight, Jeremy K., 1999. *The End of Antiquity: Archaeology, Society and Religion* AD *235–700*, Stroud: Tempus.
Koch, John T., 1982–83. The loss of final syllables and loss of declension in Brittonic. *BBCS* 30, 202–33.
Koch, John T., 1985–86. When was Welsh literature first written down? *SC* 20/21, 43–66.
Koch, John T., 1987. A Welsh window on the Iron Age: Manawydan, Mandubracios. *CMCS* 14, 17–52.
Koch, John T., 1990. Brân, Brennos: an instance of early Gallo-Brittonic history and mythology. *CMCS* 20, 1–20.
Koch, John T., 1995. The Conversion and the transition from Primitive to Old Irish *c.* 367–*c.* 637. *Emania* 13, 39–50.
Koch, John T. (ed.), 1997. *The Gododdin of Aneirin*, Cardiff: University of Wales Press.
Lambert, Pierre-Yves, 1979. Gaulois IEVRV: irlandais (*ro*)-*ír* 'dicauit'. *ZCP* 37, 207–13.
Lambert, Pierre-Yves, 1983. 'Fraudatiuus': une dénomination ancienne du 'datiuus incommodi' dans le monde celtique. *Revue de philologie, de littérature et d'histoire anciennes* 57, 39–45.
Lambert, Pierre-Yves, 1986. The new Dictionary of Old Breton. *CMCS* 12, 99–113.
Lambert, Pierre-Yves, 1989. Notes de vieux-breton. *BBCS* 36, 111–16.
Lambert, Pierre-Yves, 1990. Welsh *Caswallawn*: the fate of British **au*. In Bammesberger & Wollmann (ed.), *Britain 400–600*, 203–15.
Lambert, Pierre-Yves, 1994. *La Langue gauloise*, Paris: Errance.
Lambert, Pierre-Yves, 1995. Préverbes gaulois suffixes en -*io*-: *Ambio*-, *Ario*-, *Cantio*-. *ÉC* 31, 115–21.
Lambert, Pierre-Yves, 1995. Three Brittonic lexical notes. In Evans FS, 96–105.
Lambert, Pierre-Yves, 2000. Remarks on Gaulish place-names in Ptolemy. In Parsons & Sims-Williams (ed.), *Ptolemy*, 159–68.
Lapidge, Michael (ed.), 1991. *Anglo-Saxon Litanies of the Saints*, London: Henry Bradshaw Society.
Le Blant, Edmond, 1856–65. *Inscriptions chrétiennes de la Gaule antérieures au viiie siècle*, 2 vols, Paris: Imprimerie Impériale.
Le Blant, Edmond, 1892. *Nouveau recueil des inscriptions chrétiennes de la Gaule antérieures au viiie siècle*, Paris: Imprimerie Nationale.
Lejeune, Michel, 1980. Textes gallo-grecs. *ÉC* 17, 55–100.
Lejeune, Michel, 1982. Les noms en -*rīgos*. *ÉC* 19, 111–19.
Lejeune, Michel, 1995. Compléments gallo-grecs. *ÉC* 31, 99–113.
Lejeune, Michel, et al., 1985. Textes gaulois et gallo-romains en cursive latine, 3: Le plomb du Larzac. *ÉC* 22, 95–177.
Lewis, Henry, 1921–23. Carfan, gorcharfaneu. *BBCS* 1, 12–14.
Lewis, Henry, 1936. The honorific prefixes *To*- and *Mo*-. *ZCP* 20, 138–43.
Lewis, Henry, 1941–44. Gwair, mynwair, Caer Weir. *BBCS* 11, 82–83.
Lewis, Henry, 1943. *Yr Elfen Ladin yn yr Iaith Gymraeg*, Cardiff: University of Wales Press.
Lewis, Meinir, 1961. *Disgrifiad o Orgraff Hen Gymraeg gan ei Chymharu ag Orgraff Hen Wyddeleg*, MA, University of Wales, Aberystwyth.
L'Hour, Michel, 1987. Un site sous-marin sur la côte de l'Armorique: l'épave antique de Ploumanac'h. *RAO* 4, 113–31.
Lhuyd, Edward, ed. Morris, Rupert H., 1909–11. *Parochialia*, 3 parts, Supplements to *AC*.
Lindeman, Fredrik Otto, 1980–82. On some compound verbs in the Brittonic languages. *BBCS* 29, 504–12.
Lindeman, Fredrik Otto, 1984. On the development of some Indo-European perfect forms in Celtic. *BBCS* 31, 94–100.
Lindeman, Fredrik Otto, 1984. Welsh *dywedaf*. *BBCS* 31, 93–94.
Lindeman, Fredrik Otto, 1993. Review of McCone 1991. *CMCS* 26, 75–79.
Lindeman, Fredrik Otto, 2001. Review of McCone 1997. *ZCP* 52, 222–28.
Lindsay, W. M., 1912. *Early Welsh Script*, Oxford: James Parker.
Lloyd, J. E., 1888. The personal name-system in Old Welsh. *Cymmrodor* 9, 39–55.
Lloyd, J. E., 1939. *A History of Wales*, 2 vols, 3rd edn, London: Longmans, Green.
Lloyd-Jones, J., 1923–25. Olion sein-dawdd cyntefig yn Gymraeg. *BBCS* 2, 289–97.
Lloyd-Jones, J., 1926. Enwau Cymraeg. *Y Geninen* 44, 1–14.
Lloyd-Jones, J., 1928. *Enwau Lleoedd Sir Gaernarfon*, Cardiff: University of Wales Press.

Lloyd-Jones, J., 1931–63. *Geirfa Barddoniaeth Gynnar Gymraeg*, 2 vols, Cardiff: University of Wales Press.

Lloyd-Jones, J., 1941–44. Benŵyn. *BBCS* 11, 119.

Lloyd-Jones, J., 1947. The compounds of *gal*. In Pender, Séamus (ed.), *Essays and Studies Presented to Tadhg Ua Donnchadha (Torna)*, Cork: Cork University Press, 83–89.

Lloyd-Jones, J., 1950–52. Nefenhyr. *BBCS* 14, 35–37.

Lloyd-Jones, J., 1952–54. Rôn. *BBCS* 15, 200–2.

Lloyd-Jones, J., 1956. The compounds of **gar*. *Celtica* 3, 198–210.

Loth, J., 1890. Les anciennes Litanies des saints de Bretagne. *RC* 11, 135–51.

Loth, J., 1910. *Les Noms des saints bretons*, Paris: Champion.

Loth, J., 1910. Remarques et additions à l'*Introduction to Early Welsh* de John Strachan. *RC* 31, 129–81, 312–32, and 472–571.

Loth, J., 1911. Les Noms de Tristan et Iseut. *RC* 32, 407–21.

Loth, J., 1915–16. Remarques et additions à la grammaire galloise historique et comparée de John Morris Jones. *RC* 36, 108–85.

Loth, J., 1917–19. Remarques et additions à la grammaire galloise historique et comparée de John Morris Jones. *RC* 37, 26–64.

Loth, J., 1923. Irl. *mag*; gall. *maon*; *maith*. *RC* 40, 342–43.

Loth, J., 1923. La vie la plus ancienne de Saint Samson. *RC* 40, 1–50.

Loth, J., 1926. Gallois moyen *hydrum*; breton *trum*; vieux-breton *tromden*. *RC* 43, 409–10.

Luján, Eugenio R., 2000. Ptolemy's *Callaecia* and the language(s) of the *Callaeci*. In Parsons & Sims-Williams (ed.), *Ptolemy*, 55–72.

Mac Cana, Proinsias, 1955–56. Aspects of the theme of King and Goddess in Irish literature (part 1). *ÉC* 7, 76–114.

Mac Cana, Proinsias, 1960–62. *Vortipori. *BBCS* 19, 116–17.

Mac Cana, Proinsias, 2001. *Croesaniaid* and *Crosáin*: literary outsiders. In Jenkins, Geraint H. (ed.), *Cymru a'r Cymry 2000: Wales and the Welsh 2000*, Aberystwyth: Centre for Advanced Welsh and Celtic Studies, 19–39.

Mac White, Eóin, 1960–61. Contributions to a study of ogam memorial stones. *ZCP* 28, 294–307.

Macalister, R. A. S., 1922. Notes of an epigraphic pilgrimage in south-west Wales. *TCASFC* 15, part 40, 29–33.

Macalister, R. A. S., 1922. Notes on some of the early Welsh inscriptions. *AC* 77, 198–219.

Macalister, R. A. S., 1929. The ancient inscriptions of the south of England. *AC* 84, 179–96.

Macdonald, George, 1935–36. Two inscribed stones of the Early Christian period from the Border district. *PSAS* 70, 33–39.

MacNeill, Eoin [John], 1909. Notes on the distribution, history, grammar, and import of the Irish ogham inscriptions. *PRIA* 27 Section C, 329–70.

MacNeill, Eoin [John], 1909. Ogham inscription at Cloonmorris, County Leitrim. *JRSAI* 39, 132–36.

MacNeill, Eoin, 1930–32. Fannuci, Fanoni, Svaqqvuci [sic]. *Ériu* 11, 133–34.

MacNeill, Eoin, 1931. Archaisms in the ogham inscriptions. *PRIA* 39 Section C, 33–53.

Mahon, William, 1988. Glasraige, Tóecraige, and Araid: evidence from ogam. *PHCC* 8, 11–30.

Maier, Bernhard, 1987. Latin *sacer* 'sacred' and Welsh *hagr* 'ugly'. *Celtica* 19, 96–97.

Maier, Bernhard, 1997. *Dictionary of Celtic Religion and Culture*, Woodbridge: Boydell.

Mann, J. C., 1971. Spoken Latin in Britain as evidenced in the inscriptions. *Britannia* 2, 218–24.

Manning, Conleth, & Moore, Fionnbarr, 1997. A second ogham stone at Clara. *Peritia* 11, 370–72.

Martindale, J. R., 1992. *The Prosopography of the Later Roman Empire*, iii, *A.D. 597–641*, Cambridge: Cambridge University Press.

McClure, Edmund, 1907. The Wareham inscriptions. *EHR* 22, 728–30.

McCone, Kim, 1984. *Aided Cheltchair maic Uthechair*: hounds, heroes and hospitallers in early Irish myth and story. *Ériu* 35, 1–30.

McCone, Kim, 1985. Varia II. *Ériu* 36, 169–76.

McCone, Kim, 1991. *The Indo-European Origins of the Old Irish Nasal Presents, Subjunctives and Futures*, Innsbruck: Institut für Sprachwissenschaft.

McCone, Kim, 1997. A note on palatalisation and the present inflection of weak *i*-verbs. In

Ahlqvist, Anders, & Čapková, Věra (ed.), *Dán do Oide: Essays in Memory of Conn R. Ó Cléirigh*, Dublin: Linguistics Institute of Ireland.

McCone, Kim, 1998. 'King' and 'queen' in Celtic and Indo-European. *Ériu* 49, 1–12.

McKee, Helen, 2000. Scribes and glosses from Dark Age Wales: the Cambridge Juvencus manuscript. *CMCS* 39, 1–22.

McKee, Helen, 2000. *The Cambridge Juvencus Manuscript Glossed in Latin, Old Welsh, and Old Irish: Text and Commentary*, Aberystwyth: CMCS Publications.

McKee, Helen, & McKee, James, 2000. Review of Howlett 1998. *CMCS* 39, 77–80.

McManus, Damian, 1983. A chronology of the Latin loan-words in early Irish. *Ériu* 34, 21–71.

McManus, Damian, 1984. On final syllables in the Latin loan-words in early Irish. *Ériu* 35, 137–62.

McManus, Damian, 1986. Ogam: archaizing, orthography and the authenticity of the manuscript key to the alphabet. *Ériu* 37, 1–31.

McManus, Damian, 1991. *A Guide to Ogam*, Maynooth: An Sagart.

Megaw, B. R. S., 1946–50. The monastery of St. Maughold. *Proceedings of the Isle of Man Natural History and Antiquarian Society* 5 no. 2, 169–80.

Megaw, B. R. S., 1999. The original site of Rushen Abbey and its significance. In Davey, P. J. (ed.), *Recent Archaeological Research on the Isle of Man*, British Archaeological Reports British Series 278, Oxford: BAR, 261–66.

Meid, Wolfgang (ed.), 1970. *Die Romanze von Froech und Findabair*, Innsbruck: Institut für Sprachwissenschaft.

Meyer, Kuno (ed.), 1895. *The Voyage of Bran*, i, London: Nutt.

Meyer, Kuno, 1906. *Contributions to Irish Lexicography*, i/1, *A–C*, Halle a.S.: Niemeyer.

Meyer, Kuno, 1917. *Miscellanea Hibernica*, Urbana: University of Illinois Press.

Moon, Rosamund, 1978. Viking runic inscriptions in Wales. *AC* 127, 124–26.

Morgan, T. J., & Morgan, Prys, 1985. *Welsh Surnames*, Cardiff: University of Wales Press.

Morris, Christopher D., et al., 1999. Recent work at Tintagel. *Med. Arch.* 43, 206–15.

Morris-Jones, John, 1918. Taliesin. *Cymmrodor* 28, 1–290.

Morris-Jones, John, 1924–25. Sir John Rhys. *PBA* 11, 187–212.

Mossé, F., 1933. Sur le nom d'homme *Ketill* en Scandinave. *RC* 50, 248–53.

Motta, Filippo, 1982. Ogamica. *Studi classici e orientali* 32, 299–304.

Motta, Filippo, 1993. Gall. δεκαντεν, pitt. Δεκανται, ant. irl. -*De(i)chet*. In Brogyanyi, Bela, & Lipp, Reiner (ed.), *Comparative-Historical Linguistics, Indo-European and Finno-Ugric: Papers in Honor of Oswald Szemerényi*, iii, Amsterdam: Benjamins, 293–303.

Murphy, J. P. (ed.), 1977. *Rufus Festus Avienus, Ora Maritima*, Chicago: Ares.

Nash-Williams, V. E., 1935–37. An inventory of the Early Christian stone monuments of Wales, with a bibliography of the principal notices. *BBCS* 8, 62–84 and 161–88.

Nash-Williams, V. E., 1937. Five new Pembrokeshire monuments. *AC* 92, 325–30.

Nash-Williams, V. E., 1950–52. Medieval settlement at Llantwit Major, Glamorganshire. *BBCS* 14, 313–33.

Nesselhauf, Herbert, 1939. Neue Inschriften aus dem römischen Germanien und den angrenzenden Gebieten. *27. Bericht der römisch-germanischen Kommission 1937*, Berlin, 51–134.

Ó Corráin, Donnchadh, & Maguire, Fidelma, 1981. *Gaelic Personal Names*, Dublin: Academy Press.

Ó Cuív, Brian, 1986. Aspects of Irish personal names. *Celtica* 18, 151–84.

Ó Maolalaigh, Roibeard, 1998. Place-names as a resource for the historical linguist. In Taylor, Simon (ed.), *The Uses of Place-Names*, Edinburgh: Scottish Cultural Press, 15–53.

Ó Murchadha, Diarmuid, 1997. *The Annals of Tigernach: Index of Names*, London: Irish Texts Society.

Ó Riain, Pádraig, 1994. The saints of Cardiganshire. In Davies & Kirby (ed.), *Cardiganshire County History*, i, 378–96.

Ó Riain, Pádraig, 1999. Finnio and Winniau: a return to the subject. In Mac Cana FS, 187–202.

O'Brien, M. A., 1973. Old Irish personal names. *Celtica* 10, 211–36.

O'Hanlon, John, [1875–1905]. *Lives of the Irish Saints*, 10 vols, Dublin: Duffy.

O'Rahilly, Cecile, 1924. *Ireland and Wales: Their Historical and Literary Relations*, London: Longmans, Green.

O'Rahilly, Cecile (ed.), 1976. *Táin Bó Cúailnge: Recension I*, Dublin: Dublin Institute for Advanced Studies.

O'Rahilly, T. F., 1940–42. *Iarann, lárag,* etc. *Ériu* 13, 119–27.

O'Rahilly, T. F., 1943–46. On the origin of the names *Érainn* and *Ériu. Ériu* 14, 7–28.

O'Rahilly, T. F., 1950. Ir. *fial, gaol.* Welsh *gŵyl, annŵyl. Celtica* 1, 365–69.

O'Sullivan, Anne (ed.), 1983. *The Book of Leinster,* vi, Dublin: Dublin Institute for Advanced Studies.

Okasha, Elisabeth, 1970. A new inscription from Ramsey Island. *AC* 119, 68–70.

Okasha, Elisabeth, 1985. The non-ogam inscriptions of Pictland. *CMCS* 9, 43–69.

Okasha, Elisabeth, 1993. *Corpus of Early Christian Inscribed Stones of South-West Britain,* London: Leicester University Press.

Oliver, J. R. (ed.), 1861. *Monumenta de Insula Manniae,* ii, Douglas: Manx Society.

Olson, B. Lynette, & Padel, O. J., 1986. A tenth-century list of Cornish parochial saints. *CMCS* 12, 33–71.

Orel, Vladimir E., 1987. Thracian and Celtic. *BBCS* 34, 1–9.

Orme, Nicholas, 1992. Saint Conet: a Cornish saint. *Devon & Cornwall Notes & Queries* 37 part 2, 55–58.

Orme, Nicholas, 1996. *English Church Dedications with a Survey of Cornwall and Devon,* Exeter: Exeter University Press.

Orme, Nicholas, 2000. *The Saints of Cornwall,* Oxford: Oxford University Press.

Owen, Edward, 1896. Lewis Morris's notes on some inscribed stones in Wales. *AC* 5th ser. 13, 129–44.

Padel, O. J., 1981. The Cornish background of the Tristan stories. *CMCS* 1, 53–81.

Padel, O. J., 1988. *A Popular Dictionary of Cornish Place-Names,* Penzance: Alison Hodge.

Parry, Tom, 1939. *Mynegai i Weithiau Ifor Williams,* Cardiff: University of Wales Press.

Parry-Williams, T. H., 1923. *The English Element in Welsh,* London: Honourable Society of Cymmrodorion.

Parsons, David N., 1997. British **Caratīcos,* Old English *Cerdic. CMCS* 33, 1–8.

Parsons, David N., & Sims-Williams, Patrick (ed.), 2000. *Ptolemy: Towards a Linguistic Atlas of the Earliest Celtic Place-Names of Europe,* Aberystwyth: CMCS Publications.

Pierce, Gwynedd O., 1958–60. Enwau-Lleoedd anghyfiaith yng Nghymru. *BBCS* 18, 252–65.

Pierce, Gwynedd O., 1968. *The Place-Names of Dinas Powys Hundred,* Cardiff: University of Wales Press.

Pierce, Gwynedd O., 1985. Notes on place names: Llanynewyr (Llanyrnewydd). *Morgannwg* 29, 74–79.

Piette, J. R. F., 1970. Review of HPB. *SC* 5, 154–60.

Piette, J. R. F., 1973. *French Loanwords in Middle Breton,* Cardiff: University of Wales Press.

Plummer, Charles (ed.), 1910. *Vitae Sanctorum Hiberniae,* 2 vols, Oxford: Clarendon Press.

Pokorny, Julius, 1918. Zur Chronologie der Umfärbung der Vokale im Altirischen. *ZCP* 12, 415–26.

Pokorny, Julius, 1923. Review of Kaspers, Wilhelm, *Etymologische Untersuchungen über die mit -ācum, -ānum, -ascum und -uscum gebildeten nordfranzösischen Ortsnamen. ZCP* 14, 291–92.

Pope, M. K., 1952. *From Latin to Modern French,* 2nd edn, Manchester: Manchester University Press.

Prati, A., 1930. Ancora del nome *Orvieto. Archivio glottologico italiano* 24, 56–59.

Pryce, Huw, 1986. The prologues to the Welsh lawbooks. *BBCS* 33, 151–87.

Pryce, Huw, 2001. British or Welsh? National identity in twelfth-century Wales. *EHR* 116, 775–801.

Quesnel, Solange (ed.), 1996. *Venance Fortunat, Œuvres,* iv, *Vie de saint Martin,* Paris: Les Belles Lettres.

Radford, C. A. Ralegh, 1937. The early inscriptions. In RCAHMW, *Anglesey,* civ–cix.

Radford, C. A. Ralegh, 1949. The inscription of the Carew Cross. *AC* 100, 253–55.

Radford, C. A. Ralegh, 1957. The [Yarrow Stone] inscription. In RCAMS, *Selkirkshire,* 110–13.

Radford, C. A. Ralegh, 1969. An Early Christian inscription at East Ogwell. *PDAS* 27, 79–81.

Radford, C. A. Ralegh, 1975. *The Early Christian Inscriptions of Dumnonia,* Pool, Redruth: Institute of Cornish Studies.

Radford, C. A. Ralegh, 1983. Two datable cross shafts at Llantwit Major. *AC* 132, 107–15.

Radford, C. A. Ralegh, & Hemp, W. J., 1957. The cross-slab at Llanrhaiadr-ym-Mochnant. *AC* 106, 109–16.

Radford, C. A. Ralegh, & Jackson, K. H., 1970. Early Christian inscriptions [of Wareham]. In

RCHM, *An Inventory of Historical Monuments in the County of Dorset*, ii, *South-East*, part 2, London: HMSO, 310–12.

RCAHMW, 1921. Inventory VI, *County of Merioneth*, London: HMSO.

RCAHMW, 1925. Inventory VII, *County of Pembroke*, London: HMSO.

RCAHMW, 1937. *Anglesey*, London: HMSO.

RCAHMW, 1976. *An Inventory of the Ancient Monuments in Glamorgan*, i, part 3, *The Early Christian Period*, Cardiff: HMSO.

RCAMS, 1957. *Inventory of the Ancient and Historical Monuments of Selkirkshire*, Edinburgh: HMSO.

Redknap, Mark, 2000. *Vikings in Wales*, Cardiff: National Museums and Galleries of Wales.

Rees, William, 1932. *South Wales and the Border in the Fourteenth Century* [map], Cardiff: University of Wales Press.

Rhys, John, 1873. On some of our British inscriptions. *AC* 4th ser. 4, 74–77.

Rhys, John, 1873. Our British inscriptions. *AC* 4th ser. 4, 197–200.

Rhys, John, 1874. The Dobunni inscription. *AC* 4th ser. 5, 173.

Rhys, John, 1875. On some of our inscribed stones. *AC* 4th ser. 6, 359–71.

Rhys, John, 1877. On some of our early inscribed stones. *AC* 4th ser. 8, 135–44.

Rhys, John, 1881. The Steynton inscribed stone, Pembrokeshire. *AC* 4th ser. 12, 217–19.

Rhys, John, 1882. The Gesail Gyfarch stone. *AC* 4th ser. 13, 161–65.

Rhys, John, 1890. Traces of a non-Aryan element in the Celtic family. *Scottish Review* 16, 30–47.

Rhys, John, 1892. The inscriptions and language of the Northern Picts. *PSAS*, 26, 263–351.

Rhys, John, 1892. The Irish invasions of Wales and Dumnonia. *AC* 5th ser. 9, 56–73.

Rhys, John, 1893. Notes on some early inscribed stones in south Wales. *AC* 5th ser. 10, 285–91.

Rhys, John, 1895. Epigraphic notes. *AC* 5th ser. 12, 180–90.

Rhys, John, 1895. Goidelic words in Brythonic. *AC* 5th ser. 12, 264–302.

Rhys, John, 1895. Notes on the inscriptions on the tombstone of Voteporis, prince of Demetia. *AC* 5th ser. 12, 307–13.

Rhys, John, 1895. The Goidels in Wales. *AC* 5th ser. 12, 18–39.

Rhys, John, 1896. Epigraphic notes. *AC* 5th ser. 13, 98–128.

Rhys, John, 1897. Notes on inscribed stones in Pembrokeshire. *AC* 5th ser. 14, 324–31.

Rhys, John, 1898. The Llandrudian Stones, Pembrokeshire. *AC* 5th ser. 15, 54–63.

Rhys, John, 1899. Some Glamorgan inscriptions. *AC* 5th ser. 16, 132–68.

Rhys, John, 1902. The ogam-inscribed stones of the Royal Irish Academy, and of Trinity College, Dublin. *JRSAI* 5th ser. 12, 1–41.

Rhys, John, 1903–4. Studies in early Irish history. *PBA*, 21–80.

Rhys, John, 1904. *Celtic Britain*, London: SPCK.

Rhys, John, 1905. *The Origin of the Welsh Englyn and Kindred Metres* = *Cymmrodor* 18, 1–185.

Rhys, John, 1905–6. The Celtic inscriptions of France and Italy. *PBA*, 273–373.

Rhys, John, 1907. Epigraphic notes. *AC* 6th ser. 7, 66–102 and 309–10.

Rhys, John, 1907. The Capel Mair Stone. *AC* 6th ser. 7, 293–309.

Rhys, John, 1908. All around the Wrekin. *Cymmrodor* 21, 1–62.

Rhys, John, 1911–12. The Celtic inscriptions of Gaul: additions and corrections. *PBA*, 261–360.

Rhys, John, 1912. Three ancient inscriptions (from Wales). In Bergin, Osborn, & Marstrander, Carl (ed.), *Miscellany presented to Kuno Meyer*, Halle a. S.: Niemeyer, 227–40.

Rhys, John, 1913–14. The Celtic inscriptions of Cisalpine Gaul. *PBA* 6, 23–112.

Rhys, John, 1913–14. Gleanings in the Italian field of Celtic epigraphy. *PBA* 6, 315–69.

Rhys, John, 1918. Notes on some of the early inscribed stones of Wales, Devon and Cornwall. *AC* 6th ser. 18, 181–94.

Rhys, John, 1919. An inscription at Penmachno. *AC* 6th ser. 19, 201–5.

Rhys, John & Brynmor-Jones, David, 1913. *The Welsh People*, 6th edn, London: Unwin.

Richards, Melville, 1960. The Irish settlements in south-west Wales: a topographical approach. *JRSAI* 90, 133–62.

Richards, Melville, 1965. Early Welsh territorial suffixes. *JRSAI* 95, 205–12.

Richards, Melville, 1965. Gwŷr, gwragedd a gwehelyth. *THSC*, 27–45.

Richards, Melville, 1969. Nynnid. *AC* 118, 144–45.

Richards, Melville, 1971. Places and persons of the early Welsh church. *WHR* 5, 333–49.

Richards, Melville, 1972. *An Atlas of Anglesey*, Llangefni: Cyngor Gwlad Môn.

Richmond, I. A., & Crawford, O. G. S., 1949. The British section of the Ravenna Cosmography. *Archaeologia* 93, 1–50.

Rivet, A. L. F., & Jackson, Kenneth, 1970. The British section of the Antonine Itinerary. *Britannia* 1, 34–82.

Roberts, Brynley F., 1972–74. The treatment of personal names in the early Welsh versions of *Historia Regum Britanniae*. *BBCS* 25, 274–90.

Rodway, Simon, 1998. A datable development in medieval literary Welsh. *CMCS* 36, 71–94.

Rowland, Jenny, 1980–82. An Early Old Welsh orthographic feature. *BBCS* 29, 513–20.

Rowland, Jenny, 1990. *Early Welsh Saga Poetry*, Cambridge: Brewer.

Russell, Paul, 1985. A footnote to spirantization. *CMCS* 10, 53–56.

Russell, Paul, 1988. The suffix *-āko-* in Continental Celtic. *ÉC* 25, 131–73.

Russell, Paul, 1990. *Celtic Word-Formation: The Velar Suffixes*, Dublin: Dublin Institute for Advanced Studies.

Russell, Paul, 1993. Modern Welsh *-og* and productivity in derivational patterns. *JCL* 6, 151–56.

Russell, Paul, 1995. Brittonic words in Irish glossaries. In Evans FS, 166–82.

Russell, Paul, 1997. Review of SBCHP. *JCL* 6, 146–54.

Russell, Paul, 1998. Review of TRC. *CMCS* 35, 73–76.

Russell, Paul, 2001. Patterns of hypocorism in early Irish hagiography. In Carey, John, et al. (ed.), *Studies in Irish Hagiography: Saints and Scholars*, Dublin: Four Courts, 237–49.

Sacaze, Julien, 1880. Inscriptions inédites des Pyrénées. *BSNAF*, 157–62.

Schrijver, Peter, 1991. The development of Primitive Irish *aN* before voiced stop. *Ériu* 42, 13–25.

Schrijver, Peter, 1992. The development of PIE *sk* in British. *BBCS* 39, 1–15.

Schrijver, Peter, 1993. On the development of vowels before tautosyllabic nasals in Primitive Irish. *Ériu* 44, 33–52.

Schrijver, Peter, 1996. OIr. *gor* 'pious, dutiful': meaning and etymology. *Ériu* 47, 193–204.

Schrijver, Peter, 1997. Animal, vegetable and mineral: some Western European substratum words. In Beekes FS, 293–316.

Schrijver, Peter, 1997. On the nature and origin of word-initial *h-* in the Würzburg glosses. *Ériu* 48, 205–27.

Schrijver, Peter, 1997. Review of Evans FS. *CMCS* 34, 107–11.

Schrijver, Peter, 1997. *Studies in the History of Celtic Pronouns and Particles*, Maynooth: Department of Old Irish, National University of Ireland, Maynooth.

Schrijver, Peter, 1998–2000. Geminate spellings in the Old Welsh glosses to Martianus Capella. *ÉC* 34, 147–60.

Schrijver, Peter, 1998. The British word for 'fox' and its Indo-European origin. *JIES* 26, 421–34.

Schrijver, Peter, 1999. On henbane and early European narcotics. *ZCP* 51, 17–45.

Schrijver, Peter, 1999. Spirantization and nasalization in British. *SC* 33, 1–19.

Schrijver, Peter, 1999. The Celtic contribution to the development of the North Sea Germanic vowel system, with special reference to Coastal Dutch. *NOWELE* 35, 3–47.

Schrijver, Peter, 1999. Vowel rounding by Primitive Irish labiovelars. *Ériu* 50, 133–37.

Schrijver, Peter, 2000. Keltisch of niet: twee namen en een verdacht accent. In Hofman, Rijcklof, et al. (ed.), *Kelten in Nederland*, Utrecht: de Keltische Draak, 69–96.

Schulze-Thulin, Britta, 2001. *Studien zu den urindogermanischen o-stufigen Kausativa/Iterativa und Nasalpräsentien im Kymrischen*, Innsbruck: Institut für Sprachen und Literaturen.

Schumacher, Stefan, 1995. Old Irish *tucaid, tocad* and Middle Welsh *tynghaf tynghet* re-examined. *Ériu* 46, 49–57.

Schumacher, Stefan, 2000. *The Historical Morphology of the Welsh Verbal Noun*, Maynooth: Department of Old Irish, National University of Ireland Maynooth.

Searle, William George, 1897. *Onomasticon Anglo-Saxonicum*, Cambridge: Cambridge University Press.

Sims-Williams, Patrick, 1977–78. Riddling treatment of the 'watchman device' in *Branwen* and *Togail Bruidne Da Derga*. *SC* 12/13, 83–117.

Sims-Williams, Patrick, 1980–82. The development of the Indo-European voiced labiovelars in Celtic. *BBCS* 29, 201–29 and 690.

Sims-Williams, Patrick, 1980–82. The significance of the Irish personal names in *Culhwch ac Olwen*. *BBCS* 29, 600–20.

Sims-Williams, Patrick, 1990. Cú Chulainn in Wales: Welsh sources for Irish onomastics. *Celtica* 21, 620–33.

Sims-Williams, Patrick, 1990. Dating the transition to neo-Brittonic: phonology and history, 400–600. In Bammesberger & Wollmann (ed.), *Britain 400–600*, 217–61.

Sims-Williams, Patrick, 1990. *Religion and Literature in Western England, 600–800*, Cambridge: Cambridge University Press.

Sims-Williams, Patrick, 1991. The early Welsh Arthurian poems. In Bromwich et al. (ed.), *Arthur of the Welsh*, 33–71.

Sims-Williams, Patrick, 1991. The emergence of Old Welsh, Cornish and Breton orthography, 600–800: the evidence of Archaic Old Welsh. *BBCS* 38, 20–86.

Sims-Williams, Patrick, 1992. Review of Evans, D. Simon (ed.), *The Welsh Life of St David*. *JEH* 43, 468–70.

Sims-Williams, Patrick, 1992. The additional letters of the ogam alphabet. *CMCS* 23, 29–75.

Sims-Williams, Patrick, 1993. Some problems in deciphering the early Irish ogam alphabet. *TPS* 91, 133–80.

Sims-Williams, Patrick, 1993. The provenance of the Llywarch Hen poems: a case for Llan-gors, Brycheiniog. *CMCS* 26, 27–63.

Sims-Williams, Patrick, 1994. Historical need and literary narrative: a caveat from ninth-century Wales. *WHR* 17, 1–40.

Sims-Williams, Patrick, 1995. *Britain and Early Christian Europe*, Aldershot: Variorum.

Sims-Williams, Patrick, 1995. Indo-European $*g^{wh}$ in Celtic, 1894–1994. In Evans FS, 196–218.

Sims-Williams, Patrick, 1996. The death of Urien. *CMCS* 32, 25–56.

Sims-Williams, Patrick, 1998. The Celtic languages. In Ramat, Anna Giacalone, & Ramat, Paolo (ed.), *The Indo-European Languages*, London: Routledge, 345–79.

Sims-Williams, Patrick, 1998. The uses of writing in early medieval Wales. In Pryce, Huw (ed.), *Literacy in Medieval Celtic Societies*, Cambridge: Cambridge University Press, 15–38.

Sims-Williams, Patrick, 1999. A Turkish-Celtic problem in Chrétien de Troyes: the name *Cligés*. In Mac Cana FS, 215–30.

Sims-Williams, Patrick, 1999. Old Irish *feda* (gen. *fedot*): a 'puzzling' form in the *Cambrai Homily* and its implications for the apocope of /i/. In Meid FS, 471–74.

Sims-Williams, Patrick, 1999. The DEVORIGI inscription from Capel Eithin, Llanfihangel Ys[g]eifiog, Anglesey. *TAAS*, 146–49.

Sims-Williams, Patrick, 2000. Degrees of Celticity in Ptolemy's names: examples from Wales. In Parsons & Sims-Williams (ed.), *Ptolemy*, 1–15.

Sims-Williams, Patrick, 2001. Clas Beuno and the Four Branches of the Mabinogi. In Maier, Bernhard, & Zimmer, Stefan (ed.), *150 Jahre 'Mabinogion' – Deutsch–walisische Kulturbeziehungen*, Tübingen: Niemeyer, 111–27.

Sims-Williams, Patrick, 2002. The five languages of Wales in the pre-Norman inscriptions. *CMCS* 44.

Sims-Williams, Patrick, in press. Common Celtic, Gallo-Brittonic and Insular Celtic. In Lambert, Pierre-Yves, & Pinault, Georges-Jean (ed.), *Gaulois et celtique continental*, Paris: Publications de l'École Pratique des Hautes Études.

Smart, Veronica, 1997. *Æle-/Ale-* as a name-form on coins. In *Names, Places and People: An Onomastic Miscellany for John McNeal Dodgson*, Stamford: Watkins, 326–29.

Smith, A. H., 1956. *English Place-Name Elements*, i, Cambridge: Cambridge University Press.

Smith, William B. S., 1940. *De la toponymie bretonne, Dictionnaire Étymologique*, Supplement to *Language* 16/2.

Snyder, Christopher A., 1998. *An Age of Tyrants: Britain and the Britons A.D. 400–600*, Stroud: Sutton.

Stancliffe, Clare, 1997. The thirteen sermons attributed to Columbanus and the question of their authorship. In Lapidge, Michael (ed.), *Columbanus: Studies on the Latin Writings*, Woodbridge: Boydell, 93–202.

Steer, K. A., 1968–69. Two unrecorded Early Christian stones. *PSAS* 101, 127–29.

Stokes, Whitley, 1861. Gallische Inschriften. *Beiträge zur vergleichenden Sprachforschung* 2, 100–12.

Stokes, Whitley (ed.), 1887. *The Tripartite Life of Patrick*, 2 vols (single pagination), London: HMSO.

Stokes, Whitley (ed.), 1895. *The Martyrology of Gorman*, London: Henry Bradshaw Society.

Stüber, Karin, 1998. *The Historical Morphology of N-Stems in Celtic*, Maynooth: Department of Old Irish, National University of Ireland Maynooth.

Sweet, Henry (ed.), 1885. *The Oldest English Texts*, London: Oxford University Press.

Swift, Catherine, 1997. *Ogam Stones and the Earliest Irish Christians*, Maynooth: Department of Old and Middle Irish, St Patrick's College.

Szemerényi, Oswald, 1974. A Gaulish dedicatory formula. *KZ* 88, 246–86.

Tabula Imperii Romani, 1991. *Hoja K-29: Porto*, Madrid: Unión Académica Internacional (Comité Español).

Talbert, Richard J. A. (ed.), 2000. *The Barrington Atlas of the Greek and Roman World*, with 2-vol. *Map-by-Map Directory*, Princeton: Princeton University Press.

Tanguy, Bernard, 1984. Des cités et diocèses chez les Coriosolites et les Osismes. *BSAF* 113, 93–116.

Tanguy, Bernard, 1998. Les noms d'hommes et les noms de lieux. In *Cartulaire de l'abbaye Saint-Sauveur de Redon*, Rennes: Association des Amis des Archives historiques du diocèse de Rennes, Dol et Saint-Malo, 49–69.

Tedeschi, Carlo, 1995. Osservazioni sulla paleografia delle iscrizione britanniche paleocristiane (V–VII sec.). *Scrittura e civiltà* 19, 67–121.

Tedeschi, Carlo, 2000. Graffiti altomedievali del Tempietto sul Clitunno. *Scrittura e civiltà* 24, 413–19.

Tedeschi, Carlo, 2001. Some observations on the palaeography of Early Christian inscriptions in Britain. In Higgitt et al. (ed.), *Roman, Runes and Ogham*, 16–25.

Thomas, Charles, 1968. The evidence from North Britain. In Barley, M. W., & Hanson, R. P. C. (ed.), *Christianity in Britain, 300–700*, Leicester: Leicester University Press, 93–121.

Thomas, Charles, 1985. St Euny's Church, Redruth: a note on the inscription. *CA* 24, 173–74.

Thomas, Charles, 1991–92. The Early Christian inscriptions of southern Scotland. *GAJ* 17, 1–10.

Thomas, Charles, 1994. *And Shall These Mute Stones Speak? Post-Roman Inscriptions in Western Britain*, Cardiff: University of Wales Press.

Thomas, Charles, 1996. The Llanddewi-brefi 'Idnert' Stone. *Peritia* 10, 136–83.

Thomas, Charles, 1998. *Christian Celts: Messages and Images*, Stroud: Tempus.

Thomas, Charles, [2000?]. *Penzance Market Cross*, Penzance: Penlee House Gallery and Museum.

Thomas, Peter Wynn, 1990. The Brythonic consonant shift and the development of consonant mutation. *BBCS* 37, 1–42.

Thomas, Peter Wynn, 1995. (t): un o newidynnau tafodieithol y Frythoneg. In Evans FS, 219–43.

Thomas, R. J., 1933–35. Enwau afonydd â'r ôlddodiad -*wy*. *BBCS* 7, 117–33.

Thomas, R. J., 1935–37. Enwau afonydd â'r ôlddodiad -*wy* (*Parhad*). *BBCS* 8, 27–43.

Thomas, R. J., 1938. *Enwau Afonydd a Nentydd Cymru*, Cardiff: University of Wales Press.

Thomas, W. Gwyn, 1994. The Early Christian monuments. In Davies & Kirby (ed.), *Cardiganshire County History*, i, 407–20.

Thomson, Robert L. (ed.), 1997. *Ystorya Gereint uab Erbin*, Dublin: Dublin Institute for Advanced Studies.

Thorn, Caroline, & Thorn, Frank (ed.), 1979. *Domesday Book: Cornwall*, Chichester: Phillimore.

Thurneysen, Rudolf, 1918. Ogom *Svaqquci*. *ZCP* 12, 411–12.

Tomlin, R. S. O., 1975. A sub-Roman gravestone from Aberhydfer near Trecastle. *AC* 124, 68–72.

Tomlin, R. S. O., 1992. The Twelfth Legion at Wroxeter and Carlisle in the first century: the epigraphic evidence. *Britannia* 23, 141–58.

Tomlin, R. S. O., 1997. Roman Britain in 1996: inscriptions. *Britannia* 28, 455–72.

Tomlin, R. S. O., & Hassall, M. W. C., 1998. Roman Britain in 1997: inscriptions. *Britannia* 29, 433–45.

Tomlin, R. S. O., & Hassall, M. W. C., 2000. Roman Britain in 1999: inscriptions. *Britannia* 31, 433–49.

Tomlin, R. S. O., & Hassall, M. W. C., 2001. Roman Britain in 2000: inscriptions. *Britannia* 32, 387–400.

Toorians, Lauran, 2002. Keltisch *kagjo-; kaai, kade, Cadzand, Seneucaega en Zennewijnen. *Amsterdamer Beiträge zur älteren Germanistik* 56, 19–22.

Tovar, Antonio, 1975. Keltisch und Germanisch in Baden-Württemberg. *ZCP* 34, 30–42.

Tovar, Antonio, 1980–82. The god *Lugus* in Spain. *BBCS* 29, 591–99.

Tyers, Paul, 1996. *Roman Pottery in Britain*, London: Batsford.

Uhlich, Jürgen, 1989. *DOV(A)-* and lenited *-B-* in ogam. *Ériu* 40, 129–34.

Uhlich, Jürgen, 1993. *Die Morphologie der komponierten Personennamen des Altirischen*, Witterschlick and Bonn: M. Wehle.

Uhlich, Jürgen, 1995. On the fate of intervocalic *-u̯-* in Old Irish, especially between neutral vowels. *Ériu* 46, 11–48.

Uhlich, Jürgen, 1997. Einige britannische Lehnnamen im Irischen: *Brénainn (Brenden), Cathaír/ Catháer* und *Midir. ZCP* 49/50, 878–97.

Uhlich, Jürgen, 2000. *Kelten. CMCS* 39, 65–73.

Untermann, Jürgen, 1960. Namenlandschaften im alten Oberitalien (*Forsetzung*). *BzN* 11, 273–318.

Vallerie, Erwan, 1986. Un emprunt latin en breton: *menvent? ÉC* 23, 251–53.

Vendryes, J. 1948. Trois poèmes de Cynddelw. *ÉC* 4, 1–47.

Von Feilitzen, Olaf, 1937. *The Pre-Conquest Personal Names of Domesday Book*, Uppsala: Almqvist & Wiksells.

Wade-Evans, A. W., 1910. Parochiale Wallicanum. *Cymmrodor* 22, 22–124.

Watkin, Morgan (ed.), 1958. *Ystorya Bown de Hamtwn*, Cardiff: University of Wales Press.

Watkins, Calvert, 1963. Indo-European metrics and archaic Irish verse. *Celtica* 6, 194–249.

Watkins, Calvert, 1995. *How to Kill a Dragon: Aspects of Indo-European Poetics*, Oxford: Oxford University Press.

Watkins, Calvert, 1999. Two Celtic notes. In Meid FS, 539–43.

Watkins, T. Arwyn, 1956. Archaeology and history and the change from Brittonic to Welsh, Cornish, and Breton. *AC* 104, 166–84.

Watkins, T. Arwyn, 1964–66. Points of similarity between Old Welsh and Old Irish orthography. *BBCS* 21, 135–41.

Watson, G. R., 1952. Theta Nigrum. *JRS* 42, 56–62.

Watson, William J., 1926. *The History of the Celtic Place-Names of Scotland*, Edinburgh: Blackwood.

Webley, D. P., 1957. The Ystrad (Breckn.) ogam stone, a rediscovery. *AC* 106, 118–20.

Webley, D. P., 1958. The Nant Crew stone: a new discovery. *AC* 107, 123–24.

Weisgerber, Leo, 1931. Galatische Sprachreste. In *Natalicium Johannes Geffcken zum 70. Geburtstag*, Heidelberg: Winter, 151–75.

Weisgerber, Leo, 1969. *Rhenania Germano-Celtica*, Bonn: L. Röhrscheid.

Westwood, I. O., 1882. Further notices of the early inscribed stones of south Wales. *AC* 4th ser. 13, 40–42.

White, Richard B., 1971–72. Excavations at Arfryn, Bodedern, long-cist cemeteries and the origins of Christianity in Britain. *TAAS*, 19–51.

Williams, Ifor, 1923–25. Cynnydd, cynnif, cyni, nidro. *BBCS* 2, 299–303.

Williams, Ifor, 1923–25. Dwy gân o Lyfr Coch Talgarth. *BBCS* 2, 118–30.

Williams, Ifor, 1926–27. A reference to the Nennian Bellum Cocboy. *BBCS* 3, 59–62.

Williams, Ifor, 1929–31. Anawfedd, Blodeuwedd, -medd. *BBCS* 5, 134–37.

Williams, Ifor, 1929–31. Glosau Rhydychen. *BBCS* 5, 1–8.

Williams, Ifor, 1932. The Ogmore Castle inscription. *AC* 87, 232–38.

Williams, Ifor, 1935. The names on the Llandetty stone. *AC* 90, 87–94.

Williams, Ifor, 1935–37. Meddwyl, Hedyn, Llyngedwy. *BBCS* 8, 234–5.

Williams, Ifor, 1937. The Trescawen Stone (Llangwyllog). In RCAHMW, *Anglesey*, cix–cxiii.

Williams, Ifor (ed.), 1938. *Canu Aneirin*, Cardiff: University of Wales Press.

Williams, Ifor, 1939–41. Nodiadau ar eiriau. *BBCS* 10, 36–44.

Williams, Ifor, 1939. When did British become Welsh? *TAAS*, 27–39.

Williams, Ifor, 1941–44. Iorwerth. *BBCS* 11, 144–45.

Williams, Ifor, 1943–44. Review of CIIC i. *THSC*, 152–56.

Williams, Ifor, 1945. The lost MAILIS stone, Llanfadog. *TAAS*, p. 24.

Williams, Ifor (ed.), 1951. *Pedeir Keinc y Mabinogi*, 2nd edn, Cardiff: University of Wales Press.

Williams, Ifor (ed.), 1953. *Canu Llywarch Hen*, 2nd edn, Cardiff: University of Wales Press.

Williams, Ifor, 1954–56. Friog. *BBCS* 16, 28–29.
Williams, Ifor, 1957. *Chwedl Taliesin*, Cardiff: University of Wales Press.
Williams, Ifor, 1957. Note on the [Ystrad] inscription. *AC* 106, 120–21.
Williams, Ifor (ed.), 1968. *The Poems of Taliesin*, Dublin: Dublin Institute for Advanced Studies.
Williams, Ifor, 1969. *Enwau Lleoedd*, new edn, Liverpool: Gwasg y Brython.
Williams, Ifor (ed.), 1972. *Armes Prydein*, Dublin: Dublin Institute for Advanced Studies.
Williams, Ifor, & Nash-Williams, V. E., 1936. Two Early Christian stones from Tregaron, Cardiganshire. *AC* 91, 15–19.
Williams, Ifor, & Nash-Williams, V. E., 1937. Some Welsh Pre-Norman stones. *AC* 92, 1–10.
Williams, J. E. Caerwyn, 1954–55. Y Frythoneg a'r Gymraeg. *LlC* 3, 82–93.
Williams, J. E. Caerwyn, 1979–80. Kenneth Hurlstone Jackson. *SC* 14/15, 1–11.
Williams, J. E. Caerwyn, 1983. Welsh *drythyll, trythyll*; Irish *drettel, treitell*. *Celtica* 15, 150–57.
Williams, J. E. Caerwyn, 1990. Wysg (river-name), wysg, hwysgynt, rhwysg. *Celtica* 21, 670–78.
Williams, J. E. Caerwyn, 1991–92. Kenneth Hurlstone Jackson 1909–1991. *SC* 26/27, 202–12.
Williams, Taliesin (ed.), 1848. *Iolo Manuscripts*, Llandovery: Welsh MSS. Society.
Williams-Jones, Keith (ed.), 1976. *The Merioneth Lay Subsidy Roll 1292–3*, Cardiff: University of Wales Press.
Willis-Bund, J. W. (ed.), 1902. *The Black Book of St. David's*, London: Honourable Society of Cymmrodorion.
Wilson, Stephen, 1998. *The Means of Naming*, London: UCL Press.
Withycombe, E. G., 1977. *The Oxford Dictionary of English Christian Names*, 3rd edn, Oxford: Clarendon Press.
Wmffre, Iwan Llwyd, 1998. *Language and History in Cardiganshire Place-Names*, 2 vols., Ph.D., University of Wales, Swansea.
Wodtko, Dagmar S., 1995. *Secundäradjektive in der altirischen Glossen*, Innsbruck: Institut für Sprachwissenschaft.
Wooding, Jonathan M., 1996. *Communication and Commerce along the Western Sealanes, AD 400–800*, British Archaeological Reports, International Series, 654, Oxford: BAR.
Wright, R. P., 1962. Further notes on the Roman milestone from Aber. *TCHS* 23, 127–28.
Wright, R. P., 1962. Roman Britain in 1961: Inscriptions. *JRS* 52, 190–99.
Wright, R. P., & Hassall, M. W. C., 1971. Roman Britain in 1970: inscriptions. *Britannia* 2, 289–304.
Wright, R. P., & Hassall, M. W. C., 1972. Roman Britain in 1971: inscriptions. *Britannia* 3, 352–67.
Wright, R. P., & Hassall, M. W. C., 1973. Roman Britain in 1972: inscriptions. *Britannia* 4, 324–37.
Wright, R. P., & Jackson, K. H., 1968. A late inscription from Wroxeter. *AntJ* 48, 295–300.
Wynne, W. W. E., 1846. Notes from the records of inquisitions held for the County of Merioneth, in the reign of Edward III, Richard II, Henry VI, Henry VII, and Henry VIII. *AC*, 396–403.
Zimmer, Stefan, 1987. *Geiriadur Gwrthdroadol Cymraeg Diweddar: A Reverse Dictionary of Modern Welsh*, Hamburg: Buske.
Zimmer, Stefan, 1994. Zum britischen *s-*. *JCL* 3, 149–64.
Zimmer, Stefan, 1995. Die altkymrischen Frauennamen. Ein erster Einblick. In Evans FS, 319–35.
Zimmer, Stefan, 1995. Indogermanisch *$h_1$su-* and *dus-* im Kymrischen. *ZCP* 47, 176–200.
Zimmer, Stefan, 1997. Gallisch DIVERTOMV, kymrisch *llawer*, tocharisch A *want-wraske*. In Beekes FS, 353–58.
Zimmer, Stefan, 1999. Comments on a great book: *The Encyclopaedia of Indo-European Culture*, ed. by J. P. Mallory and D. Q. Adams. *JIES* 27, 105–63.
Zimmer, Stefan, 1999. Review of Wodtko 1995. In *ZCP* 51, 294–97.

INDEX OF FORMS DISCUSSED

This index gives references to the sections of Chapter 2 (‡) and Chapter 3 (§) where the forms, or alleged forms, in the inscriptions are mentioned. For the sake of completeness I also include some further forms (e.g. ABRAHAM) which have not been not discussed. References to other chapters may be found by looking up the inscription number in the List of Proposed Dates in Chapter 6. <u>Double underline</u> = probable Irish names; <u>single underline</u> = possible Irish names. Inscriptions outside the corpus studied in this book (such as the ogam inscriptions in Ireland and the inscriptions of Roman Britain) are indexed in the next Index.

INDEX OF OTHER FORMS MENTIONED

This index excludes forms from the corpus of inscriptions studied in this book; they are covered in the preceding Index of Forms Discussed. References are to pages. There are three sections:

Ancient forms (mostly Celtic and Latin)
Medieval and modern forms: Brittonic (also a few Pictish forms)
Medieval and modern forms: Irish (also a few Manx forms)

In the Brittonic index *k* has been normalised to *c* and the English alphabet has been followed.

Coroticus, -a 133
corvis 304
Counos 85
Cov(v)entina(e), Covintina 76 182
Critognatus 159
Crocus 233
crux 24–5 102
Cubio- 56
cultor 90
Cunaito 192
Cunaris 25–7 297–8 302
Cunedecanes 156
Cunetio 64 102 192
Cunicatus 156
Cunio- 78
Cunitius, Cunit(t)us 156
Cunobarrus 77 128 156
Cunomolius 156
Cunopennus 89
Cunoven 40
Cunovendus, -i 40 76 156
Cunovindus 40
Cunsus, -a 156
Cupidus 148
Cupinacios 56
Cupitianus 39
Cupitus, -a 39
Curcinate 160
Curcio- 164
Curcus 160
Curisius 110
Curita 48
Curitius 48

Dagorigis 62
Daili 91
Dalli 91
Dariaco 61
Darinoi 61
Darios 61
Demetia 93 283
Deomiorix 24
Deprosagilos 223
Derventio 96
Desiderius 207
Deuacnua 159
Deuorio 207
Dexsiva 24
Diaros 30
Dignus 155
Dinomogetimaro 46 65
Dis(i)derius 207
Disocno, -i 159
Diuuogna 159
Dobunna, -i 83
Doc(c)- 70

dominicus, Dom(i)nicus 57 131 150 185 231
  255 293 320
Dom(i)nus 320
Donno- 101
δρουγγος 162
Druto- 48
Dubnacus 56
Dubnoco 56
Duetil 31
Dumnouellaunus 101
Dunn- 101
Durcinate 160
Durobrivae 281

Earos 30
Eccaios 63
Ecretumarus 114
Ecrito, -us 114
Edn[50
Ἔδρου 297
Elise 190
Elvetii 130
emeritus, Emeritus, -a 42
emissarius 184 189
Enig(e)nus 155
Eppimus 31
Eppudunos 44
Equester 217
Ercauica, Ergauica 161
Eric(c)os 186
Ernodorum 99
et 135–6
Eternus 98
Etnosus 50
Etterne 135
Evalis 60
Evocati 61
Exocius 81
Exsactoris 24 29
Exsibuus 24

Fani 68
Fannac 68
Fannianus 68
Fann(i)us 68 83 202
felis, felix 25
Fer(r)ox 145
Ferna, -i 145
Ferruciacus 145 202
Ferrucio 145 274
Fessus 66
ficit 103
fig(u)linus 150
figulus, Figulus 150
flaus 25
Flavus 69 227
fraudatius 25

Medieval and modern forms: Brittonic (also a few Pictish forms)

Medieval and modern forms: Irish (also a few Manx forms)